THE PUZZLE OF
LATIN AMERICAN
ECONOMIC DEVELOPMENT

THE PUZZLE OF LATIN AMERICAN ECONOMIC DEVELOPMENT

SECOND EDITION

Patrice Franko

ROWMAN & LITTLEFIELD PUBLISHERS, INC.
Lanham • Boulder • New York • Oxford

ROWMAN & LITTLEFIELD PUBLISHERS, INC.

Published in the United States of America
by Rowman & Littlefield Publishers, Inc.
A Member of the Rowman & Littlefield Publishing Group
4501 Forbes Boulevard, Suite 200, Lanham, Maryland 20706
www.rowmanlittlefield.com

P.O. Box 317, Oxford OX2 9RU, United Kingdom

British Library Cataloguing in Publication Information Available

Library of Congress Cataloging-in-Publication Data

Franko, Patrice M., 1958–
The puzzle of Latin American economic development / Patrice Franko.—2nd ed.
  p. cm.
  Includes bibliographical references and index.
  ISBN 0-7425-2465-5 (cloth : alk. paper)—ISBN 0-7425-2466-3 (pbk. : alk. paper)
  1. Latin America—Economic conditions—1982– 2. Latin America—Economic
policy. I. Title.
HC125 .F682 2003
338.98—dc21

                                                            2002154525

Printed in the United States of America

∞™ The paper used in this publication meets the minimum requirements of American
National Standard for Information Sciences—Permanence of Paper for Printed Library
Materials, ANSI/NISO Z39.48–1992.

FOR SANDY—
STILL, AND ALWAYS

CONTENTS

Tables, Figures, and Boxes

FIGURES

BOXES

Preface

This book explores the puzzle of economic development in Latin America. Despite a similar starting point in the late 1800s, why didn't Latin America continue to grow at the pace of North America? How can we understand the economic path it took? What are the contemporary opportunities and constraints? This is not a general textbook on development, but it tries to provide tools from development, trade, and finance for students to evaluate policy outcomes in Latin America. Without ignoring the historical antecedents, the central task of the text is an analysis of contemporary problems in Latin America. It is essentially the story of the character and contradictions of the new economic model in Latin America.

The text begins with the conceptual and historical foundations of development in Latin America. After briefly raising questions about the meaning of development and issues on the Latin America economic agenda in chapter 1, chapter 2 sets a broad historical context with a focus on inputs and outputs to characterize the period leading up to World War II. The question of primary product exports as an engine for growth is a central theme. Chapter 3 takes up import substitution industrialization, providing a theoretical and applied context for state-led development policy in the region. A case study of the auto industry is provided. The debt crisis and macroeconomic stabilization attempts are treated in chapters 4 and 5. Questions of credibility and confidence return as constraints on flexible adjustment in the 1990s.

The challenge of the first part of the text was compressing into five chapters readings that used to constitute the bulk of a course on Latin American development. Beloved material is missing. But if a course on Latin America is to be one semester, we no longer have the luxury of spending two weeks on dependency theory, and then another two unraveling structuralism and import substitution industrialization. Where I used to spend nearly a month debating the debt problem and hyperinflation, if we do so there is less room for capital markets, trade integration, social policy, and the environment. Yet students need to understand the historical antecedents to appreciate the difficulties of contemporary policy. This book provides the background in a condensed approach, then moves on to the neoliberal model and contemporary challenges.

The second part of *The Puzzle of Latin American Economic Development* begins with an exploration of the role of the state in chapter 6. After discussing the downsizing of the state and efforts to enhance revenues, it takes up the question of the appropriate role of the state in Latin America, setting up a debate between the neoliberal view of a reduced state, the neoinstitutionalist prescription for institutional deepening, and a neostructuralist perspective of selective state action. This question of how much state intervention is appropriate in the economic arena arises in subsequent chapters. After discussing new capital flows to the region in chapter 7, we debate interventions by states to reduce vulnerability. In chapter 8, after a review of

trends in trade liberalization, cooperative state action in integration efforts is discussed and the potential for a free trade area of the Americas is evaluated. Chapter 9
looks at the way in which globalization and marketization have affected competitiveness of industry and associated input markets for labor and technology, while
chapter 10 takes up the contemporary challenges of agriculture. The unifying theme
of these chapters is the optimal degree of policy intervention in the face of opportunities and constraints presented by globalization of finance and production.

The final group of chapters addresses the social and environmental challenges the
region faces. After analysis of the problem of persistent poverty and inequality in the
region in chapter 11, chapters 12 and 13 grapple with the problem and promise of
health reform and education. The chapter on the environment in Latin America reinforces the environmental dimension that has run through the text. Social, gender, and
environmental issues pervade the text because they are intimately connected with
problems of stabilization, liberalization, and competitiveness in the global arena. The
chapters on poverty, education, health, and the environment focus the student on these
issues not as the effects of other policies but as profound challenges that must be
addressed for Latin America to meet the goals of sustainable, equitable development.

This book is written for students with varying economics competencies. My students often ask whether they should take this course before or after taking trade,
finance, and development. My experience is that the benefits accrue either way. If the
student has strong theoretical tools, the depth of understanding of the problem of
development in Latin America is more nuanced. However, engaging the difficult
choices facing Latin American economic policymakers provides an applied context to
acquire conceptual tools to solve the puzzle of strong, sustainable, and equitable
growth in the region. For many students the luxury of how to sequence economics
courses is a moot point. They come to a course on the economics of Latin America
after realizing through a study abroad program or through interdisciplinary course-
work that an understanding of economic trends in the region is critical to a compre-
hension of contemporary politics and society. This may be their only course in Latin
American economic development. This book therefore has no prerequisites other than
an introductory sequence of economic principles. Throughout the text terms are
explained, and box presentations provide illustrations and real-world examples.
Words in bold type are defined in the glossary at the end of the book. This is designed
to minimize the distraction to the better-equipped student eager to cut to the heart of
the development issue.

Unlike many of the fine edited collections that provide a rich array of reading
material, this text presents the fundamentals alongside the issues. An instructor may
want to use a reader or create a personalized reader from some of the terrific pieces
cited in the endnotes of each chapter. Writing this book has been a gratifying and
humbling experience. There was so much engaging work on the problem of economic development in Latin America from which to draw. It was of course always
daunting to condense a thoughtful, provocative, and well-researched book into a
two- or three-line summary. Notes have been left in throughout the text to indicate
to even the beginning student that the theory of economic development in Latin
America is the product of a mosaic of ideas and policies. The more advanced student should aggressively track down these readings to provide the nuanced texture

of the debate in the field that a single text could never hope to convey. My thanks to all upon whose work I drew, and my apologies for any errors or omissions. I look forward to hearing from readers of this book to clarify pieces that I may have misrepresented or point out works that I neglected to consult.

This book is the legacy of years of teaching bright and engaged students in my course on contemporary economic policy in Latin America at Colby College, Maine. My students pushed me with their insightful questions (some of which I hope are answered herein) and motivated me with their enthusiasm for understanding Latin American economic development. My research assistants over the past few years have been active collaborators in this book effort. Justin Ackerman, Jeana Flahive, Justin Harvey, Joanna Meronk, and Mary Beth Thomson became data sleuths and Internet wizards. In addition to work during the semester, Erwin Godoy, Luisa Godoy, Gillian Morejon, and Jill Macaferri each spent a summer helping to develop this manuscript; each has left an indelible imprint on the text. The second edition was managed by Louise Langhoft-Roos and Meg Knight; Katie Gagne, Jacqueline Smith, and Josh Schneider tracked down final details. Former assistants now with professional degrees of their own in the field—M. Holly Peirce, Marina Neto Grande, and David Edelstein—were valuable sources of information. I am very grateful for all of my students' hard work and dedication. Of course all the mistakes are mine alone. The enthusiastic and patient guidance of my editor, Susan McEachern, transformed what could have been an unpleasant struggle into a productive and energizing process. Copyeditor Luann Reed-Siegel and Assistant Managing Editor Janice Braunstein's helpful suggestions considerably improved the manuscript. My family, and especially my parents, have supported my efforts not only on this text but throughout my academic endeavors. My stepchildren and their spouses, Dana and Erik Anderson and Josh and Eden Maisel, inspire me by their own commitments to teaching and policy work. But my greatest debt of gratitude is to my husband, Sandy Maisel, who believed in my ability to see this project through even when I wasn't sure myself. He provided the pragmatic advice, personal inspiration, untiring encouragement, and steaming coffee every morning to take this project from conception to reality. He patiently adapted our travel schedule during our semester in London—where much of the editorial work of the second edition took place—due to deadlines. I dedicate this book to him with all my love.

ABBREVIATIONS

ADR	American depository receipts
ALADI	Asociación Latinoamericana de Integración
BIS	Bank for International Settlements
CACM	Central American Common Market
CBA	cost-benefit analysis
CEA	cost-effectiveness analysis
CEC	Commission for Environmental Cooperation
CEPAL	Comisión Económica Para América Latina [ECLA]
CET	common external tariff
CTM	Confederation of Mexican Workers
DRIFs	Demand-driven rural investment funds
EA	environmental assessments
EAP	economically active population
ECLA	UN Economic Commission for Latin America
ECLAC	Economic Commission for Latin America and the Caribbean
EPFZ	export processing free zones
EPI	educational performance index
ESF	emergency social fund
EU	European Union
FAO	Food and Agriculture Organization
FOSIS	Chilean Solidarity and Social Investment Funds
FTA	free trade area
FTAA	Free Trade Area of the Americas
GATT	General Agreement on Tariffs and Trade
GDI	gender development index
GDP	gross domestic product
GEF	Global Environmental Facility
GEM	gender empowerment index
GM	General Motors
GNP	gross national product
HDI	human development index
HFA	"Health for All"
HIPC	highly indebted poor country initiative
HPI	human poverty index
IADB	Inter-American Development Bank (also IDB)
IMF	International Monetary Fund
IMIP	Institute Materno–Infantil de Pernambuco
IPO	initial public offering
LAC	Latin America and Caribbean

LAIA	Latin American Integration Association
LDC	less-developed countries
MCC	Mercosur Commerce Commission
Mercosur	South American Common Market
MNCs	multinational corporations
MOH	Ministry of Health
NADBank	North American Development Bank
NAFTA	North American Free Trade Agreement
NGO	nongovernmental organization
NICs	newly industrialized countries
NIE	new institutional economics
NPE	new political economy
OECD	Organisation for Economic Cooperation and Development
OLADE	Latin American Energy Organization
PAHO	Pan American Health Organization
PHC	Primary health care
PPP	purchasing power parity
PREAL	Partnership for Educational Revitalization in the Americas
PRSPs	poverty-reduction strategy papers
PTAs	preferential trade agreements
R&D	research and development
RIAs	regional integration arrangements
SEC	Security and Exchange Commission
SIFs	social investment funds
SMEs	small and medium enterprises
SOEs	state-owned enterprises
SSI	Social Security Institutes
TNCs	transnational corporations
UN	United Nations
UNCTAD	UN Conference on Trade and Development
UNDP	United Nations Development Program
UNICEF	United Nations Children's Fund
UNT	National Workers Union [Mexico]
USAID	United States Agency for International Development
VAT	value added tax
WHO	World Health Organization
WSSD	World Summit on Sustainable Development
WTO	World Trade Organization

North and South America

Scale 1:67,000,000

Azimuthal Equal-Area Projection

| 0 | 500 | 1000 | 1500 | 2000 Kilometers |
| 0 | 500 | 1000 | 1500 | 2000 Miles |

Boundary representation is not necessarily authoritative.

802532 (R02283) 11-96

South America

Scale 1:35,000,000
Azimuthal Equal-Area Projection

0 |————| 500 Kilometers
0 |————| 500 Miles

Boundary representation is
not necessarily authoritative.

Falkland Islands
(Islas Malvinas)
(administered by U.K.,
claimed by ARGENTINA)

South Georgia and the
South Sandwich Islands
(administered by U.K.,
claimed by ARGENTINA)

802585 (R02108) 6-98

Central America and the Caribbean

CHAPTER ONE

DEVELOPMENT IN LATIN AMERICA

Conceptualizing Economic Change in the Region

Latin America contains cities of splendor . . . *(Courtesy of David Mangurian and the Inter-American Development Bank.)*

I

Latin Americans live in a complex economic system, simultaneously inhabiting the frontiers of finance and technology while also appearing hopelessly mired in a vicious circle of poverty. Consider the following stories.

Uruguayan-born financier Juan Navarro has become the buyout king of Latin America. From his modern, elegant offices in Buenos Aires, Argentina, Navarro has built his equity buyout company, Exxel Group, into one of the country's largest privately owned holdings. Since 1993, Exxel has invested more than $4.8 billion in seventy-three companies. Identifying undervalued firms in emerging markets, particularly the Mercosur countries of Brazil, Paraguay, Uruguay, and Argentina, Navarro convinced global investors such as GE, Travelers Insurance, Brown and Princeton Universities, Bankers Trust, and General Motors to invest in supermarkets, the privatization of postal services and duty free shops, a MasterCard franchise, and a music and electronics chain. With plans to expand these companies throughout the region, Navarro is taking on global giants such as the United States's Wal-Mart and France's Carrefour. Recent macro instability in Argentina, however, has rocked the company. Bankruptcy and loan defaults are plaguing Navarro.[1] But for this aggressive Latin businessman, beating the odds, and transforming underperforming companies into success stories, has become part of his game.[2]

Brazilian soccer superstar Ronaldo has reached the apex of soccer fame, becoming one of the highest-paid players in soccer history. After battling knee injuries for two and a half years, his remarkable comeback led Brazil to win its fifth World Cup title. A striker for the Spanish team Real Madrid, he has signed deals with Nike and the

. . . and pockets of poverty. *(Courtesy of David Mangurian and the Inter-American Development Bank.)*

Peruvians sign onto the Internet. *(Courtesy of David Mangurian and the Inter-American Development Bank.)*

Italian milk company Parmalat, as well as Brazil's number-one beer maker, Brahma. Born in a poor *favela* or slum, in Rio de Janeiro, Ronaldo had to quit soccer as a young boy because he didn't have the bus fare. Sixteen of Ronaldo's relatives live at the home where he grew up sleeping on the sofa with his older brother. The home is simply furnished—no telephone but a freezer and a television. Ronaldo is currently involved with a program in Brazil that takes poor kids out of the *favelas* and puts them in soccer camps to ensure that others have a chance for a future.[3]

Jessy Contreras, a cosmetology student, has long dreamed of logging onto the Internet to study the latest Parisian trends. But saving enough money for a computer and access in a poor country like Peru, where average income is less than $300 per month and few have private phones lines, seemed too far a stretch. Fortunately, Peruvians are signing on in droves through the Peruvian Scientific Fund, a network begun with $7,000 in seed money from the UN Development Fund and other cooperative arrangements with universities, hospitals, and nongovernmental organizations. Manuel Molla Madueno, a psychologist making somewhere in the range of $400–$500 a month, is able to access international journals and participate in bulletin boards. Local teachers are able to monitor Spanish culture from around the world. Unfortunately, expansion is limited by the slowness of Telefonica, the telephone company, in installing telephone circuits.[4]

Judith Yanira Viera, from El Salvador, is eighteen years old. For over a year she worked in the Taiwanese-owned Mandarin International *maquiladora* factory in the San Marcos Free Trade Zone where she made shirts for the Gap, Eddie Bauer, and

JCPenney. From Monday to Thursday her shift went from seven in the morning until nine at night. On Fridays she would work straight through the night, starting at 7 A.M. and working until 4 A.M. She and her coworkers would sleep overnight on the factory floor. The following day, they would work from 7 A.M. until 5 P.M. Despite these very long hours, the most she ever earned was 750 *colones,* about $43 per month.[5]

Blasio and Claire Lehman struggle with the help of their two teenage sons to make approximately $900 a year as tobacco farmers in Brazil. With a simple home on a small piece of land, their dream when they married twenty-two years ago was a future in tobacco. But competition in the global tobacco market has soured their dream. Small farmers are forced, in a feudal-like arrangement, to take bank loans to buy kits comprised of seeds, pesticides, herbicides, fertilizers, a plastic sheet to cover the soil, and protective gear for applying chemicals. When purchasing the kits they must pledge to sell their harvest to the companies that sold them. Fifteen percent of the payment for the first harvest is withheld to ensure complete delivery. If growers try to hold back crops because they disagree with the companies' valuation of the product, police assist the companies in seizing the crops. Illiteracy prevents farmers from mobilizing. Some farmers work in the tobacco processing plants to supplement crop income. The Lehmans' son Ismail has offered to quit school to make his family's ends meet—to save the $35 a month in bus fare. His future would brighten if the family could switch to another crop—but that would take money for start-up costs. Too bad that the fiscal incentives provided to the big tobacco companies—including Philip Morris—couldn't find their way into more affordable transportation.[6]

Economically, Latin Americans range from the very wealthy Juan Navarro to the desperately poor Judith Yanira Viera. Resources available to create working lives may be the tobacco plant or the complex strands of the Internet. International markets—for clothing, fruit, or sports—may propel some to relative affluence, but there are always the masses left behind in Ronaldo's *favela.* Economic life in Latin America is multilayered, from traditional rural life to dirty assembly factories to ultramodern skyscrapers in cosmopolitan cities. Latin American economic **development** is a puzzle. This text invites you to make some sense of this complex problem. Questions that we will explore in trying to unravel this puzzle include the following:

- How do so many fragments of different levels of economic life join to form a coherent whole?
- With a far wider income range than industrial countries, with available technologies running from a simple shovel to a sophisticated financial machine, what kind of macroeconomic policies can address the complex microeconomic structure of Latin America?
- How does this multilayered economy interface with the world market?
- How have the pressures of globalization and the international market transformed the varied lives of Latin Americans?

As an introduction to the puzzle of Latin American economic development, this book attempts to clarify the complexity of economic life in Latin America. We will try to understand the potential that Juan Navarro has been able to tap, as well as the constraints keeping many farmers and factory workers in poverty.

A Conceptual Map: What Is Economic Development?

To understand the multilayered economic home of Jessy Contreras and Juan Navarro, we first need to contextualize it within a theory of economic development. The objectives of this chapter are to explore briefly the meaning of development and to highlight selected characteristics of economic policy and performance in Latin America. In an ideal world, readers of this text would have taken courses in economic development, international trade, and international finance before embarking on a study of Latin American economics. However, many students come to understand the economic importance of Latin America late in their academic careers and simply don't have the time (or may even lack the interest) to backtrack through this important theoretical framework. The economic component may be only a small part of your broader interest in the region. For you, this section raises some of the questions that would be grappled with over a longer period of time in a course on development theory. Students with a background in development theory are invited to draw on that broader conceptual framework and apply it to the case of Latin America to answer a fundamental question of this book: How can we understand the process of economic development in the Latin American region? How can we reconcile the different lives of Ronaldo and Juan Navarro within a single economic system?

> **QUESTION FOR THOUGHT**
>
> Using the Internet site www.iadb.org/idbamerica or by going to a periodical search engine for newspapers, identify stories of the economic lives of Latin Americans. (In the search feature you might try keywords such as agriculture, environment, indigenous people, *maquilas*, poverty, and women to bring up stories of interest to you.) What contrasts can you identify in the lives of people in the region?

Characteristics of Development

What characteristics do we normally associate with developed and less-developed countries? Try ranking the United States, Mexico, Brazil, Ecuador, Canada, and France on the following measures:

- Which countries have the highest rates of urbanization?
- Which countries have the highest per capita rates of **growth**?
- Which countries have the highest weight of international trade in the economy as measured by net exports and gross domestic product (GDP)?
- Which countries have the highest per capita carbon dioxide emissions?

Clean, potable water is a step forward for the community—but its collection is part of the double duty of work that women perform in the developing world. *(Courtesy of the Inter-American Development Bank.)*

The answers might surprise you. In Brazil, 81 percent of the population live in urban areas; this is followed by 77 percent in both Canada and the United States, 75 percent in France, 74 percent in Mexico, and 64 percent in Ecuador. Average growth of per capita GDP from 1965 to 1999 ranged from 1.5 percent in Mexico and 1.9 percent in Canada and Ecuador to 2.0 percent in the United States, 2.1 percent in France, and 2.4 percent in Brazil. Trade plays the greatest role in Canada at 84 percent of GDP in 1999, followed by Ecuador and Mexico at 63 percent, France at 50 percent, the United States at 24 percent, and Brazil at 22 percent. The United States has the dubious honor of leading the list of per capita carbon dioxide emissions at 20.1 metric tons in 1997, followed by Canada at 16.6, France at 6.0, Mexico at 4.0, Ecuador at 1.8, and Brazil at 1.9.

This short exercise raises a few questions. What do we mean by a developed (versus an underdeveloped) country? Are countries neatly classifiable? What is the diversity of economic experience within Latin America itself? How can we begin to think about a development strategy with relatively divergent conditions? You might want to open the most recent *World Development Report* or log onto the World Bank homepage at www.worldbank.org to look at some of the other data within the Latin America region and comparisons between Latin America and the rest of the world. Tables 1.1 and 1.2 summarize some of these statistics. You may be surprised at the diversity you find.

Table 1.1.   Quality of Life Indicators

Country	Child Malnutrition (% of children under age five)	Under Age of Five Mortality Rate per 1,000	Female Life Expectancy at Birth	Access to Improved Sanitation (% of urban population 2000)	Household Consumption Spending (% growth 1990–1999)
Argentina	2	22	77	89	3.3
Bolivia	8	83	64	82	3.6
Brazil	6	40	71	85	1.6
Chile	1	12	79	98	7.3
Colombia	8	28	74	97	3.0
Costa Rica	5	14	79	98	5.0
Ecuador	—	35	71	70	1.6
El Salvador	12	36	72	88	5.5
Guatemala	24	52	68	98	4.3
Honduras	25	46	72	94	3.1
Mexico	8	36	75	87	1.9
Nicaragua	12	43	71	96	5.1
Panama	—	25	76	99	4.9
Paraguay	—	27	72	95	4.0
Peru	8	48	71	90	4.2
Venezuela	8	23	76	75	0.4
United States	1	8	80	100	3.2

Source: World Bank, *World Development Indicators 2001* (New York: Oxford University Press/World Bank, 2001).

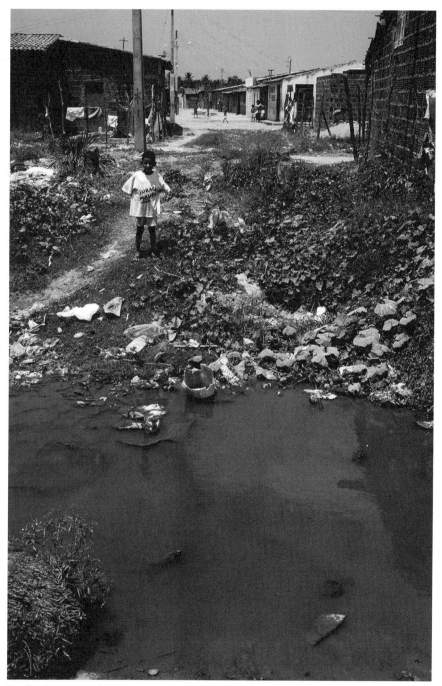

Lack of access to adequate housing leaves millions in misery. *(Courtesy of David Mangurian and the Inter-American Development Bank.)*

Table 1.2.   Communications Indicators

Country	Television Sets (per 1,000 people)	Daily Newspapers (per 1,000 people)	Telephone Main Lines (per 1,000 people)	Mobile Phones (per 1,000 people)	Personal Computers (per 1,000 people)	Internet Hosts (per 1,000 people)
Argentina	293	123	201	121	49.2	47.34
Bolivia	118	55	62	52	12.3	1.73
Brazil	333	40	149	89	36.3	38.97
Chile	240	98	207	151	66.6	33.78
Colombia	199	46	160	75	33.7	10.15
Costa Rica	229	94	204	35	101.7	24.33
Ecuador	205	70	91	31	20.1	1.67
El Salvador	191	48	76	62	16.2	1.62
Guatemala	61	33	55	30	9.9	2.54
Honduras	95	55	44	12	9.5	0.19
Mexico	267	97	112	79	44.2	50.60
Nicaragua	69	30	30	9	8.1	2.18
Panama	192	62	164	86	32.0	10.21
Paraguay	205	43	55	196	11.2	2.66
Peru	147	0	67	40	35.7	3.88
Venezuela	185	206	109	143	42.2	6.48
Latin American Average	272	71	130	82	37.7	29.62
East Asia and Pacific	252	—	82	42	17.0	3.98
Canada	715	159	655	226	360.8	590.37
United States	844	215	664	312	510.5	2,419.86

Source: World Bank, World Development Indicators 2001 (New York: Oxford University Press/World Bank, 2001).

In table 1.1, we can see that although some countries in Latin America exhibit poor performance on indicators of child malnutrition and child mortality, others perform extremely well. Honduras and Guatemala, for example, are the worst performers, with nearly one in four children malnourished, but in Chile only 1 percent of children suffer from hunger. Similarly, Bolivia, Guatemala, and Peru demonstrate tragic rates of infant mortality, whereas Chile, Costa Rica, and Argentina demonstrate strong records. In Ecuador and Venezuela, only 70 and 75 percent of the population have access to improved sanitation facilities. Guatemala, Nicaragua, Colombia, Panama, Paraguay, Costa Rica, and Chile all have rates higher than 95 percent. Throughout the region the growth of private consumption has been uneven, with slow rates in many countries reflecting small changes in the material well-being of the population. As we will see in this text, the long, hard road of economic adjustment to the debt shocks and the tough macroeconomic stabilization packages of the 1980s and the currency shocks of the 1990s have left many Latin Americans with little more in their homes than they had when they were children.

Table 1.2 gives a few measures of what you might expect to find in homes in the

Americas. There are about thirteen times as many TVs in the United States (per 1,000 people) as there are in Guatemala and about twenty-five times as many mobile phones in Canada as in Nicaragua. Chileans have access to about twice as many computers per person as do Colombians, and Mexicans lead Latin America with the most Internet hosts per person. Of course we want to be careful with these data; cross-country data are always difficult to collect, especially when you are estimating houses with access to sanitation or computers. Furthermore, we don't want to suggest that televisions or mobile phones are the bellwethers of what it means to be developed. We need to be aware of data difficulties even as we develop more sophisticated measures to evaluate progress and poverty in the region in later chapters.

What Do We Mean by Development?

When we think about the challenges of development and underdevelopment in Latin America, what do we really mean? Are mobiles and toilets the goal of development? How does "promoting development" translate into something concrete for the policymaker to target? U.S. president Harry S. Truman, in his inauguration speech in January 1949, envisioned a bold new program, based on "the concepts of democratic fair-dealing," to make the "benefits of our scientific and industrial progress available for the improvement and growth of underdeveloped areas."[7] Although the word "underdeveloped" had been introduced in 1942 by Wilfred Benson, a member of the secretariat of the International Labor Organization, development economists such as Paul Rosenstein-Rodan spoke of "economically backward areas," and Arthur Lewis characterized the emerging challenge as the gap between rich and poor countries throughout the 1940s. Truman popularized the term "underdevelopment" but did not clearly define it. Since Truman, the goal of development has been to undo the hardships of underdevelopment—without a clear statement of the positive objective. What does it mean to be developed? With the advent of the Cold War, the world was divided into industrial market economies, the communist or "second" world, and finally the rest of the globe or the "third" world. These nations were once again the residual—what was left over when the rest of the counting was done. Since the collapse of the Berlin Wall, the second world has euphemistically been referred to as "transitional economies." What exactly are they transitioning toward? What is a usable definition of the goal of "development"?

> **QUESTION FOR THOUGHT**
>
> How do you define development? List elements that you believe are important in defining a policy objective of promoting economic development.

In common language, development describes a process in which the potential of an organism is released to achieve its mature form. Dictionary definitions point to growth or expansion to bring about a more advanced state. When we think of the development of a tree or an animal, we have a clear idea of the appearance of the mature, advanced form. In economics we find ourselves in a bit of trouble. We can measure degrees of industrialization or access to a wider array of consumer products, but things become murky when we try to associate the terms "modern," "mature," and "developed" with societies having well-articulated economic infrastructures. Given the long list of ills associated with modern society, we should be clear in our understanding that more sophisticated production techniques and a wider range of electronic toys do not necessarily imply a better or happier society. In addition, we don't know which members of society have access to the gains of economic growth. More industrialization—particularly with the associated environmental costs—does not necessarily mean an increase in the well-being of citizens.

How then should we think about development? Is a developed country simply the opposite of a poor country? Is a developing country a rich country in the making? Box 1.1 presents the thoughts of development economists and practitioners on defining the term. Generally, they find it easier to agree on what constitutes the alleviation of poverty and meeting the

> **QUESTION FOR THOUGHT**
>
> Which definitions of development, box 1.1, do you find most compelling? Is there anything missing as compared to your own view of development? Can you identify ways in which the definition of development has changed over time?

basic needs of a population than on what represents the achievement of wealth or the satisfaction of material wants. This text looks at development as a process of meeting the basic human needs of the population and enhancing options for the allocation of economic resources both today and in the future to increase the choices citizens have in their daily lives. It pays particular attention to how much is produced and for whom, and it addresses the environmental sustainability of production for future generations.

Growth versus Development

From the definitions in box 1.1, we can see that most economists agree: development is far more than economic growth. It is useful, however, to clarify the difference between the two terms. Joseph Schumpeter distinguishes growth as a process of gradual change, with all quantities, such as wealth, savings, and population, increasing slowly and continuously; development is characterized as rapidly propelled by innovations.[8] Robert Lucas defines growth as the increase of income proportional to the increase of population, and development as the process whereby income increases more rapidly than population. In other words, growth does not presuppose technical change; development does.[9] For both Schumpeter and Lucas—economists of very different dispositions—development centrally engages the question of how **technological change** takes place in an economy. A key element in development is the management of technological change or how technology is used to transform the economic structure. This of course presupposes that technology is in scarce supply and its use has a price. In this sense, policy matters very much. Economic development is not simply driven by factor endowments or the quantity of resources but by how land, labor, and capital are combined in new ways to increase productivity and the choices available to a population.

New technologies require new ways of doing things. The leap from feudalism to early capitalism was propelled by technological changes—the introduction of the horse and plow as well as the three-field crop rotation system—that made an agri-

Box 1.1.   Development, Underdevelopment, and Growth: An Evolution of Definitions

WEBSTER'S DICTIONARY

"The act, process, or result of developing; the state of being developed; a gradual unfolding by which something is developed, a gradual advance or growth through progressive changes."

W. ARTHUR LEWIS (1954)

"The central fact of economic development is rapid capital accumulation, including knowledge and skills with capital."[10]

CELSO FURTADO (1964)

"Economic development, being fundamentally a process of incorporating and diffusing new techniques, implies changes of a structural nature in both the systems of production and distribution of income. The way in which these changes take place depends, to a large extent, on the degree of flexibility of the institutional framework within which the economy operates."[11]

P. BAUER AND B. YAMEY (1967)

"The widening of the range of alternatives open to people as consumers and producers."[12]

B. HIGGINS (1968)

"A discernible rise in total and in per capita income, widely diffused throughout occupational and income groups, continuing for at least two generations and becoming cumulative."[13]

THEOTONIO DOS SANTOS (1968)

"Development means advancement towards a certain well-defined general objective which corresponds to the specific condition of man and society or can be found in the most advanced societies of the modern world. The model is variously known as modern society, mass society and so on."[14]

DENIS GOULET (1971)

"Underdevelopment is shocking: the squalor, disease, unnecessary deaths, and hopelessness of it all! No man understands if underdevelopment remains for him a mere statistic reflecting low income, poor housing, premature mortality, or underdevelopment. The most empathetic observer can speak objectively about underdevelopment only after undergoing, personally or vicariously, the 'shock of underdevelopment.'"[15]

CHARLES K. WILBER (1973)

"Development itself is simply a means to the human ascent."[16]

DUDLEY SEERS (1972)

"The questions to ask about a country's development are therefore: what has been happening to poverty? What has been happening to unemployment? What has been happening to inequality? If all three of these have declined from high levels, then beyond doubt this has been a period of development for the country concerned."[17]

SIMON KUZNETS (1973)

"A country's economic growth may be defined as a long-term rise in capacity to supply increasingly diverse economic goods to its population, this growing capacity based on advancing technology and the institutional and ideological adjustments that it demands."[18]

JAMES J. LAMB (1973)

"If there is to be a possibility of choosing a human path so that all human beings may become the active subjects of their own history, it must begin at the level of new analysis. Development should be a struggle to create criteria, goals, and means for self-liberation from misery, inequity, and dependency in all forms. Crucially, it should be the process a people choose which heals them from historical trauma, and enables them to achieve a newness on their own terms."[19]

PAUL STREETEN (1979)

"A basic-needs approach to development starts with the objective of providing the opportunities for the full physical, mental, and social development of the human personality and then derives ways of achieving this objective."[20]

PETER J.A. HENRIOT (1981)

" 'Underdevelopment' is seen as the flip side of the coin of 'development.' It refers to the process whereby a country, characterized by subsistence agriculture and domestic production, progressively becomes integrated as a dependency into the world market through patterns of trade and/or investment."[21]

ORTHODOX PARADIGM (1980s)

"The view of the historical process contained in the orthodox paradigm is clear from this characterization: it is one in which developing societies move toward ever greater availability of goods and services for their citizens."[22]

WORLD COMMISSION ON ENVIRONMENT AND DEVELOPMENT (1987)

"Humanity has the ability to make development sustainable—to ensure that it meets the needs of the present without compromising the ability of future generations to meet their own needs. . . . **sustainable development** is not a fixed state of harmony, but rather a process of change in which the exploitation of resources, the directions of investment, the orientation of technological development, and institutional change are made consistent with future as well as present needs."[23]

GERALD M. MEIER (1995)

"Although requiring careful interpretation, perhaps the definition that would now gain widest approval is one that defines economic development as the process whereby the real per capita income of a country increases over a long period of time—subject to the stipulations that the number of people below an 'absolute poverty line' does not increase, and that the distribution of income does not become more unequal."[24]

(continued)

(continued)

AMARTYA SEN (1998)

"It is not hard to see why the concept of development is so essential in general. Economic problems do, of course, involve logistics issues, and a lot of it is undoubtedly 'engineering' of one kind or another. On the other hand, the success of all this has to be judged ultimately in terms of what it does to lives of human beings. The enhancement of living conditions must clearly be an essential—if not the essential—object of the entire economic exercise and that enhancement is an integral part of the concept of development."[25]

JOSEPH E. STIGLITZ (1998)

"It used to be that development was seen as simply increasing GDP. Today we have a broader set of objectives, including democratic development, egalitarian development, sustainable development, and higher living standards."[26]

cultural surplus possible. But like the transition into early capitalism, the contemporary process can be politically and socially tumultuous. Development policy can be viewed as the implementation of economic tools when political and social structures as well as economic institutions are rapidly changing. In contrast to the thrust of standard economic theory, where in principle we begin with the *ceteris paribus* condition, or "all else held constant," development policy is harder to carry out consistently due to simultaneous changes in a number of arenas. An economic policymaker in an industrialized country may be able to rely on a bit of automatic pilot under stable conditions; in the developing world, navigation is far more demanding with a variety of new challenges at each turn.

This text chronicles the development journey of Latin America. We begin by trying to understand the attempts of Latin American policymakers to promote growth and development in the region. Chapter 2 focuses on the engine of trade and Latin America's export performance in the late colonial and early independence periods. Chapter 3 looks at a growth strategy widely adopted in the region from roughly the 1950s through the 1980s: import substitution industrialization (ISI). We can see, in both cases, that the strategy centered largely on the problem of growth and made less progress in the arena of social and environmental change. In chapters 4 and 5 we discuss two unintended results of the development strategies adopted: high rates of inflation and increased vulnerability to macroeconomic shocks. The policy response to economic disequilibrium was to step back and rely more on markets and less on state intervention in the economy. Chapter 6 takes up this changed role of the state under the neoliberal model; chapters 7 and 8 look at its implications for international capital flows and trade. How industry and agriculture have fared under a more open, internationalized economic model is taken up in chapters 9 and 10. Although policies that transformed the structure of Latin American economies from closed to open markets have been largely successful in macroeconomic terms, the rest of our book explores some of the deficits in human and social development hindering sustainable growth.

Basic Human Needs versus Growth as Measures of Development

In addition to thinking about how economies change, we must raise the question of welfare and growth: who benefits from new economic opportunities? Technological change—new combinations of capital and labor to produce a surplus—does not address the general well-being of society. Does the process of economic development help the rich or the poor? A modest goal of development might be for a developed nation to meet the basic human needs of its population. Paul Streeten defines enhancing basic human needs as improving income earning opportunities for the poor, reforming public services that reach the poor, augmenting the flow of goods and services to meet the needs of all members of the household, and increasing the participation of the poor in the policy-making arena.[27] Streeten goes on to suggest why growth itself is not a good measure of economic development. Rather than generating the predicted theoretical results that growth would trickle down to the poor or that governments would extend benefits through progressive taxation or social services, Streeten argues that growth has been accompanied by increasing **dualism.** That is, when countries grow as measured by annual GDP growth rates, the rich often become richer and the poor more destitute in the process of change. We see the expansion of the modern, capitalist sector alongside a traditional, backward sector— two distinctly different worlds growing side by side. Dualism—the simultaneous existence of modern and traditional economies—complicates the policymaker's task. More important, if an economy magnetized by growth neglects the plight of the poor, people without assets are marginalized by the growth process and made even worse off. Those without land, capital, or education, like the poor peasant in feudal times who lost access to the agricultural commons, can be pushed into the margins of society. Without access to resources, the poor can become poorer. Their attempts to scrape together a subsistence existence often pressure the environment as desperation drives people to use up land or forests or dump open sewage or waste today without thought of tomorrow—for tomorrow holds little promise when they struggle with hunger or sickness.

For development economists such as Todaro, growth must be accompanied by a change in the economic and social rules of the game. Todaro defines development, in addition to raising people's living levels, as "creating conditions conducive to the growth of people's self-esteem through the establishment of social, political, and economic systems and institutions that promote human dignity and respect and increasing people's freedom by enlarging the range of their choice variables."[28] But this is a difficult task. As we will see in chapters 11–13, the social deficit in Latin America must be addressed to promote an equitable and sustainable development policy. As we investigate poverty in chapter 11, we will analyze ways of measuring human development including the **HDI** (human development index), which is a composite index comprising three indicators: life expectancy (representing a long and healthy life), educational attainment (representing knowledge), and real, inflation-adjusted GDP (representing a decent standard of living). Poverty and the associated social challenges of promoting education and health are discussed in chapters 12 and 13.

The United Nations, in its *Human Development Report,* suggests that a human development paradigm incorporates four elements—productivity, **equity,** sustainability, and **empowerment.** People must be enabled to increase their own productivity and participate as fully in the economy as their own talents allow. Gender barriers to achievement must be confronted. Economic growth is therefore a subset of human development models. To encourage fair outcomes, people must have access to equal opportunities. Economic and environmental sustainability is enhanced when all forms of capital—physical, human, and environmental—are replenished to promote access to opportunity, which must be for future generations as well as the present. Finally, development must be by people, not for them. People must participate fully in the decisions and processes that shape their lives for the benefits of genuine development.

Is There a Development Theory?

If the goal is to imitate industrial countries, is the road to a modern economy well marked by stages? Or are there different pathways to modernization? If countries are to progress economically and improve the quality of life for their inhabitants, what is the best way to do it? Is there a theory of economic development that is distinct from the economic theory we apply to our understanding of industrially advanced countries?

These are questions that economists have been grappling with for centuries. Adam Smith in *The Wealth of Nations* puzzled over how nations can best mobilize resources to produce the greatest wealth for their citizens. Box 1.2 highlights some of the conceptual guides that pioneers of development theory have offered in response to these questions. In contemporary times economists have struggled with the problem of understanding why some countries grow and others do not. This text does not assume that countries undergoing rapid economic change will necessarily follow the same pathway to achieve improvements in the quality of life. There may be different strategies to achieve the goal of raising the well-being of their citizens. The new global context for growth that Latin American economies face as we begin the twenty-first century requires a different set of policies from the ones used by the United States and Europe during the Industrial Revolution. A country's place in the region, its size, and its natural endowments may also condition its development strategy. Development theory and practice are dynamic, evolving over time.

If development is more than growth, development theory must explain not only how nations grow but also how their economic structures adapt to meet new challenges over time. If the modest goal is to meet basic needs, is growth in the developing world different from growth in industrialized countries? Are poor countries intrinsically different from rich ones? How? What are some of the defining characteristics? Can the same combination of economic tools be used to address the problems confronted by policymakers in less-industrialized as compared to more-industrialized countries? Should it be? Before we answer these questions, it will be useful to compare statistics of a Central American nation, Mexico, with those of the United States and a European nation, Spain, as a way of thinking about economic contrasts.

BOX 1.2.   PIONEERS IN ECONOMIC DEVELOPMENT

WALT W. ROSTOW (NEW YORK CITY 1916–)

Walt W. Rostow, an American economic historian, is known for his theory of the stages of economic growth. For Rostow, development was a linear process that began with traditional society, which then moved into the stage of "preconditions for take-off into self sustaining growth." The economy would then "take off," follow "the road to maturity," and finally hit "the age of high mass consumption." Rostow believed that the "takeoff" would be caused by an increase in investment, leading manufacturing sectors, and the existence of an institutional framework consistent with expansion.

PAUL ROSENSTEIN-RODAN (AUSTRIA-HUNGARY 1902–1985)

Development economist Paul Rosenstein-Rodan advanced the concept of balanced growth. He believed that in order to achieve sustained growth, an economy must develop various industries simultaneously, requiring a coordination of investment or a "big push." He was one of the first economists to emphasize market failure and the need for state intervention.

RAGNAR NURSKE (ESTONIA 1907–1959)

Ragnar Nurske, like Rosenstein-Rodan, advocated balanced growth and further elaborated upon his colleague's work. For Nurske, small market economies were victims of a vicious cycle hindering growth. The small size of the market was responsible for the limited amount of production and income, and for the perpetual poverty and stagnation. To break the cycle, an economy needed a "big push" coordinated by a government properly allocating domestic and foreign resources.

ALBERT OTTO HIRSCHMAN (GERMANY 1915–)

Economist Albert O. Hirschman provided a contrary thesis: the idea of unbalanced growth as the principal strategy for development. Building on the concept of development as a state of disequilibrium, Hirschman identified and attacked bottlenecks to growth. Like Nurske and Rosenstein-Rodan, he called for government intervention to achieve sustained growth. Yet Hirschman believed that decision making and entrepreneurial skills were scarce in underdeveloped economies. Governments should therefore concentrate this scarce resource in a few sectors rather than on the entire economy. Planners and policymakers would need to use "forward and backward linkages" between industries to attack the bottlenecks within an economy.

W. ARTHUR LEWIS (WEST INDIES 1915–1991)

W. Arthur Lewis, a Nobel Prize winner in economics in 1979, formulated a model in the 1950s known as "economic development with unlimited supplies of labor." Lewis's structure of the economy has a dualistic nature, with divisions into the subsistence sector and the capitalist sector. According to Lewis, underdeveloped economies are characterized by a large subsistence sector with surplus labor and a small capitalist sector, which contributes directly to a low savings rate. Economic growth occurs when there is an increase in the savings rate, which is made possible only when the capitalist sector expands and absorbs the surplus labor from the agricultural sector.

(continued)

(continued)

RAÚL PREBISCH (ARGENTINA 1901–1986)

Raúl Prebisch was an Argentine economist and former chairman of the UN Economic Commission for Latin America (ECLA). Prebisch is well known for the "Prebisch–Singer thesis," which claims that the export of primary products prevalent in developing countries results in a decline of terms of trade—the price of exports compared to the price of imports. There are two important implications of the thesis: first, that a decline in terms of trade results in the transfer of income from the periphery (the developing countries) to the center (the developed countries), and second, the periphery then needs to export more and more to be able to import the same quantities as before. Prebisch's pessimism on terms of trade was used to support import substitution industrialization policies in Latin America.

PAUL ALEXANDER BARAN (UKRAINE 1910–1964)

Paul Baran is known for his neo-Marxist view of development and for his contributions to the dependency school of thought. Although not completely agreeing with Marx, Baran used Marxist principles to locate the causes of underdevelopment. Countries suffer from low per capita income because the ruling classes fail to use productively the surplus extracted from peasants and wage laborers. Instead, they hold monopoly power over production and the political system. To break this monopoly power and achieve growth, a revolution must take place to replace the dominant class with one committed to social and economic development.

GUSTAV RANIS (GERMANY 1929–) AND JOHN FEI (1923–1996)

Gustav Ranis's early work focused on the economic development of Japan in the post-Meiji period and used it as a successful case of transition to modern growth. From there he began to focus on balanced growth and teamed up with another economist, John Fei, to further develop concepts used by Rostow and Lewis. For both Ranis and Fei, the process of "takeoff," as introduced by Rostow, would occur when the industrial sector absorbed both redundant labor and the disguised unemployed, using Lewis's process of absorption of surplus labor.

IRMA ADELMAN (ROMANIA 1930–)

Irma Adelman is well known for a forty-three-nation cross-country study done with Cynthia T. Morris. The results of the study show an increase in income inequality as poorer nations grow. Both women also provided a quantitative analysis of the effects of social and political factors on economic conditions. Prior to their work, social and political factors had been ignored. Adelman also worked with Sherman Robinson in the area of policy analysis and economic planning for developing countries and the application of computable general equilibrium models. Her current interests include land reform, trends in income distribution and poverty, agriculture-development-led industrialization, and the modeling of institutional change.

ANNE KRUEGER (NEW YORK 1934–)

Anne Krueger's work on foreign trade controls creating windfall gains, known as rent-seeking behavior, and its relationship to corruption in developing countries influenced a new theory in development—the new political economy. Her early work concentrated on international trade and payments theory. She is currently researching policy reform in developing countries, the political economy of policy formation, and U.S. economic policy toward developing countries.

(continued)

REFERENCES

Blaug, Mark. *Who's Who in Economics.* Cambridge, Mass.: MIT Press, 1986.
———. *Great Economists since Keynes: An Introduction to the Lives of One Hundred Modern Economists.* Totowa, N.J.: Barnes and Noble, 1985.
Blomstrom, Magnus, and Bjorn Hettne. *Development Theory in Transition: The Dependency Debate and Beyond, Third World Responses.* London: Zed, 1984.
Hunt, Diana. *Economic Theories of Development: An Analysis of Competing Paradigms.* Savage, Md.: Barnes and Noble Books, 1989.
Lewis, John P., and Valeriana Kallab, eds. *Development Strategies Reconsidered.* U.S.–Third World Policy Perspective, no. 5. Washington, D.C.: Overseas Development Council, 1986.
Meier, Gerald M. "From Colonial Economics to Development Economics." In *From Classical Economics to Development Economics.* New York: St. Martin's, 1994.
———, and Dudley Seers. *Pioneers in Development.* Oxford: Oxford University Press, 1984.
Toye, John. *Dilemmas of Development.* 2nd ed. Oxford: Blackwell, 1987.

From table 1.3 we note certain differences between a large industrial nation, the United States; a smaller industrial economy, Spain; and a largely developing economy, Mexico.[29] The size of the U.S. economy is more than ten times that of Mexico; you might be surprised to note, however, that Mexico's economy is about 7 percent larger than that of Spain. Inflation, a sign of underlying instability, is higher in Mexico than in the two industrial countries. More of the Mexican economy is engaged in industrial activity (28.8 percent) than in the United States (24.7 percent), where the service sector is dominant. As smaller economies, Mexico and Spain are more open to international trade, with imports and exports together accounting for more than 50 percent of GDP. In financial terms, we can see Mexico's greater vulnerability to international capital. Although U.S. financial markets provide 164.2 percent of domestic credit, in Mexico domestic intermediation is limited to just 28.8 percent. Mexico also lags considerably in indicators of scientific as well as basic infrastructure. The number of scientists and engineers per million inhabitants is 5.8 percent that of the United States; it has only 16.8 percent as many telephone lines to carry personal and commercial traffic. Health expenditures as a percentage of GDP are nearly one third lower than in the United States, a problem particularly for Mexico's poor. The highly unequal distribution of income in Mexico is one of the largest impediments to a sustainable development policy.

Although there is considerable diversity in terms of the performance of Latin

DATA EXERCISE

Consulting the sources for table 1.3, locate data for other Latin American countries. Select different country types (large and small) from different subregions. For example, consider the performance of Brazil, Ecuador, Guatemala, and Chile. How are they alike? Different?

Table 1.3.   Comparative Indicators of Economic Development

	United States	Spain	Mexico
Macroeconomic Indicators			
GDP (PPP value billions of U.S.$ at 2000 prices)	10,143.2	844.0	905.7
Inflation rate (consumer prices for 2000)	1.4	2.7	4.4
Unemployment (as % in 2000)	4.0	14.1	2.2
Gross domestic saving (as % of GDP for 1995)	15.0	22.0	19.0
Tax as a % of GDP	28.9	35.1	16.0
Sectoral Composition			
Agriculture (% GDP)	1.6	3.7	4.7
Industrial production growth rate (% GDP)	24.7	30.3	28.8
Services (% GDP)	73.7	66.0	66.5
Exports of goods and services (as % of GDP for 1999)	11.0	28.0	31.0
Imports of goods and services (as % of GDP for 1999)	13.0	28.0	32.0
Financial Sector			
Domestic credit provided by banking sector (as % of GDP for 1999)	164.2	108.9	28.8
Stock market (value traded as % of GDP for 1999)	202.9	124.9	7.5
Technology			
Scientists and engineers in R&D (per million people for 1987–1997)	3,676.0	1,305.0	214.0
Patenting activity for 2000	12,682.0	86.0	8.0
Communication, Transportation, and Pollution			
Telephone main lines (per 1,000 people for 1999)	664.0	410.0	112.0
Television sets (per 1,000 people for 1999)	844.0	547.0	267.0
Vehicles (per 1,000 people for 1995)	748.0	454.0	131.0
Carbon dioxide emissions (per capita metric tons for 1997)	20.1	6.6	4.0
Human Development Indicators			
Income distribution	(for 1997)	(for 1990)	(for 1996)
Lowest 20%	5.2	7.5	4.0
Second 20%	10.5	12.6	7.6
Third 20%	15.6	17.0	12.2
Fourth 20%	22.4	22.6	19.6
Highest 20%	48.3	40.3	56.7
Education expenditures, primary grade per student	6,043.0	3,267.0	863.0
Health (expenditures, private and public, as % of GDP for 1990–1998)	13.0	7.7	5.4
Total health expenditures per capita	4,373.0	1,749.0	452.0

Sources: IMF, *World Economic Outlook, 2002;* Central Intelligence Agency, *The World Fact Book,* available online at www.cia.gov; and World Bank, *World Development Indicators, 2001* (Washington, D.C.: World Bank, 2001), *The OECD Observer: OECD in Figures—Volume 2002 Supplement 1* (E-book PDF Format), www.oecd.org.

American nations on each of these indicators, comparing Mexico with Spain and the United States provides insight into some of the characteristics of economies in Latin America. As we proceed, we will see questions of macroeconomic stability, depth of markets, distributional issues, and the role of the state generating considerable controversy.

Challenges for Development Policy in Latin America

Developing countries must contend with a set of economic issues that make economic policy more difficult—and for a student perhaps more interesting—than traditional theory. Throughout this text we will analyze how these issues have been addressed in Latin America from its earliest economic history through contemporary times. It is useful to raise some of these challenges here, to help you begin to think about the dilemmas of economic policy making in the region. It is important to remember, however, that each of these challenges plays out differently in each country in Latin America; the diversity of experience is probably as great as the set of common problems.

INTERNAL VERSUS EXTERNAL MACROECONOMIC BALANCE

Developing countries, in large part because by definition they are capital poor, find themselves reliant on international capital to fuel the growth process. Unlike the United States (which until recently focused little on domestic economic policy effects on the international sector because they were relatively small), Latin American countries have had to weigh carefully the effects of changes in domestic macropolicy—traditional money supply and fiscal tools—against their effects on the external sector. There is a constant tension between internal and external balance. Lessons from economic history in Latin America will show that a one-sided focus on either the internal or the external sector results in imbalances and the deterioration of the economic plan. Integrating a nation into international capital markets raises important complexities. This may be done in the form of debt (as in the 1890s and 1970s) or through foreign direct investment in the economy, raising questions of multinational presence (such as in the control of United Fruit Company in Guatemala in the 1950s) or contemporary questions of international labor standards. Countries that orient themselves toward the international export economy—as in Chile through copper or in Ecuador through oil—may have to sacrifice domestic goals to maintain an exchange rate that is compatible with international market conditions. One response to the trade conundrum has been to pursue alternate trade regimes in the form of integration efforts such as the Central American Common Market (CACM) or the South American Common Market (Mercosur). We will be grappling with the need to achieve internal and external balance throughout this text.

Internationalization creates a wide range of opportunities, but it also introduces constraints in domestic policy making. For new entrepreneurs like Juan Navarro, it creates profit, but it may limit the relative well-being of the Lehman family. For now, remember that developing economies are especially sensitive to the internal versus external balance.

STABILITY VERSUS CHANGE: THE QUESTION OF TIMING

The process of development involves rapid structural change, yet economic agents like certainty. In traditional economic models we assume perfect information held by all agents. We know that divergence from the assumption of perfect information leads to inefficiencies in the market. How to handle economic agents' need for greater certainty and good information in an environment that is almost by definition (when it is working best) characterized by change is a challenge for policymakers in the developing world. Officials in Latin America must at once be agents of change, flexibly adapting to the dynamic needs of the economic transformation, while also acting as strict guardians of confidence and stability. The ability to walk this policy tightrope as both motivators and moderators of change often defines policy success. When governments fail to navigate and anchor the economy, they suffer a loss of confidence. Given rapid rates of change, past policy responses have often been volatile and unpredictable, creating uncertainty. Latin American governments have a smaller store of institutional credibility than, for example, the Bank of England or the U.S. Fed—where the big news might be a 0.25-percent increase in the interest rate and not the freezing of all bank accounts, the 30-percent devaluation of a currency, or the implementation of a currency peg. During Ismail Lehman's young life, for example, the Brazilian currency changed names five times. Confidence building in economic policy making is a long and slow process—one not easily achieved when the economic waters are rough and choppy. Students of Latin American economic policy always need to ask how the policy proposed is going to affect the confidence and long-run credibility of economic agents.

POLICY FOR WHOM?

Economic policy affects various groups within an economy differently. One of the fundamental challenges facing policymakers in Latin America is the deep divisions that exist in its socioeconomic structure. Latin America is characterized by high degrees of income inequality. There is a huge gap between the lives of Juan Navarro and Judith Yanira Viera. The goal is to promote not only growth but some form of equitable growth—quite a tall order. Income inequality introduces complications in the measurement of growth. If equality is important, the change in a poor person's income should carry roughly the same weight as that of a rich person. But given inequality, if a rich person earns twenty times more than a poor person, changes in the income of the wealthy receive twenty times the weight of changes in income of the poor in the national growth calcula-tion.[30] If growth is supposed to measure economic performance, even the meas-ures are far from the mark.

In many cases inequality is exacerbated by an ethnic and cultural mosaic of approaches to economic life. Traditional forms of social organization in indigenous communities may clash with the marketization of economic life. Gender also plays a key role in the assessment of policy outcomes. In a society often conditioned by traditional gender roles, policymakers sensitive to the gender divide must ask, for example, how accessible terms of credit or access to technology are to the widest range of citizens. Although these problems are not unimportant in policy making in more industrialized countries, the range of difference confronts the policymaker with hard choices. Women in Santiago, for example, may be well-educated, active economic contributors, whereas their sisters in the Altiplano live a far more tradi-tional life. In assessing policy in Latin America, do not neglect to ask: Policy for whom? Whose needs should policy be designed to meet? Judith Yanira Viera's? Or Juan Navarro's?

PRESENT VERSUS FUTURE VALUE: THE ENVIRONMENTAL DIMENSION

Promoting not only development but also **sustainable development**—or a strategy that leaves future generations as well-off as the present—may be unrealistic when more than half of a population lives on the verge of starvation or when inflation eats away at the meager earnings of the working poor. Policymakers in the developing world—like those anywhere—are constrained by political and financial capital. There are only so many things that can be done with limited energy and finances. Daily crises take precedence over long-term planning. This becomes quite evident in the environmental arena. The challenge becomes how not to forfeit future growth while confronting present dilemmas. Even in industrial market economies, charac-terized by less sensational economic twists and turns, it is hard enough to promote incentives for sustainable use of resources. Imagine the difficulties in a developing country. Enforcement of environmental laws in industrial economies, with stronger institutional and financial resources, is often lax or ineffective. Yet without an envi-ronmental sensitivity to the future, policy will not be sustainable over time. Bad choices today have costs tomorrow. Policy to promote rational environmental deci-sion making in Latin America must be carefully crafted—and perhaps supple-mented with external capital—for long-term investment in the future. Macro- and microeconomic policies must be assessed through environmental lenses to protect resources for future generations.

THE STATE AND THE MARKET: PROMOTING PARTNERSHIP

Who should be the primary development actor in the region? What should be the relative balance between the state and the market in promoting development in

Latin America? This question has framed much of the contemporary policy debate in the region. We will see that the pendulum has swung from a market-led to a state-dominated economy under ISI and bak to the market under neoliberalism. Social protest in the first years of the twenty-first century by those marginalized by growth forced a reevaluation of the belief in the return to the market. Whether or not you support a stronger role for the state in economic decision making may be conditioned by your view of the relative sophistication of economic institutions in the region. Irma Adelman and Cynthia Taft Morris, two highly respected development economists, suggest that the crucial factor affecting development is the effectiveness of economic institutions and how economic institutions mediate the way in which gains from growth are distributed.[31] Are the economic institutions—central banks, capital, land and labor markets, redistributive agents, and laws governing property rights—sufficiently strong to promote equitable and sustainable growth without much day-to-day state interference? If market institutions or the property code is weak, is policy intervention warranted? Defining where the state can and should supplement the activity of the market is an important element in crafting effective policy for development in Latin America.

Three broad schools of thought can be identified with respect to the role of the state in development policy.[32] During the 1950s and 1960s, the success of the socialist model in jump-starting industrialization in the Soviet Union led to a **planning model** that accorded a strong role to the state in promoting development. The economists within Latin America who broadly believed that state intervention was critical to promoting development were called **dependency** theorists. Since markets were viewed as incomplete and unable to send strong and accurate price signals to economic agents, the state was viewed as an essential vehicle to orchestrate the growth process. Without an interventionist state, markets alone would not spontaneously generate growth. State-run activity was seen as necessary in providing infrastructure, such as roads and railways, and public services in education and health. In addition, state activity was encouraged in the direct production of goods and services in which private initiative had failed. The state was also supposed to help to counterbalance the power of domestic and international elites. We will consider the extension of this model to Latin America in chapter 3 on import substitution industrialization. Today, the potential gains from globalization and international trade, the benefits of entrepreneurship and the profit motive, and the difficulties introduced by problems of accountability and enforcement have created a shift away from the planning model.

The second broad approach falls within the **institutionalist tradition.** Institutionalists accord a strong role to nonmarket institutions. In particular, institutionalists suggest that rather than relying solely on price signals, other forms of organization—judges, chieftains, priests, or community councils—may intervene to settle disputes arising from the conflict over scarce economic resources.[33] Economic problems must therefore be treated within the context of legal, social, and political systems. Economic outcomes were often determined as much by power as by price signals. As the wealthy would be better able to command resources, high degrees of inequality would bias development against the poor. For institutionalists, with a variety of factors influencing outcomes, development does not tend toward equilibrium but may be a bumpy and discontinuous process. As we will see in chapter 3, the planning model and dependency theorists as well as institutionalist thought informed the position of some of the structuralist thinkers and policymakers in Latin America. **Structuralists**—economists who believed that the particular structure of developing economies warranted a different policy approach—dominated regional policy from the 1940s through the 1970s. Neostructuralists suggest that the modern demands of global markets require a balancing hand of the state.

A third school of thought in development economics is the **neoclassical** tradition. Linked in part to the **Chicago School** of **orthodox** economic policies, it places the market at the center of the development equation. The orthodox key to development policy is in ensuring that economic agents face accurate price incentives without interference to make the best of all possible economic decisions. State-led activity in infrastructure and public services is seen to have a poor performance record. Well-intended short-term market interventions are argued to perpetrate unintended long-run misallocations of resources.[34] Strict neoclassical theorists therefore see a minimalist role for the state as a guarantor of rules and property rights and a provider of a limited array of public goods such as defense. The private sector, through the profit motive and Adam Smith's invisible hand, will generate the greatest good for all. Foreign trade and international prices should become the engine for growth. Under the leadership of Milton Friedman, the Chicago School was the principal articulator of the Pinochet model in Chile, and it broadly informs the neoliberal policies that have dominated development strategies in Latin America in the 1990s.

All development approaches do not necessarily fall into one of these three policy boxes. However, the three tend to define answers to the critical question: Is the market the best of all possible mechanisms to organize economic activity and promote growth, or is state intervention a necessary ingredient to development policy in Latin America? The planner would argue for the hand of the state to guide development policy, the institutionalist would suggest that mechanisms beyond the market are critical in determining economic outcomes, and the subscriber to the Chicago School would staunchly support market-based policies. As we proceed through the puzzle of development in Latin America, you will need to resolve for yourself the most beneficial mix of market, state, and complementary institutions to promote development in the region. We will address this question in chapter 6 as we take an in-depth look at the contemporary role of the state in development.

These five issues—external balance, credibility, distribution, environmental sustainability, and the role of the state—pervade our examination of development policy in the region and our treatment of contemporary issues. In chapters 2 and 3 we will see how they played out in early development theories in the region. Chapters 4 and 5 address two of the dramatic legacies of imbalances of past mistakes—hyperinflation and debt. Chapter 6 introduces the new economic model in the region and chapter 7 chronicles the return of Latin America to international capital markets. In chapter 8 we consider contemporary trade performance, and then we go on to analyze sources of industrial competitiveness as well as the potential of the agricultural sector in chapters 9 and 10, respectively. We will see the radical economic changes adopted by the region in the 1990s and evaluate their significant gains. But challenges remain. In chapter 11 we take up the problem of poverty, and in chapters 12 and 13 we assess educational and health systems in the region. Finally, although we pay attention to the environment throughout this text, in chapter 14 we look at environmental priorities in Latin America and suggest an agenda for action. We conclude in chapter 15 with an evaluation of the relative weight of the state and the market in addressing the challenges to a sustainable and equitable development strategy in Latin America.

Key Concepts

Chicago School	empowerment	planning model
dependency	equity	sustainable
development	growth	development
dualism	institutionalist tradition	technological change

Chapter Summary

Development: Definitions and Theory

- Development is a word not easily defined in the context of economic advancement. Questions arise as to what kinds of characteristics "developed" countries have or should have.
- A distinction exists between development and economic growth. Development usually presupposes technological change, and economic growth considers political and social factors.
- The goals of development extend beyond economic growth. These goals may include meeting basic human needs, increasing economic opportunities for the poor, empowering marginalized groups, and ensuring economic benefits for future generations.
- Economists have not been able to agree on a single theory of development. The development processes for less-developed nations are likely to differ from those followed by industrialized nations. Approaches to development will depend upon the location, size, and natural endowments of each country.
- Three schools of thought for development policy provide policy guides to development strategy, the planning model, the institutionalist tradition, and the Chicago School; each of these defines a degree to which the state should intervene in the development process and the extent to which the process should be left in the hands of the market.

Challenges in Development Policy in Latin America

Policymakers face five major challenges when designing development policy in Latin America. First, they must establish a delicate balance between the external sector and domestic macro policy. Second, they must be attentive to the changing nature of the global economic environment as well as preserve confidence and stability within their own economies. Third, to attain equitable growth, they must fashion policies to target different economic, ethnic, and gender groups. Fourth, their policies must balance the allocation of resources between meeting the needs of present as well as future generations. Finally, policymakers are faced with the challenge of deciding the extent to which each state should supplement the activities of its own market to facilitate equitable, sustainable development.

Notes

1. "Exxel's Shaky Empire," *BusinessWeek Online,* 24 September 2001.
2. "Exxel's Shaky Empire."
3. Excerpted from Monica Larner and Ian Katz, "It's Ronaldo's World," *Business-Week,* 22 June 1998, p. 204; and Alex Bellos, "Ronaldo's Fame Hasn't Hit Home," *Minneapolis Star Tribune,* 10 July 1998, p. 6c.
4. Calvin Sims, "A Web Entree for Peruvians without PCs," *New York Times,* 27 May 1996, sec. 1, p. 29.
5. "In the Gap and Sweatshop Labor in El Salvador," *NACLA Report on the Americas* 29, no. 4 (January–February 1996): 37.
6. Diana Jean Schemo, "Brazil Farmers Feel Squeezed by Tobacco Companies," *New York Times,* 6 April 1998. Online edition.
7. Harry S. Truman, inaugural address, January 20, 1949, in *Documents on American Foreign Relations* (Connecticut University Press, 1967), as quoted in *The Development Dictionary: A Guide to Knowledge as Power,* ed. Wolfgang Sachs (London: Zed, 1992), 2.
8. Schumpeter (1939), as presented in Paolo Sylos Labini, "The Classical Roots of Development Theory," in *Economic Development: Handbook of Comparative Economic Policies,* ed. Enzo Grilli and Dominick Salvatore (Westport, Conn.: Greenwood, 1994), 3.26. Paul Streeten, "From Growth to Basic Needs," in *Latin America's Economic Development: Institutionalist and Structuralist Perspectives,* ed. James L. Dietz and James H. Street (Boulder, Colo.: Rienner, 1987). Originally appeared in *Finance and Development* 16 (September 1979).
9. Lucas (1988), as presented in Sylos Labini, "The Classical Roots of Development Theory," 3.
10. W. Arthur Lewis, "Economic Development with Unlimited Supplies of Labour," *Manchester School* 22, no. 2 (1954). Reprinted in A. N. Agarwala and S. P. Singh, eds. *The Economics of Underdevelopment* (New York: Oxford University Press, 1963).
11. Celso Furtado, *Development and Underdevelopment,* trans. Ricardo W. de Aguiar and Eric Charles Drysdale (Berkeley: University of California Press, 1965), 47. (Originally published as *Dialectica do desenvolvimento, Rio de Janeiro* [Berkeley: University of California Press, 1964].)
12. P. Bauer and B. Yamey, *The Economics of Underdeveloped Countries* (New York: Cambridge University Press, 1967), 151.

13. B. Higgins, *Economic Development: Problems, Principles, and Policies* (New York: Norton, 1968), 148.

14. T. Dos Santos, "La crisis de la teoría del desarollo y las relaciones de dependencia en América Latina," *Boletin de CESO* 3 (1968). This article appeared in English as "The Crisis of Development Theory and the Problem of Dependence in Latin America," in *Underdevelopment and Development,* ed. H. Bernstein (Harmondsworth, U.K.: Penguin, 1973).

15. Denis Goulet, *The Cruel Choice: A New Concept in the Theory of Development* (New York: Atheneum, 1971), 23.

16. Charles K. Wilber, *The Political Economy of Development and Underdevelopment* (New York: Random House, 1973), 355.

17. Dudley Seers, "What Are We Trying to Measure?" *Journal of Development Studies* (April 1972).

18. Simon Kuznets, "Modern Economic Growth: Findings and Reflections," *American Economic Review* 63, no. 3 (June 1973): 247.

19. Kenneth P. Jameson and Charles K. Wilber, *Directions in Economic Development* (Notre Dame, Ind.: University of Notre Dame Press, 1979), 38. Originally in James J. Lamb, "The Third World and the Development Debate," *IDOC-North America,* January–February 1973, p. 20.

20. Paul Streeten, "A Basic Needs Approach to Economic Development," in Jameson and Wilber, *Directions,* 73.

21. Peter J. Henriot, "Development Alternatives: Problems, Strategies, Values," in *The Political Economy of Development and Underdevelopment,* 2nd ed., ed. Charles K. Wilber (New York: Random House, 1979), 11.

22. Jameson and Wilber, *Directions,* 7.

23. World Commission on Environment and Development, *Our Common Future* (Oxford: Oxford University Press, 1987), 8–9.

24. Gerald M. Meier, *Leading Issues in Economic Development,* 6th ed. (Oxford: Oxford University Press, 1995), 7.

25. Amartya Sen, "The Concept of Development," in *Handbook of Development Economics,* vol. 1 (Netherlands: North-Holland, 1988).

26. Boris Pleskovic and Joseph E. Stiglitz, eds., *Annual World Bank Conference on Development Economics, 1997* (Washington, D.C.: World Bank, 1998), 19.

27. Paul Streeten, "From Growth to Basic Needs."

28. Michael P. Todaro, *Economic Development,* 5th ed. (White Plains, N.Y.: Longman, 1994), 670.

29. If you would like to compare these three countries across a broader range of indicators, go to *The OECD Observer: OECD in Figures—Volume 2002 Supplement* 1 (E-book PDF Format).

30. Gerald K. Helleiner, "Toward a New Development Strategy," in *The Legacy of Raúl Prebisch,* ed. Enrique V. Iglesias (Washington, D.C.: Inter-American Development Bank, 1994), 178.

31. Irma Adelman and Cynthia Taft Morris, "Development History and Its Implications for Development Theory," *World Development* 25, no. 6 (1997): 831–40.

32. Karla Hoff, Avishay Braverman, and Joseph Stiglitz, "Introduction," in *The Economics of Rural Organization,* ed. Karla Hoff, Avishay Braverman, and Joseph Stiglitz (New York: Oxford University Press/World Bank, 1993).

33. Hoff, Braverman, and Stiglitz, "Introduction."

34. John Martinussen, *Society, State, and Market: A Guide to Competing Theories of Development* (London: Zed, 1997), 260.

CHAPTER TWO

HISTORICAL LEGACIES

Patterns of Unequal and Unstable Growth

Historical patterns of land distribution have left a legacy of high inequality in the region. *(Courtesy of the Inter-American Development Bank.)*

In *One Hundred Years of Solitude,* Colombian novelist Gabriel García Márquez warns us that Latin America recycles its past. To evaluate contemporary policy we must understand the historical legacies of the region. The economic history of Latin America, a continent with diverse national stories and richly textured social histories, is far more complicated and nuanced than this short chapter on historical legacies can ever hope to convey. Here we can only abstract some of the patterns shaping development in the region. Perhaps some of the questions raised in our study of contemporary policy in the region will motivate the serious student of Latin America to revisit the historical pattern of growth at another time.[1] Some questions we will consider include the following:

- What factors shape the growth patterns of countries?
- Why, despite relatively similar starting points, did Latin America fall behind the United States and Canada in terms of growth?
- What are the characteristics of primary product-led growth?
- What were the social forms of economic organization conditioning development patterns?
- What were the environmental implications of the early pattern of development in Latin America?

This chapter assumes the overwhelming challenge of putting contemporary development into a simplified historical framework. It explains how the colonial and early independence periods shaped later development problems by focusing on the inputs and outputs of production. This brief foray is designed to provide a context for policy making today. Like the Buendía family in the García Márquez novel, this chapter highlights the opportunities and the cyclical constraints in the development experience in Latin America.

THE PUZZLE OF COMPARATIVE GROWTH PATTERNS

What early patterns of economic organization in Latin America shaped later growth? Rather than a conventional time line, our discussion is organized around the inputs to development: availability of labor, capital, and technology to promote agricultural and industrial growth at home and abroad. How did available resources constrain and shape development? In table 2.1 we can see that in 1700, per capita gross domestic products (GDPs) in Mexico and the United States were roughly equal. As late as 1850, Argentina and Brazil enjoyed per capita GDPs higher than Canada's. Table 2.2 presents similar results based on a different study; by 1998 GDP per capita in the United States and Canada had risen to roughly five times that of Latin nations—despite starting out behind. Why did Latin America stagnate in the twentieth century while the United States and Canada surged ahead?

THINKING ABOUT INPUTS, OUTPUTS, AND ECONOMIC CHANGE

Economic development may be thought of as a process whereby the structure of the economy evolves to adapt to the changing needs of a growing population. Growth of

Table 2.1.   Historical per Capita Growth of GDP (per capita in 1985 U.S.$)

	1700	*1800*	*1850*	*1913*	*1989*
Argentina	NA	NA	874	2,377	3,880
Brazil	NA	738	901	700	4,241
Chile	NA	NA	484	1,685	5,355
Mexico	450	450	317	1,104	3,521
Peru	NA	NA	526	985	3,142
Canada	NA	NA	850	3,560	17,576
United States	490	807	1,394	4,854	18,317
		% of U.S. per Capita GDP			
Argentina	NA	NA	62.70	48.97	21.18
Brazil	NA	91.45	64.63	14.42	23.15
Chile	NA	NA	34.72	34.71	29.24
Mexico	91.84	55.76	22.74	22.74	19.22
Peru	NA	NA	37.73	20.29	17.15
Canada	NA	NA	60.98	73.34	95.95
United States	100.00	100.00	100.00	100.00	100.00

Source: Stanley Engerman and Kenneth Sokoloff, *Factor Endowments, Institutions and Differential Paths of Growth among New World Economies: A View from Economic Historians of the United States,* National Bureau of Economic Research Historical Paper no. 66 (Cambridge, Mass.: National Bureau of Economic Research, 1994).

output must outstrip population growth to improve the resources available to people. Population, or labor, constitutes one of the inputs of production. How is it organized and combined with other inputs to produce output? It is useful to think about the fundamentals shaping the structure of an economy. These in turn condition the economy's performance in meeting the requirements of society. Why do economies begin to produce certain goods? How do specializations evolve and change over time? One way to answer this is to consider the inputs available for production and the characteristics of the output market that define product demand. What inputs are available to be made into desired output? What technology is available—and who

Table 2.2.   Performance of Major Regions

	Population (millions)			*GDP (millions of 1990 U.S.$)*			*GDP per Capita (1990 U.S.$)*		
	1700	*1820*	*1998*	*1700*	*1820*	*1998*	*1700*	*1820*	*1998*
Western Europe	81	187	388	83,395	163,722	6,960,616	1,024	1,232	17,921
Eastern Europe and Russia	45	91	412	26,869	60,859	1,793,295	589	663	4,677
Western Offshoots (United States and Canada)	2	11	323	827	13,489	8,456,135	473	1,201	26,146
Latin America	12	21	507	6,371	14,120	2,941,610	529	665	5,795
Asia	402	710	3,516	229,507	411,242	12,534,571	571	622	11,675
Africa	61	74	760	24,400	31,010	1,039,408	400	418	1,368
World Total	603	1,041	5,908	371,369	694,442	33,725,635	615	667	5,709

Source: Angus Madisson, *The World Economy: A Millennial Perspective* (Paris, OECD, 2001 and www.theworld economy.org/statistics.htm).

Table 2.3.   Factors Shaping Patterns of Growth

Natural resources	Is the country resource abundant?
	Who owns resources?
Land	How is land distributed? Who decides who owns land?
	Are landholdings concentrated or spread out among small stakeholders?
	Are the claims or titles to landholdings clear?
	What is the quality of available land?
Labor resources	How abundant is labor?
	What is the skill level of workers?
	Do ethnic or racial divisions separate workers?
Financial capital	Is there a domestic surplus available for reinvestment?
	Do domestic investors find better returns at home or abroad?
	Is growth dependent on an external infusion of funds?
Technology	What is the technological base of the nation?
	Who controls the access to technology?
	Do international patents restrict the free flow of technology?
Policy environment	Is the driving force behind growth the market or the state?
	Is the policy inwardly oriented or open to the international economy?

controls it—to facilitate the process? Whose tastes and desires—local, international, rich, poor—are the target market? Looking at the factors affecting supply and demand will allow us to say something about the structure of an economy and to evaluate how policy was used historically to improve the responsiveness of an economy to the needs of its citizens. Table 2.3 summarizes some of these factors shaping patterns of growth.

What factors condition the menu of goods and services a country produces? Resources, raw materials, and the physical characteristics of land affect production possibilities. Is a country rich in natural resources? Is there a diversity of available resources? Or does the country rely on a limited number of natural commodities? Who owns resources and how they are distributed throughout the population both matter enormously. Asset ownership confers the ability to make a profit on the sale or use of that factor of production. Is the ownership of key resources concentrated in a small, powerful group, or is it evenly spread around the population? Do these assets—land or mines or timber or fish—generate a profit for the owners above and beyond subsistence needs? The development of a group of people with a profit or surplus above and beyond personal subsistence requirements creates an elite class of potential capitalists or investors. These capitalists can then reinvest the surplus to create new growth opportunities—or can send it out of the country to earn money elsewhere. If this pool of national capital falls short of domestic investment demand, the country finds itself dependent on international sources of funds for growth. The choices domestic elites make about where to invest their money also shape the available stock of technology employed in the production process. Investments in technological inputs may enhance the productivity of the labor force, or resources may be directed toward producing sophisticated products outside the reach of the common consumer. As we can see, land, capital, and labor—the primary inputs to production—help define the productive structure.

But this structure does not operate in a vacuum. Public policies fashion the productive environment. The legal structure defines property rights and social responsibilities. The policy environment may be shaped by a market philosophy limiting the sphere of government activity, or there may be a demand for the government to address collective needs or redress some of the imbalances created by economic growth. Furthermore, what a country produces, as well as how and by whom, is conditioned by what the rest of the world is doing. Borders are generally permeable to ideas, goods, services, and prices; countries view productive capabilities relative to the endowments and technological achievements of other nations. Relative advantage matters. A country's position in the international economic order also defines possible pathways to growth. A late-developing country may find that others have already cornered the market in a particular product or process. These supply characteristics of inputs, and production rules interact with demand. The most efficient producer of an undesired good goes broke. The characteristics of a product—how responsive people are to price changes, the number of substitutes, the frequency and size of purchase—as well as the internal and external market size for a country's tradable goods create the opportunity for profit.

Fundamental supply and demand conditions affect and are affected by macroeconomic variables. Supply constraints or excess demand may give rise to inflation; failure to capture a surplus for reinvestment may result in anemic or slow growth. Attempts to jump-start an economy may simply fuel inflation; policies to manipulate the exchange rate to gain competitive advantage may have unintended domestic effects. The macroeconomic environment therefore shapes the activity of producer and consumer in the market.

> **QUESTION FOR THOUGHT**
>
> Given this list of factors influencing growth, can you construct a story of the important factors shaping the pattern of growth in the country of your birth?

How have the supply conditions— land, labor, capital, and technological availability—interacted with the demand factors and the macroeconomic environment to condition historical growth in Latin America? What were the available resources? Who controlled them? What technology was available to the owners of resources? What were the rules of the market? How did demand for products from Latin America affect growth patterns? How and where were profits reinvested? Finding answers to these questions gives us a sense of the historical factors shaping growth in the region.

NATURAL ABUNDANCE: THE REWARDS OF THE EXTRACTIVE ECONOMY

In analyzing the importance of different factors of production in Latin American growth, we can see that exploitation of natural resources was at the heart of the colonial period of Latin American development. Latin America was resource rich. Exploration of the region was driven by the Spanish mercantilist search for silver and gold. The New World provided new opportunities for wealth in Europe. Monopoly control over mines and land in the New World was accorded through the ***encomienda*** system, with a share of the output, or ***repartida,*** owed in return. Under the encomienda system, rights to land were parceled out by the monarchy, with an associated portion of the profits to be shipped back to Europe. Labor, however, was scarce. In 1503 Queen Isabella of Spain "entrusted" the Indians to the landlords, requiring the heads of the estates, or ***caciques,*** to provide payment, protection, and instruction in the Christian faith in exchange for their services. Extractive activities also laid a toll on the local labor force to bring the silver and gold to Spain. Indigenous peoples were obliged to provide the labor for mining, and Indian populations were decimated by European diseases—smallpox, yellow fever, malaria, and bubonic plague. As indigenous communities were broken up in support of an emerging agricultural sector, the "biological holocaust," as some have called it,[2] claimed the lives of the large majority of the continent's indigenous population.

The Portuguese, given claim to Brazil by the Treaty of Tordesillas in 1494, were initially less driven by the search for precious metals. When the Portuguese arrived, they did not find and conquer the highly organized indigenous civilization of the Incas or the Mayans to lead them to a fabulous pot of silver or gold. Furthermore, with the indigenous population scattered throughout the vast Amazon, labor was a problem. Agriculture took hold before mining. The early import of African slaves solved labor shortages in the emerging sugar industry. The gold rush began in Minas Gerais, Brazil, in the late 1600s and continued through the middle 1700s, increasing Portuguese interest in the colony. But the relatively early development of Brazilian agriculture exerted a stabilizing influence on the early development pattern. As in the United States, importing slaves relieved the labor constraint in production.

Labor and Social Relations

The exploitation of indigenous labor supplies, the import of Africans, and European immigration radically changed the racial composition in the region. Around 1900, there were approximately twenty million Latin Americans, a regional population about equal to that of Great Britain and double that of the United States. The small national populations were seen as a constraint on development. Argentina and Brazil were the second and third most popular intercontinental destinations for European immigrants in the late 1800s and early 1900s, but they attracted only 20 percent of the immigration flow, compared to 60 percent for the United States.[3] As we can see in table 2.4, limited immigration flows set up different racial patterns in the region. In Spanish America, by 1935 blacks accounted for 13.3 percent of the population and Indians 50.4 percent; in Brazil, African Brazilians made up 35.5 percent of the population, surpassing the Indian population. Interestingly, slavery was abolished soon after independence in most Latin American nations, with little of the turmoil that accompanied the transition in the United States. Even in Brazil, where slavery lasted until 1888, racial integration has been more harmonious than in North America.

Table 2.4.   Racial Composition in New World Economies (percentages)

		White	Black	Indian
Spanish America	1570	1.3	2.5	96.3
	1650	6.3	9.3	84.4
	1825	18.0	22.5	59.5
	1935	35.5	13.3	50.4
Brazil	1570	2.4	3.5	94.1
	1650	7.4	13.7	78.9
	1825	23.4	55.6	21.0
	1935	41.0	35.5	23.0
United States and Canada	1570	0.2	0.2	99.6
	1650	12.0	2.2	85.8
	1825	79.6	16.7	3.7
	1935	89.4	8.9	1.4

Source: Stanley Engerman and Kenneth Sokoloff, *Factor Endowments, Institutions and Differential Paths of Growth among New World Economies: A View from Economic Historians of the United States,* National Bureau of Economic Research Historical Paper no. 66 (Cambridge, Mass.: National Bureau of Economic Research, 1994), table 3.

Differing racial patterns in Spanish America and Brazil as compared to the United States and Canada had a clear economic dimension. The production of export crops such as sugar and mining activities relied on imported slave labor and forced Indian labor. Although the U.S. South also solved its labor constraint through slavery, 80 percent of the population in the United States and Canada was white in 1825, whereas whites composed only between 20 and 25 percent of the population in Spanish America and Brazil. But this small white minority held extraordinary economic power. The small number of white Europeans in Latin America were granted property from the monarchies, whereas the bulk of the population were slaves or manual laborers without assets.[4] Income—derived from the ownership of assets—was highly unequal and tied to race from the start in Latin America. Mentally combine the data on per capita GDP in table 2.1 with our information about the small share of the white population. Since the per capita estimates are an average of the population, imagine how well the white European elite must have lived compared with the rest of the population.

Despite differences in the emphasis on mining and agricultural activity between Brazil and the rest of the region, early social relations in both the Spanish and the Portuguese colonies tended to be feudal. The traditional authority of the Catholic Church reinforced these social patterns. The *encomienda* system accorded property rights to a small number of landholders, concentrating ownership and crowding the indigenous and mestizo, or those of mixed heritage, onto less-productive land. This system of the *latifundia,* the feudal estates in Spanish Latin America, and the *fazenda* system in Brazil set up a highly unequal socioeconomic system. Furthermore, since internal markets were relatively small, the *latifundia* largely fostered an agricultural sector directed toward Europe. Profits were repatriated, leaving little at home for reinvestment. Those eking out a subsistence existence on the *minifundia,* the small parcels of land the peasants farmed, could do little more than feed themselves with their meager earnings. Compared to the United States, greater inequality in wealth, human capital, and political power likely promoted the evolution of weaker internal markets in Latin America.[5] The poor didn't have much money to buy goods. Elites retained positions of political power, blocking forces of economic change.

INDEPENDENCE: POLITICAL CHANGE WITHOUT ECONOMIC TRANSFORMATION

National independence, achieved regionally by 1822 (with the exception of Cuba and Puerto Rico), allowed for a change in rules regarding property rights and trade. However, the violence, lawlessness, and political turmoil of the period of independence reinforced the legitimacy of the *latifundia* as a form of political and economic organization. Lawlessness and revolt were common. People wanted security. The growing pains of nations—the difficulty in raising taxes and providing public services—highlighted the stability of the semifeudal system of social, political, and economic protection that the *coronel,* or the head of the *latifundia,* provided. The preservation of elite political interests, rather than institutional modernization favoring equal legal rights for citizens, may have had the effect of slowing growth in Latin America as compared to the North.[6]

The pattern of land tenure was perhaps unnecessarily concentrated. Although we can trace the roots of unequal land holdings to the colonial land tenure system, it is important to point out that after independence, new national governments missed opportunities to redistribute land from conquest, held by the former crowns, or further appropriated from indigenous communities. If political elites tied to this system had not been so powerful, fundamental land reforms would have created greater competition in the agricultural sector. With a larger number of small holdings, competitive pressure may have fostered activity in other sectors. Infrastructure, including transportation and energy, was also weak, making it difficult to set up local manufacturing. Thin domestic capital markets made it tough to raise money. In addition, local market demand was too small and product quality was too low for manufacturing to exploit the international sector. Political and economic structures did not help create a climate conducive to institutional change.

Contributing to the desire to maintain a political oligarchy was the fact that people were relatively well-off. By the end of the 1800s, the per capita income in Latin America was $245, at a time when it only reached $239 in North America.[7] Unfortunately for national growth, income was concentrated, and reinvestment of profits in entrepreneurial activity was limited. The lack of political change hindered economic transformation. Given the control of the political system by elites, it made little sense to venture into risky investments. The security of the *latifundia* system mitigated against economic risk taking. With political and economic gains consolidated, why embark on an investment likely to fail? As shown in table 2.5, nations tended to hitch their economic star to a dominant commodity. Coffee, sugar, bananas, and their associated feudal structures of production dominated the export profile. Exports were seen as the engine of economic growth.

Table 2.5.   Single Commodity Exports as a Percentage of Total Exports

Country	Commodity	% Total Exports, 1938
El Salvador	Coffee	92
Venezuela	Petroleum	92
Cuba	Sugar	78
Panama	Bananas	77
Bolivia	Tin	68
Guatemala	Coffee	66
Honduras	Bananas	64
Colombia	Coffee	61
Dominican	Sugar	60
Chile	Copper	52
Haiti	Coffee	51
Costa Rica	Coffee	49
Nicaragua	Coffee	47
Brazil	Coffee	45

Source: Simon Hanson, *Economic Development in Latin America* (Washington, D.C.: Inter-American Affairs Press, 1951), 107.

But there are winners and losers in the global export game. Despite the similarities in socioeconomic systems, there was a great deal of diversity in economic performance throughout the region, largely connected to the so-called **commodity lottery.**[8] The luck of natural endowment and agricultural advantage—copper and silver in Chile; sugar in Cuba; coffee in Brazil, Colombia, and Costa Rica; cattle in Argentina; bananas from Central America; guano in Peru—defined the winnings in the international export market. International demand had expanded with the opening of the British agricultural market and industrialization in Europe and the United States. In the late 1800s through the early 1900s, a broad consensus for agriculture-led export growth prevailed. This **golden age of primary product exports** in Latin America was facilitated by political stability; expansion of transportation systems encouraging geographic integration; improvements in capital markets promoting capital investment; and secondary industrialization taking place in textiles, food packing, and transportation in support of the agricultural sector. Latin America responded to new demands from the industrializing international system by providing raw materials, including key minerals and food.[9] In figure 2.1 we can see from the sampling of Latin American economies that they are more strongly export-oriented than those in Europe. During this period Central America began the export of bananas, and Brazil entered the rubber boom.

Single commodity exports, however, were an unstable basis for balanced, sustainable economic growth. Development policy was preoccupied with the needs of the export sector, with little attention to the links with domestic production and demand. In bananas, much of the production was dominated by U.S. multinationals functioning as an export **enclave** contributing little to the social development of the

Figure 2.1. Merchandise Exports to GDP, 1929

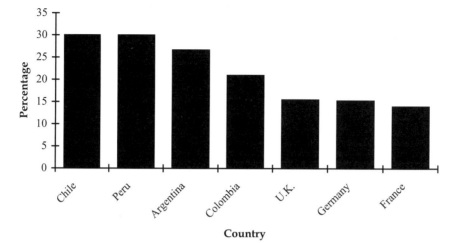

Source: Angus Maddison, "Economic and Social Conditions in Latin America, 1913–1950," in *Long-Term Trends in Latin American Economic Development,* ed. Miguel Urrutia (Washington, D.C.: IADB/Johns Hopkins University Press, 1991), table 1.13.

country. The powerful United Fruit Company, for example, did not pay a cent of tax to the Costa Rican government, and its workers bought goods imported duty-free in the company store.[10] Central American economies became inextricably linked to an international political economy beyond domestic control. As table 2.6 shows, the problems of single commodity exports were exacerbated by a high concentration in market destination. Demand for the product was essentially determined abroad. The old saying that when the United States sneezes, Latin America gets pneumonia began in this period.

The Giant Sucking Sound of Single Commodity Exports

Placing bets in the commodity casino leaves a country vulnerable to the vagaries of the international market. Commodity wealth—gold, silver, tin, coffee, rubber, sugar, oil—can exert negative effects on the process of development. With strong international demand for a particular product, national resources are sucked into the production or extraction of a single commodity. As international prices boom, so do profits at home. Given comparative advantage, it makes great sense to concentrate production on addressing international demand. Resources move to the hot sector, pressuring input prices throughout the economy. Dubbed the **Dutch disease** because of Holland's experience with natural gas, this produces a distorted pattern of development precariously predicated on the hot commodity. International resources are

Table 2.6.   Geographic Distribution of Latin American Exports, 1929 (% of total exports)

Country	United States	United Kingdom	France	Germany	Four Country Export Concentration
Cuba	76.6	12.6	2.1	0.8	92.1
Colombia	75.2	4.7	0.5	2.1	82.5
Mexico	60.7	10.3	3.9	7.6	82.5
Brazil	42.2	6.5	11.1	8.8	68.6
Peru	33.3	18.3	1.3	6.1	59.0
Venezuela	28.2	1.9	2.9	4.7	37.7
Chile	25.4	13.3	6.1	8.6	53.4
Uruguay	11.9	23.0	11.9	14.5	61.3
Argentina	9.8	32.3	7.1	10.0	59.2
Average	40.4	13.6	4.2	7.0	65.2

Source: Angus Maddison, "Economic and Social Conditions in Latin America, 1913–1950," in Miguel Urrutia, ed., *Long-Term Trends in Latin American Economic Development* (Washington, D.C.: IADB/Johns Hopkins University Press, 1991).

drawn in, overvaluing the exchange rate. When a commodity is booming, why should investors place their money in a less-lucrative outlet? If tin mining is returning high rates of profit, why invest in a dress factory? Furthermore, if profits from the boom are unequally distributed, a broader multiplier effect of the windfall income in industrial development is even less likely. Investors have monopoly or oligopoly control on the industry, and their continued access to profits or monopoly rents appears assured.

But booms have their busts. When commodity prices in the international market fall, they drag the whole economy down with them—because the commodity has essentially become the economy. For example, in 1920, sugar—a key crop for several Latin American nations—sold at 22.5 cents in May but fell to 3.625 cents by the end of that same year.[11] By the end of the decade it reached an all-time low of 1.471 cents—quite a fall for an economy revolving around "king sugar." Coffee prices dropped 40 percent from 1929 to 1930—a tough shock to national coffers.[12] Another dramatic example was the guano economy in Peru. Between 1840 and 1880, Peru's economy revolved around guano deposits left by birds on the island coasts off Peru, where it barely rains. When substitutes were found for this valued fertilizer, Peru's economy crashed. Because most governmental receipts came from taxes on foreign trade, the effect of a commodity bust was magnified by contractionary fiscal policy.

ENGEL'S LAW AND DECLINING TERMS OF TRADE

In addition to price volatility, concentration in primary product exports is also complicated by the nature of primary product demand. Primary products, particularly agricultural goods, are relatively price and income inelastic. If prices go up for coffee or sugar, as in a boom period, people cut back only slightly on their consumption of these perceived necessities. But on the downslope, with prices falling, people don't buy much more at a lower price. There is a limit to how much coffee or sugar people want. Furthermore, we observe a statistical relationship called **Engel's law,** that as income increases there is a weak increase in the demand for primary products. As world income grows and people become wealthier, the demand for agricultural products does not keep pace, unlike that for most manufactured products. If your country is an agricultural producer, compared to the rest of the world getting richer through manufactured goods, you stagnate. The net result of the **declining terms of trade** is that high rates of growth in the primary product sector may not be enough to act as a catalyst for development. **Export pessimism**—the belief that exports would not be the engine of growth—began to characterize the policymaker's mindset by the early 1900s.

The Effects of Weak Industrial Linkages and Abundant Foreign Capital

Despite declining terms of trade and export pessimism, primary product export growth is not necessarily a bad thing. Indeed, export growth can provide the opportunity for a country to capture a surplus, reinvest this profit, and reduce dependency on the agricultural product. In Latin America, however, weak links between export industries and the rest of the economy, labor shortages in the manufacturing sector, and foreign competition in industry depressed relative returns. Much export production exhibited characteristics of enclaves isolated from the rest of the economy. Linkages between commodity production and other products were relatively low. For example, coffee did not send signals back down the production chain for much in the way of capital necessary for production—a kind of **backward linkage**—nor did it generate the demand for new industries or products—a **forward linkage.** (The Starbucks coffee bar had yet to be developed!) Cattle ranching is an example of an industry that did contribute to forward linkages in leather processing and the shoe industry, but for the most part, commodity-led industrialization did not stimulate production in other sectors of the economy. In addition, with the notable exception of Argentina, immigration policies limited the labor market, creating shortages in the industrial sector. Ironically, compared to today, high-priced labor in Latin America made manufacturing costly. Domestic markets for financial capital were relatively weak, and foreign investment flowed to areas in which technological or capital constraints restricted entry of local firms.

Foreign capital was able to dominate large sectors of some economies. Tables 2.7–2.9 present data on foreign investment. Great Britain led the capital surge in Latin American in 1913 with 43.5 percent of the inflows. In Argentina about half of the capital was foreign owned, the bulk of it being British.[13] As a result of the strong inflow, we can see in table 2.8 that per capita foreign investment was much higher in Latin America than in Asian economies, tightening the link between Latin America and the rest of the world. The combination of high levels of foreign invest-

Mining projects such as this one in Bolivia have been a source of export revenues but also introduce questions of export price instability and declining terms of trade. *(Courtesy of Amanda McKown.)*

ment with commodity export economies tended to generate low returned value to the host economy, depressing possibilities for future growth.[14]

One notable exception to the weakness of domestic capital markets was the case of Brazil. It has been suggested that Brazilian coffee barons were able to underwrite the industrial base of São Paulo while continuing to expand coffee production. It is

Table 2.7.   Foreign Investment in Latin America, circa 1913

Creditor	Capital (in millions of U.S.$)	Percentage
Great Britain	3,700	43.5
France	1,200	14.1
Germany	900	10.6
United States	1,700	20.0
Others	1,000	11.8

Source: Werner Baer, "Lateinamerica und Westeuropa. Die Wirtschaftsbeziehungen bis zum Ende des Zweiten Weltriegs," in *Lateinamerica-Westeuropa-Vereinigte Staaten Ein atlantisches Dreieck,* ed. W. Grabendorff and R. Roett (Baden-Baden, 1985); cited in Walther L. Bernecker and Hans Werner Tobler, eds., *Development and Underdevelopment in America: Contrasts of Economic Growth in North and Latin America in Historical Perspective* (Berlin: Walter de Gruyter, 1993).

theorized that this took place because the coffee land was not suitable for agricultural diversification, and *fazendeiros* found themselves in the manufacturing sector in search of new profits.[15] Furthermore, coffee production itself needed so little in the way of reinvestment of surplus that profits were best placed outside the sector.[16] Table 2.9 illustrates the high rate of foreign investment as a percentage of GDP in the beginning of the century compared to later periods. When foreign capital was withdrawn during World War I, local financial systems were not sufficiently developed to intermediate capital needs. Reflecting the importance of external finance and trade, Argentina, for example, did not have a central bank until 1935. Instead, its monetary authority, the Caja de Conversión, was responsible for guaranteeing the external

Table 2.8.   Per Capita Net Foreign Capital Position, 1938

	Foreign Obligations (per capita)	Total Foreign Obligations (millions of U.S.$)
Chile	258	1,267
Argentina	230	3,154
Cuba	176	781
Uruguay	136	248
Venezuela	97	354
Mexico	93	1,759
Brazil	51	2,025
Peru	51	324
Colombia	37	320
China (including Manchuria)	3	1,787
India	11	3,441
Indochina	17	391
Indonesia	35	2,371
Korea (1941)	73	1,718
Malaya	164	695

Source: Angus Maddison, "Economic and Social Conditions in Latin America, 1913–1950," in Miguel Urrutia, ed., *Long-Term Trends in Latin American Economic Development* (Washington, D.C.: IDB/Johns Hopkins University Press, 1991), table 1.5.

Table 2.9.   Foreign Investment as a Percentage of GDP

	1900	1914	1929	1938	1950	1980	1990
Argentina	4.15	2.60	1.12	0.87	0.12	0.23	0.64
Brazil	2.55	2.96	0.92	0.70	0.18	0.32	0.36
Chile	1.88	2.11	1.56	1.63	0.49	0.27	0.40
Colombia	0.74	0.27	0.34	0.35	0.24	0.13	0.21
Mexico	1.55	1.83	1.28	0.79	0.17	0.23	0.32
Peru	1.78	1.21	0.64	0.46	0.22	0.32	0.48
Uruguay	3.14	1.62	0.67	0.59	0.18	NA	0.31
Venezuela	2.52	0.98	1.05	0.73	0.55	0.32	0.47
Average	2.29	1.70	0.95	0.77	0.27	0.26	0.40

Source: Alan Taylor, *Argentina and the World Capital Market: Saving, Investment and International Capital Mobility in the Twentieth Century,* National Bureau of Economic Research Working Paper no. 6302 (Cambridge, Mass.: National Bureau of Economic Research, 1997).

value of the currency, with no domestic lender of last resort in the system.[17] The role of foreign and domestic commercial lenders was also differentiated. Because international bankers dominated short-term, less risky portfolios, domestic institutions were left with longer-term loans in firms and real estate. When foreign banks pulled out, domestic institutions were not able to liquidate their assets quickly enough to respond to the capital shortage, and they could not respond to the needs of the local economy to finance the accumulation of physical capital.[18] International crises created local reverberations as money was withdrawn from Latin America to supplement European war chests.[19] Dependence on foreign capital has decreased over the course of the century, but vulnerability to the whims of the international capital market has remained a constant challenge for policymakers in the region.

Dependence on foreign capital also meant heightened exposure to financial collapse. Foreshadowing the debt crisis we will study in chapter 4, lending at the turn of the century was rapid, volatile, and heedless of institutional safeguards or appropriate accounting or monitoring procedures.[20] As high interest rates prior to the stock market crash of 1929 drew capital back to New York, Latin American projects were left underfunded. When markets crashed, commodity prices plunged worldwide, and protectionist barriers were erected, bringing the export engine to a grinding halt.

THE ENVIRONMENTAL DIMENSION

The environmental costs of an agricultural and extractive economy geared to export markets were substantial. Ecologically sustainable systems of communal agriculture had been practiced in Mesoamerica since at least 1500 B.C.E. The Spanish conquest succeeded in its goal of extracting natural riches and also destroyed ancient communal villages and practices.[21] After the mines were stripped, colonists cleared the land for agricultural crops. The introduction of sugar and coffee prompted vast ecological change, transforming the Central American region from subtropical forest to an agricultural export economy by clearing and planting, pushing the frontier, and exhausting the soil. Cattle were introduced, making further claims on land. Land held by the Catholic Church or publicly held Indian lands called *ejidos* came to be seen by liberal free market reformers as constraints on further development of the export economy. By 1880, every Central American country had titling laws granting coffee growers rights to land formerly held by Indian communities. Exports surged, but so did the devastation of indigenous groups. The confiscation of traditional lands led Indians to the ecologically more fragile mountains or lowlands, compounding environmental problems. When coffee estate owners faced labor shortages, the government forced communities to provide workers for the labor-intensive harvest through the *mandamiento* program, often under brutal working conditions. The expansion of banana production in the 1920s and 1930s increased pressure on the land and local food crops as firms dominated by multinationals competed with less powerful *campesinos* for the best high-nutrient soils.

Devastation was not limited to Central America. Brazilian B. F. Brandão provided one of the earliest accounts of environmental destruction in 1865 in this description of his youth on a Brazilian *fazenda:*

> At six o'clock in the morning the overseer forces the poor slave, still exhausted from the evening's labor, to rise from his rude bed and proceed to his work. The first assignment of the season is the chopping down of the forests for the next year's planting. . . . The next step is destruction of the large trees. . . . They set fire to the devastated jungle, and then they cut and stack the branches and smaller tree trunks which have escaped the fire . . . and could hinder development of the crop. . . . Centuries-old tree trunks which two months before had produced a cool, crisp atmosphere over a broad stretch of land, lie on the surface of a field ravaged by fire and covered with ashes, where the slaves are compelled to spend twelve hours under the hot sun of the equator, without a single tree to give them shelter.[22]

Initially trees were burned in a short-term effort to increase soil fertility; they were also felled because they were thought to compete with coffee for limited moisture.[23] Over time, the result was economic devastation.

In mining, industry, and some agricultural activities, local governments allowed control by foreign multinational firms. As characterized by Eduardo Galeano, Latin America's open veins of tin and copper poured into multinational coffers with little commitment to sustainable environmental policy. For example, a New York firm was granted a concession to mine in the Cerro de Pasco region of Peru's Central Andes. It constructed a network of roads, railroads, smelters, mining camps, hydroelectric plants, and haciendas to serve the mines; in 1922 it opened a smelter-refinery using timber, promoting deforestation, and polluting air and rivers with sulfuric acid and iron-zinc residues. Products were sold globally, but the devastation was local.

But foreign capital was not entirely to blame. In the 1940s Brazil's president expressed the following philosophy: "To conquer the land, tame the waters and subjugate the jungle, these have been our tasks. And in this centuries-old battle, we have won victory upon victory."[24] Resource-based growth was premised on taking advantage of the riches the land had to offer—at a clear cost to the environment. Even where an early consciousness of environmental protection existed, institutional resources for implementation were weak. The Brazilian government implemented a forest code in the 1930s, prohibiting deforestation along watercourses, limiting cutting on property, and protecting rare species. With limited financing, however, it was unenforceable.[25] Moreover, the demand for economic growth far outpaced environmental concerns.

THE ISOLATION OF THE WAR YEARS: A BLESSING IN DISGUISE?

World War I had a profoundly dislocating effect on Latin America. The fall of the gold standard fomented financial instability. Oil-producing countries such as Venezuela benefited, but the confusion surrounding world war masked fundamental structural changes taking place in the global economy. As advanced industrial products were developed, the value of agricultural trade declined. New products such as synthetics displaced traditional raw materials. The Great Depression exacerbated global commodity market instability, leaving the externally oriented development strategy without robust markets for products. Growing protectionism abroad further limited export potential. The terms of trade—what a country receives for its exports relative to what it pays for its imports—fell between 21 and 45 percent when international markets collapsed. International capital inflows to fuel industrial development virtually dried up by 1929.[26]

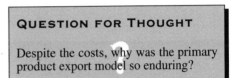

QUESTION FOR THOUGHT

Despite the costs, why was the primary product export model so enduring?

But there was a silver lining to this cloud. As a result of these external shocks to the trade-driven model, Latin America was forced to adjust. It turned inward, adopting a set of economic policies called import substitution industrialization, the subject of chapter 3, to address the cycle of instability and vulnerability it faced under the externally oriented commodity export model. Although import substitution industrialization was not the solution to the puzzle of Latin American development, new strategies to meet growing internal and external economic challenges were introduced. Unfortunately, as we will see in the following chapters, a changed focus toward internal growth did little to change the fundamental pattern of asset ownership, reinforcing the highly unequal pattern of growth in the region.[27]

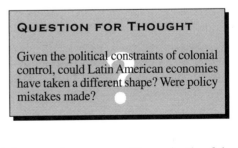

QUESTION FOR THOUGHT

Given the political constraints of colonial control, could Latin American economies have taken a different shape? Were policy mistakes made?

HISTORICAL LESSONS

To conclude our rapid tour of Latin American history, we have summarized some of the factors influencing growth in the region in table 2.10. Natural resource dependence; unequal distribution of land; and labor, capital, and technological constraints shaped early development outcomes. What kind of lessons can we draw about these historical factors affecting Latin American development? We need to be very careful about concluding too much about historical causality, especially given the diverse set of circumstances in the region, but we can point to several legacies.

First, the colonial pattern of asset distribution in the region was unequal and tied to privilege. The political and economic power of the elites was replicated in the postindependence period and set the stage for contemporary policy. Persistent and rising inequality is the defining characteristic of the region's growth. Because international capital was relatively abundant, it did not have to turn to enhancing labor productivity as a source of growth. The poor in Latin America were rarely invested in.

Second, as a region rich in resources and blessed with agricultural abundance, Latin America first pursued a strategy of export promotion. Financial resources were drawn to the dynamic export sectors, to the neglect of balanced development strategies. Colonial inequality was reinforced by the region's successful integration into the global economy and its access to relatively cheap external capital and technology. Government efforts were focused not on improving the local human capital of the peasants, but on attracting external capital as the source of growth.[28] The *encomienda* system established the pattern of depleting and not replenishing the region's human capital.[29]

Third, given the openness to world trade, Latin America was unable to protect itself from external shocks in the global economy. When the booms turned to busts and prices fell, entire economies suffered. The Great Depression and the war years produced dramatic structural changes in Latin America that forced a reconsideration of the externally oriented primary product model.

Finally, the commodity export model exacted a high environmental and social price. The dislocation of indigenous communities and devastation of the land had enduring consequences. Pristine forest lands and diverse wildlife fell under the reign of sugar-, coffee-, and banana-exporting economies. Contemporary patterns of social conflict in the region—for example, the recently ended civil war in Guatemala or the movements of the landless people in Brazil—certainly find their roots in the historical pattern of unequal land distribution.

The dissatisfaction arising from the externally oriented commodity export model gave rise to a new model of development in Latin America—import substitution industrialization. Import substitution industrialization located the answer to the question of why Latin America stagnated after the war period while Europe and the United States took off in the vulnerability of external orientation and dependency on international primary product markets. As we will see in the next chapter, the focus on substituting imports with a wider array of

Table 2.10. Stylized Characteristics of Early Growth Patterns in Latin America

Natural resources	Resource abundant although often dependent on a single commodity
	Ownership was concentrated
Land	Land was initially distributed by the crown
	Landholdings were concentrated in large *latifundia* or *fazendas*
	Peasants did not hold clear title to the land they worked
	Land quality varied; lack of title for peasants decreased incentive for investment
Labor resources	Labor in agriculture and mining was scarce; slavery and Indian labor in addition to immigration relieve the labor constraint
	Low skill level; little investment in education
Financial capital	Part of the surplus was returned to Europe; concentrated ownership protected high returns in agriculture and resources creating little incentive for domestic investment in industry
	During periods of commodity booms, high returns in agriculture make investment in industry risky
	A domestic savings gap creates international financial dependency
Technology	Weak science and technology infrastructure
	Domestic technological gaps begin to emerge between industrial North and Latin America
	Technological control by the North begins
Policy environment	The golden age of exports gives way to import substitution in the post–World War II period
	International protection through trading companies limited export options

domestically produced goods was envisioned as means of diversifying the source of growth and harnessing the emerging locomotive for growth: technological change.

Key Concepts

backward linkage	enclaves	golden age of primary
caciques	*encomienda*	product exports
commodity lottery	Engel's law	*latifundia*
declining terms of trade	export pessimism	*mandamiento*
Dutch disease	*fazenda*	*minifundia*
ejidos	forward linkage	*repartida*

Chapter Summary

Growth Patterns

- Growth patterns demonstrate that disparities between industrialized nations and Latin America did not develop until the twentieth century.
- Historical factors including natural endowments, the allocation of factors of production, policy frameworks, and macroeconomic environments have determined patters of growth in Latin America.

An Extractive Economy

- Throughout the colonial period, Spanish and Portuguese conquistadors extracted abundant natural resources from Latin America. Their exploitative techniques utilized indigenous populations and imported slaves under the *encomienda* decree as well as marginalizing peasants and concentrating land-holdings under the *latifundia* system. These methods resulted in elite control of capital and political power, a weak internal market, and severe income disparities.
- Despite the opportunity to alter rules of property rights during the period of Latin American independence, the political elite maintained concentrated land holdings. During the late 1800s and early 1900s, Latin America benefited from agricultural exports. The boom, however, was short lived. Development policy was driven by the export sector, ignoring domestic production, and demand for exports was determined abroad.
- Single commodity exports faced various problems. First, Dutch disease promoted unbalanced development. The dependence on any one export proved problematic when prices declined and revenues diminished. Secondly, single commodity exports of primary products faced inelastic demand—that is, despite significant increases in consumer income, the consumption of a particular product may only rise slightly. Growth potential is therefore limited.
- Thirdly, Latin American countries largely failed to reinvest profits from single commodity exports. Furthermore, the characteristics of export commodities did not stimulate production in other sectors of the economy through forward or backward linkages. The influx of foreign capital, moreover, failed to foster the development of domestic financial institutions.
- Finally, the environmental costs of single commodity exports in extractive economies were high. Conquistadors interrupted traditional agricultural practices and substituted environmentally unsustainable methods. World War I and the Great Depression forced Latin America to address the cycle of instability and vulnerability it faced under the externally oriented export model and to decrease its dependence on single commodity exports.

Notes

1. Bradford E. Burns, ed., *Latin America: Conflict and Creation: A Historical Reader* (Englewood Cliffs, N.J.: Prentice Hall, 1992); and Benjamin Keen, *Latin American Civilization,* 3rd ed. (Boston: Houghton Mifflin, 1974) are suggested starting points. Even a few hours dabbling in these readers will help capture the rich and complex regional history.

2. See, for example, Bill Weinberg, *War on the Land: Ecology and Politics in Central America* (Atlantic Highlands, N.J.: Zed, 1991).

3. Colin M. Lewis, "Industry in Latin America," in *Dependency and Development in Latin America,* ed. Fernando Henrique Cardoso and Enzo Faletto (Berkeley: University of California Press, 1979).

4. Stanley Engerman and Kenneth Sokoloff, *Factor Endowments, Institutions, and Differential Paths of Growth among New World Economies: A View from Economic Historians of the United States,* National Bureau of Economic Research Historical Paper no. 66 (Cambridge, Mass.: NBER, 1994).

5. Engerman and Sokoloff, *Factor Endowments,* 30.

6. John Coatsworth, "Notes on the Comparative Economic History of Latin America and the United States," in *Development and Underdevelopment in America,* ed. Walther Bernecker and Hans Werner Tobler (New York: Walter de Gruyter, 1993).

7. There is some inconsistency in the historical data. Although estimates of Latin American income at the time were almost certainly biased upward, as Bulmer-Thomas notes, "Latin America's relatively privileged status within what is now the third world at the end of the 18th century is difficult to dispute" (Victor Bulmer-Thomas, *The Economic History of Latin America since Independence* [New York: Cambridge University Press, 1994], 27).

8. Victor Bulmer-Thomas uses the term "commodity lottery" to describe the effects of export orientation in the 1800s. Much of the discussion of economic history in this chapter relies on Bulmer-Thomas's illuminating text.

9. Rosemary Thorp, *Progress, Poverty, and Exclusion: An Economic History of Latin America in the 20th Century* (Baltimore: Johns Hopkins University Press/Inter-American Development Bank (IADB), 1998), 49.

10. Daniel Farber, *Environment under Fire* (New York: Monthly Review Press, 1993), 34.

11. Simon Hanson, *Economic Development in Latin America* (Washington, D.C.: Inter-American Affairs Press, 1951), 107.

12. Hanson, *Economic Development,* 106.

13. Gerardo della Paolera and Alan Taylor, *Finance and Development in an Emerging Market: Argentina in the Interwar Period,* National Bureau of Economic Research Working Paper Series no. 6236 (Cambridge, Mass.: NBER, 1997), 8.

14. Thorp, *Progress,* 69.

15. Fernando Henrique Cardoso and Ernesto Faletto, in Lewis, "Industry in Latin America," 295.

16. Thorp, *Progress,* 56.

17. Della Paolera and Taylor, *Finance,* 12.

18. Della Paolera and Taylor, *Finance,* 18.

19. Thorp, *Progress,* 64.

20. Thorp, *Progress,* 104.

21. Farber, *Environment under Fire,* 15.

22. Burns, *Latin America,* 40.

23. Thorp, *Progress,* 57.

24. John Ryan, "The Shrinking Forest," *NACLA Report on the Americas* 25, no. 2 (September 1991): 19.

25. Thorp, *Progress,* 21.

26. Vittorio Corbo, "Economic Policies and Performance in Latin America," in *Economic Development: Handbook of Comparative Economic Policies,* ed. Enzo Grilli and Dominick Salvatore (Westport, Conn.: Greenwood, 1994), 299.

27. Thorp, *Progress,* 6.

28. Coatsworth, "Comparative Economic History," 24.

29. Timothy Yeager, "Encomienda or Slavery? The Spanish Crown's Choice of Labor Organization in Sixteenth-Century Spanish America," *Journal of Economic History* 55, no. 4 (December 1995).

CHAPTER THREE

IMPORT SUBSTITUTION INDUSTRIALIZATION

Looking Inward for the Source of Economic Growth

Many of the state-led investments under import substitution industrialization were in large-scale industries such as petrochemicals. *(Courtesy of the Inter-American Development Bank.)*

At the beginning of the twentieth century Argentina was one of the world's wealthiest nations. Why did Buenos Aires's elegant and luxurious buildings begin to seem locked in time as other nations modernized? Why did much of Latin America, despite its rich natural resources, experience slow growth? The export-led model discussed in chapter 2 did not deliver the anticipated growth. Distribution also had not improved. Why were the peasant *campesinos* stuck in a cycle of poverty? Emerging from the depression and the world wars, Latin America lagged behind its northern hemispheric neighbors. Once behind international competitors, how could Latin American nations ever hope to catch up?

Hoping to answer these questions, Latin American policymakers compared the performance of the region with that of North America and Europe; they also looked with interest at the takeoff of the Soviet Union. Two answers to the puzzle of slow growth emerged: first, an explanation for Latin America's falling behind and, second, a prescription for what to do about it. Political economists such as Paul Baran and Andre Gundar Frank suggested that Latin America was not falling behind but was being *pushed* back by the exploitative development process in the powerful industrial countries. Raúl Prebisch and those at the Economic Commission for Latin America and the Caribbean (ECLAC) defined the development problem as the need to promote growth in the face of an international system controlled by the center countries. This chapter explores these tools of inward-looking development in the policy of **import substitution industrialization** (ISI). It treats the role of the state as a developmental actor and introduces the exchange rate and trade tools used to promote industrialization. It concludes by evaluating the performance of import substitution industrialization as an answer to the puzzle of how to promote development in Latin America. The following questions form the core of our investigation:

- How did theorists make sense of Latin America's declining position in the world economy?
- How did the theory of import substitution industrialization propose to overcome the constraints on Latin American economic development?
- What were the key elements in the ISI toolbox?
- Was the approach successful in practice?

Understanding import substitution industrialization is an important step in unraveling the puzzle of Latin American development. It gives us a sense of the historical backdrop to contemporary policy and also locates one end of the policy spectrum with respect to the role of the state in development against which we can evaluate current practices.

DEPENDENCY THEORY: AN EXPLANATION FOR BACKWARDNESS

For some analysts, answering the question of why some nations were growing and others were stagnating required looking not at countries in isolation, as individual plants in a garden, but rather at how countries interacted with each other in the

Box 3.1.   Raúl Prebisch

The Argentine economist Raúl Prebisch was born in 1901 in the town of Tucuman.[1] He was strongly influential in the development of Latin American economic policy, and his contributions to development economics broke with the neoclassical. Although later criticized, his views and ideas questioned the extent to which the free market and free trade could solve the problem of underdevelopment.

Prebisch was educated at the University of Buenos Aires,[2] and during the 1920s he worked as a statistician for the Sociedad Rural, a stockbreeder's association.[3] Toward the beginning of his career, Prebisch believed in neoclassical economics, but the Great Depression and the writings of economist John Maynard Keynes shattered his faith in the free trade model.[4] Prebisch began to formulate different theoretical views in the early 1940s. This shift was first manifested in *The Economic Development of Latin America and Its Principal Problem,* written in 1949.[5] By this time Prebisch had served as director general of the Argentine Central Bank (1935–1943) and had witnessed the devastating effects of the depression on Argentina, which suffered from falling prices and debt payment difficulties. His 1949 manifesto reflected the effect of these external influences on economic development.

Prebisch divided the world in two, labeling one part the center and the other, the periphery. The center referred to advanced economies, producing primarily industrial goods; the periphery included developing countries, producers of primary products. Prebisch defined a skewed relationship between the two, with the center gaining at the expense of the periphery. For Prebisch, productivity gains in the North (the center) were translated into rising wages, not falling prices, due to the market power of business and unions. In the South (the periphery), surplus labor kept wages low, and slow productivity growth in agriculture and mining acted as a drag on the economy.[6] The unequal distribution of economic gains was due primarily to **declining terms of trade,** as developing countries would have to export more and more to be able to import the same quantities as before. It is clear that by this point Prebisch rejected the idea that comparative advantage was the answer to growth for developing countries and opted for other policy prescriptions.

In 1948, the UN Economic Commission for Latin America was created; Prebisch became its influential chairman in 1949.[7] Prebisch's diagnosis for the causes of underdevelopment led him to advocate what is known as import substitution industrialization (ISI). From 1964 to 1969, Prebisch was the secretary-general of the UN Conference on Trade and Development (UNCTAD).[8] During this time period, Prebisch put aside his theoretical thinking and formulated policies that were later ignored by both the developed and developing world. When Prebisch returned to his theoretical endeavors after the UNCTAD years, he suggested that a post-ISI policy was required, including removing protection from certain industries and encouraging nontraditional exports. He pointed to the need to develop internal savings to decrease reliance on external debt, suggested institutional changes in the labor market and financial sector, and advised budgetary reforms to consolidate change in Latin America.[9]

international system. Proponents of **dependency theory** postulated that a country did not thrive or falter simply because of its own national endowments. Rather, progress could be attributed to the power it had to set the rules of the international economic game. Center countries, or the industrialized countries, defined the rules; the periphery, or developing countries, were pawns in the international pursuit of profit. As dependency theorist Andre Gundar Frank postulated, underdeveloped countries were not developed countries in the making; rather, industrial countries had caused underdevelopment in other nations in the process of economic expansion. For Frank, underdevelopment was generated by the same historical process that produced economic development: the march of capitalism.[10] Industrialized countries had access to cheap inputs for growth through the extraction of resources, the export of minerals, and the exploitation of cheap labor in the underdeveloped world. Rich countries became rich by making other countries poor.

The owners of the resources—the wealthy in the underdeveloped region— benefited from the international market. According to dependency theorist Paul Baran, local elites formed alliances with international capitalists, hindering long-term, dynamic growth in favor of short-term profits. Baran pointed to the feudal coherence of the *latifundia* system and the monopolistic market structure as impediments to vigorous long-run growth.[11] A social glue bonding local and international elites cemented economic privilege for the upper class. Those with power had no interest in sharing it. Relatively concentrated markets weakened competitive pressures. For Baran and for Frank, while the periphery was tied to the center, there was no possibility of sustainable growth. As long as traditional elites remained in power, periphery countries would be shackled to center country interests. Revolution, therefore, was in order.

Other theorists, such as Fernando Henrique Cardoso and Enzo Faletto, disagreed with the revolutionary prescription. Although concurring with the assessment that the center countries controlled the dynamic of growth, Cardoso and Faletto argued that autonomous development was indeed possible within the periphery. It would, however, involve an active state policy to counterbalance the greedy hand of the international market. A powerful state acting in the national interest could counteract the strength of local and international economic elites to promote genuine development in the periphery.

FROM DEPENDENCY THEORY TO DEVELOPMENT POLICY: ECLA AND THE STRUCTURALIST SCHOOL

The dependency theorists' critique of the international economic system informed but did not completely define the position of the **structuralists** at the United Nations Economic Commission for Latin America (ECLA).[12] Under the leadership of Raúl Prebisch, ECLA analysts looked at the disappointing economic performance of Latin America in the first half of the century, focusing on the volatility of primary product exports, and the progressive difficulty of paying for more technologically sophisticated (and expensive) products with the limited agricultural returns.[13] Technological progress was controlled by the powerful center-industrialized countries and spread slowly into the periphery. ECLA researchers in the 1950s were also fascinated by a seeming correlation between the interruption of normal trade patterns with the industrialized countries during the war periods and accompanying robust internal growth in the Latin America region. Isolation from the international system apparently helped growth at home.

In part the disadvantaged position of periphery countries in the international system derived from the kind of goods they offered. Developing countries principally traded primary products, such as raw materials and agricultural goods, for more technologically advanced products in the international arena. Within this unequal framework, they faced what was seen as declining terms of trade for their products. There are only so many bananas that people want to eat or so much coffee that they can drink. Given the low income elasticity for agricultural products, as the global economy grows, the relative demand for primary products declines. Instead, rewards tend to accrue to those engaged in technological entrepreneurship. Technological sophistication adds value to a good, increasing its market price well beyond the cost of basic inputs. Declining terms of trade for primary products reflected the argument that as the prices of sophisticated goods rose, developing countries would need to export more and more oranges or wheat to pay for the more expensive technological machinery. Without mastering technology, countries had little hope of advancement.

In addition to the position that all goods do not generate equal rewards, structuralists also offered a view contrary to that of traditional economists on how economies functioned. Challenging the tenets of neoclassical economic theory, which assumes that rational, self-interested profit maximizers operating in open and competitive international markets will produce the greatest good for all, structuralists argued that the economy was shaped by power and politics. For the structuralists, economic activity is conditioned by interest-group politics. Markets in Latin America are controlled by concentrated oligopolies in which firms are price makers and elites establish patterns of consumption. Powerful advertising conglomerates shape global tastes; elites tend to demand sophisticated goods produced by industrial economies. Importing these items would do little to spur local growth. The promises of trickle-down economics hold no magic for the masses of the poor in the developing world. In the structuralist's eyes, the development process is not a movement toward equilibrium but rather is driven by imbalances and tension. Although the neoclassical model predicts benefits for poor countries from international trade, structuralists contend that international trade exacerbates inequality between and within nations because those countries and companies with control set the rules of the game in their favor. For the structuralist, the neoclassical model does not conform to the hard, cold facts of the international economy.

From Structuralism to Import Substitution Industrialization

The arguments of the dependency theorists and the structuralists shaped a policy package widely adopted in Latin America and known as import substitution industrialization. Perceiving the international game as stacked against them and with multiple external shocks repeatedly destabilizing the economy, Latin American policymakers turned inward to promote internal sources of

QUESTION FOR THOUGHT

Are the characteristics of Latin American economies as described by the dependency theorists and the structuralists consistent with the historical view of development portrayed in chapter 2? Are there pieces missing or overstated?

economic growth. Instead of relying on the international economy as the engine of growth, ISI policies sought to develop industries in a protected environment. The goal was to create industries capable of producing substitutes for expensive imports while simultaneously promoting industrial growth and the expansion of internal economies. The notion was that ISI would induce a process of learning driven by exposure to new ideas and processes that would dynamically spill over into the whole economy.[14] Raúl Prebisch and ECLA structuralists placed the role of technological change at the center of the development process and identified a strong role for the state in promoting national technological capabilities.[15] Without mastering technological processes, developing countries had no chance to catch up. The only economic actor strong enough to counterbalance the weight of multinational corporations was the state.

The strategy of import substitution industrialization was informed by Albert Hirschman's concepts of bottlenecks and linkages. For Hirschman, imbalances in the system, such as supply shocks and bottlenecks, were central to development as signals for investment.[16] Hirschman characterized the development process as a bottle with a thin neck. Inputs—land, labor, capital—were constrained from freely flowing from the bottle by the constricting neck of scarce complementary factors such as technology, infrastructure, or entrepreneurial capital. If the state could break the bottlenecks in crucial industries, resources would flow back up the production chain, stimulating the demand for intermediate inputs, or they would flow forward from consumption patterns to create demand for new products. Therefore, by promoting a steel sector, for example, **backward linkages** such as those to the iron ore and smelters would stimulate the growth of these supplier industries while **forward linkages** would stimulate the auto or machine industries. If the state could target those industries with the largest backward and forward linkages, it could act as an engine of development.

A strong state was critical to the structuralist program. ISI theorists pointed to a simple fact: if the market could work on its own, why had it not been successful in promoting growth in Latin America? **Market failure** to produce sustainable growth provided the rationale for state intervention. Given the weak private sector and the large economies of scale attached to industrial endeavors, an active state was viewed as a necessary complement to the market economy.[17] The ability of the state to deliver on public project investments contributed to the perceived need of governments to also meet the demand for social projects. This emanated from the highly unequal income distribution in Latin America.

The political demands of populism, of attending to the broad needs of the domestic population in the name of social peace, were consistent with the economic theory of import substitution industrialization. Populism drew on the charismatic power of leaders such as Juan Perón of Argentina or Getulio Vargas of Brazil to mobilize support within labor and industrial elites in the service of a nationalist development strategy. Traditional populist strategies encouraged support for a developmentalist model to meet the changing needs of society without explosive class conflict. By co-opting key labor and industrial groups into the quest for change, support for interventionist policies could be maintained. **Economic populism,** a term applied to the developmental strategies of the 1950s,

1960s, and 1970s, emphasized growth and redistribution of income to the neglect of internal and external constraints. That is, as long as financing was available, the state kept attempting to buy off each group in the conflictual process of development. Labor, politically powerful, was given strong protection under the law. Industrialists were favored with development schemes. State-led strategies to reduce poverty and promote infrastructure were pursued to keep local political leaders happy. But constraints on development—inflation, fiscal deficits, external imbalances—were often ignored until it was too late and crisis erupted.[18] Political demands to moderate the distributional tensions of development were consistent with the state-led ISI model.

THE ISI TOOLBOX

Import substitution industrialization relied on a variety of economic tools to achieve its aim. The toolbox can be broken down into three categories: active industrial policy, protective international instruments, and accommodationist fiscal and monetary policy complemented by a careful program of transnational participation. It is important to note that although these tools were at the disposal of all policymakers in the region, they were applied in varying degrees in each country. We will discuss these three broad tools in turn.

Active Industrial Policy: The Role of SOEs

Industrial policy was anchored in the formation of state-owned enterprises (SOEs) throughout the region. Under the assumption that the state was the only able domestic actor with the resources to produce in relatively underdeveloped markets, state firms were formed in a wide range of heavy industries, including oil, petrochemicals, telecommunications, steel, and aircraft. In some cases these enterprises were wholly owned by the state, and in others they operated as mixed enterprises, incorporating state and private capital. State firms had access to public funds for investment, research, and development. Backed by sovereign guarantees, they also had easier access to international financial markets to borrow for large development projects. State ministries could assist in the negotiation of international technology transfer packages to jump-start production. Such firms had the resources to hire some of the brightest national scientists, engineers, and managers to run operations. Additionally, the pressures of producing initial annual profits were relieved as state firms were able to extend their time horizon for investment returns.

Although public enterprise status held many advantages, there were also restrictions. Hiring and pay scales were subject to national standards, sometimes placing a ceiling on the pay for skilled labor. State firms were subject to the whims of politicians and often became agencies for employing large numbers of constituents. Furthermore, the services of industries in basic infrastructure, such as the electrical or telecommunications sectors, were often underpriced to provide cheap inputs to stimulate the growth of the private sector. Cheap inputs allowed for a local manufacturing boom; however, underpricing electricity or phone service led to losses that were absorbed by the SOEs. As resources became increasingly constrained, underpricing also resulted in underinvestment over time. Because firms were carrying losses, they couldn't afford to expand to meet the demand.

Despite the difficulties that state-owned enterprises confronted, they proliferated rapidly from the 1950s to the 1970s in Latin America. In table 3.1 we see what types of industries were most subject to state ownership and ISI policies in the case of Brazil. We see that high rates of state ownership existed particularly in industries that required significant investment, such as public goods enjoyed by all citizens and critical industries, including national security enterprises.

Table 3.1.   State Enterprise Share in the Brazilian Economy, 1973

	Proportion of Assets in State-Owned Firms
High Degree of State Participation (≥50%)	
Railways	100
Port services	100
Water, gas, and sewers	99
Telegraph and telephone	97
Electricity	79
Mining	63
Developmental services	51
Chemicals	50
Medium Degree of State Participation (20–49%)	
Water transport	45
Banking and Finance	38
Metal fabrication	37
Services	36
Air transport	22
Low Degree of State Participation (<20%)	
Construction and engineering	8
Rubber	6
Road transport and passengers	6
Agriculture and forestry	4
Nonmetallic mineral	2
Transport equipment	2
Food and beverages	1
Machinery	0
Wood products and furniture	0
Textiles and leather products	0
Tobacco	0
Printing and publishing	0
Radio and television	0
Commerce	0

Source: Peter Evans, *Dependent Development* (Princeton, N.J.: Princeton University Press, 1979), adapted from table 5.1, p. 221.

In an analysis of the cause for state intervention, Tom Trebat identifies six reasons for state enterprises: a weak private sector, economies of scale, public externalities, dynamic public managers, natural resource rents, and public historical factors. In steel, electrical energy, and telecommunications, state-owned firms were formed after private-sector failures. Particularly in Brazil, developmental nationalists believed state intervention was the pragmatic response to the failure of the free market. Economies of scale and the need for large investments to lower costs provided further grounds for state activity. In industries with clear public value, such as railroads, energy, and ports, it was argued that there were benefits to state provision of these services, especially when private providers had not emerged in the market. Because of public visibility and prestige, some state enterprises were able to attract the most dynamic managers. Finally, where industrialization was resource based, such as in oil and mining, it was argued that these resources belonged to the nation and should therefore be managed on the public's behalf.[19] Thus there was an economic rationale (although perhaps not always a compelling one) for state activity in the industrial sector.

The High Tariff Walls of ISI: Protectionism as a Tool of ISI

International economic tools facilitated the industrialization process. If your grasp of international economics is rusty, box 3.2 provides a quick review of terms. The growth of state and private enterprises was encouraged under the protection of high tariff and trade restrictions. These protective walls were designed to give less-competitive national industries, conceived of as infant industries, the chance to develop without the competition of large multinational firms. There was a perceived need for protection while an economy developed the necessary conditions to promote learning and innovation within the firm.[20] The policy objective wasn't to ignore exports; rather, the hope was that temporary protection would lead to the development of new products.[21]

We can measure the degree of protectionism by looking at tariff rates. Average nominal protection over consumer and manufactured goods was 131 percent in Argentina, 168 percent in Brazil, 138 percent in Chile, 112 percent in Colombia, 61 percent in Mexico, and 21 percent in Uruguay in 1960.[22] In the case of Mexico in 1970, the effective rate of protection—the nominal tariff rate adjusted for the protection also present in the purchase of intermediate goods used to produce the final good—was as high as 671 percent for fertilizer and insecticides, 226 percent for synthetic fertilizers, 206 percent for pharmaceuticals, 102 percent for automobiles, and 67 percent for electrical equipment. Across the board, for durable consumption and capital goods in Mexico in 1970, effective protection rates averaged 35 percent.[23] High import tariffs often induced multinational firms to set up factories within the country. In 1970 in Mexico, 62 percent of the machinery sector, 49.1 percent of transport vehicles, and 79.3 percent of electric equipment were dominated by foreign enterprises.[24] Although ownership was not national, labor learned new production techniques, and the technological level of production was raised.

Somewhat ironically, in the first stages of import substitution industrialization,

Box 3.2.   A Review of the Tools of Protectionism

export subsidy   A fiscal incentive, sometimes in the form of a tax break, for reaching
export targets. Export subsidies promote the development of export industries at
home, arguably to unfair advantage compared to the international firms.

foreign exchange controls   To restrict the quantity of imports or to direct imports to certain sectors, the government may ration foreign exchange. This generally involves
compelling exporters to sell foreign exchange to the government at a fixed price.
Selective importers of key goods are offered preferential prices for foreign exchange,
whereas importers of luxury items or those wanting to travel pay more local currency
for their dollars, yen, or pounds. Foreign exchange controls are therefore linked to a
system of multiple exchange rates. Not surprisingly, as there are therefore different
prices for the same commodity—money—a black or a parallel market often develops.
The black market price can sometimes be used as an indicator of how far the exchange
rate has been taken off course by policy distortions.

import licensing   The legal requirement to obtain a license to import a certain kind of
good. Import licensing boards evaluate national availability of goods to assess
whether the import is critical or whether the need can be met by national production.

industrial incentives   Direct payments or tax breaks to a firm engaging in a particular
line of production. These credits act as a protectionist device if an international competitor cannot meet the lower, subsidized price in the local market.

quota   A quota is a quantitative limit on imports. A quota presents a fixed limit on the
quantity of goods that may be imported. Quotas may be assigned to suppliers or they
may be auctioned, creating revenue for the central government.

tariff   A tariff, the most common type of protectionism, is a tax on imports. A tariff works
best when the demand for the good in question is elastic or price sensitive. If buyers
do not respond to the higher price, a tariff will not limit imports. With a tariff, the central government collects revenues. Nominal tariff protection is measured by looking
at the tariff rate on the final manufactured good. Effective rates of protection adjust
this rate for tariffs on intermediate inputs.

national imports usually rose. Steel, for example, could be produced only with huge
furnaces, and they had to be bought somewhere. To promote the import of these critical inputs, states tended to maintain **overvalued exchange rates,** making imports
relatively cheaper to purchase. Imports and access to this underpriced foreign
exchange were often licensed to limit imported goods to those critical to the industrialization process. As reviewed in box 3.2, import licensing boards evaluated the
quality and availability of national substitutes, their prices, and their importance in the
production process before allocating cheap foreign exchange.[25] International trade
and foreign exchange tools insulated the economy from rival foreign firms dominating the market. Box 3.3 contrasts the effects of various exchange rate regimes in
development strategies.

Additional Tools of Industrial Policy: Targeted Lending, Multinational Activity, and Passive Monetary Policy

Ownership was not the only tool of industrial policy in Latin America. Industrial
policy was accommodated by monetary and fiscal measures. The state provided

Box 3.3. Exchange Rate Policy and Development

An exchange rate is simply the price of one currency in terms of another. Ideally, exchange rates should equate the value of one nation's goods with those of another.[26]

There are three broad types of exchange rates: fixed, flexible, and crawling pegs. Under the gold standard (1870–1914) and the Bretton Woods systems (1945–1973), countries fixed their currencies to an anchor—gold or the U.S. dollar. A fixed exchange rate has the advantage of promoting stability. A critical economic price—the price of domestic goods in terms of international goods—is fixed. The rules of a fixed regime require that a country running a balance of payments deficit must clear its accounts by exporting gold or defend its rates by selling dollars or reserves. Because money supplies are anchored to dollars or gold, the decrease in money contracts the economy and few goods are imported. The economy should therefore expand only at the rate of its accumulation of real reserves—that is gold or dollars in circulation. The best way to understand this concept is to visualize the old trade rules: if France imported more from Great Britain, it had to send or "export" gold to pay for it, thus lowering the national money supply. In the next period France could buy less—and Britain more—balancing imports and exports.

Today many countries pursue a floating exchange regime. Under a floating system, if a country is running a balance of payments deficit, the price of foreign exchange adjusts or depreciates. Rather than a country exporting gold, the market changes the value of national money. The price of the currency is determined by the demand for a country's goods. As imports surge, residents sell their own currency to buy the foreign currency needed to purchase the imported goods. As a result, imports become more expensive and exports appear cheaper in international markets. If consumers are responsive to price change, flows should begin to balance. A large stock of reserves is not needed to defend the rate. Nevertheless, whereas the fixed exchange rate promotes price stability, a floating exchange rate may exacerbate inflation. Depreciation makes crucial imports more expensive, exerting an upward pressure on domestic prices.

Finally, some countries attempt to have both the stability of a fixed anchor and the flexibility of floating rates with the use of a crawling peg. Under this exchange rate system the currency is set to a central value but is allowed to fluctuate around that target in the short run.

What is the "right" exchange rate in the long run? Essentially, the same good should sell for the same price in two different markets. If it does not, and transportation costs are minimal and trade is free, some enterprising person will buy goods in the cheaper market and sell them where they are dear. Not surprisingly, using the exchange rate as a tool of industrial promotion interferes with arriving at the "right rate." Imbalances emerge that become difficult to sustain over time.

subsidies to domestic firms, and it granted tax credits and soft credit to jump-start the national industrial motor. National development banks were formed, such as Chile's Corporación de Fomento de la Producción (CORFO) and Brazil's State National Development Bank (BNDE), to target investments in the economy. A national development bank has an advantage over commercial lenders in planning strategic investment projects. As a state bank, it has a longer return horizon and is able to be active in more risky sectors because bottom-line profits are not the objective. Key industries such as machinery, automobiles, shipbuilding, and telephones were targeted as central to industrial growth. In Mexico, the Law of New and Necessary Industries provided select tax exemptions to promote growth in a limited number of unrepresented but critical sectors in the economy.

ISI contributed to the development of light manufacturing such as this Mexican knife producer. *(Courtesy of the Inter-American Development Bank.)*

Table 3.2. Foreign Share of Selected Industries, circa 1970 (percentages)

	Argentina	Brazil	Chile	Colombia	Mexico	Peru	Venezuela
Food	15.3	42.1	23.2	22.0	21.5	33.1	10.0
Textiles	14.2	34.2	22.9	61.9	15.3	39.7	12.9
Chemicals	34.9	49.0	61.9	66.9	50.7	66.7	16.5
Transport equipment	44.4	88.2	64.5	79.7	64.0	72.9	31.1
Electrical machinery	27.6	83.7	48.6	67.2	50.1	60.7	23.2
Paper	25.7	22.3	7.9	79.3	32.9	64.8	20.1
All manufacturing	23.8	50.1	29.9	43.4	34.9	44.0	13.8

Source: Rhys Jenkins, *Transnational Corporations and Industrial Transformation in Latin America* (New York: St. Martin's, 1984), excerpted from table 2.4.

In "strategic" sectors such as autos or steel, **transnational corporations** were welcomed as providers of needed technology and capital within the import substitution industrialization model. In table 3.2 we can see the significant role played by multinational corporations in manufacturing. In or about 1970, 24 percent of manufacturing in Argentina, 50 percent in Brazil, 30 percent in Chile, 43 percent in Colombia, 35 percent in Mexico, 44 percent in Peru, and 14 percent in Venezuela was under foreign control. Some of this participation predates the ISI period, but the strong involvement of transnationals, particularly in industrial production, was seen throughout the postwar ISI period.[27]

The entry of transnational corporations was somewhat paradoxical. ISI, after all, was attempting to reduce dependency on the international structure of production. However, there was also a degree of pragmatism at work. Transnationals provided critical financial capital and technology. The goal became to utilize these assets selectively, employing state bargaining power to transform the rules of the game. ISI policies set new rules: to produce and sell in the domestic market, transnational companies had to commit to technology transfer and the training of labor. Under the threat of market closure to the sale of their products, transnational firms agreed to joint ownership arrangements and the use of local inputs. In the automobile industry in Brazil, for example, GM do Brasil was a joint venture between Brazilian capital and General Motors (GM). Along with Ford, Volkswagen, and Fiat, it sparked the development of an industrial park. With high tariff rates, local production was the only viable way to sell cars nationally. Multinational firms defended market shares against the possibility of being shut out through local manufacture. If a MNC did not participate according to local rules, its international competitors would. Development of local parts suppliers was promoted by requiring 99 percent local content by weight for passenger cars produced locally.[28] Mexico was able to prod concessions in creating national joint ventures in the electrical industry by playing one multinational against another.[29] In addition to local content laws, contracts often stipulated the training of local managers to improve national managerial capacity, an assurance of technology transfer of technological processes (not simply sending the more sophisticated parts preassembled in the

United States or Europe), and limits on the repatriation of profits to promote local reinvestment of revenues. Our case study of the auto industry in the appendix to this chapter further illustrates these concepts.

A large domestic market enhanced national bargaining power in establishing contract terms with the multinationals. Clearly Brazil and Mexico had greater bargaining power than Ecuador or Paraguay, as there were many more likely Brazilian or Mexican buyers of locally produced cars. Yet, even in the Mexican and Brazilian cases, exports of locally manufactured multinational products were necessary to take advantage of economies of scale. Despite technology and export earnings, multinationals were not welcomed in all sectors. Even where bargaining power was strong, nationalist sentiments reserved strategic industries, such as oil in Mexico, to wholly local ownership.

For the most part, a loose monetary policy greased the fiscal wheels of development. From the mid-1960s to the 1980s, the dominant political system in Latin America was an authoritarian government. Developmental nationalists saw it as their mission to promote development as a critical element of security. Rules were changed to decrease the autonomy of central banks, forcing them to accommodate fiscal spending programs. Nonetheless, in areas of monetary, fiscal, or international affairs, reliable data about developing nations were sorely lacking, and many macroeconomic decisions were made by guesswork and intuition.[30]

> **QUESTION FOR THOUGHT**
>
> Given the characteristics of Latin American economies in the postwar period, would you have recommended the use of import substitution industrialization tools at the time? Would you have made any adjustments in the toolbox?

THE PERFORMANCE OF IMPORT SUBSTITUTION INDUSTRIALIZATION

How well did import substitution industrialization work? By the barometer of average annual growth rates of 5.5 percent over the period 1950–1980, one could call import substitution a successful strategy. Throughout the 1950s, Latin American economies were growing comparatively faster than the Western economies, and between 1950 and 1970 Latin American gross domestic product (GDP) tripled.

As illustrated in table 3.3, performance varied by country, with Brazil, Ecuador, and Mexico exhibiting the strongest growth rates over the ISI years of roughly 1950–1980. The production of basic consumption goods was widespread throughout the region, and some countries successfully initiated heavy-machine goods industries as well.[31] Production outstripped population growth—making progress on this problem identified in chapter 2. While the population of the region roughly doubled over the period 1945–1980, gross domestic product in real terms quintupled.[32]

Import performance was variable. Most countries did not see a decline in imports as a ratio of GDP. Brazil was more successful. Comparing 1964 with 1949, imports in the Brazilian economy decreased substantially as a percentage of total national supply, ranging from 19.0 percent in 1949 to 4.2 percent in 1964. Predictably, during

Box 3.4.   ISI Toolbox: A Summary

INDUSTRIAL POLICY

Form state-owned firms
Form mixed economic enterprises—part state, part private
Require government purchases from national firms
Require foreign firms to establish joint ventures
Pressure foreign firms to increase local content

INTERNATIONAL INSTRUMENTS

Tariffs on final goods
Quotas on imports
Exchange rate overvaluation
Exchange rationing
Import licences

FISCAL AND MONETARY POLICY

Subsidies for cheap inputs such as electricity
Subsidies for public transportation
Tax breaks in production
Preferential interest rates
Accommodating monetary policy

Table 3.3.   Percentage Growth in GDP per Capita

Country	1941–1949	1950–1959	1960–1969	1970–1979	1980–1989
Brazil	1.6	3.6	2.8	6.1	0.8
Ecuador	4.1	2.4	1.8	7.0	−0.1
Mexico	3.7	3.1	3.5	3.2	−0.3
Dominican Republic	3.0	3.4	1.4	4.6	0.7
Panama	−2.2	1.8	4.8	1.9	−0.6
Costa Rica	4.7	2.8	2.2	3.3	−0.8
Colombia	1.6	1.8	2.1	3.2	1.6
Peru	2.5	3.0	2.5	1.2	−2.1
El Salvador	9.3	1.8	2.2	1.8	−2.6
Guatemala	0.3	0.5	1.9	3.1	−2.1
Paraguay	0.6	−0.7	1.1	5.0	0.9
Argentina	2.3	0.8	2.8	1.3	−2.3
Honduras	1.5	−0.1	1.8	2.4	−1.0
Chile	1.5	1.3	1.9	0.6	1.9
Uruguay	2.5	1.0	0.3	2.5	0.1
Nicaragua	4.2	2.4	3.6	−2.5	−3.8
Bolivia	0.6	−1.7	3.2	1.9	−3.0
Venezuela	6.7	2.9	0.0	−0.1	−3.4

Source: ECLA data as found in Vittorio Corbo, "Economic Policies and Performance in Latin America," ed. Enzo Grilli and Dominick Salvatore, *Economic Development: Handbook of Comparative Economic Policies* (Westport, Conn.: Greenwood Press, 1994), 308.

the first stages of ISI in Brazil, the import of capital producer goods doubled from 1949 (15.8 b Cr) to 1959 (29.2 b Cr) as machines were needed to produce other goods. However, by 1964, imports of capital producer goods had fallen to nearly half the rate of the 1949 levels. Over the same period domestic production of consumer and producer goods rose substantially, with national production of all manufactured products increasing 266 percent from 1949 through 1964.[33]

Less-tangible gains also accrued.[34] Import substitution created forces for the development of an urban middle class, which demanded infrastructure entitlements in public utilities such as water and sewage systems. A national business class and a parallel labor union movement emerged, changing the agrarian balance of power. This coalition supporting the model, however, often intervened in policy making to thwart changes such as exchange rate valuations that might have prevented the accumulation of large fiscal imbalances.

The Crisis of Import Substitution Industrialization

Despite the apparent gains, import substitution industrialization was both unsustainable over time and produced high economic and social costs. In theory, ISI should have developed an internal momentum, expanding industrialization through interindustry linkages. Using his concept of linkages, Hirschman predicted that industrial growth should have occurred based on targeted investments. However, some contend that, given the limited size of the internal market in Latin America, ISI became "exhausted." It was postulated that as one moves to ever more sophisticated production, especially heavy machinery, the minimum plant size increases. Successful substitution would therefore be limited to sectors in which the internal demand for the good exceeded plant size—or where exports could make up the difference. The export vent, however, was largely closed due to the unfavorable exchange rates and less competitive industries. One study suggested that with such a high degree of income inequality, a massive devaluation to make Latin American exports globally competitive would have been politically and socially explosive.[35] Some programs were successful, such as the Brazilian BEFIEX (Special Fiscal Benefits for Exports) scheme, which provided incentives for exports. The benefits, however, were limited to countries and sectors with internationally competitive products. In many cases nationally manufactured goods did not meet international quality standards after growing up under protective tariffs, and firms were not forced by competition to become efficient. ECLA economists advocated economic integration within the region to expand the economies of scale, but the integration process was also stalled in its achievements. Economic performance was too varied across the region, and political differences made subregional integration difficult at times.

Others explained the crisis of import substitution industrialization in political and sociological terms. Because the industrial process was largely in the hands of elites, it failed to create a new entrepreneurial class that would have given the process greater dynamism. Given elite power, import substitution industrialization may have provided more support to industrialists than to industry.[36] Many of the tools used to manage ISI—import licenses, investment permits, and government contracts—created the possibility of profitable personal rents for those able to control them.[37] Corruption became economically expedient under the ISI model. This led to the views of the new political economists, which will be discussed in chapter 5, suggesting a minimalist role for government.

ISI exacerbated inequality in the region. With more than a third of the region's population living in poverty, internal demand was severely limited. Consumption patterns imitated those of the center elite instead of attending to the needs of the masses. Import substitution industrialization may also have been a more reactive and a less-coherently implemented strategy than is often supposed. That is, the policy-making process frequently may have been responding to balance of payments crises in erecting tariffs rather than proactive protection.[38] Finally, instead of promoting risk-taking behavior, the comfort of state ownership and international protection coddled the business culture. ISI fostered the creation of inefficient economic institutions that have persisted into the contemporary period.[39]

With resources focused on industrialization, agriculture was neglected. Necessary investments in agricultural infrastructure were not made as capital was directed to the industrial sector. Labor also gravitated toward urban industrial regions, pressuring cities. In some cases the decline in agricultural production meant an increase in the quantity of food imports, further pressuring the balance of payments. The neglect of agriculture weakened not only a source of profits but also the food security of nations. The urban, industrial bias was unsustainable. ISI was an imbalanced strategy.

Inefficiencies and inconsistencies abound under import substitution industrialization. Even Raúl Prebisch, founder of the ECLAC school, was not blind to the emerging challenges in the region in the late 1960s and early 1970s.[40] Prebisch noted that overvalued exchange rates biased growth against the export sector. Where exports are a source of international or hard currency, this introduces a foreign exchange gap to finance development. Differences in domestic expenditures and revenue in state-owned firms led either to persistent deficits or to monetary expansion that results in inflation. We will consider these inflationary biases in chapter 5. Internal and external resource gaps were met through external borrowing, adding annually to debt obligations (chapter 4). As long as international financial markets were willing to extend financing, the model could be sustained; however, once the spigots of international finance were turned off, internally driven industrialization ground to a halt.

LESSONS FOR DEVELOPMENT: WAS ISI INHERENTLY FLAWED?

Does the failure of import substitution industrialization in the 1980s mean that it was a misguided policy from the start? Some contend that the triumphant adoption of the neoliberal model throughout the region testifies to the inherent flaws of ISI. Others such as economist Werner Baer suggest that import substitution industrialization was the appropriate policy for the period but that times changed.[41] Indeed, it could be argued that the development of the industrial sector under import substitution industrialization made the dynamic private sector model possible in the 1990s. The international environment also changed substantially, with expanding globalization. After we look more closely at the neoliberal model in chapters 6–9, consider the counterfactual question for the case study of the automobile industry in Latin America that follows this chapter: Would the industry have been so successful without import substitution industrialization? Although we will come to no definitive conclusion, entertaining this question may foreshadow some of the future needs in Latin America with respect to the role of the state. Remember Gabriel García Márquez's warning (chapter 2) about the repetitious cycles in Latin American history. Before we discard the goals and tools of import substitution industrialization forever, we might do well to consider that in the future; the past may reappear, with a stronger need for the state to address some of the problems of market failure.

> **QUESTION FOR THOUGHT**
>
> Do you believe that ISI was inherently flawed or simply outlived its usefulness as domestic and international conditions changed?

But this is getting well ahead of our story. In the next two chapters we will look more carefully at some of the problems associated with the later ISI period: macroeconomic instability and the debt crisis. This will then position us for a careful look at the neoliberal model, with a strong role for the private as opposed to the public sector.

APPENDIX: THE AUTOMOBILE INDUSTRY IN LATIN AMERICA—A CASE OF SUCCESSFUL IMPORT SUBSTITUTION INDUSTRIALIZATION?[42]

The automobile industry is one of the most important sectors in many Latin American economies. In Argentina, the industry and its linkages account for 22 percent of employment. After oil, automobiles and automobile components are the second most important export in Mexico. Brazil and Argentina combined are expected to surpass Germany in automobile sales by the first decade of the twenty-first century. You may be surprised to learn that the automobile industry in Latin America is not merely an assembly operation. Full-fledged production has been in place since the early 1950s; Brazil and Mexico have become centers of innovative production. As in the developed countries, the automobile industry occupies a central role in many Latin American economies, although it has not brought the same level of development. Unlike highly industrialized economies, the Latin American automobile industry is foreign-owned. Since its beginnings, like the region, it has experienced a tendency toward stagnation. Therefore, a look at the development of the automobile industry can enhance our understanding of Latin America's economic development in the twentieth century.

The Automobile Industry and Its Role in Industrialization

As a leading sector in the development strategies of underdeveloped and developed countries, the automobile industry is credited with innovation in a number of production processes that have changed labor relations and international trade. Two such processes are Fordism and Toyotaism. Fordism—named after Ford Motor Company's production strategy—introduced the assembly line, innovated the five-dollar workday, and separated geographically the managerial aspect of production—white-collar jobs—from industrial activities—blue-collar jobs. Toyotaism or "just in time" production (named after Toyota's manufacturing strategy) has replaced Fordism's concept of an assembly line with "flexible manufacturing," using technology, robotics, and skilled labor to cut down inventory costs. Furthermore, Toyotaism integrates manufacturer and supplier to create more quality control and meet more varied consumer tastes. Both Fordism's and Toyotaism's innovations have been so successful that they quickly spilled over to other industries. It is therefore no wonder why developing countries would seek to establish an automobile industry.

Why Promote an Automobile Industry in Latin America?

The many forward and backward linkages of automobile manufacturing prompted Latin American governments to give it a central role in their development strategies. As Hirschman suggested, a large number of forward and backward linkages will stimulate development. The automobile industry creates backward linkages because it needs suppliers of steel, iron, glass, paint, rubber, and textiles. This stimulates the growth of steel mills, glass producers, rubber producers, and paint manufacturers. It creates forward linkages because automobiles need gas, oil, replacement parts, service shops, and better roads. This demand leads to private investment in oil refineries, gas stations, automobile parts, and construction companies. The result is an increase in economic growth, employment, and aggregate demand. In the mid-1950s a Brazilian admiral who was very closely involved with the promotion of the automobile industry stated, "As in the highly industrialized countries, the automotive industry will be without doubt the leading sector of the entire economy, by force of its magnitude, complexity, and dynamism."[43]

The Early Automobile Industry in Latin America

The growth potential of the automobile market led multinationals to the region. In 1916 Ford opened its first assembly plant in Argentina. In the following years operations by other automobile firms were established in Brazil, Mexico, and Chile. The market was too limited to support full production but was profitable for assembly operations. To promote expansion of locally based multinational corporations (MNCs), governments, at the request of the established foreign firms, set tariffs on fully assembled vehicles of nonresident producers to increase the profit margin of firms with local plants.

The importance of the Latin American market grew as a result of the expansion of road networks in the early 1920s. American manufacturers moved quickly at the opportunity to extend their U.S. production run of parts and components to these markets, since the European market was highly protected. By the late 1920s Argentina represented a market twice as large as Italy and a third the size of France and the United Kingdom.

The Role of the State in the Automobile Industry

A drop in commodity prices during the Great Depression debilitated the import capacity of Latin America. As available imports declined during World War II, a local parts-supply sector owned by private national capital developed to service the aging stock of vehicles. The strong demand for raw materials for war efforts boosted Latin American exports, creating huge reserves of foreign exchange.

The immediate postwar period witnessed a flood of automobile imports in response to the backlog in demand, but the availability of foreign exchange was short-lived. By 1947 vehicle imports to Argentina reached eighty thousand; in Brazil they peaked at 110,000 in 1951.[44] This surge of imports led to a balance of payments deficit and endangered the existence of local parts producers. In response, the governments of Brazil, Mexico, and Argentina—the countries with the largest automobile operations—raised trade barriers to limit the number of finished automobile imports and protected local producers by setting local manufacturing content requirements for domestic assembly operations. These state actions were crucial for the transition to manufacturing operations and reflected the beginning of a government commitment to an ISI policy. In 1956 the Brazilian government banned all imports of cars, requiring any international producers wishing to sell in the Brazilian market to establish local operations. It also required that 90 percent of parts be procured from national producers within five years, stimulating the development of a supplier industry.[45]

Foreign capital, as a source of technology and know-how, was crucial to this strategy. Since automobile corporations were among the largest and most technologically sophisticated in the world, governments had a particular interest in ensuring that they continued to invest locally. Therefore, import barriers and local content requirements were matched with high fiscal incentives. Between 1956 and 1969, the Brazilian government offered 89 cents worth of subsidies for every dollar in investment. Mexico offered 50–60 percent of the value of investment.[46] In addition, to make the market even more attractive, governments created policies to control wages. Government subsidies were important in moving from assembly to manufacturing because the small elite market limited economies of scale. Therefore, fiscal incentives made the transition to manufacturing profitable for the foreign automobile firms. As a result, by 1962 Brazil

> **QUESTION FOR THOUGHT**
>
> Given your understanding of the automobile industry and economic policy, were appropriate strategies followed throughout the course of the development of the automobile industry?

produced 191,194 vehicles per year; Mexico produced 193,000 by 1970, whereas ten years before it assembled only fifty thousand with low domestic content.[47]

Export Promotion and Debt-Led Growth

State intervention was also critical in moving from production exclusively for the domestic market to exports. Balance of payments shocks driven by the oil crisis of the 1970s prompted export promotion to relieve current account pressures. Brazil developed the Special Fiscal Benefits for Exports (BEFIEX) program in the early 1970s. Manufacturers wishing to qualify for continued fiscal benefits and reduced tariffs had to meet a dollar-value export target. Otherwise, they were subject to exorbitant import taxes for capital goods, parts, components, and raw materials. In 1977 the Mexican government issued a decree mandating automobile firms eliminate their trade imbalances by 1982. Established firms complied to fend off increased competition by Japanese firms eager to enter the market. Instead of undertaking austerity measures, the government followed a debt-led growth strategy that provided subsidies and credits for those firms that would begin exporting automobiles with a high domestic content. Given the high production costs, it was very unlikely that the Latin American industry would have generated exports without government intervention.[48]

The majority of established firms complied with the export requirements. During the second half of the 1970s and the 1980s exports from Brazil and Mexico shot up. By 1981 the proportion of vehicles produced for export in Brazil had increased to 27.3 percent, up from 2.2 percent in 1972.[49] The Mexican automobile industry by 1986 had reached a trade surplus of U.S.$1,117.7 million, over the 1977 industry deficit of U.S.$385.3 million.[50] Argentina, the third major automobile producer in Latin America, had a short-lived boom in exports during the mid-1970s. However, the coup of 1976 brought a military government with liberalization policies that led to an increase in imports, dominating 25 percent of the domestic market. Although government fiscal policies in the 1970s led to the debt crisis, the automobile industry's new capacity to export helped reduce losses from a contracted domestic market.

The Debt Crisis and a Contracting Market

During the "lost decade" of adjustment to the debt crisis, the domestic automobile market shrank. Increasing income inequality and erratic price changes made automobiles a luxury reserved for the rich. Governments eliminated many of the industry's preferential subsidies and the depressed domestic market provided little incentive for firms to add capacity. Firms shifted their exports to the United States and Europe as their developing country export markets contracted. In Mexico, the market was so depressed that in 1986 the industry was producing 43 percent less than in 1981, most of which was for export.[51] Firms with minimal investments like Renault pulled out, but the largest firms—GM, Ford, Chrysler, Volkswagen, and Fiat—had invested too much to dismiss their Latin American operations as a loss.

Austerity, Market Forces, and a Domestic Boom

During the 1990s the automobile industry experienced a turnaround. Demand in Brazil and Argentina was so high that automobile firms needed to build more plants to accommodate the booming market. Plants in Brazil operated twenty-three hours a day and could not meet domestic demand. Mexico's market, although it suffered a setback during the 1994–1995 *peso* crisis, grew by 33 percent in the first quarter of 1997.[52] In Argentina, automobile sales ran at an annual rate of four hundred thousand units, while in Brazil the yearly rate was 2.2 million vehicles.[53] Brazil and Mexico surpassed Italy, becoming the tenth and eleventh leading automobile producers in the world. In 1987, Ford and Volkswagen entered a partnership called AutoLatina to save their investments in the depressed market of the 1980s. In 1994 the partnership was dissolved because the market was once again big enough to handle the two competitors. The turn in market conditions was attributed to the sustained growth experienced by most Latin American countries. Price stability and available credit made automobile ownership a reality for many Latin American families. A study by Honda shows that more than 2.7 million households in Brazil have an annual income of $48,000 and an additional 8.6 million earn at least $24,000.[54] Argentina, which has always boasted of the largest middle class in the region, has an antiquated automobile fleet, with an average age of fifteen years, that is rapidly being replaced.

Alongside growth and an expanding market have been neoliberal policies of maintaining price stability and a self-regulating market. In the 1990s these policies, instead of fiscal subsidies, enticed automobile manufacturers to invest in the region. From 1995 to 2000, automobile manufacturers poured approximately $23 billion into new automobile factories, more than half of which were in Brazil.[55] Chrysler Corporation, which had not invested in developing countries since 1965, opened a plant in Argentina in 1997. The Japanese view Argentina and Brazil as the most lucrative markets in the world, and Toyota invested $200 million in a factory outside of São Paulo to serve **Mercosur.** Furthermore, technological spillover finally came to fruition. In the second half of the 1990s, Latin America became a locus of technological innovations in production and labor relations. Most plants are now using automation and robotics, requiring skilled labor. In 1996 Volkswagen opened a factory in Brazil that it claimed was the most advanced in the world. This factory bound VW and seven suppliers in the manufacturing and assembly process. VW supplied only two hundred workers, while the bulk of labor belonged to the suppliers. This reduced costs by 50 percent and increased worker productivity by 12 percent.[56] GM is following suit by renovating the bulk of its plants from assembly-line operations to more flexible manufacturing.

Economic Integration Allows for Economies of Scale

Aside from economic growth, economic integration and liberalization in the 1990s was responsible for the heavy investment by the automobile firms. In the 1950s and the 1960s, automobile manufacturers were reluctant to begin manufacturing operations without government incentives because the markets were too small to reap the benefits from economies of scale. The markets of Mercosur, the North American Free Trade Agreement (NAFTA), and the Andean Pact made it possible for companies like VW, GM, and Ford to take advantage of economies of scale. Mercosur member countries lowered tariffs for producers within the customs union to 35 percent. This made it possible for companies to integrate their operations to serve the entire customs union. Mexico has for a long time produced GM engines for Detroit. During the *peso* crisis, automobile production in Mexico did not fall as much as it could have because NAFTA provided an escape valve through which producers could switch from production for the domestic market to U.S. and Canadian markets. Venezuela, with its very limited automobile industry, is now enjoying investment from the American "big three" automobile producers, who use it as an export platform to markets in Ecuador and Colombia.

Economies of scale allow for cost savings. GM do Brasil has launched new, technologically advanced and affordable automobiles for the Brazilian market.[57] Another reason for falling prices and rising investment is the significant decrease in common external tariffs on imports from outside the integrated area. Imports have significantly increased, forcing the traditional producers in the Latin American economies to cut costs and prices. In Mercosur, external tariffs on automobiles were scheduled to drop to around 20 percent by the year 2000, although progress has been delayed by the Brazilian and Argentine crises until 2004.[58] Competition appears to be working to spur improvements in productivity.

Reconsidering ISI and Neoliberalism

The contemporary success of the automobile industry is forcing some economists to reconsider their judgments on ISI. Many contend that the industry's success today dates to the ISI policies of the 1950s and 1960s and the export policies of the 1970s. Producers were forced to consider the region as a profitable long-term production site. Once investments were made, they complied with government decrees to protect their privileged access into the region. In the 1980s firms had invested too much to pull out from the region. As a result, today GM, Ford, VW, and Fiat hold 99 percent of the South American market and are among the top investors.

However, the technological spillover that state officials foresaw did not bear fruit during the years of ISI. Instead, neoliberals contend that it wasn't until governments began to focus on getting prices right, downsizing the state, and liberalizing the economy that Latin America became fertile ground for technological breakthroughs in automobile production. Furthermore, neoliberal policies have reinstated growth, and market forces that have driven automobile MNCs to cut costs through technological innovations.

Key Concepts

backward linkages
declining terms of trade
dependency theory
economic populism

forward linkages
import substitution
   industrialization
market failure

overvalued exchange
   rates
transnational
   corporations

Chapter Summary

The Dependency and Structuralist School

- The dependency theory states that the center—industrialized nations—expanded at the expense of the periphery—developing nations. Capitalism therefore created underdevelopment. Local elites forged alliances with international capital, blocking development.
- The structuralist school, as defined by the UN Commission for Latin America, had two main characteristics. First, declining terms of trade hindered economic development for Latin America. Second, concentrated oligopolies and elites determined prices and consumption patterns that proved incompatible with growth for the region.

Import Substitution Industrialization (ISI)

- In response to dependency theory and the structuralist school, Latin America pursued ISI. This inward-oriented approach sought to promote and protect domestic industries through an interventionist state that would attack bottlenecks and market failure.
- ISI relied on various tools to promote industrialization:
  - active industrial policy through the use of state-owned enterprises;
  - protective international instruments such as tariffs, quotas, import licenses, foreign exchange controls, industrial incentives, and export subsidies to protect infant industries;
  - targeted lending to industries such as machinery and automobiles;
  - subsidies and tax exemptions for particular industries, including transnational corporations that provided critical financial capital and technology;
  - strict investment rules such as local content laws and minority foreign ownership;
  - and passive monetary policy to finance projects under ISI.

- Although data show that ISI had a positive effect on growth until the 1980s, there were also negative consequences. Nationally manufactured goods often failed to meet international quality standards, making them uncompetitive in the global market. ISI exacerbated inequality by preserving the power of the elite and failing to create an entrepreneurial class. In addition, the agricultural sector was neglected, which weakened a source of profit and food security. There was also a bias against export growth through overvalued exchange rates, leading to differences in domestic expenditures and revenue that contributed to persistent deficits and inflation.

Notes

1. Gerald M. Meier and Dudley Seers, *Pioneers in Development* (Oxford: Oxford University Press, 1984), 173.

2. Meier and Seers, *Pioneers,* 173

3. Ronald V. A. Sprout, "The Ideas of Prebisch," *CEPAL Review* 46 (April 1992): 178.

4. James L. Dietz and James H. Street, eds., *Latin America's Economic Development: Institutionalist and Structuralist Perspectives* (Boulder, Colo.: Rienner, 1987), 81.

5. Meier and Seers, *Pioneers,* 176.

6. Henry Bruton, "A Reconsideration of Import Substitution," *Journal of Economic Literature* 36 (June 1998): 905.

7. Meier and Seers, *Pioneers,* 176.

8. Sprout, "Ideas of Prebisch," 179.

9. Sprout, "Ideas of Prebisch," 182; and Nancy Birdsall and Carlos Lozada, "Recurring Themes in Latin American Economic Thought: From Prebisch to the Market and Back," in *Securing Stability and Growth in Latin America,* ed. Ricardo Hausmann and Helmut Reisen (Paris: OECD Publications, 1996).

10. Andre Gundar Frank, *Capitalism and Underdevelopment in Latin America* (New York: Monthly Review Press, 1967).

11. Paul A. Baran, "On the Political Economy of Backwardness," *Manchester School* 20, no. 1 (1952); reprinted in *The Economics of Underdevelopment,* ed. A. N. Agarwala and S. P. Singh (New York: Oxford University Press, 1963), and in *Political Economy of Development,* ed. Charles K. Wilber (New York: Random House, 1973). See also the classic piece written by Gabriel Palma, "Dependency: A Formal Theory of Underdevelopment or a Methodology for the Analysis of Concrete Situations of Underdevelopment?" *World Development* 6, no. 7–8 (July–August 1979): 881–924.

12. The Spanish acronym for ECLA is CEPAL, the Comisión Económica Para América Latina. ECLA later became ECLAC, with the C reflecting the incorporation of the Caribbean.

13. Enrique V. Iglesias, ed., *The Legacy of Raúl Prebisch* (Washington, D.C.: IADB, 1994).

14. Henry Bruton, "Import Substitution," in *Handbook of Development Economics,* vol. 2, 3rd ed., ed. Hollis Chenery and T. N. Srivivasan (New York: Elsevier, 1996), 1609.

15. Vittorio Corbo, "Economic Policies and Performance in Latin America," in *Economic Development: Handbook of Comparative Economic Policies,* ed. Enzo Grilli and Dominick Salvatore (Westport, Conn.: Greenwood, 1994).

16. Charles K. Wilber and Steven Francis, "The Methodological Basis of Hirschman's Development Economics: Pattern Modeling vs. General Laws," *World Development* 14, no. 2, special issue (February 1986): 181–91.

17. For a discussion of the role of the state in economic development, see Thomas Trebat, *Brazil's State-Owned Enterprises: A Case Study of the State as Entrepreneur* (New York: Cambridge University Press, 1983).

18. Rudiger Dornbusch and Sebastian Edwards, "The Political Economy of Latin America," in *The Macroeconomics of Populism in Latin America,* National Bureau of Economic Research Conference Report, ed. Rudiger Dornbusch and Sebastian Edwards (Chicago: University of Chicago Press, 1991), 9. See also Alan Knight, "Populism and Neo-Populism in Latin America, Especially Mexico," *Journal of Latin American Studies* 30 (1998): 223–48.

19. Trebat, *Brazil's State-Owned Enterprises.*

20. Bruton, "Import Substitution," 1607.

21. Rosemary Thorp, "Import Substitution: A Good Idea in Principle," in *Latin America and the World Economy: Dependency and Beyond,* ed. Richard J. Salvucci (Lexington, Mass.: Heath, 1996), 140–46. The Salvucci book is a good reader to accompany chapters 2–3 of this text.

22. Victor Bulmer-Thomas, *The Economic History of Latin America since Independence* (New York: Cambridge University Press, 1994), 280. "Nominal" refers to the tariff rate on the final good without adjusting for tariffs on intermediate inputs.

23. Adriaan ten Kate and Robert Bruce Wallace, "Nominal and Effective Protection by Sector," in *Protection and Economic Development in Mexico,* ed. Adriaan ten Kate and Robert Bruce Wallace (Hampshire, U.K.: Gower, 1980), 122, 151.

24. Tom Warts, "Protection and Private Foreign Investment," in *Protection and Economic Development in Mexico,* 198.

25. Robert Bruce Wallace, "Policies of Protection in Mexico," in *Protection and Economic Development in Mexico.*

26. This is based on the theory of purchasing power parity and the law of one price. Two sweaters should sell for the same price in two markets (adjusted for transportation costs). If they didn't, some enterprising person would buy sweaters where they are cheap and sell them where they are dear.

27. Rhys Jenkins, *Transnational Corporations and Industrial Transformation in Latin America* (New York: St. Martin's, 1984), 40.

28. Gary Gereffi and Peter Evans, "Transnational Corporations, Dependent Development, and State Policy in the Semiperiphery," *Latin American Research Review* 16, no. 3 (1981): 31–64.

29. Richard S. Newfarmer, "International Oligopoly in the Electrical Industry," in *Profits, Progress, and Poverty* (Notre Dame, Ind.: University of Notre Dame Press, 1984), 147.

30. Henry Bruton, "A Reconsideration of Import Substitution," *Journal of Economic Literature* 36 (June 1998): 910.

31. Robert J. Alexander, "Import Substitution in Latin America in Retrospect," in *Progress toward Development in Latin America: From Prebisch to Technological Autonomy,* ed. James L. Dietz and Dilmus James (Boulder, Colo.: Lynne Rienner, 1990).

32. Albert O. Hirschman, *A Propensity to Self Subversion* (Cambridge, Mass.: Harvard University Press, 1995), 156.

33. Bela Belassa, "Brazil," in *The Structure of Protection in Developing Countries* (Baltimore: Johns Hopkins University Press, 1971): table 6.2, p. 107.

34. This paragraph draws from Rosemary Thorp, *Progress, Poverty and Exclusion: An Economic History of Latin America in the 20th Century* (Baltimore: Johns Hopkins University Press for the IADB, 1998), 197.

35. James E. Mahon Jr., "Was Latin America Too Rich to Prosper? Structural and Political Obstacles to Export-Led Industrial Growth," *Journal of Development Studies* 28, no. 2 (1992): 242.

36. Alan M. Taylor, "On the Costs of Inward-Looking Development: Price Distortions, Growth, and Divergence in Latin America," *Journal of Economic History* 58, no. 1 (March 1998): 20.

37. Bruton, "A Reconsideration," 923.

38. Bruton, "Import Substitution," 1616.

39. Taylor, "On the Costs of Inward-Looking Development," 21.

40. Enrique V. Iglesias, "The Search for a New Economic Consensus in Latin America," in *The Legacy of Raúl Prebisch,* ed. Enrique V. Iglesias (Washington, D.C.: IADB, 1994).

41. Werner Baer, "Changing Paradigms: Changing Interpretations of the Public Sector in Latin America's Economies," *Public Choice* 88 (1996): 365–79.

42. This case was written by Erwin Godoy, Colby College graduating class of 1997.

43. Lúcio Meira, "A propagação dos efeitos promocionais da indústria automobilística," *Economia Brasileira* 4 (1958): 67, as quoted in Helen Shapiro, *Engines of Growth: The State and Transnational Auto Companies in Brazil* (Cambridge: Cambridge University Press, 1994), 39.

44. Jenkins, *Transnational Corporations,* 21.

45. Auto case study in McKinsey Global Institute, *Productivity: The Key to Accelerated Development Path for Brazil 1998* (São Paulo: McKinsey and Company, 1998), 2.

46. Jenkins, *Transnational Corporations,* 59.

47. Shapiro, *Engines of Growth,* 193.

48. Jenkins, *Transnational Corporations,* 191.

49. Jenkins, *Transnational Corporations,* 211.

50. Shapiro, *Engines of Growth,* 229.

51. Shapiro, *Engines of Growth,* 228.

52. "Mexico Domestic Sales Rise Sharply," *Reuters Financial Service* (LEXIS-NEXIS database), 4 June 1997.

53. Laurence Zuckerman, "In South America Car Makers See One Big Showroom," *New York Times,* 25 April 1997 (online edition).

54. Zuckerman, "In South America Car Makers See One Big Showroom."

55. Economic Commission for Latin America and the Caribbean, *Foreign Investment and the Caribbean: 1997 Report* (English summary). Available at www.eclac.cl/english/Publications/invest/summary.html.

56. David Woodruff, Ian Katz, and Keith Naughton, "VW's Factory of the Future," *BusinessWeek,* 7 October 1996.

57. GM do Brasil, www.gmb.com.br.

58. GM do Brasil, www.gmb.com.br; Mercosur Consulting Group Limited, "Recent Developments Affecting the Mercosur Economic Integration Project," vol. 42, no. 1, *Thunderbird International Business Review,* January–February 2002, pp. 1–7, www.mercosurconsulting.net.

CHAPTER FOUR

LATIN AMERICA'S DEBT CRISIS

The Limits of External Financing

The macroeconomic crisis threatened the meager savings and social security of Latin America's poor. *(Courtesy of David Mangurian and the Inter-American Development Bank.)*

The debt crisis in Latin America was a development crisis. It called into question the viability of the import substitution industrialization model of development and shaped the economic future of the region.

How did the crisis come about? Borrowing to finance development is not in itself a bad thing. Developing countries are by definition capital poor. Funding is needed for investment and growth. If a country, like a person, wants to grow or expand, borrowing provides necessary capital for change. As a student, you might be borrowing money to finance educational expenses in anticipation of a better future. This is rational behavior. Borrowing becomes a crisis when an individual or a country fails to make payments on the outstanding value of the loan. If the investment you make in your education doesn't generate a decent salary by the time your first loan payment is due, you will have a personal financial crisis. For a nation, if returns on investments don't match debt obligations when they come due, a crisis also ensues. Unfortunately, the development model in Latin America was dependent on a continuous infusion of capital, with new lending required to finance the development of long-term projects. When conditions in the international market changed dramatically in the early 1980s, Latin American economies, one after another, collapsed under the mountain of external debt. The debt crisis transformed economic policy in the region—at a very high price.

In this chapter we begin by analyzing how borrowing to support import substitution industrialization became an unstable foundation for growth. We then consider the problem of debt-led growth and why a change in external conditions brought inward-looking development to a halt. Finally, we turn to the changes in development policy that enabled economies to survive the crisis, and we analyze the economic and social costs to the region. Questions that will shape our analysis include the following:

- What fueled the accumulation of external debt?
- What role did internal and external factors play in precipitating a crisis?
- How did countries and the international financial community respond to the crisis?
- What are the legacies of the debt crisis?
- Is the Latin American debt crisis over?

THE MOUNTAIN OF DEBT: AN UNSTABLE FOUNDATION FOR DEVELOPMENT

Economic growth under the import substitution model of development was fueled by external savings. With thin domestic financial markets, by 1982 Latin America had borrowed more than $300 billion from the rest of the world. Figure 4.1 shows this accumulation of Latin American total disbursed external debt, 1980–2000. Under the import substitution model, the first stage of industrialization is driven by the import of capital goods—particularly machinery—to be used to produce goods domestically. In many cases, the capital was also used to finance large infrastructure projects such as roads, electricity, telecommunications, or water supply, all of which are vital to a nation's advancing growth. Borrowing in itself is not a bad thing. Prob-

Figure 4.1.   Total Disbursed External Debt of Latin America, 1980–2000

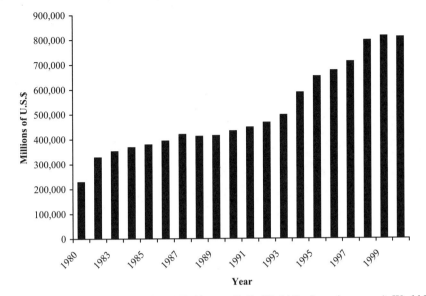

Source: World Bank, *World Debt Tables* (Washington, D.C.: World Bank, various years); World Bank, *Global Development Finance* (Washington, D.C.: World Bank, 2001).

lems arise, however, when the borrowing requirements for long-term projects outpace the ability to repay past loans. Crises may erupt due to the mechanics of borrowing or the **debt trap** (unproductive investments or investments with very long time horizons that do not generate returns in time to help service loans), internally inconsistent economic policies that impede the success of projects, or external shocks that derail the domestic economy. Let's consider these causes in turn.

It is easy to fall into a debt trap when lending is for long-term projects but obligations to repay begin in the short term. This problem is made clear with a simple mathematical example. Assume the following (rather lenient) borrowing conditions. You contract to borrow $1,000 dollars a year for a project that is going to take ten years. You agree to pay $50 a year back in principal for each $1,000 borrowed over twenty years at an interest rate of 10 percent per year on the outstanding balance of the debt. As can be seen in table 4.1, in the first year you receive $1,000 and repay $50, leaving a balance of $950. At 10 percent interest your net outflow, the interest plus the principal, is $95 plus $50 or $145. In the second year you again receive $1,000 of new money to continue your project, pay $100 in principal (the first and second $50 principal payments), leaving $185 of interest to be paid on the balance of $1,850. Your principal plus interest therefore totaled $285. Your annual net transfer, the $1,000 coming in minus the $285 going out, is $715.

This formula of new money minus principal and interest payments goes on for several years. Notice that each year, because of the obligation to pay the principal on past loans and the increasing interest burden, the net transfer—the amount of money coming in after payments have been made—substantially dwindles. Indeed, by the eighth year the $1,000 of new money doesn't even cover your payments on past obli-

Table 4.1.   The Debt Trap: Long-Term Project Lending

Year	Disbursement (new lending)	Total Debt Incurred	Principal ($50/year for twenty years)	Outstanding Debt	Interest Payment (10%)	Total Outflow = Interest + Principle	Net Transfer = Disbursement – Outflow
1	1,000	1,000	50	950	95	145	855
2	1,000	2,000	100	1,850	185	285	715
3	1,000	3,000	150	2,700	270	420	580
4	1,000	4,000	200	3,500	350	550	450
5	1,000	5,000	250	4,250	425	675	325
6	1,000	6,000	300	4,950	495	795	205
7	1,000	7,000	350	5,600	560	910	90
8	1,000	8,000	400	6,200	620	1,020	–20
9	1,000	9,000	450	6,750	675	1,125	–125
10	1,000	10,000	500	7,250	725	1,225	–225
11	1,000	11,000	550	7,700	770	1,320	–320

gations, much less fund new investment. If your multiyear project is incomplete or if it is not yet generating significant returns, you would need to borrow even more just to make payments. You have landed flat in the debt trap.

Mismatched Projects and Returns

Import substitution was fueled by regular infusions of capital not unlike our example above. In part, the import substitution industrialization model was driven by the failure of the private sector to provide critical goods and services in the economy. We remember that this took place most frequently in industries with large economies of scale and in sectors in which the complementary infrastructure was not available. This led to state investment in sectors with high capital requirements for entry as well as in large-scale projects to develop needed infrastructure in energy, telecommunications, and transportation. Unfortunately, the payback period for these multiyear investments was not always consistent with the terms of commercial lending. Furthermore, the returns to social investments by the state are not easily captured in state tax coffers for repayment of debt obligations.

Even when lending for large-scale infrastructure projects was efficient and well managed, multiyear development projects were not easily financed. If a road, for example, is constructed over a ten-year period and then it takes another ten years for businesses to move into the area and pay taxes, the project itself may not generate returns—and repayment of debt—until well into the future. Debt-generated investment should create the ability to service that debt in the future. Investments must have a sufficient rate of return within a compatible term structure. When this is not possible in huge undertakings, the government often steps in with public lending. Although it is a function of government to sequence projects and manage these flows, the magnitude of large-scale investments under import substitution industrialization left Latin American governments vulnerable to the willingness of capital markets to finance the gap between the period of investment and the long-term returns on the project. Given sovereign guarantees and the low likelihood of countries defaulting (as opposed to companies), markets were willing to lend. Debt was accumulated to service past debt.

Unsustainable Domestic Policies

In addition to the simple mathematical lesson of the debt trap, the intersection of politics and economics promoted debt-led development. Latin America has a long history of populism, or the use of political rhetoric to mobilize the masses. Old-style populists, such as Juan and Eva Perón of Argentina, charismatically co-opted labor and middle-class groups as well as domestic industrial elites to maintain power. But buying off the masses costs money. As we saw in chapter 3, **economic populism** in the 1970s emphasized growth and income redistribution and de-emphasized the risks of inflation and deficit finance, external constraints, and the reaction of economic agents to aggressive nonmarket policies.[1] The populist political culture encouraged spending, which was made possible by favorable conditions in the international financial markets.

Unfortunately, the large state-run development model also lent itself well to inefficiency and corruption in lending. In some instances, lending was for pharaonic mega-projects with limited utility for social development. The history of Latin America contains numerous stories of a state firm's payrolls padded with dead people, construction taking place only on paper, and misguided attempts at development such as the Transamazonian Highway. Debt was incurred for projects that would never generate the ability to repay.

External Shocks

Of course, at some level, politicians understood that one day the piper would have to be paid. However, extraordinarily attractive international prices for capital played into the short-term political incentive to borrow. Real international interest rates—that is, interest rates adjusted for global inflation—were negative from 1974 until 1977. As shown in table 4.2, the U.S. prime rate adjusted for inflation (the real prime rate) ranged between −2.9 and −1.4 percent. If someone asked you whether you would like to borrow money today, have the use of that money for some period of time, and repay less than what was borrowed, how would you respond? Although much of the lending was on a floating rate basis—that is, each year your interest rate would change to reflect market conditions—after several years of negative real rates and the possibility that you wouldn't even be in office when repayment time came around, the decision to borrow could be seen as a rational response to price. It would be as if the interest rates in the debt trap example presented earlier were −2 percent rather than +10 percent. At that rate it would take twenty-one years, perhaps

Table 4.2.   Real International Interest Rates, 1974–1984

Year	U.S. Nominal Prime Rate (%)	U.S. Inflation Rate (%)	U.S. Real Prime Rate (%)
1974	10.81	13.1	–2.2
1975	7.86	11.1	–2.9
1976	6.84	8.3	–1.3
1977	6.83	8.5	–1.4
1978	9.06	7.2	1.7
1979	12.67	9.2	3.2
1980	15.27	11.9	3.0
1981	18.85	10.1	8.1
1982	14.77	7.5	6.8
1983	10.81	5.1	5.5
1984	12.04	4.8	6.9

Source: ECLAC, *Economic Survey of Latin America and the Caribbean* (Santiago, Chile: ECLAC, various years); IMF, *International Financial Statistics, 1987* (Washington, D.C.: IMF, 1987), 113.

five different government administrations, for net flows to become negative. Within that time, the project may be bearing returns. Given those conditions, it would be hard for a politician to do anything but incur the loan!

Although the demand for finance was driven by developmental needs as defined by the import substitution model and the populist politics of its implementation, lending would never have taken place on such a broad scale without an ample supply of global cash. During the 1970s banks needed to recycle the proceeds from the quadrupling of oil prices, called petrodollars. Unless banks lent these petrodollar deposits, they would be unable to pay interest to the OPEC creditor nations. Many lenders simply saw it as easier and more lucrative to advance megaloans to state-owned enterprises (backed by sovereign governments) than to package small business or agricultural loans in the United States. The competition to lend was ferocious.

Distinct Patterns, Same Result: Crisis

It is important to note that Latin American countries pursued a variety of economic strategies during this time period—yet all were strongly hit by crisis. Table 4.3 compares three cases: Mexico, Brazil, and Argentina. The Mexican debt crisis was driven by an attempt to expand the oil sector while maintaining social peace at home through domestic spending programs. International bankers were only too happy to lend to Mexico because the loans were collateralized by the black gold of new oil discoveries. Domestic expansion exploded into inflation, which the government attempted to restrain through a fixed exchange rate. This exchange rate became overvalued, compromising the ability of the non-oil export sector to perform. As described below, Mexico sounded the first alert to the international community of the debt crisis in August 1982 when it announced its inability to meet its financial obligations.

Table 4.3. Debt and Distinct Patterns of Development

Policy Instruments	Mexico	Brazil	Argentina
Long- and short-term external debt (billions of 1985 U.S.$)	96.8	106.1	50.9
Fiscal policy	Overexpansion of fiscal policy driven by investments in the oil sector; new oil discoveries led to expanded investments by Pemex; fiscal deficit exploded to 17% of GDP	Respond to global recession with growth of domestic demand; maintain high protective tariffs; wages increased	Inconsistent fiscal policy; 1976 military regime adopted orthodox model
Monetary policy	Loose monetary policy with low interest rates led to massive capital flight; outflows reached $8.4 billion in 1981 and $6.6 billion in 1982; inflation soars	Economy indexed to respond to inflation; money supply passively accommodates expansionary fiscal policy	High *peso* interest rates initially generated strong capital inflow; when confidence was lost, capital flight ensued
Exchange rate policy	Maintains fixed exchange rate policy despite inflation; overvaluation results	Limited devaluation of *cruzeiro* to 50% despite inflation rates twice as high; overvaluation results	Overvalued exchange rate depressed exports and accelerated imports; acute reserve loss led to borrowing just to maintain the exchange rate
Exogenous shocks	Tightening U.S. monetary policy raised real interest rates; oil prices plunged	Oil crisis pressures balance of payments; high interest rates; commodity price shock; contagion effects from Mexico	Tight U.S. policy raised cost of capital
Comments	As an oil exporter, Mexico had access to capital; its problem derived from its attempts to limit social conflict through state spending while simultaneously expanding the oil sector	Brazil attempts to maintain state-led development model despite changes in the international economy; its large size allows it to pursue this strategy too long	Argentina pursued an aggressive liberalization policy with exchange rate priced to restrain inflation-not promote exports; the model was therefore internally inconsistent

Source: Derived from information presented in SBC Warburg Dillon Read, *The Latin American Adviser* (February 1998).

Brazil also enjoyed easy access to international finance. Because it was one of the ten largest economies in the world, lenders believed that investments in this emerging powerhouse were well placed. Loans to state enterprises were seen as backed by the **sovereign guarantee** of the government of Brazil—investors thought that the government would not default on obligations. As international financial conditions changed in the 1980s, Brazil's size also slowed the incentive for its adjustment. It was able to maintain its inward-looking model of development and turn to domestic money creation to service external debt. Inflation soared, but a sophisticated system of indexing interest rates, wages, and prices minimized the pain for economic agents. We will consider these macroeconomic responses in chapter 5. A rate of devaluation of the exchange rate slower than the rate of inflation was designed as a brake on rising prices but had the unfortunate effect of reducing export performance.

Whereas debt accumulation in Brazil and Mexico was driven by investments through state firms, Argentina's inward-looking development model ran out of steam under the populist Peronist regime. The military took over in 1976 and radically opened the economy. Unfortunately for Argentina, borrowing was used for financial purposes and did not result in an increase in the productive capabilities of the nation. Instead, a misguided attempt to maintain an overvalued exchange rate led to borrowing to defend the fixed currency price. Money flowed into the country in the form of short-term loans used to support the exchange rate, but those same dollars quickly exited in private portfolios betting against the ability of the Argentine government to restrain inflation and jump-start growth. At the crux of the Argentine problem was the fact that the overvalued exchange rate, used as an anchor for inflation, could not simultaneously promote exports. (Please see box 4.1 for a review of overvalued exchange rates.)

Despite these differences in internal development models, Mexico (an oil exporter), Brazil (a nation inwardly focused on its large domestic market), and Argentina (an economy open to the international economy) were all rocked by changes in the international economy that transformed a heavy debt profile into an insupportable burden. Unsustainable domestic policies left each nation vulnerable; external pressure exposed the fragility of the debt-led development model.

The Crisis Builds: External Shocks and Capital Flight

The accumulation of external liabilities to finance development is not a crisis. However, external conditions changed radically, and evidence began to mount that called into question the ability of governments to service their debt. In 1979 U.S. president Jimmy Carter appointed Paul Volcker as chairman of the Federal Reserve Board. Volcker's inflation-taming efforts drove the U.S. prime rate to 18.8 percent in 1981. Floating rate obligations skyrocketed to a real, or inflation-adjusted, positive 12 percent. In addition to facing escalating interest payments, countries found it difficult to generate the hard currency—usually dollars—to pay the debt. Debt in Latin America was generally dollar-denominated, since no international bank would issue a loan in *pesos* when the *peso* was likely to be devalued. To repay the

BOX 4.1. OVERVALUATION OF EXCHANGE RATES AND THE DEBT CRISIS

An overvalued exchange rate can be seen as both a cause of the accumulation of debt and an effect of the macroeconomic instability perpetuated by the debt crisis.

Before explaining the economic cause and effect of an overvalued rate, we should clarify what is meant by an overvalued exchange rate. An overvalued exchange rate exists when the currency is artificially too strong, allowing the purchase of more foreign currency than trade patterns might indicate. That is, one *peso* might buy one dollar's worth of currency (and therefore goods) when it is really only worth fifty cents. With a strong currency, people buy more from abroad. An undervalued rate is "too weak," favoring exports. Imports become prohibitively expensive, and exports cheap. Most overvaluation exists when the price of a currency is established under a fixed exchange rate system.

The Goldilocks question of figuring out which rate is "just right" goes back to a theory of exchange rate determination called purchasing power parity, or PPP. In its simplest form, PPP argues that a good should sell for the same price in two countries when prices are adjusted for the exchange rate. Holding transportation costs constant, if Costa Rican coffee does not sell for the same price in San Jose, Costa Rica, and San Jose, California, people would buy it where it is cheap (Costa Rica) and sell it where it was dear (California), driving the price up in Costa Rica and down in California. Because one would need *colones* to purchase the coffee in Costa Rica, this would drive up the value of the *colon* until the value of the two goods was identical in the two markets. If the exchange rate were set by the government (rather than being a floating market rate), the "right" price for the currency should generate one price for coffee. However, if tastes changed, and people drank less coffee and demanded fewer *colones* to buy it, an unadjusted exchange rate would become overvalued.

Alternatively, if the Costa Rican government increased the money supply, the *colon* should be worth less than the dollar. For example, if prices in Costa Rica were rising at 20 percent per year but in the United States they were only rising by 5 percent a year, this means that Costa Ricans could purchase 15 percent (20–5) less a year with the same income as those in the United States. Under a floating system, this should be reflected in a 15-percent fall in the value of the currency, or the exchange rate. Once again, if the exchange market isn't functioning smoothly or if the government intervenes to fix a currency price and does not allow the devaluation to take place, we would say that this currency is overvalued.

A look at table 4.A shows that from 1979 through 1981, currencies became significantly overvalued in Latin America. The numbers presented are indexes that set 1980–1982

(continued)

Table 4.A. Real Exchange Rate Indexes (1980–1982 = 100)

	Argentina	Brazil	Chile	Mexico	Venezuela
1976–1978	73	116	75	98	95
1979	101	96	79	98	94
1980	116	85	95	104	93
1981	107	103	108	114	100
1982	76	112	97	82	110
1983–1985	74	85	86	86	98

Source: Selected from Rudiger Dornbusch, *Stabilization, Debt, and Reform: Policy Analysis for Developing Countries* (Englewood Cliffs, N.J.: Prentice-Hall, 1993); original source Morgan Guarantee, World Financial Markets.

(continued)

as a base year. By 1981, for example, Argentina's currency was 7 percent too strong, Brazil's 3 percent, Chile's 8 percent, and Mexico's 14 percent; only Venezuela's was "just right." (We see, however, not for long.)

Why would a country allow overvaluation to take place? First, if the country is pursuing import substitution, the strong currency value allows companies to purchase intermediate inputs at a lower cost. Because the policy was often to discourage the importation of final consumer goods, import licenses at these preferential rates were sometimes required. Second, countries may choose to link their currency to a vehicle currency such as the dollar as an inflation-fighting anchor. Just as global currencies were set to the dollar under the Bretton Woods system following World War II or under the gold standard, developing countries have at times viewed the link as a stabilizing force. Currency boards have also been used to establish a one for one link, constraining the growth of the domestic money supply to the number of dollars held in reserve. Whether the link is firm or whether the government uses the dollar value as a guide to monetary policy, under a fixed exchange rate regime this should be anti-inflationary. Nonetheless, if all inflation is not immediately squeezed out of the economy, and a rate is fixed, when the local currency rate should fall to reflect inflation but doesn't due to being fixed, overvaluation is taking place.

Finally, even when a country knows that a devaluation is indicated, at times it is reluctant to do so. In addition to incurring a political cost (citizens concluding that the government was unable to control inflation), the devaluation can serve as an additional inflationary shock because imports now become more costly. The vicious circle between inflation causing the need for devaluation and then a devaluation increasing prices in the economy pressuring for a further devaluation is the economic minister's nightmare.

Capital flight makes the pressure toward devaluation worse. If indications point to the possibility of a devaluation, investors will move their assets out of the country. The rationale is clear. Say you have 1,000 *pesos* in the bank and that initially they can buy you 1,000 dollars worth of goods at a 1:1 exchange rate. Now assume that you have a 20-percent devaluation of the *peso*. This means that to buy the same U.S.$1,000-worth of goods, you will have to come up with 1,200 *pesos*. Therefore, if you think there will be a devaluation, you will sell *pesos* and hold dollars (perhaps in a Miami bank account or perhaps under your bed). Selling *pesos,* not surprisingly, weakens the *peso*. Under a fixed exchange rate, the government must intervene in the market, selling dollars and buying *pesos* to maintain the value. It is forced to sell the dollars that it holds in reserves for such foreign exchange transactions. However, a fall in reserves in the balance of payments erodes confidence. Everyone knows that reserves are dwindling and that a devaluation is inevitable because the central bank does not have infinite resources to defend the currency. Capital flight accelerates in the face of a possible devaluation, making that change in the currency value inevitable. Pressures on overvalued exchange rates resulted in many countries moving from a fixed to a floating rate.

loan, the country therefore had to earn or buy dollars. The most direct means of augmenting dollar holdings was to sell Latin American goods in the United States. Unfortunately, Volcker's inflation-fighting tools also generated recession, shrinking the United States as a market for Latin American goods. The slowdown became global, and the region found itself with increasingly burdensome obligations and a limited ability to earn the money owed.

Evidence of the unsustainability of the debt began to mount. Table 4.4 shows the capital flight from unsustainable policies in Argentina, Mexico, and Venezuela from 1979 through 1984. Capital flight as a percentage of total external debt reached 76.9 percent in Argentina, 73.3 percent in Mexico, and 131.5 percent in Venezuela. Capital flight takes place when a national makes a deposit or investment outside the home country. On one hand, capital flight is simply good international investing. A Brazilian economist once commented,

> Why is it that when an American puts money abroad it is called "foreign investment" and when an Argentinean does the same it is called "capital flight"? Why is it that when an American company puts 30 percent of its equity abroad it is called "strategic diversification" and when a Bolivian businessman puts only 4 percent abroad it is called "lack of confidence"?[2]

On the other hand, if one's portfolio preference is decidedly against domestic investment or if investors or savers actively circumvent laws to prevent scarce capital from leaving the country, capital flight has taken place. Capital votes with its feet. Many Latin American families, for example, have savings accounts in Miami to guard against the possibility that the value of all of their savings would be decimated by poor economic management, followed by a devaluation. As shown in box 4.1, overvaluation of a currency contributes to capital flight because agents do not want to be caught holding assets denominated in a currency that is likely to be devalued. In some cases corruption exacerbated capital flight. Dollars coming in as loans to state-owned enterprises found their way out of the countries in the coffers of corrupt public agents.

Capital flight further destabilizes macroeconomic management. In an attempt to bribe capital to stay at home, interest rates may be set too high and retard investment. When capital leaves the tax base, the government's ability to raise revenues is weakened. There is stronger incentive for **seignorage,** the process of printing money to cover the deficit. Because people want to sell the local currency and trade it in for dollars, the excess supply of the local currency is inflationary. We will come back to this problem in chapter 5.

Other measures of indebtedness fueled uncertainty, aggravating capital flight and the loss of confidence in economic management in the region. Since export earnings finance debt payments, it is important to look at the weight of debt to exports as well as debt service—the interest and principal that must be paid for by exports. A measure greater than 200 percent in the level of total

Table 4.4. Capital Flight from Selected Latin American Countries (billions of U.S.$)

	1979	1980	1981	1982	1983	1984
Argentina	2.2	3.5	4.5	7.6	1.3	−3.4
Brazil	1.3	2.0	−1.4	1.8	0.5	4.0
Mexico	−1.1	2.2	2.6	4.7	9.3	2.6
Venezuela	3.0	4.8	5.4	3.2	3.1	4.0

Source: Robert Cumby and Richard Levich, "On the Definition and Magnitude of Recent Capital Flight," Working Paper 2275 (Cambridge, Mass.: National Bureau of Economic Research, 1987); cited in Sebastian Edwards, *Crisis and Reform in Latin America: From Despair to Hope* (New York: Oxford University Press/World Bank, 1995), 23.

Table 4.5.   Debt Indicators for Latin America and the Caribbean, 1980–1990

Year	Total Debt/Exports of Goods and Services	Total Debt/GNP	Total Debt Service/Exports of Goods and Services	Interest/Export of Goods and Services	Interest/GNP
1980	206.0	36.2	36.9	19.6	3.4
1981	210.9	37.8	21.6	11.1	2.0
1982	269.1	46.9	47.6	30.3	5.3
1983	309.1	58.6	43.0	29.8	5.6
1984	291.4	59.3	39.9	27.2	5.5
1985	312.9	61.3	38.2	27.9	5.5
1986	376.6	63.2	43.6	27.5	4.6
1987	377.6	66.1	37.4	23.0	4.0
1988	332.6	56.7	39.6	24.1	4.1
1989	293.3	50.1	32.1	16.6	2.8
1990	277.4	45.0	26.3	13.0	2.1

Source: World Bank, *World Debt Tables* (Washington D.C.: The World Bank, various years).

external debt to exports or a debt service to export ratio over 40 percent is unhealthy, pointing to great pressure on exports for debt payments and leaving little capital for other investment. We can see in table 4.5 that by 1982 total debt over exports had reached 269 percent and that total debt service over the exports of goods and services was edging toward 50 percent. Interest payments alone ballooned to 30 percent of exports, without reducing future liabilities. Latin America was in trouble.

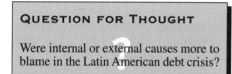

QUESTION FOR THOUGHT

Were internal or external causes more to blame in the Latin American debt crisis?

Can't Pay, Won't Pay

In August 1982, Mexico announced to the international financial community that it could no longer service its debt. When the financial community saw that the sovereign government of Mexico would not or could not make good on its obligations, confidence in all developing countries eroded. It was a crisis for Mexico that quickly spread through the region and all developing countries, and threatened the international finance system. At the time that Mexico signaled the international financial community of the severity of the crisis, exposure to debt was a problem not only for the countries but also for the banks. As can be seen in table 4.6, the exposure of the nine major banks to six highly indebted countries exceeded an average of 174 percent of shareholders' equity in the banks. Exposure to either Mexico or Brazil alone would have been approximately half of shareholders' capital.

Box 4.2. Key Debt Terms

arrears   The amount of past-due payments (interest and principal) on outstanding debt owed by any given debtor.

bilateral loans   Loans from governments and their agencies, from autonomous bodies, and from official export credit agencies. These differ from private creditors (commercial banks and bonds) who did the bulk of the lending leading to the debt crisis.

concerted lending   **Involuntary lending** by a bank. When the Mexican crisis began in 1982, large banks formed bank advisory committees to represent all banks and to keep them informed of debt negotiations. These committees, along with industrialized countries and the IMF, pressured smaller banks to continue lending to prevent defaults.

debt service   The sum of principal repayments and interest payments actually made.

disbursements   Earnings on loan commitments during the year specified.

LIBOR (London Interbank Offer Rate)   Traditional benchmark interest rate for international lending by private European banks.

loan default   A bank declaration that a borrower is not expected ever to repay its debt, usually following an extended cessation of principal and payments by the debtor.

long-term external debt   Debts with a maturity of more than one year owed to nonresidents, payable in foreign currency, goods, or services.

moratorium   A declaration by a debtor country of its intent to stop principal and interest payments to its creditors.

net flows   Disbursements minus principal repayments.

net transfers   Net flows minus interest payments during the year.

sovereign default   A government's decision to default on its external debt obligations.

REFERENCES

Biersteker, Thomas J. *Dealing with Debt.* Boulder, Colo.: Westview, 1993.

Krugman, Paul R., and Maurice Obstfeld. *International Economics: Theory and Policy.* 3rd ed. New York: HarperCollins, 1994.

World Bank. *World Debt Tables, 1995–1996.* Washington, D.C.: World Bank, 1996.

The International Monetary Fund (IMF) Approach

When Mexico rang the alarm bell on the mountain of external debt accumulated by developing countries, the depth of the problem was poorly understood. The international financial community diagnosed the difficulty primarily as a liquidity crisis. The *World Development Report 1983* noted, "Debt problems of most major developing countries are caused by illiquidity, not by insolvency."[3] Returning to the analogy of personal finances, **illiquidity** might mean that because you were laid off from your job or because you went wild with your credit cards, you cannot make your payments when due. However, with time and budgeting, you could honor your commitments and not be forced into bankruptcy or insolvency. In the banking world, the assumption was that debtors would regain creditworthiness through a combination of internal adjustments and more favorable global economic conditions.

The internal adjustments were, for most countries, tough medicine to swallow.

Table 4.6.   Exposure of Nine Major U.S. Banks to Six Highly Indebted Countries, 1984

	% of Shareholders' Equity (common and preferred)
Manufacturers Hanover	268.5
Chase Manhattan	212.7
Citicorp	206.7
Chemical	196.7
Bankers Trust	177.6
Bank of America	150.9
Morgan Guarantee	143.5
Continental Illinois	129.9
Wells Fargo	129.8
First Chicago	126.9
Average	174.3

Source: John Charles Pool, Stephen C. Stamos, and Patrice Franko, *The ABCs of International Finance,* 2nd ed. (Lexington, Mass.: Lexington Books, 1991), 113.

The presumption was that countries were living beyond their means and therefore had to reduce domestic **absorption** of resources. If fewer goods were consumed at home, more could be exported to service the debt. If we allow Y to represent national income and A to stand for the domestic consumption of goods and services (including imports), we can see in the simple formula Y – A = B that B (the balance) is the residual. A trade surplus, then, would help restore financial health by decreasing the need to finance imports, leaving the balance to pay off the debt. Absorbing less at home left more for hard currency-earning exports.

The Absorption Approach: Y – A = B

How should domestic absorption be decreased? The IMF prescription for achieving balance revolved around decreasing government and personal absorption of resources and increasing the attention to the international sector. In contrast to the state-centered import substitution strategy, the IMF recommended that states decrease spending on public works, privatize state-owned enterprises, and eliminate subsidies on goods and services. To combat inflation, monetary policy should be contractionary. If wages were indexed to a public minimum wage, it was generally suggested that wage increases be minimal. Devaluation was indicated to adjust overvalued exchange rates, and liberalization of markets through the reduction of tariffs and quotas was favored. The devaluation was designed to change the relative price of goods, making imports more expensive and exports cheaper. This creates incentives for expenditure switching by raising the opportunity cost of tradable goods. Fewer tradables will be consumed at home, and more will be released for sale abroad. Rather than borrowing, foreign investment was seen as the vehicle for the capital necessary for growth. The overriding principle was to get prices right. Resources should be directed to their most productive use through accurate price signals.

The IMF package was inherently contractionary, premised on decreasing fiscal spending and monetary emission. The hope was that the infusion of capital from abroad and initiative from the local private sector would fuel growth. The program generated a good deal of economic dislocation. Workers in bloated state-owned enterprises were laid off. Recipients of state-subsidized milk or tortillas faced dramatic price increases. The price of public transportation rose, and spending on infrastructure fell. Companies that had grown up behind the protection of high tariff walls found it difficult to compete with international firms. Tight money meant high interest rates, which retarded investment. Devalued exchange rates sent price shocks through imported consumer goods. Agricultural exports were rapidly promoted, often at high environmental cost.

QUESTION FOR THOUGHT

With the benefit of twenty years of hindsight, what do you believe should have been the policy response to the debt crisis in the 1980s?

But the bitter IMF pill was necessary if countries were to maintain access to finance. When a country found itself unable to make payments on its external obligations, banks would lend no more until the country had signed a letter of intent with the IMF to implement the tough economic policies. Targets for macroeconomic performance would be set, and if countries adopted the conditions specified to achieve these goals, IMF funding would be released. **Conditionality**—the adoption of strict fiscal, monetary, and trade policies in exchange for the release of funds—was designed to alert the private sector that substantial change in the spending habits of the country was under way. This signaled a green light for further lending.

The lending, however, was not fresh money for new projects. Instead, given the severity of the financial crisis, the loans were intended to provide the capital to make payments on past liabilities coming due. For a price—and at a higher interest rate—old loans were rolled over into new loans with maturity dates further in the future. The presumption was that when these repackaged loans came due again, the benefits of the tough economic medicine would be available to service the obligations. Called **involuntary lending,** this rolling over of obligations was designed to provide financial breathing room until payments could be made from more productive economies.

Unfortunately, international macroeconomic conditions did not cooperate. Real interest rates did not decline rapidly, and the prices that countries received for their exports—primarily agricultural commodities—were depressed. By 1985 Latin American countries had not returned to good standing in the international market. The problem was clearly more than a short-term liquidity issue. But was the IMF approach wrong?

Criticism of IMF conditionality packages centered on the IMF's diagnosis of the problem as well as the policy measures to bring about change. In Latin America, the theoretical debate was led by the structuralist school. It faulted the IMF approach as too standardized. The same IMF recipe, based upon the assessment of the need to reduce excess demand, was applied in all cases. The structuralists focused instead on the particular economic characteristics of each country. They puzzled at how a country with an unemployment rate of 15 percent and a capacity utilization rate of 75 percent could have excess demand. Furthermore, they challenged the IMF proponents to explain how a crisis triggered by the external shock of high global interest rates and expensive oil imports could be solved by domestically reducing aggregate demand. The structuralists argued that IMF programs were unnecessarily recessionary and increased inequality. They contended that the restrictive short-run targets set by the IMF exacerbated the negative impacts. Finally, the structuralists argued that the international financial community played a significant role in the accumulation of debt and should therefore bear some of the adjustment burden.[4]

Despite the standardized prescriptions, this first stage of the debt crisis was defined by a case-by-case approach to the resolution of the problem. That is, a regionwide approach was rejected by creditors. The politics of the case-by-case strategy on the part of the IMF, the World Bank, and the debtor countries may explain in part why Latin America did not default on the debt. Despite the fact that at the outset the debtor countries had some bargaining power given the exposure of money center banks, collective action was not effective. In the Declaration of Quito (1984), Latin American countries called for an immediate response from the creditor countries to ameliorate the dramatic fall in living standards. In June 1984 the Cartagena Consensus Group of debtors argued that the burden of Latin American foreign debt threatened both the very stability of the international monetary system and the emergence of democracy in the region. But the Declaration of Quito was all talk and no action. Although some countries such as Peru declared a partial moratorium, stating that it would devote no more than 10 percent of exports to debt, and Brazil announced in 1987 a unilateral moratorium on the payment of interest of $68 billion of medium- and long-term money, the carrots for good behavior—the flow of new money into countries—were sufficiently enticing to keep countries largely in line.[5]

> **QUESTION FOR THOUGHT**
>
> Given the causes, did the international financial community bear a responsibility to shoulder more of the burden of adjustment to the debt crisis?

The Market Reacts to the Continuing Crisis

While countries were engaged in difficult adjustment measures, the financial sector quietly found ways to reduce its exposure to debt. Through the process of **provisioning,** or setting aside profits before dividend payments against risky loans, banks set aside the capital to guarantee their positions in the event of a default. Banks also found means to reduce their exposure to unwanted debt through innovative new market instruments. A **secondary market** for debt developed. Because loans were assets, they could be resold to other, more risk-inclined, buyers for a discount. The

Table 4.7. Secondary Market Prices of Latin American Debt (% of face value)

Country	July 1985	January 1986	January 1987	August 1987	October 1987
Argentina	60–65	62–66	62–65	45–47	34–38
Brazil	75–81	75–81	74–77	52–54	35–40
Chile	56–69	65–69	65–68	64–66	52–56
Colombia	81–83	82–84	86–89	80–82	75–80
Ecuador	65–70	68–71	63–66	41–43	31–34
Mexico	80–82	69–73	64–57	51–53	46–49
Peru	45–50	25–30	16–19	7–10	2–7
Venezuela	81–83	80–82	72–74	72–74	50–54

Source: George Anayiotos and Jaime de Piniés, "The Secondary Market and the International Debt Problem," *World Development* 18, no. 2 (1990): 1655–60.

new holder of a million-dollar loan to Mexico might have paid only $510,000 for this asset if it were purchased in August of 1987. The value of the discount would be steeper the lower the likelihood the country would ever repay the full amount. As we can see in table 4.7, by 1987 expectations were so low that Peru would ever make good on its external obligations that its debt could be purchased for between two and seven cents on the dollar.

Beyond allowing those who were more risk-averse—particularly the medium-sized regional banks—to exit, the secondary market produced another innovation, **debt-for-equity swaps.** For example, a firm wishing to build a factory in a Latin American country could use the secondary market to purchase the debt note. In August 1987 a firm wanting to invest in Chile could purchase $100,000 worth of debt for about $64,000. The country then owed the firm instead of the bank. However, the firm could turn to the government and say "I don't need to be paid in dollars (hard earned through exports). In fact, in setting up this factory, I need *pesos* to buy supplies and pay my workers locally." In this way the debt purchased at a discount could be presented at the central bank for payment in local currencies. If the country had a strong bargaining position, such as good firm location, it too could negotiate a deal and agree to pay only $90,000-worth of *pesos* to the firm. Firms were satisfied because the secondary market gave them access to discounted funds, and governments could pay in local currency, not scarce foreign exchange.

On the surface, debt-for-equity swaps are a win-win proposal. The banks sell their poorly performing loans; the company makes a profit on the difference between the discount and the local payment; and the country, in addition to reducing its debt in hard currency, gains in jobs through the foreign direct investment. Indeed, Chile reduced 10 percent of its external obligations this way. However, it was not the perfect scheme. It is important to identify how the local currency was raised. If the central printing presses were simply run a little longer, there could be inflationary impacts. If the government borrowed internally to finance the *pesos,* indebtedness hadn't really changed—the holders just switched from international to domestic lenders. It was also questionable whether the investments by firms would have taken place anyhow—perhaps bringing hard currency into the country. Some critics raised concerns over sovereignty, charging that foreign firms were using cheap money to compete against local entrepreneurs. (Domestic firms were prevented by international banking conventions from buying back their own debt.) Finally, use of debt-for-equity swaps was a strategy suited for only the best performers. Logically, it would work only if multinational corporations wanted to operate in the host country. If economic adjustment had not been substantial, it was unlikely that foreign capital was going to be banging down the doors.

Despite these drawbacks, the appeal was strong. The secondary market was also used to facilitate **debt-for-nature swaps.** In this instance, rather than purchase materials, international organizations purchased the discounted notes and offered cancellation or partial payment in exchange for the country's promise to establish a nature preserve. As discussed in box 4.3, Costa Rica, in particular, pursued this alternative.

Beyond Muddling Through: The Baker Plan

"Muddling through" (as some called the first period of adjustment to the debt crisis) did not work to restore creditworthiness and growth to the region. Adjustment under IMF programs was largely unsuccessful. The burden of debt service had become painfully obvious. As seen in figure 4.2, high debt service costs resulted in a persistent outflow of resources from Latin America from 1982 through 1990. This loss of capital resulted in the flat growth in gross national product (GNP) seen over the same period in figure 4.3. As growth slowed, unemployment rose in the 1980s, and real wages did not increase to improve the standard of living for the masses. In figure 4.4 we see urban unemployment rising to over 8 percent in 1984, and in figure 4.5 we see wages flat or falling in all countries except Brazil.

The costs of adjustment were enormously painful. As will be discussed in later chapters, poverty increased and environmental damage was exacerbated. Political and social dislocation led to labor strikes, supermarket looting, and bus burning in

Figure 4.2.   Aggregate Net Resource Flows and Net Transfers: Latin America and the Caribbean, 1980–2000

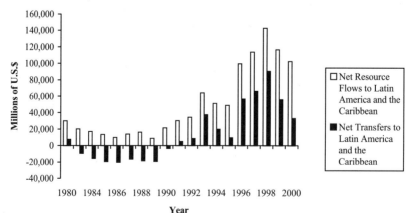

Source: World Bank, *Global Development Finance* (Washington, D.C.: World Bank, various years).

BOX 4.3.   DEBT-FOR-NATURE SWAPS

Although the debt crisis was catastrophic for Latin America, in an ironic way it turned into a blessing for international environmental nongovernmental organizations (NGOs) trying to persuade Latin American governments to adopt sustainable development policies. Third-World debt, in the form of debt-for-nature swaps, gave NGOs a bargaining tool to influence the creation of environmental measures in Latin America. Some countries were persuaded to implement environmentally sound projects and policies in exchange for a reduction in their outstanding debt.

Debt-for-nature swaps were first proposed in 1984 by the then vice president of the World Wildlife Fund, Thomas Lovejoy. Yet, it was not until 1987 that Bolivia, Costa Rica, and Ecuador engaged in this form of debt reduction. Pointing to the negative environmental effects of debt service through natural resource exploitation to earn dollars, Lovejoy and others argued for a pro-environmental policy. Debt-for-nature swaps could reduce hard currency indebtedness while making investments critical to the environment.

To carry out a debt-for-nature swap, three requirements must be met. There must be a donor, usually an NGO, who funds the initiative by purchasing a portion of a developing country's debt from the secondary market. In addition, the country's central bank must be willing to accept the debt note and able to finance the negotiated environmental programs. Finally, a private or governmental agency must carry out the environmental programs. Two types of debt-for-nature swaps have taken place: bond-based programs, where the interest on government bonds is used to pay for environmental and conservation activities, and policy programs, where the government commits to implementing a series of environmental policies. The process for both types is similar. The donor negotiates with the debtor government on the terms and then purchases debt from the secondary market at a price lower than the face value of the outstanding debt. The debtor country now owes the donor instead of the creditor. If a bond-based program was negotiated, the purchased debt is converted to government bonds issued in the name of a local NGO that receives the interest over the life span of the bond. On the other hand, if a policy program is negotiated, in exchange for the debt note, the government agrees to implement environmental policies such as creating environmental reserves or ensuring that forests are managed sustainably. Finally, the funds are transferred to a local private or government agency for the implementation of negotiated projects.

Although debt-for-nature swaps sound like fabulous deals that benefit every party involved, they have limitations. They reduce little debt. In fact, the maximum debt reduction took place in Costa Rica, where less than 5 percent of external debt was reduced. There is a fear the central bank will engage in money creation, triggering inflation. Further, conservation projects may take precedence where other, more critical sustainable development projects are more drastically needed. This also raises the question of sovereignty among nationalists who see foreign NGOs dictating the national environmental agenda.

Despite these restrictions, Costa Rica has been able to make good use of debt-for-nature swaps by making them an extension of government policy. The major reason for Costa Rica's success is the high level of government participation. To safeguard against inflationary tendencies, officials set a ceiling on the number of swaps allowed yearly. Costa Rica has demonstrated that used properly, debt-for-nature swaps can help reduce some of its external debt. More important, debt becomes an instrument to achieve another policy goal: promoting environmental sustainability.

REFERENCES

Caldwell, Laura. "Swapping Debt to Preserve Nature." *Christian Science Monitor,* 11 September 1990.

(continued)

(continued)

Patterson, Allen. "Debt for Nature Swaps and the Need for Alternatives." *Environment* 21 (December 1990): 5–32.

World Bank. "Other Financial Mechanisms: Debt-for-Nature Swaps and Social Funds." Available on the Internet at www.esd.worldbank.org/html/esd/env/publicat/edp/edp1116.htm.

response to depressed wages and higher prices. Fragile democratic regimes were threatened as people began to idealize the stability and prosperity of military rule. To promote prosperity and stability, in 1985 U.S. Treasury secretary Baker announced a plan designed to jump-start growth. The premise of the Baker plan was that countries could not continue to service their debt through contractionary policies. Growth and adjustment became linked. The Baker plan targeted fifteen less-developed countries for $29 billion of new money, $20 billion from commercial banks and $9 billion from the IMF and the World Bank.

The Baker plan was important in shifting policy from austerity to growth. It also identified a new role for the World Bank in promoting institutional change. The failure of traditional IMF measures to resolve the debt crisis changed the understanding of the debt crisis from a short-term liquidity problem (with primary responsibility lodged in the IMF) to a long-term problem of **structural adjustment.** Debt came to be understood as a development problem, and the World Bank was charged with assisting in the management of the adjustment process. As a result, the World Bank began to engage in macroeconomic policy, formerly the purview of the IMF, and the IMF was forced to design lending facilities to support long-term structural change. There was general agreement that adjustment with

Figure 4.3.   Gross National Product of Latin America and the Caribbean, 1980–2000

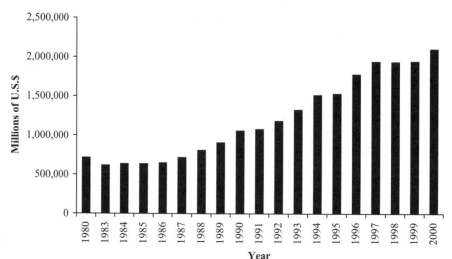

Source: World Bank, *Global Development Finance* (Washington, D.C.: World Bank, various years).

Figure 4.4.   Urban Unemployment in Latin America and the Caribbean (average annual rates)

Source: United Nations ECLAC, *Economic Survey of Latin America and the Caribbean* (Santiago, Chile: ECLAC, various years).

growth would be led by the export engine, but there was a greater appreciation for the fact that severely contractionary monetary policy would not favor investment, the deepening of markets, or democracy.

This conceptual shift was important, but the Baker plan itself was too little, too late. Twenty-nine billion dollars may have made a difference if it were targeted toward one or two countries, but given the almost trillion dollars in external obligations on the part of developing countries at the time, it was inconsequential. Furthermore, commercial banks were unconvinced that new lending to debtor countries made any sense. In their view, why throw good money after bad?

Figure 4.5.   Evolution of Real Wages

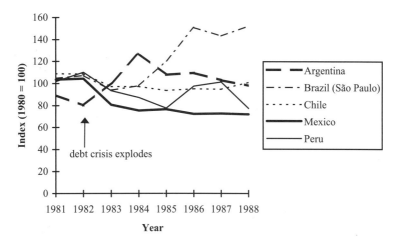

Source: James E. Wilkie, ed., *Statistical Abstract of Latin America,* vol. 29, pt. 1 (Los Angeles: UCLA Latin American Center Publications, 1992), 406.

Registering its "no confidence" vote for the success of the Baker plan, in 1987 Citicorp announced that it would allocate $3 billion from the loan loss reserves it had been setting aside against its developing country debt portfolio. Some had feared that such a move would lower Citicorp's stock value (since its assets are its loans, which were now worth less); instead, the stock market greeted the news with applause. The consensus was that the banks were prepared to take a realistic position on developing country debt: it would never be repaid in full. Accompanied by a $200 million dollar write-off in the same year by the Bank of Boston, this was seen as the death of the Baker plan. Jump-starting growth would not work until the debt burden was reduced two years later under the Brady plan.

The Social and Environmental Costs of Debt Adjustment

The burden of adjustment to the debt crisis may have fallen disproportionately on women. Several studies showed that in poor households, women were responsible for changes in work, child care, and consumption patterns. Household incomes were maintained by increasing the number of workers per home. Unlike the effects of the Great Depression in the United States, where women tended to withdraw from the work force in favor of men, in Latin America women entered the work force during austerity to help meet family needs; their entrance appears permanent.[6] Skilled men were eligible for unemployment compensation; their wives sometimes went into the informal sector to compensate for income loss. The entrance of men into the informal sector of unregulated, poorly compensated jobs tended to be inversely related to skill level.[7] Girls often assumed more domestic tasks, including child care of younger siblings, sometimes leaving school to do so. People cut back on food expenditure, eating fewer meals and consuming less protein and fresh vegetables. Health care was also postponed, often until a medical condition became severe. Households were forced to dig into savings, pawn their possessions, and borrow from relatives or loan sharks. Pressures to make ends meet took an emotional toll on families as they struggled to survive the adjustment to the debt crisis.[8]

From Adjustment through Growth to Debt Reduction: The 1989 Brady Plan

The 1989 Brady plan addressed the need for debt reduction as a necessary step toward stable growth in developing countries. The Brady plan offered three options: decreasing the face value of debt, extending the time period of obligations, or infusion of new money. Countries were officially able to decrease the face value through buybacks in the secondary market. Whereas earlier buybacks were considered cheating and not sanctioned as indicating good performance in servicing loans, countries such as Costa Rica were able to reduce official debt by $1.1 billion.[9] Alternatively, countries were able to swap old loans for thirty-year bonds with a 30–35-percent discount on the face value at a variable interest rate, or swap loans without the discount but at a fixed interest rate of 6.25 percent. The longer time period of the Brady bonds made them consistent with the long-term strategies needed for growth. A novel feature of Brady deals were the guarantees to the lender. The United States, Japan (a primary financier), and the developing country put up guarantees (usually in the form of U.S. Treasury bonds) to safeguard payment in the event of default, encouraging investor confidence. Finally, new money could be extended to cover interest in the early years and smooth the transition to the market economy. To be eligible for any of the three options, countries had to show credible political will and a strong track record in economic reform.

The Mexican Brady deal in 1989 restructured $48 billion of its liabilities by floating $20.8 billion in bonds that had been discounted from the face value at 35 percent and $22.4 billion in par value bonds at 6.25 fixed interest. In addition, Mexico received $4.4 billion in new money at the rate of LIBOR plus 13–16 percent.[10] The World Bank estimated that this debt relief reduced net transfers by $4 billion per year, nearly 2 percent of the gross domestic product (GDP), from 1989 through 1994.[11] Box 4.4 recalls the tough economic road Mexico faced up to the debt relief of the Brady plan, underscoring how crisis drove policy throughout the decade.

The commercial sector responded more enthusiastically to the Brady options than it did to the Baker plan. The former's realistic appraisal of the need to reduce the debt overhang, as well as its insurance guarantees, made it appealing. Investors found the plan pragmatic and less risky than the traditional short-term financial

---

BOX 4.4.   MILEPOSTS IN MEXICAN DEBT

Date	Event
1978–1981	Three-month London Interbank Offer Rate (LIBOR) jumps from 8.8 percent to 16.8 percent
February 1982	President Lopez Portillo vows to "defend the currency like a dog" but is forced to devalue
12 August 1982	Moratorium placed on dollar-denominated deposits held in Mexican banks
15 August 1982	Mexico announces it can no longer meet interest payments on foreign debt
Fall 1982	Mexico signs standby agreement with the IMF
1986	*Peso* devalued
October 1987	Mexican stock market collapses, losing 74 percent of its value in less than forty days; inflation at annual rate of 159 percent
December 1987	Unsuccessful Baker plan provides only $1.1 billion in debt relief for Mexico
April 1989	Mexico signs three-year, $3.64 billion loan agreement with the IMF
July 1989	U.S. Treasury secretary Brady introduces collateralized Brady bonds, reducing Mexican debt to foreign banks by U.S.$48.5 billion and cutting annual debt payments by U.S.$3 billion for next four years

Source: Helen Shapiro, *Mexico: Escaping the Debt Crisis,* Harvard Business School Case (Boston: Harvard Business School, 1991).

commitments. Table 4.8 lists the Brady deals. It is also important to note that by 1989, Latin America had already undertaken substantial reforms and was emerging as an intriguing investment arena. Brady bonds arrived as a vehicle for investment in a region that, after much painful adjustment, was beginning to be viewed as ripe for growth.

IS THE DEBT CRISIS OVER IN LATIN AMERICA?

Tough adjustments in Latin America appear to have paid off in the region. Data for the 1990s in Figure 4.2 mark the return of positive net transfers in the region. Table 4.9 shows the decline in the ratio of external debt to exports of goods and services, as well as interest as a percentage of exports of goods and services. By 2000 total external debt had reached the manageable level of 38.5 percent of gross national product, and exports, or the ability to earn hard currency, had expanded while interest rates had fallen, bringing the drain of interest payments on the export bill down to 11.8 percent. This is not to say that Latin America is no longer vulnerable to its external obligations. When international financial crises in Asia, Russia, and Brazil hit the region in the late 1990s, the burden of debt servicing increased as well. Nonetheless, crisis was averted. As we will see in chapter 7, international capital has returned to the region. Net capital inflows reached U.S.$69.2 billion in 1996 as foreign direction investment, portfolio investments, and bonds captured the attention of global investors.[12]

Latin America's recovery from the debt crisis has been a long and painful process. The turnaround in the region is quite dramatic. Many nations are emerging as major players in the world's debt and equity markets. Some countries have initiated their own stabilization and emergency funds to circumvent the need for a future return to the IMF.

These funds have been developed in response to international lenders' reluctance to deal directly with Latin American governments. Since the 1980s, financing has been restricted mostly to the corporate sector. Some of this is changing as confidence grows regarding the sustainability of stabilization programs. A 1999 agreement with the IMF shored up investor confidence that the Argentine reforms were permanent changes, able to weather the storms of the Asian and the Brazilian crises. Labor market, social security, and tax reforms will be accelerated, restoring investor faith in Argentina's ability to honor its debts.[13]

A second important sign of the maturity of Latin American markets is the shift in focus of Latin American firms to domestic markets for investment capital. Many Latin American firms are turning to the region's healthy private pension and mutual funds for financing. This explosion in private pension funds, which currently manage about $130 billion and grow about $1 billion per month, has provided Latin American markets with ample domestic funding for investment. Bankers point to the increase in privatizations in the region as another reason for the increase in loanable funds.[14] The rescheduling of Panama's private debt through the use of Brady bonds in 1996 allowed the state telecommunications company, INTEL, to return to the market with a $28-million package underwritten by Citibank.[15] The increase in

Table 4.8. Latin America Brady Deals

Country	Date	Terms of Deal
Argentina	June 2000	$3.3 billion of Brady bonds swapped $2.4 billion of new 15-year global bonds
	April 1993	$19.3 billion in debt swapped for 30-year bonds
Bolivia	May 1993	Buyback of $170 million in commercial bank debt
	July 1992	Collateralized interest-free 30-year bullet-maturity par bonds
Brazil	August 2000	$5.22 billion of Brady bonds swapped with $5.16 billion 40-year global bonds with a coupon of 11%
	April 1994	$48 billion in debt swapped for (1) 30-year discount bonds, (2) 30-year fixed interest par bonds, (3) 15-year variable interest bonds
Costa Rica	May 1990	$579 million in debt-for-bond exchange
Dominican Republic	August 1994	$107.01 billion in (1) debt buybacks, (2) discount exchange bonds, (3) past-due interest bonds
Ecuador	August 2000	$5.9 billion in debt exchanged for $3.95 billion in new 12- and 30-year global bonds
	February 1995	$7.8 billion in debt exchanged for discount and reduced-rate bonds
Mexico	September 2000	Buyback of $150 million in Swiss franc-denominated 30-year Brady bonds at a 22% discount plus any accrued and unpaid interest
	October 2000	Buyback of $1 billion in Brady bonds denominated in European currencies
	November 2000	Buyback of $385 million in Brady bonds
	March 1990	$20.5 billion in debt exchanged for 35% discount bonds, $22.4 billion for reduced interest bonds, and $5.3 billion in conversion bonds
	May 1996	$2.4 billion in Brady bonds swapped for $1.8 billion fixed-rate bond
	September 1996	Buyback of $1.2 billion in Brady bonds
Panama	September 1997	$600 million offering of 30-year uncollateralized bonds for $713 million of Brady bonds.
	April 1996	$3.9 billion public external debt exchanged for (1) discount bonds, (2) par bonds, (3) 18-year front-loaded interest-reduction bonds (FLIRBs)
Peru	November 1996	$8 billion in public external debt exchanged for (1) discount bonds, (2) reduced-interest par bonds, (3) FLIRBs, (4) discounted buyback
Uruguay	September 1999	$96 million in debt swapped for $85 million of 30-year global bonds
	February 1991	$628 million in discounted cash buyback, $535 million in collateralized debt reduction bonds, $447 million in debt conversion notes, $89 million in new money
Venezuela	September 1997	$4.4 billion in debt swapped for $4 billion of uncollateralized 30-year bonds at an interest rate of 325 basis points above the U.S. Treasury rate
	December 1990	$19.7 billion in debt exchanged for (1) 91-day short-term notes, (2) discount bonds, (3) reduced at fixed-rate-interest bonds, (4) temporary step-down interest rate bonds

Source: World Bank, *Global Development Finance* (Washington, D.C.: World Bank, 1997 and 2001).

Table 4.9.   Debt Indicators for Latin America and the Caribbean, 1980–2000

Year	Total Debt Stocks/Export of Goods and Services	Total Debt Stocks/GNP	Total Debt Service/Export of Goods and Services	Interest/Export of Goods and Services	Reserves/Months
1980	201.0	34.4	36.2	19.2	4.3
1990	254.5	44.6	24.4	12.2	3.6
1995	212.9	40.0	26.4	12.2	4.8
1996	201.0	38.0	31.3	11.7	5.2
1997	190.8	36.6	35.6	11.2	4.7
1998	212.7	41.1	32.5	11.9	4.2
1999	208.4	41.8	41.6	13.0	4.0
2000	172.6	38.5	35.7	11.8	3.5

Source: World Bank, *World Debt Tables* (Washington, D.C.: World Bank, various years).

domestic lending has also spurred a rise in foreign investment banks setting up and buying local brokerage houses within Latin America.

Finally, an important sign of the strength of Latin America markets is that these issues (both debt and equity) are being denominated in local currencies rather than U.S. dollars. Investors have placed an increasing degree of trust in Latin American currencies as countries have been able to maintain economic credibility. Internal debt, however, is also cause for serious concern. In the Brazilian case, for example, the total net public debt exploded from 30 percent of GDP in 1984 to more than 60 percent in 2002. Only about 30 percent of this debt is in dollars, but the internal obligation ties the hands of the newly elected President da Silva. His government must maintain a fiscal surplus to keep interest rates down or risk a debt-led collapse of the Brazilian economy. The key to predicting the stability of Brazilian debt is estimating the tolerance of domestic institutional investors. The debt to GDP ratio in Italy and Belgium has exceeded 100 percent. Do Brazilians have this kind of confidence that their government will honor its obligations?[16]

DATA EXERCISE

Drawing on the the World Bank's *World Debt Tables* or from the IMF statistical databases on the Internet at dsbb.imf.org, how have Latin American countries performed on external debt indicators in recent years? Do the new data confirm the trend of financial consolidation, or do any of the new numbers give cause for alarm?

These changes in the Latin American markets point to an overall increase in confidence for these developing nations. Although there is still much progress to be made, recent trends suggest that Latin America may be ready to take on a more influential position in the world market. However, underneath the shiny new exterior, the mountain of external debt still remains to be paid in full.

The return to the market has not reached the poorest countries in the region. Table 4.10 shows debt burdens by income classifications. As a result of pressure from the international community, the World Bank and the IMF launched the HIPC (or highly indebted poor country) initiative. Unlike earlier refinancing

Table 4.10.   Latin American Economies by Income Group and Indebtedness, January 2000

Income and Debt Classification	Severely Indebted (PV of Debt/XGS >220% or PV Debt/GNP >80%)	Moderately Indebted (PV of Debt/XGS >132% and <220% or PV Debt/GNP >132% and <80%)	Less Indebted (PV of Debt/XGS <132% or PV Debt/GNP <48%)
Low income pc GNP <$775	Nicaragua	—	—
Lower middle income pc GNP $756–$2,995	Bolivia, Guyana, Peru	Colombia, Ecuador, Honduras	Costa Rica, El Salvador, Guatemala, Paraguay, Suriname
Upper middle income pc GNP $2,996–$9,265	Argentina, Brazil	Chile, Panama, Uruguay Venezuela	Mexico

Source: Extracted from the World Bank, *Global Development Finance 2001,* appendix 1, table A17.

that actually increased the debt stock of poor countries, the objective of HIPC is to reduce the stock of debt to sustainable levels. A 1999 reform accelerated the relief given to countries with track records of credible reform. Countries receiving HIPC assistance must directly link debt relief to assistance to the poor with poverty-reduction strategy papers (PRSPs) developed in consultation with civil society. Comprehensive, well-targeted, and credible PRSPs include measures to achieve job-creating growth, especially in agriculture; realignment of public expenditure toward poverty reduction; improvements in access to basic health and education; action to improve governance; transparency and accountability; and processes to maintain the engagement of civil society.[17] The strategies are intended to be country-owned, developed as a result of national consultation, and implemented collaboratively with other development agencies, especially the UN system.

HIPC lending proceeds in two phases. At the end of the first period of adoption of IMF–World Bank Reforms, a decision point is reached based on an analysis of debt sustainability; if a country's debt obligations as a percentage of exports exceeds 150 percent, it qualifies for assistance. Once eligible, the country must establish a further track record of adjustment and adopt a national PRSP; further assistance will be provided at this time. The national process of consultation embodied in the PRSP is designed to promote accountability and to decrease the chances that

QUESTION FOR THOUGHT

You can access sample PRSPs at the IMF website at www.imf.org. Choose one, perhaps Bolivia. Does the condition of tying debt relief to a national program of poverty reduction make sense from an economic as well as a social perspective?

debt relief will only benefit corrupt politicians or as fungible money be used for military spending.

Early evidence suggests that the poorest HIPC-eligible countries are, for the first time in decades, spending more on social services than on debt service. Critics argue that the reduction of approximately two-thirds of outstanding debt doesn't go far enough—there should instead be a 100-percent cancellation. Others suggest that the definition of sustainable debt levels is sensitive to the volatile external market shocks that poor countries face. For example, sustainable debt to export ratios can quickly become burdensome if foreign markets dry up. The calculation process is cumbersome; the World Bank's online handbook to advise countries on document presentation runs over one thousand pages. The fear that relief is too slow and not substantial enough to alleviate the current misery of the poor also motivates opposition to HIPC.[18] Some believe that HIPC is a good step, but only a baby step given the desperate lives of those living on less than $1 a day.

In Latin America four countries qualify for HIPC: Bolivia, Guyana, Nicaragua, and Honduras. Bolivia, the first country in the world to reach the so-called completion point—the successful completion of negotiations over progress indicators—received nearly $2 billion in debt relief, reducing its external debt by one half. Debt service as a percent of exports fell from 23 to 16 percent, releasing funds for poverty programs.[19]

LESSONS OF THE DEBT CRISIS

What are the lessons of the crisis? The most salient and the most painful lesson is that strong fundamentals matter. Unlike the populist policies of the past, countries must attend to price stability and budget constraints. Responsible fiscal policy—keeping the domestic house in order—has clear effects on a country's external balance. This is perhaps more important today in highly integrated capital markets. Information travels quickly, and negative performance on critical indicators carries a high price. Maintaining the confidence of the market is a vital ingredient for success. Without credible and predictable policies, capital will quickly respond to uncertainty by fleeing to less risky instruments. Politics and market psychology are intertwined with sound economic policy.

But generating the necessary macroeconomic stability in the region was no easy task. Several countries in the region had annual inflation rates exceeding 1,000 percent. In the next chapter we will consider how governments in Latin America took on the inflation problem. Tied to the ability to restrain inflation has been a reengineering of the role of government. In contrast to the central role of the state under ISI, Latin American governments had to redefine the boundaries between the public and the private sectors. We will consider this revolution in political and economic space in chapter 6. The transformation of the inward-oriented model to an export-driven growth strategy has engendered strategic changes in the behavior of firms and states in the region. This will be discussed in chapter 8, "Contemporary Trade Policy." These radical changes in the rules and goals of the economy in Latin America have not been without cost. Poverty rose throughout the region, and the environment suffered from the natural resource export drives—the subject of chapters 10 and 14. As we explore these issues, we will see that the resolution of the debt crisis fundamentally transformed the development model in the region.

Debt Restructuring Twenty Years Later

In addition to the problems of the poorest countries, the Asian Economic Crisis of 1997–1998 forced a rethinking of conditionality. The cookie-cutter approach of reducing excess demand accompanied by changes in the size of the state simply didn't apply—and raised question of the applicability of conditionality throughout Latin America and Africa as well. Although under IMF bylaws additional financing can only be provided if necessary changes in an economy are made, the expanded scope of conditionality of the 1980s and 1990s that extended beyond macroeconomic measures to micro foundations has been reversed in the new millennium. The first principle guiding reform is ownership of policies. Success of IMF policies has been shown to be tied to domestic political support for economic reform. Although reform may still be unpleasant economic medicine, if a package is arrived at in consultation with civil society, repeated failure of packages may be avoided. Secondly, conditionality is increasingly restricted to the IMF's core areas of competence in macroeconomic reform. Privatization and social conditionality is being left to coordination with other institutions such as the World Bank. Letters of intent are more clearly drawn to reflect those necessary macroeconomic changes for release of IMF funds as opposed to recommended structural changes in a country's reform program. Overall, the average number of conditions imposed has decreased by one third. Changing conditionality will require greater flexibility and judgment on a case by case basis. Whether greater country specificity will encourage more sustainable reform will require the test of time. It is interesting to at least observe, however, that after twenty years of criticism—particularly by the neostructuralists that packages didn't address underlying national conditions—the IMF is finally beginning to listen.[20]

Changes in capital markets in the 1990s have prompted the need to rethink how to handle sovereign crises. Unlike the debt crisis of 1982, when Argentina collapsed in 2002 there was no orderly mechanism to begin creditor negotiations. Twenty years ago major creditors—primarily large banks—would negotiate collectively through a steering committee that resolved intercreditor problems, assessed debtor offers, and preserved confidentiality. Today's claimants, largely diverse bondholders rather than syndicated banks, have little incentive and ability to solve crises collectively. Bondholders holdout, free riding in hopes of receiving payments in line with original contracts. Complex financial instruments such as derivatives make the problem worse as the underlying equity value is not always transparent. Yet the failure to act promptly to resolve a debtor's problems results in a deterioration of the nation's assets—a huge economic and social loss in no one's interest.

A solution much like a corporate bankruptcy restructuring has been proposed to address the greater diversity of claims in integrated capital markets. Under a corporate reorganization model, a stay is imposed on legal actions by creditors, constraints are placed on the debtor to reorganize, incentives for new credit encourage bridge financing, and a plan approved by the majority of all creditors is binding on all. Although a sovereign nation exhibits different characteristics from a company—most importantly, one can't liquidate a nation nor take it over—these principles may promote a more orderly approach to sovereign restructuring. Changes in international law could make it possible to allow a qualified majority of bondholders to approve a restructuring that would bind all. Protection of a nation's assets during a specified period of perhaps sixty days would temporarily insulate asset values as a country prepared for credible and sustainable economic change. There may be a role for the IMF in assessing the viability of the plan and providing emergency financing, although a decentralized market plan is also possible. Allowing preferential treatment of creditors bringing fresh money to resolve the crisis might facilitate a market-based solution.

Critics of this plan worry that a sovereign bankruptcy proceeding will create a moral hazard; supporters argue that the political and economic pain a country goes through in a crash is deterrent enough. Others suggest that the plan doesn't go far enough, particularly in the case of very poor countries, in reducing the burden of unsustainable debt levels. Tough technical issues remain in determining the relative position of domestic and international creditors and in dispute resolution. However, most agree that a new approach is necessary to counterbalance the uncertainly and volatility that has accompanied access to international capital markets. In April 2002 G-7 finance ministers and central bank governors approved a plan to reduce financial crises by embodying the principle of cooling off periods and new ways for creditors to engage with debtors to improve the quality, transparency, and predictability of decision making.[21] Nonetheless, as of the September 2002 World Bank–IMF meetings, financial markets were unwilling to sign on.

Key Concepts

absorption	debt-for-nature swaps	involuntary lending
capital flight	debt trap	provisioning
conditionality	economic populism	secondary market
debt-for-equity swaps	illiquidity	structural adjustment

Chapter Summary

The Accumulation of Debt

- The debt crisis was a natural consequence of spending practices in the 1950s, 1960s, and 1970s. Careless borrowing for large-scale projects with high capital requirements was partly responsible for the accumulation of debt in Latin America. Many of these multiyear investments, with unpredictable returns, lead to a debt trap. Economic populism, inefficiency, and corruption contributed to further unnecessary and extravagant fiscal spending financed through more loans.

- Negative real interest rates and the influx of petrodollars into the banking system made borrowing attractive and easy during the 1970s. In real terms, countries had to pay back less than what they borrowed and had seemingly unlimited funds.
- As evidenced by the cases of Mexico, Brazil, and Argentina, not every Latin American country pursued the same policies. The end result of accumulated debts, however, was the same.

On the Road to a Crisis

- In 1979 the Federal Reserve Bank of the United States raised interest rates. The effects were detrimental for Latin America. While countries' interest payments for past loans increased, the U.S. market for Latin American exports fell, effectively limiting the foreign exchange needed to repay loans.
- The excess supply of local currency fueled inflation. Locals deposited their money abroad in hopes of higher returns, and capital flight ensued. Governments' ability to raise revenues was therefore greatly weakened.
- Mexico's inability and unwillingness to pay its debt signaled to the international community that the economies of Latin America were on the verge of crisis.

Responses to the Debt Crisis

- Under the assumption that Latin American countries needed to reduce domestic absorption, the IMF prescribed a decrease in fiscal spending, tight monetary policy, and strict trade policies. What has become known as IMF conditionality spurred criticism from various circles, including the structuralist school, for unnecessarily contracting the economy without changing its structural problems.
- In response to the crisis, a secondary market for debt developed. The secondary market was used to facilitate debt-for-equity and debt-for-nature swaps.
- The Baker plan was "too little, too late," representing a shift away from IMF conditionality. A new role was given to the World Bank, focusing on structural adjustment.
- The Brady plan decreased the face value of debt, extended the time period of obligations, or infused new money.

After the Crisis

- The return of international capital to Latin America, the shift toward domestic markets for financing, and an increase in the degree of trust in domestic currencies are signs of an increase in the maturity of Latin American markets.
- The HIPC initiative links debt reduction for the poorest countries with poverty alleviation measures.
- A sovereign debt restructuring plan may promote orderly responses to contemporary financial crises.

Notes

1. Federico A. Sturzenegger, "Description of a Populist Experience: Argentina, 1973–1976," in *The Macroeconomics of Populism in Latin America,* ed. Rudiger Dornbusch and Sebastian Edwards (Chicago: University of Chicago Press, 1991), 79.

2. John T. Cuddington, *Capital Flight: Estimates, Issues, and Explanations,* Princeton Studies in International Finance, no. 58 (Princeton, N.J.: Princeton University Press, 1986), 10.

3. Sebastian Edwards, *Crisis and Reform in Latin America: From Despair to Hope* (New York: Oxford University Press, 1995), 17.

4. Patricio Meller, "IMF and World Bank Roles in the Latin American Foreign Debt Problem," in *The Latin American Development Debate: Neostructuralism, Neomonetarism, and Adjustment Processes,* ed. Patricio Meller (Boulder, Colo.: Westview, 1991).

5. "'Til Debt Do Us Part," *The Economist,* 28 February 1987, 85.

6. Irma Arriagada, "Unequal Participation by Women in the Working World," *CEPAL Review* 40 (April 1990): 83–98.

7. Helena Hirata and John Humphrey, "Workers' Response to Job Loss: Female and Male Industrial Workers in Brazil," *World Development* 19, no. 6 (1991): 671–82.

8. Frances Stewart, *Adjustment and Poverty: Options and Choices* (London: Routledge, 1995), 189. Stewart summarizes results of studies published in the late 1980s.

9. U.S. Department of State, *1996 Country Reports on Economic Policy and Trade Practices,* a report submitted to the Senate Committee on Foreign Relations, the Senate Committee on Finance, the House Committee on Foreign Affairs, and the House Committee on Ways and Means, January 1997 (available at www.state.gov/www/issues/tradereports/latinamerica99/costarica96.html).

10. Edwards, *Crisis and Reform,* table 4.3.

11. Edwards, *Crisis and Reform,* 81.

12. World Bank, *Global Development Finance* (Washington, D.C.: World Bank, 1997), 89–90.

13. Bloomberg Latin America, "Argentine Markets Climb after IMF, Banks Move to Shore Up Confidence" (www.quote.bloomberg.com [accessed 14 July 1999]).

14. CANTV was partially privatized in 1991, sold to VenWorld, a consortium led by GTE Corp.

15. U.S. Department of State, *1996 Country Reports.*

16. "Brazil: Domestic Debt Dynamics and Implications," *ING Barings Emerging Markets Weekly Report,* 5 March 1999, pp. 1–3.

17. Statement of U.S. Treasury secretary Lawrence H. Summers at the Joint Session of the International Monetary and Finance Committee and the Development Committee, Prague, Czech Republic, September 24, 2000, www.imf.org.

18. Drop the Debt, "HIPC Initiative Offers No Guarantee Against Future Debt Problems," www.dropthedebt.org.

19. World Bank News Release 2001/369/S, "Bolivia: World Bank and IMF Support US$1.2 Billion in Additional Debt Service Relieve for Bolivia Under Enhanced HIPC Initiative," www.worldbank.org. Also see "Debt—Undermining Development," www.globalissues.org and www.oxfam.org.

20. Masood Ahmed, Timothy Lane, and Marianne Schulze-Ghattas, "Refocusing IMF Conditionality," *Finance and Development*, December 2001, vol. 38, no. 4 as accessed at www.imf.org.

21. Anne O. Krueger, *A New Approach to Sovereign Debt Restructuring,* Washington, D.C.: The IMF, April 2002; Ed Mayo and Romilly Greenhill, "A Bankrupt Initiative," *World Link* 15, issue 2 (March 2002): 34.

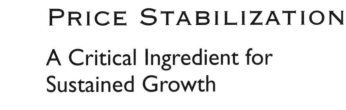

CHAPTER FIVE

PRICE STABILIZATION

A Critical Ingredient for Sustained Growth

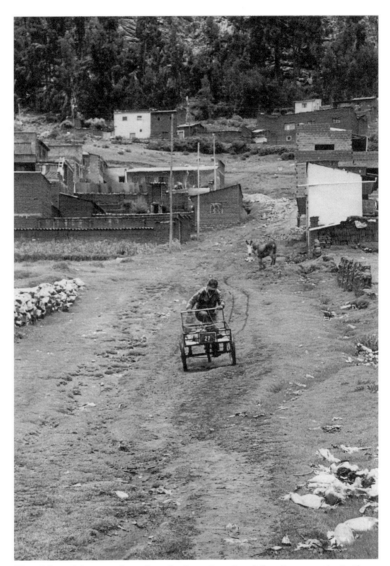

The debt crisis contributed to the lost decade of development in Latin America. *(Courtesy of Amanda McKown.)*

Inflation plagued Latin American economies from the 1980s through the first part of the 1990s. Imagine the difficulty—as was experienced in Argentina, Brazil, Nicaragua, and Peru—of living with inflation rates exceeding 2,000 percent per year! These were not isolated exceptions; as we can see in table 5.1, only Costa Rica, Panama, and Bolivia had rates under 20 percent in 1990, and as we will see, Bolivia paid a huge social price to tame inflation in the mid eighties.

Inflation exacts a high cost. Real wages—earnings after the inflationary bite—fall, thus reducing purchasing power. Inflation hits the poor particularly hard; the wealthy can insulate themselves through financial mechanisms indexed to the inflation rate. Macroeconomic instability creates uncertainty and undermines the investment climate. Inflation compromises the business environment, making long-run decision making impossible. It erodes tax earnings and reduces the ability of the government to provide public services. It promotes consumption today, reduces savings, and creates environmental pressure. Inflation hurts nearly all economic actors. Despite these costs, excessive inflation persisted in Latin America for nearly fifteen years. Our discussion in this chapter revolves around several questions:

• Why was Latin America so inflation prone?
• What caused inflationary pressures in the region?
• Why was inflation so intractable?
• What mechanisms were used to bring inflation under control in the region?

Table 5.1.   Inflation of Latin American Countries, 1990

Country	Hyper (>2000%)	High (>30%)	Medium (>20%)	Low (< 20%)
Nicaragua	7,485.0			
Peru	7,481.5			
Brazil	2,937.0			
Argentina	2,313.7			
Uruguay		112.5		
Guyana		63.6		
Ecuador		48.5		
Guatemala		41.2		
Venezuela		40.6		
Paraguay		38.2		
Colombia			29.1	
Mexico			26.6	
Chile			26.0	
El Salvador			24.0	
Honduras			23.3	
Suriname			21.7	
Costa Rica				19.0
Bolivia				17.1
Panama				0.8

Source: IADB, *Economic and Social Progress in Latin America* (Washington, D.C.: Johns Hopkins University Press, various years); and IMF, *World Economic Outlook 1997* (Washington, DC: IMF, 1997), 148.

- What worked?
- Is inflation in Latin America now gone for good? Will the collapse of the exchange rate-based stabilization plans in Argentina and Brazil result in renewed inflation in the region?

Latin America has been a virtual laboratory for macroeconomic experiments in the 1980s. This chapter will address these issues of macroeconomic stabilization, underscoring the causes and costs of inflation and highlighting the measures used to address it. It will look at the range of policies introduced to provide some insight on the difficult problem of maintaining stable prices while an economy is going through the complex and sometimes tumultuous process of economic growth.

THEORIES OF INFLATION: MONETARISTS VERSUS STRUCTURALISTS

Policies to attack inflation rest on an understanding of inflation's causes. Two broad schools of thought address the problem: the monetarists and the structuralists. For monetarists, or orthodox theorists, the cause of inflation is rather simple: too much money chasing too few goods. Monetarists such as Milton Friedman and the Chicago School look to the equation of exchange as a key to the cause of inflation. With M representing the quantity of money, V equal to the velocity or the number of times per year a unit of currency is used to purchase final goods and services, P as the price level, and Q standing for national output or gross domestic product (GDP) in real terms, monetarists argue that

$$M \times V = P \times Q$$

If the rate of growth of output and velocity are assumed to be constant in the short run, prices are determined by the quantity of money in circulation. A rising level of money in circulation causes price acceleration. Although in the short run resource price shocks or shortages may accelerate prices temporarily, monetarists perceive that inflation over time is caused by excess liquidity in the system. Understanding persistent inflation for the monetarist involves highlighting why monetary authorities would continue to make policy errors by increasing the money supply in the face of rising prices. Monetarist explanations for such excess in Latin America include irresponsible deficit financing, erosion of the tax base, and mismanagement of the debt crisis. Let's consider these in turn.

Deficit Financing

If a government is spending more than it is taking in, the deficit must be financed. This can be done in three ways: print money, issue domestic debt, or borrow from foreign sources. As John Maynard Keynes pointed out in 1923, a government can live for a long time by printing money.[1] A government's ability to buy goods and services by printing money is called **seignorage.** Indeed, if the economy is growing at a strong pace, the quantity of goods and services available increases and the price effect may be moderate. However, once growth slows down, there is too much money chasing too few goods. Deficits in Latin America imply different dynamics than in the United States. The U.S. dollar is the world's most important reserve currency. If the Federal Reserve issues more dollars—and if the world continues its appetite for dollars as a safe investment—investors throughout the world absorb the dollars and reinvest in America's sophisticated capital markets. If the Bank of Mexico emits *pesos,* a strong international demand is far less likely. The value of the *peso* erodes, confidence vanishes, and a crisis erupts. There may come a time when the demand for dollars weakens sufficiently to present binding constraints. For now it is enough to appreciate that tough budget problems in Latin America resolved by printing money are more likely to result in inflation and balance of payments crises.

The alternative to printing money is issuing debt to finance government spending. Governments are often precluded from issuing domestic debt—the equivalent of a U.S. Treasury bond—by underdeveloped local capital markets. If the public cannot be induced to hold bonds, a government must borrow externally or print money. When the debt crisis hit in the early 1980s in Latin America, the external borrowing option dried up and the simplest response to deficits was to monetize them.

We can observe the pattern of macroeconomic instability in Latin America up to the 1990s in tables 5.2, 5.3, and 5.4. In table 5.2, we note the trend of strong and persistent deficits throughout the region from 1982 to 1990. Only two countries—Chile

Table 5.2.   Overall Surplus or Deficit in Latin American Countries, 1982–1990 (as a percentage of GDP)

Country	1982	1983	1984	1985	1986	1987	1988	1989	1990
Argentina	−3.7	−10.1	−5.7	−2.9	−3.2	−4.4	−3.8	−2.6	−1.7
Bolivia	−13.7	−17.0	−18.3	−9.3	−1.7	−3.7	−5.0	−2.0	−1.3
Brazil	−3.1	−4.3	−5.0	−11.1	−14.0	−12.6	−16.3	−17.5	−6.2
Chile	−2.6	−3.7	−3.0	−1.9	−0.5	2.3	3.6	5.0	1.4
Colombia	−2.0	−1.0	−4.3	−2.7	−1.3	−0.5	−1.4	−1.7	−0.1
Costa Rica	−3.2	−3.4	−3.1	−2.0	−3.3	−2.0	−2.5	−4.1	−4.4
Ecuador	−4.4	−3.0	−0.6	1.9	−2.2	−6.2	−2.0	0.4	3.5
El Salvador	−5.9	−4.1	−3.2	−2.0	−3.6	−0.9	−3.0	−3.7	−1.5
Guatemala	−4.7	−3.6	−3.7	−1.8	−1.5	−1.3	−1.7	−2.9	−1.8
Guyana	−34.3	−40.1	−44.5	−56.1	−58.8	−42.4	−31.6	−6.6	−22.9
Honduras	−9.7	−9.0	−9.8	−7.2	−6.0	−5.8	−4.1	−6.0	−4.1
Mexico	−11.9	−8.2	−7.2	−7.6	−13.1	−14.2	−9.7	−5.0	−2.8
Nicaragua	−13.3	−30.0	−22.5	−21.3	−14.5	−16.0	−25.1	−3.5	−18.7
Panama	−11.4	−6.2	−7.4	−3.4	−4.5	−4.2	−5.2	−6.9	6.8
Paraguay	−1.5	−4.7	−3.5	−2.3	0.0	0.4	0.6	2.4	3.2
Peru	−3.1	−7.3	−4.4	−3.0	−4.3	−6.9	−3.9	−6.3	−3.5
Suriname	−1.7	−17.6	−18.4	−21.4	−26.0	−24.8	−21.3	−14.0	−6.3
Uruguay	—	−4.2	−5.8	−3.1	−1.3	−1.3	−2.0	−3.4	−0.1
Venezuela	−2.1	−0.6	2.8	2.0	−0.4	−1.6	−7.4	−1.0	−2.1

Source: IADB, *Economic and Social Progress in Latin America* (Washington, D.C.: Johns Hopkins University Press, various years).

Table 5.3.   Average Annual Rates of Growth of Money Supply in Latin America, 1982–1990

Country	1982	1983	1984	1985	1986	1987	1988	1989	1990
Argentina	154.2	362.0	582.3	584.3	89.7	113.5	351.4	4,168.2	1,023.2
Bolivia	228.8	207.0	1,798.3	5,784.6	86.1	36.6	35.3	2.4	39.5
Brazil	68.5	102.7	204.1	334.3	330.1	215.4	426.9	1,337.0	2,333.6
Chile	2.8	15.6	22.8	24.2	43.3	21.0	46.5	17.2	23.3
Colombia	25.4	23.4	24.1	10.7	—	—	25.7	—	—
Costa Rica	70.3	38.9	17.6	7.7	31.0	0.3	53.2	–2.0	3.9
Ecuador	14.0	31.9	39.6	25.6	20.1	34.7	52.7	43.8	59.0
El Salvador	3.7	–1.3	13.8	27.0	19.1	–0.4	8.1	13.5	22.3
Guatemala	1.4	6.0	4.3	54.9	19.5	9.8	14.4	20.7	33.0
Guyana	25.3	17.4	20.2	20.3	19.4	51.4	54.8	34.0	54.5
Honduras	13.5	13.6	2.5	–3.2	8.2	26.6	11.9	20.0	23.6
Mexico	62.6	40.3	60.0	49.5	67.2	118.1	67.8	37.3	63.1
Nicaragua	25.7	67.1	83.5	162.8	252.2	637.0	11,673.4	2,368.3	6,286.7
Panama	5.4	–1.8	2.2	7.5	9.8	–1.6	–31.3	1.0	41.0
Paraguay	–3.6	25.6	29.4	28.0	26.7	53.6	34.8	31.7	28.3
Peru	40.4	96.5	104.4	281.2	88.0	122.0	515.0	1,654.9	6,710.0
Suriname	17.7	8.0	26.9	52.5	39.6	27.1	24.5	11.3	4.0
Uruguay	19.8	9.0	48.4	107.6	86.1	58.1	63.7	72.9	101.0
Venezuela	4.5	25.0	27.0	8.9	5.3	40.8	22.7	22.2	54.6

Source: IMF, *International Financial Statistics 1996* (Washington, D.C.: IMF, 1996), 81.

and Paraguay—had surpluses nearly as often as deficits. Brazil's consistent deficit averaged 10 percent of GDP over the period. Although we should be careful not to over infer about the cause of the growth of the money supply, indeed we can see that in the countries with strong and persistent deficits, the average annual rates of growth of the money supply are startling. In Brazil, Argentina, Nicaragua, and Peru, the rate of growth of the money supply exceeded 1,000 percent in 1990. In an attempt to raise money internally to finance deficits as well as to stem capital flight, national interest rates in 1990 exceeded 1,000 percent in Brazil and were above 30 percent in eight countries. But this was something of a losing battle. Although these interest rates were necessary to attract money for debt servicing, they also made borrowing for business investment problematic. The result was simultaneous inflation and recession.

Deficit financing creates a vicious circle. Persistent inflation lowers the cash balances that people want to hold, because the value of the currency is declining quickly. People prefer to purchase goods to retain the value of their earnings, driving up prices in the market. Inflation therefore begets inflation. A second perverse effect has also been identified. Whereas deficit spending in most industrial countries is countercyclical, in Latin America it has largely been procyclical. That is, instead of spending to stimulate the economy during a recession, Latin American governments tend to contract during recession. This is tied to access to funds. As recession erodes the government's ability to raise money in international markets, it must reign in spending. Unfortunately, such procyclical policies, by their very nature, exacerbate macroeconomic volatility.[2]

Table 5.4.   National Interest Rates in Latin America

Country	1982	1983	1984	1985	1986	1987	1988	1989	1990
Brazil	174.0	194.0	272.0	380.0	89.0	401.0	2,282.0	38,341.0	1,083.0
Colombia	27.0	27.0	27.0	27.0	33.8	34.8	34.3	36.9	46.5
Costa Rica	30.0	30.0	28.0	28.0	27.5	31.4	31.5	31.6	37.8
Ecuador	15.0	19.0	23.0	23.0	23.0	23.0	23.0	32.0	35.0
Guatemala	9.0	9.0	9.0	9.0	9.0	9.0	9.0	13.0	18.5
Guyana	14.0	14.0	14.0	14.0	14.0	14.0	14.0	35.0	30.0
Honduras	24.0	24.0	24.0	24.0	24.0	24.0	24.0	24.0	28.2
Nicaragua	—	—	—	—	—	—	12,874.6	311.0	10.0
Paraguay	—	—	—	—	—	—	10.0	21.0	30.0
Peru	44.5	60.0	60.0	42.6	36.1	29.8	748.0	865.6	289.6
Uruguay	83.7	112.7	133.2	145.1	138.4	143.4	154.5	219.6	251.6
Venezuela	13.0	11.0	11.0	8.0	8.0	8.0	8.0	45.0	43.0

Source: IMF, *International Financial Statistics 1996* (Washington, D.C.: IMF, 1996), 96.
Note: Central bank discount rates, end of period in percent per annum.

The Tax Connection

If a government has lost credibility or if its population is very poor, tax collection as a percentage of government expenses is very low. Furthermore, as inflation rises, the real value of tax collection falls. Taxes for 1986 are due in 1987; because they are paid in 1987 dollars, they are worth less after inflation. The phenomenon by which inflation eats away at the value of tax receipts is called the **Olivera–Tanzi effect.** An extreme case was Bolivia, where by 1984 only 2 percent of government expenditure was covered by taxes.[3] More printed money was therefore needed to cover the deficits. Inflation, as a result, exceeded 8,000 percent. We will return to the problem of taxation in the region in chapter 6.

Effects of the Debt Crisis

As access to foreign loans dried up, there was more pressure to raise money domestically to service existing debt. This left printing money as the most popular action to purchase the foreign exchange to make the interest payments on debt. This was the case in Argentina after 1982.[4] Furthermore, the devaluation often required in International Monetary Fund (IMF) stabilization packages increased the value of the external debt in domestic terms. That is, as the currency became worth less, it took more of it to buy the dollars to service the external debt. This increased the temptation to print money to service the debt. Running up a down escalator may be a good metaphor for this type of policy.

Is Inflation Too Much Money?

At the center of the monetarist explanations for inflationary financing were profligate governments running budget deficits. The monetarist solution to restrain inflation in the region was therefore quite straightforward: decrease government spending. If the monetarists are right and inflation is tied to excessive government spending, the solution is clear: eliminate deficit-driven policies. Yet this was easier said than done. Deficit reduction proved politically tough.

Why do governments run large fiscal deficits despite the inflationary risks associated with them? The research in this area indicates that countries with less stable political systems are more likely to engage in deficit financing. As political instability increases, politicians see it in their own interest to buy political favor and to avoid making hard choices.[5] Politically threatened governments find it difficult to carry through on promises of fiscal responsibility. Political change can therefore make economic stabilization more problematic. Clearly this plays out in cases such as Peru or Nicaragua. Political change from an authoritarian government to a democracy was taking place over this period for countries such as Brazil and Argentina. Instability likely played a role in the capacity of states to follow sound economic programs.

In contrast to these monetarist explanations, for the **structuralists** the explanation of deficit-led instability was too simple. Structuralists do not deny that excess liquidity or budget deficits can cause inflation, but they do not believe that these are the sole or even central causes of inflation in Latin America. Attention to monetary variables is complemented by the study of a host of other factors. Because structuralists add other factors to the orthodox focus on the money supply, their policy is sometimes called **heterodox.** Structuralist or heterodox explanations focus on the structure of the underdeveloped economy as the propagating mechanism for inflation. Instead of making the equilibrium assumptions of the classical model upon which the monetarist theory is based, structuralists contend that economies in Latin America can best be understood as incomplete markets that do not automatically tend toward full employment

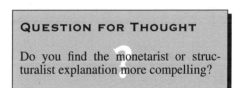

QUESTION FOR THOUGHT

Do you find the monetarist or structuralist explanation more compelling?

equilibrium. For the structuralists, bottlenecks in both the agricultural and the industrial sectors create price pressures. If input markets cannot quickly adjust to price signals to meet supply requirements, inflation will result. External price shocks from the international economy can also introduce or exacerbate instability in the domestic market.

Cost-push elements were therefore central to the structuralist explanation. Internal shortages and external price shocks such as the oil crisis interact with the structure of industry and labor organization to fuel an inflationary struggle. In contrast to the perfect competition assumption in neoclassical models, both output and labor markets in Latin America are highly concentrated. Under oligopolistic conditions, prices are sticky downward. Shortages ratchet up prices, but during periods of slack demand or recession, prices rarely fall. Furthermore, firms may engage in markup pricing to maintain profit margins. Large firms often have internal sources of capital as well, circumventing the need to pay high interest rates for capital. When prices increase, powerful labor unions demand wage increases—which firms are able to cover because they pass the cost on to the consumer. Inflation then reflects the distributive conflict between capital and labor. If all agents assume inflation, each side wants to build predicted price increases into its share of the pie.

Monetary authorities may passively accommodate the demand for money. Central banks in the region were often not independent of the executive branch and were therefore subject to political pressure. In Brazil the central bank was ordered by the military government to finance the public deficit automatically from 1971 to 1974; from 1974 until 1994, the minister of finance had overwhelming control of the central bank. In 1994 Brazil finally formed a National Monetary Council as a supervisory and coordination organ for money policy, accountable not only to the presidency but also to the congress.[6] For the structuralists, underdeveloped political systems, the lack of accountability of military governments, and later nascent democracies unable to handle competing demands contributed to inflationary tendencies.

In the structuralist model, inflation becomes embedded in the economy. People begin to anticipate inflation. Such **inertial inflation** results when economic agents come to expect inflation and automatically adjust for it in their wage demands and pricing patterns. Not surprisingly, expected inflation is a self-fulfilling prophecy as people adjust behaviors accordingly. However, for the structuralist, inflation was an unwelcome but not unexpected result of the conflicts inherent in the process of economic development. Since markets in developing countries had unique characteristics that did not favor equilibrium, the recessionary costs of forcing austerity under these circumstances were just too high. Structuralists were willing to live with inflation as a price associated with growth in the developing world. The policy challenge became reducing the costs of living in an inflationary society.

Indexation, Inflationary Expectations, and Velocity

In the 1980s structuralist thought dominated much policy making in the Latin American region. Measures were introduced to minimize the costs of inflation. Most wages were indexed to a public minimum salary that was adjusted monthly to accommodate inflation. A teacher's contract might, for example, be written for seven times the national minimum wage. As the minimum wage rose each month, salaries tracked inflation. Some prices were also indexed to inflation. If you got into a taxi in Rio de Janeiro, you would not pay the price on the meter. Rather, the meter reflected a price on a *tabela,* or list of prices, that could be adjusted by decree. In stores, clothing was tagged with letters of the alphabet. Although K might mean a Cr$50 dress one day, a week later a buyer might have to come up with Cr$65. Interest on bank accounts was also indexed. Checking accounts were interest bearing (similar to U.S. NOW accounts), and borrowers had to pay the real rate of interest plus inflation. Rents were likewise increased alongside interest and bond rates through this inflation adjustment, sometimes euphemistically called the "monetary correction."

In some periods the official rate of **indexation** was set at less than the rate of inflation to act as a brake against future inflation. But people quickly figured this out, and they took it into account in setting wage demands and prices. Ironically, although indexation was introduced as a defense against inflation, it made the transfer of inflation from the present to the future automatic, even when the government tried to manipulate expectations by lowering the percentage adjustment for inflation. Because it was built into the system, people came to expect it. Indexing made inflation easier to live with while inadvertently reinforcing its place in the economy.

Vicious Circles

Although indexation was designed to mitigate the costs of inflation, it created unintended inflationary side effects. **Inflationary expectations** became ingrained in the culture. People expected inflation, the government accommodated inflation, and the public got inflation. Inflation today was equal to inflation in the past period plus additional demand pressures and the effects of any supply shocks. As inflation accelerated, it made tax collection less efficient, pressuring fiscal balances and often leading to a further increase in the money supply. Inflation complicated exchange rate management. If the exchange rate was fixed, the erosion of the value of domestic money made it worth less relative to international or "hard" currencies. If the fixed rate was not adjusted, the currency was posted at an overvalued rate, creating a bias against exports. If the rate was devalued or if the currency was allowed to float freely, the higher prices of imported goods introduced additional inflationary pressures in the economy. To account for inflation and risk, nominal interest rates were high, often retarding investment.

The **velocity of money** changed in response to economic agents learning to live with inflation. A review of velocity will help illuminate this problem. Velocity is the number of times money turns over in a system each year. If the payment for a dinner to a restaurant owner is quickly used to purchase linens for a beach house, and those receipts are rapidly used (in concert with other receipts) by the curtain maker to buy a new sewing machine, and that revenue in turn is immediately used to pay workers, a given physical quantity of money is supporting the purchase of many goods. Velocity is a measure of how much output is supported by the stock of money, or gross domestic product (GDP) divided by the money supply (M). If velocity is increasing—that is, if a decreasing stock of money supports a given amount of output—increasing that stock of money without changing the productive capability of the economy will result in inflationary pressures.

In an inflationary economy, people have the incentive to transform their rapidly worthless currency into goods. If a worker in Brazil waited until the end of the month to buy groceries or other goods from a monthly paycheck, in 1990 the prices would have risen by approximately 70 percent by the month's end, leaving 70 percent less in the grocery basket. It made good sense to buy quickly. Of course the shortages that the "buy now" behavior created further increased prices.

The banking system may respond to the pressure to turn money over quickly, further increasing velocity. If you deposit a check and it takes three days to clear, you may not use that money for three days without bouncing another check. However, if your checks clear instantaneously, it is time to go shopping again! A higher velocity will support the purchase of more goods and services per dollar. Once a system has adapted to a higher velocity rate, modest increases in the money supply will have a stronger expansionary effect. If supply constraints prevent the rapid provision of goods and services in response to the increase in the money base, inflation will be ignited.

The velocity numbers are dramatic in the Brazilian case. During an inflationary period the velocity of money in Brazil was an astounding 125, compared to 16 in the United States. The highly efficient system of interest-bearing transactions balances allowed money holders to escape from the direct use of currency through something similar to checkable money market funds. The Brazilian money supply therefore supported a higher volume of goods and services per dollar than that in the United States. Changes in the money supply would be magnified in inflation rates.

TIMING AND ADJUSTMENT

The monetarist versus structuralist policy debate in part boils down to a decision as to how much macroeconomic imbalance is tolerable in the medium term. Monetarists argue that imbalances should be swiftly redressed. Excesses in external accounts or in fiscal deficits should not be tolerated because they will quickly aggravate inflation. Structuralists contend that it is not that simple. Given the underdeveloped nature of markets in the developing world, they expect imbalances in domestic accounts or in external spending. Harsh and rapid adjustment, for the structuralist, is too high a price. Rapid reductions in the money supply to reduce domestic absorption might also have the effect of strangling long-term growth.

Monetarists and structuralists also had different views of the degrees of freedom of countries in their abilities to isolate themselves from the effects of the "inconsistent trinity" or the "trilemma." Policymakers face inevitable tensions in balancing goals of domestic monetary policy, fixed exchange rates, and capital mobility.[7] A country cannot have all three. Under a fixed exchange rate regime, if international capital is mobile, and governments accept the rules of the game—that is, that a current account deficit will result in a decrease in money supply—autonomy in domestic monetary policy is forfeited. If a fixed exchange rate is maintained to preserve an international price anchor, capital controls and sterilization may give temporary relief, but exchange rate crises will certainly erupt if adjustment is incomplete. Governments might be tempted to pump up the money supply, but this will result in ballooning trade deficits. If nations want to pursue monetary autonomy they can certainly abandon the fixed rate and let the exchange price float, but without high credibility in international markets this is likely to introduce an inflationary bias into the economy. Unless markets believe that the government is pursuing a stable monetary policy, the expected depreciation of the currency will raise import prices and foment inflation. Facing this "trilemma," monetarists largely counseled abandoning domestic monetary policy and linking to a "hard" international currency; structuralists suggested exchange controls to preserve domestic autonomy. Rather than forfeit autonomous monetary policy or the exchange anchor, structuralists preferred to restrain capital mobility. Box 5.1 summarizes this trilemma of open economies. It is worth recalling

BOX 5.1.   MACROECONOMIC POLICY TRILEMMA

Tool	*Objective*	*Conflict*
Domestic monetary	Activist monetary policy to shorten recessions and restrain inflation	Under fixed exchange rate "rules of the game" (deficit requires decrease in the monetary money supply) weaken independent monetary policy; if domestic capital is not also mobile, central bank can perform offsetting domestic interventions (sterilization)
Fixed exchange rate	Price anchor—tie exchange rate to a firm anchor and force real adjustment	Lose monetary independence; could float exchange rate but lose price anchor; if capital is immobile, can create different domestic prices for money
Capital mobility	Encourage international investment; buoy confidence	Interest rates must be equal to international rates plus inflation; lose interest rate wedge in monetary policy; could float, but lose inflation anchor

that such capital controls were before the days when globalization and liberalized markets were the trademarks of sound policy.

How did these policies play out in practice in Latin America? Drawing in elements of both schools, Latin American nations adopted a variety of approaches to macroeconomic stabilization. The fixed versus floating rate constraint was softened somewhat in practice by using intermediate exchange rate solutions such as crawling pegs or exchange rate target zones and other forms of managed exchange rate regimes. In these cases a target is set—either pegged to a hard currency such as the dollar or set within a range, with a ceiling and a floor between which it can fluctuate. Depending on pressures on the currency, the monetary authority intervened by buying or selling to stabilize the currency but was not bound to defend a fixed price. This kind of flexibility accounted for the fact that inflation in developing countries is generally higher than in the industrial world.

Flexibility in exchange rate policy promotes competitiveness in international markets. However, if the central bank lacks credibility, inflation will resurge. The tradeoff between credibility and competitiveness has shaped exchange rate policy

Table 5.5. Advantages and Disadvantages of Fixed versus Floating Rates

	Fixed Rate	Floating Rate
Advantages	limits exchange rate risk for international transactions	neutralizes the impact of external shocks
	lowers risk premium and therefore cost of access to international financial markets	neutralizes the impact of real shocks
	decreases domestic interest rates as domestic rates need not include exchange rate premiums	neutralizes the effect of inflation on export competitiveness
	facilitates disinflation with an exchange rate anchor	cheaper export prices promote competitiveness
	impedes monetary financing of the fiscal deficit because monetary policy is impotent	price mechanism (e.g., an exchange rate depreciation) reallocates resources from the nontradable to the tradables sector
Disadvantages	credibility is fragile; subject to speculative attacks in currency markets	source of imported inflation through increasing import prices
	in case of crisis, adjustment may be costly	negative effect of strong volatility on trade and financial transactions; agents like predictable prices
	dependence on the monetary policy of the peg country; may not meet national needs	countries can engage in competitive devaluations, creating regional instability
	strong sensitivity to external and real domestic shocks; a fall in global demand, for example, must be matched by a fall in the money supply to maintain the promised peg rate	can lead to postponement of required structural adjustments; the change in prices may mask underlying rigidities
	risk of real exchange rate appreciation; if national inflation does not equal the peg's inflation rate, the local currency becomes overvalued	in case of crisis, can make the servicing of external and internal debt unpredictable; more local currency units are needed to repay obligations
	an overvalued currency creates a current account imbalance; countries would have to lower costs to maintain competitiveness	hyperinflationary past may impede necessary central bank credibility
	current account imbalances will require financing; if confidence dries up, a crisis ensues	stability is only as strong as underlying central bank institutions

Source: Helene Poirson, "How Do Countries Choose Their Exchange Rate Regime?" *IMF Working Paper* WP/01/46, April 2001, www.imf.org, adapted from table A3, 26.

Table 5.6.   Latin America and the Caribbean: Exchange Rate Regimes, 2002

Fixed, Quasi-fixed, or Dollarized	Crawling Peg or Flotation Band	Floating[a]
Belize	Bolivia	Argentina
Ecuador	Costa Rica	Brazil
El Salvador	Dominican Republic	Chile
Panama	Honduras	Colombia
	Nicaragua	Guatemala
	Uruguay	Guyana
		Haiti
		Jamaica
		Mexico
		Paraguay
		Peru
		Trinidad & Tobago
		Venezuela

Source: ECLAC, *Globalization and Development* (Santiago, Chile: ECLAC, 2002), table 5.6.
[a]Floating regimes usually involve some degree of central-bank intervention (dirty floating).

in Latin America as countries struggle to produce stable growth fueled by export engines.[8] Table 5.5 illustrates the pros and cons of a fixed versus a flexible rate. Exchange rate crises in the late 1990s have led to an increasing preference for floating systems in the first decade of the twenty-first century. Table 5.6 shows the choices of exchange rate regimes in 2002.

A crawling peg or target zone can allow for small, regular devaluations to take inflation differentials into account and prevent an overvaluation of a currency. There is some suggestion that the exchange rate regime conditions inflation. In a fixed regime, inertial factors weigh more heavily. Countries under a fixed regime should pay close attention to labor market rigidities and corporate structure. Under a floating regime, deficit financing predominates. This may lead to a resurgence of inflation in the region as more countries have abandoned fixed anchors.[9] A radical alternative to either fixed or floating is no exchange rate at all—that is simply dollarize and give up your currency. This option is discussed in box 5.2. There are rich lessons in the experience of macroeconomic stability in Latin America. Here we consider four cases: structuralist policies in Brazil, a monetarist approach in Bolivia, a change from a structuralist to a monetarist stance in Argentina, and a social compact to soften the adjustment costs to Mexico.

HETERODOX APPROACHES TO INFLATION STABILIZATION IN THE 1980S: BRAZIL

Brazilian policymakers diagnosed inflation in the 1980s as structural. The external oil price shocks of 1973 and 1978–1979 in conjunction with the interest rate shocks of the early 1980s intersected with a highly concentrated industrial sector able to pass on cost increases to the public. Maxi-devaluations of the currency in 1979 and 1983 took place because of current account pressures, fueling price increases.

Box 5.2. Dollarization

In the midst of the debate on fixed versus flexible exchange rates, one option that has gar-nered attention is abandoning national currencies—and the question of the appropriate exchange rate—and adopting the dollar.[10] Exchange rate pegs can be seen as invitations to speculative attacks, pushing countries to abandon the exchange rate anchor or float. The dollar, an international currency, is not subject to the same kind of speculative attacks and currency runs. By taking away exchange rate uncertainty—and not leaving domestic monetary policy subject to political manipulation—nations could decrease the cost of borrowing in capital markets. Proponents point to the falling cost of capital for European nations such as Italy with the adoption of the euro and suggest that, as it did in Europe, a single currency would hasten regional integration. It is even suggested that the Canadians adopt the dollar, pointing to the fact that the volume of trade among Canadian provinces is twenty times that with U.S. states, despite some geographic proximity. Dollarization would enhance credibility, making tough changes irreversible.

Dollarization is not without its drawbacks. It implies a loss of **seignorage,** the money that a government makes by issuing money. Printing money that can be used for school, roads, and hospitals is equivalent to a no-interest loan to the government. The Central Bank can also use currency, which does not bear interest, to purchase interest-bearing assets, such as foreign reserves. These show up as Central Bank profits and are trans-ferred to the government. Clearly dollarization implies a loss of monetary autonomy, including the ability of the Central Bank credit to provide liquidity to the banking system. Dollarization can also threaten competitiveness. The dollarized real exchange rate can become overvalued for the country in question. Real devaluation must be achieved through a fall in nominal wages and prices. If labor markets are not flexible, such price reduction is problematic. Finally, dollarization may be a high-risk strategy for rebellion. Trashing the local currency challenges nationalist pride.

Approaches to the process of dollarization differ. Some recommend slow, evolu-tionary dollarization. With a starting point of complementary banking, fiscal and trade reforms, dollarization would be the coronation after a long period of preparation. But those driven to dollarization by crisis may benefit from shock treatment. Rapid dollariza-tion will force labor market adjustments—there is no choice but for unions to recognize that there are few alternatives. It hardens the government's fiscal constraint. The hope is that the term structure of debt will lengthen with less risk and the country will have enhanced access to commercial credit lines. Dollarization should create synchronization of business cycles through the interest rate.

Rapid dollarization is called the Nike approach—just do it. Countries most likely to benefit from dollarization are those most highly integrated with the United States, including a wide degree of informal dollarization through dollar-based savings and transactions. The optimal currency literature suggests the best candidates include those with small size, a high degree of openness, a high degree of cross-border trade, similar shocks, and dollar-based debt structures. Williamson suggests that by these criteria the small Central American coun-tries are strong candidates for dollarization; the Andean countries are an intermediate case. Mexico, an oil-based economy, is subject to different shocks, and **Mercosur** countries in search of a monetary anchor might better think of creating their own monetary union than tie their fates to the distant dollar of the north.[11]

Panama adopted the dollar as legal tender in 1904, leaving the *balboa* as a symbolic relic. It has a low rate of inflation and low cost of capital and has eliminated exchange rate risk. But dollarization isn't a magic wand. Due to its inability to control public finances and a high rate of external borrowing, Panama unpleasantly claims the second-largest number of IMF programs in the world. No exchange rate regime—not even a non-regime—can avoid the tough problems of reconciling the demand for government services with weak revenues.

After proclaiming a few days before that dollarizing was "a jump into the abyss," Ecuador's President Jamil Mahuad switched to the greenback in January 2000. It cost him his job two weeks later, but the results have been more successful than most analysts expected. Ecuador had run out of options. It faced erratic oil prices, debilitating capital flight, bank failures, international loan defaults, and devastating floods. Nearly half its 12 million people are considered impoverished by World Bank standards. The *sucre* had plunged from 7,000 to 25,000 per US$, igniting price explosions. Without consulting the IMF, Ecuador moved to a dollar standard. Ecuador dollarized at a discount, opening the door to international competitiveness. An IMF program in 2000 consolidated the gains of dollarization and further pushed structural reform, including the fiscal accounts and banking reform. By 2001, growth hit 5 percent, inflation was under 25 percent and the people felt the benefit in the positive growth in the real minimum salary. Nonetheless, a delicate banking and financial system and vulnerability to oil prices, the weight of external debt and falling global demand leave Ecuador's recovery fragile to external shocks. The boost from the initial devaluation has weakened; competitiveness will be contingent on improvements in productivity, labor reforms, and privatization in telecommunications and electricity, very tough microeconomic changes to engineer.[12]

Orthodox policies to reduce inflation had been tried under the military governments with painful social results. Sectoral conflicts between industry and agriculture as well as social conflicts between powerful labor and industrial organizations were thereafter resolved through spending. The state itself played an active role in the economy through state-owned enterprises, especially in the provision of infrastructure such as electricity and key inputs such as steel. In these sectors prices were held down to spur development of industry, but the difference was made up in deficit spending. As inflation accelerated, bonds, credit, and wages were indexed with increasingly frequent intervals. The lack of independence of the Bank of Brazil from the Treasury left it in a passive role to accommodate expansion.

When monthly inflation hit 459.1 percent in January 1986,[13] a radically different stabilization plan was called for. The **Cruzado plan** included a general price freeze and a partial freeze on wages following an 8-percent readjustment. If the consumer price index increased more than 20 percent, wage increases would be permitted. Indexation of contracts with less than one year's duration was prohibited. A new currency was created called the *cruzado,* set equal to 1,000 *cruzeiros*. After a devaluation, the *cruzado* was fixed at 13.84 *cruzados* to the dollar. Popular favor was cultivated as Brazilian president Sarney deputized all Brazilians as *fiscais,* or price inspectors, to police the price freeze in supermarkets and shopping malls. Citizens could arrest store managers for raising prices. People felt empowered by the fight against inflation. The goal was to eliminate the inertial aspect of inflation, creating expectations for price stability rather than inflation.

QUESTION FOR THOUGHT

Does the structuralist or the monetarist approach to inflation appear most consistent with your own sense of economic theory and with the Latin American reality? Who had it right?

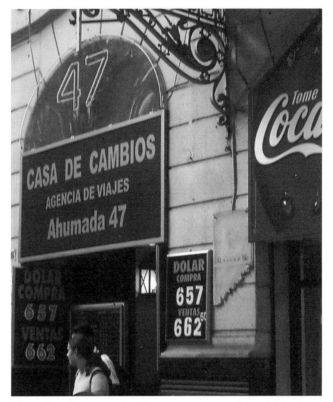

The price of currency is a key macroeconomic variable.
(Courtesy of Patrice Franko.)

The preliminary results were dramatic. By April prices actually fell 4.5 percent, and in May they rose only 1 percent. Because inflation was not eating away at paychecks, Brazilians enjoyed a real wage increase for the first time in years, and economic growth was led by the strong demand for consumer durables. However, Brazilian industry was not able to meet the surge in consumer demand, and the economy began to overheat. Shortages emerged. The sustainability of the plan was called into question. As businesses lost faith in the plan, they withheld goods from the market, anticipating that the price freeze could not last indefinitely. Fiscal reform was limited, and monetary policy accommodated the deficit pressures. With state and gubernatorial elections in the fall of 1986, politics would not permit austerity. By December 1986 monthly inflation was back in triple digits. Following the elections, adjustments were made to the price framework, and a crawling peg for the exchange rate temporarily relieved the pressure for devaluation. Contracts were once again indexed to ease the costs of inflation. But credibility was destroyed, and a year and a half after the introduction of the plan, inflation topped 1,000 percent. Although the plan worked initially to reduce inflation dramatically, when the economy was unable to respond to the increased demand, credibility eroded in the government's ability to manage the economy.

Figure 5.1. Brazilian Inflation, 1982–1995

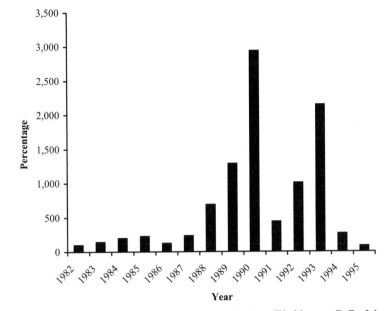

Source: IADB, *Economic and Social Progress in Latin America* (Washington, D.C.: Johns Hopkins University Press, various years).

Brazil continued its heterodox experiment with the **Bresser plan** in mid-1987. The Bresser plan also froze wages, although the caps were designed to be readjusted every ninety days to minimize misallocation and shortages. The exchange rate was managed through a series of mini-devaluations. Interest rates were targeted above inflation to keep the lid on the consumer boom that overheated the economy under the *Cruzado* plan. Finance Minister Bresser placed heavy emphasis on controlling the public deficit in theory but was unable to realign the political priorities of the Sarney administration. A follow-up "summer plan" included another revaluation of the currency, lopping off three zeros once again and calling it the *novo cruzado*. However, it did little to change the underlying politics of the Brazilian situation. Fiscal pressures continued, inflation accelerated, and confidence was low.

In 1990 a new president—the first directly elected by the people in nearly thirty years—came into office with a strong mandate to "kill inflation with a single bullet." President Collor engineered the most dramatic of stabilization plans, with both heterodox and orthodox elements. With annual inflation nearing 3,000 percent, and consistent with prior stabilization plans, Collor froze wages and prices, and once again readjusted the monetary unit, renaming it the *cruzeiro*. Agreeing with the monetarists that inflation indeed had a strong monetary component, Collor implemented a radical liquidity freeze, immediately reducing the money stock by 80 percent. All bank accounts in excess of $1,000 were frozen. Brazilians were shocked. People who had, for example, sold one house but were in the process of buying another could not go ahead with their purchases. By law, they were not allowed access to their own money. The economy—including prices—was essentially at a standstill. These drastic measures were accompanied by planned reductions in the shape of government, including privatizations and layoffs of government employees.

The plan backfired. Rather than change expectations toward a low-inflation economy, it eroded confidence in the government as a guarantor of the rules governing the economic game. If the government could step in and freeze a family's life savings, what would it not do? The powerful business lobby, represented by FIESP, the federation of industries of São Paulo, was not consulted in the plan, leaving an angry and alienated industrial sector. The plan collapsed with a loss of legitimacy; Collor himself later fell to charges of corruption and was impeached. Changing the shape of government had not addressed some of the personalistic privileges government officials had usurped. Nonetheless, this early test of Brazilian democracy led, after the interim presidency of Itamar Franco, to the election of Fernando Henrique Cardoso on the platform of price stabilization.

As Franco's economics minister, Cardoso introduced the **Real plan.** The *Real* plan was a pragmatic mix of orthodox and heterodox elements. Its premise was heterodox in spirit: eliminate the inertial elements of inflation to break out of a cycle of indexed price increases that adjusted for past inflation. The preliminary stage of the plan lasted three months. It began in December 1993 by identifying disequilibria, eliminating price distortions, and introducing emergency fiscal adjustments. In March monetary reform was introduced. All wages, prices, and taxes, and the exchange rate, were redenominated in a new accounting unit called the *urv,* or the real unit of value, roughly set at par to the U.S. dollar. The *urv* was a kind of superindex as an intermediate step on the path back to using money as the measure of value. Indexation to other rates was prohibited, and the money supply was tightened, indicating a monetarist bent. By July a new currency, the *real,* was introduced; it was tied initially one to one to the *urv* accounting unit. Once again this new currency was designed to erase the inflationary memory associated with the old unit. What was different in the case of the *real* was that the policy changes implemented in association with the *Real* plan were credible to the public. The gradual, preannounced nature of each step served to calm expectations. Furthermore, after more than two decades of unsuccessfully battling inflation, the public was simply ready to bite the bullet. Expectations of inflation were changed. As President Cardoso said on the second anniversary of the *Real* plan, "Brazil used to be like a casino. Everyone, not only banks, speculated here. This is coming to an end."[14] By 1996 the inflation rate, at 13–14 percent, was the lowest in Brazil in thirty-nine years. As we can see from the data in table 5.7, growth resumed, buoyed by consumer confidence, and unemployment did not rise.

The *real* was a stable anchor against inflation through mid-1998, but imbalances began to emerge in the Brazilian economy. Government deficits, fueled by a lack of fundamental restructuring in fiscal outlays, became alarming. Strong spending—led by workers finally able to save enough to buy consumer durables—led to trade balance problems. The *real* was becoming overvalued relative to economic fundamentals. As we will discuss in chapter 7, when currency crises shook Asia and Russia, the unstable Brazilian economy was unable to withstand the capital outflows. The

Table 5.7.   Macroeconomic Indicators for Brazil, 1982–2000

Year	Consumer Prices	Growth	Unemployment
1982	100.3	0.6	6.3
1983	178.0	−3.4	6.7
1984	209.1	5.1	7.1
1985	239.0	8.0	5.3
1986	58.6	7.5	3.6
1987	394.6	3.4	3.7
1988	993.3	0.3	3.8
1989	1,863.6	3.2	3.4
1990	1,584.6	−4.2	4.3
1991	475.8	0.3	4.8
1992	1,149.1	−0.3	5.8
1993	2,489.1	4.5	5.4
1994	929.3	6.2	5.1
1995	22.0	4.2	4.6
1996	9.1	2.5	5.7
1997	4.3	3.1	5.7
1998	2.5	0.1	7.6
1999	8.4	0.7	7.6
2000	5.3[a]	4.5[a]	7.1[a]

Source: ECLAC, *Economic Survey of Latin America and the Caribbean* (Santiago, Chile: ECLAC, various years).
[a]Preliminary figures.

government abandoned the fixed exchange rate, allowing the currency to float on international markets. The associated 30–40 percent depreciation raised fears of igniting another inflationary round in Brazil.[15]

Restraining the resurgence of inflation was a top priority. Under pressure of financial turmoil and the loss of an IMF rescue package, President Cardoso was able to extract important fiscal reforms from Congress and restrain inflation to about 10 percent, a significant achievement given the country's hyperinflationary past. This was no small task in Brazil, where the 1988 constitution hampers the president's ability to change a complex system of taxes and entitlements controlled by a powerful Congress.

Without the fixed exchange rate anchor (or its second cousin the crawling peg), Brazilian monetary authorities had to generate market confidence in their ability to manage the independent monetary policy associated with a float. The third central bank president in as many weeks, Arminio Fraga, brought his Wall Street experience to Brasilia. The Central Bank announced a transparent commitment to inflation targets. Concerned about the inflation pass-through from the devaluation (estimated to be approximately 30–40 percent), interest rates were raised to 45 percent to restrain the impact of import price escalation. Fraga hit the international financial markets with forceful international economic diplomacy, successfully garnering external financial support. Inflationary expectations fell and interest rate pressures were relieved. Panic behind it, the Brazilian Central Bank was able to lengthen the term structure of the government's domestic debt, and regularize publication of inflation targets and performance on its website (www.bcb.gov.br).[16]

To reign in public finances, Brazil passed a fiscal responsibility law in 2000 that sets limits on borrowing by states and municipalities, forbidding the expenditure of more than 60 percent of revenues on wages. Aimed at budgetary balance, unintended effects include hiring fewer doctors, teachers, and security guards. Offending mayors can be banned from office. The federal government is also forbidden to bail out states and cities in trouble. By limiting fiscal excess and promoting more efficient tax collection, Brazil hopes to promote international credibility and improve its bond ratings in international markets, lowering the cost of capital critical for growth. Nonetheless, the country remains vulnerable to market opinion. The 2002 election of "Lula," Luiz Inácio da Silva, the left-leaning workers party candidate, rocked Brazilian markets, resulting in a 40-percent depreciation of the *real* in the face of an uncertain economic direction for Brazil.

What lessons for inflation stabilization can we take from the Brazilian case? Clearly, heterodox policy alone is not enough. Simply focusing on expectations and taming the inertial component does not eliminate the imbalances creating the expectations. Fiscal and monetary fundamentals also need to be adjusted. Without reshaping the fundamentals, it is not possible to generate confidence that the imbalance in the domestic economy has been corrected. By the same token, a pure orthodox approach was not dramatic enough to generate confidence and support. In the Brazilian case, simply restraining the money supply had perverse effects. When the money supply was cut and interest rates rose as a result, economic agents perceived this as a rise in the nominal interest rate—or a signal that inflation was heating up again. They therefore increased their demands for higher wages or prices to adjust for expected future inflation. Without a change in expectations of inflation, without a clear sense of a change in the rules of the game, inertial aspects of inflation will plague the orthodox strategy. Finally, the fight for shares, the struggle to adjust to inflation by stepping on the back of other economic agents, was indeed prevalent in the Brazilian case. In an economy characterized by a high degree of inequality and structural constraints on the road to equilibrium, this battle between capital and labor cannot be ignored. With Brazil's relatively closed economy, agents did not have to look to the external sector for competitive price setting. By the same token, resolving the problem of conflict over social shares cannot be passed around like a hot potato by ineffective government. Confidence in the ability of government to mediate this conflict, to stabilize the playing field, is crucial to a compact on the part of all agents in restraining inflation. Not surprisingly, this confidence begins at home, with a transparent and credible plan for managing fiscal accounts. Solving chronic budgetary problems is the key to sustainable prices over time. Brazil's success in the short term of restraining speculative attacks on the *real* under the float will be cemented only by a long-term commitment to resolving the tough distributional issues that drive Brazil's deficits.[17]

EARLY MONETARIST APPLICATIONS: BOLIVIA

The Bolivian stabilization experience provides an interesting orthodox contrast to the Brazilian case. Bolivia had also embarked on a period of hyperinflation by

1985. External factors such as the crash of international tin prices from $6 to $3.5 from 1982 to 1985 severely contracted tax revenues. Tin export earnings fell from $234.8 million to $75.1 million. At the same time foreign debt service requirements increased from 0.4 percent of GDP in 1979 to 10.8 percent in 1983. As in other developing countries, due to the debt crisis, there was virtually no access to new funding in international markets. In addition to the fall in revenues, inflation was eating away at the value of tax receipts. Because the government was pursuing an expansionary policy, financing the internal and external deficits required monetary emissions, or increases in the money supply. By 1984 the government deficit had risen to nearly one-fifth of gross national product. The jump in the money supply, or seignorage to finance government spending, mirrored the decline in resource flows from abroad. In interesting contrast to the Brazilian case, wage and price indexation was not widespread. In a futile attempt to provide a monetary anchor, the exchange rate was fixed. Rather than price stability, the result was an overvalued exchange rate. When an exchange rate is fixed and exchange controls are imposed to restrict the amount of hard currency in the system, international currencies are strongly demanded in black—or, as they sometimes were called to reflect the openness of the transactions, parallel—markets. In Bolivia by 1985 the controlled rate was at 67,000 *bolivianos* per dollar while the free black market rate was running at 1,143,548. This 1,600-percent overvaluation made legal exports unprofitable. Underground transactions therefore emerged as evidenced by oddities in international data. Peru, for example, despite its lack of tin mines, became a tin exporter (of illegal Bolivian exports) during this period. Of course illegal exports were not taxed, further eroding the ability of the Bolivian state to finance its affairs. Speculation in foreign exchange became quite profitable. If a person could buy the overvalued official *boliviano* (sometimes illegally), money could be made in selling cheaply acquired dollars on the black market. Politically, Bolivia had a weak government trying to adjudicate increasing claims on the state to address problems of poverty and inequality. A powerful military and labor movement pressured the spending arm of the state. Falling external prices made these constraints that much more acute.

In 1985, Victor Paz Estenssoro came to power and announced the New Economic Policy to address the extreme macroeconomic deterioration (shown in table 5.8). A devaluation of the exchange rate followed by managed floating addressed the priority of getting international prices right.[18] The state-led development strategy was abandoned. Enterprises were privatized or scaled down, resulting in a reduction of the public-sector wage bill. In particular, COMIBOL, the powerful state tin producer, reduced its employment from thirty thousand in 1985 to seven thousand in 1987. Public-sector revenues were increased through tax reform. Greater confidence in the government also resulted in higher compliance with tax obligations. Debt was rescheduled, and funding from multilateral institutions and foreign governments was secured in exchange for the adoption of these orthodox economic policies. Widespread liberalization of trade and capital accounts was implemented to attract private capital inflows. An amnesty was declared for the return of dollars that had fled abroad. Dollar deposits were also legalized without proof of origin, permitting the entry of coca dollars into the economy.[19]

Table 5.8.   Macroeconomic Indicators for Bolivia, 1982–2000

Year	Consumer Prices (annual % change)	Growth Rate of GDP (annual % change)	GDP/Capita (U.S.$)	Public Deficit as % of GDP
1982	296.5	NA	1,069	–13.7
1983	328.5	–5.3	986	–15.7
1984	2,176.8	1.2	972	–17.6
1985	8,170.5	–0.1	945	–9.0
1986	65.9	–1.9	902	–1.6
1987	10.6	2.6	901	–3.6
1988	21.5	–1.3	809	–4.5
1989	16.6	3.8	822	–1.8
1990	18.0	4.6	840	–1.0
1991	14.5	5.3	864	–1.4
1992	10.5	1.7	857	0.8
1993	9.3	4.3	872	–1.0
1994	8.5	4.8	891	–4.2
1995	10.6	4.7	911	–3.8
1996	9.9	4.5	926	–1.9
1997	6.7	4.9	942	–3.3
1998	4.4	5.0	966	–4.0
1999	3.1	0.3	947	–3.8
2000[a]	3.4	2.3	948	–4.1
2001[a]	1.1	1.3	939	–4.0

Source: ECLAC, *Economic Survey of Latin America and the Caribbean* (Santiago, Chile: ECLAC, various years); IADB, *Economic and Social Progress in Latin America* (Washington, D.C.: Johns Hopkins University Press, various years)
[a]Forecast.

The immediate result of this austere package was a call for a general strike. However, after three years of hyperinflation, the public chose to support the government rather than the workers and the tough package was upheld. To minimize the social costs of adjustment, an emergency social fund (ESF), financed by the Inter-American Development Bank (IADB) and the World Bank, was implemented. It provided funds for small-scale, labor-intensive projects proposed and implemented by local NGOs. The projects financed were mostly in infrastructure; they are estimated to have created nearly 41,000 jobs and added 2 percent to the gross national product (GNP) over the period.[20] We will return to the use of social funds in chapter 11, which discusses poverty.

Despite the innovations of the ESF, the costs of inflation stabilization in Bolivia were enormous. While inflation was dramatically controlled, the price was a long period of recession. Over the period 1985–1996, the rate of growth of GDP per capita ranged from –20.33 percent to +2.86 percent in 1991. If the goal of development is to improve the well-being of its population, falling or stagnant rates of growth of GDP do not present opportunities for economic advancement. By 1994

GDP finally climbed back to the 1982 level—a lost decade of development for Bolivians. GDP per capita in 1996 did not reach 1982 levels. The Bolivian orthodox strategy eradicated inflation, but at a high price for growth.

The Case of Argentina: From the Austral Plan to the Convertibility Plan

Stabilization in Argentina was conceptually path breaking with its heterodox attempt in the 1980s and its orthodox plan in the 1990s. The Argentine **Austral plan** of 1985 provided many of the elements followed by Brazil. Inflation was diagnosed as having a strong inertial component. A decade of failed stabilization attempts taught economic agents to expect inflation and adjust for it in wage and price setting. The Austral plan therefore froze wages and prices (including the exchange rate), and introduced a new currency with a promise not to print money. Fiscal adjustment was the third element of the plan. There was a close relationship between fiscal deficits and money creation in Argentina. Eliminating deficits would stem the need for seignorage, or money printing, as the last resort for financing. Initially the plan succeeded as inflation decreased from 350 percent in the first half of 1985 to 20 percent in the second.

Nonetheless, the Austral plan collapsed as signs of disequilibrium emerged. The exchange rate became overvalued and external accounts deteriorated. The government made adjustments for price flexibility, but the credibility of the plan was undermined. Argentines needed to have their expectations grounded in a firm and credible long-run strategy. They found this in the 1991 **convertibility plan** introduced by Minister Cavallo in the Menem administration. President Menem succeeded President Alfonsín as the second democratically elected president after years of military rule. International markets held their breath because Menem was a renowned populist of the Peronist party. However, the old style of populist spending to appease conflicts between industry, labor, and the military was surprisingly transformed into a personal populism that allowed Menem to introduce one of the toughest austerity programs in the region. The convertibility plan locked the Argentine *peso* to the U.S. dollar. Through a currency board independent of the Treasury, by law the money supply could be increased only if the U.S. dollars held in reserve were to rise. This took the central bank out of the position of being the lender of last resort and removed the temptation to finance domestic deficits with new money creation. Monetary policy was nondiscretionary, fixed to the long-run performance of the external sector. Liberalization of the economy promoted exports and the inflow of foreign investment to increase the stock of dollars in Argentina. The *peso,* which formerly lost value daily, became indistinguishable from the U.S. dollar. Indeed, in bank machines in Buenos Aires one could select whether to receive cash in dollars or *pesos.* As we will study in chapters 6 and 7, fiscal adjustment was dramatic (but incomplete). The government embarked on a large-scale privatization program, putting fifty-one firms on the auction block between 1989 and 1992 and generating approxi-

Figure 5.2. Argentine Inflation, 1970–1997

Source: IADB, *Economic and Social Progress in Latin America* (Washington, D.C.: Johns Hopkins University Press, various years).

mately U.S.$18 billion.[21] Tax reform increased revenues to balance government books. Smaller government demanded less inflationary financing.

As we can see in table 5.9, inflation tumbled in Argentina from the peak of more than 3,000 percent to an astoundingly low rate of 0.1 percent in 1996. Domestic and international capital believed in the long-run commitment of the plan. International capital flowed to Argentina, convinced of the sustainability of the program and lured by the values of the privatized firms on the stock exchange. The plan was remarkably durable. Despite high social costs of 17-percent unemployment, Cavallo was tough and held firm on the convertibility plan. When the Mexican *peso* crisis of 1994–1995 rocked the international financial community's faith in Latin America, Argentina stuck to the plan even as capital temporarily fled the region. Cavallo left the administration in July 1996 with the economy contracting at a rate of 4.6 percent in 1995; nonetheless, the new economics minister, Roque Fernandez, continued to ground the Argentine *peso* firmly in the value of the dollar. Despite the recession, Fernandez attacked the budget deficit, increasing taxes and cutting spending. The costs of not erasing the inflationary memory in Argentina were simply much greater than the pain of recession.

When its trading partner, Brazil, let the *real* float in 1999, fragilities in the Argentine model were exacerbated. The accompanying devaluation of the Brazilian *real* improved competitiveness and the Brazilian trade balance; at the same time the

Table 5.9.   Macroeconomic Indicators for Argentina, 1970–2000

Year	Inflation (average annual growth of consumer prices)	Annual Growth Rate of GDP	Urban Unemployment
1970	13.6	—	—
1971	34.7	—	—
1972	58.4	3.1	6.6
1973	61.2	6.1	5.4
1974	23.5	6.5	3.4
1975	182.9	−1.3	3.7
1976	444.0	−3.0	4.5
1977	176.1	6.4	2.8
1978	175.5	−3.4	2.8
1979	159.5	7.1	2.0
1980	100.8	1.4	2.3
1981	104.5	−6.2	4.5
1982	164.8	−5.2	4.8
1983	345.0	2.6	4.2
1984	627.5	2.4	3.9
1985	672.5	−4.4	5.3
1986	85.7	6.0	4.6
1987	123.1	2.1	5.3
1988	348.3	−1.0	6.0
1989	3,080.5	−1.9	7.6
1990	2,314.7	−6.1	7.4
1991	171.7	0.0	6.5
1992	24.9	8.8	7.0
1993	10.6	5.9	9.6
1994	4.2	5.8	11.5
1995	3.4	−2.9	17.5
1996	0.1	5.5	17.2
1997	0.3	8.0	14.9
1998	0.7	3.8	12.9
1999	−1.8	−3.4	14.3
2000	−0.7	−0.6	15.1

Source: ECLAC, *Preliminary Overview of the Economy of Latin America and the Caribbean* (Santiago, Chile: ECLAC, various years); ECLAC, *Statistical Yearbook of Latin America and the Caribbean* (Santiago, Chile: ECLAC, various years); and IADB, *Economic and Social Progress in Latin America* (Washington, D.C.: Johns Hopkins University Press, various years).

strengthening dollar compounded the overvaluation of the *peso*. External accounts deteriorated, unemployment remained stuck at socially unacceptable levels in the range of 18 percent, and fiscal deficits were not brought under control. As we will see in Chapter 7, challenges from Brazil, the inability to restrain fiscal spending by the provinces, and rising external debt burst the viability of the *peso*–dollar lock in January 2002, and Argentina tumbled into economic chaos.

THE MEXICAN SOCIAL COMPACT

The case of price stabilization in Mexico is an interesting lesson in how social conflict tied to rising prices of goods and labor might be resolved. In December 1987 the Salinas government placed at the centerpiece of its reform a liberalization package to open Mexico to the international economy. Liberalization was seen as especially important in taming the power of highly oligopolistic markets. Competition from abroad would challenge domestic oligopolies. The exchange rate became a primary inflation-fighting tool to provide an anchor for the economy. Privatizations and budget cutting helped to improve the fiscal stance. The innovative feature of the Mexican plan, however, was the **Pact for Economic Solidarity** (El Pacto), explicit price agreements between business, labor, and the state to cooperate to limit price increases. Business agreed not to raise prices, and labor agreed not to push for wage increases. Wage increases became tied to productivity gains rather than past inflation. It was government's role to pursue a responsible fiscal policy and continue structural adjustment. The benefit of El Pacto was the ability to generate a social consensus on the hard choices in economic stabilization. It provided a framework for policy negotiations among key economic actors to maintain the long road toward stabilization.

As shown in table 5.10, Mexican inflation was low and stable for the first half of the 1990s. The downfall of the plan was its very success. International capital found Mexico enticing, and the inflow generated an overvalued exchange rate. The strength of the currency undermined the export drive and led to expectations of a devaluation. As the Mexican government tried to hold firm on the nominal anchor, speculators bet in the opposite direction. When political crises, including the assassination of a presidential candidate and the social uprising in Chiapas, called the effectiveness of

Figure 5.3. Mexican Inflation, 1998–2000

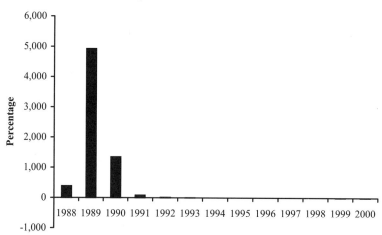

Source: ECLAC, *Preliminary Overview of the Economy of Latin America and the Caribbean* (Santiago, Chile: ECLAC, various years).

Table 5.10.   Macroeconomic Indicators for Mexico, 1988–2000

Year	Annul Growth Rate of GDP	Variations in Consumer Price Indexes	Urban Unemployment	Real Effective Exchange Rate for Imports[a]
1988	1.3	51.7	3.5	—
1989	3.4	19.7	2.9	—
1990	4.5	29.9	2.7	—
1991	3.7	18.9	2.7	74.8
1992	3.7	11.9	2.8	69.2
1993	1.8	8.0	3.4	65.9
1994	4.4	7.1	3.7	67.7
1995	−6.1	52.1	6.2	100.0
1996	5.4	27.7	5.5	89.1
1997	6.8	15.7	3.7	79.6
1998	5.1	18.6	3.2	82.3
1999	3.7	12.3	2.5	75.5
2000	7.0	9.0	2.2	69.8
2001	−0.4	4.4	2.5	66.2

Source: ECLAC, *Preliminary Overview of the Economy of Latin America and the Caribbean* (Santiago, Chile: ECLAC, various years), tables A-1, A-4, A-5, and A-8.
[a]1995 = 100.

government into question, the *peso* crisis of 1994 ensued. We will return to this crisis in chapter 7, which concerns international capital flows.

LESSONS FOR STABILIZATION

Box 5.3 summarizes the variation of the stabilization experiences we have just studied. What lessons can we draw from these cases of stabilization in Latin America? As Jeffrey Sachs notes, there are three components to inflation reduction: (1) finding a solution to chronic budgetary problems at the core of high inflation; (2) identifying a means of eliminating inertial inflation, principally wage and price indexation; and (3) introducing one or more nominal anchors to the price level at the start of stabilization to ground expectations and the behavior of central bank authorities.[22] In all the cases, without clear and credible attention to the fiscal crisis, inflation will resurge in the economy. Fiscal imbalances will prevent stabilization and the government will likely respond by monetizing the difference.

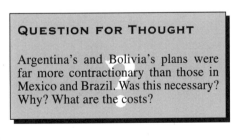

QUESTION FOR THOUGHT

Argentina's and Bolivia's plans were far more contractionary than those in Mexico and Brazil. Was this necessary? Why? What are the costs?

Restructuring the role of government in the economy has an additional benefit: creating the perception that business as usual has changed. Generating the confi-

BOX 5.3.   VARIATIONS ON THE STABILIZATION EXPERIENCE

	Brazil's Cruzado Plan 1986	Brazil's Real Plan 1994	Argentina's Convertibility 1991	Bolivia's New Economic Policy 1985	Mexico's Economic Solidarity Pact December 1987
Diagnosis of inflation	Structural; inflation is a fight over social shares; address inertial inflation	Provide nominal anchor tied to exchange rate, de-index economy, and correct fiscal imbalances	Erase inflationary memory and control expectations; provide firm price anchor	Monetary emissions to accommodate government spending; fall in tax revenue forces seignorage; exchange rate overvalued	Restrain fight for social shares to allow the effects of liberalization to work
Fiscal policy	Reform unsuccessful	Short-run emergency adjustment; long-run change stalled in Congress	Restrictive; cut expenditures; strong privatization; tax increase	Tax reform; increase public sector prices; cut state-owned enterprises (SOEs)	Austerity
Monetary policy	Increases due to fear of raising nominal interest rate giving inflation signal	Contractionary	Nondiscretionary; tied to U.S.$ reserves	Tight	
Exchange rate policy	Fixed at 13.84Cr = U.S.$1	Crawling peg set to dollar	Fixed on par with U.S. dollar; money supply tied to reserves	Establish stable, unified rate; devalue then dirty float	Consolidate exchange rate; exchange rate then becomes anchor
Wage and prices	Freeze	Flexible	Flexible	No controls	Wage indexation
Currency	1Cz = 1000 Cr	New currency real tied to *urv* loosely set to dollar	Peso interchangeable with dollar		
Political	Price inspectors			Restrain influence of labor unions	Business agrees not to raise prices; labor agrees not to push up wages
Trade	Continued internal orientation	Temporary erection of tariffs	Aggressive liberalization	Liberalization	Acceleration of trade reform

Indexation	Prohibit contracts of less than one year with indexation clauses	All indexation except to new *urv* prohibited	None		
Initial results	Inflation falls from 22 percent monthly in February to .3 in May; growth surges led by strong consumer durables	Inflation lowest in nearly forty years; consumption exploded with increase in real income; some tightening	Dramatically low inflation	Drove hyper-inflation out	Monthly inflation dropped from 15 percent in January to 1 percent in December
Persistent imbalances	Shortages, withholding of goods. Plan collapses as expectations escalate	Fiscal imbalance; real structural change awaits congressional approval	Unemployment at 17 percent	High social costs; anemic growth rates	
Balance of payments	Trade surplus shrinks; reserves fall; exchange rate held fixed too long to maintain internal–external balance	Loss of export dynamic due to overvalued currency			

dence that the government is serious about reform and will—and can—remain committed to a stable policy is critical to success. This involves erasing the inflationary memory, the backward-looking behavior of agents that reflexively drives price increases. Tying the currency to an anchor—either firmly as in the case of Argentina or loosely in terms of a crawling peg to the dollar—provides monetary restraint. But with this stability comes a loss of flexible exchange rate changes to reflect different macroeconomic conditions. Beyond these tools, the population needs to believe in the benefits of inflation fighting. In Argentina the public was so tired of struggling to live with inflation that it was willing to quit cold turkey. Much like an alcoholic, the public understood that one little ounce of price inflation would tip the economy into an inflationary binge. Over time, however, the objective of a credible anchor gave way to the need for job creation and competitiveness. Bolivians, also subject to ravaging hyperinflation, were willing to swallow the tough contractionary pill. In Mexico the support was negotiated through El Pacto, providing a framework for sharing the burden of stabilization. Brazilians have been able to stave off some of the more dramatic social conflicts, perhaps in part due to the size of their economy and the ability to insulate it to some degree from the shock of international competitiveness. Whether this will prove to be a good thing in the long run remains to be seen.

Resolving deficit financing involves putting an end to persistent deficits. Expenditures have outpaced volatile revenues in Latin America. An Organisation for Economic Cooperation and Development (OECD) study shows that industrialized countries collect an equivalent of 23 percent of GDP, while Latin American governments take in less than 15 percent—of generally smaller GDPs.[23] The ability to raise tax collection is crucial to enhancing education, health, and technology systems. Fiscal policy in Latin America also tends to be procyclical, fueling booms and protracting recession. In addition to tough questions of taxing politically powerful elites versus the penniless poor, questions of corruption and legitimacy plague reform efforts. Tax reform is a difficult balancing act, invariably asking some group to give more for the sake of the public good.

> **DATA EXERCISE**
>
> Update data for inflation, deficits, and GDP growth for our four case countries. Which countries appear to be performing best over time? Why? Try the following Internet sites:
>
> World Bank: www.worldbank.org/wdi/cd_rom/cdets.pdf
> ECLAC: www.eclac.cl/english/dstatistics/statistics.htm
> IMF: www.dsbb.imf.org/category.htm

Sustained stabilization may also involve the development of new financial markets. One of the defining features of underdeveloped economies is the lack of a long-term capital market. In part this is a self-fulfilling prophecy—instability decreases the incentive for long-term investments. But this makes macroeconomic stabilization in the short term problematic. Without long-term confidence, bond markets cannot be used as an effective instrument of open market operations to smooth cyclical variations in the economy. This lack of monetary instruments places increasing pressure on governments to use the blunt tools of decreasing fiscal expenditures to stabilize growth.[24] Banking systems are also in need of reform. Banks in Latin America are more vulnerable during crises because most deposits are short-term (due to lack of confidence in the government's policies), banking institutions tend to put a great share of assets in land, and the value of their holdings of government securities is more volatile. During crisis, banks find it hard to raise external financing; this is exacerbated by the fact that domestic capital markets are thin.[25] As banks struggle with bad loans and missed payments during a downturn, confidence in the banking system's financial health is called into question. Macro crises are exacerbated by these fragilities of banking systems. Many countries have therefore adopted reforms in the banking sector. They have tightened prudential guidelines for lending, established minimum capital requirements that banks must hold relative to their loan base, and adopted monitoring systems to assess loan quality and risk. Banks are subject to wider supervisory review and are required to provide more comprehensive financial information consistent with international standards. There is, however, a wide degree of variance in regional banking reform. Brazil's banking sector was able to withstand the pressure of the depreciation of the real in part due to reforms of the mid-nineties; Argentina and Chile are also leaders in reform efforts. Other nations need to improve supervisory capabilities, including the ability to monitor cross-border operations for those with significant offshore financial sectors.

FROM STABILIZATION TO GROWTH

The dramatic achievements in price stabilization is evidenced in table 5.11 with a fall in the increase in consumer prices from an annual rate of 440.8 percent in 1990 to approximately 8.1 percent in 2000. Imagine what that price stability means to agents trying to plan for the future. Real GDP growth accelerated to a high of 5.3 percent before falling to .2 as a result of the global slowdown in 1999; regional output grew at a slow 1.7 percent in 2001 again reflecting a sharp slowdown in global conditions. Growth in per capita GDP is lower, however, reflecting the mismatch between the rate of growth of the economy and the needs of growing populations in the region.

The process of economic stabilization has not been smooth. The IADB's 1996 report characterizes the pattern of reform in five phases: stabilization and implementation of reforms, economic recovery or boom, stress, correction or crisis, and postreform growth.[26] As in Brazil's or Argentina's first packages, successful stabilization measures discussed above created consumer and investor confidence that leads to economic recovery or boom. Growth increases at a rate 4 percent higher than normal, and the resulting increase in income tax revenues improves fiscal balances. The boom, usually lasting about three years, creates imbalances. Credit tightens and interest rates rise. Higher domestic spending leads to an appreciation of the currency, squeezing exports. The economy slows, and fiscal deficits emerge. Investors, including foreign capital, become wary. Confidence erodes, and the economy enters into a period of stress. Pressures are often exacerbated by political factors, and, as happened in Mexico in December 1994, economies can spiral into crisis. The reform

Table 5.11.   Selected Latin American Indicators

Year	Increase in Consumer Prices (%)	Increase in Real GDP per Capita (%)	Increase in Real GDP (%)
1990	440.8	−1.6	0.6
1995	36.0	−0.6	1.7
1996	21.2	2.0	3.6
1997	12.9	3.5	5.3
1998	9.9	0.6	2.3
1999	8.8	−1.1	0.2
2000	8.1	2.5	4.2
2001[a]	6.2	−1.1	1.7
2002[a]	4.9	1.5	3.6

Source: IMF, *World Economic Outlook* (Washington, D.C.: World Bank, various years); ECLAC, *Economic Survey of Latin America and the Caribbean* (Santiago, Chile: ECLAC, various years).
[a]Forecast.

process can be temporarily derailed by the crisis. However, if corrections are swift and credible, while slower growth can be expected, the downturn need not be traumatic. Chile provides an example of a country that, after more than twenty years of reform, has entered into the final stage of post-reform. This is not to say that the economy is perfectly functioning. Challenges, particularly the social challenges of poverty and inequality, require response. But policy making has achieved a level of continuity and normalcy that encourages measured, long-run responses.

THE PRICE OF PRICE STABILITY: THE CHALLENGE OF RESOLVING THE SOCIAL DEFICIT

Despite stabilization, the magic of the market has not completely fulfilled the promise of development in Latin America. It is important to recall the huge human cost of austerity measures designed to stabilize inflationary economies. Like adjustment to the debt crisis, policies to reduce inflation come at the expense of current consumption—and for the poor, reducing a thin margin means human suffering. The fragility of this model was clearly demonstrated as the repercussions of the crash of the Mexican *peso* were felt around the region. Domestic difficulties call into question the ability of governments to continue to apply tough austerity measures at home in hope of maintaining investor confidence abroad.[27] Large portions of the populations are left out of the process of growth. The social deficit—the enormous unmet need in the region for education, housing, medical services, transportation, and other public services—may not be resolved by the market. Women have borne the brunt of macroeconomic stabilization. As the guardians of the family, they are left with the task of designing strategies of survival. They must do more with less. Because they are forced outside the home for long hours to make up lost income, their daughters must fill motherly roles with younger siblings. Macro crisis can be considered a social "tax" on women's time.[28]

The road to economic reform in Latin America has been rocky. In all cases the social costs of stabilization have been the daily reality of Latin Americans. Poverty and inequality in the region rose, and human capital investments have suffered from the cuts in government programs in education, health, and social services. Macroeconomic equilibrium is seen as a necessary but not sufficient condition for development. Development, as we remember from chapter 1, revolves around the question of structural change. Several problems must be addressed to move from stability to growth. Sufficient savings must be generated and channeled into productive investment, resources must be allocated efficiently, and a setting must be developed that is conducive to generating the incentives to find new, potentially better ways of doing things.[29] The broad framework should move beyond macroeconomic policy reform to address trade liberalization, private-sector development, innovative policies for technological change, and reform of the state, focused on greater equity, efficiency, participation, and environmental sustainability.[30] We will take up these issues in the following chapters.

Key Concepts

Austral plan
Bresser plan
convertibility plan
cost-push elements
Cruzado plan
heterodox

indexation
inertial inflation
inflationary
   expectations
Olivera–Tanzi effect

Pact for Economic
   Solidarity
Real plan
seignorage
velocity of money

Chapter Summary

Monetarist Theory of Inflation

- Monetarists believe that persistent inflation in Latin America was caused by irresponsible deficit financing, the erosion of the tax base, and the debt crisis. With weak capital markets, and with foreign sources of capital drying up after the debt crisis, Latin American governments financed their deficits through seignorage, or the printing of money, inducing inflation. Unable to generate revenue with a deteriorating tax base, governments again looked at seignorage as a form of financing deficits. The debt crisis exacerbated conditions, making it difficult to finance the deficit through other means. The monetarist solution was to decrease government spending—although this was politically difficult.

The Structuralist Theory of Inflation

- The structuralists focused on cost-push elements as the main factors inducing inflation. Bottlenecks causing shortages, oligopolies, external shocks, and labor interacted to push prices up and prevented them from falling under normal market conditions. The political power of business and labor made it difficult to resist accommodating money demands. Inflation then became imbedded in the system and, for the structuralists, a necessary price for growth in the developing world.
- With ingrained expectations of inflation, some countries adopted indexation to adjust to the increase in prices. At the same time, indexation propelled inflation as price increases were automatically passed around the economy. Inflationary expectations also increased the velocity of money. With higher velocity, an increase in the money supply has a stronger expansionary and inflationary effect.
- Latin America is a laboratory of inflation-fighting policies. Brazil, characterized by a culture of inflation, began its fight against inflation with the *Cruzado* plan, which initially was successful. It failed due to a loss of credibility and political pressures. The next attempt was the Bresser plan in 1987, which fell

to shortages and balance of payments pressure. President Collor tried to bring the economy to a standstill by eliminating inflationary expectations but succeeded only in eroding credibility. Using a mix of heterodox and orthodox measures, Finance Minister (later President) Cardoso introduced the *Real* plan, which managed to bring down inflation. The fixed exchange rate aspect of the plan was abandoned, however, as international capital was wary of the lack of fundamental reform in the wake of the Asian crisis. Inflation appears to have stabilized.

• The decrease in foreign capital in the mid-1980s induced Bolivia to finance government spending through seignorage. To reduce the inflationary effects of its policies, Bolivia adopted a monetarist approach by devaluing the currency, privatizing, instituting tax reform, liberalizing trade and capital accounts, and rescheduling the debt. The austerity package brought about a general strike, but the government was able to uphold its package. Tough contractionary measures resulted in low growth throughout the 1980s and into the 1990s.

• The 1985 Austral plan to bring down inflation in Argentina initially succeeded but, like the *Cruzado* plan in Brazil, ultimately collapsed as inflationary expectations resurged. Populist president Carlos Menem surprised the country by introducing an austerity program to fight inflation in 1991. Menem tied the Argentine *peso* to the dollar to limit any increases in money supply and liberalized the economy. Though inflation came down from 3,000 percent to 0.1 percent, Argentina continues to suffer social costs of high unemployment. The convertibility plan collapsed in 2001 under the weight of fiscal deficits, weak competitiveness, and extreme debt.

• Mexico's approach to inflation differed from that of Bolivia, Argentina, and Brazil in its emphasis on social consensus. Under the Mexican Pact for Economic Solidarity, business, labor, and the state agreed to share the costs of economic stabilization. The economy was opened, encouraging competition, and the size of the state was reduced.

• Lessons for stabilization include the need for fiscal sustainability, confidence in the ability to tackle tough choices, and the development of new sources of finance. The human and environmental costs of stabilization have been high, resulting in a huge social deficit and environmental degradation.

Notes

1. Rudiger Dornbusch, *Stabilization, Debt, and Reform: Policy Analysis for Developing Countries* (Englewood Cliffs, N.J.: Prentice Hall, 1993), 19.

2. Michael Gavin, Ricardo Hausmann, Roberto Perotti, and Ernesto Talvi, *Managing Fiscal Policy in Latin America and the Caribbean: Volatility, Procyclicality, and Limited Creditworthiness,* IADB, Office of the Chief Economist Working Paper no. 326 (Washington, D.C.: IADB, 1996), 4.

3. Victor Bulmer-Thomas, *The Economic History of Latin America since Independence* (New York: Cambridge University Press, 1994), 393.

4. Dornbusch, *Stabilization,* 20.

5. Sebastian Edwards, "The Political Economy of Inflation and Stabilization in Developing Countries," *Economic Development and Cultural Change* 42, no. 2 (January 1994): 235–66.

6. G. Tullio and M. Ronci, "Brazilian Inflation from 1980 to 1993: Causes, Consequences and Dynamics," *Journal of Latin American Studies* 28 (October 1996): 635–66.

7. Obstfeld and Taylor refer to these as the macroeconomic policy trilemma for open economies. As cited in Alan M. Taylor, "On the Costs of Inward-Looking Development: Price Distortions, Growth, and Divergence in Latin America," *Journal of Economic History* 58, no. 1 (March 1998): 22.

8. Jeffrey Frieden and Ernesto Stein, *The Currency Game: Exchange Rate Politics in Latin America* (Washington, D.C.: Johns Hopkins University Press for the IADB, 2001), 9.

9. Prakash Loungani and Phillip Swagel, "Source of Inflation in Developing Countries," *IMF Working Paper 01/198* (Washington, D.C.: The International Monetary Fund, December 2001).

10. Andrew Berg and Eduardo Borensztein, "The Dollarization Debate," *Finance & Development,* March 2000.

11. John Williamson, "Dollarization Does Not Make Sense Everywhere," Institute for International Economics, Speeches 2000, available at www.iie.com.

12. ECLAC, "Balance preliminar de las economías de América Latina y el Caribe, 2001," available at www.eclac.cl/publicaciones/DesarrolloEconomico/3/LCG2153PE/lcg2153sur.pdf and IMF News www.imf.org/external/np/sec/nb/2001/nb01129.htm.

13. Inflation series from Donald V. Coes, *Macroeconomic Crises, Policies, and Growth in Brazil, 1964–90* (Washington, D.C.: World Bank, 1995), table A.10.

14. Interview with President Fernando Henrique Cardoso on the occasion of the second anniversary of the *Real* plan, as reported by the Foreign Broadcast Information Services, Latin America (FBIS-LAT-96-129, 3 July 1996), first appearing on *Rede Globo* (the Brazilian television station) at 10:30 Greenwich Mean Time, 1 July 1996.

15. The range for the depreciation depends on the day it is measured. On 30 January 1998, for example, it had depreciated 37 percent from its initial value.

16. Arminio Fraga, "Monetary Policy during the Transition to a Floating Exchange Rate: Brazil's Recent Experience," *Finance & Development* 37, no. 1 (March 2000); www.imf.org; and Victor Bulmer-Thomas, "The Brazilian Devaluation: National Responses and International Consequences," *International Affairs* 7, no. 4 (1999): 729–41.

17. Eliana Cardoso, "Brazil's Currency Crisis," in *Exchange Rate Politics in Latin America,* ed. Carol Wise and Riordan Roett (Washington, D.C.: Brookings Institution Press, 2000), 70–92.

18. "Managed floating" refers to an exchange rate policy in which the price is largely market determined; the government may intervene in the market by buying and selling currency to stabilize the value.

19. Adapted from Juan Antonio Morales and Jeffrey Sachs, "Bolivia's Economic Crisis," in *Developing Country Debt and the World Economy,* ed. Jeffrey Sachs (Chicago: University of Chicago Press, 1989).

20. Diana Tussie, *The Inter-American Development Bank,* vol. 4 of *The Multilateral Development Banks* (Ottawa: North-South Institute, 1995), 112.

21. Sebastian Edwards, *Crisis and Reform in Latin America: From Despair to Hope* (New York: Oxford University Press, 1995), 196.

22. Jeffrey Sachs and Alvaro Zini, "Brazilian Inflation and the Plano Real," *World Economy* 19, no. 1 (January 1996).

23. Federal Reserve Bank of Atlanta, "Imbalances in Latin American Fiscal Accounts: Why the United States Should Care," *Econ South,* 2, no. 1 (2000), www.frbatlanta.org.

24. José María Fanelli and Roberto Frenkel, "Macropolicies for the Transition from Stabilization to Growth," in *New Directions in Development Economics: Growth, Environmental Concerns and Government in the 1990s,* ed. Mats Lundahl and Benno J. Ndulu (London: Routledge, 1996), 46.

25. Robert Rennhack, "Banking Supervision," *Finance & Development,* March 2000: 27.

26. As characterized by Michael Gavin, "Surviving Economic Surgery," *The IDB,* December 1996: 4–5.

27. "A New Risk of Default," *Euromoney,* September 1996, p. 283.

28. Lance Taylor and Ute Piper, *Reconciling Economic Reform and Sustainable Human Development: Social Consequences of Neo-Liberalism,* United Nations Development Programme Discussion Paper Series (New York: UNDP, 1996).

29. Fanelli and Frenkel, "Macropolicies," 41.

30. Colin Bradford Jr., "Future Policy Directions and Relevance," in *The Legacy of Raúl Prebisch,* ed. Enrique V. Iglesias (Washington, D.C.: IADB, 1994), 164.

THE ROLE OF THE STATE

Defining a Desirable and Sustainable Level of State Activity

Privatization of public utilities created huge investment opportunities.
(Courtesy of the Inter-American Development Bank.)

The shape and the function of the state in Latin America changed dramatically in the 1990s. We saw the state as the engine of growth under import substitution industrialization. Coincident with a political transformation to democracy throughout the region, an economic transformation producing a smaller state sector also took place. We recall that debt crises and macroeconomic instability forced a reconsideration of the capabilities of the state. From chapter 5, we remember the pattern of deficit financing that emerged in Latin America in the 1980s. These deficits were compounded by interest rate and commodity price shocks. Capital flight contributed to the erosion of the tax base. Government spending was a source of macroeconomic instability. Fiscal reform, in terms of both decreasing expenditures and increasing revenues, was essential to macroeconomic stabilization in the region.

With greater vulnerability to international capital markets, Latin American policymakers must be able to exercise fiscal discipline more rapidly and strictly than counterparts in industrial countries.[1] Given the fiscal crisis of the state, one aspect of reform has been the downsizing of the public sector. Another element of this reform is the privatization of state enterprises, changing the shape of state activity in the region. Decreasing the financial liabilities of the state included decreasing state provision of public services. As we analyze these dramatic changes in the region, key questions emerge with respect to the new, streamlined Latin American state:

- How have decreases in the quantity of resources controlled by the state changed the role of government in the region?
- What were the mechanics of the massive transfer of resources from state-owned enterprises to the private sector? Just how are enterprises privatized without creating a garage sale, give-it-all-away atmosphere?
- What has been the record to date on privatization in the region? What remains to be done?

Driven by crisis, the first stage of downsizing—cutting aggregate public expenditure and privatizing firms—was relatively straightforward. Deficits had to be reduced to sustainable levels. The next stage is more problematic.

- What size and roles should the new, streamlined government assume?
- What should be the balance between the state and the market in Latin America?
- How have corruption and poor administrative practices affected the legitimacy of the state in Latin America?

In a sense, the first stages of stabilization were easier—by decree governments lowered tariffs, reducing gross inefficiencies and improving macro disequilibria. What lies ahead includes the tougher steps for Latin American states: an era of institution building.[2] Institutional arrangements, particularly how policymakers are elected to office and the rules of the game in allocating budgets among competing priorities, affect levels and efficiency of spending.[3]

THE NEW ROLE FOR THE STATE IN LATIN AMERICA

Privatization and fiscal stabilization revolutionized the traditional role of the strong state in Latin America. Altering levels of expenditures and mechanisms for raising revenue should be undertaken in the light of a clear vision of the appropriate role of the state in Latin America. The traditional state in Latin America was subject to a paradox; it was both omnipresent and extremely weak. Large and unwieldy, it was unable to accomplish its functions efficiently. A source of political favors and populist responses, it was also captured by numerous interest groups that competed to extract rents from the state.[4] Macroeconomic crisis brought with it unintended benefits. Internal and external shocks shook up interest group politics. Ruling coalitions broke down in many countries as exogenous shocks led to the fiscal crises of the state. What should be the new shape of the state in the region?

According to Dani Rodrik, the huge capacity gap between what the state promised and what it was actually able to deliver prompted an era of excessive pessimism with respect to state intervention in the economy. State effectiveness in delivering public goods changed the shape of the Latin American state. Rodrik suggests further that, having overcome "excessive pessimism," we are on the threshold of a serious reconsideration of the role of the state in development.[5] The question remains, however, of the character and scope of efficient and effective government intervention in Latin American economies. How should the state behave to promote economic development?

Two broad forces suggest a possible increase in state intervention: globalization and the social challenges in the region. According to Evans, international trade is increasingly organized as a flow of goods within productive networks that are structured globally rather than nationally.[6] Goods are produced transnationally, not within a single country's borders. Decisions taken in multinational headquarters are as important to workers as policy choices of the national central bank. Globalization has also increased the power of global capital markets in relation to governments. Globalization produces winners and losers. Should governments intervene to ameliorate the effects of globalization?

Rodrik finds a correlation between exposure to such global trade networks and government expenditures. More open states appear to employ greater intervention. He concludes that globalization may require larger states to insulate their citizens from the uncertainty of globalized markets.[7] In addition to the external forces of globalization, the legacy of the debt crisis and macroeconomic instability has been a huge social deficit. As we will see in later chapters, while the market may contribute to solutions, effective state leadership is critical in investing in health and education systems.

But developing countries find it difficult to decrease vulnerability to external shocks and promote human capital development at home. First of all, unless they solve the puzzle of how to raise tax revenues, they do not have the fiscal capacity to protect citizens from the costs of globalization or prepare them as healthy, educated global citizens. Second, international lending practices constrain activity by developing states. Although they are beginning to change their position on this, multilateral development institutions frown upon intervention in the national interest, favoring free market outcomes. Intervention in the domestic interest may have an international financial cost. Given conditionalities by multilateral institutions, a question arises as to where the main accountability of the state lies—with the voters in a fragile democratic system or with the external aid organizations that hold significant purse strings? As the state in Latin America shapes new roles, questions of internal and external accountability will have to be resolved.

THE MARKET FOR GOVERNMENT SERVICES

Within a restricted market for state activity, how should governments respond to different demands for services? One can think of the state as the arbiter of demands by competing interest groups. As Weingast notes, "A well functioning and stable state in which all interest groups are represented and can interact freely must exist before efficiency-enhancing policies can emerge."[8] Consolidation of democratic procedures and deepening of institutional reform is critical. Without a state apparatus that can fairly mediate competing concerns, policy will be driven by the interests of the powerful—whether or not these happen to be the majority's interest. As Evans argues, "Civic engagement flourishes more easily among private citizens and organized groups when they have a competent public sector as an interlocutor."[9] If development policy is to respond to the needs of the people, there must be some sort of political "market" where these demands can be expressed. Moves toward decentralization of power are designed to allow for bottom-up, demand-driven policies. A system of fiscal federalism can limit arbitrary behavior of the central government by introducing accountable institutions at lower levels and restricting the ability of central governments to overtax.[10] However, if local institutions are dominated by local elites, this effect can be overrun. Accountability and transparency are critical ingredients of good governance. Given the history we considered in chapter 2, this, of course, is a tall order for Latin America.

THE SHAPE OF THE STATE

What should be the responsibilities of the public sector? Economic Commission for Latin America and the Caribbean (ECLAC) suggests a **fiscal covenant** or a basic sociopolitical agreement that establishes terms of interaction with civil society.[11] Defining the fiscal covenant as the "basic socio-political agreement that legitimizes the role of the State and establishes the areas and scope of government in the economic and social spheres,"[12] it suggests five dimensions to the compact: consolidating the ongoing fiscal adjustment, raising the productivity of public management, making fiscal activity more transparent, promoting social equity, and encouraging development of democratic institutions. Consolidation of the fiscal adjustment is a critical signal to markets that irresponsible deficits are a thing of the past and fiscal policy is on a sustainable trajectory. After the size of bureaucracies has been reduced, remaining employees need to be made more efficient through adoption of better information systems and management practices. Transparency allows constituents to follow the decision-making process, conferring greater legitimacy on outcomes that are seen as procedurally fair. The state has a role in ameliorating the high degree of economic inequality that is increasingly giving rise to social tension in the region. Finally, ECLAC suggests that states must be ever-conscious of how policies affect the consolidation of democracy over time.

The 1997 *World Development Report* also takes up the question of the changing nature of the state. It revalidates the importance of the state in economic development. This is a dramatic change from the position of minimizing the state in favor of market activity. The bank suggests a principle of matching the activities of the state with its capability to carry out these roles effectively. The principle is simple: don't take on more than you can handle. Governments should first address core activities before expanding into new arenas. The report isolates five fundamental tasks: establishing a foundation of law; maintaining a nondistortionary policy environment, including macroeconomic stability; investing in basic social services and infrastructure; protecting the vulnerable; and protecting the environment. A foundation of law creates stable, predictable outcomes for economic actors. A strong system of guaranteeing property rights encourages investment today in anticipation of safe returns in the future. Macroeconomic stability enhances predictability as agents do not have to contend with wild gyrations in price. The bank suggested that the provision of basic social services and infrastructure is a central function of the state and that the state has a responsibility for improving the lives of the poor and attending to environmental concerns. Without progress in these areas, shared, sustainable poverty-reducing development is seen as impossible.

Listing areas of state intervention skirts the issue of how change should be engineered given the difficulties of raising revenue. One approach is to pursue innovations to encourage markets to do more in the public arena. The key question becomes the appropriate mix of market and government to achieve progress in these areas. The *World Development Report 1997* posits that the state and the market are complementary: state activity is essential to ensure a strong institutional foundation for markets. Back in 1944 Karl Polanyi observed that "the road to the free market was opened and kept open by an enormous increase in continuous, centrally organized and controlled interventionism."[13] Through the innovative use of

---

QUESTION FOR THOUGHT

In his address to the annual World Bank Conference on Development Economics (1996), Joseph Stiglitz, then chair of the U.S. Council of Economic Advisers, suggested that governments must work to build infrastructure in the broadest sense by promoting education, advocating technological development, supporting the financial sector, investing in infrastructure, preventing environmental degradation, and creating and maintaining a social safety net. In the following chapters we will be considering policy options in these areas. Prior to this investigation, what do you believe is the appropriate role of Latin American governments in each of these areas? How much can and should governments do?

market-based initiatives, private-sector energies can be harnessed to achieve positive social and environmental goals. Enhancing the capability of the state to undertake and promote efficient collective action in law and order, public health, and basic infrastructure through more efficient delivery systems will facilitate market confidence and growth. States can enhance capability to meet society's demand for public and social goods by strengthening rules and restraints, including judicial independence and watchdog bodies; increasing the competitive pressures for service delivery; promoting voice and partnership at the local level through deliberative councils; and local cost sharing.[14] States can facilitate the institutional framework and promote incentives for projects to encourage greater productivity in the public sector.

The absolute size of the state may not matter as much as how the state intervenes in the economy to support private-sector activity. As Enrique Iglesias of the Inter-American Development Bank (IADB) suggests, "What really matters is not the exact size of the government but how well government performs its legitimate functions (without stepping into functions that properly belong in private hands) and how well government handles its relationship to the market and to the various actors of society."[15] Some contend the state should do as little as possible; others suggest that taking the state out of development policy only works when markets are well functioning. World Bank economists indicate that states should do less in areas where markets can be relied upon, working with market forces and not against them.[16] Two criteria should be met: government actions should address serious marketplace imperfections and they should be designed such that their benefits outweigh their costs.[17] In other words, governments should intervene when markets break down, but only if government action in this arena is preferable to other uses of scarce government funds. Intervention should be selectively targeted in areas of greatest possible returns.

A successful market-based strategy relies on complementary institutions. Particularly in developing countries, where markets may not function perfectly, state-sponsored institutions can promote better flows of information, encourage standards for production, and facilitate communications and the diffusion of knowledge among firms. As illustrated in the Chilean case, this growth-enhancing collaboration between state agencies and private groups is especially important in promoting exports and diversifying production.[18] The Chilean state-owned production development corporation, CORFO, searched out the best foreign practices and fostered networks of small producers to supply large, modern processing firms in promoting agro-exports. Chile's market-based "miracle" was in part based on the knowledge sharing, quality control, and improved technical capabilities encouraged by the state that made Chilean exports competitive in international markets. PROCHILE, a state agency created in 1975, assisted firms in breaking into unknown foreign markets and cofinanced export projects with coalitions of firms. Most recently state promotion has been targeted at modernization with social equity. The Chilean example underscores that fact that achieving sustainable growth involves building economic institutions to address informational and organizational constraints in the developing world.

Good Governance: Fighting Corruption and Enhancing Transparency

To be effective, government activity must be credible and legitimate. State activity in Latin America is plagued by lack of transparency, kickbacks in contracting to civil servants and politicians, and bribes to judges and the police. Rule of law is critical to well-functioning markets. Corruption—fueled by inadequate laws, weak public administration, and weak capacity for law enforcement—contributes to the low credibility of institutions. Table 6.1 illustrates the pervasiveness of corruption in the region. Only Chile ranks among Transparency International's top twenty cleanest countries; most nations in the region find themselves in the bottom half of the global scale.

Corruption has an economic cost. One estimate for Colombia suggests that 1 percent of gross domestic product (GDP) is lost to corruption; in Brazil it is suggested that each Brazilian pays $6,000 annually due to corruption. The average Mexican household spends 14 percent of its income bribing civil servants to get a driver's license or permission to build a new house.[19] Unofficial estimates in Ecuador place the corruption burden at 11.2 percent of GDP. Estimates indicate that governments in Latin America pay corruption surcharges of 15–20 percent of their purchases, totaling forty to fifty billion dollars each year.[20]

Table 6.2 presents a measure of "opacity," or the impediments to a transparent

Table 6.1. Corruption Index for the Americas, 2001

	Rank	*Country*
Top Twenty Cleanest	7	Canada
	16	United States
	18	Chile
Top Half of Ranked Countries	35	Uruguay
	40	Costa Rica
	44	Peru
Bottom Half of Rankings	46	Brazil
	50	Colombia
	51	Mexico and Panama
	54	El Salvador
	57	Argentina
	63	Dominican Republic
	65	Guatemala
	69	Venezuela
	71	Honduras
	77	Nicaragua
	79	Ecuador
	84	Bolivia

Source: Transparency International, *Global Corruption Report 2001.*
Note: Paraguay is not ranked by the index although the accompanying text discusses corruption as systemic.

Table 6.2.   Estimates of the Level of Opacity: Latin America's CLEAR Index

	Corruption in Bureaucratic Practices	The Legal System	Government's Economic Policies	Accounting Standards and Practices	The Regulatory Regime	O-factor
Benchmark Countries						
Singapore	12.86	31.56	41.86	37.94	23.12	29.47
United States	25.46	37.35	42.15	25.00	47.66	35.53
Chile	30.05	31.93	52.01	28.10	36.17	35.65
United Kingdom	14.56	39.58	53.08	44.89	38.06	38.03
Other Countries						
Mexico	41.73	58.48	57.04	28.86	52.07	47.64
Uruguay	44.46	56.11	60.87	56.03	48.88	53.27
Peru	46.06	58.13	65.32	61.46	57.18	57.63
Colombia	48.47	66.45	77.23	54.79	54.75	60.34
Argentina	56.24	62.93	68.00	49.18	66.65	60.60
Brazil	52.64	58.76	67.78	63.13	61.95	60.85
Venezuela	52.72	67.50	79.93	50.23	66.88	63.45
Guatemala	58.99	49.21	79.85	70.83	65.67	64.91
Ecuador	60.27	71.77	78.34	67.77	61.53	67.94

Source: World Economic Forum, *The Latin American Competitiveness Report 2001–2002* (New York: Oxford University Press, 2002), 128.

economic environment in Latin America. Five variables were defined as critical to an open business environment: (C) or corruption in bureaucratic practices; (L), the legal system; (E), the government's economic policies; (A), accounting standards and practices; and (R), the regulatory regime. Within each variable a ranking system such that a low number indicates strong performance was devised. Adding all the variables together gives the CLEAR index—or the opacity factor for the business environment. With the exception of Chile, Latin American nations perform poorly on the CLEAR index, reaching a negative level approximately twice that of the best performers. Negative performance on CLEAR indicators translates into lost economic activity. High opacity ratings result in a higher cost of capital and deterred foreign investment. If Colombia, for example, were to improve its CLEAR indicators to the level of Singapore, it would be the equivalent of a 25 percent cut in corporate taxes.[21]

Corruption adds to the cost of development projects. The comptroller general of Ecuador shows irregularities in handling funds in 95 percent of projects evaluated. In Paraguay the cost of roads in rural areas increased from thirteen to twenty-four million dollars due to kickbacks. In Venezuela seven hundred ghost employees were found on the rolls of public enterprises.[22] These high costs of corruption act as a deterrent to international investors.

The perception is that bribery smooths the work of public administration, but as César Gaviria of the Organization of American States (OAS) notes, it hinders trade, growth, and development, creating disincentives to investment. An underdeveloped civil society, where a large amount of power remains in the hands of an elite, creates incentives for corruption. Combined with an inefficient bureaucracy, corruption has become accepted by society as a mechanism to expedite business. Government officials rely on bribes to supplement low state wages, and the weakness of the rule of law means that corruption generally goes unpunished.

In many countries the costs of corruption are becoming better understood. In response to public demand, governments have tried to promote clean government. Mexico's Vicente Fox set up the National Pact on Transparency and Fighting Corruption in February 2001, with special outreach to civil society. With the support of the United States Agency for International Development (USAID), El Salvador has implemented an ethics code for civil servants. In Peru, efforts to cut down on traffic ticket scams that increased costs particularly to taxi drivers included the hiring of female traffic officers—70 percent surveyed now say that traffic control has improved, in part because the women are perceived as less corruptible. In Colombia and Venezuela networks of citizen watchdog groups, including local chapters of nongovernmental organizations (NGOs) such as Transparency International (TILAC) have proliferated. Engaging the public is crucial to promoting accountability. Transparency measures supported by e-governance have helped to build credibility in public institutions. Regionwide the OAS has adopted the Inter-American Convention against Corruption; anticorruption measures have also been prominent in the Summit of the Americas meetings.[23]

Despite progress, much remains to be done. Star performer Chile finds that although its government auditing office the *Contraloria* has reigned in spending and corruption, it is important to complement clean government with measures of performance and efficiency to encourage good governance. Incentives to promote public servants' productivity are being tried to invigorate slow-moving bureaucracies. Uruguay is trying to change the tradition of patronage that handed out jobs to the one in four Uruguayans who work for the government. Government agencies were rewarded through access to special funds for labor cost savings, and employees released given access to money to start small businesses, resulting in a savings of $56 million to the Uruguayan treasury.[24] Efforts to improve the quality of public administration could be translated into a doubling of spending on health and education if squandered resources are recovered.

Enhancing the effectiveness of markets often involves strengthening the role of non-market, non-state actors: NGOs. This broader definition of the market actors includes local economic and social organizations and institutions. A concept of civil society–state synergy in which civic engagement may strengthen state institutions and effective state institutions may foster civic engagement has been proposed to strengthen market outcomes.[25] Examples of such organizations include community health cooperatives, soup kitchens, and farmers' extension groups. A key aspect of the synergy includes complementary or mutually supportive relations with a clear division of labor between public and private actors. States can provide private citizens with inputs such as health care or agricultural extension that they could not have access to on their own. However, states should allow private actors to work with these inputs and not interfere where the private sector, including nonprofit community action groups, work best. A second ingredient of the synergy thrives on bridging the state–private divide to build relationships of trust and collaboration at the community level. Embedded relations between state and society build on reciprocal trust between, for example, health extension agents and their clients, making the state agencies a part of the communities where they work.[26]

THEORETICAL APPROACHES TO STATE ACTIVITY IN DEVELOPMENT

Despite the significant statement on the part of the World Bank that the state and the market are complementary institutions, a formulaic mix of just how much state versus how much market is not provided. This echoes Adam Smith's seminal question: just how much should states do to promote the wealth of nations? In part, the answer to this policy question has to do with the assumptions about states and markets you bring in approaching the problem of economic development in Latin America. Box 6.1 outlines some of the conditions under which market solutions are optimal. As we consider the specific circumstances of state participation in the areas of international trade, finance, social policy, and the environment in the following chapters, we can look to three broad theoretical perspectives to pattern policy responses: the new political economy, the new institutionalist theory, and the neostructuralists.

The first model is loosely based on the **new political economy,** or NPE. NPE grounds its assumptions in the material self-interest and rational calculus of economic actors. A position long espoused by economist Milton Friedman and the Chicago School, NPE suggests that people make their own best individual economic choices. Intervention by the state distorts the necessary market signals for accurate decision making. Interfering with market signals by providing a soft social cushion, for example, will only prolong the long-run process of adjustment.[27] New political economists assume that self-promoting politicians and bureaucratic elites will form coalitions to control resource allocation in accord with their own narrow interests. Corruption on the part of public officials is seen as systemic because it is in their self-interest.[28] For new political economists, sometimes broadly called **neoliberals,** markets save on scarce administrative capacities. These decentralized institutions oriented by profit signals avoid the pitfalls of big bureaucracies and are more responsive to consumer needs.

New political economists do agree that outcomes in developing countries may have an internal logic inconsistent with long-run efficiency. For example, a peasant farmer may continually divide the family fields into small plots that make cultivation difficult. Although there is an associated loss of efficiency and output, the peasant rationale is simple: diversification of risks among the local community.[29] Nonetheless, the presumption of the model is that the same assumptions about individual maximization of utility adhere in the developing world as in industrial market economies. Rolling back the size of the state will facilitate the reach of the market and the ability of economies to get price signals right. Foreign trade will introduce competitive price pressure and create incentives for external orientation and transparency in public policy. For neoliberals, the free market is the best of all possible worlds.

NPE is transformed by the NIE—the **new institutional economics** associated with economists Coase, North, and Williamson—to include the importance of insti-

Box 6.1.   When Do Markets Work Best?

- Markets are most effective for goods that can be consumed by one person at a time, or when the characteristic of subtractability is present. For example, with a finite supply, one person's use of scarce water subtracts from that available to a community, but one person's use of a road does not significantly diminish its future availability for others.
- Individuals must face the threat of being easily prevented from consuming the good, or excludability, to be willing to pay. For example, people cannot be easily excluded from breathing air.
- Common pool goods such as common pastures and irrigation water are difficult because there is high subtractability but low excludability. The use of water that threads through many farms takes away from that available downstream, but it is hard to prevent one farmer from taking more than a fair share. Incentives for cooperation and persuasion through local participatory institutions work best with common pool problems. Community involvement can promote local resource management.
- When subtractability is missing, or when the use by one person does not reduce the availability to others while excludability is also low, as in the case of public goods, powerful incentives exist to free ride and not pay for resources. It is hard to get individuals to pay to clean the air, because if some individuals choose not to pay, you can't say "don't breathe." A mix of hierarchy to enforce payment and local community involvement can help solve the public good problem.
- Toll goods with characteristics of low subtractability and high excludability such as piped water not in scarce supply can be managed through a combination of market and hierarchy. Regulated private water companies, private concessions, or autonomous public corporations may be used depending on local conditions. Fair and transparent administration of private contracts to manage public resources is a key ingredient to success.
- Private markets work best when both excludability and subtractability are present. For smooth functioning of markets, a strong institutional framework ensuring private property rights is key.
- To decrease some of the conflicts generated by unfettered free markets such as pollution externalities or overuse of natural resources, the private voluntary sector or nongovernmental organizations can be effective in mobilizing grassroots energies to counter negative market effects. Lester Salamon notes that "we are in the midst of a global associational revolution that may prove to be as significant to the latter twentieth century as the rise of the nation-state was to the latter nineteenth." New institutional capital created by the voluntary sector may be a critical ingredient in holding market-based strategies together.

Source: Adapted from Robert Picciotto, *Putting Institutional Economics to Work: From Participation to Governance*, World Bank Discussion Papers, no. 304 (Washington, D.C.: World Bank, 1995).

tutions. They support the tenets of individual choice within neoclassical economics but conclude that mainstream economics has ignored transaction costs, particularly those associated with market failure. Institutions have developed to minimize transaction costs—although they may not always be efficient organizations. Institutions are defined as the rules of the game of the society and are composed of formal rules such as statute laws, common laws, and regulations as well as informal constraints including conventions, norms of behavior, and self-imposed codes of conduct. Organizational players include political bodies such as parties, city councils, or regulatory agencies; economic bodies including firms, unions, and cooperatives; and social bodies such as churches or clubs and educational bodies.[30] New institutionalists suggest that neither the state nor the market may be the best way to organize the provision of goods and services.[31] This belief is driven in part by a different view of the market. For the new institutionalists the market is not the "impersonal economic exchange of homogeneous goods by means of voluntary transactions on an equal basis between large numbers of autonomous, fully informed entities with profit-maximizing behavioral motivations able to enter and leave freely" on which neo-classical theorists build their models.[32] Instead, NIE assumes that information is rarely complete and that there are transaction costs in finding out relevant prices, negotiating contracts, and monitoring and enforcing them.[33] Economic performance depends crucially on the setting in which market transactions occur. NIE emphasizes the economic benefits of institutional arrangements that help bring down transaction costs, including transparent, effective, and accessible legal and judicial arrangements. It allows that cultural norms and values may create institutional outcomes distinctly different from those in industrial market economies, where traditional norms might mediate questions of allocation and income.

Economic modernization for the new institutionalist depends on a favorable institutional environment. A core concept is that strong market institutions make for market friendliness. North lays out four essential conditions for successful industrial development: secure property rights, effective and impartial judicial systems, transparent regulatory frameworks, and healthy institutional arrangements to promote complex interpersonal exchange, including enforcement of contracts, establishment of limited-liability corporations, and easy entry and exit of firms.[34] For the new institutionalists, capacity building in state institutions will facilitate market outcomes. Markets left alone will be inefficient; developing states need to foster the development of strong market institutions. New institutionalists do not believe that markets develop spontaneously; they must be nurtured by careful state policy.

In contrast, **neostructuralists** see a broader scope for state activity. Building upon the assumptions of the structuralists studied in chapter three that the facts describing developing economies do not conform to those of industrial market economies, they suggest a case for effective selectivity in state intervention in the economy. Calling for a modernization strategy that would respond to socioeconomic backwardness and excessive vulnerability, neostructuralists recognize a vital role for the state in making up for market failures. They specifically suggest intervention to promote or simulate missing markets (such as long-term capital markets), strengthen incomplete markets (including technology), eliminate or correct structural distortions (heterogeneous production structures, concentration of property), and eradicate or compensate for the most significant market imperfections arising from economies of scale, externalities, and learning.[35] They part with their intellectual fathers in the dependency school in placing greater emphasis on outward-looking export development as opposed to inward-directed import substitution and place less faith than the new institutionalists (and certainly than the new political economists) in the ability of markets to meet the difficult challenges of development without significant state activity. The neostructuralists believe that markets alone—even relatively efficient ones—will not solve intractable problems such as poverty or the environment or meet the challenge of promoting dynamic technological change in a globally integrated world, for the markets are a necessary but not sufficient condition for economic development. Instead, an effective state is key to sustainable development.

This is not to say that neostructuralists naively believe that all state intervention is positive. In a typology of states, one can distinguish between states that are captured by elite constituencies and those able to maintain policy independence. The first type has been called a factional state; it may be either democratic or authoritarian. The second has been characterized as autonomous. The autonomous state may be seen as either guardian or predatory. A guardian state may attempt to maximize the welfare of its subjects or despotically create its own rules under the assumption that it is more enlightened than its constituency. The predatory state focuses on the extraction of resources from the population for its own benefit. Gains may accrue to a single ruler or to enhance the power of state bureaucracy.[36] Clearly the goal is to establish parameters for public policy that would encourage the development of an autonomous guardian state responding to the will of the people.

Some neostructuralists have suggested a non-Washington consensus in counterpoint to the policies of recent years.[37] Such a package would include an appreciation for fiscal equilibrium but add an additional focus on the links between the fiscal, foreign, and savings gaps with a particular eye to the distributional and political aspects of fiscal equilibrium. The non-Washington consensus advances the position that getting prices right is neither easy nor without cost and that wage reductions resulting from economic reforms adversely affect human capital development. The orthodox interpretation of sound macroeconomic policy backfires into an anemic state and economic stagnation, and privatization in itself is not desirable. Investment in a better-educated, better-paid, and healthier labor force is a long-term process with limited payoffs in short-run economic expansion. Finally, preset blueprints for macroeconomic policy do not apply to all cases. Each country has its own set of historical circumstances and institutional norms that need to be taken into consideration when designing policy. State economic policy must be carefully crafted to local conditions.

Not surprisingly, new political economists disagree with many of the neostructuralist prescriptions. New political economists might agree that markets will not generate perfect outcomes, but in their eyes government, even when acting in a benevolent fashion, does not know more than markets in terms of the "right" intervention schemes. Government does not have enough information or sharp-enough tools to minimize the costs of intervention and maximize the benefits. Market prices—the quintessential magnification of disaggregated decision making—are a better guide to resource allocation.[38] New political economists contend that markets will move the economy toward the best of all possible levels of economic growth. New political economists, consistent with their orthodox roots, suggest that intervention in the market will only divert the economy from its long-run efficient equilibrium. Under the guise of making things better in the short run, intervention will only leave the economy worse off over time. Furthermore, when policy interventions are possible, agents are encouraged to engage in rent-seeking behavior to influence outcomes. Nonmarket activities such as lobbying or offering bribes become a mechanism for securing preferences by the state.[39]

As we continue in our text to investigate development challenges in Latin America, the broad framework of the new political economists, the new institutionalists, or the neostructuralists may guide your policy perspective. Do you believe that the market alone will generate the best of all possible outcomes? Do you support the proposition that transaction costs might interfere with the efficient workings of the market, warranting different institutional arrangements? Or do you subscribe to the view that the state has a legitimate role as an actor in economic development in the region? Clarifying your position on the appropriate mix of market and government activity will facilitate your ability to formulate coherent policy positions.

THE SIZE AND STRUCTURE OF THE LATIN AMERICAN STATE

As you consider the conceptual framework for the role of the state, it is important to understand the realities and contemporary trends of state activity in Latin America. You may be surprised to know that the public sector in Latin America is roughly half the size of the typical industrial country government. Accounting for approximately 20 percent of GDP, the Latin American state spends less on social security, defense, health, and education than European counterparts, which spend approximately 40 percent. Interest payments on debt constitute 3.5 percent of GDP for both Latin American and industrial countries, but because the size of government is smaller, Latin American nations spend nearly twice the industrial average of 8 percent of central government expenditure on interest payments.[40] It is also important to note that less spending is not necessarily better for the market. As Carol Wise points out, Chile's successful performance has been correlated with one of the largest investments on the part of a state. The Chilean experience points to the need to invest in institutions and links to civil society to support broad market-based reforms.[41]

Why are Latin American states relatively small? The small size of the Latin American state is in part driven by its more limited capacity to raise revenues as compared to an industrial country government. This limited capacity stems from the region's large informal markets, which largely escape taxation, and from a weak bureaucratic structure for tax collection. Tax evasion is high, imposing higher costs on those complying with tax obligations. The administration of tax collection is weak, on average relying on one tax official per 6,649 inhabitants versus an average for industrial countries of one per 1,835.[42] Without an increased capacity to raise revenue, and lacking the financial capacity to run persistent deficits, Latin American governments must limit the functions of the state. The tough lessons of overblown state sectors without the financial capacity to sustain them were made clear to Latin American governments in the high costs of debt service and macroeconomic instability.

Progress on reducing the fiscal deficit in Latin America has been far more dramatic than changes in the fiscal stance of industrial countries. Both began the 1970–1995 period with deficits of nearly 4 percent of GDP; isolating 1990–1995, Latin America had slashed its deficits to 2 percent with little change in industrial country deficits. Debt, the accumulated deficits of past years, was lower than the Organization for Economic Cooperation and Development (OECD) average for six Latin American countries and higher for eleven. Nonetheless, because domestic credit markets are more shallow in Latin America, governments are more vulnerable and exposed than in industrial countries. Relative to the size of the domestic financial system, Latin American deficits were three times the OECD average for the 1970–1994 period.[43] Furthermore, the public is less interested in holding government debt when more secure international investment vehicles are available. The difficulty in raising money domestically pressures local interest rates and introduces macroeconomic disequilibrium. The downsizing of the Latin American state has left little room for further decreases in expenditures. Sustained macroeconomic stabilization is contingent on the ability of the state to increase revenues.[44]

INCREASING REVENUES: THE TAX PROBLEM

The challenge in Latin America is generating a sustainable increase in fiscal resources, permitting the provision of needed services. Increasing spending on social services such as health, education, or environmental protection without provoking macroeconomic instability is contingent upon increasing government revenue. How might this be done? Tax revenue derives from a number of different sources. Liberalization has made reliance on international trade taxes problematic and forced a shift toward domestic taxes. Tax reform in Latin America has been oriented toward the reduction of rates and the simplification of the individual income tax system as well as the widespread use of withholding.[45] With respect to direct income and property taxes, the threshold limit for income taxes has been raised and the maximum lowered for individuals (from 47 to 28 percent) as well as for corporations (from 43.3 to 35.5 percent).[46]

The dismantling of import substitution industrialization prompted a dramatic revision of the source of tax revenue. International trade taxes—tariffs on imports or taxes on exports—constituted 27.7 percent of total tax revenue in 1980; this ratio fell to 20.5 percent for the 1991–1995 period.[47] Most dramatic was the case of Argentina, where in 1980 international trade taxes accounted for 45.8 percent of total tax revenue; by the first half of the 1990s this had fallen to 5.6 percent.

There is an apparent preference in the region for indirect taxation such as the VAT, or **value added tax.** Advantages of the VAT include its domestic, international, and intertemporal neutrality and its self-monitoring nature.[48] The VAT is seen as improving the likelihood of tax compliance. By 1995, twenty-one countries in Latin America used the VAT. The VAT is a consumption tax. It is assessed at various levels of the production process, with each buyer of an input paying a percentage. It is therefore self-policing in that it is in the interest of the buyer to ensure that the tax at the previous level has been fairly paid to receive credit on the already taxed input. A large number of goods, including foodstuffs and most services, are excluded from the VAT.

Goods with negative externalities—such as alcoholic beverages, tobacco, and fuels—are generally taxed at a higher rate. VAT rates can also be used as an instrument to promote gender equality because men and women tend to purchase different items. Those services that might decrease the burden of the double day that women face in the home and the marketplace might, for example, be taxed at a lower rate.[49]

In contrast, an income tax is difficult to administer because it is spread among a variety of activities, the number of potential taxpayers is large (but compliance low), and the administrative tax collection process does not generate a self-policing paper trail. Income tax collection relies on a process of withholding—a procedure that is thwarted by a large number of unregistered small firms or individuals in the informal sector. Low literacy rates complicate filing individual tax returns, and weak administrative capacity makes evasion widespread. The average income tax revenue for Latin America and the Caribbean is 4.3 percent of GDP, compared to 7 percent in Asia. Given difficulties in income tax collection, the VAT, which encourages the next agent in the chain to certify that the tax was paid at the stage before, is often seen as preferable.

Throughout Latin America the concept of decentralization—of redirecting state functions from centralized bureaucracies in state capitals to the local level—has taken hold. However, this is problematic in that decentralization has weakened the capacity to promote fiscal balance. The absence of accountability on borrowing at lower levels of government and the incentives for subregions to generate their own funds suggest that a decentralization of administration of tax services must accompany the political process of devolution of authority to the local level. Local politicians may be more prone to corruption. In Colombia, for example, many local governments are controlled by guerrilla groups or drug cartels.[50] Decentralization can also exacerbate inequalities by enhancing regional disparities in income. Wealthier regions can raise revenues while poor areas fall further behind in the provision of health care and education to a needy population. Increasing regional inequality may be a long-run constraint on sustained national development.

Despite advances in deficit reduction, fiscal reform in the region is incomplete. Policy alternatives include combating tax evasion, increasing direct taxation (especially the income tax), introducing green taxes to promote environmental compliance, and readjusting central versus local revenue-raising capabilities.[51] Mexico provides an example of decreasing the rate of evasion. In 1989 it introduced a tax on assets. Many firms did not pay income taxes, declaring a loss or no profits for the taxable period. In this case, if the firm had not paid taxes equal to 2 percent of its assets, it would be liable to that limit; credit would be given against the asset taxes for tax paid on profit.[52] Only by generating a stable and predictable level of revenue will the state be able to execute an active, developmental role.

THE PROMISE OF PRIVATIZATION

Beyond fiscal balance, privatization in Latin America has become a dramatic and visible symbol to the international community of the depth of the commitment to a new economic model. Selling state-owned enterprises to the private sector signals a long-term commitment to the market model. But simply privatizing might not resolve some of the market inefficiencies that gave rise to the perceived need for state ownership in the first place. As Douglas North noted in his Nobel Prize acceptance speech, "Transferring the formal political and economic rules of successful Western market economies to third world economies is not a sufficient condition for good economic performance. Privatization is not a panacea for solving poor economic performance."[53] Changes in rules must accompany changes in ownership. Key questions must be resolved. Is a private monopoly any better than a state monopoly? Can the provision of important public services be guaranteed by market magic? What are the distributional implications of privatization? Will workers or consumers be hurt? Some of the concerns surrounding privatization can be addressed if the privatization process is carefully planned. How should that be done? This section will discuss the privatization record in Latin America with an eye to key complementary policies—particularly competition—that will reduce the costs and enhance the gains of privatization.

THE MECHANICS OF PRIVATIZATION

Privatization can be achieved in a variety of ways. An enterprise might be sold to the private sector by issuing stock in the corporation, a concession for the provision of public services can be auctioned off, or the regulations grounding economic activity might be changed. These three types of privatization—sale of assets, contracting for services, and deregulation—are very much conditioned by the type of good or service produced and the existing market structure. If the market is relatively competitive, the outright sale of assets is most likely. Sometimes deregulating the market can enhance competitiveness. If the newly private firm will enjoy considerable market power, the state might choose to retain ownership and contract private services or introduce public regulations to make the private monopoly accountable to the public good. This may be appropriate in the case of natural monopolies. It is important to note, however, that privatization does not take place in a vacuum, but is integrated as part of a comprehensive package of reforms. The success or failure of the privatization is intertwined with the overall progress of reforms.

The first wave of privatizations in Latin America in the 1980s generated significant resistance. At the time, state firms accounted for approximately 12 percent of GDP in Latin America.[54] Not surprisingly, managers and workers in state firms were threatened by the potential loss of jobs. Nationalist sentiments ran strong, contending that foreign capital would purchase the country's patrimony at bargain-basement prices. The military was concerned about the vulnerability of strategic industries, and the state itself did not want to lose the political power that control of jobs and production conferred.

Nonetheless, the potential gains from privatization were compelling. Many state-owned enterprises were inefficient and operating at a loss. Privatization, it was argued, would increase efficiency and decrease the pressure on state coffers. Whether the productivity gains and the desired macroeconomic effects were achieved was very much influenced by how the privatization was conducted. Privatization is a process involving a range of complementary measures. Simply selling shares in a corporation does not guarantee competitiveness. Furthermore, particularly if a state-owned company was already relatively efficient, the revenue gains from the sale have only a one-time fiscal effect. That is, it is much like selling grandmother's silver to finance a vacation. The deficit may be helped temporarily, but once the heirloom is gone it carries no asset value.

The success of privatization is shaped by the measures taken before the sale as well as the broader economic environment. Efforts to improve the efficiency of enterprises prior to the sale increase the value of the firm on the market. Conglomerate restructuring, administrative reorganizations, personnel cutbacks, debt rescheduling, and liquidation of nonviable operations contribute to the firm's attractiveness. To prevent shares from being sold at below their worth, valuations of the firm (usually using a net present value calculation) provide a minimum reference price below which shares are not sold. How shares are offered on the market can have distributional and efficiency consequences. If the firm had been owned by the public, should the citizenry continue to have an interest in the corporation through widely distributed shares, or does a tightly held corporation make more sense? Several methods can be employed: sale of stock to workers, private individuals, and corporate entities; sales of stock on an exchange; and competitive bidding through public auctions.[55] The selection of which method to use depends in part on the sophistication of markets and their ability to distribute shares in a fair, efficient, and transparent manner.

The speed of privatization matters. Rapid, comprehensive privatization signals strong political will to adhere to the market. However, if complementary measures such as market deregulation to promote competition cannot be implemented at the same pace, privatization efforts are likely to falter. Market structure may indeed be more important than ownership in explaining the comparative performance of companies. Where privatized firms become natural monopolies without regulatory reforms, consumers may be no better off. Large private powerhouses can extract monopoly rents and provide low-quality services to consumers. Trade liberalization encouraging international competition may help mitigate monopolistic abuses.

To promote successful, sustainable service to the population, privatization may need to be accompanied by measures to promote competition. In the privatization of utilities, telecommunications, water, and sewage, for example, state monopolies may become private monopolies without appropriate rules to govern behavior. In the Chilean case, it was found that although privatization of these sectors led to improvements in the quality and quantity of services, without an enforceable regulatory structure, prices did not fall with the privatization of services.[56] In energy, losses were cut from 23 percent to 7 percent, and the number of clients per worker doubled. In telecommunications, the number of phone lines tripled, and the phone line per worker ratio rose from 74 to 235 from 1987 to 1995. As monopolists, firms were able to charge the highest price the market would bear. The only areas experiencing falling prices were those where competition emerged. Long-distance telephone rates, for example, fell 50 percent as new competitors entered the market; monopolized local rates rose by 35 percent. In a noncompetitive setting, efficiency gains have not been passed on to the consumer in the form of lower prices. An alternative to competition policies is a strong regulatory role for the government. Regulation of utilities tends to be problematic given the classic problem of public regulation: asymmetry of information. Only the firm knows the true cost of services; there is an incentive to inflate costs if the regulator's price formula is based on costs. Increasing competition between firms acts as a natural brake on price increases and avoids the problems of regulation.

The rules for both national and international actors must be perceived as fair to build public support. The transition from state-owned enterprises to a competitive private market may be facilitated by multilateral support in preparing bids for sale, developing new management plans, or downsizing the workforce. International participation—either through a public agency such as the World Bank or a private concern such as an international consulting firm—is important in safeguarding transparency and generating credibility in the fairness of the process. In the absence of transparency, the perception that private firms are "stealing" from what had been the national patrimony is fostered. Domestic political commitment at the highest level is critical to sustain privatization;[57] otherwise, the losers from the process will stonewall progress.

Privatization may include measures to reduce short-term labor costs. Measures may be introduced as part of the package to delay employment reduction or spread it over a longer period of time. Often the deal includes temporary protection of the labor force for a specified period after privatization. Fair severance packages and early warnings for mass layoffs can help cushion the blow to workers when jobs are not protected. Bonuses can induce voluntary layoffs to secure political support and the cooperation of unions in the privatization process. The state may also facilitate the movement of laid-off workers into other forms of employment through job search and mobility assistance, retraining, or vocational education programs. Political support for privatization can be expanded if it is construed as part of a wider process of increasing democratic participation in public decision making on issues such as whether to spend more on loss-making public enterprises or instead increase spending on health and public education. Consultation by government and the incoming private management with workers is critical in minimizing the social costs of adjustment in privatization efforts.[58]

WHO HAS PARTICIPATED?

Generating sufficient investor interest in a wide array of newly private activities may be problematic when capital markets are thin. Foreign capital has been a significant source of privatization revenues, accounting for 39.7 percent regionwide for the 1990–1995 period. In 1994 and 1995 foreign revenue jumped to 71.4 and 76.7 percent, respectively. In Bolivia, Peru, and Uruguay, more than 80 percent of the privatization revenues flowed from abroad. A new trend has been intraregional foreign direct investment through privatization. Latin Americans are now investing in other countries in the region. The Argentine steel producer SOMISA, for example, was acquired by a consortium composed of the Argentine group Technit,

Chilean CAP (Compañia de Acero), Brazilian USIMAS, and CVRD. Investment is coming not only from industrial countries but also from within the region.

For most countries, privatization revenues come in the form of **foreign direct investment** (FDI). Notable exceptions are Mexico, Argentina, Brazil, and Colombia, where more sophisticated capital markets allow for portfolio investors. Although portfolio investors such as mutual funds and insurance companies have invested in these markets heavily, they have no significant day-to-day control. In contrast, foreign direct investors acquire sufficient shares to control the strategic direction of the firm. Additionally, foreign direct investment generates additional FDI flows to modernize plants and equipment. There may also be spillover effects beyond the particular company as the privatized firm improves the provision of key services and raises the profitability of investments in other sectors. One study found that worldwide, each dollar of FDI privatization revenue generates an additional 88 cents of FDI transactions outside the privatization.[59] Privatization therefore has the potential to generate future capital flows as the business climate improves in a country. We will return to the role of foreign investment in chapter 7, as we evaluate its effects on economic performance.

THE PRIVATIZATION RECORD

Privatization generated much excitement in Latin America in the 1990s. Seventy-seven percent of all privatizations in developing countries in 1998 took place in Latin America; in 1999 the region accounted for more than half of such privatizations.[60] Ambitious programs of privatization in Latin America were undertaken in Chile, Argentina, and Mexico. Chile has the longest regional track record in privatizations. In 1973 state-owned enterprises accounted for nearly 40 percent of Chilean GDP.[61] From 1974 to 1992, more than five hundred firms were privatized, primarily under the supervision of the state holding company CORFO. The first stage of the privatization, from 1974 to 1982, was largely debt led, with workers and other buyers taking advantage of relatively cheap credit to finance purchases. The Chilean crisis in 1982 resulted in the failure of many of these vulnerable firms, and the second stage involved more equity than debt and was accompanied by sweeping regulatory reform. Public enterprises not privatized in the first wave were given a mandate to behave "as if" private and were forced to face competition in liberalized markets. Many of these firms were privatized in a later stage, reducing state ownership to 16 percent of GDP by 1989, or 6.6 percent if Codelco, the copper giant, is excluded from the count. In the case of the Chilean electric firms CHILGENER and ENERSIS, privatization contributed to higher profitability, improved productivity, and increased investment. The loser was the Chilean government, which was no longer able to appropriate the quasi-rents from electrical sales. The sale of CTC, the Chilean telecommunications monopoly, resulted in increased foreign investment, expansion of services, and improved labor productivity with a net gain to state coffers. A comparison of the two sectors underscores that the positive fiscal effect is a function of whether the firms were profitable or not in the first place. Furthermore, Chile was able to enhance the gains from privatization by requiring that foreign investors commit to investments to improve services. Workers gained in both sectors through participation in the ownership and appreciation of the shares they acquired. On balance, privatization improved the well-being of society.[62]

Privatization in Argentina has been extensive, including television, petroleum, trucking, gas and electric, water and sewage, railroads, ports, the postal service, manufacturing enterprises, telecommunications, and the airlines. International participants in Argentine privatizations included Chile (6 percent), Spain (15 percent), the United States (12 percent), Italy (9 percent), and France (7 percent).[63] One of the largest privatizations to take place in emerging markets was of the Argentine oil company YPF. Prior to privatization YPF had been a huge conglomerate including hospitals and schools in addition to an array of energy-related businesses. Not only was it poorly run, but it was also bled by other state agencies benefiting from underpriced energy and unpaid bills. Before the IPO, or initial public offering, YPF was downsized, trimming the firm to its core activities where it had competitive advantage. It was then restructured, with a focus on upstream exploration and production, downstream refining and marketing, and well-defined business units for information processing and personnel. The capital was distributed such that the federal government retained 20 percent of the shares, provincial governments were accorded 11 percent, workers were given 10 percent, and the balance was offered in national, U.S., and international tranches. Despite a relatively weak oil market, the launching of the stock exceeded expectations, in large part due to enhanced efficiency prior to the sale. YPF has gone on not only to become a regional player, building upon a strong understanding of the South American business environment and the growth of trade in **Mercosur,** but also to acquire a U.S.-based subsidiary, Maxus Energy Corporation. Despite adverse economic conditions in Argentina from the 1995 Mexican *peso* crisis, YPF was able to turn itself and Maxus around to post historically high profits in 1997. In 1999 YPF was sold to Repsol of Spain for $13 billion.

Nonetheless, beyond the YPF success story, nationwide measures to promote competition were sacrificed in the name of speed. This was perceived as necessary because President Menem used the privatizations as a bold signal to the global market of the transformation of the Argentine economy. Deregulation of markets followed at a slower pace. Free competition opened in the Argentine telecom market in November 2000. Although the privatization of the national phone company created two geographically divided companies that have increased the number of lines from three to seven million, calling rates in this duopolistic market structure remain high by international standards due to the lack of competitiveness. The introduction of up to eight competing international companies was designed to increase service and lower prices in the local, long-distance, and cellular markets.[64] However, Argentina's macroeconomic collapse in 2002 derailed progress. Telecommunications operators suspended payments in debt incurred for expansion; some international participants have withdrawn from participation.[65]

Mexico has recently privatized between 2.1 and 3.2 percent of GDP, reserving strategic industries such as petroleum for national control. The state sector had grown to 1,155 enterprises accounting for 12.6 percent of GDP and 38 percent of investment.[66] By 1994 the number of state firms in Mexico was reduced to eighty.[67]

Privatization enjoyed more political support in Mexico than in other Latin American countries, in large part because it was tied to a tripartite agreement between labor, business, and the government. Labor ownership came to play a large role in the privatization effort. Foreign participation played only a minor role in the Mexican case. The success of the Mexican privatization effort can be attributed to strong commitment at the highest levels of Mexican government and transparency in the rules governing the process such that all parties could fairly evaluate conditions of sale. A big success story was the privatization of Teléfonos de México, the monopolistic provider of local and long-distance service, whose stock value soared from 25 cents a share to U.S.$7 a share after privatization. The negotiations governing the sale included commitments to expand the number of lines in service, increase coverage of small towns, add significantly to the number of public telephones, and improve the speed of repairs. Service and access dramatically improved along with profitability. Aeroméxico, a big money loser, was made profitable through privatization, in contrast to the privatization of another state airline, Mexicana, where productivity gains were not realized in the divestiture. One study of 218 privatized Mexican state-owned enterprises (SOEs) showed that the output of privatized firms increased by 54.3 percent, largely through incentive-related productivity gains. Although employment in privatized firms was cut in half, wages rose for remaining workers, and the need for subsidies, equal to 12.7 percent of GDP, was virtually eliminated.[68] Overall, divestiture in the Mexican case met its most important goal: cutting the budget deficit to facilitate macroeconomic stabilization.

Brazil came late to the privatization game with legal changes in 1990. Before the process began, the state held 100 percent of sales in public utilities, 67 percent of steel, 67 percent of chemicals and petrochemicals, 60 percent of mining, 35 percent of transportation services, 32 percent of gasoline distribution, 26 percent of fertilizers, and 21 percent of transportation equipment.[69] Raising 71 billion dollars from 1990 to 1999, progress has been substantial.[70] Privatization in Brazil is very much tied to the increase in capital inflows that we will study in the next chapter. Initial efforts were in the steel, petrochemical, and fertilizer industries. Privatization has been extended to transportation, including railways and the energy sector.

CVRD, Compania Vale do Rio Doce—the world's largest iron ore exporter, Latin America's biggest producer of gold, Brazil's largest exporter, and the biggest foreign exchange earner in Brazil—was placed on the auction block in 1997. The privatization took place in three stages. In the first, the government released 45 percent of voting shares, out of its holdings of 51 percent, to enable a small group of strategic investors to gain control. Employees were allowed to buy 10 percent of the firm, facilitated by BNDES loans to acquire stock, with the rest sold through a global stock offering.[71]

Merrill Lynch did the valuation, with a minimum price set at $9.8 billion. The government held a golden share for the first five years, to be able to veto decisions. No single investor could hold more than 45 percent of equity, with no one firm holding more than 10 percent to prevent monopoly control. The CVRD privatization was the biggest privatization deal since the $3 billion offering of Argentine oil conglomerate YPF. Following the sale costs were reduced by 30 percent, 4,500 people were let go, and new management systems contributed to profitable performance.[72] During the first nine months of 2001, the CVRD experienced a nearly 51-percent increase in profits over the same period in 2000, with $2.1 billion in gross revenue.[73]

Telebrás, Brazil's national telecommunications network, was auctioned off in twelve restructured pieces for $19.1 billion, topping London's privatization of British Telecom in the early 1990s. Despite protests from labor unions, the historically poor service of the company created public support for the sale. With just eleven phones and three mobiles per one hundred inhabitants and a two-year waiting list for phones in some areas, the telecom sale in the world's eighth-largest economy was characterized as a sale of "repressed demand" of the huge unanswered market of Brazilian talkers. The Spanish firm Telefónica won the crown jewel, São Paulo's Telesp, and MCI picked up another key piece, EMBRATEL, Brazil's long-distance and international carrier.[74] We will return to the implications of improvements in the efficiency of the privatized Telebrás when we consider infrastructure deficits in chapter 9.

The sale of power sector and telecommunications companies has led privatization activity in Central America. Interestingly, despite an early start, Costa Rica is the least-privatized economy in the region; El Salvador has gone furthest in privatization efforts.[75] Nicaragua has had the furthest to go in restructuring after the central planning system of the Sandinista government. In Central America, the small size of capital markets has not allowed for widespread public offerings of privatized stock, resulting in less transparency and competition, two keys to privatization success. El Salvador's complementary policies to deregulate markets to promote additional competition compensated for few bidders in the sale itself. In Guatemala the lack of credible efforts to promote competition and irregularities in the bidding process compromised the privatization program.[76]

Despite difficulties throughout the Central American region, privatization has at least improved the climate for foreign direct investment, leading to great investor interest. Privatization has also relieved pressures on cash-strapped governments. Nonetheless, the level of state ownership of enterprises is still high—8, 4, and 3.5 percent of GDP respectively for Costa Rica, Nicaragua, and Honduras, leaving room for gains in efficiency and profitability in moving firms into a well-regulated, competitive private sector.

Despite the strong success in transforming public enterprises into private sector ventures, it is important to note the limitations of privatization. As shown in table 6.3, there has been a great deal of variation in privatization across the region—between countries and from year to year within countries. Privatization revenues tend to be lumpy. That is, the sale of a single large state firm such as a telecommunications entity has a big impact on the numbers. The other interesting number to analyze in table 6.3 is the ratio of privatization to FDI. The steady attraction of foreign direction investment is an important source of growth over time. If, however, foreign direct investment is driven primarily by privatization, there are diminishing returns to how many state enterprises are left on the auction block. Furthermore, although there may be important productivity gains in key sectors with private ownership, privatization does not reflect "greenfield" investment—that is, invest-

Table 6.3. Privatization Revenues in Latin America and the Caribbean, 1990–1999 (millions of U.S.$)

	1990	1991	1992	1993	1994	1995	1996	1997	1998	1999	Total	Privatization/ FDI (% 1999)	% Total Revenue from Privatization, 1990–1999
Argentina	7,532	2,841	5,741	4,670	894	1,208	642	4,366	510	16,157	44,561	67.5	25.06%
Bolivia	NA	NA	9	13	NA	789	34	40	10	151	1,046	14.9	0.59%
Brazil	44	1,633	2,401	2,621	2,104	992	5,770	18,737	32,427	4,400	71,129	13.5	40.00%
Chile	98	364	8	106	128	13	187	NA	181	1,053	2,138	11.4	1.20%
Colombia	NA	168	5	391	170	NA	2,075	2,876	518	NA	6,203	NA	3.49%
Mexico	3,160	11,289	6,924	2,131	766	167	1,526	4,496	999	291	31,749	2.5	17.85%
Peru	NA	3	212	127	2,840	1,276	1,751	1,268	480	286	8,243	14.5	4.64%
Venezuela	10	2,278	140	36	8	39	2,017	1,387	112	46	6,073	1.4	3.41%
Other	71	147	120	393	1,289	132	140	726	2,447	1,231	6,696		3.77%
Total	10,915	18,723	15,560	10,488	8,199	4,616	14,142	33,897	37,685	23,614	177,839		100.00%

Source: World Bank, *Global Development Finance 2001*, 186.
[a]% total 1991–1999.

ment in new economic activity. Ownership patterns have changed, productivity may rise, but there is not a net addition to production.

The Special Case of the Banking Sector

Privatization has also extended to the banking sector. Under import substitution industrialization (ISI), state banks were used to finance activities that were not attractive to the private sector but had developmental promise.[77] The Brazilian BNDES, for example, was instrumental in financing both state enterprises and private activity. Bank privatization presents a special case because of links with the international financial sector and domestic financial intermediation. States still have a strong incentive to maintain control. The experience of bank privatization in the region is mixed. Privatization has led to systemic financial instability in cases where new forms of regulation did not accompany the privatization. The nature of banking also results in a relatively concentrated market structure after privatization.[78] Early privatizations in Chile and Argentina suffered from coincident macroeconomic crises, leading to liquidity problems and bank rescues.

In part this has to do with the problems of **adverse selection** and **moral hazard** in lending that are exacerbated in a newly liberalized environment. Adverse selection is an asymmetric information problem, that is, a situation where one side of a deal has more information than another, leading to the selection of an undesirable outcome. For example, people who are conservative and risk averse are less likely to gamble on a chancy venture. Therefore, loan applicants are, as a group, likely to be risk takers. This results, over time, in banks lending less money because there is a smaller chance of getting a good loan candidate in the borrowers' pool. Moral hazards also stem from asymmetric information. Borrowers have more information than lenders about their own likely behavior after the sale. If sufficient collateral is not secured prior to the loan, the borrower has an incentive to pursue high-risk behavior because the gains will be high if the project succeeds but will be shared by the lender if it fails.[79]

Good information gathering on the part of the bank or predictable borrowing on the part of state-run firms can mitigate banking risks. With deregulation and privatization, however, the informational advantage further shifts from the bank to the private sector. Mexican banks that were nationalized in 1982 had directed roughly 50 percent of their lending to the government. Privatization in the early 1990s left the banks without formal credit bureaus to monitor and assess risk on household and small business loans. As the demands of the now burgeoning private sector intensified, bank lending escalated from 10 percent of GDP in 1988 to more than 40 percent in 1994, quickly exceeding monitoring capabilities. An interest rate spike in January 1995 exacerbated the adverse selection problem, leaving only the most venturesome in the market for loans. With the *peso* crisis, increased uncertainty in stock markets and in firm balance sheets skewed the fundamental values upon which the loans were originally based. With the *peso* halved in value from December 1994 to March 1995, inflationary pressures escalated. Interest rates were ratcheted up to 100 percent to stem the bleeding, and the Mexican stock market fell 60 percent in dollar terms. International investors fled—particularly those with limited knowledge of the Mexican market—exacerbating the financial crisis. Many firms and households could not meet bank debt obligations, and a banking crisis ensued as their balance sheets deteriorated.

The collapse of the banking system was forestalled by government intervention to provide funds to protect depositors. (Remember that it was the depositors' money lent out to the now failed firms.) However, unlike an industrial country government, which can reflate the economy in a crisis, developing economies must guard against the perception of resumed inflation eroding confidence. Reflating the economy may also precipitate depreciation of the currency, and with many loans denominated in dollars, the debt burden on the firm in the developing country is extended. When the U.S. government injected liquidity into the economy following the 1987 stock market crash, there was little fear of inflation. However, recovery in a fragile and internationally dependent developing country is more complicated and fraught with pitfalls. Although bank privatization was not the root cause of financial instability in Mexico, the lack of a strong bank supervisory system coupled with rapid changes throughout the economy left the economy more vulnerable to a free fall. Independent, transparent, well-funded agencies need to be able to enforce adequate accounting and disclosure practices on the part of borrowers and the banking community to safeguard against banking crises. If an appropriate regulatory institution is not in place prior to privatization and deregulation, failure is likely.[80]

Identifying the need for prudent supervision does not mean that national banks bring efficiency gains to economies. One study shows, for example, that extensive state ownership can retard the development of the financial system and slow economic growth rates due to low productivity. Nevertheless, banking privatization and supervision is an art.[81]

THE GAINS FROM PRIVATIZATION

What have been the welfare consequences of privatization? A fair evaluation of the consequences of privatization for society involves an analysis of the particular market structure, the variables used to measure performance, and a control group of contrasting cases. The degree of competitiveness in input and output markets will determine whether gains accrue to society or are appropriated as monopoly rents to large, now private, firms. The employment effects of privatization are ambiguous. It is difficult to separate the effects of privatization from other changes in the economy. Some argue that privatization will increase the capacity of the economy to create jobs through a more efficient use of capital and labor.[82] Others, however, suggest that privatizing existing industries will reduce the number employed in state agencies, which, as a political goal, had inflated employment. Studies show devastating short-run effects, decreasing employment by 40 percent in Argentina, 36 percent in Mexico and 55 percent in Peru. In the long run, however, employment is forecasted to rise over time through re-hiring and indirect job generation.[83] Profitability as a measure of performance may not always be consistent with long-run productivity gains or the social and environmental externalities generated through production. Some critics of privatization suggest that increased profitability derives from the ability to charge higher prices in an unregulated environment, although this may only be a partial explanation. Although efficiency based on sales per worker rose between 88 percent in Chile and 112 percent in Peru, state firms may have served other social objectives such as employment generation.[84] An evaluation of the divestiture process must take into account the trade-off that private firms might perform more efficiently, but that the private means and ends might not be in the social good. Finally, because a controlled experiment with both public and private enterprises operating in the same market under the same macroeconomic conditions cannot be run, it is difficult to attribute gains to privatization as opposed to liberalization or lower inflation.[85]

Special care should be taken in infrastructure privatization to evaluate the potential welfare effects on the poor. Questions of access and pricing are important equity considerations. Will a privatized firm have the incentive to expand telephone lines or water pipes in the poorest of neighborhoods? How will the poor, who may have piggybacked on water or electrical supplies without paying, react to stronger enforcement of illegal connections? Research suggests that competition, in conjunction with prudent supervision, can actually improve access. As evidenced by statistics in the Chilean case prior to privatization, only 2 percent of the poorest fifth of households had access to electricity, and only 3 percent had access to telephones. A decade later only 5.5 percent lacked electricity, and 60 percent lacked telephones.[86] With competition the price of services also dropped in Chile and Argentina by more than 50 percent—a benefit to the poor.

CONCLUSION

Redefining the role of the state in Latin America has included elements of fiscal austerity, tax reform, and privatization to reduce the drag of deficits and the restructuring of the ownership role of the state. Reform of the state sector is a balancing act between a desirable and a sustainable level of state activity. We began our chapter with a discussion of the three schools of thought: the new political economists, the new institutionalists, and the neostructuralists. Because the new political economists believe that a small state is the most efficient outcome, reducing deficits and eliminating state responsibilities for production and provision of services should free the public sector from the need to raise additional money through taxes. Trimming the size of the state and improving its efficient delivery of a limited array of services is the focus of reform. Financing expenditures is more problematic for the new institutionalist and the neostructuralist. At least until market institutions mature and transactions costs are lowered, new institutionalists would call for a stronger mediating role for government in the marketization of the economy. They are concerned about the regulatory capabilities of states to oversee privatized monopolies.

> **QUESTION FOR THOUGHT**
>
> What do you believe is the appropriate role of the state in Latin America? How do you propose matching state roles with financial means to support state activity?

Regulation and supervision are not free, necessitating some new finance for public activity. Neostructuralists must match an active role for government as it supplements the activity in the market with an enhanced capacity to pay and to deliver needed services more efficiently. Committed to the notion that the state is an important actor in promoting equitable development, especially where markets are imperfect, neostructuralists face the challenge of convincing constituencies of the necessity to pay for public goods. For the neostructuralists, however, the long-run payoff of decreased poverty and improved education and health is well worth the investment.

Key Concepts

adverse selection	moral hazard	new political economy
fiscal covenant	neostructuralists	value added tax
foreign direct investment	new institutional economics	

Chapter Summary

The New Role of the Latin American State

- What should be the new role of the Latin American state? The state must balance accountability to multilateral organizations and voters. ECLAC suggests a social covenant in which the state establishes a socioeconomic agreement with civil society. The World Bank in 1997 suggested that states should only engage in those activities in which they have the capacity to be effective, such as investing in basic social services.

The Theoretical Framework for State Intervention

- The theoretical framework for state intervention can be divided into three main schools of thought: new political economy, new institutionalist economics, and neostructuralism. New political economists believe that state intervention will interfere with market signals; therefore, the role of the state should be minimal. New institutionalists claim that neoclassical economics ignores transaction costs. The principal tenet behind new institutionalist economics is that market actors rarely receive perfect information. There is a need for institutional norms such as transparent, effective, and accessible legal and judicial arrangements to reduce transaction costs. Unlike the new institutionalists and new political economists, neostructuralists are not optimistic about the market's ability to enhance development. Neostructuralists call for effective state intervention when the market fails.

A Weak Public Sector

- The Latin American public sector is on average half the size of that of industrialized countries. Its small size stems primarily from a weak tax bureaucracy and a large informal sector that is difficult to tax.
- There has been a shift in the source of tax revenue from custom duties to domestic taxes. The most popular tax instrument has been the value added tax (VAT) because of its self-regulating mechanism. The next steps for Latin America are to combat tax evasion and increase revenue from direct taxes and green taxes.

Privatization

- Privatization of generally inefficient state-owned enterprises requires a complementary set of policies and their swift implementation. During privatization governments should promote competition to maximize the value of the sale by improving the efficiency of the firms prior to the sale. Foreign financing has played a major role in privatization in Latin America.
- Chile led the wave of privatization in the late 1970s and early 1980s. Although these initial attempts encountered difficulties, subsequent privatization efforts proved more successful because complementary policies were introduced to increase efficiency.
- Privatization of the banking sector presented a different kind of problem, one of asymmetric information where the borrower has the advantage. Successful banking sector privatization must be accompanied by an appropriate regulatory institution.

Notes

1. Ricardo Hausmann and Ernesto Stein, "Searching for the Right Budgetary Institutions for a Volatile Region," in *Securing Stability and Growth in Latin America,* ed. Ricardo Hausmann and Helmut Reisen (Paris: OECD Publications, 1996), 247.

2. Shahid Javed Burki and Sebastian Edwards, *Latin America after Mexico: Quickening the Pace* (Washington, D.C.: World Bank, 1996).

3. Ernesto Stein, Ernesto Talvi, and Alejandro Grisanti, *Institutional Arrangements and Fiscal Performance: The Latin American Experience,* National Bureau of Economic Research Working Paper no. 6358 (Cambridge, Mass.: National Bureau of Economic Research, 1998).

4. Shahid Javed Burki and Sebastian Edwards, *Dismantling the Populist State* (Washington, D.C.: World Bank, 1996), 23.

5. Dani Rodrik, in Peter Evans, "The Eclipse of the State?: Reflections on Stateness in an Era of Globalization," *World Politics* 50 (October 1997): 83.

6. Evans, "Eclipse," 66.

7. Dani Rodrik, "Why Do More Open Economies Have Bigger Governments?" *Journal of Political Economy* 16, no. 5 (1998).

8. Barry Weingast, in Hans P. Binswanger and Klaus Deininger, "Explaining Agricultural and Agrarian Policies in Developing Countries," *Journal of Economic Literature* 35 (December 1997): 1978.

9. Evans, "Eclipse," 80.

10. Binswanger and Deininger, "Explaining Agricultural and Agrarian Policies," 1987.

11. ECLAC, *The Fiscal Covenant: Strengths, Weaknesses, Challenges* (Santiago, Chile: ECLAC, 1999), 1.

12. ECLAC, *The Fiscal Covenant,* 9.

13. Takashi Hikino and Alice Amsden, "Staying Behind, Stumbling Back, Sneaking Up, Soaring Ahead: Late Industrialization in Historical Perspective," in *Convergence of Productivity: Cross-National Studies and Historical Evidence,* ed. William Baumol, Richard R. Nelson, and Edward N. Wolff (New York: Oxford University Press, 1994), 290.

14. World Bank, "Overview," in *World Development Report 1997* (New York: Oxford University Press for the World Bank, 1997).

15. Enrique V. Iglesias, "The Search for a New Economic Consensus in Latin America," in *The Legacy of Raúl Prebisch,* ed. Enrique V. Iglesias (Washington, D.C.: IADB, 1994), 93.

16. John Martinussen, *Society, State, and Market: A Guide to Competing Theories of Development* (London: Zed, 1997), 266.

17. Joseph E. Stiglitz, "The Role of Government in Economic Development," in *Annual World Bank Conference on Development Economics 1996* (Washington, D.C.: World Bank, 1997), 12.

18. Paola Perez-Aleman, "Learning, Adjustment and Economic Development: Transforming Firms, The State and Associations in Chile," *World Development* 28, no. 1 (2000): 41–55.

19. Robin Emmott, "Bribery Costs Mexicans up to 14% of Income," *Financial Times,* October 31, 2001, www.ft.com.

20. "Lousy Deal," *IDB America,* May–June 2000: 2.

21. Peter Cornelius, Thomas Hall, and Joel Kurtzman, "Opacity, Foreign Direct Investment, and Economic Growth," *The Latin American Competitiveness Report 2001–2002,* ed. Joaquín Vial and Peter Cornelius (New York: Oxford University Press, 2002), 128–29.

22. Transparency International, *Global Corruption Reports 2001,* www.transparency.org.

23. See www.oas.org for information on the convention and summit measures.

24. "Just Don't Call It Downsizing," *IDB America,* September–October 2000: 10–11.

25. Peter Evans, ed., "State–Society Synergy: Government and Social Capital in Development," *World Development* 24, no. 6, special edition (June 1996).

26. Evans, "State–Society Synergy," 185.

27. Mick Moore, "Toward a Useful Consensus," in "The Bank, the State, and Development: Dissecting the World Development Report, 1997," *IDS Bulletin* 29, no. 2, special edition (1998): 41.

28. Martinussen, *Society, State, and Market,* 262.

29. Popkin, as cited by Martinussen, *Society, State, and Market,* 244.

30. Douglas C. North, "The New Institutional Economics and Third World Development," in *The New Institutional Economics and Third World Development,* ed. John Harriss, Janet Hunter, and Colin M. Lewis (London: Routledge, 1995), 23.

31. John Harriss, Janet Hunter, and Colin M. Lewis, "Introduction: Development and Significance of the NIE," in *The New Institutional Economics and Third World Development,* ed. John Harriss, Janet Hunter, and Colin M. Lewis (London: Routledge, 1995), 1.

32. Barbara Harriss-White, "Maps and Landscapes of Grain Markets in South Asia," in *The New Institutional Economics and Third World Development,* ed. John Harriss, Janet Hunter, and Colin M. Lewis (London: Routledge, 1995), 87.

33. Harriss, Hunter, and Lewis, "Introduction," 3.

34. North, as cited by Martinussen, *Society, State, and Market*, 254.

35. Osvaldo Sunkel, *Development from Within: Toward a Neostructuralist Approach for Latin America* (Boulder, Colo.: Rienner, 1993), 7.

36. C. Gunnarsson and M. Lundahl, "The Good, the Bad, and the Wobbly," in *New Directions in Development Economics: Growth, Environmental Concerns, and Government in the 1990s*, ed. Mats Lundahl and Benno J. Ndulu (London: Routledge, 1996), 256–57.

37. As synthesized by Nader Nazmi, *Economic Policy and Stabilization in Latin America* (New York: Sharpe, 1996), 7–8.

38. Anne Krueger uses the term "benevolent social guardian" to characterize a well-intended but inefficient state. As described in Gunnarsson and Lundahl, "Good, Bad, and Wobbly," 256.

39. Gunnarsson and Lundahl, "Good, Bad, and Wobbly," 260.

40. Gunnarsson and Lundahl, "Good, Bad, and Wobbly," 109.

41. Carol Wise, "Latin America and the State–Market Debate: Beyond Stylized Facts," paper presented at the Latin American Studies Association, Miami, March 16–18, 2000: 22.

42. Wise, "Latin America and the State–Market Debate," 84.

43. Michael Gavin, Ricardo Hausmann, Roberto Perotti, and Ernesto Talvi, *Managing Fiscal Policy in Latin America and the Caribbean: Volatility, Procyclicality, and Limited Creditworthiness*, IADB, Office of the Chief Economist Working Paper, no. 326 (Washington, D.C.: IADB, 1996), 4.

44. José María Fanelli and Roberto Frenkel, "Macropolicies for the Transition from Stabilization to Growth," in *New Directions in Development Economics: Growth, Environmental Concerns, and Government in the 1990s*, ed. Mats Lundahl and Benno J. Ndulu (London: Routledge, 1996), 41.

45. Guillermo Perry and Ana María Herrera, *Public Finances, Stabilization, and Structural Reform in Latin America* (Washington, D.C.: Johns Hopkins University Press/IADB, 1994).

46. ECLAC, *The Fiscal Covenant*, 13.

47. IADB, *Economic and Social Progress in Latin America, 1995 Report: Overcoming Volatility* (Washington, D.C.: Johns Hopkins University Press, 1995), table 3.1, p. 126.

48. IADB, *Latin America after a Decade of Reforms: Economic and Social Progress 1997 Report* (Washington, D.C.: Johns Hopkins University Press/IADB, 1997), 72.

49. Ingrid Palmer, "Public Finance from a Gender Perspective," *World Development* 23, no. 11 (1995): 1984.

50. Vito Tanzi, *Fiscal Federalism and Decentralization: A Review of Some Efficiency and Macroeconomic Aspects*, presented at the World Bank Conference on Development Economics, World Bank, May 1995. (As summarized by *The Economist*, 3 June 1995, p. 74.)

51. ECLAC, *Fiscal Covenant*, 14.

52. Carlos Elizondo Mayer-Serra, "Tax Reform under the Salinas Administration," in *The Changing Structure of Mexico*, ed. Laura Randall (Armonk, N.Y.: Sharpe, 1996).

53. Douglas C. North, "Economic Performance through Time," acceptance lecture, 1993 Alfred Nobel Memorial Prize in Economic Sciences, published in *American Economic Review* 84, no. 3 (1994).

54. Rolph Van der Hoeven and Gyorgy Sziraczi, *Lessons from Privatization* (Geneva: International Labour Office, 1997), 4.

55. M. Sánchez, R. Corona, L. F. Herrera, and O. Ochoa, "A Comparison of Privatization Experiences: Chile, Mexico, Colombia, and Argentina," in *Privatization in Latin America*, ed. M. Sánchez and R. Corona (Baltimore: Johns Hopkins University Press, 1994).

56. Eduardo Bitran and Pablo Serra, "Regulation of Privatized Utilities: The Chilean Experience," *World Development* 26, no. 6 (1998): 945–62.

57. Emanuel Delovitch and Klas Ringskog, *Private Sector Participation in Water Supply and Sanitation in Latin America* (Washington, D.C.: World Bank, 1995), 3.

58. Van der Hoeven and Sziraczi, *Lessons from Privatization,* 12–17.

59. Sader (1993) as cited in chapter 5, "Privatization," in *Economic and Social Progress in Latin America 1996 Report* (Washington, D.C.: IADB), 179.

60. The World Bank, *Global Development Finance 2001,* appendix 4.

61. Ahmed Galal, Leroy Jones, Pankaj Tandon, and Ingo Vogelsang, "Divestiture: Questions and Answers," in *Welfare Consequences of Selling Public Enterprises* (Washington, D.C.: World Bank, 1994), 184.

62. Galal et al., "Divestiture," 288

63. This is in 1992. *World Investment Report 1994* (New York: United Nations, 1994), 93.

64. Clifford Krauss, "Argentina to Hasten End of Phone Monopoly," *New York Times,* 11 March 1998, p. D4.

65. Elizabeth Mooney, "South American Economic Crisis Hits Telecom Operators," *RCR Wireless News,* April 2002, p. 25.

66. Galal et al., "Divestiture," 407.

67. Sebastian Edwards, ed., *Crisis and Reform in Latin America: From Despair to Hope* (New York: Oxford University Press, 1995).

68. La Porta, Lopez-de-Silanes, and Shleifer, 1999, as summarized in William Megginson and Jeffry M. Netter, "From State to Market: A Survey of Empirical Studies of Privatization," *Journal of Economic Literature* XXXIX (June 2001): 349.

69. Werner Baer and Annibal V. Villela, "Privatization and the Changing Role of the State in Brazil," in *Privatization in Latin America,* ed. Werner Baer and Melissa Birch (Westport, Conn.: Praeger, 1994).

70. World Bank, *Global Development Finance 2001,* 186, table A42.

71. "Privatization," *Euromoney,* September 1996, p. 294.

72. "Brazil's Iron King," *Financial Times,* 29 June 1998, p. 13.

73. Michael Kepp, "Refining Mining," *Latin Trade,* April 2002, p. 30.

74. "Telebras Sold for US$19.1b," *Latin American Weekly Report,* 4 August 1998, p. 352; and Seth Schiesel, "Brazil Sells Most of State Phone Utility," *New York Times,* 30 July 1998, p. D1.

75. Felipe B. Larraín and Luis F. López-Calva, "Privatization: Fostering Economic Growth through Private Sector Development," ch. 13 in Felipe B. Larraín, *Economic Development in Central America. Vol. 2: Structural Reform* (Cambridge, Mass.: Harvard University Press, 2001), 68.

76. Larraín and López-Calva, 96.

77. Baer and Villela, "Privatization," 2.

78. Kenneth P. Jameson, "The Financial Sector in Latin American Restructuring," in *Privatization in Latin America,* ed. Werner Baer and Melissa Birch (Westport, Conn.: Praeger, 1994), 120.

79. This section draws extensively on Frederick Mishkin, "Understanding Financial Crises: A Developing Country Perspective," in *Annual World Bank Conference on Development Economics 1996* (Washington, D.C.: World Bank, 1997), 28–30.

80. Mishkin, "Understanding Financial Crises," 28.

81. La Porta, Lopez-de-Silanes, and Shleifer, 2000, as summarized in William Megginson and Jeffry M. Netter, "From State to Market: A Survey of Empirical Studies of Privatization," *Journal of Economic Literature* XXXIX (June 2001): 333.

82. Van der Hoeven and Sziraczi, *Lessons from Privatization,* 11.

83. "The Privatization Paradox," *Latin American Economic Policies,* Inter-American Development Bank, vol. 18, 2002, 3.

84. IADB, "The Privatization Paradox," 3.

85. Galal et al., "Divestiture," 13–14.

86. Antonio Estache and Danny Leipziger, "Utilities Privatization and the Poor: Lessons and Evidence from Latin America," *World Development* 29, no. 7 (2001): 1181.

New International Capital Flows

The Benefits (and Hidden Costs) of Latin America's Return to Markets

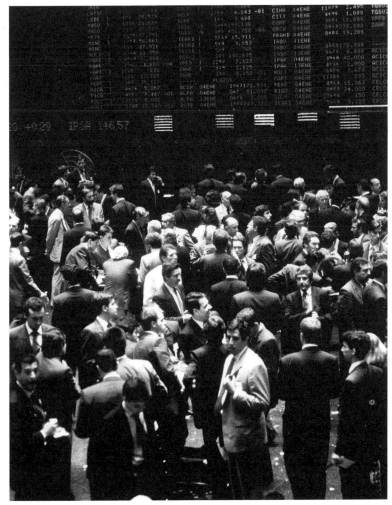

Foreign capital has flooded regional stock markets. *(Courtesy of David Mangurian and the Inter-American Development Bank.)*

After the long period of painful structural adjustment to the debt crisis, Latin America became a magnet for international finance in the mid-1990s. Macroeconomic stability, opening of closed economies to international markets, lucrative privatizations, and subregional integration made potential returns in Latin America enticing to foreign capital. By 1995 capital flows had tripled their 1990 level. After a decade of isolation, Latin America was again a darling of international investors. Peaking in 1998, capital flows have still remained strong throughout the region, despite four financial crises. What have been the causes and the consequences of sustained capital flows to the region?

Although new capital is of course a welcome way to spur growth, rapid inflows raise questions about the ability of economies to absorb international funds productively. Are funds being channeled to improve the productive capacity of the region or are they fueling asset bubbles or consumption booms? A lesson of the debt crisis was the vulnerability of regional economies to changes in international liquidity. The Mexican *peso* crisis of 1994–1995, the Asian currency crises of 1997–1998, the Brazilian crisis of 1998–1999, and the Argentine crisis of 2001–2002 underscore the fragility of developing economies in highly integrated international capital markets. What if Latin America is once again cut off from capital inflows? Policy must carefully appraise not only the huge growth potential but also the possible pitfalls of the new capital flows to Latin America.

The following questions will guide our discussion of new capital flows to the region:

- Why has capital returned with such intensity to the region?
- How do the different kinds of capital—short- and long-term portfolio investments as well as long-term **foreign direct investment** (FDI) through multinational corporations—affect development prospects in the region?
- Does this new reliance on international capital make Latin America vulnerable once again to swings in global markets?
- Are there ways of minimizing vulnerability while maintaining the confidence of international capital?

Understanding the changing nature of capital flows to the region will enhance our understanding of the promise and the limitations of liberalization as a strategy for Latin American economic development. Like trade, which we will study in the next chapter, the free flow of capital brings opportunities for growth but may be accompanied by an increase in uncertainty and volatility. Unlike the inward-looking model of import substitution industrialization, financial and trade liberalization make a nation more sensitive to changes in the global economy—the good *and* the bad.

AN INTRODUCTION TO THE BEHAVIOR OF CAPITAL FLOWS

The neoliberal market model places private capital flows at the center of development finance. Capital, it is argued, will flow to its most productive uses. Tough aus-

Figure 7.1.   Net Resource Flows

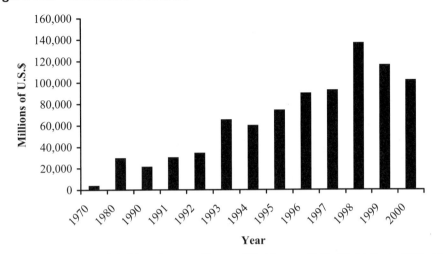

Source: World Bank, *Global Development Finance* (Washington, D.C.: World Bank, 1998, 2000, and 2001).

terity measures that transform the productivity of an economy should therefore be rewarded by improved access to international capital markets. This has, to some extent, taken place in the Latin American region. We can see in figure 7.1 that capital flows in the 1990s are dramatically higher than in earlier periods; flows in 2000 were nearly twenty-five times as large as 1970. This is an extraordinary vote of confidence on the part of international markets in Latin American economic reform.

It should be pointed out that foreign capital inflows are not a solution for all countries. Although private capital flows to all developing countries have risen dramatically, they are concentrated in a few countries. In 2000 private flows to developing countries exceeded $200 billion, four times official flows and three times levels at the beginning of the decade. However, 75 percent of the flows went to twelve countries, and fifty countries received virtually no private flows.[1] At the same time, official aid flows to poor countries have been diminishing quickly—at $38.6 billion in 2000 they were more than a third less than their 1990 level.[2]

Although the trickle of capital to poorer countries is problematic, ironically the rapid infusion of international capital to hot countries may also have economic costs. International capital is an undependable friend. It can flow out as quickly as it comes in, following the highest rate of return. How permanent are capital flows to Latin America? How predictable? Rapid inflows may be too much of a good thing, distorting asset and foreign exchange prices.

To understand the implications of rapid capital flows it is useful to analyze what drives the demand for foreign assets. As we have noted, the restructuring of Latin American economies created new growth potential. Remember that investors buy today in anticipation of returns in the future. Unlike buying a car or a computer, where you can pretty well predict what the asset will be worth next year, financial investments carry an uncertain future value. Purchases are made based on *expected* value. Do you think the value of the asset will rise or fall over the term of the investment? This applies to investments in stocks, bonds, or commodities such as copper or tin. If there is a high degree of uncertainty as to the future performance of an asset, investors must be compensated for additional risk. If the asset is denominated in a foreign currency, the possibility that the currency may lose value over the term of the investment must also be taken into account. Stability, confidence, and predictability are key to promoting sound financial investments.

Because international investment decisions are made one versus another—that is, investors evaluate *relative* returns—the policy or performance in Latin America may not be the sole factor. Relative returns on other assets—perhaps the dollar or maybe investments in Europe or Asia—could become more lucrative. Latin America may be interesting because returns in other regions are low. But a country can't control what is happening in the rest of the world. Capital flows must therefore be looked at not only for their investment potential today, but also for their sustainability in promoting long-term development. This chapter will analyze these flows and address policies Latin American governments have introduced to tame their volatility in the region. It will also look at interactions with other macroeconomic variables, especially the exchange rate. If capital—say, dollars—is flowing in, this will increase the supply and decrease the price of the dollar relative to the national currency. If the national currency as a result becomes stronger, this may compromise the ability of the country to pursue an aggressive export drive. As we will see, capital's helping hand may also choke off the growth of exports. The gains to financing in the internal market may not be consistent with the external requirements of the economy. We will explore whether policy instruments are needed to balance capital flows in emerging markets.

Explaining Capital Flows to Latin America

A variety of factors explain the increase in global private capital flows and the new interest in Latin America relative to other regions. Beginning with the supply side, international flows have responded to changes in international markets, following global integration. Technological changes facilitating the transfer of money and ideas have made the world a smaller place, reducing transaction costs for international investment. With better information and changes in the U.S. legal code, new groups of institutional investors such as pension and insurance funds have internationalized investment opportunities.[3] The aging of the baby boomers created a pool of capital in search of high returns. Low interest rates in the United States in the early and mid-1990s made domestic investments less attractive. There is simply more international money to be invested. These external supply factors, including developments in international financial markets, have been shown to be the primary determinant of capital flows to the region.[4] More investors are looking for productive opportunities around the globe.

Why invest in Latin America instead of other regions? In addition to the factors that have increased the global supply of capital, structural changes in Latin America have pulled financing into the region. Tough austerity measures improved financial solvency. In most countries changes in investment codes and macroeconomic policy are perceived to be permanent. National exchange rate regimes are less susceptible to mega devaluations. Investors have greater confidence in their ability to predict the long-term macroeconomic environment for business. Legislation has favored international investment, and privatization has created new investment opportunities. Simultaneous political reform and the deepening of democracy reduced the political risk—although examples of Venezuela and Argentina show how quickly things can change. We can summarize these factors by saying that the relative yield of countries' assets as well as financial solvency has improved, while political instability and potential losses due to devaluation or nationalization have declined. In short, Latin America has become a good investment risk.[5] Nonetheless, it is important to remember that no matter how well structured Latin America's reforms are, international capital chooses a home based on *relative* appeal: opportunities for profit not only have to be good, but they must be better than expected returns adjusted for uncertainty and risk everywhere else.

The policy environment in each country may also explain capital flows. Latin American country officials see expanding foreign direct investment as a key policy tool for growth. How can countries, particularly those that have not been the largest beneficiaries in the past, attract foreign direct investment? How does the policy environment affect the location decision of multinational companies? Policy recommendations for attracting productive new international investment include lowering trade costs, improving export processing zones, investigating the further use of incentives, promoting dialogue with investors on business climate, and investing in education.[6] Foreign firms must have some advantage in producing abroad that justifies additional coordination costs and risks in a foreign business climate.

Country size as expressed by gross domestic product (GDP) adjusted for the "effective market"—those consumers that can be reached with strong infrastructure such as good roads or ports—and distance from investors are two additional factors that influence foreign direct investment decisions.[7] Distance works as a pro and con, depending on whether the company wants to sell goods or infrastructure services in the foreign market (local production cuts down on transport costs) or desires to re-export (where proximity to the target market is key.) Whether a company is attracted to produce abroad is a function of the type of FDI—export-oriented, host-market serving, or infrastructure. Export orientation reflects low labor, transport, and tax outlays; host-market serving investment is largely a function of size; and infrastructure investment depends on the regulatory environment in providing for after-contract services in areas such as telecommunications or water management.[8]

It is important to note that low wages are not in themselves a draw; the key is total compensation (which includes indirect costs from labor legislation) per unit of output. Low wages for low productivity are not a bargain. Legal codes that guarantee intellectual property right protection and investment dispute settlement mechanisms are important in decreasing a country's risk profile. The degree of transparency in a country's institutions is an important factor. One study suggested that on average a country could expect a 40-percent increase in FDI with a one-point increase in its transparency rankings.[9] Rather than grease the wheels, corruption adds to the burden of taxes and capital controls.

The United States is still the principal investor in the region, concentrating on manufacturers in Mexico and services such as electricity and gas distribution and telecoms in **Mercosur.** European firms are a growing presence, located in Mercosur and Chile in telecoms, energy financial services, automotive, agro-industry, and retail trade. The new kid on the block, Spain, is a significant presence in telecoms, financial services, electricity generation and distribution, and petroleum—although the Argentine crisis hit it hard. Japan has not exerted a large presence in the region.[10] Firms seeking efficiency gains and lower wages tend toward the automotive and electronics sectors in Mexico and the Caribbean Basin. Natural resource-seeking investors are attracted to Venezuela, Colombia, Argentina, Chile, and Peru. Those seeking market access in manufacturing are interested in Argentina, Brazil, and Mexico, and firms taking advantage of liberalization and privatization of services have moved in throughout the region.[11]

Worldwide, U.S. multinationals sell about two-thirds of their output in the host country, suggesting that cheap labor only motivates exports in a small number of cases. In the Andean region host-market serving and infrastructure arguments are even more compelling. U.S. manufacturing affiliates reach a striking 90 percent in Peru and Venezuela and average 75 percent for other nations, indicating that export orientation as a rationale for investment is limited.[12] This constrains foreign investment, because the number of consumers is relatively small. Despite a good deal of activity in natural resource-related activities, Andean countries will be limited by market size in attracting technology-based investment in manufacturing.

Characteristics of Latin American Markets: What Is the Absorptive Capacity?

The fact that capital is flowing to Latin America doesn't mean that investments there are always productive. Can Latin America productively absorb the capital flowing into the region? Understanding the absorptive capacity involves an appreciation of the types of capital coming into the region. The flow of capital into the region takes four forms: foreign direct investment, bond purchases, portfolio equity flows, and lending directly to support trade.[13] Figure 7.2 shows the net increase in all types of capital flows to the region from 1990 to 1999. Foreign direct investment increased more than tenfold, portfolio equity 3.5 times, and **portfolio bonds** 188 times. Coping with the rapid influx of short-term or hot money is a source of policy concern. We will explain the role each type of capital plays in turn.

Portfolio bonds and **equity investments** can be transitory. Portfolio bond flows are bond issues purchased by foreign investors. These might be government bonds similar to U.S. Treasuries to finance public investments, or they might be corporate offerings. Remember that bonds are essentially a promise to pay in the future. Equity investments are the sum of country funds, depository receipts,[14] and direct purchases of shares by foreign investors. Short-term (less than one year) capital

Figure 7.2.   Net Private Capital Flows

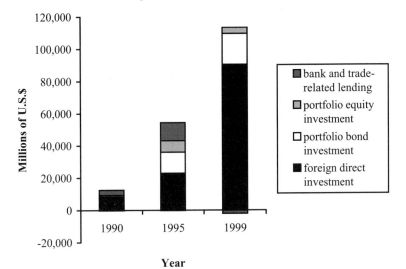

Source: World Bank, *World Development Indicators* (Washington, D.C.: World Bank, 1997 and 2001).

with the exception of loans to finance trade is broadly characterized as speculative or "hot" money. It is this stateless, agile capital that concerns policymakers. As we learned in the chapter on the debt crisis in the 1980s, financing long-term development on short-term capital is a risky venture. Portfolio flows create problems for long-term sustainability.

Equity investments, or the purchase of stocks, are also considered liquid, short-term capital, particularly if the holder maintains less than a 10-percent share. Nonetheless, equity or stock investments are less risky to a company than bonds. If an economy or a firm experiences a downturn and the stock value plummets, stockholders lose. When hard times hit a company that has financed expansion through bonds (or through commercial bank loans), the firm or nation must still make good on that obligation or face the ramifications of default. Stocks, therefore, spread risk from firms to investors. We can measure market capitalization or market value by taking the share price times the number of shares outstanding on an exchange. Market size is an important predictor of a country's ability to mobilize capital and diversify risk. The level of stock market development closely tracks a country's overall development level. Finance in less-developed economies tends to be dominated by commercial banks, rather than stock exchanges. The growth of stock markets may increase liquidity and diversify risk.[15] As shown in table 7.1, stock markets in Latin America, as measured by the ratio of capitalization to GDP, are small compared with those in developed countries.[16] The outlier is certainly Chile: its sophisticated market was 101 percent of GDP in 1999, comparable to that of France. The markets are modest; only Brazil's market value comes close to the European country of Spain. With fewer shares traded and fewer participants, small stock markets can be overwhelmed by foreign participation. Furthermore, Latin American

Table 7.1.   Market Capitalization

Country	1990 Value (millions of U.S.$)	1995 Value (millions of U.S.$)	2000 Value (millions of U.S.$)	% Rate of Growth 1990–1995	% Rate of Growth 1990–2000	% of GDP 1999
Argentina	3,268	37,783	166,068	1,056	4,981	29.6
Brazil	16,354	147,636	226,152	803	1,283	30.3
Chile	13,645	73,860	60,401	441	343	101.1
Colombia	1,416	17,893	9,560	1,164	575	13.4
Ecuador	69	3,627	704	5,157	920	2.2
Mexico	32,725	90,694	125,204	177	283	31.8
Panama	226	831	3,584	268	1,486	37.5
Peru	812	11,795	10,562	1,353	1,200	25.8
France	314,384	522,053	1,475,457	66	369	103.0
Spain	111,404	197,788	431,668	78	287	72.4
United Kingdom	848,866	1,407,737	2,933,280	66	246	203.4
United States	3,059,434	6,857,622	16,635,114	124	444	181.8

Source: World Bank, *World Development Indicators* (Washington, D.C.: World Bank, 1997 and 2001), table 5.3.
Note: Market capitalization is the share price multiplied by the number of outstanding shares; it is also known as market value.

equity markets are relatively concentrated. Ownership is highly entrenched among a small number of participants in closed and family-owned corporations such that markets are not easily contestable.[17] Nonetheless, they have exhibited substantial growth in the past five years. As box 7.1 shows, some believe there is greater potential for smaller investors. While market size is small, growth has been rapid. Average growth from 1990 to 2000 was 1,384 percent, roughly three times that of the vibrant U.S. market.

LONG-TERM INVESTMENT: THE ROLE OF MULTINATIONAL CORPORATIONS

In contrast to short-term bond and equity flows, foreign direct investment largely represents a long-term capital flow with a commitment to local manufacturing. It is generally measured by acquiring a lasting management interest or 10 percent of the voting stock or by establishing a subsidiary or production branch. On average, foreign direct investment in Latin America accounts for approximately 2.2 percent of a country's GDP.[18] Foreign direct investment is less risky than borrowing because if a project fails it is the shareholders and not the citizens that bear the cost. We can see in figure 7.3 that foreign direct investment grew enormously throughout the 1990s, with an increasing diversity of recipients. Flows for 2000 were 536 percent greater than for 1991, even adjusting for a downturn due to the Asian crisis. Multinationals from Spain, the Netherlands, Switzerland, and the United States snatched up cheaply priced Latin American firms in the telecommunications, banking, electric utility, and consumer finance sectors to strengthen their stakes in key markets in Brazil, Argentina, and Chile.[19] Inflows to Mexico and Argentina in the beginning of

Box 7.1.   The New Entrepreneurs—Not Just for Big Players: Stock Markets Could Open the Door to Entrepreneurs

Latin America's stock markets are still dominated by a relatively small number of large corporations. But according to Jorge Roldán, chief economist for the Inter-American Investment Corporation (IIC), medium-sized and even small companies could soon tap this rich source of low-cost, long-term capital. Roldán spoke to *IDB EXTRA* about the future of financing for Latin American entrepreneurs.

Q. Have small companies benefited from the billions of dollars in foreign investment that have flowed into the region in recent years?

A. Yes, but to a very limited degree. Most of the money has gone to established corporations listed on the stock exchanges of countries with larger economies, such as Mexico, Brazil, Argentina, Chile, Colombia, Peru, and Venezuela.

Traditional private venture capital funds make equity investments in established companies and help them to upgrade technology and management expertise in order to become internationally competitive. The typical investment is between $20 million and $80 million in a company worth from $50 million to $300 million. Once the company reaches the desired volume of business, the venture fund typically cashes out. Unfortunately, in some cases, the fund may pull out at the first hint of a downturn, either in the company itself or in the economy of the country.

Q. How does the IIC fit into this picture?

A. We have a development-oriented investment strategy. We specialize in much smaller companies and allocate a large part of our portfolio to the countries that private investors tend to overlook. Our typical loan or equity investment ranges between $2 million and $10 million, and we're willing to make a longer commitment, usually in the ten-year range.

We work very closely with the managers of the companies we invest in to help them adopt new technologies that improve productivity and competitiveness. We also have a very strict commitment to environmental protection. We won't invest in companies that don't have a viable plan for ameliorating the environmental consequences of their activities.

Q. Small companies in Latin America have traditionally depended on debt financing to expand. Should they be looking to local stock markets as an alternative way to raise funds?

A. Absolutely. Interest rates on bank loans remain prohibitively high in many of the region's countries. Issuing stock or bonds on a local securities market can be a much cheaper way to obtain long-term financing, even for a relatively small firm. We have a project in Guatemala, for instance, where a developer placed $2 million in bonds on the local stock exchange to help finance a new hotel.

The problem is that most smaller companies are not used to the rigorous financial reporting requirements that investors demand before they are willing to buy stocks or bonds. So one of our principal goals is to help companies put their house in order and get to the point where they can be listed on an exchange.

Along with the Multilateral Investment Fund, the IIC has been working to help regional governments modernize their stock markets and harmonize reporting requirements. This is especially important in the smaller countries, where there isn't enough of a critical mass to sustain individual markets. In Central America and the Caribbean, for example, we are helping to coordinate regulatory and reporting standards in order to create regional exchanges. That way an investor in Honduras could easily buy stock in a Costa Rican company, for instance.

Our board has just approved a very innovative line of credit to a Brazilian bank, Credibanco, that is going to assist medium-sized companies to go through the process of

(continued)

(continued)

preparing to go public. Our credit facility will be used to purchase dollar-denominated bonds issued by medium-sized enterprises. This will give a number of companies access to longer-term financing for much less than they could hope to get by borrowing. Beneficiary companies will be required to register with the local securities and exchange commission. In Brazil, this is the first step in the process of becoming publicly listed.

Ultimately, we think local stock markets will be the best way to channel domestic savings towards entrepreneurs and small companies. There are several countries where public pension reforms based on individual retirement accounts are quickly creating a huge pool of savings that needs to be invested. We have already seen the benefits of that approach in Chile. Now we want to extend it to other countries.

Source: IDB Extra, June 14, 1998. Online edition.

the decade have been supplemented by investment in Brazil, Venezuela, and other Latin American countries. Nevertheless, the investment in the smaller countries of the region is about half that of Mexico or a quarter of Brazil's. In Ecuador, for example, foreign investors have shunned the unstable political and economic environment, with ventures largely limited to the oil sector.[20] Foreign direct investment has also slowed in response to dramatic swings in global markets. After a decade of extremely strong performance, foreign direct investment (FDI) into Latin America

Some multinationals contract with smaller local producers for piecework to export. *(Courtesy of David Mangurian and the Inter-American Development Bank.)*

Figure 7.3. Net Foreign Direct Investment

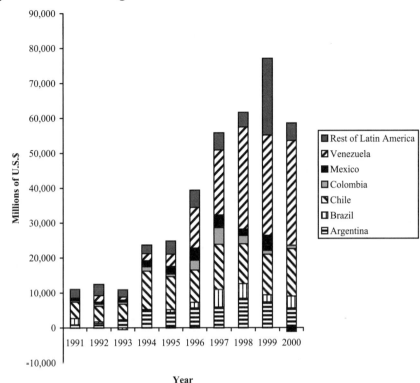

Source: ECLAC, *Preliminary Overview of the Economies of Latin America and the Caribbean, 2000,* table A-13.

and the Caribbean fell from U.S.$105 billion in 1999 to U.S.$80 billion in 2001. The two-year decline may be exacerbated by the region's increasing instability, as exemplified by recent events in Argentina and Venezuela. Nonetheless, net inflows for this type of investment still remain above average for the past five-year period. Mexico was a big winner in 2001 with a 10 percent increase in FDI. And, as a region, the 10-percent decline during 2001 compares favorably to a 50 percent reduction in global flows.[21] Latin America's share of global FDI at 11 percent has remained surprisingly stable in the face of the worldwide slowdown.[22]

Although the importance of single firms such as Chiquita Brands or General Motors in the economies of the subregion is not inconsequential, foreign direct investment is not the solution for all countries that want to spur development. That is, multinationals do not necessarily want to produce where conditions are unstable or the infrastructure is incomplete. They are also attracted to large markets such as Brazil or Mexico to sell the cars or machines produced there and avoid transport costs. Foreign direct investment can be seen as preferable to short-term capital flows in that it reflects a long-term commitment to the nation. It should in fact translate into an increase in a country's productive potential—but it may work best

Table 7.2. Top Multinationals in Latin America

Corporation	Country	Sectors	1999 Sales (millions of U.S.$)	Operations in
Telefónica de España	Spain	Telecommunications	12,439	Argentina, Brazil, and Chile
General Motors	USA	Automotive	12,425	Argentina, Brazil, Chile, Colombia, and Mexico
Volkswagen	Germany	Automotive	11,902	Argentina, Brazil, and Mexico
DaimlerChrysler	Germany	Automotive	9,746	Argentina, Brazil, and Mexico
Carrefour Group	France	Commerce	9,561	Argentina and Brazil
Ford Motor Company	USA	Automotive	8,252	Argentina, Brazil, Colombia, and Mexico
Repsol-YPF	Spain	Petroleum	8,109	Argentina, Brazil, Chile, and Colombia
Fiat Spa	Italy	Automotive	7,659	Argentina and Brazil
Royal Dutch Shell	UK/Netherlands	Petroleum	6,449	Argentina, Brazil, and Chile
Exxon	USA	Petroleum	6,403	Argentina, Brazil, Chile, and Colombia
IBM	USA	Electronics	5,479	Argentina, Brazil, and Mexico
Endesa Espana	Spain	Electricity	5,475	Argentina, Brazil, Chile, and Colombia
The AES Corp.	USA	Electricity	5,182	Argentina, Brazil, and Chile
Wal-Mart	USA	Commerce	4,816	Argentina, Brazil, and Mexico
Nestle	Switzerland	Food	4,766	Argentina, Brazil, Chile, Colombia, and Mexico
Renault/Nissan Motor	France	Automotive	4,179	Argentina, Brazil, Chile, Colombia, and Mexico
Unilever	UK/Netherlands	Food	4,126	Argentina, Brazil, Chile, Colombia, and Mexico
Motorola	USA	Electronics	3,817	Argentina, Brazil, Colombia, and Mexico
Cargill	USA	Food	3,541	Argentina and Brazil
Intel	USA	Electronics	3,540	Brazil

Source: Unit of Investment and Corporate Strategies, ECLAC, 2000.

where the country's industrial base is already relatively developed. On, the negative side, however, multinational investment raises other questions with respect to balanced development, dependency, and domestic entrepreneurship.

Multinational corporations (MNCs) are extraordinarily powerful, accounting for one-third of world production, with total sales exceeding the value of world trade. Table 7.2 shows the activity of the top twenty MNCs in the region. Worldwide, ranked by output, fifty-one of the top "countries" are multinational corporations. In addition, more than half of world trade consists of transnational firm trading activity, largely of an intrafirm nature.[23] That is, half of world trade is associated with firms like Coca-Cola or Nike sending subassembly materials and final products among their own subsidiaries.

Box 7.2 summarizes the debate on the pros and cons of multinational production. Multinationals may provide technology, improve efficiency, and create jobs. They encourage the adoption of best production practices across borders. Some

---

BOX 7.2. IS MULTINATIONAL PRODUCTION GOOD FOR DEVELOPING COUNTRIES?

Pros	Cons
• With a technology gap, the farther behind you are, the faster you can pick up the leader's innovations to catch up. Multinational corporations (MNCs) provide a positive contagion effect[24]	• Traditional dependency arguments—powerful international capital exploits workers, maintains control of technology, and preempts local development of production
• Spillover efficiency even if the MNC does not directly share technology with local firms, it may have positive productivity effects through competition, as domestic firms are given an incentive to catch up; through training of labor and management; and through effects on local suppliers including higher standards of quality and delivery[25]	• MNC production is culturally inappropriate, introducing products unsuited for local conditions
• Source of capital for investment (if not squeezing local capital out of domestic markets)	• MNCs engage in human rights abuse, unfairly taking advantage of female and child labor
• Employment source of jobs that generally pay higher wages than local firms[26]	• MNCs circumvent international law in the environmental arena
• Provides needed management skills to the economy	• Global production causes job loss in home economy—although one study shows that U.S. multinationals compete only at margins with affiliates[27]
	• MNCs are production enclaves—there is a low level of linkages with local suppliers; evidence on this is mixed, depending on the type of MNC[28]
	• Net capital outflow—after initial injection of capital, MNC may remit more in profits than it put in
	• Use of technology inappropriate for local conditions—more capital intensive than appropriate. Big gap between local and MNC forestalls spillovers
	• Reliance on foreign technology retards local development, causing negative effects on productivity[29]

multinationals invest abroad to take advantage of cheaper labor or less stringent environmental standards. Producers of textiles, for example, have long moved to where unskilled workers, often women, can be paid a tenth of the going wage in the United States. Profits—made in part through the exploitation of cheap labor—are remitted to the home country rather than supporting growth in the local economy. Environmentalists worry that companies set up shop in countries with lax pollution laws, a phenomenon called environmental dumping. Governments, afraid of losing jobs and investment, may retreat from stricter environmental codes, promoting a race to the bottom of the environmental ladder. Evidence on this theory is incomplete; there is some suggestion that pollution costs are not a critical factor in location decisions and that at the national level governments tighten regulations as income rises.[30] We will return to the social impacts of multinationals in our discussion of labor in chapter 9.

The good news is that globalization of information systems has decreased the ability of multinationals to get away with social and environmental abuse. As the Internet and CNN bring corporate activities into stockholders' living rooms, firms have been forced to comply with new standards. For example, after celebrity Kathie Lee Gifford was charged with exploitation of female workers in Central America in the production of her clothing line for Kmart, the negative publicity generated a fall in the stock price. The firm was forced to adopt codes of corporate conduct that improve the lives of workers. As dismal conditions and low wages have become well documented, college students across America have pressured for changes in sweatshop practices and adoption of a fair labor code by boycotting bookstore apparel.[31] Globalization of production has increased the multinational's reach but has made its activities more transparent.

Does the surge in multinational investment improve the productive capabilities of Latin American economies? As Latin America has moved away from protected state-run industries to allow greater multinational participation, how has productivity changed? One study of foreign production in Mexico shows that a high multinational presence is correlated with an increase in productivity in locally owned firms and that the rate of catch-up with international productivity standards is positively associated with the degree of foreign concentration in the industry. This suggests spillovers from multinational production to less-efficient local firms. Multinational firms may act as a catalyst to productivity growth, speeding up the convergence in productivity levels between developing and industrialized countries.[32] The authors warn, nonetheless, of extrapolating too much from the Mexican case because there is extensive movement of labor and capital between Mexico and the United States, especially in border production. Other studies of the Mexican case point out that the technology transferred may be too capital intensive and that subsidies provided by the Mexican government to attract firms may divert scarce resources from social investments.[33] Box 7.3 summarizes Mexico's long love–hate affair with foreign capital, and box 7.4 gives an example of multinational activity that has minimized the costs and maximized the benefits of foreign direct investment in Peru.

The gains and the costs of multinational production should be evaluated on a case by case basis. The effects of multinational production vary with the purpose of

Box 7.3. Mexico's Long Love–Hate Affair with Foreign Direct Investment

Mexico has progressed through a variety of positions in terms of the role of foreign direct investment in its economy, reflecting different views—sometimes simultaneously—of foreign investment in Mexico. Opposition to foreign intervention was a hallmark of early Mexican history since the days of the Spanish conquest. Nonetheless Porfirio Díaz and his científico advisers espoused liberalization policies and encouraged foreign investment during the Porfiriato, 1876–1911.

The Revolution to 1944 was marked by the establishment of state ownership, particularly in the mining sector and the 1938 nationalization of petroleum companies. The formation of the Banco de Mexico took the role of financing from foreign commercial banks. Ownership rules were defined by sector in the 1930s: strategic industries, including primary product exports and utilities, were dominated by state ownership. Manufacturing, under import substitution industrialization, drew on FDI, and the early *maquilas* used cheap labor to re-export goods to international markets.

Fears of foreign takeover of the Mexican economy led to the 1944 law requiring majority Mexican ownership except with permission of the Secretariat of Foreign Relations. "Mexicanization" extended to radio, cinema, domestic airlines, buses, soft drink bottlers, publishing, and tires. Paradoxically, at the same time efforts were made to recruit foreign investment to fill the capital needs of industrialization. National ownership in banking, finance, and extractive industries was secured while foreign investment boomed in areas of manufacturing.

The *Maquila* program was introduced in 1965, allowing firms to import inputs tax free if they were to be transformed into exports. Mexico benefited through employment and foreign exchange, while the transnationals found high profit margins with cheap labor. In contrast, the 1973 Law to Promote Mexican Investment and Regulate Foreign Investment diverted policy inward, regulating foreign entry and enforcing Mexicanization and local majority ownership.

Capital constraints with the debt crisis again prompted a change of policy, including a 1989 liberalization law to encourage investment. Mexico acceded to the General Agreement on Tariffs and Trade (GATT) in 1985, lowering tariffs and reducing import controls. Signature of the North American Free Trade Agreement (NAFTA) formalizes this open investment regime and symbolizes Mexico's firm commitment through an international treaty to encourage international investment.

Source: Michael J. Twomey, *Multinational Corporations and the North American Free Trade Agreement* (Westport, Conn.: Praeger, 1993), 27–34.

the investment. As shown in table 7.3 and discussed earlier in this chapter, multinationals may be attracted by efficiency gains (through a cheaper labor platform, access to raw materials, or access to a market). One study showed that the positive effects of multinational transfer of technology were strong only when there was already a well-developed human capital base.[34] Some of the issues we consider in later chapters on social development and education may therefore play a key role in shaping costs and benefits. Government policy in establishing the rules of the game for multinationals is important in evaluating outcomes. The size and number of other firms in a market also condition multinational behavior. If a multinational company is the only employer in a small town, it is less likely to treat workers well.

BOX 7.4.   BEST PRACTICES: A POSITIVE CASE OF MULTINATIONAL INVOLVEMENT

AGAINST THE ODDS: HOW A SEEMINGLY HOPELESS ENERGY PROJECT BECAME A MODEL FOR INVESTORS

BY DAVID MANGURIAN

The plan that Maple Gas Corp. of Dallas, Texas, took to prospective investors seemed a long shot at best.

It was 1993, and the company was proposing to drill gas wells in a remote section of the Peruvian jungle that was controlled by antigovernment subversives. The gas would fuel an electric power plant to be built next to a town controlled by cocaine drug traffickers. And all of this would happen in a country that was just getting its yearly inflation rate below three digits and was still an outcast to the world's financial community.

Furthermore, the proposed facilities would be built east of the Andes mountains, meaning that thousands of tons of equipment and material would have to be shipped 3,200 km up the Amazon River by freighter, then off-loaded onto barges and hauled another 800 km up the smaller Ucayali River during the four-month rainy season when the river was deep enough for barges to reach their destination. Then the equipment would be trucked to the project sites on washboard-surfaced, potholed dirt roads that turned to mud when it rained.

The price tag? A quarter of a billion dollars. Not an easy sell. The idea might have seemed far-fetched, except that the economic case for the project was overwhelmingly strong. Peru's electricity demands were growing 9 percent a year. The country desperately needed more low-cost power, and the gas was just 2,500 meters under the jungle floor. The project's payback period was calculated at less than eight years and the profit potential was excellent.

It looked like a perfect opportunity for Maple Gas. The company had just sold off most of its assets in the United States to concentrate on developing a more lucrative foreign venture. At the same time, Peru had started privatizing its energy sector and was preparing to award concessions to commercialize existing hydrocarbon reserves. Among the properties the government was putting up for bid was the Aguaytía gas field, which had been discovered by Mobil Oil in 1961 in the jungle west of Pucallpa. The field had never been developed because of the high cost of building a pipeline to transport the gas over the Andes to Peru's coastal cities.

Maple executives saw a different way to tackle the problem of getting the energy from the wellhead to the consumer. They proposed building a gas-powered electricity generating plant at Aguaytía and running transmission lines across the Andes, figuring that this alternative would cost much less than a pipeline.

In 1993, Maple outbid other companies in a public auction to win a 30-year concession to develop and commercialize the Aguaytía gas field. As soon as the concession papers were signed in early 1994, and long before Maple had any guarantee of financing, the company began planning for construction. In fact, Maple became so confident of success that it began putting most of its money into the Aguaytía project.

The first thing Maple did after it won the concession was to run tests on the wells drilled in the Aguaytía field 33 years earlier to confirm the results. Maple hired a burly, retired Peruvian special forces commander, Jorge Meza, to assemble a security team to protect people working in the project area. Although the Peruvian government had by then made substantial progress in controlling guerrillas and drug trafficking, security was still a very real problem.

"It was still an area of high risk from subversives," recalls César Valderrama, area operations manager for Maple Gas. "We practically had a regiment of marines at the well site. It looked like a battlefield. We were surrounded by soldiers."

Meza and others also recommended a community action program to develop long-term relationships with residents near the project's multiple sites, and thereby help avoid local opposition that might delay construction. Maple sent medical teams into villages to immunize children and teach basic hygiene, and the company sponsored programs with local schools.

SEARCH FOR INVESTORS

The well tests proved positive: there was enough gas to fuel a new 155,000 kW power plant as well as Pucallpa's existing 20,000 kW power plant for at least 28 years. In addition, gas liquids could be processed into bottled gas for cooking and gasoline to generate further income. Maple now had a viable "integrated" gas and electricity project to sell potential investors.

But investors were skeptical, particularly when they saw the local conditions. Meza recalls one instance: "I drove a group of Americans across the route of the [planned] transmission lines. No car had been there for 30 years. We had to spend the night in a very poor hotel high in the Andes. These were investors used to five star hotels. So I told them: 'Tonight you'll be staying at a hotel with more than five stars. You'll be at a hotel with all the stars of the heavens.'"

But as the months passed, the strengths of Maple's proposal became increasingly apparent. By 1996 the company had put together a group of equity investors and banks willing to commit a total of $254 million to the project, including a $60 million loan from the IDB. The financing arrangement broke new ground and drew accolades from international project finance experts.

In Peru, the project was seen as a resounding vindication of the government's privatization program. "Aguaytía is the first private sector 'Test' of Peru's economic reforms," stated the IDB loan document.

Construction began in August 1996, and was to be completed in just 18 months. Contractors would be charged substantial penalties for each day of delay. The company hired some 2,200 construction workers. Conditions in the jungle were tough: high humidity, temperatures up to 45 degrees (C), tarantulas and poisonous snakes, and frequent, thundering downpours that mired trucks and equipment in mud.

Planning had to be meticulous because of the extremely complicated logistics. If the giant generators, transformers and other pieces of heavy equipment and machinery were not built and shipped on time, they would not make it the 4,000 km up the Amazon and Ucayali rivers to Pucallpa before the river level dropped to unnavigable levels.

The equipment started arriving in January 1997. "We unloaded the last shipment on the last day Pucallpa's port was open," recalls Valderrama. Now the 122-ton generators, 86-ton transformers and other equipment had to be hoisted off the barges and onto the trucks for their arduous trip overland to Aguaytía. This would be the job of a 140-ton crane, which was trucked in from Lima in six pieces, a 785-km trip that took four days.

"If you had a heavy load on a truck and it rained, you had to wait for hours after the rain stopped for the road to dry before you could move on," says Naef. The 300 km of pipelines for natural gas and natural gas liquids, and 400 km of electricity transmission lines were routed alongside existing roads in order to minimize the impact on the environment. Maple employed a team of archeologists to ensure that important sites were not

(continued)

(continued)

disturbed by construction of the transmission lines across the Andes. These and other environmental measures added $10 million to the project's cost.

This March, gas operations are to begin and one of the two gas turbines at the Aguaytía electric power plant is to begin operations. Full commercial operations are expected by April 1.

"The officers of Maple Gas had to have a lot of tenacity to sell this project to investors," says Valderrama. "Most were afraid. Aguaytía was one of the first large private investments in Peru."

Much has changed in Peru since Maple Gas arrived on the scene. The country has consolidated sweeping economic reforms and is becoming a magnet for investors. In 1997 the inflation rate dropped to 7 percent and private foreign direct investment hit $7 billion, four times the 1993 level.

The Aguaytía project now looks like a superb investment, not the risky venture of five years ago. "It has become an example for other companies to follow," said Valderrama.

Source: IDB América, March 1998; available online at www.iadb.org.

If, however, it is in competition with a large number of firms, it is more likely to provide good working conditions. An ethical dilemma arises in considering labor standards for multinational production. Should home country or host country labor codes be employed? Labor standards in poor countries may approximate conditions in industrial countries fifty years ago. Should U.S. multinationals meet U.S. safety and health standards in a Guatemalan plant? Some contend that best practices should apply worldwide; others suggest local standards as a baseline while developing countries catch up. Proponents of foreign direct investment contend that although standards and wages may not match industrial country standards, they most often exceed the conditions and the pay in local factories. Sorting out the effects of multinational production poses tough ethical and policy dilemmas. Are workers worse off than they were without the new paychecks? How far can governments go in insisting on higher standards without driving investment and jobs away?

Foreign direct investment, particularly in services, has been an important part of the privatization boom that we studied in chapter 6. Liberalization of global trade rules under the General Agreement on Trade in Services also encouraged foreign direct investment in telecommunications and financial services. We noted that the gains from the privatization of state monopolies were greatest when competition could be introduced or an effective regulatory structure implemented to limit private monopoly pricing. Yet the challenges for effective regulation and competition policy in markets dominated by large transnationals are especially difficult for developing-country officials.

QUESTION FOR THOUGHT

Can you think of ways to minimize the costs and maximize the benefits of multinational production in developing countries?

Regulators in developing countries must deal with multiple social objectives. They are still struggling with issues such as improving access to phones in rural and poor areas and guaranteeing basic levels of quality. The international dynamism in mobile

Table 7.3. Latin America and the Caribbean: Strategies of Transnational Corporations in the 1990s

| Sector | Corporate Strategy | | |
	Efficiency Gains (labor costs)	*Raw Materials Access*	*National or Regional Market Access*
Primary Products		**Oil/gas:** Argentina, Bolivia, Brazil, Colombia, Venezuela **Minerals:** Argentina, Chile, Peru	
Manufacturing	**Automotive:** Mexico **Electronics:** Caribbean Basin, Mexico **Clothing:** Caribbean Basin, Mexico		**Automotive:** Mercosur **Agribusiness:** Argentina, Brazil, and Mexico **Chemicals:** Brazil **Cement:** Colombia, Dominican Republic, Venezuela
Services			**Finance:** Argentina, Brazil, Chile, Colombia, Mexico, Peru, Venezuela **Telecommunications:** Argentina, Brazil, Chile, Peru **Electric power:** Argentina, Brazil, Central America, Chile, Colombia **Natural gas distribution:** Argentina, Brazil, Chile, Colombia, Mexico

Source: ECLAC, *Globalization & Development* (Santiago, Chile: ECLAC, 2002), table 6.6.

cellular communications and Internet services introduces a whole set of complicated regulations. With generally weaker institutions, less experience, and fewer resources, regulatory agencies in developing markets must carry out traditional and new tasks. In doing so regulators come up against some of the titans of the global marketplace—large and powerful megacorporations. In many cases—particularly those of the early privatizers—the rush to privatization granted long periods of exclusive operation to foreign investors in exchange for commitments to expand basic services. As these frameworks expire, the regulatory challenge will be to develop coherent sectoral strategies to achieve national policy goals as well as corporate objectives through an upgrading of the regulatory institutions themselves.[35]

REWARDS AND RISKS OF NEW CAPITAL FLOWS TO LATIN AMERICA

Despite the complexity of multinational production, its commitment to production is generally of a long-term nature, especially where the firm located for better access to the local market or to provide infrastructure services. This stands in contrast to hot money flows, or short-term capital investments, which, while used to finance investments and spur growth, introduce questions of volatility. What are the implications of short-term capital flows to Latin America? New capital flows to the region are the financial rewards for the painful process of structural adjustment. Greater global integration can be seen as a movement toward the more efficient worldwide utilization of capital. For advocates of new capital flows, maintaining access to international financial markets is simply the result of sound domestic economic management. They see international inflows as complementary to national capital. The infusion of funds will spur growth, which will then encourage savings.

Is money moving to the region because it is most efficiently employed in Latin America as compared to other investment alternatives? To evaluate the arguments of proponents of capital inflows, it is important to situate the theoretical argument in the context of the reality of Latin American markets. Latin American markets are not exactly like the Wall Street variety. If markets are relatively thin and uncompetitive, efficiency gains will be limited. Furthermore, the price signals driving capital to certain markets may be flawed. Informational bottlenecks and the institutional peculiarities of investors may interfere with market efficiency. Many new investment instruments are complex and not completely understood by participants, increasing the underlying risk. Transactions in many markets are unregulated, accounting standards are lax, balance sheets are inscrutable, and financial disclosure is not as strictly enforced as in the United States. With incomplete information, the globalization of capital may not generate as much efficiency as claimed.[36] Capital may be more fickle and less efficient than is sometimes assumed. Some policymakers in Latin America are wary of long-run dependency on the new capital flows, particularly **short-term money,** because of its volatility and how it affects other variables. Because the decision to invest is made on relative rates of return, a country continuing to pursue a sound policy course might find itself out of favor in the international market as another nation or region becomes the Wall Street flavor of the month. A long history of negative effects of external price changes—such as the oil price and interest rate shocks precipitating the debt crisis of the 1980s— make policymakers nervous concerning external vulnerability. Uncertainty is built into the structure of current financing. For example, bonds with an average maturity of four years are a major source of capital supporting infrastructure expansion. What if they are not renewed at expiration?[37] Can development planning be creatively financed with short-term inflows?

In addition to volatility, capital inflows may adversely affect other economic variables. In particular, some economists are concerned about the degree to which capital inflows are consistent with sustainable levels of the exchange rate and the interest rate. Because capital inflows change the supply of money available for investment, they also change the price of money—both nationally, as measured by the domestic interest rate, and relatively, as measured by the exchange rate. If inflows are strong, finance becomes cheaper, and the interest rate falls. International money is more abundant, and therefore the local currency, relatively scarcer than it was before, appreciates. Low interest rates could have a negative effect on national savings rates, discouraging local sources of financing. An appreciated exchange rate may stand in the way of pursuing an export orientation. In particular, if financial markets are shallow and uncompetitive, they may not be able to intermediate the capital surges, effectively exacerbating instability. If capital surges accelerate demand beyond the capacity of the economy, they may also create inflationary pressures. For some countries, the boom in capital flows is a high-risk venture that threatens national control over key monetary variables.

Financial innovation and international capital flows have decreased the degrees of freedom available to Latin American policymakers.[38] The speed of international capital markets requires greater flexibility in economic instruments; paradoxically, it also demands stability. Instantaneous movement of capital implies that markets are overly responsive to small policy mistakes, increasing the tendency toward instability.[39] The policymakers' tightrope is more threatening in international markets. Capital inflows, while acting as a spur to development, can also have a high cost.

INTERNATIONAL CAPITAL FLOWS AND DOMESTIC BANKING

A strong banking system can serve to dampen domestic macroeconomic instability. Under a sound banking system, if domestic investors decide to sell long-term financial assets, they can move into domestic bank deposits. That is, if in the United States you are uncertain about the performance of the stock market or long-term mutual funds, you might opt for the safety of a certificate of deposit or CD. As people move into CDs, the greater availability of funds makes it easier to lend to companies, and expansion is encouraged, counteracting the downward trend in the market. However, if there is a lack of confidence in the banking sector, the substitute is international instruments or **capital flight**.[40] When banks fail to provide domestic intermediation, the effects of crises are magnified. Furthermore, as has been demonstrated in the Asian financial crisis of 1997–1998, if domestic loans to large conglomerates—or, in the Latin case, *grupos*—sidestepped sound accounting procedures, a downturn may result in a resounding crash. The Chilean crisis in 1982–1993 and the Mexican crisis were exacerbated by loans made to huge conglomerates riding high on overinflated asset prices without corresponding real collateral to secure the megaloans. When the crisis hit in each country—and later in Asia—the high percentage of nonperforming loans magnified the contractionary effects on the economic system. Weak banks exacerbated rather than minimized the crisis.

The banking sector in Latin America was relatively fragile in the beginning of the 1990s. Years of high inflation and fiscal mismanagement had weakened the sector. **Capital controls** during the 1980s restricted competition, technological advances lagged, and most banking relationships were driven by personal or political ties.[41] The 1990s heralded a new era of openness, but institutional development is often slow. Privatization in Mexico, for example, led to a high degree of concentration, with fifty-eight institutions consolidated into eighteen commercial banks, of which six were considered national, with the balance regional. The presence of foreign banks is also increasing. Spain's BSCH, Banco Santander Central Hispano, is the dominant transnational bank in the region, followed by Citibank (United States), Banco Bilbao (Spain) and BankBoston (United States).[42] As noted in chapter 6, the speed of privatization—a bank was sold every three weeks—led to improper asset valuation, sloppy accounting, and a tendency toward political expediency in sales.[43]

Few developing countries can muster the institutional resources necessary for a strong, functioning, independent regulatory authority.[44] Paradoxically, liberalization of capital markets decreases the ability and increases the need for sound government oversight at the national and international levels of lending practices of banks.[45] Opening up too fast may overwhelm institutional capacities to behave as financial watchdogs.

To deepen capital markets, necessary ingredients include macroeconomic stability, a sound legal framework, an efficient and reliable clearing and settlement system, an adequate accounting system, an efficient microstructure for trading securities, and a proper regulatory and supervisory framework.[46] However, this kind of institution building may take time. Some have suggested that financial liberalization may have taken place too quickly, not giving markets enough time to develop appropriate institutions.[47] In the Mexican case, for example, reprivatization of banks was simultaneously accompanied by lifting constraints on credit expansion. Overzealous lending without adequate supervision may have contributed to the depth of the ensuing financial crisis. Time and timing of changes matter. In the interim, the policy question becomes how to decrease the vulnerability of domestic financial systems to crisis and instability while strengthening financial institutions.

THE MEXICAN *PESO* CRISIS

The Mexican *peso* crisis of 1994–1995 highlights the problematic effects of international capital flows for internal macroeconomic stability. It underscores the conflict between domestic stabilization and the concerns of international capital in policy making. How should authorities balance national domestic concerns such as inflation and unemployment against external constraints of exchange rate stability and current accounts when there are two different judges of success: voters and international capital?

Mexico had become a darling of the international community. A poster child for liberalization, the country had, since the 1982 debt crisis, undertaken tough reform measures including fiscal stabilization, privatization, and the opening of internal markets to international trade. Markets were eager to lend to this nation that had battled budget deficits and revamped the rules of doing business. Unlike conditions during the debt crisis of the 1980s, much of the lending was in the private sector. Between 1987 and 1994 commercial credit expanded by more than 100 percent, with credits for housing ballooning 100 percent and consumption credit growing by 450 percent. GDP growth was strong, and prices were steady. Two-thirds of the $91 billion inflows were portfolio investments, quickly attracted to high returns in the new Mexico. Implementation of the North American Free Trade Agreement (NAFTA) promised new gains in markets and productivity. Relatively low interest rates in the United States made the returns in Mexico particularly lucrative. Mexican markets were hot.

This optimism created an asset price boom in Mexico, as investors were attracted to high returns; others, afraid to miss out on the rising market, jumped on the bandwagon. Incentives in the investment industry tend to draw clients in on an upward trend. Brokers are more frequently fired for missing a great opportunity than for crashing when everyone else around them is also falling.[48] Upward trends tend to reinforce themselves, overshooting real values, creating a divergence between the true investment potential and the asset bubble. Of course, the further the investment gets from its fundamental value, the harder is the landing when the market corrects itself. Small events can lead to major speculative attacks as investors who jumped on the bandwagon knowing little about the investment overreact without taking the time to get better information. Unfortunately, those who pay the highest price for the crash—like the poor Mexicans who must bear the brunt of adjustment—are not necessarily those involved in creating the speculative bubble.

Oddly, in the midst of Mexico market euphoria, the true performance of the Mexican economy was below the glowing predictions. Although both multilateral agencies such as the IMF and private-sector firms such as Bear Sterns painted a rosy picture, actual performance fell short of potential. While Mexico was being certified as low risk, investment-grade potential by J. P. Morgan and being heralded as a success story by the World Bank, real exchange rate appreciation caused by capital inflows was sending the wrong signal to the productive sector, eroding competitiveness.[49] The same price for the exchange rate was not clearing both financial and tradable goods markets.

Warning signs of unsustainability of the Mexican situation and an impending crisis appeared on the horizon. The Mexican *peso* began to appreciate substantially as a result of capital inflow. Adjusted for inflation differences with the United States, some estimated it was overvalued by 30 percent. Others, including those within the Mexican government, contended that the appreciation was warranted by the improved productive potential of the Mexican economy. They argued that the currency was not overvalued but reflected stronger GDP growth. Why, they reasoned, would private capital continue to flow in if the underlying fundamentals weren't sound?

Nonetheless, there was a clear cost to the external account imbalance. Figure 7.4 shows that by 1994 Mexico's ballooning current account deficit had nearly reached 8

Figure 7.4. Mexico's Current Account Deficit, 1985–1994

Source: Stephany Griffith-Jones, "The Mexican Peso Crisis," *CEPAL Review* 60 (December 1996): 155–75.

percent of GDP. Was this sustainable? We remember that deficits on the current account, composed primarily of an excess of imports over exports, must be financed by surpluses on the capital account. Indeed, if imports are used to enhance productive potential (as opposed to luxury consumption), and if international capital is willing to finance these investments, trade deficits are not necessarily a bad thing. The question of sustainability revolves around the willingness of international markets to continue to supply funds to cover the deficits. If investors continued to believe that Mexico's future performance outpaced other alternatives, deficits could be sustained. Because inflows were largely private—albeit short-term—capital, Mexican authorities contended that they were a simple market reflection of Mexico's new growth potential.

Whether or not this argument was accurate, it was certainly politically expedient. The ruling party of Mexico, the PRI, was facing its first real electoral challenge from both the Right and the Left since the Mexican Revolution. Selling economic stability and the success of the Mexican liberalization plan were central to reelection efforts.

In hindsight we can see the folly of this argument. We can analyze current account sustainability through a simple formula:

$$C/y = gk*$$

C, or the current account, as a percentage of y, gross domestic product, should be equal to the real growth rate of the economy, called g, times k*, or international investors' willingness to expose themselves to that nation's financial instruments, also as a percentage of GDP. The logic of this formula comes from the balance of payments rule that to be sustainable, a current account deficit must be financed by capital inflows. The allowable size of the deficit will vary with the growth rate of the country and foreigners' interest in holding that nation's liabilities. This willingness, as expressed here by k*, is largely determined by investors' assessment of the risk involved in holding the securities as well as the difference in expected returns between investments at home and abroad. A Mexican treasury bond is seen to be riskier than one issued by Uncle Sam; therefore, the Mexican government will have to offer higher interest rates to compensate investors for risk.

If we assume that initially a country is in a steady state, and we observe in this case that foreigners are interested in holding liabilities equal to 50 percent of GDP, and if the growth rate of GDP is 4 percent, a current account deficit of 2 percent of GDP is sustainable. (Fifty percent or one-half of 4 percent is 2 percent.) If, however, investors believe that risk has decreased or that expected returns have risen, say to 75 percent, the same rate of growth will sustain a 3-percent deficit. (Three-quarters or 75 percent of 4 percent is 3 percent.) Indeed, at their peak, foreign holdings of Mexican securities were in the 50 percent range, and growth was under 4 percent. By this formula, Mexico should have had a current account deficit of between 2 and 3 percent, not the nearly $50 billion, or 8 percent, shown in figure 7.5. Moreover, not only were deficits too high, but exchange rates overvalued by capital inflows indicated that they would continue to rise. Again in figure 7.5, we see a fall in the real exchange rate, indicating an overvaluation on the order of 30 percent.

Authorities ignored these signs and struggled to maintain market confidence, continually pointing to the soundness of the Mexican economy. Because disequilib-

Figure 7.5.   Current Account Deficit (CAD) and the Real Exchange Rate (RER)

Year

Source: Ricardo Ffrench-Davis, "Policy Implication of the Tequila Effect," *Challenge* (March–April 1998): 36.

rium in accounts was lodged in the private sector, they contended that private-market price signals should eventually correct this distortion. We don't know whether this self-correction would have taken place in the long run. In the interim, political crises spooked markets. In January 1994, an armed uprising in the poor southern region of Chiapas by insurgent rebels panicked investors. Presidential candidate Luis Donaldo Colosio was then assassinated in the March before the August elections. The selection of lesser-known Ernesto Zedillo Ponce de Leon as candidate did little to quell suspicions of Mexico's instability. Pressing social and political problems threatened economic gains. Investors began to wonder if Mexico was a political backwater or a strong emerging nation.

International capital began to vote with its feet. Because capital moves faster than trade patterns can adjust, Mexico's balance of payments deficits were being financed by dwindling international reserves. As importers went to the central bank to get dollars to pay suppliers, fewer dollars were available. To maintain the exchange rate, the central bank was forced to supply dollars from reserves. Mexico reportedly spent U.S.$10 billion from March through May attempting to defend the *peso* in the wake of the Colosio assassination, although lags in the release of data decreased the transparency of events to the international community. The exchange rate, set using a crawling band, was under severe pressure, yet the government did not want to fuel inflationary expectations with a devaluation.

Nonetheless, knowing that the Bank of Mexico did not have the capacity to stem the outflow, both domestic and international investors came to expect a large devaluation to correct the trade imbalance. At the same time, the government didn't want to raise interest rates to keep capital at home, because this would have a recessionary effect on the domestic economy. Because the risk premium for holding foreign securities includes foreign exchange rate risk, investors needed to be compensated for the fact that if the devaluation took place, their assets would be worth less. If you are holding a financial instrument denominated in *pesos* and the *peso* is worth less, your asset value falls by the same proportion. To entice capital to stay, the government began to offer dollar-denominated treasury bonds, called ***tesobonos,*** to replace the *peso*-denominated *cetes*. In creating this option, the Mexican government essentially internalized the currency devaluation risk, simultaneously trying to send a signal that it perceived that the crisis was caused by short-term political factors. These would soon blow over, it argued, rendering a mega-devaluation unnecessary.

Ruling-party PRI candidate Zedillo was elected president in August, and to the surprise of many in the international financial community, the government did not alter the exchange rate or the monetary or fiscal stance. With the support of business and labor under Mexico's El Pacto, President Salinas and President-Elect Zedillo forged ahead. The hope was that business as usual would reassure markets that the turbulence was temporary and Mexico was ready to resume course. Mexican officials declared that a devaluation was out of the question.

But markets were unconvinced. By the end of November, reserves of $12.5 billion were insufficient to cover even half of the $27 billion short-term public debt, 70 percent of it in dollar-denominated *tesobonos*. When reserves reached critically low levels of around $6 billion in December, the government had little choice but to devalue. It adjusted the band on the *peso* by 15 percent. However, this attempt to release a little steam exploded. Investors felt they had been deceived by Mexican authorities. Although instruments were dollar denominated, there was a lack of confidence that the government would be able to honor its obligations. The devaluation was not accompanied by any policy changes to assure markets that the disequilibrium would be addressed, and capital took a fast flight out of Mexico. After the Mexican government lost $4 billion in one day trying to defend the *peso,* it had no choice but to let it float—or, more appropriately, let it sink like lead—in international markets.

Emergency measures were taken to rescue the Mexican economy. An agreement with U.S., Canadian, and European banks allowed for $7 billion of financial guarantees to back the maturing short-term *tesobonos* coming due. Belated measures were taken to restructure the economy. The pace of privatization was quickened in railroads, satellites, and ports. The banking system was opened to foreign investment, labor unions agreed to hold down wages, and the government cut spending. Interest rates rose to 55 percent to hold investors at home, but this created a recessionary drag on the economy. Investor confidence further deteriorated, and uncertainty was extended to other Latin American economies. This so-called tequila effect created regional pressure, especially for Argentina with its currency board, to readjust internal accounts. Other Latin American countries were guilty by association.

Mexican adjustments were too little, too late. The initial devaluation had been announced in a policy vacuum, creating a panic disproportionate to the underlying fundamentals in the economy. As a result of consulting domestic business and labor prior to the devaluation, capital anticipated the devaluation, further depleting reserves. Timing was bad. The announcement of the devaluation took place on a Tuesday, prior to Christmas. Fridays are better bad news days, giving investors the weekend to calm down before markets reopen for the week. Furthermore, holiday markets were thin, so there were fewer engaged in fishing the bottom for great deals to counter the downward market trend. Finally, the new administration's finance minister had yet to solidify ties with the international financial community.

When panic erupted, there were few calming voices of reason because hardly anyone had the inside scoop as to the government's intentions. Credibility and confidence were shaken.

After conditions deteriorated further, the United States proposed a rescue package in January to assist its southern neighbor. Isolationist forces in the U.S. Congress resisted, and President Clinton, not willing to see the positive gains Mexico had achieved through liberalization evaporate, used his own emergency authorities to provide loan relief. The IMF and the Bank for International Settlements (BIS, the banker's bank) came up with $17.8 billion and $10 billion in loans, respectively, all of which was collateralized by Mexico's oil reserves. With a concerted international rescue, markets settled, and Mexico began another long and painful climb to economic recovery.

Several lessons emerged from the crisis. First is the importance of maintaining sustainable current account performance. Given confidence and economic growth, a sustainable deficit should not exceed 3 percent of GDP.[50] The composition of capital inflows to sustain the deficit is critical. Short-term capital inflows are extremely sensitive to political events. Changes to rely less on short-term international capital and more on internal sources of savings will encourage longer-term stable growth. Finally, the inflexibility of the exchange rate as an inflation anchor can be dangerous as economic fundamentals move out of line. The anchor becomes something of an albatross weighing down the process of flexible adjustment.

THE CHILEAN CASE: REGULATING GLOBAL INFLOWS

The rise and fall of the Mexican economy in the mid-1990s prompted a search for alternatives to the volatility of hot capital flows. Portfolio investments are tied to stock prices, reflecting increases in the real value of firms, and short-term capital flows or hot money respond to interest rate differentials or the expected appreciation of the currency—in Chile's case, the *peso*.[51] Speculative portfolio inflows rose in the early 1990s, concerning policymakers. Much attention was paid to the Chilean case. In Chile, net capital inflows ranged from 11 percent to 18 percent of GDP from 1979 to 1981. Over the period 1990–1993, the low was 1.9 percent and the high was 7.6 percent.[52] The composition of flows changed markedly as well, moving from medium- and long-term loans in the earlier period to foreign direct investment and Chilean investment abroad as well as portfolio investments and hot money in the 1990s. Laws governing foreign direct investment in Chile are highly favorable to foreign capital. The bulk of FDI in Chile has been in the export sectors, with over half in mining alone. Laws governing the outflow of capital were liberalized in 1991, leading to significant investment abroad. In a new twist, Chilean companies poured billions into the rest of Latin America, the bulk of which flowed into just three countries: Argentina, Bolivia, and Peru. In Argentina, Chileans command a large share of the privatized electricity business as well as owning assets in ceramics, disposable diapers, bottled gas, welded products, caddies, cables, and industrial oils. They operate the railways in Bolivia. In Peru,

Chileans direct the fast-expanding pension fund industry and make everything from copper wire to spaghetti.[53]

Although new capital flows may appear to be beneficial, the effects on the exchange rate are the dark side of the inflow of speculative money. The Chilean development model is driven by the export sector. Throughout Latin America, structural adjustment was led by the export sector, yet paradoxically, good performance was rewarded by capital inflows that appreciated the currency and retarded export performance. Accounting for more than one-third of GDP, the diversified export sector has been a source of dynamism in Chilean growth. To the degree that capital inflows appreciate the *peso,* these financial flows undermine efforts in the real economy.[54] Ironically, countries can be hurt by their own successful adjustment. As the international market sees the assets of a country as a good investment, inflows appreciate the exchange rate, choking off the export drive that made for the success in the first place. The real exchange rate appreciation caused by capital inflows works against international competitiveness.[55]

The policy dilemma becomes balancing external sector growth and internal stability. What should be done to offset these negative effects of financial flows? The Chilean central bank and Ministry of Finance utilized a combination of pragmatic measures designed to reduce short-term inflows. These included regulating short-term movements through reserve requirements, quotas, and fees; foreign exchange market intervention; and sterilizing the monetary effect of foreign exchange.[56] The goal of this policy has been to expand the leeway for domestic monetary policy by increasing domestic savings and decreasing the flow of international hot money.[57] Pragmatic management of the exchange rate has reduced Chile's vulnerability to capital swings, allowing it to pursue a more stable path in a highly liberalized market regime. The Chilean government has employed a crawling band system pegged to three international currencies; the *peso* has performed at the bottom of the band, indicating that appreciation would have been larger without intervention.[58] This is a case of government policy augmenting the stability of markets—and not the kind of zealous free market wizardry often associated with the Chilean model. The Chilean government also promoted foreign direct investment, in both traditional and nontraditional exports. Four out of the five largest fruit companies (which together account for one-half of fruit exports) are transnational corporations. Several new mining projects involve transnational corporations (TNCs). Capital continues to enter Chile, but it is on Chilean terms.

The downside to capital controls includes the fact that they are difficult to enforce, may signal risk and therefore drive up capital prices, and, if effective in the short term, may delay needed economic reforms. Furthermore, few countries have the long track record of adjustment demonstrated by Chile. Whereas the Chilean government has the accumulated credibility to apply brakes without coming to a screeching stop, other economies could be devastated by a chilly signal to international markets. No clear consensus has emerged on the overall effectiveness of capital controls, especially in affecting long run levels of investment.[59]

THE ASIAN ECONOMIC CRISIS AND THE CONTAGION EFFECT IN LATIN AMERICA

The dilemma of how to slow capital inflows may be a moot point in the face of new apprehension about emerging market investments in the wake of the Asian crisis. In the summer of 1997, the currencies of Thailand, Malaysia, and Korea came under attack. The loss of confidence in the once heralded "Asian Tigers" quickly spread not only throughout Southeast Asia but to all emerging economies. Beset by the contagion effect, Latin America was confronted with a crisis not of its own making. Despite nearly two decades of adjustment since the eruption of the debt crisis in 1982, regional economies were challenged by a global loss of investor confidence in developing economies. The nosedive in stock and bond markets throughout the region had little to do with underlying economic fundamentals. Capital frightened of any emerging market risk indiscriminately pulled out of the region, leaving governments to sustain policies structured around open markets and the infusion of capital from abroad. Governments were forced to raise domestic interest rates as a means of bribing capital to stay at home. High domestic interest rates had contractionary effects on growth and increased unemployment. International commodity prices have also fallen as a result of global recessions. Sugar prices fell 21.14 percent, copper was down 22.7 percent, coffee declined 29.35 percent, and oil lost 32.6 percent with weakened Asian markets.[60] For commodity exporters such as Chile, this translated into balance of payments problems on the current account. The 30-percent devaluations of East Asian currencies also made manufactured goods from Korea, Malaysia, Thailand, Indonesia, and the Philippines more competitive in world markets, where they compete against goods from the larger Latin American industrial producers in Brazil and Mexico. Adjusting for the overvaluations throughout Latin America, the real cross-rate devaluations for South Korea, for example, range from 78.8 percent for Venezuela to 45.8 percent for Brazil. This is a hefty price difference for Brazilian or Venezuelan firms competing in international markets![61] Unfortunately, competitive devaluations by Latin American governments may lead to a feared resurgence in inflation.

When the Russian ruble collapsed in 1998, eyes turned to the last bulwark against total collapse in emerging markets: Brazil. In Brazil, the black market rate for dollars rose from the normal range of two cents over the official exchange rate to thirty cents, evidencing the stronger demand to convert into dollars, perhaps to send to bank accounts in Miami. Reserves fell by between $500 million and $1 billion a day in the wake of the uncertainty created by the Russian ruble.[62] The timing of the crisis was particularly unfortunate. President Fernando Henrique Cardoso, the architect of the Brazilian *Real* plan, was engaged in a contest for reelection with left-leaning "Lula," the nickname for contender Luiz Inácio da Silva. Having already raised domestic interest rates, Cardoso was reluctant to further clamp down on the economy and irritate the vote of labor. Although he won the election, the margin was thin, reflecting national frustration with stabilization-induced high unemployment. After the election, Cardoso announced a fiscal austerity plan, including $20 billion in budget cuts. Devaluation, a key to increasing exports and jobs, was feared because of the possibility of reigniting inflation. The international community, perhaps belatedly, recognized the importance of Brazil, with an economy larger than those of South Korea, Thailand, and Malaysia combined.[63] It made ready a $41.5 billion-dollar IMF standby package to avoid seeing Brazil and the $800 billion Brazilian economy join Indonesia and other Southeast Asian nations in the international intensive care ward.[64]

The Asian crisis highlighted the fickle nature of international capital flows. Apart from the problem with commodity prices, the difficulties facing Latin America in large measure stemmed from a change in global risk aversion. Based on the fall of Asian markets, investors became wary of emerging market investments, without making distinctions for country performance. Said Chilean Finance Minister Eduardo Aninat, "It's the packaging effect. Analysts don't differentiate between regions, countries, or sectors anymore."[65] The difficulties facing Asian economies—especially the closed nature of business dealings dominated by cronyism—had already been in large part addressed through the painful adjustment of the 1980s and 1990s. Yet the rewards for good market behavior were not forthcoming.

International investor uncertainty was intensified by the reluctance of Brazilian politicians to pass Cardoso's budget. The ballooning government deficit had reached 8 percent of GDP and pushed domestic short-term interest rates above 40 percent in October 1998. A preliminary rejection of a key component of the plan, an increase in private contributions to the generous state-supported pension fund, frightened already jittery investors in early December. Local political feuds exacerbated uncertainty as the governor of a powerful state (and former president of the country Itamar Franco) declared a unilateral moratorium on obligations owed to the federal treasury. Fearing that Brazil would not be able to meet its financial obligations, investors began pulling out. Capital outflows accelerated. As international reserves plummeted, the government found it impossible to defend the Brazilian *real* and engineered an 8-percent devaluation on January 13 to relieve the pressure. Investors, having been burned by Asian devaluations, interpreted this as a sign of weakness and fled even faster. As we studied in chapter 5, the Brazilian government was forced to abandon the *Real* plan, which had anchored the economy from inflation since 1994, and simply floated the currency on world markets. The currency fell another 20 percent, although stock markets in Brazil rallied on the news that the government would not continue to be bled of reserves in an uphill battle to defend the currency.

The price shock to Brazilians was dramatic. Imagine a Brazilian family with a child in an American university. Within days, the cost of tuition increased 30–40 percent. Many Brazilians who traveled during the holidays returned home to credit card bills now inflated by one-third or more. Import prices for medicines and supplies rose.[66] As the new, higher costs worked their way through the supply chain, the specter of inflation rose on the Brazilian horizon. Tough contractionary measures, however, resulted in recession. Congress passed painful tax increases and cut government workers, although much tough work remained on the fiscal front. Auto workers in Brazil's multinational factories were laid off. The Brazilian government was able to weather this economic storm, but at considerable social cost. Capital flows, while they had brought strong investment and jobs, also carried costs associated with international volatility and vulnerability to external events.

The Argentine crisis of 2001–2002 presents a slightly different lesson. Argentines relied heavily on international capital flows to finance the gap between national spending and domestically available capital under the convertibility law of 1991. Powerful provincial governors thwarted the weak federal administration of President de la Rua from reducing fiscal deficits. The Brazilian devaluation of the *real* in 1998 pressured external accounts as Argentina's export competitiveness eroded in the face of the cheaper Brazilian currency. When Argentina's international exposure became alarmingly high, international capital pulled out, leaving the nation to face default. The surprise in the Argentine crisis is the degree to which international markets appear to differentiate the problems of Argentina from the region's stronger performers. Contagion to other Latin American financial markets was limited, although Argentina's trading partners did suffer from real declines in exports.

LESSONS FOR CAPITAL MOBILITY: QUESTIONS OF FINANCIAL SECTOR REFORM

The vulnerability of Latin America to the Asian and Russian crises renewed questions with respect to the sustainability of the externally driven model versus the need to promote stable domestic growth. Maintaining strong capital inflows over time will require either higher interest rates for bonds or loans or improved profitability of equity investments. Higher interest rates have a clear domestic cost. If higher rates are offered to attract capital, the domestic cost to borrowers—the firms that want to use this capital to expand—is necessarily higher. This also increases the cost to the government of servicing publicly held domestic debt.[67] Higher interest rates therefore act as a drag on productive domestic investment. They may also create pressures to appreciate the currency, making it more difficult for exporting firms and pressuring the balance of payments. Once again the exchange rate paradox emerges, because one indicator of country risk is a trade deficit.

> **QUESTION FOR THOUGHT**
>
> Do you believe that capital controls should be used to manage short-term capital flows? Or should international capital flows be left alone? Look at recent financial data for Mexico and Chile to substantiate your point.

Playing with the price of money is therefore unlikely to work in the long run. For capital inflows to remain stable, financial investments must be translated into real gains in productivity. If a disproportionate share of investments is directed toward the stock market or consumption, asset bubbles and imbalances will emerge.[68] Firms can be made more profitable through productivity improvements, but this is tough work. The "easy" stage of reorganization driven by privatization efforts is coming to a close. Firms will be forced to focus on long-run efforts to improve productivity, including human capital investments in health and education. Unfortunately, these take time and are not costless.

To escape the vicious circle of external vulnerability and internal recession, two other domestic policy possibilities emerge. Decreasing consumption in favor of domestic savings may lower the reliance on capital inflows for growth. Savings rates in the region have remained flat, at levels incompatible with sustainable growth. One of the reasons Latin American countries have been so vulnerable to international capital flows is the underdeveloped nature of long-term capital markets. Domestic savings in the region was 20 percent of GDP in 2000; savings rates in Asia range around 30 percent.[69] Increased reliance on domestic savings would reduce volatility, making them less vulnerable to the sudden withdrawal of foreign money. Changing savings rates, however, is a difficult long-term process. Rather than save, many Latin Americans have chosen to consume, particularly as overvalued exchange rates encouraged the purchase of imports. Weaning a country off capital flows requires substituting domestic for foreign savings to maintain growth. Encouraging savings may be accomplished by changing the relative opportunity cost of consuming today as compared to saving for tomorrow. Nevertheless, it is rarely popular with voters.

The second alternative is to promote tradable goods (exports) over nontradables, to strengthen the balance of payments. However, where the exchange rate is fixed in terms of the dollar, and thus represents a real and psychological anchor against inflation, changing relative prices between imports and exports becomes problematic.[70] Furthermore, primary product exports have their own source of instability. We will turn to the possibilities and limitations offered by the tradable goods sector in the next chapter.

In addition to changes that developing countries themselves might implement, others have suggested that the architecture of the global economy needs revision. Some contend that the IMF is too weak to grapple with the force and the ramifications of international capital flows, and that the lending authority of the IMF may be too limited to deal with the needs of large countries such as Brazil or Mexico. They argue for an effective lender of last resort, much like the U.S. Federal Reserve system for domestic banks. International financier George Soros, believing that "international capital movements need to be supervised and the allocation of credit regulated," has called for the establishment of an international credit insurance corporation.[71] Diagnosing financial instability as in part caused by a "great asymmetry between an increasingly sophisticated and dynamic international financial market and the existing institutional arrangements, which are inadequate to regulate it," the Economic Commission for Latin America and the Caribbean (ECLAC) has called for a new institutional framework.[72] Arguing that the international community helps to create speculative crises, with risk-rating agencies drawing attention to "hot" countries, thus creating bubbles bound to burst, ECLAC urges negotiations to establish an institutional framework capable of providing accurate information in an increasingly sophisticated and dynamic international financial world.[73]

Others suggest, however, that an expansion of lending capabilities of the IMF or a new financial institution would create a moral hazard. That is, countries might act irresponsibly knowing that the IMF would be there to bail them out. This contention, however, is countered by those who say that governments would not risk paying the political price of austerity measures for some short-term emergency capital. The costs of adjustment are simply too high. At issue in policy circles is whether a new framework to provide enhanced international stewardship through improved early warning and data collection, as well as greater accountability to strengthened international regulations and accounting practices, might smooth the volatility—and its associated costs—in the international financial system.[74] The IMF itself is working to promote better transparency and dissemination of data, especially on short-term debt, but as Deputy Managing Director Stanley Fischer points out, change can be accomplished only with the full support of the IMF's 182 member countries.[75] The IMF has encouraged members to release public information notices, letters of interest, and policy framework papers that accompany IMF consultations; indeed, with member consent, some of these documents can be found posted on the IMF webpage.[76] The IMF is also encouraging better dissemination of private banking data through expanded coverage of the BIS data and addressing gaps in banking supervision and adoption of standards. These efforts can be seen on the BIS homepage at www.bis.org. As noted by the managing director of the IMF, Michel Camdessus, in an era of intense integration of global capital markets, the most challenging aspect of reform has been the question of involving private sector actors in forestalling and resolving crises.[77] The proposal for an international debt restructuring mechanism, discussed in chapter 5, may also serve to calm markets.

What to do about the problems of the instability and crises associated with international capital flows may be thought of using our three policy perspectives. A pure neoliberal or new political economy approach would suggest that interfering with the market allocation of private capital would promote inefficiency. Although the neoliberal might acknowledge the costs of volatility, intervention would only slow the path of adjustment. The best policy response would be to leave the market alone. The only warranted intervention might be to strengthen and clarify regulations and standards of reporting in domestic and international financial markets such that participants could make decisions on the best available data. A neoinstitutionalist would perhaps look to see if any of the transactions costs in global capital markets might be reduced. In particular, the neoinstitutionalist might suggest that while institutional deepening is pursued, countries should pursue countervailing measures to lessen the domestic costs of short-term capital. This may, for example, include a tax on short-term international capital flows along the lines of a Tobin tax of 0.1 percent of the value of a transaction to slow the wheels of international finance until markets could be made more efficient. The neostructuralist would be more concerned with the distributional implications of the international financial casino. The state might be called upon as a financial intermediary to generate domestic sources of savings, leaving countries less exposed to international capital flows. For example, special investment funds could be set up by the government and incentives created to promote opportunities to invest in small and medium-sized firms, increasing both savings and income flowing to smaller businesses.[78] Your vision of the appropriate role of the state may guide you in outlining preferred policy options. The roles you assign to the state and the market may have something to do with the relative weight you place on each of three objectives of financial system reform: fostering efficiency and growth by allocating capital to areas of highest returns, reducing the risks of financial crises, and softening the impact and equitably sharing the burden of adjustment when crises hit.[79]

Key Concepts

capital controls	foreign direct investment	short-term money
capital flight	portfolio bonds	*tesobono*
equity investments		

Chapter Summary

Capital Flows and Latin America

- In the 1990s, after the debt crisis, there was an influx of foreign capital. The new interest stemmed from changes in international financial markets as well as structural changes within Latin America that have made it a good investment risk.
- Capital inflows into Latin America can be divided into short-term and long-term capital. Short-term capital includes portfolio bonds or equity investments, which are more volatile than foreign direct investment. However, foreign direct investment has both pros and cons. FDI can represent a source of technology, increase efficiency, and generate employment with higher wages. Yet multinational corporations have also been responsible for human rights abuses and infringement of sovereignty. Production in enclaves with low levels of linkages to the local economy may do little for long-run growth. Whether a multinational is helpful or harmful is best measured on a case by case basis.
- Capital flows can spur growth and, subsequently, savings. However, imperfect information and thin markets may lead to inefficiency. An influx of short-term money, such as portfolio bonds, depresses interest rates, discourage domestic savings, and appreciate the exchange rate, discouraging exports. It may also create inflationary pressures.
- With the liberalization of financial markets, an appropriate institutional framework is needed to provide supervision and oversight. The fragile banking sector contributed to instability after liberalization. Strong banking institutions are critical to mediate capital inflows.

The Mexican Peso Crisis

- After engaging in a fiscal stabilization, privatization, and the opening of internal markets to international trade, Mexico was perceived as a safe haven for investors. The optimism in the Mexican economy induced high levels of capital inflows and an appreciation of the Mexican *peso*. The appreciation exacerbated the current account balance, which was already at unsustainable levels, financed mostly by volatile capital inflows. After the uprising in Chiapas and the assassination of presidential candidate Luis Donaldo Colosio, investors panicked. The Mexican government, in its attempt to defend the exchange rate, saw reserves rapidly dwindle. In response to the imminent crisis, the government began to offer *tesobonos,* dollar-denominated treasury bonds, refusing to raise interest rates or devalue the currency. The markets were unconvinced by the attempt, and the Mexican government was forced to let the currency float and, hence, devalue. To bail out Mexico from the crisis, the Clinton administration, along with the IMF and the BIS, provided loan relief. Three main lessons stemmed from the Mexican *peso* crisis: a sustainable current account balance is important, short-term capital is volatile, and the inflexibility of the exchange rate as an inflation anchor can be dangerous.

Regulating Capital Inflows: Chile

- A strong export-oriented economy such as Chile's is generally rewarded with capital inflows. As capital flows increase, the currency appreciates, choking the export sector. As a response to this dilemma, Chile established reserve requirements, quotas, and fees, as well as engaging in foreign exchange market intervention and the sterilization of the monetary effect of foreign exchange. Its aim was to reduce portfolio inflows and increase domestic saving.

Effects of the Asian and Russian Crises on Latin America

- The Asian economic crisis and the collapse of the Russian ruble had negative repercussions on Latin American economies. The loss of confidence in the Asian Tigers spread to the Latin American region, leading to significant capital outflows, an increase in interest rates, and a loss of competitiveness for Latin American goods against cheaper Asian goods. The hardest hit country was been Brazil. It was forced to float its currency, abandon the *Real* plan established in 1994 as an anchor for inflation, and subsequently experience a large devaluation.

Lessons for Capital Mobility

- It is clear that capital inflows incur a cost for the domestic economy. The higher interest rates needed to attract investors also represent a higher price for domestic borrowers, hurting investment. They also increase the cost of servicing the publicly held domestic debt and lead to pressure for an appreciation of the currency. Two possible solutions have been suggested to deal with this dilemma. The first is decreasing current consumption in favor of domestic saving, which may reduce the reliance on capital inflows. The second is promoting tradable goods over nontradable goods. On the global scale, a form of international credit insurance corporation has been proposed. All of these have their limitations, especially where they undermine confidence in free markets and raise the cost of capital.

Notes

1. James D. Wolfensohn, remarks to the Board of Governors of the World Bank Group, 1 October 1996. LEXIS-NEXIS database.

2. The World Bank, *Global Development Finance, 2001,* chapter 4, "Making International Aid More Effective," table 4.1, 87 (Washington, D.C.: World Bank, 2001).

3. As of October 1992 U.S. authorities approved increasing the number of institutional investors, including pension plans and insurance funds, allowed to invest in privately placed securities. Standardization of legal and accounting practices between the United States and Mexico has also helped.

4. Sebastian Edwards, *Capital Flows into Latin America: A Stop-Go Story?* National Bureau of Economic Research Working Paper no. 6441 (Cambridge, Mass.: National Bureau of Economic Research, 1998), available at www.nber.org/papers/w6441. Edwards cites a 1993 IMF staff paper by Calvo and a 1997 World Bank study on capital flows.

5. Adapted from José Angel Gurría, "Capital Flows: The Mexico Case," in *Coping with Capital Surges: The Return of Finance to Latin America,* ed. Ricardo Ffrench-Davis and Stephany Griffith-Jones (Boulder, Colo.: Rienner, 1995), 189.

6. Howard Shatz, "Expanding Foreign Direct Investment in the Andean Countries," *CID Working Paper* no. 64 (Cambridge, Mass: Center for International Development at Harvard University, March 2001): 3.

7. Shatz, "Expanding Foreign Direct Investment," 7.

8. Shatz, "Expanding Foreign Direct Investment," 11.

9. Zdenek Drabek and Warren Payne, "The Impact of Transparency on Foreign Direct Investment," IMF Staff Working Paper ERAD-99-02, (Geneva: The World Trade Organization, 1999).

10. ECLAC, slide presentation on the Internet, 18 April 2001.

11. ECLAC, 18 April 2001.

12. Shatz, "Expanding Foreign Direct Investment," 31.

13. Lending directly to support trade includes bank letters of credit that provide financing for exports in transit until the importer pays for the goods, as well as commercial bank lending.

14. Depository receipts represent purchases made through another exchange. A depository receipt is a security issued by a U.S. bank in place of the foreign shares held in trust by that bank. Essentially, it is a mechanism for listing on the U.S. exchange. For example, American depository receipts (ADR) could represent shares of Brazilian Telebras bought on the U.S. stock exchange. Each Telebras ADR that is traded on the New York Stock exchange represents 1,000 preferred shares held by the bank of New York. An advantage of the ADR is that the liquidity and visibility of the stock increase. Some American retail investors by their own rules are not permitted to buy emerging market shares but can purchase an ADR. In some countries, to control capital inflows and outflows, only qualified institutional buyers approved by the central bank can invest in local shares. To qualify for an ADR the foreign firm must file with the SEC (Security and Exchange Commission) and abide by SEC rules. The costs associated with filing (e.g., registration, lawyers, and investment bankers) are high, and the requirements for listing in terms of transparency and reporting are stringent. However, the gains in increasing market size are often worth the cost.

15. World Bank, *World Development Indicators, 1997* (Washington, D.C.: World Bank, 1997), table 5.3, "About the Data."

16. John Welch, "The New Face of Latin America: Financial Flows, Markets, and Institutions in the 1990s," *Journal of Latin American Studies* 25 (1993): 1–24.

17. Welch, "The New Face of Latin America," 18.

18. This is unweighted by the share of a country's GDP in regional GDP; it is a straight average of foreign direct investment taken as a percentage of 1995 GDP. World Bank, *World Development Indicators, 1997.*

19. Ian Katz, "Snapping up South America," *BusinessWeek,* 18 January 1999, p. 60.

20. Nader Nazmi, "The Internationalization of Capital in a Small and Vulnerable Economy: The Case of Ecuador," in *Foreign Direct Investment in Latin America,* ed. Werner Baer and William R. Miles (New York: The Hayworth Press, 2001), 119–39.

21. ECLAC, "Foreign Investment in Latin America and the Caribbean Falls," Presentation by ECLAC Executive Secretary, José Antonio Ocampo (at www.eclac.org), 17 June 2002.

22. The United Nations Council on Trade and Development (www.unctad.org), *Foreign Direct Investment 2002.*

23. Alejandro C. Vera-Vassallo, "Foreign Investment and Competitive Development in Latin America and the Caribbean," *CEPAL Review* 60 (December 1996).

24. Richard E. Caves, *Multinational Enterprise and Economic Analysis,* 2nd ed. (Cambridge: Cambridge University Press, 1996), 230.

25. Mangus Blomström and Edward N. Wolff, "Multinational Corporations and Productivity Convergence in Mexico," in *Convergence of Productivity: Cross-National Studies and Historical Evidence,* ed. William Baumol, Richard R. Nelson, and Edward N. Wolff (New York: Oxford University Press, 1994), 265.

26. Blomström and Wolff, "Multinational Corporations," 228.

27. S. Lael Brainard and David Riker, "Are U.S. Multinationals Exporting U.S. Jobs?" National Bureau of Economic Research Working Paper no. 5958 (Cambridge, Mass.: National Bureau of Economic Research, 1997).

28. Brainard and Riker, "Are U.S. Multinationals Exporting U.S. Jobs?"

29. Blomström and Wolff, "Multinational Corporations," 265. For a general discussion of multinationals, consult Thomas J. Biersteker, *Distortion or Development? Contending Perspectives on the Multinational Corporation* (Cambridge, Mass.: MIT Press, 1978).

30. David Wheeler, "Racing to the Bottom? Foreign Investment and Air Pollution in Developing Countries" (Washington, D.C.: World Bank, Environmental Division).

31. Aaron Berstein, "Sweatshop Reform: How to Solve the Standoff," *BusinessWeek,* 3 May 1999, p. 186.

32. Blomström and Wolff, "Multinational Corporations," 276.

33. James Cypher and James Dietz, *The Process of Economic Development* (New York: Routledge, 1997), cited by Miguel D. Ramirez, "Foreign Direct Investment in Mexico and Chile: A Critical Appraisal," in *Foreign Direct Investment in Latin America,* ed. Werner Baer and William R. Miles (New York: The Hayworth Press, 2001).

34. E. Borenstein, J. De Gregorio, and J. W. Lee, "How Does Foreign Investment Affect Economic Growth?" *Journal of International Economics* 45 (1998): 115–35.

35. ECLAC, *Foreign Investment in Latin America and the Caribbean, 2000,* "Introduction: A Regulatory Challenge," 27–31.

36. Robert Devlin, Ricardo Ffrench-Davis, and Stephany Griffith-Jones, "Surges in Capital Flows and Development: An Overview of Policy Issues," in *Coping with Capital Surges,* ed. Ricardo Ffrench-Davis and Stephany Griffith-Jones (Boulder, Colo.: Rienner, 1995), 234, 243–44; and "Some Mutual Funds Go Back Full Throttle to Emerging Markets," *Wall Street Journal,* 12 November 1996, p. A1.

37. Devlin, Ffrench-Davis, and Griffith-Jones, "Surges in Capital Flows and Development," 243–44.

38. Comment by Agustín Carstens and Moises Schwartz in *Securing Stability and Growth in Latin America,* ed. Ricardo Hausmann and Helmut Reisen (Paris: OECD Publications, 1996), 128.

39. Comment by Charles Wyplosz in Hausmann and Reisen, *Securing Stability,* 132.

40. Liliana Rojas-Suarez and Steven R. Weisbrod, "Building Stability in Latin American Financial Markets," in *Securing Stability and Growth in Latin America,* ed. Ricardo Hausmann and Helmut Reisen (Paris: OECD Publications, 1996), 140.

41. Walter Molano, *Financial Reverberations: The Latin American Banking System During the Mid-1990s,* Working Paper, SBC Warburg, April 1997, 2.

42. ECLAC, *Foreign Investment in Latin America and the Caribbean, 2000,* table I.12, 65.

43. ECLAC, *Foreign Investment in Latin America and the Caribbean, 2000,* 27.

44. Ethan Kapstein, "Global Rules for Global Finance," *Current History,* November 1998, p. 358.

45. Robert Wade, "The Asian Crisis and the Global Economy: Causes, Consequences and Cure," *Current History,* November 1998, p. 362.

46. Comment by Jans Blommestein in Hausmann and Reisen, *Securing Stability,* 171.

47. Stephany Griffith-Jones, "The Mexican Peso Crisis," *CEPAL Review* 60 (December 1996): 156–57.

48. Griffith-Jones, 155–75.

49. Sebastian Edwards, "The Mexican Peso Crisis: How Much Did We Know? When Did We Know It?" *World Economy* 21, no. 1 (1998): 1–7. Much of this section follows the argument Edwards makes in this article. Also see James T. Peach and Richard V. Adkisson, "Enabling Myths and Mexico's Economic Crises (1976–1996)," *Journal of Economic Issues* 31, no. 2 (June 1997).

50. Shahid Javed Burki and Sebastian Edwards, *Latin America after Mexico: Quickening the Pace* (Washington, D.C.: World Bank, 1996), 5.

51. If the interest rate in Chile adjusted for risk is higher than in the rest of the world, capital will flow to that higher return. If people expect an appreciation, they will purchase the currency today when it is still cheaper, making money on the transaction when it strengthens. Of course, such expectations are self-fulfilling. If the market believes a currency will rise in value, it is purchased, and its price, or value, not surprisingly increases.

52. Ricardo Ffrench-Davis, Manuel Agosin, and Andras Uthoff, "Capital Movements, Export Strategy and Macroeconomic Stability in Chile," in *Coping with Capital Surges,* ed. Ricardo Ffrench-Davis and Stephany Griffith-Jones (Boulder, Colo.: Rienner, 1995), 104.

53. Jonathan Friedland, "Their Success Earns Chileans a New Title: Ugly Pan-Americans," *Wall Street Journal,* 3 October 1996, p. A1; and Ffrench-Davis, Agosin, and Uthoff, "Capital Movements," 114.

54. The inflow of foreign capital increases the supply of, for example, dollars. The price of dollars falls, and that of *pesos* rises. Remember as well that dollars coming into Chile are also purchasing Chilean assets—which increases the demand for (and the price of) *pesos.*

55. Edwards, *Capital Flows into Latin America.*

56. Sterilization involves an offsetting action on the part of the central bank. If, under a fixed exchange rate, foreign capital flows in, thereby increasing the money supply, the central bank can draw money out of domestic circulation to offset the capital flow.

57. Eduardo Aninat and Christian Larraín, "Capital Flows: Lessons from the Chilean Experience," *CEPAL Review* 60 (December 1996).

58. Edwards, *Capital Flows into Latin America.*

59. Felipe B. Larraín, ed., *Capital Flows, Capital Controls and Currency* (Ann Arbor: University of Michigan Press, 2000), 12.

60. Warburg Dillon Read, "The Impact of the Asian Crisis on Latin America," 14 July 1998, p. 2. Fax newsletter.

61. Warburg Dillon Read, "The Impact of the Asian Crisis," 5.

62. Diana Jean Schemo, "Brazilians Fret as Economic Threat Moves Closer," *New York Times,* 20 September 1998. Online edition.

63. Paul Lewis, "Latin Americans Say Russian Default Is Hurting Their Economies," *New York Times,* 6 October 1998. Online edition.

64. Mac Margolis, "Hat in Hand," *Newsweek,* 12 October 1998, p. 32B.

65. Lewis, "Latin Americans," p. A13.

66. "Brazil's Affluent Are Hurt by Crisis," *Washington Post,* 25 January 1999, p. A18.

67. Remember that a Latin American government—just like the U.S. Fed or the Bank of England—issues domestic debt to finance fiscal expenditures. If the Fed raises the interest rate, the cost of financing the U.S. debt goes up; correspondingly, when a Latin American government raises interest rates, it increases the cost of financing domestically held debt.

68. Ricardo Ffrench-Davis, "Policy Implications of the Tequila Effect," *Challenge,* March–April 1998, p. 36.

69. www.eclac.org, Economic Survey of Latin America and the Caribbean, 2000–2001.

70. This problem is discussed in José María Fanelli and José Luis Machinea, "Capital Movements in Argentina," in *Coping with Capital Surges: The Return of Finance to Latin America,* ed. Ricardo Ffrench-Davis and Stephany Griffith-Jones (Boulder, Colo.: Rienner, 1995), 183.

71. In Richard N. Haass and Robert E. Litan, "Globalization and Its Discontents," *Foreign Affairs* 77, no. 3 (1998): 4.

72. José Antonio Ocampo, "Towards a Global Solution," *ECLAC Notes* 1 (November 1998): 2.

73. Communiqué of the ECLAC on the international financial crisis, 15 September 1998. Available at www.cepal.org.english/coverpage/financialcrisis.htm.

74. *Current History,* November 1998, includes a set of accessible articles on the global financial crisis.

75. Stanley Fischer, "Reforming World Finance," *The Economist,* 3–9 October 1998. Reproduced at www.imf.org.

76. See, for example, the May 1999 Argentine letter of intent at www.imf.org/external/np/102/1999/051099.htm.

77. Michel Camdessus, "The Private Sector in a Strengthened Global Financial System," remarks at the International Monetary Conference, Philadelphia, 8 June 1999, as posted at www.imf.org/external/speeches.

78. Lucy Conger, "A Fourth Way? The Latin American Alternative to Neoliberalism," *Current History,* November 1998, pp. 380–84.

79. Michael Mussa, as reported in "Involving the Private Sector and Preventing Financial Crises," *IMF Survey* 28, no. 12 (21 June 1999): 195.

CHAPTER EIGHT

CONTEMPORARY TRADE POLICY

Engine or Brakes for Growth?

Liberalization of trade has encouraged production and processing of nontraditional exports. *(Courtesy of the Inter-American Development Bank.)*

Trade liberalization has been at the center of economic reform in Latin America. In contrast to import substitution industrialization's (ISI) internal approach, Latin America now looks to the global market as the source of dynamic growth. In part this change in orientation was motivated by the debt crisis. Without external financing, the internal orientation of ISI was not viable over time. International trade rather than the state has become the engine for growth. Yet even without the financing constraint, many analysts argued that an open trading regime is preferable to a closed model. As globalization of trade, finance, and production came to define the international agenda, an external orientation was widely adopted as the only strategy compatible with global trends. This chapter provides the theoretical underpinnings for the free trade argument. But some of the concerns of the ISI period about the vulnerability of less-powerful nations competing in a trading arena dominated by industrial giants remain. This chapter will consider these objections and analyze policies consistent with an open trading regime that may mitigate some of the costs. To enhance the gains from trade, some advocate economic integration with other regional partners. We will therefore consider the benefits of subregional integration as well as the progress toward a hemispheric free trade agreement. Different strategies have different risks and opportunities. Free trade with a large number of partners should be weighed against the possible trade diverting effects of integration. The effects of trade policy choices on the environment and equitable growth will also be considered.

The following questions will orient this chapter:

- What are the theoretical benefits of free trade?
- What concerns do some analysts have with the free trade model?
- What has been the record of liberalization in the region?
- Who trades what and why?
- Why have countries entered into subregional trading arrangements?
- Is a hemispheric free trade agreement desirable and feasible?

THE THEORETICAL BENEFITS OF FREE TRADE

Economists have long been enamored with the gains from free trade. In 1776 Adam Smith posited trade as the answer to a central development question: How do nations become wealthy? In contrast to the mercantilist, state-centered policies of the seventeenth and eighteenth centuries in Europe, Smith countered that nations become wealthy through open trade with each other. For Smith, open markets encouraged individuals to pursue greedy self-interest—the surplus of which could be traded for overall gain.

David Ricardo, in the nineteenth century, provided the conceptual underpinnings for the theoretical argument for free trade: the **theory of comparative advantage.** In a classical model, where all factors of production can be reduced to the labor required to produce them, Ricardo showed that if each country produces the good it is relatively best at producing, world output would increase. Even if a country is absolutely better in both growing wheat and producing engines, if in comparison to another country it is relatively better at engine production, it should build engines and leave wheat to be grown elsewhere. The gains derive from the benefits of specialization.

To understand the gains, first imagine there is no trade. Each country must produce both wheat and engines. Given scarce resources (a fixed supply of labor), a certain number of each good can be produced. Because there are only two goods in this hypothetical model, we can create an internal trading price of how much wheat it would take to buy an engine. For example, we might find that each engine costs one hundred bales of wheat, or each wheat bale trades for 1/100 of an engine. Now drop our imaginary trade barriers. In another country each engine might cost two hundred bales of wheat or each wheat 1/200 of an engine. An engine costs more here, but wheat costs less—1/200 rather than 1/100 of an engine. By specializing in the product you are relatively better in, you can produce that product more cheaply than in the other country. Furthermore, your country may produce both goods more efficiently than the other. In this case it should produce the good it is relatively best at; because you are not using scarce labor to produce the good that you are only second best at, your labor can focus on engines, your star performer.

This is analogous to the often told story of the lawyer who can type faster than her secretary. Should the lawyer type her own briefs? The answer is no, because the secretary can't appear in court to try the cases. With each person doing what she is relatively best at, the law firm will make more money. The same logic is extended to countries. Even if the United States can produce textiles and cars more cheaply than Guatemala, if textiles can be produced relatively less expensively in Guatemala, there are gains from trade.

The **Heckscher–Ohlin theorem** extends the concept of comparative advantage to a two-factor model. In the H–O model, factor proportions determine the direction of trade. A country relatively well endowed with labor should produce and export labor-intensive goods; the country with a larger proportion of capital than labor should focus on capital-intensive products. Relative costs once again drive the two-factor model. In a country where labor is abundant relative to capital, the excess supply of labor will make for lower wages and the scarcity of capital will exact higher interest rates. Producing labor-intensive products will allow the labor-abundant country to bring the cost advantage of the cheaper labor to the international market.

Two corollaries to the H–O theorem extend its range to include distributional implications. The **Stolper–Samuelson effect** indicates that if a labor-abundant country produces cheap labor-intensive goods, over time the increased international demand for these goods will raise their price and by association the price of their key input, labor. The Stolper–Samuelson effect therefore predicts that trade will initially benefit the least well-off—the poor workers. As more people in the world demand Guatemalan textiles, workers should share in the rewards. A second corollary, the **factor price equalization** theorem, suggests that as wages increase in the labor-abundant country (and fall in the capital-rich country), international prices of labor and capital will each converge. Therefore, at least in theory, there should be greater equality of prices for each factor in the international economy: both wage rates and interest rates should be nearly equal in all markets. Of course this implies that there may be a social price, including unemployment, in the country where wages are rising. Although consumers will benefit from the cheaper price of imports, trade policy, including worker retraining, might be indicated. Empirical research underscores the theoretical lesson of the free trade argument. Separating out globalizing developing countries in the period 1970–1990, those with open trade regimes grew at 5.0 percent per capita; nonglobalizing developing countries struggled along at 1.4 percent. The conclusion of this body of work indicates that trade does seem to create higher growth.[1]

THE CRITIQUE OF LIBERALIZATION

Free trade advocates therefore contend that by producing in accord with comparative advantage, global output and income distribution will improve. In May of 1978, Carlos Díaz Alejandro, a Colombian economist, wrote an article in the *American Economic Review* questioning the theory of free trade in practice.[2] Using the construct of a Martian landing on earth, he challenged readers to explain why, if the theory of free trade is so compelling, haven't the gains from trade been more apparent in developing countries? Why were countries still so poor? Why were the poor workers in these countries still suffering? Why hadn't the prices of capital and labor equalized?

> **QUESTION FOR THOUGHT**
>
> How would you explain the results of the contemporary trading system to Díaz Alejandro's Martian?

Problems with applying the free trade model to the real economy motivated ISI. The developing world believed that free market trade theory wasn't benefiting the least well-off. Indeed, the theory itself doesn't predict necessarily *which* country will gain from the increased production in trade, but simply that there will be gains to global welfare. In practice, developing countries perceived that the gains were accruing to the powerful industrial countries, leaving the periphery further and further behind. In particular, we remember from the discussion in chapter 2 on dependency theory the problem of declining terms of trade; control of technology in the center made it more and more difficult for the periphery countries to export a sufficient quantity of goods to purchase the high-tech products. For the South, trade was therefore impoverishing. Dependence on commodity exports left countries open to export price instability. Furthermore, rather than trade improving the lives of poor workers, the belief was that multinational corporations were exploiting the cheap labor in the periphery and keeping the additional profits for themselves. Export pessimism caused nations to turn inward, developing domestic industrial sectors to attend to the needs of the population.

In addition to the dependency critique, two other negative assessments of the results of trade emerged: the environmental and the gender dimensions. Environmentalists fear that specialization in accord with comparative advantage further encourages countries to base their economies on agricultural export crops such as timber, bananas, or coffee that can be environmentally damaging.

Environmentalists are also concerned that in an open global trading system, companies seeking to reduce production costs will flee to those countries in the developing world with the lowest environmental standards or lax enforcement. Those concerned about the gender implications of free trade point to the cases of multinational production exploiting a cheap female labor force in the developing world. Because women, with double obligations in the home and in the factory, find it difficult to organize, low wages and poor working conditions result.

WHY LIBERALIZATION? GAINS FROM TRADE IN THE 1990S

Despite concerns, liberalization is on the agenda of nearly every nation in the region. Why? Economic imbalances had built up under import substitution industrialization. The overvalued exchange rates typical of the period resulted in a bias against exports. As we can see in table 8.1, by 1981 regional current account deficits had reached $42 billion annually. In 1982, no country had a positive current account balance. If you import more than you export, someone has to pay for it. As capital dried up due to the debt crisis, current account deficits became unsustainable without external financing.

In contrast to deteriorating performance in Latin America stood the successful export-oriented growth model in Asia, which was capturing the attention of multilateral agencies as well as governments. Although the Asian model also relied in good part on an active role for the state, the International Monetary Fund, the World

Table 8.1. Current Account Balance for Latin America, 1980–1985 (millions of U.S.$)

Country	1980	1981	1982	1983	1984	1985
Argentina	−4,784	−4,712	−2,353	−2,495	−2,495	−952
Bolivia	7	−465	−173	−138	−174	−282
Brazil	−12,793	−11,751	−16,312	−6,837	42	−273
Chile	−1,971	−4,733	−2,304	−1,117	−2,111	−1,413
Colombia	−204	−1,961	−3,054	−3,003	−1,401	−1,809
Costa Rica	−663	−409	−267	−280	−151	−126
Dominican Republic	−720	−389	−443	−418	−163	−108
Ecuador	−670	−988	−1,196	−115	−273	76
El Salvador	31	−251	−120	−28	−54	−29
Guatemala	−164	−573	−399	−224	−377	−246
Honduras	−317	−303	−228	−219	−316	−220
Mexico	−10,753	−16,061	−6,307	5,403	4,194	1,130
Nicaragua	−411	−592	−514	−507	−597	−726
Panama	−322	−360	−207	337	133	123
Paraguay	−277	−374	−375	−248	−317	−252
Peru	−104	−1,728	−1,609	−872	−233	92
Uruguay	−709	−461	−235	−60	−133	−99
Venezuela	4,731	4,000	−4,246	4,427	4,651	3,327
Latin America	−30,176	−42,633	−41,784	−8,199	−939	−2,298

Source: Inter-American Development Bank, *Economic and Social Progress in Latin America* (Washington, D.C.: IADB, various years).

Bank, and the Inter-America Development Bank came to promote trade liberalization as an engine of growth. It is also important to note the change in the global context. The process of globalization—the integration of production and trade structures, the expansion of international financial markets, and the information revolution that knows no borders—had transformed the way states and firms participated in the international economy. The world had changed, and Latin America needed to change with it. The game was global.

In addition to the predicted gains in resource allocation from trade in accord with comparative advantage, new protrade arguments began to dominate the liberalization debate. Openness to the international market brings with it better access to technologies, inputs to production, and a wider array of intermediate and final goods. An economy producing for the international market is also better positioned to take advantage of economies of scale in production. Also very important is the fact that opening borders to the influx of new products and investment by multinational firms encourages competition in the domestic market. Oligopolistic power to set prices enjoyed by large firms in protected domestic markets is pressured by the competition of international markets. Production under conditions of competition not only encourages lower prices but also provides incentives to produce goods more efficiently. The shake-up of domestic industries from the challenge of international competition may create a Schumpeterian effect as firms adapt to the new business environment.[3] Participation in the international market opens firms to new ideas and the transfer of knowledge that defines success in the global economy. Indeed, improvements in productivity rates have been correlated with periods of liberalization in Latin America.[4]

How Should Liberalization Be Implemented?

No country has grown over time by turning its back on trade and capital flows. However, simply opening up to trade without building institutions to manage its social and environmental costs is a risky approach.[5] Despite the gains from liberalization over time, there are also short-run costs. Tearing down trade barriers can decimate inefficient firms, putting large numbers of employees out of work. The time path of liberalization is therefore important. How quickly should it proceed? Should industries gradually adapt to international price signals, giving them time to modernize or become more efficient? In contrast, does a gradualist approach prolong the agony of adjustment, suggesting that a quick, tough shock, although painful, might be preferable? Some research indicates that a staged process of reduction works best. In the first stage tariffs might be brought down to a uniform rate of, say, 50 percent. After industries adapt to this structure, tariffs could be lowered to an across the board 10-percent rate. However, others suggest that a quick and thorough opening of the external sector is an important element in establishing credibility in the seriousness of the reform process.

In addition to the question of the time path, liberalization should be seen in the context of a package of policies to maximize its benefits. Trade liberalization without an appropriate exchange rate is dangerous. If a currency is or becomes overvalued and trade barriers are low, the country will face an explosion of imports and exporters will find it difficult to sell goods internationally. Trade liberalization may also need to be accompanied by short-term incentives from the state (perhaps financed through multilateral agencies) for export promotion. The Asian export model does not indicate a free market, but one in which the state selectively promoted the growth of the export sector. In particular, firms that have been producing for domestic consumption need to learn international marketing. They may also need state assistance in the form of trade missions and financing to establish themselves abroad. Finally, trade liberalization works best when it is preceded by fiscal reform. If internal consumption—either public or private—is too high, the surplus for export disappears. Relieving pressures on the internal balance facilitates the generation of an external equilibrium. Without fiscal reform, internal interest rates may become too high, attracting short-term financial capital, leading to an appreciation of the exchange rate and thwarting export efforts. It is clear that trade liberalization must be seen in the context of overall structural reform.

THE RECORD OF LIBERALIZATION IN LATIN AMERICA

Average tariff rates in Latin America declined significantly following the debt crisis. The average tariff for the region was nearly 50 percent in 1985, with rates as high as 80 percent in Brazil and Colombia. By 1999, average tariffs in the region had come down to just above 12 percent, a radical transformation in the structure of the economies. There is far less dispersion in rates, signaling the consensus view that open economies are more conducive to growth. In table 8.2 we can see the high rates and variability in the tariff structure in the pre-reform period. Although Argentina, Brazil, Mexico, and Peru retain higher than average tariff rates, they are relatively close to the low tariff countries of Bolivia, Chile, and Paraguay. Most of the reductions were introduced gradually over the period to soften the adjustment effects on industries, but in cases such as Peru, the tariff surgery was radical and swift, with rates falling from 68.05 percent in 1990 to 17.63 percent in 1992.

Lower tariffs and free access of goods to the region were accompanied by a surge in growth of exports of goods and services from the region. We note in table 8.3 the explosive growth of trade in the 1990s. In contrast to negative performance in the 1980–1985 and 1985–1990 periods, in the 1990s Latin America exceeded the global boom in trade. Indeed, from 1995 to 2000, regional exports expanded at twice the rate of the rest of the world. Star exporters include Costa Rica, Mexico, and El Salvador. Mexico's clear-cut commitment to global trade is evidenced by its strong performance over the two decades. As can be seen in table 8.4, exports as a percentage of GDP averaged 19 percent in 2000, representing a significant change from the precrisis export to GDP ratio of 10.7 percent. With tariff liberalization it is not surprising that the average annual rate of growth of imports to GDP has also risen. Indeed, this can be seen as a positive effect if the goods coming into the country introduce new technologies or better production techniques. Imports were severely curtailed during the period of adjustment imposed by the debt crisis to a rate of growth of 0.6 percent; this increased to 19 percent in 2000. A concern with

Table 8.2. Average Tariff in Latin America: Selected Years, 1985–1999 (percentage)

Country	1985	1986–1987	1988	1989–1990	1992	1994	1995	1998	1999
Argentina	28.0	39.5	43.7	21.0	14.8	19.3	14.0	13.9	13.5
Bolivia	20.0	21.9	18.6	13.4	9.8	9.7	9.7	9.7	9.7
Brazil	80.0	74.1	50.6	32.4	17.6	11.3	12.6	14.6	14.3
Chile	36.0	20.2	15.1	14.9	11.0	11.0	11.0	11.0	9.8
Colombia	83.0	46.4	47.6	23.2	11.6	11.4	11.4	11.6	11.6
Costa Rica	53.0	26.0	NA	NA	NA	NA	11.7	NA	NA
Ecuador	50.0	41.4	39.9	33.0	11.3	11.4	11.2	11.8	11.5
El Salvador	NA	23.0	NA	NA	NA	NA	9.2	NA	NA
Guatemala	50.0	25.0	NA	NA	NA	NA	10.8	NA	NA
Honduras	NA	NA	NA	41.9	NA	NA	17.9	NA	NA
Mexico	34.0	27.8	10.6	13.1	13.1	12.8	13.7	13.2	16.2
Nicaragua	54.0	21.0	NA	NA	NA	NA	17.4	NA	NA
Panama	NA	NA	NA	NA	NA	NA	NA	NA	NA
Paraguay	71.7	19.3	19.3	16.0	9.2	8.0	9.4	9.5	11.4
Peru	64.0	63.0	67.8	68.1	17.6	16.3	16.3	13.5	13.7
Uruguay	32.0	35.7	27.0	27.7	18.3	14.8	9.6	12.2	12.3
Venezuela	30.0	30.6	33.8	19.0	11.8	11.8	11.8	12.0	12.0
Latin America	50.0	38.2	34.0	25.6	13.3	12.5	12.4	12.1	12.4

Source: Data from IADB. Available online at www.iadb.org.

Table 8.3.   Merchandise Exports, 1980–2000 (billions of U.S.$)

	1980	1985	1990	1995	2000	% Share in World Trade	
						1980	2000
World[a]	2,035.17	1,950.56	3,441.54	5,078.09	6,424.62	100.00	100.00
North America	293.56	309.98	521.78	777.37	1,058.87	14.42	16.48
Canada	67.73	90.95	127.63	192.20	276.64	3.33	4.31
United States	225.57	218.82	393.59	584.74	781.92	11.08	12.17
Latin America	109.74	108.55	146.76	229.34	358.62	5.39	5.58
Argentina	8.02	8.40	12.35	20.97	26.30	0.39	0.41
Bolivia	0.94	0.62	0.93	1.10	1.23	0.05	0.02
Brazil	20.13	25.64	31.41	46.51	55.09	0.99	0.86
Chile	4.71	3.80	8.37	16.02	18.16	0.23	0.28
Colombia	3.92	3.55	6.77	10.13	13.04	0.19	0.20
Costa Rica	1.00	0.98	1.45	3.45	5.87	0.05	0.09
Cuba	5.58	5.98	5.10	1.60	1.64	0.27	0.03
Ecuador	2.48	2.91	2.71	4.31	4.93	0.12	0.08
El Salvador	0.97	0.68	0.58	1.65	2.94	0.05	0.05
Guatemala	1.52	1.06	1.16	2.16	2.70	0.07	0.04
Guyana	0.40	0.21	0.25	0.46	0.57	0.02	0.01
Honduras	0.83	0.78	0.83	1.22	1.32	0.04	0.02
Mexico	18.03	26.76	40.71	79.54	166.42	0.89	2.59
Nicaragua	0.45	0.30	0.33	0.53	0.63	0.02	0.01
Panama	0.36	0.33	0.34	0.63	0.86	0.02	0.01
Paraguay	0.31	0.30	0.96	0.92	0.87	0.02	0.01
Peru	3.90	2.98	3.23	5.58	7.03	0.19	0.11
Suriname	0.51	0.33	0.47	0.48	0.44	0.03	0.01
Uruguay	1.06	0.91	1.69	2.11	2.30	0.05	0.04
Venezuela	19.22	14.44	17.50	18.46	31.80	0.94	0.50

Source: The World Trade Organization. International Trade Statistics available online at www.wto.org.
[a]Includes significant re-exports.

liberalization is that import growth not outpace export performance, leaving the country to struggle with a current account deficit.

Chile provides an interesting example of trade liberalization. From an average level of 105 percent at the time of the military coup in 1973—with some tariffs reaching more than 700 percent—Chile unilaterally implemented a 10-percent tariff rate within four years of the Pinochet government. How did such a radical and rapid restructuring of the economy take place?[6] Five stages distinguished the Chilean process. After a dramatic reduction of trade barriers as part of a comprehensive stabilization package including a real exchange rate devaluation in the first period (1974–1978), the second stage was characterized by exchange rate overvaluation when the *peso* became the anti-inflationary anchor. During the third stage (1983–1985) Chile suffered through a temporary reversal during a deep economic crisis, while in the fourth, from 1985 to 1990, liberalization accompanied recovery. With the transition to democracy in the fifth stage, Chile began its turn to preferential trading agreements to complement its unilateral liberalization.

Foreshadowing later reform efforts in the region, economic crisis drove the

Table 8.4. Latin America: Exports and Imports, 1990–2000 (percentage of GDP)

Country	1990 Exports/ GDP	1990 Imports/ GDP	1995 Exports/ GDP	1995 Imports/ GDP	2000 Exports/ GDP	2000 Imports/ GDP
Argentina	8	2	9	8	11	10
Bolivia	15	16	15	18	16	23
Brazil	6	3	7	7	9	8
Chile	23	16	25	22	32	21
Colombia	11	8	11	14	13	12
Costa Rica	21	20	30	32	45	44
Ecuador	16	15	25	23	24	22
El Salvador	15	21	17	33	29	38
Guatemala	13	15	15	21	22	27
Honduras	40	32	37	40	47	64
Mexico	13	14	22	20	34	39
Nicaragua	18	37	26	47	34	60
Panama	80	58	77	84	60	72
Paraguay	23	24	50	54	29	31
Peru	10	8	10	14	15	13
Uruguay	12	9	12	15	15	18
Venezuela	25	14	27	17	31	23
Average	11	8	14	13	19	19

Source: ECLAC, *Statistical Yearbook 2001* (Santiago, Chile: ECLAC, 2001), tables 135, 292, and 294.
Note: At constant 1995 prices.

adoption of a new model. Views of economists trained at the University of Chicago—later called the Chicago boys—gained ascendancy in the Pinochet regime. Criticism of the distributional implications of the open trading model were carefully voiced by economists opposed to the authoritarian regime. Nevertheless, when these economists came to power in the democratic transition in 1990, it became clear that the open trading model would not be altered. The consistency of policy was made possible through a variety of compensation schemes designed to buy off the losers in the liberalization and stabilization process, including owners of import-competing industries, nontradable goods industries, and labor. Export promotion schemes and assistance in export diversification channeled private-sector energies from import substitution toward the external economy. Accompanying

DATA EXERCISE

Prepare a report card comparing 1995 and the early years of the new millennium on trade performance in Latin America. What has happened to current account balances? The export to GDP ratio? The import to GDP ratio? Can you explain these trends? For trade and current data, you might want to consult the following Internet addresses:
ECLAC at www.eclacl.cl/english/ statistics/statistics.htm
IMF at dsbb.imf.org/category.htm

financial-sector reforms reduced the prices of credit for domestic entrepreneurs. Repression of labor unions made restructuring easier on firms, albeit at a high political price. Although organizing activity was repressed, by law real wages were maintained in labor contracts. Subsidies eased the transition in the agricultural sector. The Chilean example surprisingly contains some of the elements we discussed in chapter 6 with respect to the role of government in an internationalized economy. Chilean performance confirms Rodrik's proposition of the need for an enhanced role for the state in an open economy.

COMPOSITION OF GOODS

The type of goods Latin America is exporting to the rest of the world has changed over recent decades. As can be seen in table 8.5, although primary products composed 60.1 percent of exports in 1965, by 1990 they accounted for 42 percent, and with liberalization they accounted only for 34.1 percent of exports. Although their total value did increase marginally over the period, the surge in both traditional and nontraditional industrial exports account for the changing composition of trade. Nonetheless, traditional primary products still play a large role in the export profile of the region. As can be seen in table 8.6, bananas comprise 25 percent of Ecuador's exports, 23 percent of Costa Rica's, 14 percent of Honduras's, and 7 percent of Guatemala's. Similarly, coffee accounts for 38 percent of exports in El Salvador, 28 percent in Honduras, 25 percent in Guatemala, 20 percent in Colombia, 19 percent in Nicaragua, 14 percent in Costa Rica, 6 percent in Peru, and 5 percent in Brazil. It is interesting to compare table 8.6 with table 2.5 to see how single-product dependency has changed over time. Among Central American nations, Costa Rica has had the most success with nontraditional exports, which make up 40 percent of exports and include products such as fresh shrimp, lobster, plantains, pineapple, and macadamia nuts.[7]

The historical problems of geographic market concentration and export price instability discussed in chapter 2 continue to plague the region. Of exports in 2000, nearly 17 percent went to the region and 61.4 percent to North America, with Japan and Asia accounting for 6 percent and the European Union (EU) 11.6 percent.[8] There is, of course, considerable variation by country in the regional export numbers. For example, Chile, a Pacific Basin country, exports 14.6 percent of its goods to Japan, with another 12.8 percent going to other countries in Asia. The European Union is its next largest Chilean trading destination with 26.2 percent, with the United States lagging at 18 percent. Mexico, a North American Free Trade Agreement (NAFTA) partner of the United States, sells 88.4 percent of its goods to its northern neighbor, with only 1.0 percent going to Asia and 3.6 percent to the European Union. In contrast, Brazil's largest export market is the European Union at 25 percent of exports.[9] Table 8.7 shows the dramatic changes in commodity prices over time. In inflation-adjusted dollars coffee and cocoa in 2001 generated about a third as much income as they did in 1980. Cocoa, maize and soybean prices have fallen by half; coffee and copper to a third of 1970 levels. For small farmers, losing 50 to 65 percent of income is devastating.[10]

Table 8.5. Latin America and the Caribbean (excluding Mexico): Exports of Goods Traded According to Category, 1965–1999 (millions of U.S.$)

Exports	1965 Value	1965 %	1970 Value	1970 %	1980 Value	1980 %	1990 Value	1990 %	1995 Value	1995 %	1999 Value	1999 %
Primary Goods	5,954	60.1	7,219	52.9	34,987	46.8	39,806	42.0	45,388	33.1	49,972	34.1
Agriculture	3,252	32.8	4,018	29.5	14,391	19.2	15,665	16.5	23,109	16.9	23,900	16.3
Minerals	671	6.8	1,082	7.9	4,316	5.8	5,150	5.4	7,184	5.2	6,941	4.7
Energy	2,032	20.5	2,119	15.5	16,280	21.8	18,991	20.0	15,095	11.0	19,130	13.1
Industrialized Goods	3,828	38.6	6,330	46.4	39,365	52.6	54,353	57.3	90,231	65.8	94,788	64.7
Traditional	1,548	15.6	2,649	19.4	15,435	20.6	21,058	22.2	34,437	25.1	34,540	23.6
Food, beverages, and tobacco	1,285	13.0	2,023	14.8	9,771	13.1	11,788	12.4	18,616	13.6	19,172	13.1
Other	263	2.7	625	4.6	5,664	7.6	9,270	9.8	15,821	11.5	15,369	10.5
Scale-intensive	2,198	22.2	3,393	24.9	19,090	25.5	25,360	26.7	41,323	30.1	38,832	26.5
Durables	14	0.1	47	0.3	1,765	2.4	2,565	2.7	5,840	4.3	6,630	4.5
Diffusers of technical progress	68	0.7	241	1.8	3,076	4.1	5,371	5.7	8,632	6.3	14,786	10.1
Other Goods	125	1.3	93	0.7	478	0.6	706	0.7	1,474	1.1	1,704	1.2
Total	9,907	100.0	13,641	100.0	74,830	100.0	94,864	100.0	137,093	100.0	146,463	100.0

Source: ECLAC, *Indicadores Económicos* (Santiago, Chile: ECLAC, 2001), table A.4a, 18.

Table 8.6.   Exports of Primary Products from Latin America and the Caribbean

Product	% of Exports of Principal Exporters
Iron and Steel	Brazil 13%
Copper (mineral)	Chile 42%, Peru 16%
Zinc (mineral)	Bolivia 16%, Peru 9%
Estano (mineral)	Bolivia 8%
Gold	Peru 10%, Bolivia 9%
Petroleum	Venezuela 83%, Ecuador 29%, Colombia 24%, Argentina 11%, and Mexico 10%
Sugar	Uruguay 13%, Nicaragua 6%
Shrimp	Ecuador 17%, Nicaragua 9%
Bananas	Ecuador 25%, Costa Rica 23%, Honduras 14%, Guatemala 7%
Wheat	Argentina 5%
Rice	Uruguay 9%
Corn	Argentina 5%
Coffee	El Salvador 38%, Honduras 28%, Guatemala 25%, Colombia 20%, Nicaragua 19%, Costa Rica 14%, Peru 6%, Brazil 5%
Fish flour	Peru 15%
Soy	Paraguay 43%
Soy flour	Bolivia 9%, Argentina 9%, Brazil 5%
Vegetable oils	Argentina 8%
Natural fibers	
Cotton	Paraguay 6%
Wool	Uruguay 8%

Source: ECLAC, *Panorama de la Inserción Internacional de America Latina y El Caribe, 1998,* Santiago, Chile: ECLAC, 1998, 37.

EXCHANGE RATE PERFORMANCE

A critical price in promoting trade is the exchange rate (see table 8.8). Two factors have limited the ability to use a competitive exchange rate as an export promotion tool: inflation fighting and the performance of the U.S. dollar. Several regional currencies have used an exchange rate fixed to the U.S. dollar as a means of introducing credibility and stemming inflationary fears. A devaluation of the currency would raise inflationary expectations and derail stabilization. Indeed, rather than devaluing vis-à-vis the rest of the world, as the dollar has gained strength, so did the linked currencies. For example, in 1997 the Brazilian *real* was up 7 percent against the German *mark* and 8.1 percent against the Japanese *yen,* pressuring the balance of payments. Until 2002 Argentina maintained a one-to-one parity, and the Brazilian *real* was linked to the dollar through 1998. Resulting

> **QUESTION FOR THOUGHT**
>
> Review the objections Latin American structuralists had to export-led growth prior to ISI. Do the new global conditions change their prescriptions? What do you recommend as a trade policy for the region?

Table 8.7. Commodity Prices in Constant 1990 Dollars

Commodity	Unit	Actual				
		1970	*1980*	*1990*	*2000*	*2001*
Crude oil, average	$/bbl	4.3	46.8	22.9	29.0	25.4
Cocoa	c/kg	240.6	330.5	126.7	93.1	111.4
Coffee, other milds	c/kg	408.8	440.0	197.2	197.3	143.2
Soybeans	$/mt	416.8	376.0	246.8	217.7	204.2
Maize	$/mt	208.2	159.0	109.3	91.0	93.5
Bananas	$/mt	592.1	478.9	540.9	435.7	608.1
Copper	$/mt	5047.0	2770.0	2661.0	1863.0	1645.0

Source: World Bank, *Global Development Finance 2002* (Washington, D.C.: World Bank, 2002), table A5.10.

trade imbalances prompted a sweeping change in exchange rate regimes across the region, with most countries moving to a floating exchange rate system.

TRADE IMBALANCES

Liberalization of trade does not, of course, imply that a country's trade accounts will be balanced. Improvement in exports, if outpaced by an increase in imports, will result in a deteriorating trade balance. Unless this trade deficit is matched by

Table 8.8. Latin America and the Caribbean: Index of Real Effective Exchange Rate of Exports

Country	1980	1985	1990	1991	1992	1993	1994	1995	1996
Argentina	58.7	94.7	100.0	83.3	77.5	74.0	78.4	87.0	89.0
Bolivia	72.8	50.4	100.0	108.3	116.3	117.6	125.1	126.5	120.5
Brazil	141.7	149.9	100.0	119.7	128.4	113.5	92.6	70.5	65.0
Chile	50.5	71.2	100.0	98.9	95.3	97.5	96.5	92.4	88.1
Colombia	52.2	59.6	100.0	101.0	90.0	85.6	74.8	74.5	71.6
Costa Rica	64.7	90.0	100.0	108.3	103.0	100.4	101.0	98.8	98.9
Ecuador	48.4	62.3	100.0	95.2	94.7	83.5	78.2	78.5	80.0
El Salvador	139.0	75.9	100.0	98.4	98.2	88.0	83.9	80.9	75.6
Guatemala	57.0	47.2	100.0	87.9	87.0	88.9	85.1	82.6	82.5
Honduras	66.4	53.4	100.0	107.9	102.4	112.5	125.3	112.3	114.7
Mexico	76.2	95.3	100.0	91.1	84.1	79.7	81.9	121.1	109.4
Nicaragua	243.4	70.1	100.0	104.6	105.2	108.3	113.3	118.8	117.1
Paraguay	50.4	80.8	100.0	86.9	90.6	93.9	97.4	106.8	104.3
Peru	220.2	232.6	100.0	82.1	80.9	89.1	84.6	85.6	82.4
Uruguay	59.5	78.0	100.0	88.1	84.1	786.8	76.6	79.4	80.4
Venezuela	45.9	52.2	100.0	93.9	88.5	88.9	92.5	10.6	90.0

Source: ECLAC, *Indicadores Económicos* (Santiago, Chile: ECLAC, 1997), 38.
Note: A rise in the index implies a depreciation.

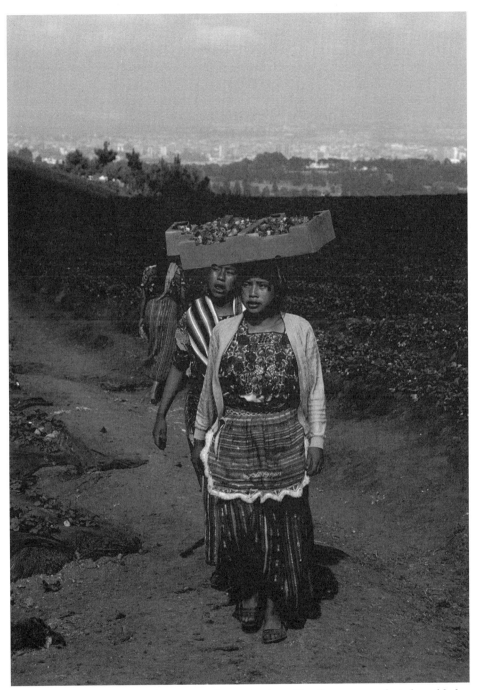

Nontraditional export crops have opened new opportunities for women—but also added to their burden *(Courtesy of the Inter-American Development Bank.)*

strong inflow of capital to finance them, the country may quickly find itself with balance of payments problems. As we can see in table 8.9, the strong increase in exports of goods was accompanied by continued demand for the import of services, leaving the region with a negative balance on goods and services. Financial inflows compensated for this balance in 1995 and 2000; one of the fears associated with the decline in capital flows discussed in chapter 7 is the restructuring this will require in the balance of payments. Promoting a sustainable global balance that does not draw down reserves or necessitate International Monetary Fund (IMF) interventions is a delicate process. External variables, including the performance of the global economy, play havoc with national accounts. One mechanism to attempt to decrease some of the extraregional effects of trade disturbance has been to pursue regional trade integration. However, as we will see below with the effects of the Brazilian currency crisis on **Mercosur,** there may be some unintended effects in the transmission of disturbances within the region.

REGIONAL TRADING ARRANGEMENTS: THE THEORY OF TRADE INTEGRATION

Beyond opening their borders to trade, countries may choose to negotiate trade agreements with other nations. There are four broad categories of trade integration: a **free trade area,** a **customs union,** a **common market,** and an **economic union.** In a free trade area, or FTA, trade restrictions are abolished between participating countries, but each country maintains an independent trade policy and separate tariff rates with the rest of the world. In a bit of an ironic play on words, a free trade area is actually a step away from pure free trade. Economists define free trade as an open, multilateral system in which countries do not define preferences for partners but simply buy the cheapest goods available in the global market. A free trade area

Table 8.9. Regional Balance of Payments (millions of U.S.$)

	1980	1985	1990	1995	2000
Exports of goods	91,590.8	97,499.6	136,316.4	229,584.8	357,134.1
Imports of goods	−92,461.5	−63,237.2	−105,161.2	−225,910.5	−353,213.6
Exports of services	15,274.8	15,255.1	25,076.2	36,448.5	48,650.8
Imports of services	27,135.8	−20,608.6	−33,251.2	−51,811.4	−66,159
Balance on goods and services	−12,731.7	28,908.9	22,979.8	−11,688.6	−13,588.4
Current account balance	−29,882.2	−2,717.5	−2,153	35,240.5	−46,154.3
Financial accounts, including errors and omissions	29,207.6	−16,042.9	−4,844.9	28,946.2	59,878.0
Global balance	—	—	—	—	14,569.3
Reserves and related items	—	—	—	—	−14,568.5

Source: ECLAC, *Statistical Yearbook for Latin America and the Caribbean 2001* (Santiago, Chile: ECLAC, 2001), 432–33.
Note: An outflow of reserves is reflected by a positive number (export of capital) and an inflow by a negative number (import of capital).

negotiates preferential status for member countries, diverging from pure unfettered trade. A customs union takes preferential arrangements a step further, establishing a common external tariff for the group, and a common market advances cooperation in other policy-making measures, such as agriculture and the social sector. Full economic integration, including a common monetary policy and a common currency, is an economic union. Because trade integration tends to occur on a regional basis to take advantage of geographic proximity, the different forms are sometimes lumped together under the term regional integration arrangements (RIAs) or preferential trade agreements (PTAs).

Why pursue economic integration? Economic integration may create special opportunities to take advantage of economies of scale, allowing export diversification by producing for a larger market. Absent trade restrictions and in the presence of a stable currency, trade might proceed as if it were between Massachusetts and Connecticut. This may be particularly useful in broadening the markets for nontraditional exports, where global markets themselves remain relatively protected. Where labor training, technology, and long-term capital are scarce in developing markets, economies of scale may offer new opportunities to strengthen markets and create new sources of international competitiveness.[11] Regional trading arrangements may also be a means of moving beyond opening markets for goods to promote "deep integration" in trade in services, harmonization of regulatory regions, and the coordination of macroeconomic policies.[12]

A free trade agreement can work to open protected markets, creating new sales opportunities. Countries with similar tastes and cultural predispositions as well as common language ties may find invigorating marketing opportunities. Opening to trade through regional integration may meet less political resistance than unilateral tariff reductions. The perception of neighborliness and reciprocity may serve to soften the price of sectoral reform. As new competitors emerge in the regional context and as the dislocation that always accompanies the change in the trading rules of the game dissipates, new players may be better positioned in the global economy. The learning curve in terms of international marketing and shipping infrastructure can be extended to the world marketplace.

Integration may also have an effect on the expectations of investors, promoting credibility in the permanence of reforms. This is due to the difficulty of rolling back trade liberalization after it has been locked in by a treaty with another country. For example, when Mexico suffered from the 1994–1995 *peso* crisis, it raised tariffs on 550 products—except for those exported to NAFTA partners. The political costs of abrogating a treaty may exceed the short-term pain of economic adjustment.

The gains or losses from economic integration may be assessed in light of the existing distance from a free trade ideal. If a free trade agreement opens a country further, it is said to have a trade creating effect. If a country trades more—and in the process makes more efficient use of its own resources—welfare will increase. If, however, the treaty serves to create an economic enclave, it is trade diverting, as purchases are now made from a partner, not the most efficient global producer. Some have suggested that trade integration in the region has diverted trade from its most efficient sources. Traditional suppliers of textiles from the Caribbean countries, for example, may have suffered from Mexico's improved access to the U.S. market under NAFTA.[13]

The free trade ideal may not, however, be the most practical benchmark to assess efforts. One of the difficult parts of assessing the impact of regional trading arrangements is figuring out what would have happened in its absence. Would there have been more movement toward the pure trade model, or greater protectionism? Analysis of regional economic integration parallels the joke about the economist who is asked "How is your love life?" and replies "Relative to what?"[14] Evaluating integration involves a benchmark: should the benchmark be the free trade ideal or increasing global isolation?

In promoting integration in the area, the Economic Commission for Latin America and the Caribbean (ECLAC) has embraced a concept called **open regionalism.** This concept refers to a coupling of regional integration with overall liberalization of trade barriers to nonmember countries. Countries accompany lower tariffs to integration partners with a general opening of the economy to world trade. In characterizing contemporary trade agreements, ECLAC's Enrique Iglesias notes that "One difference between our earlier integration experiences and those of today is that the latter, as a general rule, have a more limited scope in terms of the countries, sectors and interests involved in them, as well as greater flexibility, greater sensitivity to market signals and a less preprogrammed approach."[15] Where the old schemes were protectionist and supported state-led development, new regionalism embraces an outward focus, encourages foreign investment and has encouraged strategic participation in hemispheric and world forums.[16] The new regionalism is market driven, and relies on a scaled-down institutional architecture. In this sense intraregional trade may be considered a complement to and not a substitute for an open global trading arena. Let us turn to consider the wide range of integration efforts in the region to evaluate this proposition.

THE NORTH AMERICAN FREE TRADE AGREEMENT

In 1991 the United States, Canada, and Mexico began negotiating the North American Free Trade Agreement, or **NAFTA,** which was then signed in 1994. NAFTA was the first formal regional trading agreement to involve both developed and developing countries. The centerpiece of NAFTA is the gradual elimination of tariffs over a ten-year period, including the elimination of restrictions in textiles and apparel in the United States and Canada.[17] Intellectual property rights were also strengthened. To prevent the abuse of the free trade status by nontreaty countries, the legislation includes tough rules of origin specifying what proportion of the value of a product must be added locally and imposing strict domestic content rules for the purchase of inputs. Computers, for example, could not be assembled in Mexico with imported components from around the globe and qualify for NAFTA trade preferences.

Key elements of the NAFTA accord include changes in agriculture, manufacturing, and services. The accord provides for liberalization of the export of fresh fruits and vegetables from Mexico into the United States as well as that of corn and other grains from the United States to Mexico. It promotes lowering of tariffs and quotas on textiles and apparel. It removes tariffs on cars imported into Mexico over a five- to ten-year period, and it opens the Mexican telecommunica-

Trade is dependent on export infrastructure such as this port in Paraguay. *(Courtesy of the Inter-American Development Bank.)*

tions and government procurement markets. Finally, it speeds implementation of the General Agreement on Tariffs and Trade (GATT) intellectual property rights and provides national treatment to investors of other NAFTA countries.[18] Unlike the European Union, NAFTA makes no provision for the free movement of labor within the bloc. It is notable that the only sectors where the new regime explicitly benefits Mexico are concessions in the U.S. markets for fruit, textiles, and clothing. The more industrialized partners realized significant gains in lucrative telecommunications and government markets. In an effort to gain credibility with international investors, Mexico may have given up more than it got in the NAFTA negotiations. Liberalization with industrialized partners came at a relatively high price for the Mexicans.

The signing of NAFTA generated a great deal of controversy. In the United States and Canada, opponents were concerned about the potential loss of jobs as manufacturers moved south of the border to take advantage of cheaper labor. Environmental advocates were also fearful of the motives of big business in relocating to avoid tougher environmental regulations in the North. In Mexico there was the apprehension that the *yanquis* would invade again, exploiting Mexican labor and putting Mexican corporations out of business.

Some of these fears were unfounded. It is important to note that Mexico had already engaged in substantial liberalization, such that the decrease in tariff rates was not particularly dramatic, with the exception of changes in agriculture and government services. Those opposing NAFTA failed to point out that international capital was already well dispersed throughout Mexico through the *maquiladora* program. Begun in 1965, for thirty years this twin-plant program has allowed foreign firms to import components without duty so long as the final product was reexported. Capital that wanted to be in Mexico because of the cheap labor platform largely was already there. In fact, foreign direct investment from the United States to Mexico did not increase much with NAFTA, and Mexico's share of total U.S. foreign direct investment declined.[19]

Furthermore, in assessing the effects of cheap labor, it must be remembered that low wages do not magically guarantee a profit. Low wages may be the result of low levels of productivity such that the cost per unit of product is not reduced. In fact, although wages in the United States are roughly eight times the wages paid in Mexico, U.S. workers produce 8.2 times as much as Mexicans in *maquila* plants. This is not to say that *if* cheaper Mexican workers can be made more productive with better education and equipment, Mexico wouldn't be more of a threat, but rather that the claims for the widespread job loss in the United States, given Mexican productivity levels, were somewhat exaggerated. Profit increases only when productive labor is paid less than it is worth.

In the United States, the AFL-CIO, an organization of affiliated labor unions, charged that NAFTA helped keep inflation-adjusted average hourly wages of U.S. workers flat, at approximately $12 per hour. What NAFTA may do is make the threat of plant relocation to Mexico more real to American workers, and therefore depress wage demands in collective bargaining. One study found that 60 percent of union organizing efforts after NAFTA were met by the threat of plant closings, compared to 29 percent before.[20] Nonetheless, NAFTA does not change the fact that multinationals could always threaten to move abroad. As we just noted, *maquiladoras* have been around for thirty years. If it wasn't Mexico, it would be Malaysia.

Jobs may also be created through integration. Transportation sector jobs such as trucking have also benefited, as goods are moved over land between the NAFTA countries. In cases such as the U.S. Fisher-Price Corporation, a job-creating effect of NAFTA was relocating production from Hong Kong to Monterey, because firms such as Celadon Trucking, which move goods from Mexico into the U.S. market, must hire drivers.[21] There is the possibility that NAFTA created as many jobs as it may have lost. Overall the impact of NAFTA on the U.S. economy has been relatively small and does not support the view that the agreement has been largely trade diverting.[22]

Job creation or job loss is difficult to measure in part because you can't tell which workers are dedicated to "NAFTA production" and which are making goods sold elsewhere. We know that employment has fallen over the first eight years of NAFTA, but this can hardly be attributable to the accord. We also know that when workers are laid off from jobs due to firms moving to Mexico, they may register for benefits under the NAFTA Transitional Adjustment Assistance. As of March 1997, a total of 177,000 workers (about 39,000 per year) qualified; this is a very small share of the annual job losses totaling about 1.5 million per year in the United States. So if NAFTA has had a role in job loss, it is unnoticeably small on a national level.[23] We might also expect that job loss would be concentrated the most in the areas where the greatest deficit exists in U.S.–Mexican trade. From table 8.10, we can see this deficit in the machine transport or automotive sector. Nevertheless, few auto workers have filed. Perhaps Mexican imports are a complement to U.S. production, boosting the competitiveness of U.S. firms as they market their goods around the world. For the most part, it is macroeconomic conditions and not trade agreements that determine the level of employment in an economy.[24] National levels of income determine aggregate demand; changes in the sectoral distribution of which country is producing each item will not determine an overall job loss.

Table 8.10.   U.S.–Mexican Trade (millions of U.S.$ at 2000 prices)

	Exports to Mexico	*Imports from Mexico*
Food and live animals	4,620.57	4,520.74
Beverages and tobacco	126.71	1,299.02
Crude materials, inedible, except fuels	3,137.72	817.00
Mineral fuels, lubricants, and related materials	4,303.37	12,763.31
Animal and vegetable oils, fats and waxes	303.19	28.84
Chemicals and related products, N.E.S.	8,944.48	1,783.06
Manufactured goods classified chiefly by material	15,789.53	9,127.73
Machinery and transport equipment	57,143.57	79,478.75
Miscellaneous manufactured articles	12,332.01	20,219.51
Commodities and transactions, N.E.S.	5,019.72	5,872.57
Total	111,720.88	135,910.53

Source: U.S. Census Bureau, official statistics. Available online at www.census.gov/foreign-trade/ sitc1/2000.

Unfortunately, where jobs are lost the damage is geographically concentrated in communities devastated by plant closing. The pain is magnified on a local level.

Another reason the aggregate job loss hasn't been as high as predicted is the domestic content regulations. Where firms, particularly those that had set up in the *maquiladora* zones before NAFTA, had imported components from Asia, now they must purchase from American suppliers. Exports to Mexico may have been higher had the *peso* crisis not sent the Mexican economy into a tailspin.[25] By 1999, Mexico had indeed become the second-largest U.S. export market after Canada, surpassing Japan. By 2000, two-way trade had reached a record $248 million; Mexico has been the fastest growing U.S. market for the past seven years. As shown in table 8.10, U.S. exports to Mexico reached 111.7 billion, a 28-percent increase over the previous year. Imports rose by 24 percent in 2000, leaving the United States with a trade deficit with its southern partner. Mexico's duty on American goods has fallen from its pre-NAFTA rate of approximately 10 percent to less than 2 percent, allowing 80 percent of U.S. goods to enter duty free. Mexico is the U.S.'s third most important agricultural market.[26] From 1994 through 2000 Mexico's annual average capital inflow reached 11.7 billion, three times the amount in the years prior to NAFTA. Half of Mexico's job creation is in the export sector; jobs here pay 40 percent more than the national average. U.S. employment supported by exports to NAFTA countries reached 2.9 million jobs, these paying 13–18 percent more than the average U.S. wage.[27]

Environmental dumping under NAFTA was also a concern for both sides. The border between the United States and Mexico had long suffered environmental deterioration from sewage problems in Tijuana, inadequate waste disposal from *maquilas,* and copper smelting in Sonora and Arizona. NAFTA heightened fears. U.S. firms in conformance with environmental regulations did not want to be put at a disadvantage with respect to firms located in Mexico, and Mexicans themselves did not want to breathe dirtier air or drink more polluted water courtesy of multinational capital. As a result of tough lobbying, NAFTA also includes important side agreements concerning labor and the environment. The nations agree to an upward harmonization of environmental standards, but give no authority to any country to enforce domestic environmental standards beyond its borders.[28] Under the United States–Mexico Border XXI Program, five-year goals were set for achieving a cleaner environment. Nine binational groups were created to work on reducing vehicle emissions at border crossings, tracking transport of hazardous wastes, minimizing the risk of chemical spills, reducing solid waste, monitoring children's health risks from pesticide exposures, and reducing the impacts of growth on fish and wildlife resources. Two institutions were set up under NAFTA to promote sustainable environmental practices: the Border Environment Cooperation Commission and the trinational Commission for Environmental Cooperation (CEC). An interesting innovation in the international legislation makes it possible for citizens and nongovernmental organizations (NGOs) to make direct complaints to the CEC.

Unfortunately, dissatisfaction remains as to the efficacy of the environmental agreements in practice. Box 8.1 summarizes some of the strengths and weaknesses. Some have argued that the institutions are underfunded and that the political attention in Mexico given to macroeconomic stabilization took away from progress on

---

Box 8.1.   NAFTA AND THE ENVIRONMENT

Strengths	*Weaknesses*
• Establishes a norm of cooperation • Creates new institutions • Prompted consolidation of environmental legislation in Mexico • New initiatives championed • Encouraged public participation by institutionalizing citizen input and making data available • Self-regulation and adoption of voluntary standards • Citizens have a complaint mechanism • Dispute settlement for persistent non-enforcement	• Governments are ineffective outside of geographic jurisdictions • New institutions are underfunded • Enforcement lags, in part due to budget cuts in Mexico • Many promises unfulfilled due to lack of financing • Inefficiencies make NGO use problematic • Compliance is incomplete • Delays and lack of sanctions impede transforming outcomes • Unwieldy dispute mechanism design discourages use

Source: Jeanne M. Logsdon and Bryan W. Husted, "Mexico's Environmental Performance under NAFTA: The First Five Years," *Journal of Environment and Development* 9, no. 4 (December 2000): 370–83; and Gary Hufbauer and Diana Orejas, "NAFTA and the Environment: Lessons for Trade Policy," Institute for International Economics, Speeches & Testimony online at www.iie.com.

---

the environmental front. One critic noted that only 1 percent of the $2 billion in cleanup funds promised under NAFTA has been spent.[29] The NADBank, or North American Development Bank, which was set up to finance capital requirements of environmental projects, has been slow to review project proposals and has approved funding for only a handful of projects. Environmental conditions along the border are making people sick. Rates of hepatitis, diarrheal diseases, and gastroenteritis are two to six times the Texas state average—and things are worse on the Mexican side. With a doubling of the border population in the past decades, sanitary services are pressed beyond capacity.[30] New mechanisms may be needed to facilitate lending, as the bank's charter limits it to projects viable on commercial terms. It may need a special concessional window to attend to the needs of the poorest and most vulnerable communities, expanding projects to include some of the structural causes of environmental degradation such as housing and poor sanitation.[31] Finally, some analysts are concerned that under NAFTA institutions basic principles such as "polluter pays" are absent. Although a fine may be levied, it is not calculated on the basis of environmental damage, and it is paid by the government as opposed to the industry.[32] Nonetheless, the environmental side agreement within NAFTA can be seen as an accomplishment in that it exists at all; it is the first to go beyond World Trade Organization (WTO) provisions to address ecological interests. Institution building in environmental cooperation is important; nonetheless, this first "greening" of a trade agreement is far from coherent and effective.[33]

The jury is still out on the overall effects of NAFTA. It is, in a certain sense, a work in progress. Since 1991, NAFTA has created more than $250 billion in trade between the United States and Mexico each year.[34] Table 8.10 also shows U.S.–Mexican trade by commodity. It is difficult to separate out the direct effects of the trade agreement, the unrelated negative macroeconomic effects of the *peso* crisis and its aftermath, and the historically positive binational atmosphere NAFTA has generated. Isolating the effects of the trade agreement from a 45-percent devaluation of the *peso,* a 7-percent drop in Mexican output, and a 22-percent fall in Mexican real wages staggers even the economists' imagination.[35] At the same time, the spirit of NAFTA worked to encourage both business confidence and a willingness to work together on binational issues.

Perhaps the greatest gains in NAFTA have been the indirect effects of an improved climate of negotiations between the two countries. One example of this spillover from the economic realm to the policy plate has been in the area of immigration policy. As noted, NAFTA has no provisions for the free movement of labor. What it has created, however, is a better climate for negotiations concerning tough issues surrounding migration policy, particularly along the border area. Whereas these negotiations had always been contentious and crisis oriented, a binational U.S.–Mexican commission on immigration is an example of the spirit of cooperation NAFTA promoted.[36] In 2001, President Vicente Fox of Mexico and President Bush put immigration reform on the table. The White House and Congress, it seems, are finally ready to entertain discussion over changing immigration laws in favor of illegal Mexican migrants. Although negotiations were stalled by changing U.S. priorities following September 11, Fox still hopes to conclude an immigration deal.[37]

Beyond NAFTA, numerous free trade agreements were signed in the 1990s. As is shown in table 8.11, a network of free trade agreements links the region, consistent with ECLAC's concept of "open regionalism." The web of bilateral agreements is loosely coordinated through the Asociación Latinoamericana de Integración (ALADI), the successful organization established in 1980 to replace the Latin American Integration Association (LAIA). We will discuss three of the regional arrangements in depth: **Mercosur,** the **Andean Community,** and the **Central American Common Market.**

> ### QUESTION FOR THOUGHT
>
> NAFTA has been called an "iterative process." That is, it is a document flexible enough to allow for change. What priorities would you define to strengthen North American trade?

MERCOSUR

The second-largest trading agreement in the region after NAFTA is Mercosur. The groundwork for Mercosur began with a bilateral program signed in July 1986 between Argentina and Brazil for industrial integration. Extending from Brazil's tropical jungles to the sub-Antarctic zone of Argentina in Tierra del Fuego, Mercosur countries account for approximately half the Latin American land mass and GDP, 43 percent of the population, and 33 percent of regional trade. Because Mercosur countries include some of the world's richest agricultural and mineral resources, there are

Table 8.11. Trade Agreements in the Americas in the 1990s

Agreements in Force	Date of Signature	Entry into Force
Caribbean Community (CARICOM)	1973	1973
Chile–Mexico	1991	1992
Central American Common Market (CACM)	1960	1961
Chile–Venezuela	1993	1993
North American Free Trade Agreement (NAFTA)	1992	1994
Colombia–Chile	1993	1994
Southern Cone Common Market (Mercosur)	1991	1995
Costa Rica–Mexico	1994	1995
Group of Three (G-3)	1994	1995
Bolivia–Mexico	1994	1995
Chile–Ecuador	1994	1995
Andean Community	1969	1969
Chile–Mercosur	1996	1996
Canada–Chile	1996	1997
Bolivia–Mercosur	1996	1997
Mexico–Nicaragua	1997	1998
Chile-Peru	1998	1998
CACM–Dominican Republic	1998	1999
CARICOM–Dominican Republic	1998	1999
Mexico–European Union	1999	2000
CACM–Chile	2000	2001
Mexico–Northern Triangle	2000	2001
Chile–United States	2003	2003/4

Source: Robert Delvin and Antoni Estevadeordal. "What's New in the New Regionalism in the Americas?" IADB, Working Paper no. 6 (Buenos Aires, 2001). Available online at www.iadb.org/intal/pub.

ample opportunities for growth and production. The 1991 Treaty of Asunción, including Uruguay and Paraguay, expanded this bilateral agreement to include progressive, automatic tariff reduction; a CET (common external tariff) of 20 percent for 85 percent of goods; and harmonization of macroeconomic policies. Exceptions were made for four years to the free trade in textiles, steel, automobiles, and petrochemicals.

Chile initially did not join the agreement because it wanted to maintain a lower external tariff than the Mercosur countries, although in 1996 it signed a bilateral agreement with the union as an associate member. Bolivia became an associate member in 1997. Mercosur places fourth among the world's economic blocs, with more than $750 billion in GNP and more than 220 million inhabitants. In 1999, Mercosur and the EU commenced talks that could lead to a free market agreement, perhaps edging the United States out. The EU's two-way trade with Mercosur totaled U.S.$47 billion in 2000. In particular, Europe is active in the infrastructure arena, buying telephone companies and utilities in Brazil, Chile, Peru, and Argentina. Seven of the ten largest private companies in Brazil are European owned; only two are dominated by Americans.[38]

Administratively, Mercosur is governed by six institutions. The council, a political leadership group, is composed of the foreign relations and economics ministers of the four member states and oversees all other Mercosur institutions, with decision-making authority over member state institutions. The Common Market Group, or the executive organization of the community, has both policy-making and administrative responsibilities. The Mercosur Commerce Commission (MCC) is divided into eleven working groups charged with monitoring the common commercial policy, including the common external tariff and competition policy. The joint Parliamentary Commission is an advisory commission representing national legislatures; the Forum, a consultative body, reflects the views of various sectors such as producers, consumers, workers, and merchants; and a small secretariat with a permanent staff of about thirty professionals headquartered in Montevideo, Uruguay, completes the list. In comparison to the autonomy built into EU institutions, political control in Mercosur resides in the hands of the member states. In the European Union, "European" delegates are elected; in Mercosur, institutions are staffed by national representatives.

Mercosur is not yet a true common market. Although members have achieved a customs union, full market status targeted for 2006 awaits progress in the coordination of economic, legislative, environmental, infrastructure, and technology policies. Member countries face the hard task of harmonizing standards and establishing a supranational bureaucracy beyond the national control of member states. Evaluated by the criteria of common market, Mercosur is still a bit thin. Nonetheless, the achievements of Mercosur are important, particularly in locking in progress toward free trade in the region.[39] It is also important to remember that economic unions such as the EU have been decades in the making; slow progress in negotiating tough international issues is rather predictable.

Trade within Mercosur quadrupled since 1990, growing from approximately U.S.$4.1 billion in 1990 to more than U.S.$17.6 billion in 2000. Argentina sells more than one-third of its exports—especially agricultural and natural resource products—to Brazil, making Brazil Argentina's largest trading partner after the United States. Brazilian multinationals have set up shop in Argentina. International automakers have taken advantage of the new scale economies to expand auto production in the region. Investments in the auto sector were expected to be close to $20 billion for 1994–2000, a vote of confidence in the potential of the region's economies.[40] As shown in table 8.12, trade within the Mercosur subregion accounts for more than 20 percent of the countries' total net trade. This is large compared to any of the other subregional arrangements, in part due to the large internal market presented by Brazil. Cost margins have come down, there has been some rationalization of production patterns to take advantage of larger scale, and there has been an increase in total factor productivity growth with increased trade. Once again, however, we are confronted with the problem of simultaneous changes. It is unclear whether these improvements are caused by Mercosur policies or by the concurrent process of trade liberalization and economic restructuring aggressively pursued by the countries.[41] Some have also questioned whether the cross-border production, particularly in heavy goods, is trade diverting and therefore lowering efficiency.[42] Others suggest that overall trade in Mercosur countries has increased productivity.[43]

Harmonization of monetary and tax policies has had less success, partly due to the late stabilization of Brazil under the *Real* plan. Imbalances in the Brazilian

Table 8.12.   Western Hemisphere: Total Intraregional Exports, 1990–2000 (millions of U.S.$)

	1990	1995	2000	Average Annual % Growth, 1990–2000
Western Hemisphere				
Total Exports	632,702.0	994,328.0	1,308,489.0	
% growth	8.3	15.8	7.6	7.5
Intra-Hemispheric Exports	302,322.0	522,419.0	799,711.0	
% growth	9.5	12.1	9.9	10.2
Intra/Total	47.8	52.5	61.1	
LAC				
Total Exports	136,177.0	220,411.0	340,079.0	
% growth	10.4	20.7	20.7	9.6
Intra-LAC Exports	16,917.0	41,782.0	52,155.0	
% growth	9.0	19.5	19.8	11.9
Intra/Total	12.4	19.0	15.3	
Andean Community				
Total Exports	31,751.0	38,259.0	57,236.0	
% growth	29.0	11.7	32.5	6.1
Intra-Andean Exports	1,324.0	4,735.0	5,191.0	
% growth	33.0	38.2	31.8	14.6
Intra/Total	4.2	12.4	9.1	
CACM				
Total Exports	4,046.0	6,864.0	12,765.0	
% growth	13.1	24.6	14.2	12.2
Intra-CACM Exports	658.0	1,456.0	2,571.0	
% growth	14.9	18.5	12.3	14.6
Intra/Total	16.3	21.2	20.1	
Mercosur				
Total Exports	46,402.0	70,402.0	84,659.0	
% growth	-0.3	13.3	13.9	6.2
Intra-Mercosur Exports	4,127.0	14,384.0	17,698.0	
% growth	7.6	20.3	16.7	15.7
Intra/Total	8.9	20.4	20.9	
Mercosur, Chile, and Bolivia (MCB)				
Total Exports	55,617.0	87,977.0	104,120.0	
% growth	0.5	17.6	14.0	6.5
Intra-MCB Exports	6,455.0	20,074.0	24,539.0	
% growth	3.1	22.0	18.6	14.3
Intra/Total	11.6	22.8	23.6	
NAFTA				
Total Exports	537,226.0	853,694.0	1,134,834.0	
% growth	8.0	15.7	5.9	7.8
Intra-NAFTA Exports	229,930.0	393,113.0	643,140.0	
% growth	9.5	10.9	9.9	10.8
Intra/Total	42.8	46.0	56.7	

Source: IADB, Statistics and Quantitative Analysis Unit and Integration (INT/STA), Trade and Hemispheric Issues Division (INT/ITD). "Periodic Note on Integration and Trade in the Americas," Dec. 2001, table 3.

economy in 1997, in part driven by its policy of using a strong currency to control inflation, resulted in temporary import limits against Mercosur partners. Common industrial policies to direct resources toward new areas have also lagged. The asymmetrical nature of the economies makes noncompliance difficult to address. Brazil's economy overwhelms that of Argentina. For example, just the increase in output in one year of Brazil's beer giant Brahma was equal to Argentina's entire consumption of brew. Given its size, Brazil can act without much regard for the effects a policy may have on Mercosur partners. Relatively weak enforcement institutions make unilateral actions on Brazil's part unpunishable.

Economic instability has rocked Mercosur. Brazil's move to a floating exchange rate in 1999 pressured the already fragile Argentine economy. The collapse of the Argentine convertibility plan in 2001–2002 and its ensuing economic chaos has led to a sharp decline in intraregional trade. After expanding an average 16 percent a year during the 1990s, such trade declined by almost 10 percent in 2001, with all four Mercosur countries recording negative growth. Mercosur's extraregional exports did well, in part driven by Brazil's currency depreciation.[44] Mercosur holds promise but also pitfalls for participant countries. In the wake of the Brazilian crisis of 1998–1999 and the Argentine collapse of 2001–2002 Mercosur may be behaving slightly more like a free trade area than a common market, turning outward to European and U.S. markets as a source of dynamism. Mercosur countries, in light of the crisis, pushed for reductions on tariffs in industrial countries on agricultural policies, with the hopes of easing recession through traditional export markets.[45] Internal economic disruptions have made multilateralism the short-term trade strategy. This, however, underscores that fact that multilateralism, or working through the WTO, can be a complementary strategy to the new regionalism, encouraging a flexibility in moving forward in the global arena.

OTHER REGIONAL TRADING AGREEMENTS

The **Andean Community** has a long but uneven history. A modern realization of independence hero Simón Bolívar's vision of unification, the treaty was signed in 1969. It provided for free commerce between Bolivia, Colombia, Ecuador, Venezuela, and Peru, with a common external tariff adopted.[46] The hope was that subregional production would overcome the limitation of economies of scale faced under import substitution industrialization. Problems in the early stages of the Andean Pact derived in large part from political disputes as well as very different domestic economic policies and goals. An ambitious emphasis on industrial planning and joint industrialization was more than the meager sums dedicated to the projects could support, particularly as disputes arose between the more powerful countries and the smaller nations. Policies governing foreign capital were also controversial. International investment disputes led nations to ban foreigners from investing in activities that would compete with existing firms; strict controls were also placed on foreign ownership and profit remittances.[47]

With greater contemporary homogeneity in economic policies, there are improved prospects for the development of subregional trade. Exports within the

Andean Community have increased at an average annual rate of 12.9 percent from 1990 to 1999. Accomplishments in the 1990s include establishing a free trade area among four of its five member countries;[48] negotiating a common external tariff (CET): and the adoption of sectoral policies in foreign investment, intellectual property rights, and air transportation. **Trade creation** seems to dominate **trade diversion** in an assessment of the impacts of the union. The regional market appeared to play a key role in promoting export expansion. Scale economies in intra-industry trade between Andean partners are preparing firms for competition in the global marketplace.[49] The Andean free trade area is largely complete, with Peru committed to eliminating remaining barriers to intraregional trade by 2005. Progress toward a CET, however, is stalled, although the Andean presidents pledged to transform the community into a common market by 2005. Economic and political setbacks among member nations have led to the use of unilateral, trade-distorting measures, pressuring the system. Nonetheless, the commitment to a common market agenda is widespread, supported by both business and labor.

The **Central American Common Market,** formed in 1960, has had a rocky history. Progress in the 1970s was set back by geopolitical struggles and civil war in the region. Although by 1970 intraregional trade had reached 26 percent, small market size and social revolutions turned the clock back. The 1990s, however, saw new resolve to exploit the economies of scale offered by integration. Both business and civil society have taken leadership roles in propelling integration efforts forward. Given that most countries in the Central American region have already pursued trade liberalization, convergence at a low CET between 0 and 20 percent was achieved. Countries have liberalized capital accounts, and investment is returning to the region. Nonetheless, progress by mid-decade was stalled by macroeconomic instability, weak infrastructure, and unskilled human capital. Priorities of the new regional economic integration (REI) program include strengthening the legal and institutional framework; joint actions to reduce debt; and promoting cooperation on sectoral issues such as upgrading infrastructure in transport, energy, and telecommunications. Mexico and the Central American countries have announced an infrastructure strategy "Puebla-Panama Plan" that would also incorporate social and environmental dimensions.[50] The prospect of a free trade agreement with the United States, announced in January 2002, has given new impetus to breaking down barriers not only with their largest market to the north but also among themselves. Trade is seen as the regional catalyst for growth.

> **QUESTION FOR THOUGHT**
>
> What have been the costs and benefits of subregional trade organizations? What measures should be considered to strengthen integration efforts?

TOWARD A HEMISPHERIC FREE TRADE AGREEMENT?

Should subregional hemispheric efforts be linked in a regional free trade agreement? Would a hemispheric free trade agreement benefit the United States? Latin

Figure 8.1.   U.S. Trade by Region, 2000

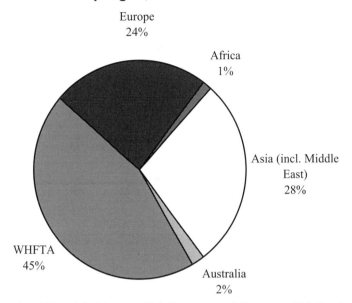

Source: International Trade Administration, U.S. Department of Commerce, *U.S. Foreign Trade Highlights* (Washington, D.C.: U.S. Department of Commerce, 2001). Available at www.ita.doc.gov/industry/otea/usfth/aggregate/HL00T06.txt.

America is a growing market for U.S. exports. From the perspective of the United States, the answer in part depends on the economic importance of the hemisphere. Figure 8.1 shows U.S. trade broken down by trading region. The Western Hemisphere Free Trade Agreement (WHFTA) member countries accounted for 45 percent of U.S. trade. The United States sells more to Chile than to India and more to Central America than all of Eastern Europe.[51] Brazil, with its large population, is seen as a huge potential market; the United States currently sells more there than in China. Table 8.13 gives a more detailed breakdown of U.S. trade.

Of particular importance to the United States are oil imports from the region. A strong argument for improving relations in the hemisphere is protecting energy security. Over one-third of U.S. oil imports come from Latin America; as shown in table 8.14, Mexico and Venezuela in 2001 were among the largest suppliers. OLADE, the Latin American Energy Organization, was formed to promote cooperative efforts for conservation, sales, and development of oil resources in the region. Given the shorter distances to transport oil compared to the East, Latin American oil sources are more secure, with shorter, less-congested routes to travel. After the decontrol of many state-owned oil companies, there has been an increased trend in cross-border ventures, particularly with Venezuela. As shown in table 8.14, in 2001, Venezuela was the second leading source of foreign crude oil for the United State (following Canada), with 13.2 percent of U.S. imports; Mexico ranked fourth.[52] The oil sector gives the United States a strong incentive for enhanced integration in the Latin American region.

Table 8.13.   U.S. Exports, Imports, and Balance of Goods by Selected Countries and Geographic Areas, 2002 (not seasonally adjusted, millions of U.S.$)

	Balance	Exports	Imports
U.S. Total Balance of Payments Basis	−132,679	224,538	357,217
North America	−28,181	83,279	111,459
Canada	−16,387	52,495	68,882
Mexico	−11,793	30,784	42,577
South/Central America	−3,390	16,722	20,113
Argentina	−468	467	934
Brazil	−274	4,161	4,435
Chile	−704	870	1,574
Colombia	−539	1,166	1,705
Western Europe	−22,531	53,584	76,116
European Union	−21,138	48,986	70,124
Finland	−463	584	1,046
France	−2,853	6,784	9,637
Italy	−4,209	3,239	7,447
United Kingdom	−1,341	11,516	12,857
Eastern Europe/FSR	−2,309	3,716	6,025
Russia	−807	805	1,611
Pacific Rim Countries	−61,753	55,802	117,555
China	−26,536	6,250	32,786
Japan	−22,913	16,424	39,337
Hong Kong	−1,284	3,986	2,703
Korea	−4,259	7,001	11,261
Singapore	841	5,489	4,647
Taiwan	−4,541	5,448	9,988
OPEC	−9,926	5,630	15,556
Indonesia	−2,190	756	2,946
Nigeria	−1,209	373	1,583
Saudi Arabia	−2,225	1,349	3,574
Venezuela	−2,356	1,451	3,807

Source: Report FT900, Bureau of the Census, Foreign Trade Division, June 2002, exhibit 6. Available online at www.census.gov/foreigntrade/www.press.html.
Note: This exhibit is not additive. Selected countries are included in more than one area grouping. Venezuela is included in both OPEC and Other South/Central America.

Many other factors contribute to making Latin America a natural market for U.S. business. These range from historical ties in the Andean region, where the United States holds 35 percent of the market share, to dominance of the U.S. media in Central America, where consumers have a preference for American products. The U.S. Department of Commerce is strongly encouraging U.S. business to invest

Table 8.14.   U.S. Oil Imports from Latin America and Selected Countries, 2001 (% of U.S. total oil imports)

Country	Amount	Ranking among Top 20
Venezuela	13.2	2
Mexico	10.1	4
Colombia	2.9	10
Argentina	1.1	14
Brazil	1.1	15
Ecuador	1.0	17
Trinidad & Tobago	0.9	18
Canada	14.4	1
Saudi Arabia	12.4	3
Nigeria	8.5	5

Source: International Trade Organization, *Top 20 Suppliers of Petroleum Products to the U.S. in 2001,* 8 April 2002. Available at www.ita.doc.gov/td/industry/otea/usfth/aggregate/H01t33.pdf.

in the region because it expects the real growth rate of the region to equal or exceed that of any other region by the year 2010.

At the Summit of the Americas, held in Miami in December 1994, regional presidents agreed to negotiate a Western Hemisphere Free Trade Agreement by the year 2005. It should be noted that negotiations are not implementation: the agreement may be phased in over a period of fifteen or twenty years. The idea behind the FTAA, the Free Trade Area of the Americas, is the consolidation of the nearly twenty-five free trade pacts already operating in a region of nearly eight hundred million inhabitants. Is this a feasible notion? Widely different levels of economic development as well as divergent interests make this process fraught with difficulty. For the FTAA to move forward, argues Enrique Iglesias, head of the Inter-American Development Bank (IADB), a second generation of structural reforms must take place, in areas such as education, pensions, health, modernization of the state, and financial regulation, to promote competitiveness on the part of Latin America. Hemispheric integration should drive structural reform.

Is an FTAA the best approach to deepening trade ties in the region? Some contend that subregional units should be the building blocks. Brazil has been a strong proponent of this approach. Iglesias rejects the either/or nature of this question. He argues that the process of subregional integration in the formation of subregional blocks is complementary to a hemispheric agreement.[53] Others think that trading blocs—hemispheric or subregional—are trade diverting. On the other hand, proponents of the FTAA suggest that the FTAA is "WTO-plus." That is, it moves beyond the issues on the worldwide trade agenda to push barriers in services, intellectual property, and government procurement.[54]

In a May 1997 meeting of trade ministers from thirty-four countries, little progress was made, in part due to divergent interests on the part of some Mercosur members. Their position has been that consolidation of Mercosur prior to a hemispheric agreement will strengthen Latin America's bargaining position vis-à-vis the United States. On the part of the United States, President Clinton was denied congressional authorization in November 1997 for fast-track authority to negotiate the FTAA. Fast-track authority (renamed trade promotion authority by President Bush) would have permitted the president to negotiate a package to present to Congress for an up or down vote. Because trade agreements are complicated and different constituencies would like to pick them apart after they are constructed, fast-track authority improves the likelihood of the final passage of an agreement. President Bush was granted fast-track authority in 2002, although the redirection of administration energies toward counterterrorism following September 11 and economic turmoil in Latin America call into question achieving a Free Trade Area of the Americas agreement by the deadline of 2005. Nevertheless, some progress has been made. The movement toward a free trade agreement in the hemisphere can be seen as a process of dialogue among hemispheric partners on key international issues. Interestingly, the initiatives of the April 1998 hemispheric summit in Santiago, Chile, had little trade content, focusing on issues of technology, education, gender, and the environment. Table 8.15 illustrates the range of issues included in the 2001 Quebec Plan of Action—reflecting work on key labor, environmental, gender, and cultural issues along with trade negotiations.

There was limited attention in either the Santiago Summit or the Quebec Plan of Action directly related to trade. Consistent with the recommendation of the Inter-American Bank's Enrique Iglesias, advances first need to be made on the social and environmental agendas before meaningful integration can take place in the hemisphere. Whether these goals will be realized will be a function of whether political will toward integration is strong enough to overcome regional, political, social, and economic differences.

From a business perspective, an FTAA with Latin America may bring direct and indirect benefits. In addition to the elimination of tariffs and other restrictions on goods and services and changes in rules governing investment practices, the FTAA provides an opportunity to design mechanisms to ensure that governments do not divert from existing environmental, health, safety, or labor measures to gain competitive advantage in trade or investment. It also aims at increasing transparency in both government policies and practices in areas affecting business, particularly in establishing standards and regulatory requirements, improving intellectual property protec-

> **QUESTION FOR THOUGHT**
>
> Is a hemispheric free trade agreement good for Latin America? Which countries are likely to benefit most? Which countries are likely to have high costs? What are the lessons from NAFTA?

tion rights, and adhering to Organization of American States (OAS) and Organisation for Cooperation and Economic Development (OECD) accords to combat corrupt business practices.[55] In this way, the FTAA provides a negotiating forum for issues that are created by the process of globalization of trade and finance, but are outside pure market mechanisms for resolution.

Table 8.15. Summit of the Americas—Quebec Plan of Action (selected issues)

Making democracy work better	Share best practices and technologies to increase citizen participation and enhance electoral mechanisms. Promote audit and oversight of public accounts.
Human rights and fundamental freedoms	Integrate fully the human rights of women and children into the work of hemispheric institutions and develop additional policies to combat violence against both groups.
Justice, rule of law, and security of the individual	Support public and private initiatives to educate people about their rights relating to access to justice.
Hemispheric security	Continue strengthening hemispheric efforts against drugs and develop inter-American strategies to combat drug trade. Encourage hemispheric cooperation to prevent, combat, and eliminate all forms of terrorism.
Civil society	Promote participation of all minority groups in forging a stronger civil society and develop education programs to provide democracy and human rights education.
Trade, investment, and financial stability	Ensure the transparency of the FTAA negotiating process and full participation of all Latin American countries in the FTAA, taking into consideration the differences in the levels of development and size of the economies of the Hemisphere.
Infrastructure and regulatory environment	Modernize national laws to reflect a pro-competitive approach and encourage greater productivity of all sectors through distance education, tele-health, and Internet-based industries.
Disaster management	Develop the capacity to forecast, prepare for, and mitigate the potential impacts of natural and man-made hazards.
Environmental foundation for sustainable development	Promote the adoption of urgent actions toward sustainable forest management and reaffirm a commitment to advancing environmental stewardship in the area of energy.
Labor and employment	Continue to work toward the elimination of child labor and promote and protect the rights of all workers, particularly those of working women.
Growth and equity	Acknowledge the need for development financing, including aid from bilateral donors and commit to developing and maintaining access to international capital markets. Support the formation of business incubators, joint projects, national competitiveness programs, and credit unions.
Education	Support and promote lifelong learning by providing the use of information and communications technology; enhance the performance of teachers by improving their conditions of service.
Health	Intensify efforts and promote best practices to reduce maternal and infant mortality and provide quality reproductive health care and services for women, men and adolescents. Commit, at the highest level, to combat HIV/AIDS and its consequences.
Gender equality	Recognize that women's full and equal participation in development is central to the reduction of poverty.
Indigenous peoples	Promote and enhance, particularly in the area of education, the understanding of the contribution made by indigenous peoples in shaping the national identity of the countries in which they live
Cultural diversity	Recognize that respect for cultural diversity contributes to social and economic dynamism and positively promotes good governance, social cohesion, human development, human rights, and peaceful coexistence.

Source: Summit of the Americas, *Quebec Plan of Action,* Third Summit of the Americas, Quebec City, Canada, April 20–22, 2001.
Note: For a full set of issues, refer to Quebec Plan of Action, available online at www.summit-americas.org.

Free Trade and Trade Integration Revisited

Latin America has radically reoriented its trade approach in the past two decades. It has gone from a relatively inward-looking to an outwardly oriented development model. Much of this has taken place through unilateral changes in accord with global trading rules. A second wave of trade reform was prompted by the movement to subregional trading arrangements. These arrangements have encouraged countries to negotiate some of the tougher issues of market access and management of externalities. A spirit of neighborliness is evolving in the region, where collective goals figure prominently on the agenda of the hemisphere's leaders. Whether the countries of the hemisphere will be able to capitalize on this momentum to create a regional trading system is uncertain. Neighborliness is somewhat easier at the subregional level, where countries may share common economic characteristics or have a clear incentive to solve common border problems. In the spirit of cooperation, we should also not forget to ask again whether such a regional regime is desirable. Will a hemispheric agreement increase trade or divert trade from other, more efficient suppliers in the world? Nevertheless, in the end it may, like NAFTA, be a story less of pure economic effects and more of the ways in which a genuine trade partnership may open the door to solutions on tough problems facing the region on the social and environmental agendas. The initiatives of the Santiago Summit and Quebec Summits indicate a willingness to pursue the social agenda. After we look at the effects of the new economic model on sources of competitiveness in the industrial and agricultural sectors in chapters 9 and 10, we will turn to these difficult issues of poverty, human capital formation, and environmental degradation that require remediation for the nations of the region to pursue genuinely sustainable and dynamic integrated development.

Key Concepts

Andean Community
Central American
    Common Market
common market
customs union
economic union

factor price equalization
free trade area
Heckscher–Ohlin
    theorem
Mercosur
NAFTA

open regionalism
Stolper–Samuelson effect
theory of comparative
    advantage
trade creation
trade diversion

Chapter Summary

The Theory of Free Trade

- The theoretical underpinning of free trade is the theory of comparative advantage, which states that countries should trade those goods they can most efficiently produce to maximize global output. Neoclassical trade theory posits that trade will benefit the least advantaged through raising the price of labor in developing countries as well as bring factor prices into global equilibrium.

- Critics of free trade contend that, in practice, there are few gains from trade for developing countries. From a dependency, gender, and environmental standpoint, critics believe that free trade can actually damage a country's overall welfare by perpetrating trade in commodities with low value added, produced through exportative means that pressure fragile environments.

- Although Asia prospered from export-oriented growth during the 1980s, Latin America experienced deteriorating current account deficits. Based on Asia's success, trade liberalization was promoted by the international community as a way of improving growth conditions in Latin America.

- Policymakers pursuing trade liberalization should consider an adequate time frame, appropriate exchange rates, trade adjustment assistance, and fiscal reform.

- Reduced tariffs in Latin America have effectively increased the flow of exports and imports in the region. The composition of goods has changed somewhat, although primary products continue to play a dominant role in the export sector.

Integration

- There are four ways a country can integrate its markets: by establishing a free trade area, a customs union, a common market, or an economic union. Integration encourages economies of scale, opens markets, and promotes credibility within the region. If trade diversion occurs, however, the costs of integration may be high.

- NAFTA, a regional trade agreement among the United States, Canada, and Mexico, sought to decrease tariffs over a ten-year period and thereby increase trade in the region. The controversy surrounding the agreement was based upon fears that NAFTA would lead to job loss in the North, contribute to environmental degradation, and put domestic corporations out of business in the South.

- Mercosur is a customs union comprised of Brazil, Argentina, Uruguay, and Paraguay, with Chile and Bolivia as associate members. Since its inception, trade has increased not only among the member states but with the European Union as well. Harmonization of policies has, however, proved difficult. Two other regional agreements, the Andean Community and the Central American Common Market, have been less successful in promoting intraregional trade.

- The increased importance of Latin America as a trading partner for the United States has led many to negotiations for a Free Trade Area of the Americas. Despite the increase in interest among many Latin American countries and the United States, achieving the FTAA by the target date of 2005 could prove difficult due to political tension, social inequality and economic instability.

Notes

1. David Dollar and Aart Kraay, "Trade, Growth and Poverty," Development Research Group, the World Bank, June 2001, Research paper posted at www.worldbank.org.

2. Carlos Díaz Alejandro, "International Markets for LCDs: The Old and the New," *American Economic Review,* May 1978, pp. 254–69.

3. Schumpeter argued that shocks to an industry, like crises in the life of an individual, might force the sector to grow and adapt. Industries, like people, he suggested, sometimes need to be pushed to try something different.

4. Sebastian Edwards, "The Opening of Latin America," in *Crisis and Reform in Latin America: From Despair to Hope* (New York: Oxford University Press, 1995).

5. Dani Rodrik, "The Global Governance of Trade as If Development Really Mattered," United Nations Development Programme, October 2001, accessed at www.undp.org.

6. This section summarizes the findings of Sebastian Edwards and Daniel Lederman, *The Political Economy of Unilateral Trade Liberalization: The Case of Chile,* National Bureau of Economic Research Working Paper no. 6510 (Cambridge, Mass.: National Bureau of Economic Research, 1998). Available at www.nber.org/papers/w6510.

7. Andrew Zimbalist, "Costa Rica," in *Struggle against Dependence: Nontraditional Export Growth in Central America and the Caribbean,* ed. Eva Paus (Boulder, Colo.: Westview, 1988), 26.

8. WTO, Merchandise exports of Latin America by destination, 2000, www.wto.org.

9. All data are from Commission Economica Para America Latina, *Indicadores Económicos* (Santiago, Chile: Comisión Económica Para América Latina, 2001).

10. Warburg Dillon Read, *The Latin American Adviser,* 9 July 1998, p. 16 (fax newsletter).

11. Ricardo Ffrench-Davis, comment on L. Allan Winters, "Assessing Regional Integration," in *Trade: Towards Open Regionalism,* proceedings of the 1997 World Bank Conference on Development in Latin America and the Caribbean (Washington, D.C.: World Bank, 1998), 73–74.

12. Sarath Rajapatirana, *Trade Policies in Latin America and the Caribbean: Priorities, Progress, and Prospects* (San Francisco: International Center for Economic Growth, 1997), 15.

13. Jagdish Bhagwati, "The FTAA Is *Not* Free Trade," in *Trade: Towards Open Regionalism,* proceedings of the 1997 World Bank Conference on Development in Latin America and the Caribbean (Washington, D.C.: World Bank, 1998).

14. L. Allan Winters, "Assessing Regional Integration."

15. Enrique V. Iglesias, "The Search for a New Economic Consensus in Latin America," in *The Legacy of Raúl Prebisch,* ed. Enrique V. Iglesias (Washington, D.C.: IADB, 1994), 97.

16. Robert Devlin and Antoni Estevadeordal, "What's New in the New Regionalism in the Americas?" INTAL Working Paper no. 6, Inter-American Development Bank, Integration and Regional Programs Department, May 2001, 7–8.

17. Domestic lobbies in both countries kept the tariffs on textiles high.

18. Arvind Panagariya, "The Free Trade Area of the Americas: Good for Latin America?" *World Economy* 19, no. 5 (1996): 496.

19. Magnus Blomström and Ari Kokko, *Regional Integration and Foreign Direct Investment,* National Bureau of Economic Research Working Paper no. 6019 (Cambridge, Mass.: National Bureau of Economic Research, 1997). The U.S. Foreign Direct Investment stock went from U.S.$13,370 million in 1992 to U.S.$14,037 million; this represents a decline from 2.73 percent of total U.S. foreign direct investment to 1.97 percent.

20. "NAFTA: Where's That Giant Sucking Sound?" *BusinessWeek,* 7 July 1997, p. 45. Cites study by Kate Bronfenbrenner of Cornell University.

21. "NAFTA: Where's That Giant Sucking Sound?"

22. Anne Krueger, "NAFTA's Effects: A Preliminary Assessment," *World Economy,* June 2000, p. 762

23. "NAFTA: Where's That Giant Sucking Sound?" and Jeffrey J. Schott, "NAFTA: An Interim Report," in *Trade: Towards Open Regionalism,* proceedings of the 1997 World Bank Conference on Development in Latin America and the Caribbean (Washington, D.C.: World Bank, 1998).

24. Employment Policy Foundation, "Open Trade: The 'Fast Track' to Higher Living Standards," *Contemporary Issues in Employment and Workplace Policy* 111, no. 10 (October 1997). Internet publication available at epfnet.org.

25. Sidney Weintraub, "In the Debate about NAFTA, Just the Facts, Please," *Wall Street Journal,* 20 June 1997, p. A19.

26. *2001 National Trade Estimate Report on Foreign Trade Barriers* www.ustr.gov/html/2001_mexico.pdf.

27. USTR, Report, *NAFTA at Eight: A Foundation for Economic Growth,* May 28, 2002 www.ustr.gov/naftareport/nafta8_brochure-eng.pdf.

28. Claudia Schatan, "Lessons from the Mexican Environmental Experience: First Results from NAFTA," in *The Environment and International Trade Negotiations: Developing Country Stakes,* ed. Diana Tussie (New York: St. Martin's Press in association with International Development Research Center, 2000).

29. Congressman David Bonior, "I Told You So," editorial, *New York Times,* 13 July 1997.

30. Sam Howe Verhovek, "Pollution Problems Fester South of the Border," *New York Times,* 4 July 1998. Online edition.

31. Data from Lustig's comment on Jeffrey J. Schott, "NAFTA: An Interim Report," 127.

32. Schatan, 178.

33. Schatan, 184.

34. "Fox, Bush promote closer U.S.-Mexican partnership," Inside Politics, Sept. 2001, available online at www.cnn.com.

35. Data from Lustig's comment on Jeffrey J. Schott, "NAFTA: An Interim Report," 125.

36. Report on the Binational Commission, International Studies Association meetings, Washington, D.C., 20 February 1999.

37. Tony Karon, "Person of the Week: President Vicente Fox," available online at www.TIME.com, June 13, 2002.

38. John Templeman, "Is Europe Elbowing the U.S. Out of South America?" *BusinessWeek,* 4 August 1997, p. 56.

39. *Argentina Business: The Portable Encyclopedia for Doing Business with Argentina* (San Rafael, Calif.: World Trade Press, 1995).

40. "Auto Industry Delivers Vote of Confidence in Brazil and Mercosur," *Latin American Weekly Report,* 3 February 1998, p. 49.

41. Danny Lepziger, Claudio Frischtak, Homi J. Kharas, and John F. Normand, "Mercosur: Integration and Industrial Policy," *World Economy* 20, no. 5 (1997): 596.

42. A study by Alexander Yeats at the World Bank caused an uproar when it argued that Mercosur lowered efficiency. Michael Phillip, "South American Trade Pact Is under Fire," *Wall Street Journal,* 23 October 1996.

43. World Bank, *Towards Open Regionalism* (Washington, D.C.: World Bank, 1998).

44. INTAL, *Periodic Note on Integration and Trade in the Americas,* December 2001.

45. Diana Jean Schemo, "A Latin Bloc Asks U.S. and Europe to Ease Trade Barriers," *New York Times,* 23 February 1999. Online edition.

46. Venezuela joined in 1973; Chile was a member between 1969 and 1976.

47. Devlin and Estevadeordal, "What's New in the New Regionalism in the Americas, 24.

48. Peru does not participate.

49. Juan José Echavarría, "Trade Flow in the Andean Countries: Unilateral Liberalization or Regional Preferences," in *Trade: Towards Open Regionalism,* proceedings of the 1997 World Bank Conference on Development in Latin America and the Caribbean (Washington, D.C.: World Bank, 1998), 95.

50. Eduardo Lizano and José M. Salazar-Xirinach, "Central American Common Market and Hemispheric Free Trade," in *Integrating the Hemisphere, 1997: The Inter-American Dialogue,* ed. Ana Julia Jatar and Sidney Weintraub (Santa Fé de Bogotá, Colombia: Tercer Mundo, 1997).

51. Thomas F. McLarty, "Hemispheric Free Trade Is Still a National Priority," *Wall Street Journal,* 26 May 1995, p. A11. Facts confirmed in *U.S. Total Exports to Individual Countries, 1991–1997.* Available at www.ita.doc.gov.

52. International Trade Administration, Top 20 Suppliers of Petroleum, www.ita.gov.

53. As reported in "The Key Points of the FTAA Agenda," *Latin American Weekly Report,* WR-97-20 (1997), p. 230.

54. Paulo Wrobel, "A Free Trade Area of the Americas in 2005?" *International Affairs* 74, no. 3 (1998): 547–61.

55. Robert Mosbacher, chairman, Council of the Americas, "Trade Expansion within the Americas: A U.S. Business Perspective," remarks at the Chile–United States Issues Round Table, Crown Plaza Hotel, Santiago, Chile, 17 April 1998.

INTERNATIONAL INDUSTRIAL COMPETITIVENESS

Improving the Quality of Labor, Technology, and Infrastructure

CHAPTER NINE

Increasing labor productivity is a key challenge to compete in global markets.
(Courtesy of David Mangurian and the Inter-American Development Bank.)

263

Competitive participation in global markets that promotes equitable growth in Latin America demands radical changes in how inputs are combined to create output in the region. As shown in table 9.1, Latin America scores poorly on international competitiveness rankings. Latin America has been through a wrenching structural transformation from inward to outward-looking growth and grueling macroeconomic stabilization policies. Yet these changes have not positively transformed the lives of most Latin Americans. Growth rates in Latin America have not been sufficiently strong to lift its population from poverty. Despite a strong global economy, average annual regional growth only hit 3.3 percent. This modest change only improved average income by 1.5 percent. If regional growth had matched the 3.5 percent rate of some groups of Asian countries, eighty million of the 170 million poor would have been lifted from poverty.[1] If income distribution hadn't worsened in the region, another forty-five million would have escaped the indignity of living on less than $2 a day. Social and political protest around the region underscores the dissatisfaction with the results of the new economic model. The puzzle becomes how to promote dynamic, equitable growth.

Human capital is at the center of enhanced productivity. Yet as we will see in later chapters, there has been an underinvestment in health and education in the

Table 9.1.   Growth Competitiveness Rankings of the Americas, 2001–2002

Country	World Ranking
United States	2
Canada	3
Chile	27
Costa Rica	35
Trinidad & Tobago	38
Mexico	42
Brazil	44
Uruguay	46
Argentina	49
Dominican Republic	50
Jamaica	52
Panama	53
Peru	55
El Salvador	58
Venezuela	62
Colombia	65
Guatemala	66
Bolivia	67
Ecuador	68
Honduras	70
Paraguay	72
Nicaragua	73

Source: World Economic Forum, *The Latin American Competitiveness Report 2001–2002* (New York: Oxford University Press, 2002).

region. Furthermore, labor market rigidities have slowed the response to new global demands. Although labor markets have become more flexible to adapt to global production requirements, unemployment in the region is persistently high. Complementary assets of capital, technology, and infrastructure are also understocked. Technological change defines the production frontier, and complementary infrastructure is critical for rapid communication and transportation of goods. Bottlenecks in both technology and infrastructure slow growth.

Increasing trade and openness have not translated into sufficient improvements in national well-being. In chapter 8 we learned that trade theory indicated that labor-abundant countries should export labor-intensive goods. You may be surprised to learn that relative to other developing countries, Latin America is not labor abundant. Unfortunately, neither has it been able to improve the skill level of its labor to compete effectively and efficiently in the middle technology niche. Clearly the quality of the labor force will affect efficiency and the relative cost of goods. Simply having abundant and cheap labor is not enough to win in the global trading game. With the entry of low-wage countries such as China into the world trading system, Latin America can't compete on a cheap wage basis. More importantly, the path to equitable growth is not to drag wages and incomes down in a race to the bottom. The goal is to improve the productivity of labor; this will contribute to lower unit costs of production rather than poverty wages. Labor must be combined with effective capital investment, dynamic technological systems, and smoothly functioning infrastructure. To make the most of labor in a dynamic technological setting, firms must also have adequate transportation and telecommunications infrastructure to promote global competitiveness.

This chapter will survey some of the changes in input markets, with a focus on labor, technology, and infrastructure. We will explore both how policy changes have affected inputs and ways in which the improvement of input quality might enhance growth. Our questions for consideration include the following:

- How has internationalization affected labor markets?
- Has an external orientation improved the position of workers, or has it made them worse off?
- What are the technological requirements of global competitiveness?
- How can less-technologically advanced economies compete in the international arena?
- With a decrease in the role of the state, who should be investing in technology and infrastructure?
- What investments are needed to provide an adequate infrastructure for growth?
- Will new global technologies such as the Internet accelerate the pace of growth in the region—or increase the divide between Latin America and the industrialized world?

The chapter will look at some of the changes that have already taken place in the 1990s but will also identify deficiencies in input quality and an agenda for further development of sources of competitiveness in the global arena.

Human Capital: Investment in Labor

Latin America's advantage in the international market does not lie in cheap labor. Wage competitiveness is relative; wages in Latin America will never fall to levels such as those in China. Poised between two worlds, export performance has lagged. Latin America has an abundance of workers with primary education—and a huge deficit of those with secondary schooling and developed skills. As shown in table 9.2, international shares of world trade, Latin American nations have increasingly exported goods in the midlevel technology range. Mexico and the Caribbean have especially broken into export markets based not in natural reserves but in technology and skilled labor. Rather than low wages, the key to competitiveness is investment in human capital, leading to higher labor productivity. The objective is to create conditions for business development that are better than what might be predicted by the income level of the country. That is, if wages correlate with national income levels, success rides on firms becoming more productive than the average cost of wages. Wages need not be low if exceeded by productivity gains. Export success relies on productivity-adjusted labor costs—not on reducing the welfare of the workers.

But Latin American nations lag on productivity measures. The International Institute for Management Development weights a set of economic performance, government and business efficiency, and infrastructure indicators to arrive at the World Competitiveness Scorecard. Chile is the only nation to place in the top 20; Brazil barely scoots in at 35, followed by Mexico (41), Colombia (44), Venezuela (48), and Argentina (49) scraping into the top 50.[2] Labor productivity is determined by the quality of human capital as well as complementary physical and social infrastructure. Low savings rates have lead to underinvestment in the physical capital in plants; poor performance in education fails to deliver workers skilled for global competition. Most Latin American nations have been pushed out of the low wage bracket but have not gained broad entrance to the skill sets to compete successfully in the global arena. In the following chapters we will study the social investments in health and education necessary for productivity gains. For now we will turn to other impediments to flexible and fair labor markets.

Labor markets in Latin America have not delivered. As shown in table 9.3, unemployment rates have nearly doubled from 1980 to 2001, rising from a regional average of 6.41 percent prior to the debt crisis in 1980 to 11.03 percent in 2001. There is a wide degree of variation; persistently poor performance is registered by Venezuela, Uruguay, Panama, Argentina, and Colombia. Mexico stands out with its low unemployment record. The variation in employment performance is driven both by the structure of labor markets and the importance policymakers placed on employment generation in structural adjustment. Brazil, for example, was able to maintain more expansive growth policies because of its large internal market, while Argentina was held to strict external conditionality.

In addition to unemployment generated by the legacy of economic crisis, the relatively young age structure of the population in the region requires substantial new job creation. The employment problem is compounded by the need not only to find jobs for existing workers but also to accommodate new members of the eco-

Table 9.2.   Latin America and the Caribbean: International Shares of World Trade, 1985–1998 (percentages)

	1985	1990	1995	1998
I. Share of the International Market				
South America	3.3	2.7	2.7	2.8
Mexico and the Caribbean	2.1	1.7	2.2	2.8
Market share in natural resources				
South America	7.1	7.6	8.9	10.0
Mexico and the Caribbean	5.0	3.6	3.3	3.7
Market share in manufactures based on natural resources				
South America	5.0	4.3	4.6	4.6
Mexico and the Caribbean	1.4	1.2	1.3	1.5
Market share in manufactures not based on natural resources				
South America	1.2	1.1	1.1	1.2
Mexico and the Caribbean	1.2	1.4	2.2	3.0
II. Export Structure (contribution)	100	100	100	100
Exports relying on natural resources				
South America	49.2	44.3	43.6	44.0
Mexico and the Caribbean	54.1	33.3	20.0	16.2
Exports relying on manufactures based on natural resources				
South America	29.2	28.3	27.6	25.7
Mexico and the Caribbean	13.1	11.9	9.7	8.6
Exports relying on manufactures not based on natural resources				
South America	19.7	26	27.1	28.5
Mexico and the Caribbean	29.9	51.3	66.9	71.9
Exports relying on low technology				
South America	8.2	10.5	10.1	9.0
Mexico and the Caribbean	7.1	13.8	18.0	20.1
Exports relying on midlevel technology				
South America	9.9	13.5	15.1	16.7
Mexico and the Caribbean	14.6	25.7	33.1	32.8
Exports relying on high technology				
South America	1.5	1.9	2.0	2.8
Mexico and the Caribbean	8.2	8.0	15.8	9.0
III. Three Main Exports by Contribution				
South America	27.4	21.6	20.3	19.7
Crude petroleum oils	12.3	10.0	11.2	11.1
Animal feed	4.4	4.4	4.7	4.3
Petroleum products, refined	10.7	7.2	4.4	4.3
Mexico and the Caribbean	35.6	23.3	19.0	17.6
Passenger motor vehicle	0.6	4.4	7.6	7.5
Crude petroleum oils	33.2	15.6	7.6	6.2
Electricity distribution materials	1.8	3.3	3.8	3.9

Source: ECLAC, *Foreign Investment in Latin America and the Caribbean, 2000,* tables I.6 and I.7.

Table 9.3. Latin America: Urban Unemployment (average annual growth rates in percent)

Country	1980	1985	1990	1995	1996	1997	1998	1999	2000	2001[a]
Argentina	2.6	6.1	7.5	17.5	17.2	14.9	12.9	14.5	15.1	17.4
Bolivia	7.1	5.8	7.3	3.6	3.8	4.4	4.1	6.1	7.6	—
Brazil	6.3	5.3	4.3	4.6	5.4	5.7	7.6	7.6	7.1	—
Chile	11.7	17.2	6.5	7.4	6.4	6.1	6.4	10.8	10.0	9.5
Colombia	10.0	13.9	10.5	8.9	11.2	12.4	15.3	19.4	17.2	18.5
Costa Rica	6.0	6.7	5.4	5.7	6.6	5.9	5.4	6.2	5.3	5.8
Ecuador	5.7	10.4	6.1	7.7	10.4	9.3	11.5	14.4	9.0	10.9
El Salvador	—	—	10.0	7.0	7.5	7.5	7.6	6.9	6.5	6.1
Guatemala	2.2	12.1	6.5	4.3	3.7	5.0	3.8	—	—	—
Honduras	8.8	11.7	7.8	6.0	6.5	6.4	5.2	5.3	—	6.3
Mexico	4.5	4.4	2.7	6.3	5.5	3.7	3.2	2.5	2.2	2.5
Nicaragua	3.2	7.6	11.1	18.2	16.0	14.3	13.2	9.8	9.0	10.7
Panama	9.9	15.6	20.0	16.2	16.7	15.4	15.2	14.0	15.2	16.9
Paraguay	4.1	5.2	6.6	5.3	8.2	7.1	6.6	9.4	10.7	—
Peru	7.1	10.1	8.3	8.8	8.0	9.2	8.4	9.1	8.5	9.5
Uruguay	7.4	13.1	9.2	10.8	11.9	11.5	10.1	11.3	13.6	15.4
Venezuela	6.0	13.1	11.0	10.9	11.8	11.4	11.3	14.9	14.0	13.9

Source: CEPAL, *Statistical Yearbook for Latin America and the Caribbean, 2001* and *Balance Preliminar de las Economías de América Latina y el Caribe,* appendix. Published each year in December and available at www.eclac.org.
[a]Forecast.

nomically active population (EAP). A growing proportion of workers concentrated in the urban sector further compounds this problem. The industrial sector must create jobs not only faster than the rate of growth of the population but also fast enough to absorb those fleeing rural poverty and land degradation.

New types of growth in Latin America have had a limited effect on job creation. Even Chile, following its first recession after fifteen years, found itself in 1999 with a more than 50 percent increase in unemployment; its unemployment rates have remained stuck at historically high levels through 2001 despite economic recovery. The failure of globalization to deliver jobs has led to social protest and strikes across the region.

Official unemployment rates obscure much of the story of inadequate job creation in Latin America. Open unemployment refers to those officially counted by governments as actively searching for jobs. Imagine the data difficulties in counting the unemployed in poor countries. Furthermore, most unemployed workers in the region cannot afford the luxury of waiting in line at the unemployment office. With weak unemployment safety nets, people must find whatever work they can to scrape by. White-collar unemployed take blue-collar jobs. You may be surprised at the level of underemployment, for example, if you ever have occasion to debate politics or philosophy with your overeducated Buenos Aires cabdriver. Many are subsisting with jobs for which they are extremely overqualified. The informal sector, the topic of our next section, has also claimed large numbers of the unemployed. As the number trying to eke out a living in this sector increases, many turn to petty street crime and social violence to survive.

Unemployment is a result of a greater number of new entrants to the market than new jobs. It has been exacerbated by the severe contraction of state employment under the neoliberal model.[3] Both privatization and the downsizing of central government have released workers. But the fall in public-sector employment is not the whole story. Workers in all sectors of the economy may be confronting conditions of "precarious" employment where, compared to past regimes of labor guarantees and state jobs, employment for some has become less remunerative, less regulated by government, and less subject to collective control of workers.[4] An International Labor Organization survey shows that two-thirds of all workers in the region are worried or very worried about losing their jobs.[5] Competition for export assembly in the global arena has decreased worker and community leverage with respect to employment conditions. Economic crises and associated adjustments such as the currency crisis in Mexico have resulted in lower wages and poorer conditions for workers. In 1995 minimum wages adjusted for inflation were 70 percent of their 1980 levels. Imagine if your family income had declined nearly one-third while you grew up. A worsening of formal-sector conditions has contributed to the poor progress on poverty reduction in the region.[6] A weakening of labor rights increased insecurity in the labor market.

Women's participation in the labor force has also changed. Long-term forces including technological changes, advances in educational attainment, decreases in fertility, progress in women's rights, shifts in the structure of households, and intensified consumerism have pushed more women into the workplace. But women have also responded to short-term cyclical changes. Labor force participation by women increased from an average of 28 percent in the 1970s to 41.4 percent by 1998.[7] The good news for the future is that as women have entered the workforce, population growth rates have fallen from 2 percent a year in the late 1980s to 1.6 percent in the late 1990s. There is, however, wide variation as population rates continue to grow in Central America.[8] Overall, this means that in the future, there is less pressure for the economy to grow faster than population increases.

The growth of female participation is concentrated at the low end of the income structure, indicating that necessity has pushed women into the workplace.[9] Once at the bottom of the labor market, women tend to stay there. Labor market segmentation, or the stereotyping of jobs suitable for women, has a profound impact on employment potential in the region. A World Bank report found that 60 percent of the earnings differential between men and women in a study of fifteen Latin American countries was attributable to cultural aspects segmenting the market and limiting the suitable jobs for women.[10]

Why haven't labor markets created sufficient job opportunities? Basic supply and demand suggests that excess unemployment should be addressed in a free market with falling wages that induce an increased demand for labor. Table 9.4 shows that for many countries real salaries were stagnant over the 1990s—yet unemployment was persistently high. The average industrial wage increased 1.8 percent from 1990 to 2000; why aren't labor markets adjusting? Some blame rigidities in wage adjustments and job security. High unemployment and structural rigidities in the labor market contribute to a large **informal sector,** characterized by low wages and poor working conditions, that reaches levels as high as 60 percent of

Table 9.4. Real Industrial Wages, 1990–2000

Country	1990	1995	2000	Rate of Growth (% 1990–2000)
Argentina	75.0	75.6	77.4	0.3
Bolivia	86.7	94.3	93.3	0.7
Brazil	96.7	124.2	128.8	2.9
Chile	105.8	133.1	155.5	3.9
Colombia	114.8	123.6	136.1	1.7
Costa Rica	109.7	122.9	150.3	3.2
Ecuador	74.1	113.3	97.8	2.8
Honduras	73.4	73.9	87.7[a]	—
Mexico	59.6	62.1	59.5	0.0
Panama	97.8	99.7	135.3	3.7
Paraguay	102.4	98.8	98.3	–0.4
Peru	34.4	43.5	42.4	2.1
Uruguay	110.8	115.5	117.5	0.6
Venezuela	57.0	46.0	48.0	–1.7
Average	85.7	94.2	103.1	1.8

Source: International Labor Organization, regional office for Latin America, *Panorama Laboral 2001,* table 9-A, 69.
[a] 1999 data.

the labor force in Bolivia. In part the high rate of unemployment can be attributed to a mismatch between skilled and unskilled labor as the economy has opened to international competition. Labor unions, while protecting the rights of workers, can also contribute to inflexibility and unemployment. We will consider these issues in turn with an eye to policy suggestions to improve labor's contributions to global competitiveness.

Labor Policy: Job Security versus Job Creation

Latin American countries have long used labor legislation as a tool of social policy.[11] Minimum wages and measures to protect jobs, such as heavy required severance packages or laws against hiring replacement workers, were seen as political vehicles for income transfers and the protection of the poor. The unintended result, however, was labor market rigidity. Labor market distortions in Latin America include government intervention in setting wages, high costs of dismissal, high payroll taxes, and the nature of labor–management relations. There is a long tradition of protecting job security. Workers may contest dismissals in court and may be awarded large severance packages. All these factors reduce the flexibility of management and make restructuring difficult. Studies show that an increase in job security results in a decrease in economy-wide employment.[12] Furthermore, the impact more squarely falls on the employment prospects of young, female, and unskilled workers, contributing to rising inequality. The policy dilemma becomes how to protect income security for the employed—who tend to have political power—and simultaneously open labor markets to new entrants.

Union activity is concentrated in the urban formal sector. The union movement in Latin America is often the path to political power, and many government officials are leaders in the union movement. Labor unions along with the military have historically been among the few interest-group power centers with the organizational structure, leadership capacity, and defined objectives to affect policy outcomes.[13] However, labor union influence has varied historically. Beginning in the 1920s, many Latin American governments began enforcing workers' rights. Legislation and public controls to address employment issues and resolve labor conflicts fit with the populist political paradigm. Governments were directly involved in collective bargaining, promoting a close alignment between political parties and labor. Through legislative changes, formal sector employees obtained a number of guarantees, most important among them job security. Ground was lost in the 1970s when military governments restricted labor organizing. The return to democracy in the 1980s was also accompanied by austerity, limiting gains on the labor front. Trade liberalization in the 1990s has further constrained labor's bargaining power. Union membership declined in industrial countries from 39.7 percent of the workforce in the 1980s to 31.2 percent in the 1990s; in Latin America the fall was from 24.6 percent to 15.5 percent.

Beyond union power, labor laws impede flexibility. In most countries in the region, dismissing a worker after one year carries a severance penalty of more than one month's wage; with ten years' seniority, the cost rises to between six months and one year's salary. Temporary hiring practices have traditionally been constrained in the interest of job security; this interferes with firms' ability to meet cyclical global demand. Finally, in the absence of strong social legislation, health, social security, and unemployment compensation schemes have been directly tied to wages. In Argentina, Brazil, Colombia, and Uruguay this tax tops 30 percent of labor costs; throughout the rest of the region it ranges between 15 and 30 percent.[14] High social taxes on labor distort whatever trade advantages abundant labor might confer. On average, the costs of mandatory job security provisions in Latin America were nearly three months of wages; this is nearly double the average Organisation for Economic Cooperation and Development (OECD) level.[15]

Formal-sector workers are required to contribute to social security funds, which generally provide workers with pensions, health care, and accident insurance. The difficulties with these funds include their encouragement of early retirement, payments unrelated to individual contributions, and expensive health care packages that exclude the nonworking poor. Pension systems in the region tend to be organized on a pay-as-you-go basis, placing the burden for payments on current enrollees in the system. In Chile a program of mandatory payments into individual accounts with minimum benefits guaranteed by the government has replaced the pay-as-you-go scheme. Workers may choose among different investment accounts, generating competition in the market. Similar schemes have been adopted in Argentina, Colombia, Mexico, and Peru.[16] Using the market to create the individual incentive to save for retirement may not only take the burden off firms but also raise national savings rates and decrease reliance on capital inflows, a point we made in chapter 7.

Labor market reforms have not followed a uniform direction in the region. Some countries, such as Colombia, Nicaragua, Argentina, and Venezuela, have worked to increase flexibility. Others such as Chile have traded measures for decreasing the costs of labor to the firm (such as the use of private retirement accounts) for greater protection for workers, including part-time and seasonal workers. President Lagos of Chile pushed through the labor reform bill of 2001, which reduced the workweek and extended labor protection, arguing that Chile must have labor legislation in step with the modern world in order to enter into trade agreements.[17] This tension between labor market flexibility and international standards is a difficult national problem.

Nations are therefore working to promote job creation rather than job protection. These programs tend toward labor-intensive public works projects or subsidies to private firms to hire more workers. They are financed by central governments, and often executed by local agents, either public or private through nongovernmental organizations (NGOS). The difficulty with employment-generating schemes is that they are not countercyclical; it is difficult to synchronize spending with an economic downturn. Furthermore, workfare can distort private labor markets and supplements to private firms may simply subsidize hires that would have taken place anyway. Training programs are also popular. Chile Joven, a pioneering youth training program combines scholarships for classroom training with private-sector apprenticeships. But training programs tend to be expensive on a per-beneficiary basis, and they may in fact attract youth away from continuing formal education. For those that otherwise would be working, scholarships must be set low enough so that they don't discourage job search. Finally, both employment generation and training schemes often don't reach the poorest of the poor—those without the basic requisites for labor market entry.

Labor relations in Latin America are relatively inflexible. The right to representation is assigned to union officials by the government. For example, in the case of autoworkers negotiating with General Motors in Brazil in 1995, when union–management relations broke down, a labor court mediated the outcome. Strikes are permitted as a manner of political expression. Under the old economic model a focus on job creation and solidarity undergirded the socioeconomic order.[18] Labor was an important political player.

Mexico provides an interesting example of how political change and economic liberalization are affecting the power of unions. For decades union effectiveness through the Confederation of Mexican Workers (CTM) was tied to the political power of the PRI, the dominant political party in Mexico. As the power of the PRI was challenged by new political parties in the 1990s, space was created for independent breakaway unions. Changes in labor laws have been proposed by upstart labor foundations such as the UNT, or the National Workers Union, to decrease government's control over the unions. New organizations are also benefiting from the North American Free Trade Agreement (NAFTA). U.S. and Canadian unions, fearful of being undercut by cheap Mexican labor, have been working to strengthen an independent labor movement in Latin America. International media attention has been called to cases of union bashing in the *maquila* sector. Oddly, internationalization may work to strengthen the hand of labor in the region.

Globalization may transform the role of unions in Latin America. "Reinventing" the labor movement as an inclusionary, democratic movement that promotes accountability is a challenge for the future.[19]

BOX 9.1.   A SEAT AT THE TABLE: UNION LEADERS URGE IDB TO INCLUDE WORKERS' CONCERNS IN REFORM PROGRAMS AND FREE TRADE NEGOTIATIONS

It was the sort of meeting that presumably never takes place.

At the IDB's Washington, D.C., headquarters last February, senior Bank officials spent a day listening to some of their most legendary critics: labor union leaders from Latin America and the Caribbean . . . including John J. Sweeney, president of the American Federation of Labor-Congress of Industrial Organizations (AFL-CIO), Luis Anderson, president of the Inter-American Regional Workers Organization (ORIT), and top union federation officials from Argentina, Barbados, Brazil, Canada, Chile, the Dominican Republic, Mexico, Venezuela and the United States.

"Much of the mistrust that existed between us before has now disappeared," said ORIT's Anderson. But while he praised the IDB for its willingness to talk with labor leaders, Anderson said most of the region's governments have refused to consult organized labor prior to adopting economic reforms that are promoted by the IDB.

Anderson said this lack of consultation is inexcusable, particularly on issues such as regional integration and trade liberalization, because workers are the first to feel the consequences of these changes. "We've never debated whether or not we agree with economic globalization and integration, because we know it's a reality," Anderson said. "We know that great wealth is being created [thanks to integration], but at the same time we see that poverty is increasing, the number of jobs is decreasing, and the informal sector is growing. So we believe there is a problem in the distribution of the benefits of these reforms."

Anderson and other labor leaders at the meeting said they generally support efforts to open local economies to greater foreign competition, but they warned that governments that fail to address the inequitable distribution of wealth and exclude labor unions from the trade policy debate risk a backlash from voters. . . . As a step in the right direction, Anderson suggested that the IDB promote the creation of a forum for labor consultations as part of negotiations leading to the creation of the Free Trade Area of the Americas (FTAA).

In his remarks at the meeting, IDB President Enrique V. Iglesias agreed that the economic reforms that have swept Latin America in recent years have come at a cost for the regions' workers, and that the problem of unemployment has reached "new dimensions" in many of the region's countries. He also concurred that relations between labor, government, and business have not been as productive as they should, saying there is a need to "improve the quality of the dialogue" between these groups.

Labor participants at the meeting also criticized what they described as a widespread failure to enforce worker rights codified in the various conventions of the International Labor Organization (ILO). The ILO conventions, which most Latin American and Caribbean countries have ratified, set forth a variety of basic workers rights, including the right to organize and bargain collectively, and protections against child labor and on-the-job discrimination based on gender.

Stan Gacek, the AFL-CIO's assistant director for international affairs, said the failure to enforce labor protections stems from a broader refusal by most governments to link social rights to trade policy. He argued that this refusal is difficult to justify when capital rights, such as those protecting intellectual property and trademarks, are explicitly addressed and defended in trade accords. "Governments that violate copyright protections get harsh treatment," Gacek said, "but what about those who violate labor protections?"

On a different note, other union participants at the meeting acknowledged that labor movement leaders have not always kept up with the changing demands of the market. "We recognize that the trade union movement isn't prepared adequately to deal with new tech-

(continued)

(continued)

nologies and globalization," said Nair Goulart, a Brazilian who is president of ORIT's Women's Committee. Participants praised an IDB program that paid for selected union leaders to take university courses on labor economics, and they encouraged the IDB to consider additional programs in labor leadership training.

Gustavo Márquez, a labor specialist in the Office of the IDB Chief Economist, said today's union leaders also need to be more understanding of the demands of increasingly specialized and competitive labor markets that require flexible workers to meet evolving production processes. He said many of the labor disputes in Latin America today revolve around outdated work rules that limit the ability of employees' to adapt to these changes. He urged new rules that safeguard worker rights while allowing for greater competitiveness and productivity.

"We have different starting points, different jargon, and a different history," IDB Executive Vice President Nancy Birdsall told participants at the conclusion of the meeting. "But we need more of these meetings because it is clear that we also have a great deal in common. We support open negotiations between business and labor. We support social protections, developing better safety nets and better unemployment insurance arrangements."

Source: Paul Constance, www.iadb.org, 14 June 1998, from *IDB América,* April 1998.

Box 9.1 illustrates a productive approach to labor–management relations in the region. In many countries, contract negotiations have moved from an industry-wide, national level to decentralized collective bargaining at the company level. This allows firms greater flexibility in negotiating contracts that better reflect local conditions and productivity levels. While this of course also decreases the power of the unions to shut down production, greater flexibility has created new employment options economy-wide.[20] To deal effectively with the question of unemployment and poverty tied to informal-sector employment, however, unions may no longer be enough. Collective social action that includes measures to improve training, productivity, and work organization is important. NGOs have become active participants in reaching down into the informal market to promote labor reform.[21]

THE RISE OF THE INFORMAL SECTOR

One result of inadequate job growth in the private sector has been the expansion of the informal sector. Survival strategies have sent workers scrambling for subsistence in a sector not covered by insurance, benefits, or regulations. The informal sector acted as the main source of job creation in the 1990s, rising from 51 percent of nonagricultural employment to 57 percent by 1997. Eighty-four out of every one hundred new jobs were in the informal sector, while formal-sector employment shrank from 15.3 percent to 13 percent of total employment.[22] Informal sector growth has been strongest in Bolivia, Panama, Paraguay, and Venezuela.[23]

Informality can describe any number of jobs ranging from the street vendor of nail files and the family maid to the small restaurant owner and the corner mechanic. The informal sector has three main areas: microenterprise employment, own-account workers, and domestic service. Microenterprises have been the fastest growing area, at 5.2 percent per year, accounting for 22.5 percent of total employment in the region. Own-account workers have been increasing at 4.4 percent per year, making up 26.5 percent of the region's total working population. Domestic service employment has increased by 3.9 percent, with workers of this sector making up 7.1 percent of the EAP. Domestic service and own-account work are the lowest productivity occupations, acting as a drag on overall productivity growth.[24]

The lack of a clear definition for the informal sector makes measurement problematic. Some basic guidelines that characterize informality include a low ratio between capital and labor, small-scale, worker-owned means of production, family-based operations involving children, and the virtual impossibility of accumulation of capital. The list of informal jobs with these characteristics is extensive, including mobile vendors, taxi drivers, small business owners, artisan manufacturers, maids, subcontractors, other services providers, and illegal businesses such as contraband or drug trafficking and professionals who work for themselves.[25] The informal sector is an easy solution for the unemployed because there is little in the way of money, capital, or qualifications needed to become involved. It is also an important source of employment for women and children. Box 9.2 illustrates the promise and the problems of small firms in export markets.

There is overwhelming evidence to suggest that urban poverty and informal employment are closely related. The proportion of working poor in the informal sector varies in each country: Bolivia has 66.2 percent, Brazil 66.4 percent, Costa Rica 63.5 percent, Guatemala 93.3 percent, Honduras 84.9 percent, Panama 87.1 percent, Paraguay 64.7 percent, Uruguay 18.3 percent, and Venezuela 57.4 percent. In Costa Rica in 1982, 75.8 percent of the poorest among the poor were in the informal sector, compared with 53.5 percent of the "not-so-poor" and 31.7 percent of the "nonpoor." In urban Panama in 1983, 67 percent of the urban poor population was in the informal sector.[26]

Informality tends to be associated with unskilled workers. As a large majority of the labor force, the unskilled have difficulty finding formal-sector employment. Limited educational opportunity and an unequal social structure constrain workers from investing in their own human capital. With little education, workers land in low-skill jobs—jobs that in a vicious circle are associated with limited on-the-job training opportunities. Furthermore, a low-quality and low-skilled labor force can act as a deterrent to investment if investors need an experienced labor force.

Poverty and inequality in the informal sector appear to be self-perpetuating. The broad income gap between highly skilled workers and those in low-skilled, often informal occupations increased from 40 percent in 1994 to 60 percent in 1996. Skilled labor incomes are increasing while wages for workers outside the modern sector have not experienced growth.[27] As seen in table 9.5, incomes of professional workers have largely risen while those in the low-productivity sector suffered declining growth. Because those at the bottom have even less to invest in their own human capital, they fall further and further behind. Professional and technical wages in Chile, Paraguay, Uruguay, and Venezuela increased sharply; in contrast, wages of unskilled workers fell in Bolivia and Brazil. In Colombia, Mexico, Paraguay, and Venezuela, where a rise in professional and a drop in unskilled wages occurred, the

Box 9.2.   The New Entrepreneurs: Preparing the Ground for Small Business

For Eugenia Kleiman and Martha Gámez of Monterey, Mexico, it began as a whim. "We wanted to build something beautiful, something different," said Kleiman, a former shoe shop owner. So in 1990, she teamed up with Gámez, an interior designer, to create Margen Arteobjeto, a workshop that would make home furnishings from wrought iron.

Using personal savings, the two rented a small garage, hired a craftsman and began displaying their plate holders and lamp stands at regional fairs. Buyers were impressed, and orders began to trickle in. The products also caught the eye of an official from Bancomext, Mexico's export promotion bank, who encouraged the pair to show their wares at trade fairs in the United States. Before long, major department stores were placing bulk orders.

"At first our U.S. customers were hesitant, because they had a bad image of Mexican producers," said Kleiman. "But we made it our business to erase that image through quality and service. Now our U.S. customers say, 'Why should we buy from Southeast Asia when you folks are right here?'"

By late 1996, Margen had grown to some 300 full-time employees operating in three round-the-clock shifts. Annual sales had reached $6 million and are set to top $8 million in 1997, at a time when most of the Mexican economy is still recovering from the effects of the 1995 peso crisis. Most recently, Margen was named one of the four most successful export-oriented companies in Mexico by Bancomext.

THE RIGHT MIX

Margen's story illustrates just how quickly entrepreneurs can germinate when the environment for growth is right. Many economists hoped this environment would emerge naturally from the structural reforms that have reduced the economic role of the state in the region's countries over the last decade. Indeed, privatization programs, financial reforms and trade liberalization have opened whole sectors of the economy to competition, and a new generation of political leaders has embraced the notion that private enterprise should be the engine of growth and development. In some countries most notably Chile these macroeconomic reforms did have the desired effect, stimulating a flowering of start-up companies and new growth among existing small enterprises. But in many other countries, the benefits of reform have accrued primarily to large, well-established corporations, while activity among the small companies has remained stagnant.

Why have these outcomes been so uneven? The principal reason, according to many observers, is that entrepreneurs need much more than a positive macroeconomic environment to take root and thrive. Indeed, a number of less visible factors, including access to credit, access to nonfinancial services such as market research, and the quality of government institutions that regulate business activity, can ultimately have a much bigger impact on entrepreneurs.

The scarcity of bank credit for small borrowers in Latin America has been a perennial problem. "Small businesses justifiably complain about the lack of access to medium- and long-term financing, high interest rates, the difficulty in finding required collateral, excessive red tape, and a general lack of sensitivity shown by banks toward small firms," says Juan Llisterri, an economist in the IDB's Infrastructure and Financial Markets Division.

Kleiman is a case in point. Like many of the region's small entrepreneurs, she simply assumed that commercial banks would not be interested and didn't even bother seeking credit for the first three years after launching Margen. When Kleiman finally did approach a bank, officials seemed more concerned with her gender than with her ability to offer collateral. "The banks didn't think we knew what we were doing because we are women," Kleiman said. Margen's business record eventually persuaded a lender, however, and the company now easily obtains credit.

Although some of the region's commercial banks are in fact beginning to target the small business market segment, the high transaction costs associated with managing multiple small loans still keep most banks from lending to first-time entrepreneurs. As a result, many potential businesses must resort to informal sources of financing at usurious rates that make it difficult to compete.

Even when a start-up enterprise does obtain credit, it often faces additional costs related to official paperwork. In some countries, simply registering a business and obtaining the required government licenses can take months. Moreover, if regulatory institutions are poorly managed and have weak controls, unofficial "service fees" are often necessary to obtain documents and licenses. While large companies can afford to hire intermediaries to navigate bureaucracies and handle paperwork, entrepreneurs can find these transaction costs prohibitive. In fact, as Peruvian economist Hernando de Soto reported in his landmark study, "The Other Path," many small entrepreneurs claim that the cost of dealing with the government is so high that they must operate illegally (in the informal sector) in order to survive.

But entrepreneurs who opt for informality suffer permanent disadvantages compared to their legal counterparts. They cannot request municipal services or utilities, obtain titles to property, apply for credit, or sign enforceable contracts, to name just a few limitations.

Even for entrepreneurs who do operate in the formal sector, the lack of effective legal protections can be crippling. In countries where law enforcement is weak and the judicial system is hampered by inefficiency and corruption, small companies have little recourse against delinquent customers, broken contracts, or other commercial disputes. Large companies compensate for weak legal protections by forging informal agreements with suppliers and partners based on family contacts and friendships. But these closed, inflexible networks make it difficult for entrepreneurs to break into a market.

MANY INGREDIENTS

A strong, open economy, access to financing, transparent and efficient regulations, and effective legal protections: all these conditions must be present for small entrepreneurs to prosper over the long run.

Source: IDB América, 1997, available at www.iadb.org.

income gap doubled. Those in the informal sector are also more vulnerable in that the majority lack coverage in national social security and health systems. As we see in table 9.6, roughly a quarter of informal sector workers in 2000 had coverage.

Although it holds limited promise for advancement, the informal sector does serve as a social net for the poor and unskilled and has therefore helped to rescue families from deprivation. Where there are weak social safety nets and limited unemployment insurance, the informal sector is employment of last resort.[28] Beyond poverty and survival, there are other motives for participation in this sector. Sometimes individuals take advantage of profitable opportunities in market niches waiting to be exploited. This may take place by offering tailored services that large enterprises may not find attractive or possible. Also, the informal sector allows businesses to avoid compliance with regulations. Labor legislation in many countries defines not only basic legal rights but also detailed conditions of employment including wages, job security, the number of vacation days, and employer obliga-

Table 9.5.   Percentage Growth of Average Incomes and Labor Income Disparities

Country	Year	Professional and Technical Workers	Workers in Low Productivity Sector
Bolivia	1989	7.6	3.4
	1994	7.2	2.3
Brazil	1987	7.7	3.4
	1993	7.5	2.3
Chile	1990	6.6	3.9
	1994	8.4	4.1
Colombia	1990	6.7	3.3
	1994	7.9	2.7
Costa Rica	1990	7.2	3.2
	1994	8.2	3.6
Honduras	1990	6.5	1.5
	1994	4.5	1.4
Mexico	1989	5.5	4.0
	1994	6.3	3.1
Paraguay	1990	3.9	2.4
	1994	6.7	2.0
Uruguay	1990	6.0	2.7
	1994	9.6	3.1
Venezuela	1990	4.2	3.6
	1994	6.3	3.3

Source: ECLAC, *The Equity Gap: Latin America, the Caribbean and the Social Summit, 1997.*

tions. In Brazil, for example, taxes and labor laws can add up to 70 percent of the base salary. By law, formal-sector workers are also entitled to large severance packages. Many businesses therefore remain unregistered or unlicensed to avoid costly compliance with regulations. However, there should be a distinction made between those who are capable of paying the cost of regulations and those who cannot because their incomes are too low. Many nonpoor—who could, for example, be paying taxes—also form part of the informal sector.[29]

The large, untaxed segment of the working population in the informal sector creates challenges for fiscal stabilization. Some, such as analysts within the Economic Commission for Latin America and the Caribbean (ECLAC), contend that it has widened the wage gap, increased inequality, and lowered average productivity, hampering competitiveness.[30] However, this may be blaming a symptom and not a cause. According to the International Labor Organization, the informal sector arose as a response to the inability of the modern sector to provide sufficient jobs. Urban employment would have to grow more rapidly than the number of new labor market entrants to reduce open unemployment—a daunting objective in the short run. The burden of employment generation therefore falls on the informal sector—not a first best solution.

Given its usefulness in absorbing workers, the challenge is to improve produc-

Table 9.6.   Salaried Workers Who Have Coverage in Social Security (percentage of population)

Latin America		*Total*	Informal Sector		*Formal Sector*	*Total*
			Domestic Service	*Small Firms*		
1990	Total	29.2	17.6	34.7	80.6	66.6
	Men	32.5	35.5	32.5	79.1	68.4
	Women	27.0	16.6	39.5	82.8	65.1
1995	Total	24.2	19.1	28.3	79.3	65.2
	Men	24.4	32.0	24.8	78.2	66.6
	Women	24.0	18.0	37.5	81.1	65.7
2000	Total	26.9	23.1	29.3	79.0	64.2
	Men	26.5	31.9	26.5	77.6	65.6
	Women	27.8	22.6	37.5	81.2	62.5

Source: ILO, *Panorama Laboral 2001,* table 8-A, 67.

tivity and incomes in the informal sector. There may be hidden opportunities within the informal sector. Job creation was accomplished through micro activity without government subsidy in a hostile policy environment. Informal-sector activity is in fact market-friendly. It provides a wide array of services cheaply and efficiently. For example, many firms are recyclers, collecting and disposing of garbage in cities in a cost-efficient manner. Also, the bulk of low-income housing is produced in the informal sector. These and other arguments indicate that it may be possible to work with and not against the urban informal sector to promote employment and incomes.[31]

Nonetheless, low productivity drags the rest of the economy down. Because the informal sector is by definition capital poor, this is not surprising. Productivity levels in the formal sector, on the other hand, have been advancing, although the increase in the number of jobs has been slow. Thus, the productivity gap between the two sectors has been increasing.[32] Paralleling the productivity gap, the income gap between the formal and informal sectors has also been increasing.

Chile stands as an exception to the rising trend in informal-sector activity, with the largest drop in informal-sector activity as a proportion of total employment. Four elements contributed to this decline: rapid growth of the economy; the introduction of private retirement accounts, limiting the burden on the firm for social insurance; increased flexibility in labor legislation; and a strengthening of the legal infrastructure of the state.[33] Consideration of these factors may point to areas of future development in other Latin American countries looking to increase formal-sector engagement. We will return in chapter 11 to the problem of the informal sector as it relates to poverty.

QUESTION FOR THOUGHT

How should the employment–informality trade-off be resolved in the region?

Input Markets: Productivity and Technology

An important drawback to informal-sector activity is its low rate of productivity. Enhancements in productivity—increasing the output of workers—are the key to improving material welfare in society. **Labor productivity** in Latin America is between one-fourth and one-third of the prevailing U.S. level.[34] Table 9.7 shows relative labor productivity versus that of the United States. Without productivity enhancement, if a benevolent dictator simply gave everyone a raise, more money would simply be chasing the same quantity of goods. Advances in material life take place when technological changes allow for the production of more goods with a given set of resources. The three-field crop rotation system and the use of the horse in agriculture to yield an agricultural surplus facilitated the transition from feudalism to capitalism. At the heart of the development challenge is a question of technological change. How can the quality of inputs be improved and the combination of inputs be transformed to raise production? This, by definition, is the role of technology.

Technological change confers advantage on those who discover new ways of combining inputs to create outputs. Technology is a commodity bought and sold in markets; those nations owning it tend to erect high barriers to its open purchase in the international arena. For a developing country, the challenge is twofold: how to catch up with the dominant technological paradigm and how to carve out a particular niche in the international arena to trade competitively in items produced with new technologies. In table 9.8 we can see how far behind Latin America is compared to other country groupings in science and technology indicators. As a percentage of gross domestic income (GNI), Latin America dedicates roughly half as much to research and development as East Asia and the Pacific and roughly a quarter of high-income country levels. When countries are ranked according to international competitiveness, Latin America has the worst scores for science and technology; the six most-

Table 9.7.   Latin America: Evolution of the Relative Labor Productivity Gap in Manufacturing between Latin America and the United States (manufactures as a whole) (U.S. = 1.00)

Country	1970	1980	1990	1996
Argentina	0.42	0.41	0.55	0.67
Brazil	0.28	0.26	0.29	0.37
Chile[a]	0.25	0.24	0.23	0.20
Colombia[b]	0.29	0.25	0.37	0.34
Costa Rica[b]			0.15	0.14
Mexico[c]	0.32	0.30	0.44	0.38
Peru	0.33	0.25	0.16	0.15
Uruguay[a]	0.35	0.22	0.20	0.22

Source: Jorge Katz, "Structural Changes and Productivity in Latin American Industry, 1970–1996," *CEPAL Review* 71 (August 2000): 69.
[a]Data only up to 1995.
[b]Data only up to 1992.
[c]Data only up to 1994.

Table 9.8. Science and Technology Indicators

Country	Scientists and Engineers in R&D (per million persons)	Technicians in R&D (per million persons)	Science and Engineering Students (% of total tertiary students)	Scientific and Technical Journal Articles	Expenditures for R&D (% of GNI)	High-Technology Exports (millions of U.S.$)	Manufactured Exports (%)	Royalty and License Fees (receipts millions of U.S.$)	Payments (millions of U.S.$)	Patent Applications Filed Residents	Non-residents
Argentina	660	154	28	2,119	0.38	557	8	19	442	861	5,459
Bolivia	172	59	30	27	0.50	296		2	5		
Brazil	168	233	27	3,908	0.81	3,453	13	133	1,283	2,535	48,331
Chile	445	112	42	850	0.68	93	4	99	51	189	1,771
Guatemala	104			15	0.16	71	9			11	196
Honduras		74	24	10		6	3	0	0	11	140
Mexico	214		32	1,915	0.33	24,070	21	42	554	472	44,249
Latin America and the Caribbean		193	30	10,093	0.62	31,706	16	503	2,710	4,003	241,989
East Asia and Pacific	492		43	14,817	1.32	136,271	31	558	4,147	65,506	284,777
High income	3,166	147	25	437,303	2.36	776,133	22	66,201	57,786	679,822	2,837,232
United States	3,676		19	166,829	2.63	184,239	35	36,467	13,275	141,342	121,445

Source: 2001 World Development Indicators.

Table 9.9.   International Comparison of Investment in Science and Technology

Country	Total S&T (millions of U.S.$)	Public Sector S&T (millions of U.S.$)	Public as % of Total S&T	Private Sector (millions of U.S.$)	Private as % of Total S&T
United States	184,300	66,822	36.26	117,478	63.74
Japan	76,004	22,573	29.70	53,431	70.30
Germany	37,149	14,785	39.80	22,363	60.20
France	26,721	11,788	44.12	14,933	55.88
South Korea	12,200	3,282	26.90	8,918	73.10
Spain	4,376	2,464	56.31	1,912	43.69
Brazil[a]	5,888	4,107	69.75	1,850	31.42
Mexico[a]	1,114	1,039	93.27	75	6.73
Argentina[a]	1,353	984	72.73	369	27.27
Chile[a]	398	310	77.89	88	22.11

Source: Argentina, GACTEC (1997); Daniel Chudnosky, "Science and Technology Policy and the National System in Argentina." *CEPAL Review* 67 (April 1999).
[a]Corresponds to total expenditure on science and technology, which covers more than expenditure on research and development.

advanced countries in the region rank in the lowest third of the forty-three countries evaluated.[35]

Table 9.9 presents international comparison of investment in science and technology for some of the best performers in Latin America—yet even these are dismally far from European and Asian competitors. Developing countries may measure success differently. Core innovators require a substantial scientific base; strong noncore innovators, however, have the capacity to absorb and adapt new technologies. This requires strong linkages between universities and the business sector. But these links are weak. In contrast to industrial countries, the state sector takes the lead in technological development, with nearly 80 percent of expenditures. The private sector in Latin America does not appear to be a dynamic source of technological change. Unlike developed countries, in which businesses themselves account for more than 50 percent of national investment in research and development (R&D), in Latin America the private sector finances less than 20 percent.[36] In comparison with developed economies, ECLAC finds a productivity gap in Latin America due to the use of outdated equipment, obsolete production methods, deficient organization of labor, a failure to improve quality, unsystematic marketing techniques, and outdated after-sales services. This gap widened in the postwar era.[37] It is particularly acute for small and medium-sized firms, pointing to a clear need to promote the dissemination of information systems, personnel training, and the outreach of sectoral technology centers to small businesses.[38]

The need for public financing may be explained by market failure. Basic scientific knowledge can be considered a public good that the state must provide to promote new activity. With such a low level of basic science and technology infrastructure, it is expensive for firms to span the gap between basic science and industrial applications. With few firms engaging in R&D, there are limited externalities or synergies created by a core of high-tech firms. It would be as if the high-tech corridor in Silicon Valley were distributed one firm at a time across the poorest counties in the mountains of Appalachia. Not only would low levels of educational attainment hinder innovation, but the clustering of suppliers and skilled labor would disappear. The challenge clearly has become how to overcome constraints of training and size to improve productivity in the region.

There is also a science and technology gap among countries in the region. Argentina, Brazil, Chile, Mexico, and Venezuela are relatively advanced. Colombia, Costa Rica, and Uruguay have recently generated significant national capacity, but in the rest of the region there is an absence of policies and institutions for science and technology development. In technology generation, the number of patents granted ranged from eleven in Guatemala to 2,535 in Brazil.

Meeting the productivity challenge involves a clearer understanding of the nature of technology. Neoclassical theory tends to see technology as exogenous to the production system, a tradable recipe or input that incurs a short-run cost in production. Technological progress is viewed as continuous and cumulative, in a single-track race for dominance. Neostructuralists view technology differently. Relying in part on the views of Schumpeter, an economist who dedicated much of his work to thinking about technological change, neostructuralists see technology as tacit knowledge not easily transferred, a result of interactive learning and a synergistic process between producers and users. Progress is seen as both continuous and discontinuous, with windows of opportunity for acquisition opening but abruptly shutting at critical junctions in the process of technological change.[39] The policy ramifications of the different views on technology are complex. Can technology be purchased like any input of production to increase output, or are institutional changes required to promote technological absorption into Latin America economic systems?

No matter your theoretical perspective, the problem of catching up with the technological frontier involves the question of technological acquisition. Technology is an asset; it must be procured somewhere. Technology may be acquired through foreign direct investment, through licensing or turnkey plants, or through the promotion of national technological parks. Technological acquisition is often asymmetrical. The seller of a technology naturally has more information about the new product or process than the buyer. In the case of hard technologies (incorporated into machinery and equipment) as well as soft technologies (new management techniques, quality control, industrial relations, and just in time production)—the seller of the technology may be the only agent that knows fully the nature of the commodity.

In a developing country, the next task is the assimilation of technology. Here our question of institutional change comes into play. Simply installing a modern factory does not result in technological acquisition. Technology can remain a black box poorly understood and unsuitable for adaptation and innovation. Improving productivity in an economy involves both appropriating information about technological systems and assimilating this knowledge and disseminating applications beyond the first user. Absorption of technology requires not only obtaining a machine but also training a labor force to run it. Sometimes companies are reticent to make such expensive investments in human capital, as well-trained people often leave the firm. Workers themselves, when poor, may not be able to afford the educational investments to become productive in the international economy. Financing of technological acquisition is also risky—investments often do not pan out. Thin capital markets in the developing world make it far more difficult to finance a good idea. Institutions—

the set of rules and enforcement mechanisms that shape the behavior of organizations and individuals in society—do not effectively promote technology in Latin America. Poor regulatory quality, weak rule of law, corruption, and ineffective governance contribute to the widening productivity gap between Latin America and the rest of the world.[40] The capabilities of governments to promote technological change are limited not only by financing but also effective governance.

Given these challenges of technology in developing countries, who should invest in a national technological infrastructure? Under the import substitution industrialization regime, investments in technological development were principally made by the state. Publicly funded research and development centers were promoted to support the needs of national businesses to link the domestic supply and demands for science and technology services. The state also intervened with private multinational capital to negotiate positive terms for technology transfers through multinational corporations. A smoothly functioning technological system was an interface between universities and national industry in identifying priority projects for technological investments. That system meets the needs of the final user of technology by effectively organizing research and development facilities in the public and private sectors. Unfortunately, the challenge of technological development was beyond the capabilities of most states, and most nations in Latin America fell further and further behind in the global arena. The private sector has not risen to fill the technology gap. Incentives must be changed to promote technological change in the region.

Given fiscal constraints, states must focus more on structuring incentives for private-sector investment in technology rather than directly invest in technology. Tax incentives favorable to R&D and strong laws protecting intellectual property rights are crucial in promoting a business environment conducive to the development of a science and technology infrastructure. Regulatory frameworks to encourage firms to finance and undertake more R&D must be designed. The state can also act as an arbiter of information, disseminating information about best practices. Box 9.3 illustrates the way Uruguay's agriculture ministry helped improve farming techniques. It might also work to promote dynamic cooperation between research communities, universities, and the private sector. Collaboration can maximize the use of scarce resources. The state can work directly to redirect public resources in education to improve the quality of human capital. It can take a leadership role in monitoring and assessing the national stock of technological assets.

Attention should be paid to the gender implications of investments in infrastructure and science and technology education. Gender-aware planning in infrastructure might take the location of housing, workplaces, and nurseries into account; it would pay attention to peak and off-peak transportation networks.[41] Good science and engineering indicators are crucial to informed adjustments in science and technology policy.[42] State promotion of investments in science and technology may help transform the problems of economies of scale and limited time horizons that firms face in allocating resources to technological activity. By adjusting incentives, risk may be minimized for these investments, which tend to have uncertain long-term payoffs.

Latin America has traditionally been plagued by a splintering of capacity in science and technology systems. Businesses, universities, research institutes, and state

Box 9.3.   Just-in-Time Fruit: Technology Makes the Difference for Award-Winning Apple Growers in Uruguay

By Christina MacCulloch

When Felipe Reyes and Osvaldo Moizo formed a partnership in the early 1980s to grow apples and pears in the Melilla region near the Uruguayan capital of Montevideo, they never imagined that they would have to compete with producers around the world.

But with the 1990s came the new era of open markets, when even medium-scale farmers like Reyes and Moizo would have to keep up with the latest technical innovations and consumer demands. If their 39-hectare farm, called Zanja Honda, were to succeed, they would have to learn about the best crop varieties and the latest production systems, and search out buyers at home and abroad.

Luckily, one of the world's premier fruit producing countries was practically next door, so Reyes and Moizo traveled to Chile on a fact-finding mission. Back home they applied what they learned with such success that their operation caught the attention of officials in Uruguay's Ministry of Agriculture who were running a new initiative called the Program for Farm Conversion and Development (PREDEG). The IDB-financed program was established to provide technical assistance and marketing support to small and medium-size farms, such as Zanja Honda, as well as to agroindustries and nurseries.

That same year, PREDEG awarded Reyes and Moizo a prize for innovation and quality, particularly citing their success in integrating production and marketing. "These producers stand out for their technological capabilities as well as for their business management," declared Carlos Sammarco, PREDEG chief, at the awards ceremony.

Encouraged, Reyes and Moizo set out to change over from the traditional orchards to high-density plantings with quick-growing, early-ripening varieties that would result in higher yields and less damaged fruit. With financing from PREDEG, Reyes and Moizo traveled to Italy, France and Spain to learn about new fruit varieties with the best flavor, color and texture, and get a feel for potential markets. "The trip marked the starting point for a new approach to raising fruit, a trip to the future," recalled Reyes. "The fruit producer of the future is the person who can rapidly adapt to change with new varieties and cutting-edge production systems. It is the only way," he added.

Soon, the two partners had joined a group of other Uruguayan farmers to import 12,000 Australian hybrid apple plants from a supplier in Brazil. Called "Pink Lady," the crisp, flavorful new variety was specifically developed for high-density planting and early maturity.

"Things are changing so fast that in two years we won't have any fruit trees left that we had when we won the PREDEG prize," said Reyes. The full-size apple trees used in years past were spaced the traditional distance apart and would begin producing fruit after five years at the rate of 15 boxes per tree. With the new variety, 15 small, early-maturing trees are planted in the same space that would have been taken by a single tree in the previous production system. Each new tree produces one box of fruit at much lower cost and higher quality in a shorter period of time.

"It is incredible, but the apples that I have on my table today are the first fruit from a tree we planted three months ago," said Reyes. But while the Pink Lady variety is well received by growers and consumers alike, it comes with strings attached. Royalties must be paid to the Australian Ministry of Agriculture for each tree purchased. Further payments must go to the Pear and Apple Export Association of Australia for each apple sold. But by using the latest varieties and production systems, Reyes and Moizo have met the competitive challenge.

(continued)

(continued)

The PREDEG program that helped Reyes and Moizo to compete came at a crucial moment for Uruguay. "Our farm sector was lagging," said Sammarco, "and after our domestic producers lost tariff protection, they became vulnerable to competition, particularly from neighboring countries."

PREDEG currently works with some 3,000 farmers organized into 260 producers' groups along with 900 individual fruit producers. It provides the farmers with training and cofinances innovative operations, such as the establishment of new plantings and drip irrigation systems. The program also provides technical assistance and marketing support to some 30 agroindustrial firms and commercial agents and 25 nurseries. In a pilot program that now includes some 200 producers, PREDEG is helping farmers to reduce the use of agrochemicals by introducing alternative disease-control methods.

For more information, contact PREDEG at PREDEG@adinet.com.uy or choose Rural Development under www.iadb.org/sds.

Source: www.iadb.org/idbamerica/Archive/stories/2000/eng/APR00E/e400f5.htm, March–April 2000.

providers of financing do not interact in a smooth technological system. Jorge Sabato conceived of a smoothly functioning technological system as a triangle in which industry, basic educational institutions, and science and technology centers constantly interact. Latin America has been plagued by gaps among these institutions, such that there is little communication between the private sector and the university or even between state-run research institutes and academic researchers. Clearly, with limited resources in the area, incentives toward public–private partnerships might allow for exploitation of economies of scale in technological innovation and adaptation.

An interesting example of effective investment in human capital to attract high-technology production is the case of Intel in Costa Rica. Intel's 1996 investment in a microprocessor plant in Costa Rica was a function of an ample supply of well-educated workers across the technical, maintenance, engineering, and management levels. The Intel decision is seen as the culmination of a policy begun in the 1960s to invest in technical education. In 1974 Costa Rica, with Inter-American Development Bank (IADB) assistance, formed the National Council for Scientific and Technological Research (CONICIT) and the Costa Rican Technological Institute (ITCR) to promote technical training. Regional centers of technical training were built in the late 1970s. Inter-American Development Bank funding in part supported the training of researchers, as it did throughout the region. The IADB also set up a technology development fund in Costa Rica (as well as in Argentina, Brazil, Chile, Colombia, Mexico, and Uruguay). A private Costa Rican Foundation in concert with UN and United States Agency for International Development (USAID) money promoted computer literacy at the elementary level. Costa Rica supports a science and technology program that funded 239 postgraduate fellowships, many of whose recipients are currently teaching in Costa Rican technical institutions. As a small country, Costa Rica decided early on to focus on a limited number of technologies: information systems, environmental sciences, and the agricultural and forestry sectors. It has transformed these narrowly defined investments into international comparative advantage in these fields. It has done a good

**BOX 9.4.   A SCIENTIFIC SUCCESS STORY:
STRATEGIC RESEARCH INVESTMENTS IN SÃO PAULO**

FAPESP, the scientific and research institute of the State of São Paulo, is setting new standards for research in the Third World. The number of citations by Brazilian scientists has grown at three times the global level since 1996, and the institute has been instrumental in promoting a world-class biotechnology industry which has been the first anywhere to decode the genome of a plant pathogen that infests oranges and other citrus fruits. The goal of the institute is to work on the frontier of science—but science with direct social and economic relevance for Brazil. Success has led to international cooperation—including a request from the U.S. Department of Agriculture for research on the sequencing of a gene of a bacterium that afflicts vineyards in California.

What has made FAPESP successful? Funding, autonomy, and strong linkages to the university and the business community are keys to its accomplishments. By law, since 1962, the State of São Paulo allocates 1 percent of total tax revenue to FAPESP to fund scientific and technological research. A quick scan of its website shows the range of projects funded. But FAPESP has few staff. Law prohibits it from assembling its own corps of scientists; instead it must work through university and commercial labs. Research grants and fellowships strategically target the development of young scientists and new projects. Its administrative costs are limited to 5 percent of its investment in research, and governance is through a twelve-member board with fixed terms. This virtual institute identifies opportunities—and expects accountability. It avoids the brain drain problem of many developing countries by requiring that scientific grantees return to teach in the university for at least four years—or pay back the salary earned. Unlike research in industrial countries the model among the scientists is more cooperative as opposed to competitive. Although competition among multiple-funded groups may create rapid results, it is not seen as the best use of very limited resources. Private industry is a research partner; for example, it shares the costs in a project to sequence the genomes of the eucalyptus tree, which is cultivated by the paper and cellulose industry.

The approach appears to be working, generating research with a practical return relevant to the Brazilian economy. This niche, often ignored by research institutions in industrialized countries, creates dollars and hope. FAPESP is currently working on a program to identify the genes of the worm that causes a parasitic infection afflicting millions around the world. The hope is that this research—and other projects—will lead to the development of drugs targeted at tropical diseases such as malaria and Chagas. Given FAPESP's record, success is more than a dream.

Source: Larry Rohter, "Model for Research Rises in a Third World City," *New York Times,* 24 April 2001; and FAPESP's website watson.fapesp.br/begin01.htm.

job of balancing investments at the levels of both basic and higher education. Costa Rica is seen as an example of the gains of smart, modest investments in the technological arena generating long-term rewards.[43]

The Costa Rican case is one example of what can be achieved in a small country. Small and poor countries must be highly selective in targeting research and development dollars. In addition to promoting sectors such as information systems that don't require huge capital investments, countries might consider innovations in agriculture, health, and environmental resource management, in which fields of scientific study may also have social benefits. In box 9.4 we show how the Brazilian

Poor roads and mountains such as these in San Jose, Bolivia, create obstacles
to transportation. *(Courtesy of David Edelstein.)*

research institute FAPESP has successfully managed technological change with
social gains. Over time, however, a clear plan to move up the technological ladder
is required such that countries aren't caught forever in a narrow range of low-level
technological specialization.[44] Medium-sized and large countries should use the
state arm to create incentives for technological innovation in business, facilitate
linkages between universities and the private sector, and consolidate or close obsolete institutions. All countries must address the question of financing. Investments
in technology are risky and take place over time. Judicious investments in research
and development institutions are required, and instruments to reduce risk and
encourage investment by private actors must be encouraged to jump-start Latin
American technological systems. Multilateral institutions such as the Inter-
American Development Bank have in the past contributed to the training of some
twenty thousand researchers in one hundred universities in the region. However,
more needs to be done to promote the formation of competent personnel within a
healthy regional science and technology infrastructure. In smaller countries, assistance can be directed to laying solid foundations; in larger countries that already
possess these institutions, consolidation and modernization can be facilitated.[45]

INFRASTRUCTURE: A CRITICAL COMPLEMENTARY INPUT

In addition to weak technological systems, Latin America faces an infrastructure gap
that undermines gains in productivity. Underinvestment, particularly during the 1980s

Better roads will facilitate bringing goods to market for peasant farmers. *(Courtesy of David Mangurian and the Inter-American Development Bank.)*

and the debt crisis, led to a need for $60 billion annually in injections in telecommunications, roads, and ports.[46]

Infrastructure development in Latin America must confront an unfriendly geography. Although long coastlines are a plus, high mountains, dense jungle, dry deserts, and isolated urban centers pose enormous challenges. International ranking of transportation infrastructure places Latin America in the bottom seventy-fifth percentile. A movement from the bottom to the top quarter is the equivalent of a reduction of 9,000 miles measured in transportation costs. Traversing the Andes between Santiago and Buenos Aires is equivalent to nearly quadrupling the distance from 1,129 to 4,700 km; transport costs rise as a function of closed passages in winter and the costs of driving at high altitudes. Trucks must detour about 1,500 miles around the Argentine pampas in the worst of winter. The Amazon consumes infrastructure. Intense rains wash out roads; only 30 percent of investments Peru made in jungle roads in 1980 remain paved today. Overall the ratio of paved roads in the region is the lowest in the world at just 20.2 percent. The global average is 55.3 percent; in the European Union 99 percent of the roads are paved.[47] Table 9.10 presents data on air and road density in the region with comparisons to the European Union and NAFTA. The accompanying photos in this chapter shows just how tough road conditions are in Latin America!

Given poor roads, travel by sea is the preferred transport mode. Yet the potential of rivers for intra-Latin trade is under realized due to poorly connected river basins. Latin America has some of the most inefficient ports in the world, better only than

Table 9.10.   Air and Road Density

Region	Paved Road System (km)	Airports with Paved Runways	Road System Density		Airport Density	
			per 1,000 km²	per 1,000 inhab.	per 100,000 km²	per 100,000 inhab.
South America	347,703	1,096	20.4	1.0	6.4	0.3
Andean Community	65,913	326	14.4	0.6	7.1	0.3
Mercosur	270,778	708	23.0	1.2	6.0	0.3
European Union	3,888,046	1,542	1241.8	10.3	49.2	0.4
NAFTA	4,147,349	5,922	204.3	10.9	29.2	1.6

Source: World Economic Forum, *The Latin American Competitiveness Report 2001–2002* (New York: Oxford University Press, 2002).

South Asia and West Africa. One index of port efficiency places Europe at 5.41 and Latin America at a weak 3.37. Yet Latin ports charge almost twice as much for this poor handling service. Central America's proximity to the huge North American market confers advantage; delays, nevertheless, equal to 40 percent of travel time add to costs. Table 9.11 shows the average number of days to clear customs in ports for Latin American nations and comparison countries. Poor customs procedures, lack of electronic data processing, lack of coordination at crossings, confusing documentation, and poorly trained personnel impede trade. One can see from the table, however, that good port performance in Latin America is possible—Chile and Costa Rica, for example, already achieve fast clearing rates to facilitate their export focus.

Investments in infrastructure can support economic growth, reduce poverty, and make development environmentally sustainable.[48] In considering reforms in infrastructure, three policy guidelines emerge: infrastructure should be managed like a business, not a bureaucracy; competition should be introduced; and stakeholders should have a strong voice and real responsibility.[49] In infrastructure reform there is a clear need for a public–private partnership. Profit opportunities create incentives for private participation to increase productivity and reduce costs. But incentives from the public sector are critical in reducing risks that make private-sector activity alone prohibitive.

Throughout the world, public-sector services no longer need to be conceived of as natural monopolies. Revolutions in telecommunications and in provision of electrical and energy services have made a smaller scale possible. Natural monopolies can be opened to the forces of competition, unbundling portions of the service or breaking up service areas geographically. Clearly this must be done with an eye to equity. Profit-oriented telecoms, not surprisingly, are more interested in servicing high-priced business areas rather than low-income neighborhoods or rural sectors. Private activity in one area may need to subsidize access for all.[50]

In the power and gas sector, population concentrations in urban areas make private investment lucrative. Indeed, Latin America has become a leader in electricity infrastructure privatization. Brazil, Argentina, and Colombia lead the list of developing countries in terms of private investments in the electricity sector. Cost savings are significant. In Bogota, Colombia, the private CODENSA electricity distribution

Table 9.11. Delays in Customs Clearing in Ports

	Average Days
Region	
East and South Africa	12.0
East Asia and the Pacific	5.6
Eastern Europe	2.4
Latin America and the Caribbean	7.1
North Africa	5.5
North America	3.5
West Africa	11.7
Western Europe	4.0
Latin American Country Performance	
Argentina	7.0
Bolivia	9.5
Brazil	10.0
Colombia	7.0
Costa Rica	4.0
Chile	3.0
Dominican Republic	7.0
Ecuador	15.0
El Salvador	4.0
Guatemala	7.0
Haiti	15.0
Honduras	4.0
Mexico	4.0
Nicaragua	5.0
Panama	5.0
Peru	7.0
Uruguay	5.0
Venezuela	11.0

Source: World Economic Forum, *The Latin American Competitiveness Report 2001–2002* (New York: Oxford University Press, 2002).

company halved its losses from 24 percent to 12.5 percent, increased customers per employee from 800 to 1,900, and reduced the frequency of service disruption 30 percent within two and half years.[51] But other countries such as Mexico and Venezuela have been resistant to privatization and foreign participation in national electricity production. Privatization may also be uneven outside the cities.

In transport, possibilities for private road concessions and maintenance are being pursued. In water and waste, public municipalities are accepting bids for lease contracts to private services. However, state activity is critical in providing technical and financial assistance to the solid waste and wastewater disposal firms.

Public–private partnerships in infrastructure are beginning to provide lessons of how complementary efforts can enhance productivity. In Argentina, with the privatization of the telephone company Entel, phone service requests can now be met in forty-eight hours, as compared to the five- to ten-year waits common in the 1980s.

Overall, privatization has increased the number of main line and mobile phones by about 7 percent and waiting lists for service by 60 percent.[52] But consumers have new complaints: high prices. The cost of local telephone service has risen by about 14 percent. One estimate suggests consumers are overpaying by about $1 billion per year—with excess profits going into the coffers of Telecom and Telefónica owners in Italy, Spain, and France. In Brazil the prices of electricity, telephone, and water rose by more than double the increase in general prices from 1995 to 2001.[53] Private monopolies may need regulation or the introduction of competition policies to restrict price gouging.[54]

There are, unfortunately, unintended consequences to privatization. Rural inhabitants are more likely to see their service remain under public ownership, given the higher costs of servicing remote areas. In urban centers market concentration has worked against price decreases. Monopoly rents are accruing to private agents, often based in other nations. Blackouts in Brazil and Chile have raised questions about security of supply and who is ultimately responsible for the delivery of this critical input. Regulatory policies are incomplete, best by lack of transparency and bureaucratic complication.[55]

The private sector alone may not work; the case of Mexican roads is illustrative. In Mexico, 3,600 miles of highways were built from 1988 to 1994 at a cost of $15 billion. These high costs resulted in government bailouts of forty-eight out of the fifty-two concessions granted.[56] Outrageous tolls scared away traffic, making cost recovery problematic. The tolls from Mexico City to Acapulco were a whopping $63! The government stepped in, cutting average tariffs by 60 percent. In part the lesson of Mexican road concessions concerned the short time frame. Given contract periods of between ten and fifteen years, firms were attempting to recover costs too quickly with exorbitant prices. A longer concession period reduces these pressures, making the concessions more profitable.

A more successful outcome of privatization was in the case of Argentine waterworks.[57] In 1992 a consortium led by Lyonaise des Eaux was given a thirty-year contract to run water and sewerage for Buenos Aires. It was able to make post-tax profits of $52 million on $355 million of revenues. The Argentine consortium worked in part because its predecessor, Obras Sanitarias de la Nación (OSN), was hugely inefficient. OSN facilities used to leak half of the water, and the agency was heavily overstaffed. It was therefore relatively easy to make changes. The workforce was cut from 7,500 to 4,000. New meters and new pipes were installed. As part of the public–private partnership, the Argentine government financed a retirement scheme for workers, allocating 10 percent of the shares in the company to employees, giving them a stake in the success of the venture.

Brazilians are looking for productivity gains in the privatization of Telebrás, Brazil's huge telecommunications firm. Telebrás was created as a state enterprise in 1972 under the Ministry of Communications. Although its initial stages registered strong growth, as measured by a 16-percent increase in access lines and a 26-percent fall in the congestion rate, the period of the debt crisis brought underinvestment and dismal performance. It was reorganized in the early 1990s, positioning it for privatization in 1998. International bidders were attracted by the unmet potential of the Brazilian market. As the world's fifth most-populous nation, Brazil had a two-year waiting list for phones in some areas. The total sale—which was split among eight groups of investors paying more than $19 billion—was roughly 13 percent larger than London's privatization of British Telecom in the early 1990s.[58] Competition will be encouraged, initially regulating prices but then moving to free prices as more firms are established in the market. One benefit of late investments in the industry is the ability to leapfrog over existing technologies to develop a low-cost, high-productivity sector.[59] With investments in infrastructure and associated productivity enhancements in industry and labor, one forecast projects a possible 6 percent per year growth rate, leading to a doubling in GDP per capita over a ten-year period.[60] Productivity—enhancing the performance of labor, infrastructure, and industry—is clearly the key to raising living standards in the region.

The Business Environment: The Emerging Shape of the Latin American Industrial Sector

Macro instability and the contractionary effects of the debt crisis had a profound impact on industrial performance in Latin America. High rates of inflation and associated uncertainty thwarted long-term strategic decision making and investments in the capital stock. Capital formation was stalled by the lack of available finance. Survival depended on financial ingenuity, not investments in plant and equipment. During this period, dramatic changes in information technologies transformed the frontiers of business practice, largely leaving Latin American firms behind. The technological lag in automated production as well as new inventory systems set firms at a competitive disadvantage. Sluggish domestic demand forced a new orientation toward the export sector as opposed to production for the domestic market, but the focus was on agriculture and natural resource-based products. Industries that process raw materials have been more successful than those relying on labor or engineering services. Trade liberalization and associated import competition have had negative effects on textiles, footwear, and the metal and machinery branches.[61] Small and medium-sized enterprises were hard hit, in part because of difficulties in securing bank guarantees critical to exports.[62] Some weathered the crisis by becoming subcontractors to large transnational firms.[63] One study suggests that in the manufacturing sector, the expected dynamic results of liberalization have been muted. At least through the 1980s, manufacturing still suffered from limited competitiveness and a concentration in traditional exports.[64] As shown in table 9.12, lagging institutional environments for business—large bureaucracies creating delays in registering businesses—create inefficiencies. Insertion into the international economy as a competitive exporter not only involves sound macroeconomic policies and the change toward export orientation but also depends upon institutional change in domestic markets for labor, technology, and infrastructure.

The effect of export-led growth varies by sector. The most efficient of the natural resource processors need few workers. Because they are newly automated, the labor they do use tends to be skilled management and not unskilled line workers.[65] As noted by Gert Rosenthal, head of ECLAC, it would be an irony to return to the primary product production pattern that left Latin America vulnerable to external

Table 9.12. Bureaucratic Controls

	Number of Procedures to Start New Business	Time to Complete Procedures (days)
Argentina	12	71
Bolivia	20	82
Brazil	15	67
Chile	12	78
Colombia	17	55
Ecuador	12	141
Mexico	15	112
Panama	7	14
Peru	14	171
Uruguay	9	105
Venezuela	15	124
Average LAC	13.5	92.7
Average non-LAC countries	9.6	57.9

Source: World Economic Forum, *The Latin American Competitiveness Report 2001–2002* (New York: Oxford University Press, 2002).

shocks and commodity price instability.[66] One of the objectives is to move in the direction of what ECLAC calls "changing production patterns"—products with a higher value added and stronger growth potential. To do so, however, will require changes in labor, technology, and infrastructure.

EXPORT PROCESSING FREE ZONES: GOOD INVESTMENTS OR A WASTE OF MONEY?

The benefits of export processing free zones, EPFZ, sometimes called foreign trade zones or free economic zones, are controversial. EPFZs are designed to attract foreign direct investment into a nation, with intended spillovers to stimulate manufacturing production. Imports of raw materials, equipment, and intermediate production are normally exempted from customs duties, and customized infrastructure such as roads or electricity are usually provided. Special tax incentives or exemption from profit repatriation rules are often offered to lure business to the area, and labor laws are sometimes held in abeyance.

Although these zones have been shown to contribute to employment and the entry of foreign capital, many charge that they operate as enclaves with limited linkages to the broader economy. As such, little technological learning takes place, and the incentive for diversification of production is limited. EPFZ activity tends to be restricted to manufacturing assembly, in a vertically integrated transnational production structure. Jobs are created, but little value is added in production. Because profits are repatriated and taxes forgone, the country may be left with little in the way of foreign contribution to economic activity.[67]

The proliferation of EPFZs in Central America has led to fierce competition to attract foreign capital.[68] One zone in El Salvador, in San Bartolo, includes a wide array of products such as textiles, clothing, shoes, paper bags, cardboard boxes, electronic components, and jewelry. Tax incentives and profit repatriation leave wages as the primary contribution to the economy. However, given the transnationals' preference for inputs from their own subsidiaries, there were few linkages with other industries. Low-skilled employment did little to raise the level of human capital.

Deep in the Brazilian Amazon, one of South America's largest industrial parks—with about five hundred corporations, including Toshiba, Philips Electronics, and Xerox—is found alongside traditional river people.[69] Providing environmentally friendly employment for the indigenous population and settlers to the region, the free trade zone gives people an alternative to survival strategies that contribute to deforestation. But the cost to the Brazilian economy is enormous. Imports of components for electronic assembly accounted for $3 billion of Brazil's $8 billion trade deficit in 1997. The government's $2.4 billion annual subsidy to the free trade zone is the equivalent of $50,000 for every job created there—roughly ten times the value of the wage paid to the workers. Local Amazonian firms are irked by the subsidies to multinationals; one ice cream producer is frustrated by the thoughts of how he could expand the sale of exotic Amazonian fruit flavors in the Brazilian ice cream market if he had a small portion of the government incentives given to outsiders.

Production in the jungle is subject to regular electricity blackouts and exorbitant freight costs. There isn't much comparative advantage in electronic production in a system defined by biological diversity and fragile ecosystems. TVs produced in the zone are $100 more expensive than those in international markets. The logic of the Manaus free trade zone traces back to import substitution industrialization. When domestic production was protected behind high tariff walls, assembly in desperately poor Manaus made some sense. People were drawn in from the jungle, decreasing the population that the ecosystem supported and concentrating them in the city. Others were drawn to the region from the overpopulated Northeast. This was consistent with the military's plan to strengthen the northwestern frontier of Brazil.

Reduction of tariff walls under liberalization makes production uneconomical without continuing incentives and tax holidays. Why maintain these subsidies? High unemployment will prompt a return to the forest; it will also create opportunities for inroads from the Colombian drug cartels to the north. Alternatives are problematic. Under a development plan called the "Third Cycle," state planners hope that Manaus's colonial rubber boom and contemporary electronics-based economy will be followed by an agro-industrial structure that will sustainably develop the region's rich natural base. But politicians with the purse strings may not follow the lead of the planners. It is far easier to attract jobs through the visible entry of a shiny new assembly plant than to engage in the long and difficult process of changing the shape of the Manaus economy.

INFORMATION TECHNOLOGIES, THE INTERNET, AND E-COMMERCE IN LATIN AMERICA

Successful participation in the global economy requires tying into the information age. Businesses are linked through the web, e-mail, and intranets to produce, gather, distribute, consume, and store information. The Internet transmits information

Table 9.13. Network Access

	GDP per Capita 1999 (PPP)	Telephone Lines per 100 Inhabitants	ISPs	Hosts per 10,000 Inhabitants, January 2000	Internet Users (thousands)	Internet Users (% of population)	Estimated PCs per 1000 Inhabitants, 1999
Argentina	12,277	20.1	47	47.3	900	2.5	49.2
Bolivia	2,355	5.8	5	1.7	35	0.4	12.3
Brazil	7,037	14.9	197	39.0	4,000	2.4	36.3
Chile	8,652	18.6	26	33.8	625	4.2	66.6
Colombia	5,749	16.0	13	10.2	600	1.6	33.7
Costa Rica	8,860	20.4	2	24.3	150	3.9	10.7
Dominican Republic	5,507	9.3	1	9.2	25	0.3	—
Ecuador	2,994	9.1	8	1.7	20	0.2	20.1
El Salvador	4,344	7.6	2	1.6	40	0.7	16.2
Guatemala	3,674	5.5	7	2.5	65	0.6	9.9
Honduras	2,340	4.4	14	0.2	20	0.3	9.5
Jamaica	3,561	18.7	6	2.3	60	2.4	43.0
Mexico	8,297	11.2	167	50.6	2,453	2.6	44.2
Nicaragua	2,279	3.0	5	2.2	20	0.4	8.1
Panama	5,875	16.5	3	10.2	45	1.6	32.0
Paraguay	4,384	5.5	4	2.7	20	0.4	11.2
Peru	4,622	6.7	15	3.9	389	1.5	35.7
Trinidad & Tobago	8,176	20.6	5	41.9	25	1.9	54.2
Uruguay	8,879	27.1	5	107.3	250	7.6	99.6
Venezuela	5,495	10.9	11	6.5	400	1.7	42.2

Source: World Economic Forum, *The Latin American Competitiveness Report 2001–2002* (New York: Oxford University Press, 2002).

quickly, efficiently, and cheaply. It is hard to imagine that only a decade ago the Internet was the purview of a group of intellectual shut-ins. Today it is broadly used to connect people, businesses, and governments to each other. Internet use has soared in Latin America—yet in 1999 only .5 percent of the region's residents had access.[70] Table 9.13 presents data on network access in the region. Some worry that despite its potential to enhance productivity and open new markets, the Internet is also creating a digital divide among countries and between rich and poor within countries.

Access to the Internet conveys benefits. Companies and governments can use the web for e-procurement, enhancing transparency and choice. Coupled with just-in-time delivery systems, the fast transmission of orders allows companies to hold less-costly inventory systems. Marketing systems can be efficiently expanded.

Latin America is an interesting market for e-commerce. The demographic bubble, with 50 percent of the population under age thirty-five, defines a group open to new marketing techniques. Twenty percent of the population is highly desirable to multinational marketers as it controls 65 percent of the wealth. Among this wealthy class, per capita GDP is equal to that of residents of Germany and the United Kingdom. Unlike the multiple languages of Europe, however, the dominance of Spanish and Portuguese facilitates marketing. On the negative side, the lack of Internet infrastructure is daunting. Fewer than 13 percent of households have fixed phones lines, and there is a low computer ownership rate. Low credit card penetration as well as the distrust of security for online purchases limits the market. High telephone charges and underdeveloped delivery systems also impede the spread of the Internet.

Nonetheless, strong potential exists. Latin America's e-commerce purchases were only $194 million in 1999, but they are estimated to grow to $8.3 billion by 2005.[71] Internet startups are emerging, although financing is limited by thin local-capital markets and the global dot.com bust. Greater competition in the telecom sector is introducing new actors. As more public and private organizations implement the Internet, network effects—the gains from having larger number of people linked with the same technologies—create greater momentum. Governments are developing new ways to help firms, schools, government agencies, and NGOs adopt efficiency-enhancing net-based systems. In Brazil, the computer industry signed on media tycoon Silvio Santos, host of the Brazilian version of "Who Wants to Be a Millionaire," for a promotion "the computer of the million," a package of PC, printer, and software subsidized by hardware and software companies.[72] A low-cost Brazilian start up, Metron, has soared in sales as it offers a machine for $250 less than Compaq, complete with installation services. With 70 percent of buyers first-time computer purchasers, support is important. But the biggest constraint is household income. The fifteen million Brazilian households interested in having a computer can only afford an average monthly payment of $25, including the price of the Internet. Sustained GDP growth per capita is necessary to spread the benefits of the technological revolution to all.

EMERGING INDUSTRIAL COMPETITIVENESS

The terms of competitiveness are changing in the region. Stability on the macro front, a new external orientation, and the stimuli of global competition are transforming the industrial landscape of the region. The emerging productive structure can be characterized by three dimensions: changes in the organization of firms at the firm level, changes in the structure and behavior of markets, and changes in the relative contributions of various activities to each nation's development.[73] Enterprises that are aggressively engaging the global market are integrating within the globalized productive system as subsystem producers. Stronger use of imported as opposed to locally supplied parts (particularly where quality is superior) has created cheaper, more marketable products. Entrepreneurial processes are exhibiting increasing dualism. On the one hand, there are a large number of sectors—such

> **QUESTION FOR THOUGHT**
>
> Given the state of labor and technology markets and the existing infrastructure in Latin America, what role do you believe the state should play in promoting industrial competitiveness?

as automobiles in Mexico, Brazil, and Argentina; domestic appliances in Chile; ceramic and leather industries in Uruguay; and textiles and clothing in Colombia and Central America—that are engaged in an intensive process of modernization. The

Table 9.14. Ten Commandments of Competitiveness Policy

I	Create a stable and predictable legislative environment.
II	Work on a flexible and resilient economic structure.
III	Invest in traditional and technological infrastructure.
IV	Promote private savings and domestic investment.
V	Develop aggressiveness on the international markets (exports) as well as attractiveness for foreign direct investment.
VI	Focus on quality, speed, and transparency in government and administration.
VII	Maintain a relationship between wage levels, productivity, and taxation.
VIII	Preserve the social fabric by reducing wage disparity and strengthening the middle class.
IX	Invest heavily in education, especially at the secondary level, and in the lifelong training of the labor force.
X	Balance the economies of proximity and globality to ensure substantial wealth creation, while preserving the value systems that citizens desire.

Source: International Institute for Management and Development, *World Competitiveness Yearbook,* www02.imd.ch/wcy/factors.

Internet and e-commerce have grown enormously. However, in other sectors, technological modernization is slow and international competitiveness is declining.

A change in competition policy, or the body of laws and regulations surrounding business practices—including agreements between firms, abuse of market power, monopolization, and mergers and acquisitions—has promoted industrial activity. Emerging competitiveness is as much contingent on human resources and technological capacity as it is on wage costs or natural resources.[74] Linkages and a better flow of information among private agents and between the public and private sectors must be improved to reduce the risks of new investments.[75] The question is how this should proceed. Will this take place spontaneously as more firms are subject to the pressures of the global market? The new political economists would suggest that the market itself is the best way to solve this problem. The neoinstitutionalists would contend that market institutions are underdeveloped and in need of state intervention to provide adequate information to firms. The neostructuralists would suggest that the state assume a more strategic role, guiding business toward developing new areas of comparative advantage. Table 9.14 summarizes the policy menu advocated by the International Institute for Management and Development to promote competitiveness. It is clear from this table that competitiveness is grounded in the interaction between economic performance, effective governance, smoothly functioning markets, coherent legal institutions, an equitable social compact, and a robust infrastructure—a tall order for Latin America, but a necessary one.

Key Concepts

informal sector   labor productivity

Chapter Summary

The Labor Market

- Contemporary labor markets in Latin America are characterized by three main factors: powerful trade unions, an expanding informal sector, and high levels of unemployment. Latin Americans have historically emphasized job security; this strict labor legislation has led to market rigidity. In recent years, union participation has begun to fall under pressures from the globalized economy.
- The unemployment rate alone does not give a clear indication of the problems encountered in the labor market in Latin America; underemployment or people working below their skill levels is also problematic. Furthermore, unemployment rates have increased in many countries due to privatization, government downsizing under the neoliberal model, and an increase in the labor force participation of women. To combat unemployment, the number of jobs must grow at a faster rate than the increase in the economically active population of a country—a difficult feat.
- The informal sector has increased dramatically as a result of inadequate job growth in Latin America. It can be divided into three main categories: microenterprise employment, own-account workers, and domestic service. Its attractiveness to the unemployed, especially the unskilled worker, stems from the minimal requirements of capital, money, and qualifications needed to enter the sector. The informal sector appears to be a solution to the lack of employment generation in the private sector, but it is hardly the best solution. It has led to an increase in income inequality, low-productivity sector, and tax evasion. Yet, it has proved to be a social net and prevented deprivation where the private sector has failed.

Technology

- Compared to the industrialized countries, Latin America is technology poor; increased technological innovation is needed to improve the productivity of workers. Closing the technology gap has become a central issue. Technology must be acquired, perhaps through foreign direct investment, but it must also be accompanied by institutional changes. Due to fiscal constraints, the state can no longer invest as much in research and technology, but it can still play an important role in establishing incentives and regulatory frameworks.

Infrastructure

- Limited investment in infrastructure in the 1980s led to higher costs and a loss of competitiveness. Latin American geography presents enormous challenges to infrastructure integration. Investment in infrastructure with a well-defined partnership between the public sector and the private sector is needed. The three main guidelines to be kept in mind for reform are the following: infrastructure should be managed like a business, not a bureaucracy; competition should be introduced; and stakeholders should have a strong voice and real responsibility.

- The industrial sector in Latin America has been thwarted by several forces. Though some sectors have managed to modernize, others have remained behind. To improve in competitiveness, Latin America needs reform in infrastructure, technology, and improving the flow of information among private agents and between the private sector and the public sector.

Notes

1. IADB, *The Business of Growth: Economic and Social Progress in Latin America 2001 Report* (Washington, D.C.: The Inter-American Development Bank, 2001), 1.

2. Source: International Institute for Management and Development, *World Competitiveness Yearbook,* Scorecard 2002, www02.imd.ch/wcy/factors/.

3. Richard Tardanico and Rafael Menjívar Larrín, "Restructuring, Employment, and Social Inequality: Comparative Urban Latin American Patterns," in *Global Restructuring, Employment, and Social Inequality in Urban Latin America,* ed. Richard Tardanico and Rafael Menjívar Larrín (Miami: University of Miami North-South Center Press, 1997).

4. Tardanico and Larrín, "Restructuring," 244.

5. "Creating Jobs Is Main Headache," *Latin American Weekly Report,* 5 January 1999, p. 2.

6. Tardanico and Larín, "Restructuring," 252.

7. Sonia Montaño, "Women Now Work More," *ECLAC Notes,* November 1999.

8. World Bank, *Labor and Economic Reforms in Latin America and the Caribbean: Regional Perspectives on World Development* (Washington, D.C.: World Bank, 1995).

9. *Labor and Economic Reforms in Latin America,* 253.

10. Psacharopoulos and Tzannatos (1992), as presented by Rosemary Thorp, *Progress, Poverty, and Exclusion: An Economic History of Latin America in the 20th Century* (Baltimore: Johns Hopkins University Press/IADB, 1998), 31.

11. Shahid Javed Burki and Sebastian Edwards, *Latin America after Mexico: Quickening the Pace* (Washington, D.C.: World Bank, 1996), 19.

12. James J. Heckman, Carmen Pages, Working Paper 7773, NBER Working Paper Series, www.nber.org/papers/w7773, June 2000: table 2 [Summary of existing evidence on the impact of job security in Latin America], 15.

13. Sebastian Edwards and Nora Claudia Lustig, eds., *Labor Markets in Latin America: Combining Social Protection with Market Flexibility* (Washington, D.C.: Brookings Institution, 1997), 32.

14. IADB, *Latin America after a Decade of Reforms: Economic and Social Progress 1997 Report* (Washington, D.C: Johns Hopkins University Press/IADB, 1997).

15. IADB, *The Business of Growth,* 113.

16. World Bank, *Labor and Economic Reforms in Latin America.*

17. Mark Mulligan, "Chile Labour Reform Secures Backing," *Financial Times,* September 5, 2001, Internet edition.

18. Victor E. Tokman, "Jobs and Solidarity: Challenges for Post-Adjustment in Latin

America," in *Economic and Social Development in the XXI Century,* proceedings of the 1997 IADB Conference, ed. Louis Emmerij. Available at www.iadb.org/exr/pub/xxi/sec4.htm.

19. Burki and Edwards, *Latin America after Mexico,* 20.

20. Tokman, "Jobs and Solidarity."

21. Tokman, "Jobs and Solidarity."

22. ECLAC, *The Equity Gap,* 60–61.

23. ECLAC, *The Equity Gap,* 61.

24. ECLAC, *The Equity Gap,* 66.

25. Vanessa F. Cartaya, "El Confuso mundo del sector informal," in *Nueva Sociedad Marginalidad* 90 (July–August 1987): 81–84.

26. International Labor Organization, headquarters homepage: usa.ilo.org/news.

27. ECLAC, *The Equity Gap,* 70.

28. Jaime Mezzera, "Abundancia como efecto de la escasez. Oferta y demanda en el mercado laboral urbano," *Nueva Sociedad* 90 (1997): 106–17.

29. International Labor Organization, skills development for the informal economy, www.ilo.org.

30. ECLAC, *The Equity Gap,* 65.

31. International Labor Organization, skills development.

32. ECLAC, *The Equity Gap,* 60.

33. Díaz, cited in Tardanico and Larrín, "Restructuring," 249.

34. Tokman, "Jobs and Solidarity."

35. *World Competitiveness Report 1994,* as cited by Román Mayorga, *Closing the Gap,* IADB Working Paper SOC97–101 (Washington, D.C.: IADB, 1997), 9.

36. Mayorga, *Closing the Gap,* 15.

37. ECLAC, *Policies to Improve Linkages with the Global Economy* (Santiago, Chile: ECLAC, 1995), 149.

38. Mayorga, *Closing the Gap,* 15.

39. Hubert Schmitz and José Cassiolato, *Hi-tech for Industrial Development: Lessons from the Brazilian Experience in Electronics and Automation* (London: Routledge, 1992), 9.

40. IADB, *The Business of Growth,* 3.

41. Caroline Moser, "Gender Planning in the Third World: Meeting Practical and Strategic Gender Needs," *World Development* 17, no. 11 (1989): 1799–825.

42. Lauritz Holm-Nielsen, Michael Crawford, and Alcyone Saliba, *Institutional and Entrepreneurial Leadership in the Brazilian Science and Technology Sector,* World Bank Discussion Paper no. 325 (Washington, D.C.: World Bank, 1996).

43. Case taken from Paul Constance, "A High Technology Incubator," *IDB América* 1997. Available at the Inter-American Development Bank homepage at www.iadb.org.

44. Mayorga, *Closing the Gap,* 24.

45. Mayorga, *Closing the Gap,* 4, 45.

46. World Bank, *Meeting the Infrastructure Challenge in Latin America and the Caribbean* (Washington, D.C.: World Bank, 1995), 10–11, gives data on infrastructure deficits.

47. Statistics in this section from Jeffery Sachs and Joaquin Vial, "Can Latin America Compete," in *Latin American Competitiveness Report* (New York: Oxford University Press, 2002).

48. World Bank, *World Development Report 1994* (New York: Oxford University Press/ World Bank, 1994).

49. World Bank, *Meeting the Infrastructure Challenge.* Information on the energy sector is available at www.eia.doe.gov/emeu/cabs/argentina.html.

50. World Bank, *Economic Growth and Returns to Work* (Washington, D.C.: World Bank, 1995), 17.

51. IADB, *The Business of Growth,* 166.

52. IADB, *The Business of Growth,* 186.

53. Richard Lapper, "Policy under Pressure," *Financial Times,* October 56, 2002, weekend I.

54. Juan Manuel Valcarcel, "Calling Someone in Argentina: Dial M for Monopoly," *Wall Street Journal,* 16 August 1996, p. A11.

55. IADB, *The Business of Growth,* 166.

56. "Tequila Freeways," *The Economist,* 16 December 1996, p. 66.

57. "Water Works in Buenos Aires," *The Economist,* 24 February 1996, p. 66; Emanuel Idelovitch and Klas Ringskog, *Private Sector Participation in Water Supply and Sanitation in Latin America* (Washington, D.C.: World Bank, 1995).

58. Seth Schiesel, "Brazil Sells Most of State Phone Utility," *New York Times,* 30 July 1998, p. D1.

59. McKinsey Global Institute, *Productivity: The Key to Accelerated Development Path for Brazil 1998,* Telecom Case 9 (São Paulo, Brazil: McKinsey and Company, 1998).

60. McKinsey Global Institute, *Productivity.*

61. José Miguel Benavente, Gustavo Crespi, Jorge Katz, and Giovanni Stumpo, "Changes in the Industrial Development of Latin America," *CEPAL Review* 60 (December 1996): 62.

62. A firm will typically secure a bank letter of credit to finance goods in transit. The bank loans the firm money while the goods are in transit, before they arrive and are paid for by the importer.

63. Benavente, Crespi, Katz, and Stumpo, "Changes," 63.

64. John Weeks, "The Manufacturing Sector in Latin America and the New Economic Model," in *The New Economic Model in Latin America and Its Impact on Income Distribution and Poverty,* ed. Victor Bulmer-Thomas (New York: St. Martin's, 1996), 271–94.

65. Benavente, Crespi, Katz, and Stumpo, "Changes," 65.

66. Gert Rosenthal, "Development Thinking and Policies: The Way Ahead," *CEPAL Review* 60 (December 1996).

67. Summarized from Teresa S. Weersma-Haworth, "Export Processing Free Zones as Export Strategy," in *Latin America's New Insertion in the World Economy,* ed. Ruud Buitelaar and Pitou Van Dijck (New York: St. Martin's, 1996), 90.

68. Weersma-Haworth, "Export Processing," 90.

69. Adapted from Matt Moffett, "Deep in the Amazon, an Industrial Enclave Fights for Its Survival," *Wall Street Journal,* 9 July 1998, p. A1.

70. This compares to 30 percent of U.S. residents at this time (IADB, *The Business of Growth,* 205).

71. U.S. Department of Commerce, *ExportIT Latin America,* International Trade Administration, June 2000.

72. Jennifer L. Rich, "Computers for the People in Brazil," *New York Times,* January 7, 2002, Internet edition.

73. ECLAC, *Strengthening Development: The Interplay of Macro and Microeconomics* (Santiago, Chile: ECLAC, 1996), 37.

74. ECLAC, *Strengthening Development,* 71.

75. ECLAC, *Strengthening Development,* 72.

CHAPTER TEN

AGRICULTURAL POLICY

Sowing the Seeds of Equitable, Sustainable Growth in Latin America

Large-scale farms have increased Mexican agricultural exports. *(Courtesy of the Inter-American Development Bank.)*

Due to its unique characteristics, the rural sector presents policymakers with some of the most intractable challenges in development. Agriculture is more than coffee and bananas, wheat or cattle. It is a complex, interrelated set of markets for land, labor, capital, and technology embedded in a socioeconomic web of traditional and corporate farming practices producing for both domestic and international consumption. Successful agriculture must paradoxically meet the need for low-cost national food security as well as provide a sufficient income for rural families. It is increasingly relied upon as an export engine by developing nations in search of comparative advantage, yet it faces relatively high import barriers to agricultural products in the developed world. Agricultural export drives may strain environmental resources, undermining the future productivity of the sector. Agriculture is full of promise yet requires careful tending to maximize the benefits of socially, environmentally, and economically sustainable growth.

In this chapter we will consider the opportunities and constraints in agricultural development in Latin America. We will explore the following questions:

- What are the characteristics of agricultural markets in Latin America? In particular, what are the dimensions of the market for land, labor, capital, and technology? Do agricultural markets behave differently from other markets? How are complementary inputs with respect to infrastructure and transportation provided?
- How have past development strategies shaped agricultural performance in Latin America? What is the legacy of feudal land patterns and/or import substitution industrialization?
- What was the experience with **land reform** to redress some of the inequality in asset distribution in this sector? Was it successful?
- How has the neoliberal model changed agricultural policy? Has it been effective?
- What challenges remain for agriculture in Latin America?

CHANGING PATTERNS OF AGRICULTURAL PRODUCTION IN RURAL LATIN AMERICA

Agriculture in Latin America spans a wide diversity of crops and climates. From the plains of the Argentine pampas to the hilly Guatemalan highlands, from traditional crops such as cattle and coffee to new boom products such as soya and kiwis, the plurality of agricultural systems in the region presents challenges to thinking clearly about agricultural practice. Nonetheless, we can generalize with respect to dominant modes of agricultural production and consider agricultural strategies that will help overcome common constraints of regional production.

Two types of landholdings dominate agriculture in Latin America: relatively small-scale, traditional peasant agriculture and large-scale corporate farming. This pattern of small and large landholdings is a legacy of the colonial *latifundia,* in which large tracts of land were deeded to Spanish or Portuguese descendants.

Although intermediate-sized producers exist, policy has been driven by this **dualistic structure of production** in agriculture.

The agricultural sector has gone through dramatic changes not only in terms of its relative importance in the economy but also in its internal structure. The share of agricultural in total gross domestic product (GDP) has been slipping over time; in countries such as Brazil and Chile it is 10 percent or less, although in Guatemala and Honduras it is more than 20 percent.[1] The *latifundia* or *hacienda* system has more or less disappeared, but its large scale has been retained by modern capitalist farming. The nature of agricultural production has changed. Whereas the large oligarchic estates had a certain socioeconomic cohesion, the divide between modern commercial farmers and peasant producers is large. Under the *latifundia* system, labor for coffee, sugar, and cotton production was tied to the estates through sharecropping, credit, and personal obligations to create a framework of paternalistic relations.[2] With the dissolution of this social structure, although large commercial farms have largely flourished, peasants are marginalized from land, labor, and credit markets. In the 1990s land use under cultivation for wheat, coffee, and cotton—products grown primarily by small and medium-sized farms—lost ground with an increase in commercial production.[3] Box 10.1 illustrates the problems that small coffee producers have faced in international markets.

BOX 10.1.   A BITTER CUP: THE COFFEE CRISIS IN LATIN AMERICA

International coffee prices are at historic lows, having fallen by almost 50 percent from 1999 to 2002. A production glut—driven in part by new entrants into the international coffee market such as Vietnam—has driven global prices down. World exports were a record 88.7 million bags in 2001, sold at the lowest prices in fifty years. Coffee growing accounts for 8.2 percent of the GDP in Honduras, 7.2 percent in Nicaragua, 4.2 percent in Guatemala, 2.5 percent in El Salvador, and 2 percent in Colombia. Forty-four percent of the region's cropland is used to grow coffee. Indirect activities, including commerce, banking, storage, and transportation, are also affected by the crisis; at the macroeconomic level states must cut back public spending due to lower tax revenues.[4]

It is estimated that 300,000 have lost their jobs in Guatemala due to the coffee crisis; in El Salvador coffee exports are down 40 percent. The situation in Central America is made worse by a severe drought in some parts of the region; 220,000 rural Nicaraguan families are estimated to be suffering from food shortages and abandoning their land to search for work in Costa Rica. Coffee farms have been seized by banks. Health officials estimate a growing number of Nicaraguans dying from hunger due to the lack of jobs, income, and food created by the coffee crisis. Acute child malnutrition has risen. Beggars from shantytowns line the roads, pleading for help. It is a desperate time. In September 2002, Nicaraguan protesters held government negotiators hostage in exchange for food, medicine, and debt relief for workers. Anger is erupting across the region against what is perceived as an unjust global market that does not give small farmers a chance. Coffee farmers receive a global average of 24 cents a pound for their produce; consumers pay $3.60 a pound. Ten years ago coffee-producing companies got approximately one third of every dollar spent on coffee; now they get about 8 cents.[5]

(continued)

(continued)

Figure 10.A. Average of Monthly Coffee Prices—Composite of Different Blends, 1982–2001

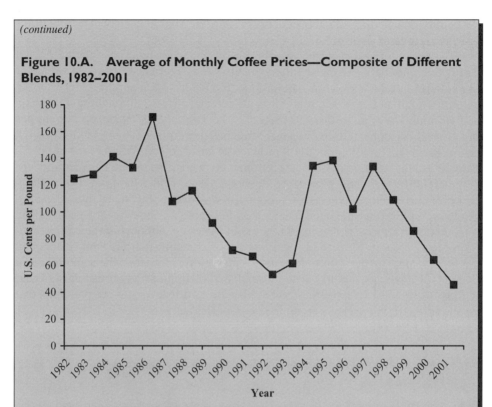

Source: International Coffee Association, www.ico.org.

What can be done? Fair trade coffee is the response of an international movement that helps businesses buy directly from rural coffee cooperatives, eliminating middlemen and providing double the price to small farmers. Guatemala is using the Internet to auction its specialty beans as an alternative to selling them on the New York market under the supervision of PricewaterhouseCoopers.

Small farmers are urged to move into designer coffee; organics have been increasing by 20 percent a year. International aid agencies are promoting restructuring for small farmers, especially in lowland areas, to switch to other crops. The Organization of American States (OAS) is helping Central American and Colombian farmers experiment with medicinal plants such as sarsaparilla, which can be grown alongside or instead of coffee.[6] Nonetheless, steep hillsides, poor infrastructure, lack of information, and remote villages thwart such a transition. Hopeless farmers in Colombia are increasingly pushed into the illegal coca market.

Brazil, the world's biggest producer and exporter of the bean, is attempting to add value to current production by doing more of the processing, aiming to roast and grind more beans and produce more instant coffee. Embrapa Café, the coffee research arm of the Brazilian agricultural research agency, is working to make the often delicate bushes more resistant to disease and sharp changes in temperature.[7]

The International Coffee Organization (ICO), representing fifty producer countries, is launching a quality standard that aims to remove five million bags a year of low quality coffee from the market. Oxfam, the international NGO, is campaigning to spend $100 million of aid from rich countries to destroy five million more bags of stock.[8] Addressing the coffee crisis will certainly take both local and global solutions.

In some countries, agribusiness has grown rapidly. The primary focus has moved from production for local consumption to nontraditional products for exports. Although manufacturing has assumed increased importance in the export profile of the region, agricultural products still account for 25 percent of the value of Latin America's exports. Countries of the region have expanded production beyond traditional crops of sugar, cocoa, bananas, and coffee into high-value products such as fruits, vegetables, flowers, nuts, and oils.[9] Brazil has become one of the world's five "food powers" through increasing productivity generated by investments in mechanization. Brazilian farmers have expanded beyond their own borders, planting 33 percent of the soy in Bolivia and Paraguay and owning 4 percent of Uruguay's land.[10]

Mexico's agricultural exports began in the 1960s, promoted by transnational corporations. Strawberry and tomato exports boomed in the 1970s and 1980s, resulting, in conjunction with export of other fruits and vegetables, in more than a doubling of agricultural exports in two decades. Guatemala supplied 80 percent of the snow peas coming into the U.S. market in 1991, roughly double its market share of 1988. Between 1983 and 1993, the share of Central American melons rose from 5 to 58 percent of the U.S. market. Colombia has become known for its cut flowers, becoming the second-largest exporter of flowers after the Netherlands. Ecuador has also become a cut-flower exporter, increasing global sales fifteenfold from 1985 to 1991.[11] Overall, nontraditional exports constitute 15 percent of agricultural exports from Latin America.

Reverse seasons from North America make Latin American production complementary to the U.S. and Canadian markets. As Americans replace meats with more fruits and vegetables, demand has risen year-round. Innovations in packaging and refrigerated cargo handling have facilitated long-distance transport. Chilean fruit and wine have become common items on North American tables. Melting Andean snows water rich land in Chile's central zone, supporting new varieties of grapes and pears that are most welcome in northern countries in midwinter. Chilean wines are now winning international competitions. Poor farmlands converted into forest plantations have shown handsome dividends. Agriculture and forestry have contributed to Chile's trade surplus to the tune of more than $2 billion per year.

The transition to nontraditional, high-value exports has been facilitated by development agencies and governments as part of structural adjustment packages. In particular, USAID, the United States Agency for International Development, has been an active supporter of private incentives in the agricultural sector. The Commonwealth Development Corporation, the World Bank, and the Inter-American Development Bank (IADB) also provide support for agricultural export growth.[12] Unfortunately, in the second half of the 1990s Latin America's share of these dynamic growth markets had slowed, losing competitiveness to new entrants in the global market.[13] Nonetheless, despite efforts to promote nontraditional exports by peasant farmers, the successes are due primarily to large corporate farming. Indeed, the expansion of agricultural exports often has been at a cost to small farmers and the production of subsistence foods for domestic consumption.

Alternative Production: Organic Farming

Organic farming is appealing to small-scale producers in the region because of the minimal use of expensive fertilizers and the high prices organic products obtain in international markets. Global sales of organic fruit and vegetables have been increasing at annual rates between 20 and 30 percent in the last years of the 1990s.[14] Yet organic farming is not problem-free. Small farmers still need to find reliable buyers, be able to meet volume and quality requirements, and find affordable and timely transportation to avoid spoilage. They also confront a new kind of nontariff barrier: certification. All organic produce must be certified by an organization such as the Organic Crop Inspectors Association for compliance to strict standards. For an illiterate farmer to provide documentation that a field has been chemical free for at least three years is a daunting task.[15] Farmers must also pay for inspections. Local agricultural organizations help. Cooperatives can create economies of scale in marketing and transportation. In Costa Rica, through a small blackberry farmers' association, APROCAM, berries plucked from mountain bushes at dawn arrive on Miami grocery shelves by that same afternoon. In Guatemala some of the larger farms are selling organic produce directly to supermarket chains such as Fresh Fields. Organic coffees have exhibited more stable (and 20-percent higher) prices due to consumer tastes for designer, chemical-free coffees. In Mexico, a confederation of coffee-producer organizations, UNCAFESUR, through an organization called La Selva, is working with small-scale *ejido* farmers to switch to organic production.[16]

Organic production not only has a stronger market but also is better suited to the needs of the small farmer. It rejects the chemical cocktail of expensive fertilizers in favor of labor-intensive natural composting and weeding by hand.[17] La Selva is working to teach terracing techniques, organic composting, intercropping of bananas to provide shade, and developing nurseries for seedlings. The InterAmerican Foundation, in conjunction with a private foundation and a Dutch coffee broker, supported the transition costs. Although nearly half of the initial harvest was lost to the violence in the Chiapas region, marketing efforts exceeded all expectations, with three North American companies—Aztec Harvests Coffee Company, Ben & Jerry's, and United Airlines—featuring coffee grown by La Selva producers. A potential downside is that the more labor-intensive methods of organic farming have drawn women further into agricultural production, adding to their already burdensome dawn-to-dusk routines. Nonetheless, the additional demand for labor has decreased the degree of migration of males and older children in search of work. Furthermore, organic methods are environmentally sustainable, creating an economic incentive to produce without using inputs that interfere with the ecosystem.[18] Box 10.2 provides an example of how, with funding, green methods have boosted yields and markets in El Salvador.

Extralegal Production: Coca

Despite the gains from crop diversification and organic farming, access by peasant farmers to inputs and good land as well as international market conditions limit

Box 10.2.   Organic Crops Gain Ground in El Salvador

IDB Program Assists Farming Cooperatives That Supply Local Restaurants and Supermarkets
By Carlos Gonzáles, La Palma, El Salvador

Organic food, like fancy bottled water, is often portrayed as a luxury for well-heeled people in rich countries. The assumption is that only people with means can afford to buy food produced without chemical pesticides, synthetic fertilizers and other agricultural inputs that have become the mainstay of farmers around the world.

But in El Salvador, a number of forward-looking farming cooperatives have discovered a market for organic fruits and vegetables at their doorstep. Under a project partly financed by the IDB's Multilateral Investment Fund, these cooperatives are selling fruits and vegetables to health-conscious restaurants, hotels and supermarkets right in the capital of San Salvador. Better yet, the cooperatives are generating new, better-paying jobs for rural men and women while helping to protect and restore scarce farmland.

One such cooperative operates out of a large shed in the Salvadoran municipality of La Palma, just a few kilometers from the border with Honduras. On a typical workday, women stand at stations inside the shed, sorting piles of carrots, spring onions, tomatoes, strawberries and passion fruit, all of which has been delivered there by local organic farmers. All the produce is washed, graded and bagged. Some of the fruit, such as strawberries, is processed and bottled as jam and bar-coded so that checkout machines at supermarkets can identify it.

"We have been working in various localities, and several cooperatives are now implementing expansion plans," says Mario Urrutia, coordinator in El Salvador of the Cooperative League of the United States of America (CLUSA), one of two executing agencies running the project. CLUSA provides technical and marketing assistance to participating cooperatives along with Proexsal (Producers and Exporters of El Salvador), an agricultural marketing company based in San Salvador that is the project's other executing agency. "We come in once the farmers have begun to produce organic crops and want to penetrate the local market," explains Godofredo Pacheco, manager of Proexsal. "Our pitch is simple: high-quality, organically grown Salvadoran products." Together, the two organizations help qualified cooperatives to become financially and ecologically sustainable businesses.

GREEN METHODS BOOST YIELDS

The case for organic farming in El Salvador goes beyond rising consumer demand. One of Latin America's most densely populated countries, it already faces a shortage of high-quality agricultural land. The intensive use of pesticides and chemical fertilizers can often hasten the degradation of land in tropical climates, so farmers who correctly implement organic methods can actually increase yields and lower their production costs over time.

Scarce land is just one of the challenges facing El Salvador's farming cooperatives, however. Many of these were founded 20 years ago, when the government instituted an agrarian reform program in response to long-standing conflicts over land tenure. Most of the farmers who acquired land thanks to the reform had little or no experience managing businesses, and as a result many new cooperatives saw their production decrease. The country's commercial banks have also proved unwilling to finance most cooperatives; even when loans are available, interest rates remain prohibitively high.

The new project aims to help cooperatives deal with all these obstacles. "CLUSA is helping us with the production of organic cacao and sesame, and strengthening the coop-

(continued)

(continued)

erative," says Rafael Pineda, chairman of La Carrera cooperative. "We are learning about how to run a business and the different types of credit." Proexsal's Pacheco says La Carrera is learning to handle the kind of strategic and planning decisions that all businesses face. "Now they're trying to come up with a brand name for their chocolate bars," he says. "But first, they have to learn about the features of the market and use efficient processing and packaging techniques so that they can compete."

As recent earthquakes and hurricanes have shown, Salvadoran farmers also face a disproportionately high risk of natural disasters. In the Lempa River basin, the river is once again threatening to flood, as it did in 1998 when Hurricane Mitch struck. "Now we are more aware of the danger the Lempa River represents," says José Santos, chairman of the Los Navegantes cooperative, "but our situation has changed a great deal in two years. Even though there were many promises of support for development of the region after Hurricane Mitch, we have not received any significant aid. Since April, CLUSA has been providing us with advisory services," says Santos, "and we have been very encouraged by what we can learn."

"They came to us," says CLUSA's Urrutia, "because they had heard about the progress other cooperatives have been making with the program. So we explained to them that CLUSA and Proexsal could help them, but that they would have to follow the official procedures and commit to the program. In just four months of work, the first farmers are already experimenting with demonstration plots of organic crops and the cooperative members are immersed in institutional and technical training."

One of the more interesting aspects of Los Navegantes is that 56 percent of the cooperative members are women. "Many of us are parents," notes member Sonia Hernández, "and we need a strategy to help us improve our lives. That need motivated many of us women to join the cooperative."

Pacheco and Urrutia say the ultimate proof that organic farming is viable in El Salvador is the fact that several cooperatives are starting to compete effectively with imported conventional food products. They say the market for organic produce also tends to be more stable than the general agricultural market, a factor that helps cooperatives to maintain a steady revenue stream.

Source: www.iadb.org/exr/idbamerica/English/MAY01E/may01e6.html, June 2001.

widespread benefits. Planting coca is easier. As an agricultural crop, coca is versatile and lucrative. It grows in a wide range of conditions, may be harvested from three to six times per year, and can have a gestation period as short as eighteen months. Four-fifths of the coca is grown in the Upper Huallaga Valley of Peru and in the Chapare of Bolivia. Earnings for coca range from ten times that of cacao, to nineteen times that of citrus, to ninety-one times that of rice. There are three markets for coca: traditional, for uses in medicine and folk remedies; licit, for markets controlled by governments for production for cola and pharmaceuticals; and illicit production. Before coca is brought to the illicit market, its leaves are mashed and mixed with chemicals to become paste. The paste is then treated with sulfuric acid and potassium permanganate to form a cocaine base that can range in purity from 90 to 92 percent. It is then transported and cut before reaching the $110 billion international market, double the combined profits of all Fortune 500 companies.

Production is extremely mobile; illegal narcotics have become Latin America's true multinational. The technology is fairly straightforward, low cost, and relatively barrier-free. South American traffickers earn between $5 and $6 billion in the U.S. market. It is also labor-intensive, engaging growers, processors, and distributors in the production chain. The value added at higher levels of production graduates from $500 to $1,000 for an average kilogram through $160,000 to $240,000 as it hits the street. Small coca farmers can earn a few thousand dollars a week to pay employees and feed, clothe, and house their families—and unlike traditional crops, have some left over to buy goods. Efforts at eradication have cut global production of coca from 201,600 in 1994 to 183,000 in 1999, but dramatic declines in production in Peru and Bolivia have been nearly countered by a five-fold increase in Colombia.[19] Former president Paz Estenssoro of Bolivia once remarked that "cocaine has gained an importance in our economy in direct response to the shrinking of the formal economy; it is perhaps the only wealth in our history that benefits an important sector of the Bolivian population." In 1986 the aggregate value of coca production was 20 percent of farm income; in the Upper Huallaga Valley and Chapare, the proportion hits 90 percent. Peru's Alan García once called cocaine "our only successful multinational." For peasants, coca cultivation can be the margin between subsistence and a decent standard of living.

But coca can promote imbalanced growth through conspicuous consumption, potential inflationary effects from the infusion of money, the displacement of domestic food production as more land is dedicated to coca, and environmental damage, especially through chemical processing. The political price of narco-terrorism, the threat to democratic institutions, and international pressure is relatively high. The governments of the region, under pressure from the United States, have promoted alternative development by drawing producers toward new crops, but many peasants find the dollar lure of illicit crops irresistible. Furthermore, falling prices for agricultural products have turned back limited progress on alternative development schemes. Said one Colombian *cocaleiro,* "We grow coca for survival, not because we like it."[20]

PITFALLS OF SUCCESS

As farmers moved into nontraditional and illicit crops and corporate farming has dominated the sector, producers of traditional crops such as wheat, maize, sugar beets, and milk have suffered. In particular, smaller *campesino* producers have been hurt. Recall the story of the Lehmans from chapter 1, who were squeezed by competitive global tobacco companies. The number of commercial farms has risen by 22 percent, accounting for an additional 30 percent of the land. Smaller producers find it difficult to overcome credit and finance constraints; economies of scale in marketing, packaging, and transport; import regulations and inspections in foreign markets; and production challenges with respect to pest control, soil management, and pesticide use. The result has been a bimodal agricultural sector in which the rich agroexport firms are edging out traditional producers. Many former farmers now find themselves in orchards and packaging plants. Prospects for peasant farmers are dim unless investments in microtechnologies are promoted by the state to bring peasant farmers into small-scale commercial sectors such as the cut flower industry.[21] Transnational corporations command a large proportion of agroexports. Chiquita (United Brands), Del Monte, and Dole (Standard Fruit) continue to exert substantial influence in Central America, using their base in traditional bananas to capture 25 percent of all **nontraditional export production.** Three of the four top firms leading the Chilean boom are transnational.[22] Agriculture is big business in Latin America—sometimes to the detriment of the small farmer.

Not surprisingly, corporate farming has transformed relations between peasants and landowners in the region, resulting in a complex structure of agricultural production. With a decline in feudal land forms and a rise in corporate farming, we see several changes with respect to labor. Traditional clientelistic social relations have been replaced by a wage labor system. Capital is increasingly substituted for labor. In table 10.1 we can see that by the mid-1990s, in most countries the percentage of irrigated land has increased, as has the use of fertilizer and farm machinery. The amount of land farmed in the region grew from 86 to 98 million hectares during the 1980 to 2000 period, primarily driven by the cultivation of corn and soybeans.[23] In Costa Rica, for example, fertilizer consumption has more than tripled, and the number of tractors has increased by more than 25 percent. Mechanization has not advanced evenly in every subsector, benefiting large-scale corporate crops over small and medium enterprises.

A major shift has taken place in the agricultural labor force. Over the last twenty years, the workforce available to farms fell from 35 percent to 21 percent of the region's total workforce.[24] As machines and fertilizers replace workers, we can see the share of the labor force in agriculture declining in most countries. Table 10.2 groups countries by the magnitude of the shift in the share of labor force employment. Imagine the degree of change in the social structure: in the relatively short span of ten years, there is a 20–50 percent shift in agriculture's share of employment. For anyone who has traveled in Latin America and was amazed at the influx of poor workers from the countryside, perhaps this number is not startling. Landless workers are searching for survival in cities. There is also an increase in the migrant laborers called *volantes*—those who fly between the rural sector and the outskirts of the urban sector as labor demand changes. These are workers without permanent jobs or homes, generally leading lives of misery, contributing to both urban and rural poverty. In Mexico, twenty-six villagers were killed in 2002 in a clash over land, a longstanding feud ignited by dwindling resources for survival.[25]

Box 10.3 chronicles the incredible obstacles and devastating human cost faced by those struggling for land in Bolivia. Similarly in Brazil, landless workers desperate for survival erupted into violence in 1998, looted stores, and commandeered government buildings in an attempt to call government attention to their plight. Organized by Brazil's landless movement, MST (Movimento Sem Terra), the group has, with the support of churches and international groups, occupied (or invaded) unproductive ranches to pressure for land reform in a country where 3 percent of the richest farmers own 66 percent of the land. Killings by police defending the land have made land reform in Brazil an international human rights issue. By forging connections between the rural and urban sector, the MST has been able to transform itself into the largest social movement in the region. It has developed an

Table 10.1. Key Agricultural Inputs

	Arable Land (hectares per capita)		Irrigated Land (% of arable land)		Fertilizer Consumption (hundreds of grams of nutrient per hectare)		Agricultural Machinery (tractors per 1,000 agricultural workers)	
	1979–1981	1996–1998	1979–1981	1996–1998	1979–1981	1996–1998	1979–1981	1996–1998
Argentina	0.89	0.70	5.7	5.7	46	330	132	190
Bolivia	0.35	0.24	6.6	6.2	23	53	4	4
Brazil	0.32	0.33	3.3	4.1	915	1,020	31	58
Chile	0.34	0.14	31.1	78.4	338	2,225	43	52
Colombia	0.13	0.05	7.0	13.7	601	1,077	8	6
Costa Rica	0.22	0.16	7.7	20.7	812	2,826	8	6
Ecuador	0.20	0.13	24.8	28.8	471	955	6	7
El Salvador	0.12	0.10	4.3	4.4	1,376	1,619	5	4
Guatemala	0.19	0.13	5.0	6.6	726	1,604	3	2
Honduras	0.44	0.28	4.1	3.7	163	720	5	7
Mexico	0.34	0.27	20.3	23.8	570	658	16	20
Nicaragua	0.39	0.53	6.0	3.2	392	198	6	7
Panama	0.22	0.18	5.0	4.9	692	753	27	20
Paraguay	0.52	0.43	3.4	2.9	44	233	14	24
Peru	0.19	0.15	32.3	28.9	381	498	5	3
Uruguay	0.48	0.39	5.4	13.5	564	1,102	171	173
Venezuela	0.19	0.12	10.0	15.4	711	1,058	50	59

Source: The World Bank, *World Development Indicators, 2001* (Washington, D.C.: The World Bank): 130–32.

Box 10.3.   Bolivian Landless Give Birth to a Movement

By Peter Lowe, Tarija, Bolivia

Leading two tired kids by the hand and carrying her youngest in a cloth on her back, Juana Ortega arrived on foot in this southern Bolivian provincial capital, the destination of a 175-mile protest march. "My children are heavy," she said, not even mentioning the one she had been carrying *in utero* for almost nine months. "But I do this out of necessity. We need land."

Ortega, 31, and her children had been riding in a crowded truck or walking in the sweltering sun for six days since leaving their hut in Pananti, one of eight landless settlements on the Chaco, a low-altitude plain east of here. The Ortegas were among 150 families that converged from the settlements for the march, organized by Bolivia's two-year-old Landless Rural Workers Movement (MST), which took its name and many of its tactics from the Brazilian group famous for occupying idle farmland.

In Tarija, the marchers demanded titles to their parcels. But the government ignored them for a week, until they occupied a National Institute of Agrarian Reform office March 6. Officials quickly called the police, who fired tear gas and clubbed protest leaders.

As Ortega ran from the building, she stumbled and fell hard. Four days later, back in her hut in Pananti, her pregnancy ended in a stillbirth.

The death was just the most recent tragedy for the settlement. Last October, Ortega was among 350 women and children who lived along a parched riverbed without food or shelter for three days after dozens of landowners and paramilitary thugs tried to dislodge landless communities in the area. The following month a paramilitary gang massacred six settlers in Pananti. Despite Bolivia's 50-year-old agrarian reform law and recent government promises, Pananti residents don't expect titles for their plots anytime soon, leaving them vulnerable to more attacks.

Conditions are similar in the other landless settlements on the Chaco, the poorest part of South America's poorest country. But the MST is pressing forward. "What we're doing here in Bolivia is not illegal," says Ermelinda Fernández, president of the group's Chaco chapter. "We're struggling together, on the basis of our reality, to recuperate what has always been ours—the land."

Bolivia's landless movement follows a half-century of dashed rural hopes. In 1952 a revolutionary government banned forced labor and gave some land to *campesinos*. Since then, however, most Bolivian regimes have favored export farming and large estates while ushering in transnational firms such as Syngenta, the Swiss seed and chemical giant. Free-market policies have kept most of Bolivia's 8 million inhabitants in poverty.

Former President Gonzalo Sánchez de Lozada's 1993–1997 administration banned large estates that serve no social or economic purpose, attempted to reduce corruption in the agrarian-reform agency and streamlined the legal framework for redistributing abandoned land. Despite the reforms, the Sánchez government did not manage to wrest a significant number of plots from large landholders, known here as *latifundistas* and *patrónes*. His successors, Hugo Banzer Suárez and Jorge Quiroga Ramírez, who assumed the presidency last August, have not done much better. "On the Chaco," Fernández says, "agrarian reform has only strengthened the hold of the *patrónes* and not resulted in the distribution of land to those who work it."

Today 4.5 percent of the nation's landowners own 70 percent of its agricultural acreage, according to the Bolivian Documentation and Information Center, a nongovernmental organization based in the central city of Cochabamba. As they wait for the value of their idle parcels to increase, an estimated 100,000 landless agricultural workers live in extreme poverty. "There are still haciendas where 30 peons work from sunrise to sunset for a completely inadequate salary," Fernández says, citing daily pay as low as $1.41. "They have no alternative because they have no land of their own."

Perhaps nowhere in Bolivia is the problem more glaring than in Yacuiba, the municipality that includes Pananti and runs along the Argentine border. Just 25 families own 80 percent of the municipality's land, according to the Permanent Assembly of Human Rights (APDH), a Bolivian nongovernmental organization. Another 3,000 families have no land.

The disparity prompted the Gran Chaco Campesino Federation, the local arm of the Bolivia Rural Workers Union (CSUTCB), to start organizing landless workers to occupy underused plots instead of waiting for government action. In the first takeover, the Ortegas and 140 other landless families occupied Pananti, an abandoned 235-acre property, in May 2000. Most of the families had lived and worked for years on plantations nearby. The MST was formed at a conference the following month in Yacuiba, the municipality's largest town, 25 miles south of Pananti.

Since then, landless workers have founded seven other settlements on the Chaco, and the MST has organized new chapters in the provinces of La Paz, Potosí and Santa Cruz. MST President Angel Durán says another is in the works in Cochabamba.

Headquartered in La Paz, the capital, the MST has coordinated actions with farmers battling U.S.-backed coca eradication programs in the Chapare, a jungle region in central Bolivia. The group also cooperates with trade unions, indigenous organizations and others interested in social justice for *campesinos*.

And the MST is developing ties with Brazil's Landless Rural Workers Movement, the world's largest and most successful agrarian-reform group, which has grown to an estimated 500,000 families since forming in 1984 (see Stage Might). The Brazilian group is planning to send a delegation to Tarija in June for the Bolivian MST's annual meeting.

Bolivian *latifundistas* aren't happy about the movement. One of their groups, the Gran Chaco Stockbreeders Association (Asogachaco), has called for violence against landless people.

The Chaco settlers, in turn, have fought off eviction attempts by police and soldiers. Last October about 80 landowners and at least seven masked paramilitary thugs, wearing military uniforms and carrying military weapons, burned down huts in a landless community called Los Sotos. Then they threatened settlers in Pananti. Neither the landowners nor the masked men were punished, says Fernández, the local MST leader. "The authorities did nothing."

That was just a warm-up. Shortly after dawn November 9, as unarmed Pananti settlers walked to their fields to prepare for corn planting, paramilitary gunmen ambushed and killed six of them and wounded 21. The injured included Ortega's husband, Mario. Later that day, some of the survivors fatally beat a man they had identified as a ringleader of the attack.

Responding to the incidents, authorities arrested nine landless *campesinos* and five people linked to area landowners. The five were quickly released, while the landless remained in jail. (Fernández herself was jailed December 18, just three days after giving birth. She was released on bail three days later.)

Bolivia's interior minister, Leopoldo Fernández, ordered an investigation of nearby police and army troops who failed to prevent or stop the violence. And a communiqué from NGOs that work with Bolivian *campesinos* alleged that a variety of government officials and institutions were complicit in the massacre for failing to resolve land conflicts quickly. On November 20, the government promised to release the jailed MST activists and grant landless people titles to 21,000 acres, including Pananti.

But attacks on landless settlers have continued. On December 11 army troops fired on

(continued)

(continued)

campesinos occupying an estate in Santa Cruz Province, just north of the Chaco. Human rights activists say at least two *campesinos* died in the violence.

The terror in Pananti disrupted corn planting, so the community has no harvest this year. Ortega's husband and many of the family's neighbors are working as low-paid day laborers on nearby farms. MST lawyers, meanwhile, have started a slow legal process to win land titles for the settlement. "We've had to work very hard to recuperate the community's stability," Fernández says.

A few days before losing her baby, Ortega explained why she had joined the march with her three children. "I decided to do it for them," she says, "for the land they will need to survive."

Source: Printed with the kind permission of Peter Lowe. You may find this article online at www.americas.org/country/Bolivia, May 2002.

---

alternative socioeconomic development model that places people before profits, transforming the face of the Brazilian countryside and its politics.[26]

The movement to less labor-intensive means of production has indeed produced gains in output. Table 10.3 shows the gains in agricultural production. From a baseline of 1979–1981, we can see that several countries—Chile, Argentina, Paraguay,

Table 10.2. Labor Force Employment in Agriculture

	1980	1999	% Decline in Agriculture's Share
Moderate Shifts in Labor Force Employment			
Argentina	13.37	9.25	30.81
Bolivia	60.91	47.71	21.67
Chile	22.34	16.42	26.50
El Salvador	46.22	32.30	30.12
Guatemala	65.67	50.65	22.87
Panama	31.83	21.34	32.96
Paraguay	49.23	35.14	28.62
Peru	36.77	26.95	26.70
Uruguay	16.47	12.40	24.71
Dramatic Shifts in Labor Force Employment			
Brazil	35.64	16.73	53.06
Colombia	40.33	22.06	45.30
Costa Rica	35.64	20.27	43.13
Ecuador	42.33	25.39	40.02
Honduras	62.75	31.87	49.21
Mexico	36.35	21.53	40.77
Nicaragua	42.16	20.83	50.59
Venezuela	15.64	8.51	45.59

Source: ECLAC, *Survey of Agriculture in Latin America and the Caribbean* (Santiago, Chile: ECLAC, 2002) 48; ECLAC, *Statistical Yearbook 2001* (Santiago, Chile: ECLAC, 2001), 712.
Note: Labor force employment in agriculture for 1999 is calculated using economically active population for the year 2000.

Table 10.3. Crop Productivity Index

Country	Crop Productivity Index 1979–1981	Crop Productivity Index 1998–2000	Change in Index
Argentina	83.5	159.5	76.0
Bolivia	71.6	151.0	79.4
Brazil	75.3	121.6	46.3
Chile	70.7	126.3	55.6
Colombia	84.1	100.0	15.9
Costa Rica	70.6	133.6	63.0
Ecuador	78.2	122.4	44.2
El Salvador	120.4	108.5	−11.9
Guatemala	89.6	120.9	31.3
Honduras	90.4	116.5	26.1
Mexico	86.5	121.6	35.1
Nicaragua	124.1	134.2	10.1
Panama	97.1	97.2	0.1
Paraguay	58.7	110.4	51.7
Peru	82.2	162.9	80.7
Uruguay	86.8	149.7	62.9
Venezuela	76.3	105.7	29.4

Source: World Development Indicators 2001, 134–36.

Peru, Uruguay, Bolivia, and Costa Rica—have logged relatively rapid growth in the agricultural sector. By 2000 the change in the index of agricultural production in these countries exceeded 50 percent, above the 30-percent change in the index of world agricultural production. A second group of countries—Ecuador, Mexico, and Brazil—roughly approximated the change in the world index. Other countries in the region did not fare as well. Not surprisingly, domestic conflict in El Salvador and Nicaragua contributed to low growth rates in agriculture. In most cases the conflict itself had roots in highly unequal patterns of land distribution. The outbreak of fighting was the manifestation of social conflict over control of land, a precious commodity. Policy measures must resolve the underlying unequal conditions of production to generate a sustainable and strong pattern of agricultural growth. Simply improving output without improving the lives of rural residents is not sustainable as a development policy.

But aggregate growth rates don't tell us who the largest regional producers are or how the value of agricultural production fared. Table 10.4 shows that as a percentage of regional output, Brazil, Mexico, Colombia and Argentina top the list in agricultural production. Although to some degree this is to be expected, given endowments of land and population, it is important to remember because these countries have become players in global agricultural markets. It should be noted, however, that strong output does not necessarily translate into healthy revenues. Because revenues are determined by both the quantity produced and the price charged, the gains from agricultural production are highly sensitive to price changes. Agricultural prices of Latin America's major commodities, measured in constant

Table 10.4. Gross Domestic Product of Agriculture at Constant Market Prices (millions of U.S.$ at 1995 prices)

Country	1990	1995	2000	2000 Share of Latin American Output
Brazil	45,471	53,025	61,099	42.6
Mexico	17,053	18,171	19,877	13.8
Colombia	11,732	12,967	13,599	9.5
Argentina	10,497	12,734	13,622	9.5
Venezuela	3,488	3,695	3,882	2.7
Chile	3,357	4,566	5,228	3.6
Peru	3,301	4,153	5,616	3.9
Guatemala	2,722	3,132	3,586	2.5
Ecuador	1,852	2,138	2,123	1.4
Paraguay	1,836	2,071	2,184	1.5
Uruguay	1,195	1,531	1,490	1.0
Costa Rica	1,156	1,473	1,726	1.2
El Salvador	1,185	1,270	1,322	0.9
Bolivia	842	998	1,126	0.8
Honduras	686	817	861	0.6
Nicaragua	536	629	880	0.6
Panama	538	602	672	0.5
Total	109,818.6	126,219.7	139,634.7	100.0%

Source: ECLAC, *Statistical Yearbook for Latin America and the Caribbean, 2001*, 202–3.

dollars, fell to their lowest level of the century during the 1990s.[27] In part the fall in agricultural prices was driven by a fallacy of composition. As debt-laden countries across the globe adopted the neoliberal focus on agricultural exports, markets were saturated. Excess supply drove prices down. Furthermore, protectionist measures in the developed world limited export opportunities. Although the Uruguay round of trade talks were supposed to reduce agricultural subsidies in the industrialized world, little progress has been made. As a percentage of production, subsidies remain stubbornly stuck at 40 percent, ranging from lows of 2 percent and 6 percent in New Zealand and Australia to 65 percent in Japan, 73 percent in Switzerland, 24 twenty-four in the United States, and 49 percent in the European Union.[28] According to the World Bank, rich countries support their farmers with $350 billion a year in subsidies, seven times the amount spent on international development aid. The United States and the European Union are the biggest subsidizers, providing $50 and $100 million respectively. High tariffs compromise the competitive advantage of agricultural exports from the region. Subsidies depress global prices by flooding markets with low-priced agricultural products.

Revenues and production are also sensitive to the exchange rate. Recall that under import substitution industrialization the overvalued exchange rate biased development against the agricultural sector. Overvalued exchange rates worked against the development of comparative advantage in external markets. Industrial protection distorted the internal terms of trade between the domestic sectors. Very often, agricultural protection of competitive commodities was directly taxed as a means of raising revenue to support industrial expansion. One estimate places indirect taxation through industrial protection and macroeconomic policies at 22 percent of agricultural output. To offset this drain, politically powerful agricultural elites were sometimes able to garner favors in terms of subsidies or infrastructure support—but rarely did these benefits trickle down to the small producers.[29]

A real exchange rate depreciation is important in maintaining agricultural exports. Between exchange rate biases, industrialized country tariffs, and subsidies, agriculture faces significant distortions. But simply getting prices right will not work unless adequate rural infrastructure is available, including irrigation, roads, power, and telecommunications as well as credit, market information, research, extension, and farmer education and health.[30] If the farmer—particularly the small producer—does not have the necessary complementary inputs, production and revenues will not rise. We now turn to look at the structural constraints in agricultural production.

CHARACTERISTICS IMPEDING SUSTAINABLE GROWTH IN THE AGRICULTURAL SECTOR

The rural poor are either landless farm workers in commercial farming areas or small holders in areas of low productivity. They lack adequate access to roads, potable water, electricity, communications, secondary schools, and public health. As a result of tough macroeconomic adjustment strategies, the proportion of destitute in the rural sector rose from 28 to 31 percent. Overall poverty—not the poorest of the poor—claimed more than half of rural inhabitants. In Guatemala and Nicaragua, 85.67 and 76.1 percent of rural inhabitants lived in poverty. Rural poverty has clear connections to environmental degradation. Those without assets find it hard to invest in the land through sustainable agricultural practices. The lack of attention to environmental considerations in the early stages of macroeconomic adjustment further resulted in a high degree of environmental degradation.[31] The intensification of agriculture has also had environmental costs. Attempts to increase agricultural output through intensive application of fertilizer and pesticides have contributed to environmental and human costs. Illiteracy and poor health training among uneducated workers have resulted in the poisoning of workers who spread pesticide by hand and then ate without washing. One investigation showed that 39 percent of pesticide applications were undertaken without protective clothing, and 18 percent of workers admitted to not washing after completing the chore. Mothers in Nicaraguan cotton regions were found to have DDT in breast milk, and some blame agro-chemicals for the region's malaria epidemic.[32] Environmental degradation is a constraint in expanding agricultural output.

Women are the sometimes invisible contributors to agricultural production. Nicaraguan census data report only 5 to 12 percent of women involved in farming, yet an IADB study found 50 percent of the labor of corn and bean production being carried out by women. Out of their sixteen-hour daily workload, women usually dedicated an average of four hours to farming. The rural woman's day is consumed

Small traditional farmers, many using sustainable techniques, have been squeezed out by large agro-enterprises. *(Courtesy of Amanda McKown.)*

by food preparation, collection of water and firewood, care of vegetable gardens and domestic animals, clearing and plowing land, weeding, cultivating, milking cows, processing milk and other foods to sell at market, and acting as business managers for the family enterprise.[33] Unlike men, whose crops tend to be seasonal, they work year-round to provide food for their families. When men migrate to the cities in search of work, women are left completely in charge of the farms. The transition to export crops has also opened up new employment opportunities for women. Large agro-industries employ predominantly female labor forces, because women tend to be more readily available to work on a seasonal basis for lower wages.[34] Older daughters in a household take on additional tasks, releasing women for remunerated labor.[35] This naturally calls into question traditional roles in the rural family. Without changes in the social division of labor in the family, women's increased work in the commercial sector is on top of an already long day in the rural home. Sound agricultural policy must take the problems of rural poverty, its environmental dimensions, and its gendered characteristics into account.

Why has agriculture failed to generate an adequate income for most rural inhabitants? A variety of reasons explain failure. Politically, governments have viewed agriculture as a declining sector with falling prices. The rural poor have little political power; urban elites have therefore pursued polices disadvantaging agriculture. Past policies on the part of multilateral organizations have been overly centralized, with top-down integrated rural development schemes ignoring the needs of rural inhabitants. Credit was directed to specific crops and often concentrated in the hands of the rural elites. Frontier settlements contributed to environmental degradation, and many large-scale irrigation projects carried unforeseen environmental costs.[36]

Beyond these policy mistakes, structural characteristics of the agricultural market create challenges for successful policy. The agricultural sector is often characterized by missing or **incomplete markets** for products, labor, and finance, and by high risk, in terms of both crop failure and pricing. Market failures result in inefficient or inequitable outcomes. They often result from inadequate property rights and underpriced or unpriced resources, as well as unwise government regulations and subsidies.

Property rights in the rural sector are often poorly defined, with official records frequently incomplete or nonexistent. A lack of computerization, insufficient staffing, or inappropriate storage facilities may contribute to poor record keeping. Conflicts emerge between nationally registered systems and de facto rights of occupancy by local squatters or customary rights of traditional communities.[37] Indigenous land rights are sometimes mapped but not recognized. Settlers with guns have usurped traditional rights and crudely marked boundaries.[38] Transferability or sale of rights is limited when land records are absent or conflicting, or when a functioning legal system with enforcement capabilities is missing. Secure land titles are often a prerequisite to obtaining credit. Poor judicial and police enforcement may make it difficult to exercise legal claims to land. Uncertainty in retaining property rights over time promotes underinvestment in the land and reduces the incentives to use land efficiently and sustainably. A farmer facing the possibility of eviction is less likely to invest in reforestation or conservation, because there is great uncertainty about reaping the benefits of the investment. For the farmer with tenuous land rights, environmental irresponsibility is economically rational.

Developing countries typically have **segmented credit markets** such that different borrowers are charged different prices. Formal credit markets intermediated by state and private institutions generally charge a low rate of interest that is often government subsidized. But lack of access to collateral to guarantee formal-sector loans forces smaller holders to rely on kinship circles, friends, landlords, or professional moneylenders, often at higher than market interest rates. Agricultural lending is more difficult than commercial lending. The seasonal nature of agricultural activity yields products only at harvest season. Because the same adverse weather conditions affect all borrowers, diversification is problematic. Several factors complicate lending: a high cost to serving geographically dispersed customers, frequent deficits of collateral, problems in contract enforcement, and a lack of trained and motivated financial personnel in the rural sector.[39] There is an informational constraint as well, because less is usually known about a large number of little farmers. The typically high rates of interest in the informal sector can be traced to the ways these factors affect different groups of farmers. Small producers with uncertain harvests and a lack of collateral are less likely to find formal-sector lending than large, mechanized farms. Without credit, the investment in orchards that bear fruit years later, or even in vegetable farming with no returns until the end-of-season harvest, is extremely difficult for the small family farmer.

In addition to credit, the allocation of **water rights** is another important element of incomplete or inefficient agricultural markets. Typically, surface water rights systems accrue based on seniority. Under this system, there is little incentive for those with first rights to conserve water to increase the availability to others. For groundwater, incentives need to be developed to prompt efficient use today and conservation for the future. In the case of surface water in rivers or streams, a market for water rights could be developed. Under this system, if those with prior rights were given a greater number of shares in a water rights system to head off political opposition, they could trade these shares, also prompting more efficient allocation of this scarce resource.[40]

Agricultural Policy Options

Policy remedies for incomplete markets include securing transferable property rights, creating enforceable contracts, removing subsidies, implementing market-based initiatives as opposed to command and control regulations, adopting green accounting methods and peer monitoring, and co-signing loans to decrease risk. In credit markets, mechanisms have been employed to reduce the risk to lenders of bad loans through relying on local leaders or group lending schemes.[41] Positive incentives such as interest rebates for timely repayment and access to new benefits including longer time horizons may enhance enforcement of repayment. Negative sanctions such as legal proceedings may be useful, but the large number of small producers makes enforcement tough and costly. Local governance structures to promote repayment are more promising, such as cooperative lending. Such nonconventional rural finance can also facilitate the growth of horizontal civic rural institutions, enhancing the sustainability and equity of rural finance.[42]

Policy measures can once again be broken down as neoliberal, new institutionalist, and neostructuralist. Pure marketeers will focus on removing governmental restrictions in the agricultural market, eliminating subsidies, and opening markets to free trade. They would also push to strengthen and clarify contractual property rights. New institutionalists would focus on the high transaction costs imposed by incomplete markets and would revamp agricultural credit systems.

For neostructuralists, policies designed to improve the functioning of the market that ignore a class and gendered understanding of market actors face likely failure. In Latin America, agricultural reform is about more than markets. It involves the power of elites to influence policy outcomes.[43] In a case of imperfect factor markets, in which different-sized farms face different prices for labor, capital, or technology, the strongest—the largest—are most likely to benefit from policy changes. For example, in the macroeconomic changes accompanying neoliberal reforms in the Chamorro government in Nicaragua—a nation that pursued aggressive redistributive land reform—small farmers were shown to fail in tough times, selling between 6 and 13 percent of the land back to large-scale owners or wealthy individuals.[44] Policy must take the market structure into account.

But this doesn't mean that neostructuralists will advocate large size. Although small-scale farmers are more vulnerable to external policy shocks, it is not clear that large farmers are necessarily more productive than small farmers. Evidence suggests that with the exception of plantation crops such as sugar or cotton, or where market imperfections such as access to credit or information about international marketing exist, there are few economies of scale in agriculture for farms larger than a family can operate with its own labor. One historical study contrasted the relatively small landholdings in the United States under the Homesteading Acts, with limits of 160 acres, to large-scale allocations of land in Brazilian agriculture of plots no smaller than 988 acres. It showed that large size forced Brazilian farmers to rely on wage labor, with the resulting inefficiencies in supervising hired labor, as opposed to the incentives for the family farmer to rely on productive family labor.[45] Furthermore, to supplement meager wage earnings on the large Brazilian farm, a system of sharecropping emerged that later introduced its own fears in terms of evictions in the face of possible land invasions or impending land reform. Large landowners evict poor sharecroppers because they are afraid of land invasions from squatters exercising the right of occupancy.

The cost of unequal landholdings may be high. Some evidence suggests that the legacy of unequal landholdings can pose a serious barrier to growth over the long term. One study shows that initial land distribution and associated low primary education for sixteen developing countries explain variation in national growth rates. Other empirical investigations also point to this inverse relationship between land inequality and economic growth.[46] As demonstrated by Southeast Asian nations, small family farmers supplemented by investments in rural infrastructure appear to fare better in terms of long-run growth. In contrast, the unequal land distribution from colonial times in Brazil, Colombia, or Guatemala, as worsened by a policy mix of industrial protection under import substitution industrialization and agricultural taxation, constrained dynamic growth in the agricultural sector.[47]

Experience with Land Reform

For the neostructuralist, unequal landholdings correlate with unequal power and unfair access to resources. Land reform has been used in Latin America to address asset inequality in the rural sector. The land reform movement in Mexico and Bolivia was revolutionary; throughout the rest of the region it was a legislated process. Extensive land reforms were undertaken in Chile, Ecuador, El Salvador, Nicaragua, and Peru—although they have generally failed to reduce the poverty of the peasantry. Several issues inform the process. What is the optimal size of farms? As farms are broken up, will small peasant farmers have access to credit, technology, and new equipment to increase productivity? If the nation does not have idle land, whose land should be taken, and what kind of compensation should be offered? When the easy stage of capturing idle or uncolonized land is over, how will the confiscation affect the credibility of property rights in the economy? Should the process take place quickly to send signals of resolve, or does a slower, more measured program allow for the development of complementary infrastructure? How nations have resolved these questions defined the nature of their land reforms. We will now consider the cases of Mexico, Bolivia, Peru, and Chile.

Given high inequality, Mexican agriculture was strongly characterized by the bimodal agricultural production system. In response to high inequality, Mexican land reform was a legacy of the Zapatista agitation in 1917. Based on the constitutional recognition of community rights to land, it created a system of small landholdings called *ejidos*. In practice the *ejido* was farmed individually, but the land could not be sold. Despite this land reform, some of the best lands remained under the control of wealthy farmers. Today the large-farm sector produces 70 percent of all marketable food and nearly half the exports. The *ejidos,* poorly integrated into the marketplace, suffer from a lack of roads and marketing networks, producing corn and beans for peasant subsistence.[48] Attempts were made by various administrations to assist peasants. During the 1970s, under the Echeverria administration (1970–1976), state marketing agencies bought peasant commodities at subsidized prices to support small-scale agricultural production. President de la Madrid (1982–1988) confronted the problem of land fragmentation without complementary resources, and his successor, President Salinas (1988–1994), called for the modernization of the *ejido* through privatized joint ventures—without fundamentally altering the *campesino* way of life.[49] Nevertheless, the primary purpose of the policies was, too often, to support the political arm of government, the PRI (Mexican Revolutionary Party) and not to improve the peasants' lives.

Reduction of subsidies under the neoliberal model, as well as the opening of agricultural markets to imports, has further impoverished the peasantry. The 1994 Chiapas rebellion in Mexico can be seen as evidence of the rural crisis exacerbated by the opening to international markets.[50] An Economic Commission for Latin America and the Caribbean (ECLAC) study showed approximately 11 percent of *ejido* agricultural producers in Chiapas to be commercially viable; 58 percent are diversified producers that barely eke out an existence on the land, earning a surplus of about $300 per year, and 31 percent are subsistence farmers on the margins of economic life unable to obtain basic necessities from their efforts.[51] In contrast to the *ejido* farmers is the commercialized private sector. Large commercial landowners control the most productive assets while Indians and peasants are forced to the margins. Such poverty and inequality is ripe ground for rebellion. Reprivatization of rural institutions of credit and technology and a sharp decline in public investment in the sector have left the Mexican peasantry without access to institutional resources to improve productivity. Small and middle-sized farmers would benefit from the promotion of producer organizations for self-delivery of services and lowering of transactions costs of bringing goods to market. A transition program orchestrated by governmental and nongovernmental organizations (NGOs) and the private sector is necessary to preserve the economic viability of this important sector.[52] The World Bank and the government of Mexico are collaborating on developing decentralized approaches to enhance small-scale social and productive infrastructure.[53]

In Bolivia, land reform was designed to address problems of increasing violence in the countryside due to the unbalanced nature of landholdings. Beginning in 1952, 80 percent of land was affected by the redistribution process. Eighty-two percent of farmers—largely poor—holding 1 percent of the land began to invade large estates and claim property. Often the expropriation was spontaneously undertaken by *campesinos,* without governmental assistance. This later created problems of legal title to the land, and settlement of property rights has taken decades. Furthermore, the process was not accompanied by a program of capital assistance to the peasant farmers. Although the Bolivian reform was a political success, economically it did little to improve the lives of the peasantry. Ironically, a residual of the poorly orchestrated reform process is that cocaine production is easily maintained on a large number of small plots without much in the way of technological assistance.

In Peru, the process of land reform was guided by clear political objectives: to bring social justice to the rural areas, to support an enlargement of the internal market, and to contribute to the capital formation critical for rapid industrialization. The revolutionary military government of General Juan Velasco initiated an ambitious program in 1969 that expropriated between 40 and 50 percent of agricultural land. Land was subject to expropriation if it was between 150 and 200 hectares on the coast and 150 to 330 on the sierra; land could also be subject to expropriation if certain conditions were not met, such as provision of satisfactory living conditions for workers. Workers were also supposed to receive 50 percent of the profit, own 50 percent of the capital, and receive 20 percent of net income.[54] Land was reorganized as CAPs, or agrarian cooperatives. This decision, geared to maintain scale economies and allow cooperative farming, did not translate into improving productivity and incomes.[55] The Peruvian land reform experience was state directed as opposed to spontaneously driven by peasant demands. Problems with compensation for expropriated lands bogged down the process, resulting in delays that undermined legitimacy. Later, revolutionary groups such as Sendero Luminoso in the highlands were better able to provide the support peasants needed for survival. As in Mexico and Bolivia, failed Peruvian land reform has had a high political cost.

The Chilean land reform process has been reversed to some degree by the effects of the agro-export boom. Data show that nearly half of the *parceleros,* the small-scale farmers given land under reform measures, completely sold their farms between the late 1970s and 1991, leading to a reconcentration of land in medium to large holdings. Forty-seven percent of *parceleros* in the fruit boom region became completely landless by 1990, excluding these smaller farmers from the direct benefits of the agro-export boom. However, this exclusionary model was somewhat offset by an increase in labor absorption of the boom, providing employment for the landless peasants.[56] The experience in Guatemala demonstrates different results with agro-exports, with small farmers benefiting from the boom in nontraditional exports. The differences between the Chilean and Guatemalan experiences reflect differential impacts of crop choice on small farmers. Small farmers tend to be more risk averse, fearful that the adoption of new technologies or crops could, if unsuccessful, wipe out their livelihood. They tend to face higher prices for inputs and lower prices for outputs than larger farms that are able to take advantage of economies of scale. In particular, they are poorly connected to marketing and transportation networks. Small farmers often have a difficult time gaining access to credit, and they have been able to invest less in their own human capital. These biases against small farmers interact with crop choice. Orchard crops for fruit exports in Chile require multiyear investments; vegetable crops in Guatemala may advantage smaller producers because they are relatively labor intensive. Small-scale farmers did not find themselves in competition with large-scale producers for land or resources.[57] But this is not to say that the land problem is solved in Guatemala. Two percent of landowners hold two-thirds of the country's land.[58]

Several lessons can be distilled from the experience with land reform. First, the easy stages of redistributing unproductive land are over. Land is in short supply, so that redistribution now has a clear economic opportunity cost. The goal of increased production may be harmed because taking land away from large owners may result in less land available for export sectors. Second, land reform has not helped the poorest of the rural poor. Those who were relatively better off were able to take advantage of changes in policy; those on the margins of existence were less adept at working with authorities to transform property rights. Third, land reform works best when accompanied by ample credit and technical assistance. Simply owning land without the complementary inputs does little to raise productivity or incomes. To succeed, land reform therefore requires a comprehensive strategy for rural development. Fourth, policies adopted may have differential effects on small and large landowners. A policy package that reduces biases toward large holders and secures property rights of small peasants may help reduce rural poverty. This package could be supplemented with public investments to develop infrastructure and promote better exchange of information among small farmers to encourage broader-based growth. Picking labor-intensive crops to promote may direct growth toward the small farmer.[59] Fifth, this strategy must incorporate environmental as well as economic dimensions of reform. Environmental deterioration is closely tied to **insecure property rights,** inadequate credit, and poorly designed public infrastructure for water use, waste disposal, or transportation of goods to market.

Agricultural reform is more than land reform. It requires changes in law as well as public and private investments. Public resources for an **integrated rural development strategy** might come from increased taxation of agricultural land, particularly unproductive land. Higher taxation of larger parcels might encourage private market sales to small-scale producers. Revenues from taxation can be used for public infrastructure as well as financing loans to prospective buyers. Multilateral and bilateral international assistance in agricultural reform can help in project lending for infrastructure, and NGOs can facilitate grassroots access to poor farmers to promote extension services well suited to local conditions. Box 10.4 describes a project to increase the income of the rural poor in Guatemala. In one

Box 10.4.   The Rural Development Challenge in Guatemala: A USAID Program Response

Guatemala is the largest Central American country in terms of population and economic activity, but its largely rural, Mayan population lives in some of the most difficult conditions found in the Central American region. Distribution of land, income, and other wealth is highly skewed toward a small share of Guatemala's Spanish-speaking population. An estimated 75 percent of Guatemalans live in poverty, and the roughly five million Mayans are isolated socially, economically, and politically due to geographic and language barriers. The country's social indicators are among the worst in the hemisphere, and national averages mask even sharper inequalities between ethnic groups and gender. Overall adult literacy is estimated at 48 percent, but literacy among Mayan women is estimated as low as 10 percent. Less than half of rural Guatemalans have access to running water, only a quarter have access to electricity, and less than one in ten have access to modern sanitary facilities. Infant, child, and maternal mortality rates are among the highest in Latin America, despite decreases in recent years. These indicators reflect the country's persistent underinvestment in social services and basic rural infrastructure, as well as past practices of political and socioeconomic exclusion of the indigenous population.

To expand economic and social opportunity for the rural poor through programs that will increase incomes, improve the nutritional status of food aid program participants, and improve access to and quality of intercultural bilingual education, USAID—in conjunction with the Guatemalan Ministries of Agriculture, Food, and Livestock (MAGA), Public Finance (MOF), and the Economic Planning Secretariat (SEGEPLAN) and with the support of nongovernmental organizations—signed a $16.5 million, five-year agreement to increase productive incomes for the rural poor by expanding access to credit and training and strengthening intermediary organizations. Local and international nongovernmental organizations currently assisting in program implementation are Guatemala's National Coffee Association (ANACAFE), the Banco de Desarrollo Rural, CARE, Catholic Relief Services, and World Share. Earlier, USAID supported the Ministry of Finance and the National Development Bank in the design of a trust fund that is providing credit to micro enterprises and small-scale farmers in rural areas. Sustainability and expansion of activities into the poorest rural areas remains problematic, primarily due to the inability of local organizations to manage credit and to provide direction, leadership, and training to their members.

The USAID-supported program for increasing the incomes of the rural poor targets on- and off-farm income generation, expanded economic opportunities for micro entrepreneurs and small-scale farmers, and expanded capacity of local organizations and institutions to provide financial and technical assistance services. The delivery network of private voluntary organizations (PVOs) will continue to focus activities on the most marginal rural communities. The nutritional aspects of the program target maternal and child health by increasing the level of understanding of the nutritional and health needs of the family. The program supports small-scale community activities and the development of sustainable agricultural production technologies to encourage income generation and increase food production.

As a result of USAID activities and committed partners, support has been provided to over 55,000 small farmers and nearly 50,000 microentrepreneurs. Four Internet business centers were established in remote communities allowing women microentrepreneurs and others to develop new market opportunities. Eleven new microfinance offices were opened in the Peace Zone during 2001, and a commercial bank receiving technical assistance from USAID created a full-service bank division for micro and small business.

The activities implemented by PVOs continue to form the primary basis for outreach

(continued)

(continued)

to the rural poor under this program. During fiscal year 2001, over 42,500 mothers and nearly 76,000 children were provided a monthly food ration and education in health and nutrition. In addition, Food for Work rations were provided to nearly 37,000 workers and their dependents. These interventions tend to emphasize sustainable agriculture and microenterprise development, and they all provided a series of income generation and education interventions that enhance food security as a means of improving the families' livelihood.

Source: Abstracted from the USAID FY 1999 and 2002 Congressional Presentation Document (CPD) for Guatemala. (The CPD is the document the agency transmits to Congress to explain past use of funds and present the coming year's programs. You may find the current CPD at www.info.usaid.gov.)

IADB project in Brazil, rural families are being helped in their efforts to create self-sufficient communities through improving infrastructure, providing social services to settlers, and establishing a set of procedures to transform settlements into economically viable units.[60] Carefully crafted policies with clear results are important to demonstrate the benefits of infrastructure investments as well as gain the confidence of small farmers in new techniques for small-scale production. Concrete achievements will build confidence in the rural reform process. Moving beyond input markets for land or output markets for products, we will now turn to some of the systemic agricultural changes being implemented in the region.

RAISING PRODUCTIVITY: THE KEY TO RAISING RURAL INCOMES

A strategy to spur rural development must take a broad focus, moving beyond the narrow agricultural sector to include the entire rural productive system.[61] The management of natural and human resources, infrastructure development, and social development must be woven into a comprehensive strategy. Past policy mistakes derive in part from a narrow focus. Rather than simply look at irrigation and drainage, questions of resource allocation and comprehensive watershed management must be addressed. Instead of a focus on crop production, forestry, or livestock management, attention must be given to management of natural resources in a sustainable production system. Human capital development, infrastructure, and community-based decision making form the basis of an equitable, sustainable strategy. Stakeholders must be involved in the development and execution of projects.[62]

The greatest challenge in any agricultural strategy is to create equitable pathways to rising farm productivity. Farmers need incentives to produce more with fewer inputs. Cheap food for burgeoning urban populations is often a key policy objective. Yet if the price of foodstuffs falls without a decrease in the costs to the farmer, farm income is likely to suffer. Maintaining rural incomes while supporting urban populations can best be resolved by either increasing export quantities or decreasing costs through improvements in technology. But export-driven models do not guarantee benefits to the poor, and technological change costs money. If the dynamism in the rural sector is going to extend beyond large corporate farms, a system of peasant credit is necessary to support advances in small-scale farming. Technological change is also risky: if a peasant is living on the margins of subsistence, although change might have a large production payoff, it could also fail dismally, and the family would likely starve. Policies to improve productivity for peasant farmers must acknowledge the risk-averse nature of small-scale producers and provide flexible, extended terms to smooth the potential losses in any one year.

AGRICULTURAL EXTENSION PROGRAMS: GETTING FARMERS INVOLVED

Simply getting prices right is clearly not enough. **Agricultural extension programs** must speak to the family and cultural needs of the farmer. Improvements in productivity are driven by encouraging farmers to adopt new agricultural practices. This has historically been accomplished through agricultural extension programs. The World Bank estimates that global extension services have reached one million direct beneficiaries—an unsatisfactory record given the number of rural poor.[63] However, many farmers find agricultural extension programs ineffective. Problems with free extension services included budget pressures, poorly defined objectives, low motivation, a lack of accountability to clients, and little interest on the part of farmers in obtaining quality service. Centralized systems are also costly and inefficient delivery vehicles for services. In an era of fiscal tightening, expensive, centrally directed extension programs are unsustainable. In contrast, demand-driven services operate on the market concept that extension is an economic input that, if effective, may generate additional income that farmers would be willing to pay for. Free services may result in under or overuse.[64]

As a measure of their effectiveness, when extension services were cut in Nicaragua in December 1995, no one went on strike. Yet when university financial support was cut, strikes were widespread. In part this had to do with an outdated centralized extension system in which information was delivered to peasants and not developed and appropriated by them. Extension can also have a gendered dimension, because in some cultures it is inappropriate for a male outside the household to work closely with a female. Peasant farmers need to be involved in determining the necessary changes in farming practices to solve local problems. Extension should be thought of not as the transfer of knowledge, but as the development of agriculture systems to promote innovation and sustainable growth. One program shows promise in Nicaragua—a demand-driven accountable extension system through the Agricultural Technology and Land Management Project (ATLMP), financed by the World Bank and the Swiss government. Through a demonstration of a willingness to pay, farmers shape the services of the extension agent. Providers of extension services compete for contracts; because dissatisfied farmers can cease to be clients of extension agents, this creates a stake on the part of the agents to be more attentive to the needs of the farmers.[65] Despite initial objections, through small group meetings with farmers, extension agents overcame the lack of confidence of clients. In a voluntary pilot test, they were convinced that it was to their benefit to pay for services. An NGO provided credit to purchase the extension services. In addition, half the crop increase would go to the extensionist, with half retained by the farmers. The extension agent was to visit the site at least once a week. Although measurement of output was somewhat suspect, with overreporting of historical yields and underreporting of current production, the success of the program was defined by a uniform willingness to sign new contracts for the following season. Similarly, in a Costa Rican project to address the needs of poorer farmers, government vouchers are awarded for extension services to farmers on the basis of farm type.[66] Farmers trade vouchers for the services of extension agents, building up a corps of private extension agents accountable to local clients. As farmers see the gains from effective extension services, gradually vouchers will be eliminated and private provision of services will take over.

DECENTRALIZATION AND COMMUNITY CONTROL

In part, the difficult challenge of agricultural policy derives from the fact that farmers are not simply workers or owners but are inhabitants in a rural system with different practices from those in urban commercial markets. Agricultural policy—far more so than industrial policy—must be community based. **Demand-driven rural investment funds** (DRIFs) are an instrument for improving local control of agricultural development. Through DRIFs, central governments transfer funds to local governments and communities to address their own priorities within a carefully constructed set of guidelines. Beneficiaries include neighborhood associations, women's groups, and producer associations or cooperatives. Specific eligibility requirements must be met, including cost limits, and beneficiaries are required to contribute to the project cost either directly or through in-kind work. In Mexico, for example, communities must contribute a minimum of 20 percent of the project costs. Communities decide for themselves what type of technical assistance is required and then receive the funding to pay for it. The Mexican experience with DRIFs has extended to 30,000 subprojects with average costs 30 to 60 percent less than traditional centralized funding mechanisms. The economic sustainability of the projects is also higher, because local groups are vested in the project from the start.[67]

AGRICULTURAL ROLE OF THE STATE

Where should the state intervene directly in agricultural policy? A state role is critical in dealing with common property and environmental sustainability issues. Public institutions are preferable when benefits are diffuse, when the public policies require change, or when enhanced equity is a central goal. A public–private mix works best when the ability to achieve responsive and flexible management is contingent on political influence. A strictly private provision of services is superior when direct and continuous interaction with users is required.[68] The appropriate mix of state and market is therefore a function of local conditions. The agricultural sector may be an example where the temptation to employ our neat policy prescriptions of

BOX 10.5.   STRATEGIC CHECKLIST FOR RURAL DEVELOPMENT

- Macroeconomic and sectoral policies are stable. The foreign exchange, trade, and taxation regimes do not discriminate against agriculture, but are similar for rural and urban sectors.
- The growth of private agriculture is encouraged by minimizing distortions among input and output markets and by market development for agricultural and agro-industrial products, both at home and abroad.
- Public investment and expenditure programs for economic and social infrastructure, health, nutrition, education, and family planning services do not discriminate against rural populations or the rural poor.
- Large farms and large agro-industrial firms do not receive special privileges and are not able to reduce competition in output, input, land, or credit markets.
- The agrarian structure is dominated by efficient and technologically sophisticated family operators, who rely primarily on their own family's labor. The rights and needs of women farmers and wage laborers are explicitly recognized.
- Access to and security of land and water rights is actively promoted. Restricting land rentals hurts the poor. Where land distribution is highly unequal, land reform is needed. Decentralized, participatory, and market-assisted approaches to land reform can achieve this much faster than expropriations by land reform parastatals.
- Private and public sectors complement each other in generating and disseminating knowledge and technologies. Public-sector financing is particularly important for areas of limited interest to the private sector, such as strategic research, smallholder extension, and diffusion of sustainable production systems and techniques.
- Rural development programs mobilize the skill, talents, and labor of the rural population through administrative, fiscal, and management systems that are decentralized and participatory, and through private-sector involvement.
- Rural development programs are designed so that the rural poor and other vulnerable groups are fully involved in the identification, design, and implementation of the programs. Otherwise, rural elites will appropriate most of the benefits.
- Sustainable rural development requires multidisciplinary and pluralistic approaches to poverty, social and gender equity, local economic development, natural resource management, and governance.
- An agricultural focus is necessary but not sufficient for sustainable rural development; key are integrated approaches to infrastructure, technology, and building institutional capacity.
- Solutions in rural development must be based on participation, empowerment, and rural governance in contrast to earlier programs of top-down, noninclusive approaches.
- A holistic agricultural strategy must also foster growth of the private-sector and market mechanisms for financial sustainability.

Source: Adapted from World Bank, *Rural Development: From Vision to Action,* Environmentally and Socially Sustainable Development Studies and Monograph Series no. 12 (Washington, D.C.: World Bank, 1997); and World Bank Rural Development Strategy: *Reaching the Rural Poor,* draft posted at www.worldbank.org, June 2002.

neoliberal, neoinstitutionalist, or neostructuralist may lead to policy failure unless we are clear on the local characteristics of the market.

Agricultural policy reform has paralleled broader changes in development policy in the 1990s. The broad elements of reform, as captured by a World Bank directive in 1982, combine the use of markets and prices with strengthening property rights and regulatory institutions to promote productivity increases in the agricultural sector.[69] In part the answer to the new mix between state and market in the agricultural sector depends on the type of good or service being delivered. If the good is a plantation product such as sugar, a new tractor, or new seed, the private sector can probably address the need. If, however, the constraint is in practices such as farm management or marketing, some combination of public and private efforts is most likely to bear fruit. Finally, in areas affected by externalities and uses of common resources, government intervention is critical to provide incentives for cooperative voluntary action. In the agricultural sector the new role for the state is to create enabling environments for private and voluntary action—not to deliver the goods or the technologies, as in the past.[70] Enhancing the voice of farmers in a demand-driven approach may result in a more efficient and equitable agricultural system.

Consistent with neoliberal market approaches, agricultural loans supported by the new strategy with the World Bank are structured to help eliminate price controls, replacing generalized subsidies with targeted interventions. They are geared to develop competitive local markets for inputs and outputs and to reduce state interventions in international trade. In terms of agricultural trade policy, the goals are to replace quantitative restrictions with tariffs and to abolish state marketing boards. Improvements in the legal and regulatory system should include land tenure, export regulations, phytosanitary procedures, and the licensing of commerce. Finally, a stronger emphasis on food security might include targeted spending on food and nutrition programs. For example, Mexico was given a World Bank loan to support trade, price, privatization, and other policy reforms and reduce the government's role in the production, planning, marketing, storage, and processing of agricultural products and inputs. In Honduras support was given to modify the land reform law, improve property rights, permit the development of land markets, and reorient forestry practices toward protection and conservation of the environment.[71]

Overall, the key to a strong agricultural policy is to raise productivity while simultaneously including the poor. In doing so it is essential to triage the really poor, providing emergency relief. From there, working with community organizers to resolve land tenure issues, define emergent farmers, and identify technologies appropriate to local practices and conditions will facilitate rural development. A complementary program between the agricultural and nonagricultural sectors will help stem the migration from the farm to the cities. Providing off-farm activities for those unable to make it in farming will also help reverse the demographic tides toward urbanization. Nonetheless, coordination of an agricultural policy with other aspects of reform may require a super ministry, or a national coordinator with authority over other ministries, and a great deal of political will. Box 10.5 provides a strategic checklist for government rural development policy. The key to the millennium rural development strategy at the World Bank is a better recognition of the needs of the poor, with a focus on the neglected political voice of

> **QUESTION FOR THOUGHT**
>
> Identify policy initiatives to increase productivity in the rural sector. Are these initiatives consistent with programs to improve the incomes of the rural poor?

the rural poor.[72] Addressing these issues should facilitate a better balanced development strategy that provides sustainable resources for a greater portion of the agricultural population in the region.

Key Concepts

agricultural extension
 programs
demand-driven rural
 investment funds
dualistic structure
 of production

incomplete markets
insecure property rights
integrated rural
 development
land reform

nontraditional export
 production
segmented credit markets
water rights

Chapter Summary

- The agricultural sector in Latin America is characterized by its dualistic nature: corporate farming and small-scale, traditional peasant agriculture. The trend in many Latin American countries has been a shift away from production for local consumption to production for exports. Commercialization for exports has marginalized peasant farmers and increased migration from the rural sector into the cities.

- Though some Latin American countries have experienced slow growth in agriculture, many have seen moderate to rapid growth in production. Nevertheless, falling prices, international trade barriers and subsidies, overvalued exchange rates, and other forms of indirect taxation have placed constraints on the agricultural sector.

- Agriculture has not been able to generate sustainable incomes for the rural majority. Rural poverty contributes to a number of problems such as environmental degradation or harmful use of pesticides. Women's contributions to agricultural production are many times unaccounted for, yet women play a major role in the agricultural sector. Weak capacity in agricultural ministries has led to poor input in integrating agricultural policy with an overall development policy. A fragile private sector cannot fill the gap as governments have moved out to make room for the market.

- The failure of the agricultural sector to generate adequate incomes for the rural poor is due to several factors. Previous policies and incomplete markets have been biased against the peasant farmer and in favor of the rural elite. Ambiguity with property rights, common in the region, has led to underinvestment, barriers in obtaining credit, and inefficiency in the use of land. Peasant farmers face more obstacles in obtaining much-needed credit due to their lack of collateral and the nature of agricultural activity. Policies to remedy the problem must use nonconventional forms of allocating credit for the small farmer and address the issue of unequal landholding.

- Historically, many Latin American countries have engaged in land reforms to address the issue of inequality. The experience in the region has shown that land reform has done little to improve the quality of life of the rural peasant. Its failure is due to a lack of complementary policies that will address problems such as the biases disadvantaging the poor relative to the elite, the problem of credit, and environmental sustainability.

- Agricultural policy must be multidimensional. Farm productivity must be raised, but policy needs to take into account the concerns and behavior of the poor small farmers, who tend to be risk averse. Polices that consider factors such as migration to urban sectors, infrastructure, credit, and landholding patterns will tend to be more successful in the long run.

- Decentralization through demand-driven rural investment funds has increased local control and participation in agricultural development. Communities must usually meet certain requirements before the funds are distributed. This type of fund allocation allows different groups to set their own priorities and address their own needs.

Notes

1. ECLAC and IICA, Survey of Agriculture in Latin America and the Caribbean, 1990–2000, December 2001, at www.eclac.cl, 36.

2. Johan Bastiaensen, "Non-Conventional Rural Finance and the Crisis of Economic Institutions in Nicaragua," in *Sustainable Agriculture in Central America,* ed. Jan P. de Groot and Ruerd Ruben (New York: St. Martin's, 1997).

3. ECLAC and IICA, 17.

4. "Worst Ever Coffee Crisis Hits Latin America," *Cepal News* vol. XXII, no. 4 (April 2002).

5. T. Christian Miller and Davan Maharau, "Coffee's Bitter Harvest," *Los Angeles Times* Staff Writers, as circulated by CENTAM-L@LISTSERV.BUFFALO.EDU, 7 October 2002.

6. Oxford Analytica, *Latin America Daily Brief,* Thursday, September 12, 2002, prodept@oxford-analytica.com.

7. "Brazil: Aiming to Add Value," *Latin American Economy & Business,* LAEB-02-03, March 2002, p. 22.

8. *Mugged: Poverty in Your Cup.* Oxfam International 2002, www.maketradefair.com.

9. Lori Ann Thrupp, *Bittersweet Harvests for Global Supermarkets: Challenges in Latin America's Agricultural Export Boom* (Washington, D.C.: World Resources Institute, 1995), 17.

10. James Brooke, "Home, Home on the Range, in Brazil's Heartland," *New York Times,* 26 April 1995.

11. Thrupp, *Bittersweet Harvests,* 18, 58.

12. Thrupp, *Bittersweet Harvests,* 24.

13. ECLAC and IICA, 196

14. Canute James, "Caribbean Banana Producers See Future in Organic Farming," *Financial Times,* November 13, 2001, Internet edition.

15. Jim Adriance, "Living with the Land in Central America," *Grassroots Development* 19, no. 1 (1995): 15.

16. *Ejidos* were created by the Mexican government following the 1910 revolution. The structure adapted a pre-Columbian farming practice of communal landholdings, requiring the Mexican government to cede tracts of land to Mexican peasants. Each *ejido* comprises between twenty and two thousand *ejidatarios* and is governed by a general assembly and an elected administrative council. Although the individual *ejidatario* cannot sell, mortgage, or rent the land, he may pass it on to his spouse, children, or other relatives. The 1992 agricultural law has worked to privatize *ejidos*.

17. "Green, as in Greenbacks," *The Economist,* 1 February 1997, p. 42.

18. Ellen Contreras Murphy, "La Selva and the Magnetic Pull of Markets: Organic Coffee-Growing in Mexico," *Grassroots Development* 19, no. 1 (1995): 27–34.

19. United Nations Office for Drug Control and Crime Prevention, *World Drug Report 2000*, Oxford University Press, 2000, Annex 1, www.odccp.org/pdf/world_drug_report_2000/report_2001-01-22_1.pdf.

20. Monique Stauder, "Colombian Cocaine Runs through It," *The Christian Science Monitor,* June 13, 2001, 12–13.

21. "New Farms for Old," *The Economist,* 10 January 1998, p. 30.

22. Thrupp, *Bittersweet Harvests,* 67.

23. ECLAC and IICA, 152.

24. ECLAC and IICA, 46. The total number of agricultural workers had flattened at 43.3 million by 1999; the economically active population during this period increased from 125.2 million to 210.2 million.

25. Tim Weiner, "16 Arrested in Killings of 26 over Land Disputes in Mexico," *The New York Times,* June 2, 2002, Internet edition.

26. James Petras, The Rural Landless Workers Movement, *Z Magazine,* March 2000 on the MST website at www.mst.org.br.

27. John Weeks, "Macroeconomic Adjustment," as noted in "Latin America's Export of Manufactured Goods," a special section of *Economic and Social Progress in Latin America 1992 Report* (Washington, D.C.: IADB, 1992), 68.

28. ECLAC and IICA, 141.

29. Maurice Schiff and Alberto Valdes, "The Plundering of Agriculture in Developing Countries," 1994 draft paper, available at the World Bank homepage at www.worldbank.org/html/extpb/PlunderingAgri.html. Also Krueger, Schiff, and Valdes (1991), cited in Hans P. Binswanger and Klaus Deininger, "Explaining Agricultural and Agrarian Policies in Developing Countries," *Journal of Economic Literature* 35 (December 1997): 1958–2005.

30. Jacob Meerman, *Reforming Agriculture: The World Bank Goes to Market* (Washington, D.C.: World Bank, 1997), 38.

31. Michael Redclift, "The Environment and Structural Adjustment: Lessons for Policy Intervention," in *Structural Adjustment and the Agricultural Sector in Latin America and the Caribbean,* ed. John Weeks (New York: St. Martin's, 1995).

32. Andy Thorpe, "Sustainable Agriculture in Latin America," in *Sustainable Agriculture in Central America,* ed. Jan P. de Groot and Ruerd Ruben (New York: St. Martin's, 1997), 42.

33. IADB, "Invisible Farmers," in *IDB Extra: Investing in Women* (Washington, D.C.: Inter-American Development Bank, 1994).

34. Cristóbal Key, "Rural Development and Agrarian Issues in Contemporary Latin America," in *Structural Adjustment and the Agricultural Sector in Latin America and the Caribbean,* ed. John Weeks (New York: St. Martin's 1995).

35. Elizabeth G. Katz, "Gender and Trade within the Household: Observations from Rural Guatemala," *World Development* 23, no. 2 (1995): 327–42.

36. World Bank, *Rural Development: From Vision to Action,* Environmentally and Socially Sustainable Development Studies and Monographs Series no. 12 (Washington, D.C.: World Bank, 1997), 33.

37. Karla Hoff, "Designing Land Policies: An Overview," in *The Economics of Rural Organization,* ed. Karla Hoff, Avishay Braverman, and Joseph Stiglitz (New York: Oxford University Press/World Bank, 1993), 231.

38. Michael Richards, "Alternative Approaches and Problems in Protected Area Management and Forest Conservation in Honduras," in *Sustainable Agriculture in Central America,* ed. Jan P. de Groot and Ruerd Ruben (New York: St. Martin's, 1997), 147.

39. Avishay Braverman and J. Luis Guasch, "Administrative Failures in Government Credit Programs," in *The Economics of Rural Organization,* ed. Karla Hoff, Avishay Braverman, and Joseph Stiglitz (New York: Oxford University Press/World Bank, 1993), 53.

40. Fared Shah, David Zilberman, and Ujjayant Chakravorty, "Water Rights Doctrines and Technology Adoption," in *The Economics of Rural Organization,* ed. Karla Hoff, Avishay Braverman, and Joseph Stiglitz (New York: Oxford University Press/World Bank, 1993), 478.

41. Bastianensen, "Non-Conventional Rural Finance," 199.

42. Bastianensen, "Non-Conventional Rural Finance," 199.

43. Robert L. Paarlberg, "The Politics of Agricultural Resource Abuse," *Environment* 36, no. 8 (October 1994).

44. Jon Jonakin, "The Interaction of Market Failure and Structural Adjustment in Producer Credit and Land Markets: The Case of Nicaragua," *Journal of Economic Issues* 31, no. 2 (June 1997): 355.

45. Binswanger and Elgin (1989), cited in Binswanger and Deininger, "Explaining Agricultural and Agrarian Policies," 1968.

46. Roderick (1994), as described in Carlos Acevedo, Deborah Barry, and Herman Rosa, "El Salvador's Agricultural Sector: Macroeconomic Policy, Agrarian Change and the Environment," *World Development* 23, no. 12 (1995): 2153–72.

47. Johan van Zyl et al. (1995), cited in Binswanger and Deininger, "Explaining Agricultural and Agrarian Policies," 1964.

48. Michael Foley, "Agenda for Mobilization: The Agrarian Question and Popular Mobilization in Contemporary Mexico," *Latin American Research Review* 26, no. 2 (1991): 66.

49. Foley, "Agenda for Mobilization," 61.

50. Roger Burbach and Peter Rosset, "Chiapas and the Crisis of Mexican Agriculture," *Food First Policy Brief,* no. 1 (San Francisco: Institute for Food and Development, 1994).

51. As cited in Burbach and Rosset, "Chiapas and the Crisis of Mexican Agriculture."

52. Alain de Janvry and Elisabeth Sadoulet, "NAFTA and Mexico's Maize Producers," *World Development* 23, no. 8 (August 1995): 1349–62.

53. Mexico, "Municipal Development in Rural Areas Project," July 2002, www.worldbank.org.

54. David Lehmann, ed., *Agrarian Reform and Agrarian Reformism: Studies of Peru, Chile, China, and India* (London: Faber & Faber, 1974), 51–59.

55. Michael Carter and Dina Mesbah, "State-Mandated and Market-Mediated Reform in Latin America," in *Including the Poor,* ed. Michael Lipton and Jacques van der Gaag (Baltimore: Johns Hopkins University Press/World Bank, 1993).

56. Michael Carter and Bradford Barham cite Dina Mesbah in "Level Playing Fields and Laissez Faire: Postliberal Development Strategy in Inegalitarian Agrarian Economies," *World Development* 24, no. 7 (July 1996): 1136.

57. Carter and Barham, "Level Playing Fields," 1136–38.

58. H. Byrnes and B. Spencer, "U.S. Must Aid Guatemala's Shift to Peace," *St. Louis Post-Dispatch,* 20 December 1996.

59. Carter and Barham, "Level Playing Fields," 1144–48.

60. Nora Lustig and Ruthanne Deutsch, *The Inter-American Development Bank and Poverty Reduction: An Overview* (Washington, D.C.: IADB, 1998). Available at www.iadb.org.

61. World Bank, *Rural Development.*

62. World Bank, *Rural Development,* 17.

63. Julio A. Beredegué and Germán Escobar, "Agricultural Knowledge and Information Systems and Poverty Reduction," World Bank AKIS working papers, January 2001.

64. Gabriel Keynan, Manuel Olin, and Ariel Dinar, "Cofinanced Public Extension in Nicaragua," *World Bank Research Observer* 12, no. 2 (August 1997): 230.

65. Keynan, Olin, and Dinar, "Cofinanced Public Extension," 226.

66. Keynan, Olin, and Dinar, "Cofinanced Public Extension," 227.

67. World Bank, *Rural Development,* 83. Excerpted from box 6.10.

68. Rogers, as cited in Charles Ameur, *Agricultural Extension: A Step beyond the Next Step,* World Bank Technical Paper no. 247 (Washington, D.C.: World Bank, 1994), 12–13.

69. Meerman, *Reforming Agriculture,* 2, 40–41.

70. Robert Picciotto and Jock Anderson, "Reconsidering Agricultural Extension," *World Bank Research Observer* 12, no. 2 (August 1997): 254.

71. Meerman, *Reforming Agriculture,* 53.

72. World Bank Rural Development Strategy: Reaching the Rural Poor, draft posted at www.worldbank.org June 2002.

CHAPTER ELEVEN

POVERTY AND INEQUALITY

Addressing the Social Deficit in Latin America

Extreme poverty forces children to scavenge at dumps to contribute to meager family incomes—although this does promote sustainable recycling. *(Copyright Pan American Health Organization.)*

The social challenges of poverty and inequality constitute the greatest obstacle to sustained growth in Latin America. One in three inhabitants of the region—approximately 150 million people—live below the **poverty line.**[1] Poverty constrains human beings from investing in the education and health necessary for productivity. Inequality skews opportunities toward the rich, not those who desperately need it. When people lack the ability to invest in the future, they are forced to deplete natural resources to survive today. Despite this need, programs to address poverty have failed dismally, in part due to the fact that the poor themselves have not participated in their design or implementation. For poverty programs to do more than simply ward off starvation or malnutrition, the people themselves must be involved. As the president of the World Bank said,

> The lesson is clear: for economic advance, you need social advance—and without social development, economic development cannot take root. For the Bank, this means that we need to make sure that the programs and projects we support have adequate social foundations by designing more participatory country strategies and programs, reflecting discussions not only with governments, but also with community groups, nongovernmental organizations and private businesses, by putting more emphasis on social, cultural and institutional issues, with their interplay with economic issues and in our project and analytical work, and by learning more about how the changing dynamics between public institutions, markets and civil society affect social and economic development.[2]

Discrimination against women and ethnic minorities limits their full potential as economic actors. Poverty exacts a toll on the environment as people lack the assets to invest in their future. Poorly nourished children will not grow up to be productive members of the global workforce. Reducing the depth of poverty in the region is key to long-term, sustainable development.

This chapter will focus on the question of development for whom and ask how marginalized groups can more fully participate in the benefits of growth. The following questions will shape our understanding of the issue:

- How do we measure poverty? Is Latin America poor?
- How do we measure inequality in the region? What are trends in inequality?
- How do poverty and inequality define living standards?
- What effects do gender and inequality have on economic well-being in Latin America?
- How did macroeconomic performance affect poverty?
- What are areas for action to reduce poverty and the social deficit in the region?

IS LATIN AMERICA POOR?: A PROFILE OF POVERTY

Is Latin America poor? As measured against the typical North American family, the answer is yes. Compared to the images of starvation from the most destitute countries of the world, Latin Americans are relatively well-off. How is poverty defined? This is a controversial question. Poverty in a major metropolis such as Buenos Aires will differ from that in a small remote village in the Andes. We somewhat arbitrarily define the poor as the portion of the population unable to meet basic needs such as food, health care, education, and shelter. The poverty line is determined as the minimum income needed to purchase socially determined essentials for living.[3]

International comparisons of poverty are complicated by cultural differences in defining human needs, the variety of local goods available at different prices, and divergent government policies including transfer payments, exchange rates, and inflation. Counting the poor is extremely difficult, especially for those without permanent residences. Unlike the people enumerated in data generated by income tax payments, census takers, or those in formal public support programs, the very poor are often nameless. The data should therefore be interpreted with caution. Setting a dollar benchmark is also controversial. The World Bank uses $50 per month as a rule of thumb; the Economic Commission for Latin America and the Caribbean (ECLAC) uses $60, categorizing those making less than $30 per month as living in extreme poverty. Moderate poverty is therefore roughly $2 per day, with those living in extreme poverty subsisting on $1 per day. Different studies also generate different outcomes. For example, reputable studies on poverty in Mexico generated ranges from 19.7 to 46 percent—certainly creating a divergent picture of the degree of poverty in the country![4] Since poverty can be a subjective concept that depends on culture and development levels, it is natural to have a range.

Once a poverty line is established, the **headcount ratio** estimates those who fall below it. We can see from the data in table 11.1 that in 1997, 36 percent of Latin Americans lived in poverty, with extreme poverty concentrated in the rural sector.[5] Fifteen percent of the population lives in conditions of extreme poverty. They are not able to meet their nutritional requirements even if they spend everything they have on food. Analyzing country experience, we find that there is a wide degree of diversity in terms of progress on poverty in the 1990s, with some Latin America nations reducing poverty and others stagnating. Poverty in the region has risen slightly since the 1980s and has become increasingly urbanized, with 30 percent of city dwellers living in poverty. The urbanization of poverty has made the problem more visible as cosmopolitan residents must face the tragic contradictions of development on street corners, on hillsides, or in rings of shacks and squalor at the city limits.

We should, however, look at trends in poverty line data with some caution. Temporary macroeconomic factors affect the numbers. Recession increased the

Table 11.1.   Changes in the Extent of Poverty, 1980–1997

Year	Poverty (millions and percentage)			Extreme Poverty (millions and percentage)		
	Total	Urban	Rural	Total	Urban	Rural
1980	135.9 (35)	62.9 (25)	73.0 (54)	62.4 (15)	22.5 (9)	39.9 (28)
1990	200.2 (41)	121.7 (35)	78.5 (58)	93.4 (18)	45.0 (12)	48.4 (34)
1994	201.5 (38)	125.9 (32)	75.6 (56)	91.6 (16)	44.3 (11)	47.4 (34)
1997	204.0 (36)	125.8 (30)	78.2 (54)	89.8 (15)	42.7 (10)	47.0 (31)

Source: Ruben G. Echeverria, "Opciones para reducir la pobreza rural en América Latina y el Caribe," *CEPAL Review 70* (April 2000): 147–60.

Table 11.2.   Poverty Gap

Country	Survey Year	Average % Shortfall from Poverty Line of $2 per Day	Survey Year	Households below Poverty Line	Rural Households below Poverty Line
Uruguay	1989	1.9	1997	NA	NA
Chile	1994	5.9	1998	18	23
Costa Rica	1996	10.1	1997	20	23
Panama	1997	10.2	1997	27	34
Colombia	1996	11.6	1997	45	54
Bolivia	1990	13.5	1997	57	72
Venezuela	1996	15.7	1997	42	NA
Peru	1996	17.1	1997	37	61
Mexico	1995	18.1	1998	38	49
Paraguay	1995	18.8	1996	NA	NA
Ecuador	1995	21.2	1997	NA	NA
El Salvador	1996	24.7	1997	48	62
Guatemala	1989	36.6	1989	63	72
Honduras	1996	36.9	1997	74	80

Source: World Development Report 2000/2001, 280–81.

number of poor in the 1980s. Furthermore, although the headcount ratio gives us a sense of the number living in poverty at any point in time, it does not measure the extent of immiseration. A person making $45 and a person making $20 per month would each count as one poor person despite tragically different lives. A second measure of poverty therefore calculates the size of the income shortfall or the amount of money it would take to raise the person to the poverty line. This **income gap** measures the depth of poverty a nation faces. In table 11.2 we can see that in Honduras, Guatemala, and El Salvador, on average, people's income falls short of the poverty line by 36.9, 36.6, and 24.7 percent, respectively. This says that in Honduras it would take a 36.9-percent increase in a poor person's income to raise the individual out of poverty. This is in contrast to Uruguay or Chile, where on average the poor are short of the poverty line by 1.9 or 5.9 percent. The experience of the 1990s was that although growth and macroeconomic instability allowed most countries to make some progress on reducing poverty, those that remained poor were poorer than at the beginning of the decade.[6]

Quality of Life

Even with the income gap statistic, we really don't know what $60 can buy given different living standards. Measures that count the poor are best complemented by statistics that capture the quality of their lives. The 1997 *Human Development Report* introduced a new measure, the HPI, or human poverty index. The HPI concentrates on three dimensions of poverty: vulnerability to death at an early age, exclusion from global communications as measured by literacy rates, and a decent standard of living as approximated by the percentage of people with access to health services and safe water and the proportion of malnourished children under five. As a weighted composite of deprivation, the HPI gives us a comparative basis to judge the extent of human poverty. The data for the HPI in Latin America show that Uruguay, Costa Rica, Chile, and Cuba have made significant progress in reducing poverty, ranking 1 to 4, respectively, on the 2002 HPI index. Uruguay and Chile had reduced the level of those living on less than a dollar a day to under 2 percent of the population. Colombia, Mexico, Panama, and Brazil fall into the next cluster, with rates hovering in the 10–15 percent level. Honduras, Bolivia, Nicaragua, and El Salvador have more than one quarter of the population falling below this line.[7]

Life for the Poor in Latin America

The living conditions of the poor constrain their human potential. Poverty and inequality interact to limit the opportunities for the less fortunate. Poverty is a complex, multidimensional phenomenon. How do the realities of their daily lives constrain them from pursuing better options? If you ever have the opportunity to observe life in a poor neighborhood—a *favela* in Brazil, a *villa miseria* in Argentina, or a *callampas* (mushroom) in Chile, where roughly one in four Latin Americans live—you will notice that nearly everyone is working hard to survive. Why aren't these tremendous energies transformed into a better quality of life for people?

Quality of life statistics can give us an appreciation for the standard of living in the region. The UN *Human Development Report* also calculates the HDI, or human development index, as a composite of life expectancy at birth, educational attainment (measured by adult literacy and school enrollments), and income. The GDI, or gender development index, discounts the HDI for gender inequality in life expectancy, educational attainment, and income, by assigning a penalty for inequality. The greater the gender disparity, the lower the GDI. The GEM, or gender empowerment index, concentrates on economic, political, and professional participation by incorporating variables such as female share of income, access to professional and managerial jobs, and seats in public office. The GEM therefore measures the degree to which opportunities are open to women in society. It should be noted that these indexes also have their drawbacks. Although as composite indexes they take attention away from gross domestic product (GDP) as a measure of human development, the measures of life expectancy, education, and income do not take the distribution of the population around the average into account, covering considerable variation in performance.[8] We will return to the difficult problem of inequality in Latin America in a moment.

Table 11.3 presents the HDI, GDI, and GEM for Latin American countries. Some interesting results appear. The best performers in quality of living include Argentina, Uruguay, Chile, and Costa Rica, although Argentina is likely to slip considerably as poverty increases with economic crisis. The positive numbers in the column "real GDP per capita minus HID rank" indicate that performance on social indicators exceeds that predicted by the nation's income. In contrast, the standard of living in Brazil, El Salvador, and Guatemala is worse than their income ranking would indicate. As weighted

Table 11.3.   Indicators of Standards of Living in Latin America, 2001

Country	HDI	HDI Rank	Real GDP per Capita Rank	Real GDP per Capita Minus HDI Rank	GDI	GDI Rank	GEM	GEM Rank
Argentina	0.840	34	44	10	0.833	34	NA	NA
Uruguay	0.828	37	46	9	0.825	37	0.491	42
Chile	0.825	39	48	9	0.817	39	0.445	49
Costa Rica	0.821	41	47	6	0.813	41	0.571	23
Mexico	0.790	51	51	0	0.782	49	0.507	37
Panama	0.784	52	67	15	0.782	50	0.475	44
Venezuela	0.765	61	71	10	0.759	57	0.439	51
Colombia	0.765	62	68	6	0.760	56	0.507	36
Brazil	0.750	69	57	−12	0.743	64	0.470	n/a
Peru	0.743	73	81	8	0.724	73	0.516	33
Paraguay	0.738	80	85	5	0.725	72	0.407	57
Ecuador	0.726	84	103	19	0.711	79	0.482	43
El Salvador	0.701	95	86	−9	0.694	87	0.440	50
Bolivia	0.648	104	111	7	0.640	94	0.425	55
Nicaragua	0.635	106	113	7	0.628	95	NA	NA
Honduras	0.634	107	112	5	0.623	96	0.449	47
Guatemala	0.626	108	92	−16	0.610	98	NA	NA

Source: Human Development Report, 2002 (New York: Oxford University Press, 2002), tables 1, 21, and 22; www.hdr.undp.org/reports/global/2002.

by the degree of inequality between the sexes in access to resources, Argentina is the best regional performer. Nonetheless, in terms of women's participation in economic and political life, Costa Rica and Peru top the list.

Measures such as housing, communications, and basic infrastructure help fill out the picture of poverty in Latin America. Housing in the region is woefully inadequate. Adequate housing is critical to the development of individual capability and to fostering family and community ties. Table 11.4 shows that although there has been progress in extending electricity to most homes in the region, almost half are unconnected to sewers. These deficits have significant implications in terms of health, in that access to running water and appropriate treatment of waste water is critical to reducing disease. ECLAC estimates that between 20 and 30 percent of children in Latin America grow up in conditions of overcrowding, with three or more people per bedroom, a condition closely associated with poor school performance. In Bolivia, Peru, El Salvador, and Nicaragua, 20 percent or more of the dwellings are beyond repair, a threat to health and life. Some rural indigenous workers in Bolivia and in Brazil are kept in a state of virtual slavery as employers charge them more for room and board than they earn. The most extreme housing deprivation is to be homeless. In Brazil, more than 200,000 children are growing up on the streets without the protection a home affords. Box 11.1 sadly illustrates life on the streets in Guatemala. The waste of young lives to poverty is a tragic result of slow growth and limited opportunity.

Two measures of literacy and the effect of the media on public consciousness are the number of newspapers sold daily and televisions per one hundred people.

Housing in Latin America is woefully inadequate, leading to construction solutions that make ingenious use of scarce supplies and limited space. *(Courtesy of Helena Tubis.)*

Table 11.5 gives a sense of the role of the media in shaping people's worldview. It is not surprising that the more affluent nations sell more newspapers. Literacy is correlated with wealth. Furthermore, if a newspaper costs fifty cents, for those making two or three dollars a day, it is quite a luxury. During the periods of macroeconomic crisis in Brazil, even upper-middle-class families would get together in a buying group for *Veja,* the Brazilian equivalent of *Time* magazine. Indeed, if you walk the streets in a Latin American city, you are likely to find people standing around the newspaper kiosk reading the headlines of papers for sale because they are too expensive to buy. The number of televisions has exploded in the region, although not quite approaching the industrial country average of one television for every two people. Television transforms culture. Many American TV shows are translated and rebroadcast. The contradiction of

Table 11.4. Occupied Private Dwelling Units by Type of Services Available

Country	Total Dwelling Units[a]	Piped Water (%)			Sewage Disposal (%)			Electric Lighting (%)		
		1980	1990	1999	1980	1990	1999	1980	1990	1999
Argentina	8,515,441	86.0	92.5	98.7	—	71.6	82.9	—	94.0	99.5
Bolivia	1,614,995	—	57.5	71.1	22.7	44.0	59.2	59.3	55.5	67.4
Brazil	34,734,715	54.9	82.6	85.6	27.7	52.8	64.6	68.5	97.6	94.8
Chile	3,101,356	81.4	88.2	94.3	—	69.9	77.3	84.6	88.1	96.8
Colombia	5,266,581	70.5	94.5	89.7	59.4	84.2	84.3	—	99.4	94.4
Costa Rica	500,030	86.9	94.7	—	—	—	—	83.1	98.8	—
Cuba	2,306,590	74.1	—	—	—	—	—	82.9	—	—
Ecuador	211,121	51.8	62.7	—	51.1	62.4	—	62.1	77.7	—
El Salvador	—	—	—	54.4	—	—	40.1	—	—	81.6
Guatemala	1,102,281	52.3	58.2	63.6	18.6	—	32.6	37.2	86.8	64.1
Honduras	762,117	—	63.1	85.2	—	20.4	31.9	—	39.6	69.7
Mexico	16,035,233	70.7	79.4	83.8	43.7	52.2	60.5	76.5	87.5	95.0
Panama	524,284	75.4	72.8	—	33.2	44.2	—	64.8	72.8	—
Paraguay	913,079	20.5	25.4	30.8	9.5	7.2	8.3	38.8	54.1	86.4
Peru	4,904,219	37.9	46.7	59.1	28.9	40.0	50.0	44.9	54.9	69.2
Uruguay	980,567	86.5	92.3	86.6	44.2	56.1	52.0	88.4	97.2	94.2
Venezuela	3,534,507	85.3	81.4	93.1	—	63.1	72.6	88.6	93.1	98.8

Source: ECLAC, *Statistical Yearbook for Latin America and the Caribbean, 2001*, table 52.
[a]ECLAC, *Social Panorama of Latin America and the Caribbean 1999–2000*, table 384.

Box 11.1. Casa Alianza: An NGO Helping Street Children in Guatemala

More than five thousand children live on the streets of Guatemala City. Some are as young as seven. Most are addicted to glue or other poisonous solvent-based products. Many resort to petty robbery and prostitution to survive. Each year, scores of children are abused, tortured, or killed by police or other authorities. Some are assaulted by other street children. Others take their own lives out of utter desperation. Most have chosen the streets to escape family abuse. Many number among the 250,000 children who have been orphaned by a brutal thirty-year civil war that has displaced an estimated one million people. They are children of "street families" who come to the city in search of a "better" life—and end up hawking cigarettes, candy, and food on street corners. With many mouths to feed, parents abandon their children to their fate.

ABOUT GUATEMALA

With the largest population in Central America, estimated in 1990 to be 9.9 million and growing at a rate of 3.1 percent each year, Guatemala has one of the youngest populations in the world, with 55 percent less than nineteen years old. In Guatemala today, 80 percent of the population lives in poverty; 54 percent of those who live in poverty are children. In 1991, the per capita gross national product was $930 per year; however, many people, especially the indigenous, earn far less. With 40 percent of its population now living in cities, Guatemala's urban population is soaring, with a growth rate of 3.5 percent. The urban growth rate in the United States is 1.2 percent; Canada's is 1.3 percent; Germany's 0.5 percent; and the United Kingdom's 0.2 percent.

More than 40 percent of the total population does not have access to safe drinking water or adequate sanitation, and only 34 percent have access to health services. The mortality rate for children below the age of five is estimated at 76 per 1,000 live births—the second highest in Latin America, after Bolivia. With less than half the population able to read, Guatemala ranks second behind Haiti among countries in the region with the highest illiteracy rates. Only 36 percent of those who enroll in the first grade complete primary school. More than 80 percent never make it to secondary school. Poverty and rapid urbanization are the reasons why Guatemala City's 224,000 children live in shantytowns and 789,000 children live in extreme poverty.

These problems, along with a high rate of family disintegration, have forced 27 percent of Guatemala's children between the ages of ten and seventeen to work to supplement their families' income.

CASA ALIANZA GUATEMALA

Casa Alianza began operating in Guatemala in 1981 as a refuge for children orphaned by the civil war. In 1986, the organization expanded its focus to street children. Currently, about 330 children are in Casa Alianza's residential programs in Guatemala, and street educators and other staff attend to the needs of about one thousand street children per year.

Here is the story of one of the street children Casa Alianza is helping. Other stories are available at: www.casa-alianza.org.

> My name is Gabriela. I am thirteen years old. I've been on my own for three years now. I used to beg for money, but now I am working. I am a prostitute. I don't like to say that, because it's not who I am inside. I dream of my village, and the fresh mountain air there, and the smell of the freshly turned earth. But here in "El

(continued)

(continued)

Hoyo," it smells like a dirty toilet, and the diesel smoke from the buses turns my stomach. I hate this place. I hate the men who I sleep with. All I can do when they touch me is think of something else—of the walks I used to take through the fields with my sister Juliana on Sunday mornings. I think of the good things I loved at home. It makes it all a little easier.

You may wonder why I still do this, even though I hate it. I don't know, really. Somehow it works. Marta, the lady who owns the bar where the men come for me, she takes care of me. When I have a bad night, she'll let me cry and stroke my head, and give me some warm milk—and then I'm ready to work again. She's the closest thing to a mother I've got now. You see, my father killed my mother the day I left home. He was drunk and was hitting her, like he always did, but she fell backwards and slammed her head, and never got up again. All I could do was scream when I saw her, and run. I was afraid he'd kill me too. I hated it when he drank. But when he was sober, I was his little girl. I remember his big hands, and the smell of cows that stuck on his clothes. He'd give me a big hug with his big hands, and I felt so warm and safe inside. But now, if I saw him, I'd want to chop off those hands for what they did to Mama.

There are a bunch of other girls who work with me. Aida, Mercedes, and Silvia. Aida is eighteen. She showed me how to wear makeup, and how to look at men so they'd want me. She's real good at it. But she has been sick a lot lately. She doesn't want to get up in the morning, always has some kind of problem, she's got so thin, and she's got these marks growing on her face. I'm worried about her. Someone said she might have this bad sickness called AIDS. But she's so sweet. It was always the off-duty soldiers who would like Aida—they would pay her about 10 quetzals (U.S.$2) a time. But if she got sick, I wonder if some of the soldiers did too?

Mercedes is like my sister. We make each other laugh about the men we see. We have nicknames for each of them. You don't want to hear them, though. If Mama were still alive, she'd wash my mouth out with soap if I uttered any of them. Mercedes got pregnant once, which is really bad for work. When any of us girls get pregnant we kick her in the stomach several times. It hurts a lot, but it's a way of getting unpregnant. It didn't work with Mercedes, though, and she got an abortion. It was terrible. She went to a friend of Marta's—they call her La Carnicera, the Butcher—because the girls always bleed so much after they see her. She's not a doctor or anything. She just does it—with a hanger, I think. Some girls have died. But we don't talk about that. La Carnicera helps us. It's not her fault that some girls can't take the pain, I guess. I hope I never have to see her.

Sometimes I wish I could meet a nice boy. I don't like these men. I want a boy to play with. But it's hard here. All of the boys in "El Hoyo" are so dirty and crazy. All they do is sit around and sniff that stupid glue all day, and fight with each other. It makes them so stupid. Sometimes they also "work" the street—like me, selling their bodies so they can buy food and glue. Sometimes terrible things happen to them, too. The police come and they pour the glue over the boys' heads. Oh, it looks so terrible. They even kicked to death one of Francisco's best friends— Nahamán. When the police went to pour the glue on his head, he resisted—and God, it was terrible. You could hear his shrieks from blocks away. Poor Nahamán, he was so sweet. He was my age. I never told anyone, not even Mercedes, but I liked Nahamán. We kissed one night, it was so beautiful—so different from the ugly kisses of the men who come for me. Nahamán. When I say his name now, all I want to do is cry. Why did they have to do that? Why?

Sometimes I dream of another life—the one my grandmother told me about. She was a beautiful, wise woman, and she knew how to make such a beautiful

(continued)

Huipul. Yes, she was an Anciana. To be hugged by her was to know the hug of God for the world. She knew the secrets of all good things. She died before Mama. Thank God. I wish she were here now, to tell me something good—to give me one of her hugs. Everything would be better then, I know.

But I'm here, in El Hoyo, and if I don't get to work soon, I won't have enough money for Marta. I need to pay her, otherwise I'll be out on the street. She takes care of me. Sometimes I wonder if she'd do this to her own daughter, though, if she had one. I wouldn't want this life for mine.

Oh God, I'd love to have a baby of my own someday. But not here, not in El Hoyo. It's not a place for a kid. Oh God, no, it's no place for me, either.

Marta's calling. Okay, okay, Marta, I'm coming. I'm coming, now. Got to go.

Source: Casa Alianza, Covenant House, www.casa-alianza.org/children/child.htm.

walking into a *favela,* or poor *barrio,* and seeing an imported sitcom on the lives of the rich and famous is startling. In countries where literacy is not universal, the ability to communicate (or miscommunicate) through the media is a powerful social and political tool. Without widespread literacy, people do not have the

Table 11.5.   Communications Indicators

Country	Television Sets (per 1,000 people)	Daily Newspapers (per 1,000 people)	Telephone Main Lines (per 1,000 people)	Mobile Phones (per 1,000 people)	Personal Computers (per 1,000 people)	Internet Hosts (per 10,000 people)
Argentina	293	123	201	121	49.2	47.34
Bolivia	118	55	62	52	12.3	1.73
Brazil	333	40	149	89	36.3	38.97
Chile	240	98	207	151	66.6	33.78
Colombia	199	46	160	75	33.7	10.15
Costa Rica	229	94	204	35	101.7	24.33
Ecuador	205	70	91	31	20.1	1.67
El Salvador	191	48	76	62	16.2	1.62
Guatemala	61	33	55	30	9.9	2.54
Honduras	95	55	44	12	9.5	0.19
Mexico	267	97	112	79	44.2	50.60
Nicaragua	69	30	30	9	8.1	2.18
Panama	192	62	164	86	32.0	10.21
Paraguay	205	43	55	196	11.2	2.66
Peru	147	0	67	40	35.7	3.88
Venezuela	185	206	109	143	42.2	6.48
Latin American Average	272	71	130	82	37.7	29.62
East Asia	252	—	82	42	17.0	3.98
Canada	715	159	655	226	360.8	590.37
United States	844	215	664	312	510.5	2,419.86

Source: World Bank, *World Development Indicators 2001* (New York: Oxford University Press/World Bank, 2001).

opportunity to evaluate competing arguments, and they come to accept pronouncements made on television as truth. Internet penetration is extremely low, limiting access to important opportunities for e-learning and international communication.

Health statistics not only paint a picture of human misery but also are a proxy for the shortfall in resources for investment in human capital. Poor people find it difficult to purchase health care. It is estimated that 130 million people, or one in three Latin Americans, do not have routine access to health services. Maternal and child health programs are deficient. More than ten million children under five suffer from malnutrition in Latin America; 12 percent of the total population is under nourished. PAHO, the Pan American Health Organization, evaluated 1,700 lab services and hospitals in eighteen countries and found eighty unsatisfactory.

Education is lacking. Despite strong enrollment rates, repetition and dropout rates are high. Income and educational attainment are clearly correlated. In Guatemala, for example, a poor child is likely to complete only one year of schooling, while a wealthy child on average will finish seven. Even in Costa Rica, one of the region's best performers on social indicators, as many as one in three school-age children do not attend school; about 20 percent of those between seven and ten are absent, primarily among the poor and the rural communities. This contrast is maintained in the wealthier countries as well. In Chile, a poor child might complete 6.1 years of schooling, while a wealthy one will likely complete 11.6. Both cause and effect are at work here. Wealthy individuals have lower opportunity costs for education, and the higher level of education helps improve their income. For the poor, the additional wages of children are important to family incomes. Because the poor complete fewer years of school, their income is likely to be lower. Education is the greatest explanatory variable in both income inequality and the probability of being poor. Differences in educational attainment account for nearly 25 percent of the total income inequality in the region. Improving education will not only improve the distribution of income but also improve the standard of living of the poor.[9] In chapters 12 and 13 we will take up these important issues of health and education in depth.

> **QUESTION FOR THOUGHT**
>
> In this section we have provided a regional composite of indicators of standards of living. Select two countries and compare them directly. What likenesses and differences do you observe? Why do you imagine this to be the case?

In considering definitions of poverty we have focused on minimum income measures that allow consumption purchases as well as access to infrastructure and public goods provided by the state, sometimes in partnership with the private sector. It is important to note that these relatively narrow definitions of public and private consumption shortfalls ignore metrics for access to assets as well as qualitative measures of dignity and autonomy.[10] Poverty as a multidimensional phenomenon should be considered in the context of the broad definitions of development introduced in chapter 1.

Figure 12.1.   Intersectoral Cooperation: The Health–Development Framework

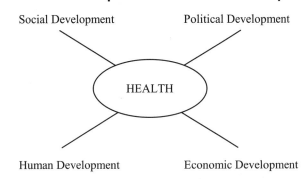

Source: Rosalia Rodriguez-García and Ann Goldman, eds., *The Health–Development Link* (Washington, D.C.: PAHO, 1994), 38.

cant health deficits among the poor. The level of economic development in part determines the social resources available for health care as well as individuals' ability to invest in their own well-being. A poor person has little control over the external environment of open sewage, polluted water and air, or safety from violence. A poor country has limited resources to provide health services and transform the social infrastructure into one that provides basic human needs for all. Avoidable mortality—deaths that could be prevented by improvements in basic health conditions—hover in the 45 percent range in the region. A startling 1.5 million persons under the age of sixty-five are dying each year from avoidable causes.

Health priorities for Latin America include health and the environment (including water supply and sewage disposal); food and nutrition issues; maternal and child health; control and elimination of preventable diseases, with particular attention to lifestyles and risk factors; AIDS; worker health; substance abuse; population control; mental health; and violence. AIDS has now spread to all countries in Latin America, with the risk of transmission highest among the poor. It is estimated that at least 1.3 million adults, or one in one thousand, is infected with HIV. Nearly six hundred people are infected every day. Forty-two percent of reported AIDS cases in Latin America are in Brazil, with between 430,000 and 650,000 people infected, giving Brazil the dubious distinction of ranking second to the United States in terms of AIDS cases in the hemisphere. (The UN provides low and high estimates at www.unaids.org.) Transmission is primarily sexual; in Mexico a man having sex with another man faces a one in three chance that his partner is HIV positive. The epidemic is concentrated among the poor; 60 percent of those with HIV/AIDS have not completed primary school. IV drug users are another group at risk; in Mexico between 3 and 11 percent are infected; in Brazil and Argentina the rate reaches nearly 50 percent. The epidemic has spread to include women, who now account for one-fourth of all reported AIDS cases.[1] In Central America unprotected sex between men and women remains the primary mode of transmission. In Brazil, the AIDS epidemic has begun to spread to indigenous communities. In Santos, a city outside São Paulo, a condom social-marketing strategy is generating

BOX 12.1. SOCIAL MARKETING

Social marketing uses commercial marketing techniques to influence social behaviors. Playing to the market, it creates important information about the demand for a given product. People appear to value things they must pay for, even if the payment is very modest. Paying customers demand more from services, making providers more attentive to clients. Advertising campaigns can be used to change the tastes of the target audience to promote socially beneficial choices for society. If marketing can sell Pepsi, why not prophylactics?

Social marketing began in the 1970s as public health professionals realized that programs needed to be attentive to the needs and desires of recipient communities. This technique has since been successfully used in international health programs, especially in the areas of contraceptive distribution and oral rehydration therapy (ORT) for infants. Social marketers follow the four Ps: product, price, place (distribution), and promotion. Products can be tangible items such as condoms or rehydration salts, or services (medical exams and education) and practices (breast-feeding). Prices for these products and services are very low, often below production costs, to service the needs of the poor. These low prices are made possible through heavy subsidization. Most programs are funded by organizations such as USAID, with as much as 80 percent of the costs covered. These programs, which are often run by private providers, work with or alongside government-run programs to promote social health to a broad portion of the general public.

One example of a successful program in Latin America is in Mexico, which has in recent years had a surplus of doctors. Start-up funding has allowed these unemployed doctors to set up health clinics in previously underserved communities. The Fundacion Mexicana para la Planeacion Familiar (MEXFAM), with support from USAID and the International Planned Parenthood Federation, has helped 175 doctors set up clinics in the past ten years. These clinics provide family planning and child health services in small towns and poor urban areas. With subsidies from MEXFAM, after two years the doctor is able to buy the office and medical equipment from MEXFAM for half of its original setup cost. MEXFAM continues to provide contraceptives and training after the two-year period.

Source: Weinreich Communications, *The Social Marketing Place*, www.members.aol.com/weinreich/whatis.html; and Population Reports, *Johns Hopkins University Population Information* 19, no. 4 (November 1991): 14.

positive results. Supported by the United States Agency for International Development (USAID) and the Ministry of Health, the program aims to use marketing to change social behavior and encourage responsible sexual practices. Box 12.1 further describes social marketing.[2]

Beginning in 1996, Brazil implemented what is now considered "the most successful AIDS treatment program in the developing world."[3] Brazil has started a virtually free drug distribution program.[4] In response to high-price of antiretroviral medicines available largely in the United States, domestic companies in Brazil began the production of generic HIV drugs at low costs. According to Brazil's health ministry, by 2001, the policy had resulted in savings of roughly 422 million dollars to the Brazilian government. More importantly, the number of deaths from AIDS is estimated to have been slashed in half.[5] Hoping to emulate the success of Brazil in coping with the epidemic under financial constraints, South Africa has adopted a similar program of its own. While many international health agencies have heralded Brazil's treatment program, it has also been the subject of ongoing controversy. The U.S. government has launched legal proceedings against both countries, claiming that the production of generic HIV drugs breaks international laws on patent production. In April of 2001, and after months of debate, thirty-nine international pharmaceutical companies dropped their lawsuit against South Africa. One month later, the United States withdrew its patent complaint against Brazil. Oxfam has initiated a program to cut the cost and drive down the price of HIV drugs. Both cases sent strong messages to the international community. If Western governments are to commit themselves to reducing the AIDS epidemic and improving world public health, drug companies must take moral responsibility by providing affordable drugs to the less-developed world.[6]

Violence, especially domestic violence, has risen to become one of the most serious health problems in urban areas of the region. The homicide rate for males for 1990–1995 increased 65 percent compared to that from 1980 to 1985.[7] The leading cause of death in Colombia, for example, is homicide.[8] The explosion of violence sweeping the continent has complex causes. In Colombia and El Salvador it may be linked to historical conflicts over land. Rapid urbanization in the context of huge disparities between rich and poor may exacerbate social violence. Traditional values practiced in the countryside are lost on the new generation of tough urban youth often lured by alcohol and drugs. Rising unemployment associated with globalization may also be a contributing factor. As police capabilities are overwhelmed and judicial systems choked, repression and brutality are more common than prevention and reform. Such violence exacts a high human and economic cost. One World Bank economist estimated that the net accumulation of human capital was cut in half because of the increase in crime and violence since the mid-1980s.[9]

Nonetheless, progress has been made in overall health in the region. Over the period 1960 through 2000 (table 12.1) we can see a dramatic improvement in health in the Latin American region. Life expectancy, a general proxy for health, has improved by almost fourteen years—but this mirrors worldwide trends. Death by diseases most often associated with poverty and deficient living standards—infectious, nutritional, and birth-related diseases—declined significantly from 7.6 deaths per thousand to 1.9 in 2000.

Table 12.1. Mortality by General Causes in Latin America, 1960–2020

	1960	1970	1980	1990	2000	2010	2020
Life expectancy at birth in years	57.1	61.2	65.4	68.7	71.1	73.2	75.0
Mortality by cause (rates per 1,000)							
Infectious, nutritional, and birth-related diseases	7.6	5.0	2.9	2.1	1.9	1.5	1.2
Noninfectious Diseases	4.9	4.7	4.5	3.8	5.0	6.4	8.1
Intentional and unintentional lesions	0.8	0.8	0.9	0.9	1.1	1.3	1.4

Source: Rafael Lozano, *Cambios en el Perfile epidemiologico en America Latina: Desigualdades, alcances, y retos* (presented at LASA 1997, Guadalajara, Mexico, April 17–19, 1997), 15.

Infant mortality fell from 125 per 1,000 live births in 1950–1955 to 30 in 1999.[10] The extraordinary success of Chile in bringing down infant mortality from 109 per 1,000 live births in 1960–1964 to 14 in 1990–1994 illustrates the possibility for improvement through concerted policy efforts.[11] But progress on basic health concerns is met by new challenges. The region is going through an **epidemiological transition,** reflecting new causes of death associated with the ills of modern living, which include noninfectious disease such as heart failure and cancer. Accidents and violence as measured by intentional and unintentional lesions are expected to increase. Health systems are easily overwhelmed by confronting traditional and emerging health concerns simultaneously. Health becomes a battle on two fronts: continuing to address the basic health deficit and making progress on new threats such as AIDS, violence, and cardiocare.

As Latin American nations have experienced major transitions in health profiles, occupational health concerns have become a leading cause of morbidity among adults in the region. People spend more than a third of each day at work; conditions in the workplace clearly impact health. There are between twenty and twenty-seven million work-related accidents annually in Latin American and the Caribbean, 90,000 of which are fatal. Despite impacting more than two hundred million workers and their families, occupational safety and health have been largely ignored. The existing data underestimate the problem, and the institutional capacity to address concerns is weak. Heavy physical workloads; hazards such as noise or radiation; dangerous conditions; toxic chemicals; exposure to asbestos or coal dust; risk of cancer; and exposure to viruses, fungi, and molds as well as social conditions can damage workers' health. In the rural sector acute pesticide poisoning is a major health problem. Workers do not wear appropriate protective clothing (perhaps because the heavy rubber is designed for colder climates) or follow safety directions. Miners suffer from falls, electrocution, lung disease, and neurological damage from exposure to chemicals such as mercury. Informal-sector employment, accounting for nearly 50 percent of the labor force in the region, increases health risks in that small firms, high turnover, absence of monitoring of conditions, and lack of insurance generate a higher incidence of health problems. Child labor is still widespread in the region, and children are more vulnerable to workplace risk. The fifty-six million women in the workforce face a dual burden: the stress of low-paying jobs and the double duty of their second workday in the evening at home. *Maquila* workers, primarily women, suffer from repetitive stress disorders on the musculoskeletal system. Latin America and the Caribbean's fatality rate in the workplace is approximately twice that of Canada's. This may even understate the data, as reporting in the informal sector is weak as well as the fact that in the formal sector insurance rates in the region are often tied to injuries. The economic cost of occupational health hazards is high; the International Labor Organization (ILO) and the WHO estimate the total burden to reach as much as 10 percent of GDP of developing countries, more than three times the estimated occupational health cost of the United States.[12] Despite the enormous burden of occupational health costs, extending regulation is problematic because of the need to create jobs and the weak institutional capacity for enforcement.

There is a great deal of diversity in health performance in the region. As can be seen in table 12.2, life expectancy ranges from a low of sixty-two years in Bolivia to

Table 12.2. Health Statistics by Country

Country	Life Expectancy at Birth		Infant Mortality Rate per 1,000 Live Births		Doctors per 1,000 Population	Hospital Beds per 1,000 Population	Health Expenditure Total % of GDP	Health Expenditure ($) per Capita
	1980	1999	1980	1999	1990–1998	1990–1998	1990–1998	1990–1998
Argentina	70	74	35	18	2.7	3.3	10.3	852
Bolivia	52	62	118	59	1.3	1.7	6.4	69
Brazil	63	67	70	32	1.3	3.1	6.6	309
Chile	69	76	32	10	1.1	2.7	5.9	289
Colombia	66	70	41	23	1.1	1.5	9.3	227
Costa Rica	73	77	19	12	0.9	1.7	6.8	267
Cuba	74	76	20	7	5.3	5.1	9.1	83
Ecuador	63	69	74	28	1.7	1.6	3.6	59
El Salvador	57	70	84	30	1.0	1.6	7.2	143
Guatemala	57	65	84	40	0.9	1.0	4.4	78
Honduras	60	70	70	34	0.8	1.1	8.6	74
Mexico	67	72	51	29	1.6	1.1	4.7	202
Nicaragua	59	69	84	34	0.8	1.5	12.2	54
Paraguay	67	70	50	24	1.1	1.3	5.2	86
Peru	60	69	81	39	0.9	1.5	6.1	141
Uruguay	70	74	37	15	3.7	4.4	9.1	621
Venezuela	68	73	36	20	2.4	1.5	4.2	171
Latin America and Caribbean	65	70	61	30	1.6	2.2	6.5	272
High Income	74	78	12	6	2.8	7.2	9.7	2,702

Source: World Bank, *World Development Indicators 2001* (Washington, D.C.: World Bank, 2001).

a high of seventy-seven in Costa Rica. Bolivia and Guatemala are the worst performers on infant mortality, while Chile and Cuba have achieved low child-mortality
rates. Hospital beds are scarce relative to high income countries. In countries with
either the political will or the money, significant strides have been made in creating
health systems to treat these diseases. Countries such as Cuba and Costa Rica have
gone through an epidemiological transition and have health profiles similar to developed countries. The least developed countries, like Bolivia, have truncated transitions and suffer primarily from infectious diseases, such as malaria, and diseases of
deficiency, such as malnutrition. The middle- and high-income countries, such as
Ecuador and Brazil, which have begun their epidemiological transition, suffer from
an accumulation of both the infectious and deficiency diseases found in the less-
developed countries and, as a result of the demographic transition toward a more
urbanized and aging society, also have high levels of emerging, chronic, and degenerative diseases.[13] This situation is known as an **epidemiological backlog.** This
double health burden puts a strain on social welfare budgets. These systems must
solve the problems of poorer countries while also being challenged by the health
concerns of the wealthier world. Table 12.3 classifies countries by disease type,
underscoring the prevalence of deficiency and infectious diseases in poor countries.

Countrywide data should, however, be interpreted with caution. Income inequality
skews access to health care. If you are an affluent Mexican, for example, chances of
your baby dying in infancy are 13.4 per 1,000 live births; if you are poor the odds esca-
late to a tragic 109.76. Rural Peruvian babies are about three times as likely to die as
those in Lima. Malnutrition in Ecuador among children under five ranges from 8 to
42.6 percent, depending on the socioeconomic district. In Peru, a mother with no education is three times more likely to have her child die than a mother with a secondary
education or higher. A rural inhabitant in Brazil can expect to live twenty fewer years
than a wealthy cousin in the city.[14] Divergent rural and urban standards of living result
in widely different health profiles. Health ministries must therefore make tough
choices about where to invest the nation's health resources. Should investments be
made in cities to confront new challenges to health with technologically sophisticated
systems? Or should resources be placed in the poorest rural sectors to address traditional threats of disease?

GENDER, ETHNICITY, AND HEALTH

In addition to biological differences, gender inequalities in health care are driven by
differences in men and women's social roles and in their access to family and community resources. The denial of reproductive rights results in death:[15]

- 23,000 women die each year in Latin America of pregnancy and birth-related
  causes
- 25,000 die of cervical cancer
- 25 percent give birth without the assistance of a skilled attendant
- 27 percent have no access to prenatal care

Table 12.3. Diseases of the Americas—The Epidemiological Transition

	Poorest Latin American Countries: Bolivia	Middle-Income Latin American Countries: Ecuador	High-Income Latin American Countries: Brazil	Latin American Countries with a Strong Safety Net: Costa Rica/Cuba	Developed Countries: United States/Canada
Deficiency					
Intestinal disease	X				
Intestinal infections	X				
Malnutrition	X				
Infectious					
Changes	X				
Malaria	X	X			
Influenza				X	X
Parasitic					
Pneumonia				X	X
Respiratory infections		X	X		
Tuberculosis	X	X	X		
Emerging					
Cancer					X
Heart disease				X	
Malaria			X		
Parasitic		X	X		
Chronic Diseases					
Pulmonary infections					X
Tuberculosis					
Malignant Tumors				X	
Tumors					
Degenerative					
Cancer					X
Cerebrovascular				X	
Malignant tumors					
Strokes					X
Tumors					
Congenital					
Heart Disease		X	X		
Birth defects					X
Congenital anomalies				X	
Diabetes		X	X		
Heart attacks					
Environmental					
Accidents		X	X	X	X
Homicides					X
Parasitic					
Tumors			X		

Source: PAHO (1989 and 1993 data) and the Ministry of Health Ecuador.

Maternal malnutrition is a leading cause of both maternal and infant mortality. Without adequate prenatal care, an infant will not receive important nutrients for growth. Breast-feeding by well-nourished mothers transfers needed antibodies to their children to fight viral and bacterial infections such as diarrhea and pneumonia, rashes, and allergies. In urban areas, many women, however, have been substituting more "modern" infant feeding practices for breast-feeding, leading to a decline in infant health.

An important element in health care is a woman's ability to control her own fertility. Table 12.4 presents reproductive health statistics for the region. A Save the Children/Bolivian mothercare project found that women identified their most urgent health problem as having too many children.[16] All countries in the region are significantly above the high-income fertility ratio of 1.7 children per couple. According to the Inter-American Development Bank (IADB), one third of all women have their first child before age twenty; in Guatemala, the rate is one half.[17] As women have entered the marketplace in increasing numbers, the opportunity cost of children has risen. As some market women note, customers want to be waited on quickly and not be distracted by crying babies.[18] Use of contraceptives ranges from 77 percent in Brazil to less than 40 percent in Guatemala; demand (including unmet needs) is between 50 and 80 percent.[19] The most widely used method of contraception in the region has been female sterilization. According to the Brazilian health ministry, 21 percent of women between ages twenty-five and twenty-nine have been sterilized, reflecting a failure to provide other methods of contraception. Family planning, however, remains somewhat controversial, given both religious preferences and the position of some multilateral donor agencies. For some indigenous women, the thought of (mostly male) doctors poking inside them prevents them from seeking medical advice on family planning methods. Traditional men sometimes fear that contraception will encourage promiscuous behavior among their wives and daughters. Tragically, unwanted pregnancies are often terminated with self-induced abortions that threaten the lives of the mother or leave deformities in the child should it be born. Some alliance between ethnomedicine (traditional healers) and biomedical practitioners might help alleviate the difficulties in providing health care to indigenous women. Biomedical practitioners need to better understand the role of patient attitudes and responses in improving the delivery of health services in traditional areas. Husbands need to be included in educational efforts at family planning to dispel widely held myths concerning the negative effects of family planning.

Violence against women is also a critical concern. The United Nations defines violence against women as an act of gender violence that results or is likely to result in physical, sexual, or psychological harm or suffering to women. The Panos Institute reports that gender violence causes more death and disability among women in the fifteen to forty-four age category than cancer, malaria, traffic accidents, or war. The costs extend to families; children of abused women in Nicaragua drop out of school four years earlier and were one hundred times more likely to be hospitalized than children of non-abused women. A Costa Rican survey showed that 95 percent of pregnant girls age fifteen or younger were incest victims. According to one Honduran health worker, overburdened health care providers often don't have the time

Table 12.4. Reproductive Health Statistics by Country

	Total Fertility Rate (births per woman)		Adolescent Fertility Rate (births per 1,000 women, ages 15–19)	Women at Risk of Unintended Pregnancy (% of women, ages 15–49)	Contraceptive Prevalence Rate (% of women, ages 15–49)	Births Attended by Skilled Health Staff (% of total)	
	1980	1999	1999	1990–1999	1990–1999	1982	1996–1999
Argentina	3.3	2.5	63	—	—	—	—
Bolivia	5.5	4.0	80	26	49	—	59
Brazil	3.9	2.2	71	7	77	98	88
Chile	2.8	2.2	44	—	—	92	100
Colombia	3.9	2.7	84	8	72	—	—
Costa Rica	3.6	2.5	76	—	—	—	96
Dominican Republic	4.2	2.8	12	13	64	—	—
Ecuador	5.0	3.1	73	—	66	62	90
El Salvador	4.9	3.2	104	8	60	—	—
Guatemala	6.3	4.7	109	23	38	—	55
Honduras	6.5	4.0	108	11	50	—	—
Mexico	4.7	2.8	70	—	65	—	65
Nicaragua	6.3	3.6	130	15	60	—	—
Panama	3.7	2.5	77	—	—	80	—
Paraguay	5.2	4.0	81	17	57	—	71
Peru	4.5	3.1	65	12	64	30	56
Uruguay	2.7	2.3	66	—	—	—	—
High Income	1.8	1.7	25	—	75	—	—

Source: World Bank, *World Development Indicators 2001* (Washington, D.C.: World Bank, 2001).

to talk to patients in diagnostic exams; many women will not discuss household violence unless directly asked. A Pan American Health Organization (PAHO) study ties violence against women in the Americas to a macho culture that reinforces male control over wealth and decision making in the family.[20]

The health and nutritional levels of indigenous communities in Latin America are well below national averages. Viral diseases, including influenza, measles, dengue, and respiratory infections, frequently become epidemics under poor sanitary conditions in indigenous communities. Activities such as mining and oil exploration exact high costs in terms of the health of otherwise isolated indigenous groups. In addition to disrupting the environment, workers introduce diseases for which indigenous communities have not developed immunities. In the Amazon Basin countries, the most important challenges to the health of indigenous communities come from the overexploitation of resources. In Bolivia, indigenous people report more than twice the number of illnesses and injuries, and miss twice as many work days, but receive less medical care than the general population. Life expectancy for the indigenous in Colombia is about ten years lower than national averages.[21] Cultural differences between health care dispensed in hospitals and traditional practices promoted by healers and midwives in indigenous communities also create a health services gap, particularly in practices such as childbirth, which are highly sensitive to custom and tradition. In Guatemala, for example, the maternal mortality rate in the indigenous population is 83 percent higher than the national rate. For the indigenous peoples, humans are inseparable from nature; health care must therefore involve a holistic approach. To be effective, health delivery systems must be sensitive to cultural practices. The 1993 PAHO workshop on Indigenous Peoples and Health held in Winnipeg, Canada, set out guidelines for health promotion, advocating community participation, preservation of habitat and traditional lifestyles, evaluation and monitoring of the health status and living conditions of indigenous peoples, and formulation of national health policies to address the problems of indigenous communities. Nonetheless, as the communiqué initiating the meeting characterized, the health of indigenous peoples is "perhaps the most technically complex and difficult health issue of the day."[22] Interim evaluation of progress on indigenous health care improvements indicates the need for supplemental funding for nongovernmental organizations (NGOs) to reach indigenous populations, improvement of the database on indigenous health concerns, better preparation of health care workers in multicultural communities to attend to the needs and to respect the traditional practices of indigenous peoples, and improved dissemination of program efforts to illustrate best-case practices for other countries.[23] Policy measures will require patience and perseverance for success.

THE IMPORTANCE OF PRIMARY HEALTH CARE

The first step in improving health indicators and the well-being of citizens is universal access to basic health services. **Primary health care** (PHC) is the essence of the "Health for All" (HFA) strategy adopted at the 1978 Alma Alta joint WHO–UNICEF conference and endorsed by the WHO Assembly in 1981. The landmark document outlined programmatic health objectives as part of a new model for health care based on comprehensive primary health care. These included water, sanitation, food supply, nutrition, mother and child care (MCC), family planning, immunization, control of local diseases, essential drugs, and education. Health for All encourages culturally sensitive plans that employ appropriate treatment and technology. Health should be integrated into national development plans to improve the social and economic development of the community. Education and active participation are seen as the keys to the promotive, preventive, curative, and rehabilitative services of PHC. The primary health care approach is aimed at mobilizing individuals and communities to improve health systems to provide fair and equitable delivery of needed services. The issue of inequality is particularly important in Latin America; PAHO sees overcoming inequality as the major constraint in meeting the goal of universal access to basic health services for the inhabitants of the region.[24]

The strategies for achieving HFA and the subsequent emphasis on PHC are based on three pillars: participation, equity, and intersectoral cooperation. PHC emphasizes social justice, a broadly defined concept of health that includes lifestyle and environmental components, intersectoral integration, and community participation. PHC employs a holistic approach, embracing the individual's relationship with community and family. Participation is central to the implementation of effective health plans. It can be viewed as the first step toward the decentralization of local health systems.[25] Equity is threefold: between the First and Third Worlds, rural and urban areas, and genders. The call for equity is grounded in the fundamental right to health care. Intersectoral cooperation[26] refers to the need to link health and development plans, as seen in PAHO's "health in development" and WHO's "health as a conditionality for economic development" strategies.

Investing in PHC can at times involve tough choices. In Brazil, the Institute Materno–Infantil de Pernambuco (IMIP) faced such a tough trade-off. IMIP, a winner of a UNICEF award for a child-friendly hospital, had to decide whether to maintain its pediatric intensive care unit or engage in community outreach. With 95 percent of its financing coming from the Brazilian Ministry of Health, it had to match costs to average revenues set by the government. The intensive care unit cost more than the government was willing to pay. Furthermore, the children sent to the unit from all over northeastern Brazil were so sick and malnourished that the mortality rate remained high despite the expensive interventions. A more cost-effective strategy to saving children's lives was pursued: close the intensive care unit and expand the network of small community health posts in slum neighborhoods of the major city of Recife. Indeed, infant mortality declined from 147 to 101 per 1,000 live births in those neighborhoods.[27] Box 12.2 demonstrates another case of effective delivery of preventive health services in Brazil. Local control and local initiative can work to reverse the devastating effects of neglect on children and families in poor rural regions.

Most countries have some elements of PHC in their Ministry of Health (MOH)

QUESTION FOR THOUGHT

Given limited funding, how would you propose that the health care dollar be spent in Latin America? Does focus on primary health care leave Latin America further behind or a step ahead?

BOX 12.2.   PREVENTIVE HEALTH CARE IN CEARÁ: REVERSING A HEALTH NIGHTMARE

Prior to decentralization of health care, Ceará, Brazil, had some of the worst health indicators in the region. Fewer than a third of the state's municipal districts had a nurse; most people had never seen a doctor. Infant mortality was twice the Brazilian average, and only one in four children had been vaccinated against measles or polio. A new preventive health care system, called the Health Agent System (Programa de Agentes de Saúde, PAS), radically transformed the health profile of the state. Infant deaths declined 36 percent, vaccination coverage is nearly complete, and each of the districts has a nurse and a public health program. The program cost was about $1.50 per person served—markedly lower than the $80 per capita cost of Brazil's existing health care system. How was this minor medical miracle—with such tangible gains to so many Brazilians—accomplished?

Starting PAS as an employment-generating program in the drought-stricken Northeast in 1987, the state committed to funding it permanently in 1989. The program supported a small army of public health agents who went from house to house (sometimes, in more distant areas, traveling by bicycle, donkey, or canoe) to teach families good health practices. Agents were paid more than teachers or the wage paid to male agricultural labor, although this sometimes did not amount to the national minimum wage. In an area in which nonagricultural opportunities were rare, the jobs were seen as highly prestigious positions. The work was rewarded by warm public support, as the effects were demonstrable to the community. Standards were high. Unlike many government jobs, these were without tenure, and the community (especially those not selected as agents) was told to report lax behavior on the part of the extensionists. People were told to expect a visit once a month to their homes, and for health agents to be a part of the communities in which they worked. Nurse supervisors brought in to train agents and administer the program were, through their success, accorded more control, respect, and admiration than they had received in poorly run city hospitals. Administratively, the program was efficient and cost-effective.

At first agents confronted mistrust from rural inhabitants unaccustomed to government programs and comfortable with traditional medicines and faith healers. Agents used curative tasks such as oral rehydration techniques for a baby seemingly near death to convince mothers of the benefits of modern medicine. With the baby playing happily a few hours after nearly dying, the mother was more amenable to hearing about the benefits of breast-feeding, hygienic food preparation, and water filtration systems. Agents developed a bond of trust with often lonely and overburdened mothers, sometimes helping with cooking or child care. The decentralization of services and the empowerment of 7,300 never-before salaried rural women through training and extension services have truly transformed the health profile in Ceará.

Source: This box is based on the study by Judith Tendler, *Good Government in the Tropics* (Baltimore: Johns Hopkins University Press, 1997), 21–45.

delivery systems and have decreased emphasis on the medicalization of health as well as the engineering model, which saw the body as a machine and good health a question of getting it tuned correctly. However, due primarily to budgetary and political reasons, selective PHC programs, as opposed to comprehensive PHC programs, have been implemented. Weaker versions, limited to growth monitoring, oral rehydration, breast-feeding, immunization, family planning, food production, and female education, have been the norm. The poor have had an increasing burden of paying for health

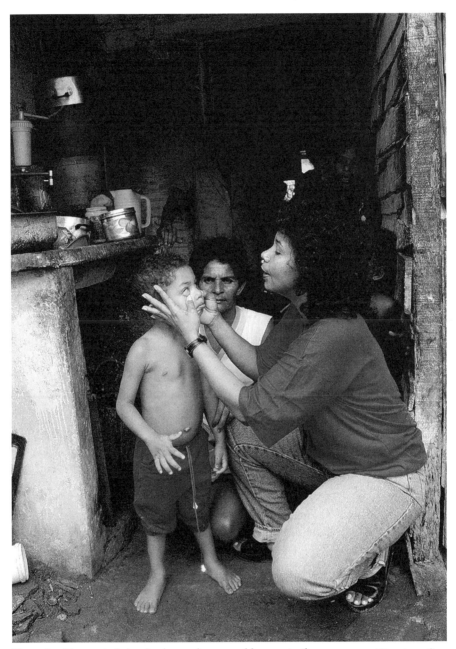

Home health agents bring basic services—and hope—to the very poor. *(Courtesy of David Mangurian and the Inter-American Development Bank.)*

services out of pocket. With budget cuts, many health posts can no longer provide basic services. In Ecuador, for example, spending on health has come to absorb between 12 to 17 percent of the family budget. Those unable to afford private-sector service are left without critically needed curative care and rarely invest in preventive care.[28] Public and private international donor agencies, led in part by WHO and PAHO, can facilitate a broader adoption of PHC programs through partnerships with state and local governments to bridge the fiscal gap.

HEALTH CARE SYSTEMS IN LATIN AMERICA

In addition to choices about the level of sophistication of health care, improvements in health require changes in systems of delivery. The health status of the people of Latin America is affected not only by extant diseases and each country's socioeconomic status but also by institutions and systems established to provide health services for the populations and the environments in which these institutions operate. The challenges to Latin American health care delivery systems are numerous and require a redefinition of the traditional health care system. Old or accumulated challenges include insufficient coverage of the population, poor technical quality, inadequate patient referral, and deficient management of institutions. New challenges to health delivery systems are composed of cost escalation, financial insecurity, and technological expansion in light of their opportunity costs in terms of primary health care.

Rural health care poses particular challenges for 25 percent of the hemisphere's population. In some rural areas, health care can be a four- to eight-hour bus ride or a one- to two-hour walk away. Between 50 and 80 percent of all health expenditures go to hospitals located near urban centers. Inaccessible health facilities make prenatal and other types of preventive primary health care particularly problematic. Shifting from hospital-based to community-based health systems can help direct resources toward the needs of the local population rather than urban patterns of demand. Although a hospital has the advantage of being a physically distinct unit in which health services can be coordinated under one roof, it can also be a center of power and influence that drains resources from community health systems. Major resources may be tied up in plant, equipment, and services that come at an opportunity cost to meeting people's primary health care needs. Unless the hospital is integrated into a community health care system, when patients are discharged they may find little continuity of care and suffer from a fragmentation of health services.[29] Health care must extend into the community.

The organization of health care varies across the region. Although each Latin American country has a unique mixture of social security facilities, private practitioners, and government ministries responsible for health, generalizations can be made. Health care systems have two service factors: finance and delivery of service. Financing refers to how, and by whom, services are paid for. Delivery refers to the actual provision of services. Each factor can be provided either by the public or by the private sector. For example, financing could be public, through universal health insurance, but rely on the services of private practitioners. Alternatively, some financing— especially for the poor—might be public, with a mix of public hospitals and private providers. In Cuba, both financing and provision are public. The Costa Rican model is also largely public, with its nearly universal state coverage, although private-sector services are available. Paraguay and Argentina are closer to the U.S. model, which is a mixture of private health insurance that includes out-of-pocket expenditures and public resources. The United States is a pure example of this model. In Brazil, public financing is nearly universal and the services are contracted out.

Moving from financing to delivery of health services, the most common structure in Latin America is a mixed system. Three main health sectors in Latin America are present: the Social Security Institutes (SSI)[30] (*cajas de seguro social*) for formal-sector employees, the private-sector for those who can afford private insurance and those who are uninsured and choose to seek private services, and the Ministry of Health (MOH) for the poor. The formal sector finances and provides health care services to its employees. The MOH is responsible for the coordination of health care service delivery for approximately 70 percent of the population but has only approximately 40 percent of the financing.

Figure 12.2 illustrates the breakdown of health coverage for Bolivia in 1995. The Ministry of Social Provision and Public Health orchestrates curative and preventive care through 101 general and regional hospitals, 896 health centers, and 1,210 rural health outreach posts. Although it is officially responsible for covering 75 percent of the population, it reaches only about 38 percent. The Bolivian SSI covers formal sector employees with pension, sickness and maternity, work injuries, and family allowance programs. The SSI operates its own health facilities in the urban areas and

Figure 12.2.   Bolivian Health Care Coverage, 1995

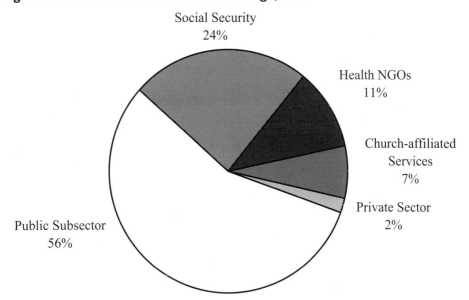

Source: Pan American Health Organization, *Basic Country Health Profiles, 1999.* Available online at www/paho.org/English/SHA/prflbol.htm.

frequently uses private contractors for users outside the cities. In 1995, 24 percent of the population had access to Social Security. Private health providers cover about 2 percent of the population, with another 4–5 percent receiving health care through the five hundred NGOs at work in Bolivia. Foreign donations and foreign loans compose roughly 22.5 percent of the public health budget, with user fees covering 9.4 percent and central government budget and transfers making up the balance. USAID provided over 5 percent of the total central government financing in 1991, with other funds coming from the World Bank and the United Nations Development Program.[31]

> **QUESTION FOR THOUGHT**
>
> Go to the PAHO website at www.paho.org or to the Center for International Health Information site at www.cihi.com. Select two countries, one a relatively poor country (perhaps Guatemala) and the other a relatively affluent country (such as Chile). How do the specific health problems and risks differ? How are health services organized? What do you see as the health priorities for each country?

There are numerous problems with this common Latin American health care model. Because many institutions provide similar services to different client bases, there is unnecessary duplication of services, especially of costly high-tech items. Services are concentrated in urban areas. There are concerns of quality, especially for the lower classes who utilize the resource-poor MOH facilities. Health care reflects broader social patterns in the region, defined by a high degree of class inequality. Better use of health resources will require a restructuring of the delivery systems in the region while tackling tough issues of social inequality.

REFORMING HEALTH SERVICE DELIVERY: THE CHALLENGE TO POLICY

Health care policy is determined by a number of critical choices a nation faces. How much should people pay for health care? How should the trade-off between high-quality, sophisticated treatment and increased access to basic health and nutrition be resolved? Should health services be provided by the public or the private sector? How should governments resolve the tension between hospital-based urban care and comprehensive rural coverage? What kind of health insurance schemes will meet society's goals? Policies to improve health care in Latin America include improving the choices households face, transforming the pattern of public spending on health, and changing the structure of the health care market.

Households are constrained by income and education in the choices they make about health care. Governments should consider pursuing policies that improve choices, particularly among the poor. This includes expanded investments in the link between education and health, particularly for girls. Girls in the region play important roles in the care of younger siblings. An example of public education is a radio program in Bolivia directed toward eight- to thirteen-year-old children providing lessons on food preparation, sanitation, diarrhea prevention and oral hydration, cholera, and immunizations to improve family health practices. Women are an important target group. The pattern of public spending might be oriented toward the financing of public health interventions and community health services that deliver the greatest improvements in health care per dollar spent, rather than expensive investments in tertiary care for the wealthy. The use of health promoters—members of the community trained and practicing under a doctor's supervision—can extend the medical reach. Promoters engage in preventive medicine and health education, as well as carry small medical kits to deal with wounds, infections, and simple medical problems such as diarrhea. As members of the community themselves, health promoters have the trust of their clients, travel to remote areas, and often help bridge the gap between modern medicine and traditional healing practices.

The direction of health policy should in part be shaped by the local demand for health care. The perceived need for medical care—generally determined by medical experts—may diverge from the demand for health care based on a community's assessment of its own health conditions and socioeconomic circumstances. Demand for health care might be influenced by cultural norms and traditional medical practices, income, and prices that include not only monetary fees paid for services but also the travel time and forgone income to seek care.[32] Perception of illness also varies across cultures. If an illness becomes a way of life for a community, fewer members might seek treatment than in a community in which the same disease is rare. Tourists, for example, rarely forget their malaria shots and pills or their diarrhea remedies; inhabitants in some tropic communities may simply find these diseases part of the natural cycle of life—and sometimes death. Education and literacy also condition the demand for health care. Sadly, what people don't know can kill them. Estimating local demand for health services is important to direct funds away from underutilized services and toward unmet needs. A process of health education at the community level can facilitate grassroots participation in the determination of the demand for health.

Paying the Bill for Health

Who should pay for health services? Traditionally, health services in Latin American have been controlled by central governments. Consistent with the changes of the neoliberal model, in Latin America there has been a move to limit governmental responsibility for health. There are three variants to this reform: privatization, decentralization, and contracting. Privatization has been especially popular in reference to the SSIs, as seen in Chile. Decentralization involves the devolution of previously centralized responsibilities to the local level. In Chile, responsibility for health care was brought down to the municipal level; the budget for primary health care and 50 percent of the health staff were transferred from the national health service to local governments. Chilean workers, with a mandatory 7-percent deduction from their paychecks, were given a choice of enrolling in either public or private health insurance plans.[33] To overcome limited Ministry of Health budgets and improve equity, participation, and intersectoral cooperation, Colombia's decentralized contracting system appears to be a viable model for reforming Latin American health care systems. Multinational companies such as Aetna and Cigna are entering the Latin

American market as partners to local providers of private health insurance. In Argentina, international investors are funding the development of Excell Corporation, the booming health maintenance organization (HMO) insurance enterprise of Juan Navarro, the entrepreneur we met in chapter 1 of this text. Argentina's move to market-based providers has been facilitated by a $350 million loan from the World Bank to restructure health care debt in the interest of improving competitiveness in the sector. Box 12.3 discusses reforms in Mexican health care in greater depth.

> ### QUESTION FOR THOUGHT
>
> Table 12.A gives data on spending on health care in selected countries in the Western Hemisphere. Given the social and economic priorities we have addressed thus far in this text, is Latin America investing enough in health care?

In addition to the question of who should pay for health services, the question of "how much" arises. Given fiscal constraints, some evidence suggests that even the poor can and should pay for at least a part of services rendered. The very poor can be given vouchers to cover expenses; payment for service sets up greater accountability at the local level. In some areas user fees have been introduced to stretch scarce public resources in the health field. Some research indicates that even the poor are willing to pay for health services, if the introduction of fees is accompanied by an improvement in quality.[34] In cases such as El Salvador, where user fees have been instituted, evidence suggests that cost was an inconsequential factor in determining why rural residents did not seek health care.[35] The additional income can be used to increase the stock and variety of effective drug treatments. In contrast to tax-funded "free" health services from the central government, payment at the local level establishes a direct relationship between quality of services delivered and fair compensation. It may encourage cost savings and more efficient delivery of health services.

Nevertheless, some Third World medical experts are wary of user fees, especially in very poor areas where barter practices and lack of cash income limits the ability to pay for health services. User fees can also be seen as a form of regressive tax by which the poor pay proportionately more of their income for health than the rich. Unfortunately, there may be few alternatives. With a fixed budget for public health, governments must make tough choices about the allocation of resources. Market-oriented reforms may be needed as a key element of system overhauls. Cost-effectiveness is a criteria that guides many decisions in the health care field.

The market, however, is not enough. Some services (e.g., aerial spraying to reduce dengue carrying mosquitoes) would simply not take place without government. The market alone is not sufficient as an allocator of health services. Without proper state guidance and oversight, the market often fails to provide equity and, in many cases, does not yield the expected improvements in efficiency. Even insurance magnate Navarro himself notes the need for market regulation in managed care to provide a framework for prices and services.[36] The market for health services involves a complicated array of interconnected markets, including health care professionals, pharmaceuticals, medical equipment, and education. Market failures in health delivery bedevil sophisticated industrial economies.[37] Marketization of

Box 12.3. Reform of Mexican Health Care

While the overall health of the Mexican people has improved significantly, including an increase in life expectancy from sixty-two to seventy years from 1980 to 1994, compared with industrial economies there is considerable room for improvement. Modern health problems of Mexico's NAFTA neighbors coexist with the epidemiological characteristics of low-income countries. Mexicans still face problems of infectious diseases, malnutrition, and concerns related to insufficient mother and infant care, while simultaneously confronting the needs of a more urbanized and aging population. Challenges to the Mexican health system include extending coverage, particularly in rural areas; reducing disparities in health status among regions; responding to the needs of a more urban and higher-income group; and preparing for the coming needs of an elderly population. Systemic reform is crucial to meeting divergent challenges.

Mexico's health system is segmented into various social security schemes covering insured workers in the formal sector, public health services provided by the Ministry of Health, and a private sector that is largely unregulated. Those falling in the public sector are a heterogeneous group including rural inhabitants and those in marginal urban zones. Some in the social security sector overlap, also using private-sector services; provision for the poor is clearly separated from that for the working class and the rich. In reality some ten million Mexicans have access to little or no health care. Coordination between the different segments of the system is typically low, resulting in a duplication of services. There have been few systemic incentives to improve efficiency or extend coverage.

Improving equity in health services is a goal of the Mexican government. Deficiencies in infrastructure, lack of trained health professionals, long waiting times, large distances to services, lack of medication at clinics, and poor supervision are common complaints. Deficient public health services force the poor to spend meager savings on vital care. As a proportion of their income, the bottom 40 percent of the population spends 5 percent, as opposed to 3 percent in the upper half of the income distribution. Mexico allocates between 5.0 and 6.5 percent of GDP on health care, an amount within the normal range given its income level.[38] The problem in Mexico is not necessarily the level of spending but rather the large unmet needs and regional disparities in the health system.

The Mexican health system may exhibit tendencies from the worst of two options in health care, relying on elements of the public integrated model and the private contract model. Much of the population falls under the national health system, and the social insurance schemes are subject to the quasi-monopoly power of providers, with no effective consumer choice. Because the provider of services is also the regulator, supervision and quality control are erratic. The private sector of the market must attend to those dissatisfied with public services.

Table 12.A. Health Care Spending

Country	Per Capita (U.S.$)	% of GDP
United States	4,403	14.1
Argentina	675	7.3
Chile	364	6.2
Uruguay	318	5.7
Venezuela	293	6.5
Brazil	288	5.8
Mexico	171	3.8

Source: Wall Street Journal, 6 August 1998.

(continued)

(continued)

Systemic reforms aim to increase public access, make service provision more efficient, and contain future cost escalation. One element of the reform is to bring informal-sector workers with prepayment abilities—those in small firms and family businesses—into the social security scheme. A voluntary affiliation scheme will allow unaffiliated individuals to buy into the social security plan. The plan allows for user choice of primary physicians. Regional decentralization is also being pursued to better meet local health demands. It is designed to reduce duplication of services at the national and local levels while addressing equity through a formula for funding that accounts for health needs, poverty, and financial capacity of state governments. Nonetheless, experience shows that decentralization should be phased in gradually to avoid a deterioration of services in poorer regions. Ensuring that local providers meet national standards will be the responsibility of the National Health Council (Consejo Nacional de Salud, CNS) and the Ministry of Health. A program targeted to those in extreme poverty financed by federal transfers is focused on twelve primary health services selected for their cost-efficient nature. This program benefited some six million people by 1997. The federal government will maintain the normative, coordination, planning, and evaluation functions under the new health plan.

The ambitious reform of the health care sector embarked upon by the Mexican government creates the potential for better delivery of health services to millions of Mexicans. In the new health model, preventive strategies dominate over curative approaches, covering the life cycle from reproductive health through aging. Success, however, will depend on the political will to overcome resistance to vested interests in the old, inefficient system of delivery.

Source: The Reform of the Mexican Health Care System, Organization for Economic Cooperation and Development Economic Surveys: Mexico (Paris: OECD, 1998).

health care may also lead to a fragmentation of services.[39] In Chile, for example, as funding chased the quantity of services offered, quality suffered. Decentralization negatively affected the excellent preventive care that had traditionally characterized the Chilean system, in which funding was targeted to curative as opposed to preventive purposes.[40] Furthermore, as workers were given a choice between private and public plans, the healthier participants were drawn to the private sector; those unable to get coverage from risk-averse private insurers were left on the public rolls. Finally, marketization is unlikely to work for those most severely affected by the health crisis in Latin America: the poor, particularly the indigenous, outside the market economy.

The challenge for policy in Latin America is to achieve a workable balance between private-sector participation and public-sector control to address critical health challenges in the region. It is unlikely that the state or the private sector alone will be able to meet what are seen as the ten common and urgent health problems faced by health institutions in the Americas[41]:

- health and the environment (including water supply and sewage disposal)
- childhood and nutrition
- maternal and child health
- control and elimination of preventable diseases, paying particular attention to lifestyles and risk factors

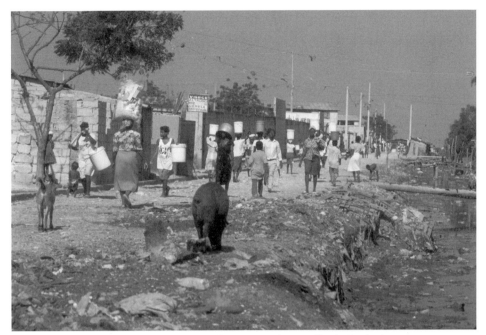

Contaminated water is a leading cause of disease and mortality in Latin America. *(Copyright Pan American Health Organization.)*

- workers' health
- substance abuse
- AIDS
- population control
- mental health
- violence

Partnerships among governments, multilateral lending agencies, and the non-governmental community represent the key to health sector reform. It is important to keep in mind that health care policies must be designed not only for nations but also for multiethnic communities within nations that may have differing health needs. Participation of communities with different traditional practices is critical in the design of health care policies.

Key Concepts

epidemiological backlog	epidemiological transition	HFA primary health care

Chapter Summary

Health Care

- Health is an essential component of human development. Health indicators from 1960 through 1990 suggest an improvement in health in Latin America. Despite improvements, however, each Latin American country still faces critical health matters.
- The World Health Organization has promoted the HFA2000—a comprehensive primary health care plan that includes participation, equity, and intersectoral cooperation. Budget constraints make enacting such a plan difficult.
- Inadequate health care institutions are major detriments to health performance in Latin America. Health care is most commonly delivered by a system made up of SSIs for formal sector employees, the private sector, and a Ministry of Health for the poor.
- Policies to improve health care in Latin America should include increasing the health care choices made available to households, raising public financing to reflect local demand for health care, and striking a balance between the public and private sectors' roles in health care.

Notes

M. Holly Peirce, Ph.D. (Colby College graduating class of 1990), collaborated in the conceptualization and writing of this chapter.

1. WHO, *Report on the Global HIV/AIDS Epidemic, June 1998* (Geneva: UNAIDS, 1998). Available at www.who.int/emc-hiv.

2. USAID Congressional Presentation Document (CPD), Brazil, US FY 1999. Available at www.info.usaid/pubs/cp99/br.htm. U.S. agencies must present past-program achievements and new fiscal year's objectives to Congress in the spring of each fiscal year to justify its annual budget. An agency's CPD is a good source of information on U.S. policy.

3. Seth Amgott, spokesman for Oxfam, quoted by Barbara Crossette, "US Drops Case Over AIDS Drugs in Brazil," *New York Times,* 26 June 2001, vol.150, issue 51796.

4. This section was authored by Margaret Knight, Colby College graduating class of 2002.

5. Gavin Yamey, *British Medical Journal,* "US trade action threatens Brazilian AIDS program," 17 February 2001.

6. "South Africa's Moral Victory," *The Lancet,* vol. 357, 28 April 2001.

7. PAHO, "Health Situation in the Americas," CD421.6, 18 August 2000.

8. PAHO, *Strategic and Programmatic Orientations, 1995–1998,* presented at the Inter-American Meeting, Washington, D.C., 25–27 April 1995. Available at www.paho.org.

9. Robert L. Ayres, *Crime and Violence as Development Issues in Latin America* (Washington, D.C.: World Bank, 1998).

10. World Bank, *World Development Indicators 2001.*

11. Juan Antonio Casas, J. Norberto, W. Dachs, and Alexandra Bambas, "Health Dispar-

ities in Latin America and the Caribbean," in *Equity and Health: Views from the Pan America Security Bureau, PAHO* (Washington D.C.: PAHO, 2001), 27.

12. William Savedoff, Antonio Giuffrida, and Roberto Iunes, "Economic and Health Effects of Occupational Hazards, IADB, Sustainable Development Department, June 2001, www.iadb.org.

13. Emerging diseases are new diseases such as Lyme's disease; chronic diseases develop slowly and persist over a period of time and are generally related to lifestyle; and degenerative diseases involve decay of the structure or function of tissue.

14. PAHO, *Strategic and Programmatic Orientations, 1995–1998.*

15. IADB, "Reproductive Rights," Technical Notes no. 8, 30.

16. Barbara Kwast, "Reeducation of Maternal and Peri-natal Mortality in Rural and Peri-urban Settings: What Works?" *European Journal of Obstetrics and Gynecology and Reproductive Biology* 609 (1996): 49.

17. *Women in Development,* Technical Note no. 9.

18. Sidney Choque Schuler and Ruth Choque Schuler, "Misinformation, Mistrust, and Mistreatment: Family Planning among Bolivian Market Women," *Studies in Family Planning* 25 (1994): 214.

19. Miriam Krawczyk, "Women in the Region: Major Changes," *CEPAL Review* 49 (April 1993).

20. Markjke Velzboer-Salcedo and Julie Novick, "Violence against Women in the Americas," *PAHO Perspectives in Health,* 5, no. 2 (2000), available at www.paho.org.

21. Casas, Dachs, and Bambas, "Health Disparities," 37.

22. PAHO, *PAHO Resolution V: Health of Indigenous Peoples,* Series HSS/SILOS, 34 (Washington, D.C.: PAHO, 1993). Available at www.paho.org.

23. Anonymous, "Health of Indigenous Peoples," *Pan American Journal of Public Health* 2, no. 25 (1997): 357–62.

24. Visit PAHO's website at www.paho.org to read more about PAHO's goals and strategic plans.

25. PAHO, *Implementation of the Global Strategy: Health for All by the Year 2000,* vol. 3 (Washington, D.C.: PAHO, 1993), 10.

26. Also referred to as multisectoral cooperation or collaboration and the health-development link.

27. "Cost Information and Management Decision in a Brazilian Hospital," *World Development Report* (1993): 60.

28. World Bank, *Poverty Reduction and the World Bank: Progress in Fiscal 1996 and 1997.* Available at www.worldbank.org.

29. WHO, *Integration of Health Care Delivery: Report of a WHO Study Group,* WHO Technical Report Series 861 (Geneva: WHO, 1996), table 5, "The Role of the Hospital in the District Health System."

30. It is important to remember that in most cases we are talking about more than one Social Security Institute. Often each public sector will have its own insurance fund and facilities, leading to unnecessary duplication within the sector, not to mention across sectors.

31. Center for International Health Information, *Country Health Profile/Bolivia* (Arlington, Va.: Center for International Health Information, December 1996). Available at www.cihi.com.

32. Catherine Overholt and Margaret Saunders, *Policy Choices and Practical Problems in Health Economics: Cases from Latin America and the Caribbean,* Economic Development Resources Series (Washington, D.C.: World Bank, 1996).

33. For an overview of the evolution of the Chilean health care system, see Jorge Jimenez de la Jara and Thomas J. Bossert, "Chile's Health Sector Reform: Lessons from Four

Reform Periods," in *Health Sector Reform in Developing Countries: Making Health Development Sustainable,* ed. Peter Berman (Cambridge: Harvard University Press, 1995), 199–214.

34. Harold Alderman and Victor Lavy, "Household Responses to Public Health Services: Cost and Quality Tradeoffs," *World Bank Research Observer* 11, no. 1 (February 1996): 3–22.

35. Ricardo Britan and Keith McInnes, *The Demand for Health Care in Latin America,* Economic Development Institute Seminar Paper no. 46 (Washington, D.C.: World Bank, 1993).

36. David Swafford, "A Healthy Trend: Health Care Reform in Latin America," *Latin Finance* 83 (December 1996).

37. William C. Hsiao, "Marketization—The Illusory Magic Pill," *Health Economics* 3 (1994): 351–57.

38. PAHO, "Mexico," in *Health in the Americas,* vol. 2 (Washington, D.C.: PAHO, 1998), 370.

39. WHO, *Integration of Health Care Delivery.*

40. WHO, *Integration of Health Care Delivery.*

41. Adapted from Yvette M. Delph, "Health Priorities in Developing Countries," *Journal of Law, Medicine, & Ethics* 21, no. 1 (1993): 18.

CHAPTER THIRTEEN

EDUCATION POLICY

The Source of Equitable, Sustainable Growth

Education of indigenous children presents special challenges of language and culture. *(Courtesy of the Inter-American Development Bank.)*

Education is seen as the key to promoting equitable, sustainable growth in Latin America. Education raises the level of human capital, enhancing a nation's productivity. Reducing poverty rests upon upgrading basic skills as well as increasing the number of technologically sophisticated workers in the economy. A more informed citizenry is better able to participate in democratic decision making, demanding that government be accountable to the people. A better-educated populace will make more informed decisions about health and family planning, and it can participate more fully in environmentally sustainable development practices.

Few dispute the promise of education in enhancing the quality of life in Latin America, yet the record is dismal by nearly any standard. Although there have been gains in universal access, quality suffers. Segments of the population are excluded from higher education by a primary and secondary school system that encourages repetition and dropping out rather than excellence. Public primary education has been emaciated as dollars are funneled into public university systems. Teachers are poorly trained and managed. Inadequate statistics provide little guidance or incentive for reform. Education is a catalyst for equitable development. Yet paradoxically, unequal access to education perpetuates exclusion and marginalization of the poor, rural citizens and the indigenous.

This chapter discusses the discouraging state of education in the region and assesses efforts and prospects for reform. Questions we will explore include the following:

- What is the current evidence on educational performance in Latin America?
- What are the causes of the **educational deficit** in the region?
- What is the role of the market in educational reform?
- What other structural reforms are necessary to improve educational performance in the region?

THE RECORD: EDUCATIONAL ACHIEVEMENTS AND DEFICITS

Education in Latin America has made great strides in recent decades, increasing access to segments of the population that previously had no formal schooling. As shown in table 13.1, literacy rose on average from 74 to 87 percent from 1970 through 1998, although the lows of about 67 percent in Guatemala and about 68 percent in Nicaragua are cause for great concern. Enrollment rates at the primary school level grew by nearly 50 percent, placing nearly 90 percent of age-eligible starters in the primary school classroom. Two-thirds of secondary-age children are now in the classroom, as opposed to just over one third in 1960. Opportunities for higher education have been extended to four times as many students in the 1990s as compared to the 1960s. Latin America appears on track to meet the global goal of the Jomtiem, Thailand, international conference of universal access to primary education.[1] The diversification of the postsecondary educational network has expanded to include polytechnic training institutes, traditional universities, and new universities (public and private). Through the explosion of the Internet as well as interna-

Table 13.1. Adult Literacy Rate

Country	Adult Literacy Rate (%)	
	1970	1998
Argentina	93	97
Bolivia	57	84
Brazil	66	85
Chile	89	95
Colombia	78	91
Costa Rica	88	95
Cuba	87	96
Ecuador	72	91
El Salvador	57	78
Guatemala	44	67
Honduras	53	73
Mexico	74	91
Nicaragua	n/a	68
Panama	81	91
Paraguay	80	93
Peru	71	89
Uruguay	93	98
Venezuela	75	92
Latin America average	74	87

Source: United Nations Development Program, *Human Development Report 2000* (New York: Oxford University Press, 2000), 157–59.

tional exchanges, universities have become linked to their international counterparts, spurring internal reorganization of faculties and upgrading of degrees and skill bases. Regionwide networks of private research centers such as FLACSO, or the Facultad Latinoamericana de Ciencias Sociales, entirely separate from the universities, have also flourished, producing an important body of scholarship on Latin America, in part through funding from international donor agencies such as the Ford Foundation.[2]

But these successes are not nearly enough in today's global economy. Education in Latin America is deficient. Compared to other regions of the world, the fewer than six years of schooling Latin American children receive is roughly half that of their counterparts in the United States, Japan, and Germany and two-thirds of those in the Asian newly industrialized countries, or NICs.[3] Early leavers reflect poor quality; for many the value added in education is not worth the wages lost in the market. Twenty percent of the population aged twenty-five to twenty-nine in urban areas has only completed between zero and five years of education; in the rural sector nearly 60 percent struggle by with fewer than five years of education.[4] In contrast, nearly all students in Egypt, China, and the Asian tiger nations reach grade five. In El Salvador and Colombia, a quarter or more of first graders don't even make it to second.[5] In Colombia, Guatemala, Nicaragua, and Bolivia (no data are reported for El Salvador) more than 20 percent of school-age children are out of school.[6]

Table 13.2. Average Years of Education for Twenty-Five-Year-Olds, by Income Decile

	Overall	1	2	3	4	5	6	7	8	9	10
Argentina	9.44	7.04	7.48	7.74	7.71	8.52	8.82	8.99	9.91	11.13	13.57
Bolivia	8.80	5.96	6.45	7.23	7.67	7.58	8.32	9.15	9.29	10.38	13.12
Chile	8.79	6.24	6.88	7.09	7.40	7.69	8.16	8.47	9.80	10.88	12.83
Panama	8.68	4.31	5.36	6.30	7.07	7.53	8.16	8.78	9.90	10.88	13.57
Uruguay	8.02	6.03	6.31	6.54	6.49	6.79	7.34	8.00	8.68	9.74	11.87
Peru	7.20	3.87	4.17	4.95	5.69	6.60	7.05	7.66	8.28	9.04	10.80
Venezuela	7.15	4.66	4.94	5.27	5.72	6.23	6.68	7.20	7.78	8.58	10.81
Ecuador	7.12	3.39	4.39	5.07	5.61	5.64	6.85	7.74	8.23	9.19	11.83
Costa Rica	6.94	4.08	4.88	5.39	5.54	5.91	6.31	6.75	4.65	8.62	11.53
Mexico	6.23	2.14	2.95	3.78	4.15	4.78	5.66	6.06	7.24	8.89	12.13
Paraguay	6.06	3.37	3.67	3.88	4.59	4.81	5.46	5.96	6.62	7.88	10.72
Brazil	5.22	1.98	2.49	2.97	3.41	3.66	4.40	4.99	5.98	7.43	10.53
El Salvador	4.88	1.63	2.14	2.40	2.75	3.27	3.99	4.73	5.90	7.11	10.27
Honduras	4.74	2.07	2.33	2.47	3.06	3.59	3.90	4.70	5.76	6.86	9.58
Nicaragua	4.74	2.17	2.05	2.65	3.33	4.11	4.55	4.94	5.46	6.46	8.49
Average	6.93	3.93	4.43	4.92	5.35	5.78	6.37	6.94	7.57	8.87	11.44

Source: Partnership for Educational Revitalization in the Americas, *Lagging Behind: A Report Card on Education in Latin America, 2001*, table A.12.
Note: Lowest income decile is 1 and highest is 10.

There is an even greater deficit in secondary education. More than 70 percent of the region's urban population between the ages of twenty and twenty-four has fewer than twelve years of schooling—the level considered necessary to lead to employment generating acceptable levels of well-being. Only four countries in the region have secondary enrollments above 50 percent, below the 75 percent target set at the 1998 Summit of the Americas. Rather than invest in secondary education, Latin American nations poured money into university systems. Asian countries targeted their educational dollar toward universalizing secondary education, while Latin America allowed its children to leave after primary school, choosing instead to expand university coverage for the few.[7] As shown in table 13.2, years of schooling vary greatly by income level. Twenty-five-year-olds in the bottom 10 percent of the population have 3.9 years of school; in the top 10 percent the average is 11.4.

Although classical illiteracy or the inability to write one's name as a sample message has fallen, many remain functionally illiterate, unable to read and respond to written instructions. Close to 80 percent of low-income students in Latin America cannot understand written messages after six years of schooling. Furthermore, the content delivered by educational systems is isolated from the investments in human capital demanded by global society.[8] Despite the fact that one out of ten persons in the continent is estimated to have some form of a disability, little attention is paid to the educational needs of the disabled. Rural migrant workers' children are rarely incorporated into educational systems. There is a radical separation between the region's educational systems and its growing development needs in competitive, open democracies.

Table 13.3. Educational Performance Index

Country	EPI Rank among LDCs	Per Capita Income Rank/LDCs	Difference
Cuba	5	50	45
Uruguay	10	20	10
Costa Rica	18	25	7
Mexico	21	18	–3
Chile	24	13	–11
Panama	31	24	–7
Venezuela	35	17	–18
Paraguay	37	46	9
Argentina	41	15	–26
Ecuador	46	34	–12
Brazil	48	32	–16
Peru	50	44	–6
Bolivia	54	56	2
Nicaragua	59	71	12
Honduras	62	63	1
Colombia	68	23	–45
El Salvador	69	58	–11
Guatemala	88	48	–40

Source: Oxfam, *The Oxfam Education Report, 2000,* available at www.oxfam.org.

Educational performance varies widely by country. Table 13.3 provides an educational regional scorecard. Cuba, Uruguay, Guyana, and Costa Rica rank in the top 20 of global developing country performers as measured by the **educational performance index** (EPI) of Oxfam, an international nongovernmental organization (NGO). This index captures the extent of educational deprivation by incorporating measures of enrollment, gender equity, and completion rates. Bolivia, Nicaragua, Honduras, Colombia, El Salvador, and Guatemala don't even make it into the group of the global top 50, finding themselves in the company of countries such as Vietnam, Nigeria, and India. What is perhaps most intriguing about this index is the lack of correlation between per capita income ranks and the EPI index. Colombia, for example, has an EPI rank of 68, but its per capita income rank is 23. This 45-point negative difference indicates that despite having a relatively high level of wealth for a developing country, it has fallen behind in educational performance. This might be contrasted to Nicaragua—also a poor performer by the educational index, but doing relatively better than its per capita income level would indicate, with a positive difference of 12. This divergence between income levels and educational performance suggests that educational outcomes are driven by more than simply money. How educational systems are organized, the quality of inputs, and the political will behind reform efforts influence how many students stay in school and for how long.

The weak relationship between income and educational outcomes indicates that *how* money is spent is as important as *how much* is spent. On average Latin American nations spend 4.52 percent of gross national product (GNP) on education, but spending is disproportionately concentrated at the university level. As shown in table 13.4 there is a wide divergence in spending. In contrast to the Asian NICs, which allocate 1.5 percent of GNP for primary education, Latin American nations spend 1.1 percent of GNP on primary schooling. If a goal is global competitiveness, Latin America must devise a way for educational outcomes to exceed expenditures. As a percentage of gross domestic product (GDP), Costa Rica—one of the best performers in the region—spends approximately as much as the United States, 5.6 percent. However, a smaller absolute GDP and a larger cohort of children combine to reflect lower spending per student. The United States on average spends more than $6,000 dollars per pupil on primary and secondary education; Costa Rica only edges over $1,000. This data is already adjusted for the fact that a dollar may go farther in Costa Rica. The dismal fact is that at the bottom of the rung, Guatemala, Peru, and El Salvador spend less than $250 per pupil.

Public spending on education fell during the lost decade of the 1980s in twelve of the eighteen countries in the region.[9] The structural adjustment policies of the period forced ministries to cut back on spending—including investments in education. Nicaragua spends five times as much paying debts as it does teaching its children. Despite the goal of improving competitiveness, structural adjustment has also had negative effects on teacher salaries and class size in some countries. Mexico's teachers in 1993 made 40 percent of their 1981 salaries; those in El Salvador fell to 32 percent of the 1980 level by 1992. Chile, Colombia, and Uruguay run counter to this trend, increasing teacher salaries to attract competent professionals.[10] Short-term budget balancing measures of the 1980s will have long-term consequences in

Table 13.4.   Student–Teacher Ratios and Public Expenditure on Education

Country	Year	Pupil–Teacher Ratio Pre-primary	Pupil–Teacher Ratio Primary	Pupil–Teacher Ratio Secondary	Public Expenditure on Education as Percentage of GNI
Argentina	1998–1999	21	21	14	4.14
Argentina	1999–2000	24	22	11	4.65
Bolivia	1998–1999				5.67
Bolivia	1999–2000	42	25	21	5.79
Brazil	1998–1999	20			
Brazil	1999–2000	19	27	23	5.15
Chile	1998–1999		27	23	3.84
Chile	1999–2000		33	29	4.26
Colombia	1998–1999	17	23		
Colombia	1999–2000	18	24	18	
Costa Rica	1998–1999				
Costa Rica	1999–2000	19	27	18	5.53
Cuba	1998–1999	34	14	11	6.81
Cuba	1999–2000	34	11	12	7.67
Ecuador	1998–1999	18	27	17	3.32
Ecuador	1999–2000	15	23	12	2.46
El Salvador	1998–1999				2.35
El Salvador	1999–2000				2.40
Guatemala	1998–1999				
Guatemala	1999–2000	26	38	13	1.60
Honduras	1998–1999				4.19
Honduras	1999–2000				
Mexico	1998–1999	22	27	21	4.35
Mexico	1999–2000	22	25	20	4.55
Nicaragua	1998–1999				4.76
Nicaragua	1999–2000	26	34	25	3.95
Panama	1998–1999				
Panama	1999–2000			16	6.28
Paraguay	1998–1999	25	20	10	4.52
Paraguay	1999–2000				4.81
Peru	1998–1999	29	25	17	3.29
Peru	1999–2000				3.45
Uruguay	1998–1999	31	21	17	2.58
Uruguay	1999–2000	31	20	15	2.82
Venezuela	1998–1999				
Venezuela	1999–2000				
United States	1998–1999	22	15	15	5.00
United States	1999–2000	21	15	15	5.04
Average		24.68	24.50	17.25	4.27

Source: Unesco Institute for Statistics.

terms of the future productivity in the region. Redressing the educational deficit is critical to new political and economic opportunities. As shown in table 13.4, public spending on education as a percentage of total government expenditures in the region recovered somewhat in the late 1990s, although countries suffering from economic instability, such as Ecuador, were forced to cut back on expenditures.

Class size, particularly at the primary level, is large in all countries with the exception of Cuba.

UNEQUAL EDUCATION

Rather than promoting opportunity and class mobility, education has perpetuated inequality in Latin America. The paradox of education in Latin America is that the principle of opportunity in public schooling has resulted in unequal outcomes. Primary and secondary schooling continue to be segregated by class. The poorest 20 percent of the population are allocated 16 percent of total public spending on education while the richest 20 percent receive a share of 24 percent.[11] At the Santiago Summit of the Americas, in 1998, the region's leaders characterized education's split personality, noting that "students from the region's top private schools perform at levels comparable to schools in industrialized countries. Public school students, in contrast, perform dismally by any standard. Latin America's future will be bleak until all its children are provided real opportunities for decent education."[12] Public funds have flowed disproportionately to the upper class, reflecting elite political power. Wealthy Latin Americans wanted world-class universities. Private producers could not meet this need, because university systems require costly investments in faculties, libraries, and laboratories. In response to powerful constituents' demands, governments chose to expand secondary and higher education, leaving little left over for the primary level. The best universities in the region are public (and often free)—but it takes a high-priced private education to pass the matriculation tests for admission. The 2000 World Conference on Education in Dakar, Senegal, called on governments to identify strategies for reducing inequalities in education.[13]

> ### QUESTION FOR THOUGHT
>
> Links for educational resources for the Americas can be found at the IADB's www.iadb.org/exr/topics/education.htm. Scroll down to Approved Project Documents—Education at www.iadb.org/exr/doc98/apr/apeduc.htm. Identify two educational initiatives addressed at the primary school level. How do these programs contribute to reducing the country's educational deficit? What problems or limitations can you observe in the program?

Neglected, primary education in Latin America is plagued by a high rate of **grade repetition.** Of the nine million six- or seven-year-olds entering first grade in the region, approximately four million fail the first time around. In total, 29 percent of all primary students repeat their grade annually. As shown in table 13.5, a startlingly low 1 percent of Brazilians reach the sixth grade without repeating. Latin America spends U.S.$2.5 billion—or nearly one-third of total public expenditure on primary education in the region—teaching repeaters. High repetition, especially in the lowest grades, is mainly an indicator of inadequate learning, prompted in large part by the low quality of inputs into the system.[14] Students cannot reach grade level norms without sufficient books, pencils, and trained teachers. Rural students often find themselves unable to complete a school year due to harvest seasons and

Table 13.5.   Repeaters

Country	Percent of First Grade Repeaters, 1990	Percent Graduating from Sixth Grade without Repeating, 1989
Argentina	29.8	17
Brazil	55.7	1
Chile	19.6	41
Colombia	33.9	26
Costa Rica	23.4	31
Guatemala	35.9	9
Mexico	29.3	23
Nicaragua	54.8	NA
Peru	30.0	21
Venezuela	19.7	14

Source: Jeffrey M. Puryear, "Education in Latin America: Problems and Challenges," *PREAL*, 7 May 1997. Available at www.preal.cl.

must repeat the same grade in the fall. Reducing repetition rates would release resources for new educational opportunities.

With primary school enrollments exploding from 50 percent of age-eligible children to nearly 90 percent from 1960 to 1990, facilities were overrun with students.[15] Latin America has the highest proportion of workers in developing economies with some primary education but is second to sub-Saharan Africa with the lowest number of workers with some secondary education.[16] Nearly all children in South America start school, but by the fifth year 40 percent of the poor have dropped out while 93 percent of the rich remain in school. The figures for Central America are more dismal, with nearly two-thirds of students leaving by fifth grade.[17] In many cases schools are operating two or three shifts daily, leaving fewer than three and a half hours per day in the classroom.

Students in Latin America score poorly on internationally standardized tests. Academic performance is below that of industrial and East Asian countries. Only those students who have benefited from elite private schools are on par with international levels.[18] Chile alone agreed to participation in the 1999 Third International Mathematics and Science Study, placing 35 out of 38, well below Asian competitors—and Chile is one of the best performers on education in the region.[19] Teaching materials are poor (when they even exist), and some teachers haven't even graduated from high school themselves. Rural students are most deprived, with unprepared teachers, scarce resources, and limitations on the number of grades offered.[20] Teachers are woefully underpaid, resulting in frequent strikes as well as low morale.[21] Low salaries make it more difficult to recruit young talent into education, depressing future educational opportunity.

Malnutrition, poor health, and easily remedied problems such as a need for eyeglasses limit poor children's educational success. The poor attend inadequate public schools at the primary and secondary levels while the wealthy place their children in better-equipped private schools.[22] Many of the poor can't afford school at all, because even public schools have associated private costs. With the direct cost of education for books and transportation amounting to 4 percent of a family's income per child, as well as the accompanying opportunity costs of lost income from the child, many poor children become poor adults without the means to invest in their own human capital. Expanding educational access at the primary level is a concrete achievement in the region over the past thirty years; inequality remains entrenched, however, in the way students advance throughout the system.

The highly stratified educational system impedes social mobility. The effects of educational inequality are compounded by the time the students get into the workforce; better-educated (and wealthier) workers make ten times the amount of their poorer counterparts. The high degree of income inequality we studied in chapter 11 is perpetuated by unequal educational opportunities. Because the wealthy benefit from access to a strong public university and the poor generally lack the sophistication, information, and power necessary to influence policy, the social demand for education reform is weak.[23]

The good news is that with respect to gender equity, Latin America scores fairly well. With the exception of indigenous communities, there is little difference between boys and girls in their likelihood to attend or complete schooling. Investments in girls' education is critical due to connections between low levels of female education and overall health levels. An increase of between one and three years of a mother's schooling can reduce infant mortality by 15 percent; the comparable rate for men is 6 percent. In Peru, it was shown that an addition of six years of schooling cut infant mortality by a dramatic 75 percent. In addition to having better income-earning capabilities, women with education make greater use of prenatal health services and are generally healthier themselves.[24] Evidence suggests that for countries of similar labor force and capital stock, if the ratio of female to male at given levels of education falls below 0.75, GDP growth is likely to be 25 percent lower. Investment in girls' education clearly has public returns. Nonetheless, in terms of income forgone and relatively low levels of economic opportunity, the private costs of education are high. Girls are needed in the home and on the farm to help in chores and supervise younger siblings. Many families simply cannot afford the indirect costs of schooling.[25]

THE INDIGENOUS AND EDUCATION

The gravity of the educational deficit is greater for the indigenous in Latin America. The direct and indirect costs of education to the poor—the clothes, shoes, books, transportation, or perhaps room and board in the nearest large village for middle or high school as well as the forgone earnings of the child—are compounded by a frequent inability to speak Spanish. Ten percent of Mexicans do not speak Spanish. In Guatemala, 60 percent of the indigenous people have no education.[26] On average, the number of years of schooling for indigenous Guatemalan males is 1.8 years and for females 0.9 year as opposed to their non-indigenous counterparts with 4.5 and 4 years each. The scant evidence available indicates that working-age adults with indigenous or African backgrounds in Peru,

Guatemala, Brazil, and Bolivia have three fewer years of education compared to their white counterparts.

Particularly for those in the agricultural sector, the opportunity costs of children's labor is high. In Bolivia, the incidence of no schooling for monolingual indigenous is 77.9 percent, bilingual indigenous 11 percent, and nonindigenous 2.8 percent, indicating that basic education is not equitably distributed over different ethnic groups.[27] In Peru the difference between indigenous and nonindigenous education levels is narrowing to approximately 20 percent. Nevertheless, when analyzed by gender, indigenous females continue to receive less than half the education of their nonindigenous counterparts, perhaps reflecting the difficult investment decisions families face with respect to education. Given scarce resources, the indigenous poor may choose to invest in their male children who have a greater probability of remaining in the labor market than in their sisters for whom the cultural perception is that they will return to the home.[28]

More education, however, is not the simple answer. Education in the indigenous communities may also have unintended cultural effects. Educational programs may work to obliterate the distinctive languages and customs of the indigenous. Participation of indigenous leaders is critical to ensure the transfer of traditional customs and practices as part of the child's educational experience. Bilingual education can facilitate this process of preserving cultural practices. Change should be respectful of local cultures but open up opportunities for the indigenous poor. Educational policy must be informed by the needs of the target group.

> **QUESTION FOR THOUGHT**
>
> Recall the discussion in chapter 11 on the indigenous and poverty. Can you think of ways to promote education among the indigenous populations? Are there other complementary programs in addition to education to improve the welfare of indigenous communities in Latin America?

WHAT ARE THE CAUSES OF THE EDUCATIONAL DEFICIT IN LATIN AMERICA?

The educational deficit in Latin America is the result of ineffective demand by poor families and deficient quantity and quality of the supply offered by school systems. With clear positive returns to education, why don't families elect to invest in more years of schooling? In addition to the direct costs of clothing, books, and other supplies, unfortunately, for many families, the opportunity costs of education are high. In many parts of the region, children's income is an important contribution to the family's survival. School calendars often do not accommodate children's work schedules, particularly around harvest times in the agricultural sector. In the urban sector, one estimate places children's participation in the informal sector between 20 and 30 percent of family income.[29] Families found it even harder to give up earnings from children—often amounting to a third of household income—during the periods of macroeconomic instability, causing a slowdown in education accumulation since the 1980s.[30] When survival is at stake, education appears to be a luxury. The demand for education must be seen in the context of the price of day-to-day living.

The supply of a quality education has also deteriorated. The lost decade of the 1980s took its toll on education in Latin America. The goals of eliminating illiteracy, extending basic education from eight to ten years, and improving the quality of basic education in the "Mexico Declaration" signed by the region's education ministers were stalled by the lack of available resources. Although per capita expenditures on education increased from 1975 to 1980 by 4.29 percent, they decreased by 6.14 percent between 1980 and 1985.[31] The rate of growth of students receiving preschool education fell from 10.6 percent for the 1970–1980 period to 4.7 percent for 1985–1988. Likewise, the rate of growth of primary education was more than halved from 4 percent prior to the crisis to 1.5 percent in the late 1980s.[32] The economic slowdown stalled progress on education.

In addition to constrained choices families make about the economic opportunity costs of education and falling expenditures, the management of educational systems in Latin America has led to inferior outcomes. Education has traditionally been managed by central governments insulated from local demands. Teachers have normally been employed by state governments rather than municipalities or individual schools. In Venezuela, for example, the Ministry of Education is the country's largest employer. Bureaucratic educational machines become overly involved in their own interests to the detriment of the student. Often geographically distant and powerless, families have little effective involvement in educational policy at the ministerial or school level.[33]

With policy efforts focused on expanding access to schools, quality suffered enormously. This was acutely felt in the qualifications and training of teachers in the region. National systems of pay, put in place by powerful teachers' unions, leave principals little recourse in local-level administration. Political and administrative obstacles impede much-needed reform. Teachers' unions have resisted **decentralization** and enhanced parental choice. Salaries absorb more than 90 percent of the total educational budget in fifteen of twenty-one countries for which data was available.[34] Politicians fear the loss of control over patronage jobs they can offer, and university students and their families have been able to defend their subsidies for higher education. Politicians would rather channel funds to a new building than contend with reforms in teacher training and performance. As a leading analyst of education in Latin America noted, "You don't see primary-school students protesting in the streets, like university students do."[35] Teachers and elites present a formidable coalition of interests for a poor community to come up against. This intersection of weak demand and inferior supply comes at a high cost to the development of human capital in the region.

BENEFITS OF EDUCATIONAL REFORM

The political roadblocks explain poor outcomes and sluggish reform in education in Latin America. Globalization may, however, be creating a new set of conditions. International competitiveness demands a highly skilled, educated workforce. The educational deficit in Latin America has a high social cost. As noted in an Inter-American Development Bank (IADB) report, education is by far the main factor in determining whether a working individual is poor.[36] There is a strong correlation between national investment in education and economic growth. A better-educated work force will be more productive and competitive in the global economy. As noted by Alejandro Foxley, former Chilean minister of the economy and Organization of American States (OAS) coordinator on education issues for the OAS, "The issue of a well trained labor force is critical to maintaining a path of economic development that is sustainable."[37] Education strongly influences farmer productivity, encourages a reduction in fertility, and results in improved health and nutrition.

No country has made significant economic progress without a strong educational infrastructure. A recent study of economic returns by education level in fourteen Latin American and Caribbean countries showed that the social rate of return of primary education averaged over 17 percent—a high rate of return for any social investment.[38] It has been estimated that an increase of one year in Latin America's average educational level of the workforce over current trends would increase long-term economic growth by 1 percent on average in the next decade. An additional year increases productivity by 0.8 percent annually. Evidence from Honduras, Guatemala, and El Salvador shows that an additional year of education translates into a 5 to 10 percent increase in informal-sector earnings. Another study in the case of Brazil dramatically shows an additional year of education adding between 5 and 20 percent to real output.[39] In a world in which competitiveness is increasingly defined by technology, well-skilled workforces are critical to managing growth. Increasing the educational attainment in the region, with its associated gains in productivity, would bring the region in line with East Asian levels.[40] Education is estimated to account for 40 percent of the divergence in growth rates between Latin America and East Asia.[41] Women with a secondary education are three times as likely to attend political meetings. Global interests have created new incentives for elites to demand better public education systems. The new coalition of interests driven by global competition may have broken the logjam on educational policy change. The million dollar question is how should this be done?

STATE AND MARKET IN THE REFORM EFFORT

Educational policy reform, like other areas of social investment, must address the question of the role of the state versus the role of the market. Given scarce resources, what should be the level of state spending for education? Is there a complementary role for the private sector? What direction should investments in education take?

Does education fit the neoliberal prescription for market-based policies? The case against the reliance on the market and for the public provision of education rests on several arguments: education creates **externalities,** is considered a **merit good,** has long lead and lag times, has equity implications, may suffer from principal/agent problems, and exhibits scale economies that allow for decreasing costs.[42] Let's consider this list in turn. Improving literacy creates externalities in lowering the transaction costs between individuals in society. Instructions at work can be written, not only spoken; social and environmental campaigns can take place in the print media. Literacy may contribute to improving the health profile and fertility control because health education is often disseminated in print. With positive externalities, one person's welfare is enhanced by increasing the educational status of another. Essentially, this position argues that the social rate of return to education, particularly at the primary level, exceeds the individual's investment.

Education is also considered a merit good. The direct benefits of education may be worth more to individuals than they themselves are aware. Purchasers of education may estimate the benefits in terms of a better job, for example, but may not be able to anticipate the effects on family health and nutrition. As a result, they might demand less education than the whole family's return on the investment would indicate. Given long gestation times, the signals for increasing educational investments may be slow to reach the buyers.

Equity concerns inform the educational investment debate. The poor are unable to invest in education, particularly if credit markets do not reach down the economic ladder for student loans. Finally, a principal/agent problem plagues decisions about individual investments in education. The parents act as the agent of the child. The returns to education are primarily in the child's future; the cost comes to the parents today. Underinvestment in education may therefore be a rational response to immediate family needs as weighed against uncertain future returns. Principal/agent problems may be magnified in the case of girls' education or the enrollment of indigenous children. Given traditional norms, parents may choose to underinvest on behalf of their children. On the supply side of the equation, with economies of scale in higher education—the libraries, scientific equipment, and computer facilities necessary—the provision of higher education may be economically feasible only through the visible hand of the state.

> **QUESTION FOR THOUGHT**
>
> Should educational reform in Latin America be market driven?

In counterpoint to these arguments for the public provision of education, neoliberals point to the need for private-sector participation. Advocating a much reduced role for the state, they point to the benefits of market allocation of education. Governments, they contend, have failed to provide quality public education. Resource constraints, coupled with systematic misallocation of funds, point toward the market solution. Policy prescriptions offered by neoclassical economists include the adoption of user fees, student loans, and the encouragement of private schooling. Particularly at the higher levels of education, parents should become responsible for educational expenses, with scholarships offered to students without the means to pay. Student loans, as opposed to outright subsidies, could facilitate educational opportunity. Private education is seen as more cost-effective and quality conscious, with the saving generated redirected toward deficient primary school education.

STAGE ONE OF EDUCATIONAL REFORM IN LATIN AMERICA

Educational reform has been motivated by three factors: competitiveness, finance, and equity.[43] Changing demand for labor driven by globalization has created an impetus for better training to compete in world markets. Given the constraints of less government spending, education spending in Latin America has been redirected from the university and secondary levels to focus on primary education. Secondary and higher education have increasingly become privatized or financed through user fees. With equity as a goal, education is seen as an instrument to improve social mobility. Equity-driven reforms tend to focus on acquiring basic literacy skills, increasing school supplies in the poorest areas, and reaching groups such as women and the indigenous populations that have lagged behind in educational performance. To improve equity considerations, the state must assume a central role. Given the complementary goal of increasing competitiveness under fiscal constraints, the private sector has been increasingly involved. Competitiveness-driven reform can be facilitated by market-based mechanisms.

To improve equity, educational reform must attend to the constraints on the most disadvantaged. In particular, the high opportunity costs of sending children to school must be addressed. The Colombian Escuela Nueva program offers an innovative approach to formal education. Working from the assumption that children in rural areas need flexible schedules to accommodate agricultural work, it operates under a multigrade, independently paced framework. Using problem solving rather than rote learning, semiprogrammed modules allow students to work alone when necessary to catch up with the class. Because the modules are relevant to the problems students are facing at home, academic learning is reinforced by practical application.[44] Pilot studies indicate that Escuela Nueva students have performed better and stayed in school longer than students attending traditional institutions.[45]

As an example of how the private sector might assist, financed by a small private international organization, Mayan girls in Guatemala are offered a small scholarship—$6 per month—to provide pencils, notebooks, and shoes as well as cover some of the money the girls may have provided to the family. A small but inspiring result of this program was the achievement of two girls in a small mountain village entering the fifth grade: the first ever in the community to do so.[46] A discussion of educational efforts in Guatemala is presented in box 13.1. In Mexico, two million very poor families in Chiapas and other rural areas receive $25 monthly from the government if children attend classes, are promoted, and get regular medical checkups.[47]

Community involvement in educational reform is critical. One of the trends in educational reform in the region has been decentralization of educational policy to the local level. This doesn't necessarily mean less government but rather a different combination of levels of government. Local input and control can reduce educational inefficiency. If decisions are made at the local level, greater responsiveness to local needs should result. In Chile under the Pinochet military government, educational reform moved decision making from a central bureaucracy to the municipalities. The central government continued to finance education and provide technical support, but there was greater autonomy at the local level in how to spend the money.

BOX 13.1.   WILL SHE MAKE IT? GUATEMALA FINDS NEW WAYS TO KEEP GIRLS IN SCHOOL

BY CHRISTINA MACCULLOCH

In a cramped two-room house in Villa Nueva, a working-class district south of Guatemala City, seven-year-old Gabriela González Hernández is getting ready for her first day of school. Although she probably does not consider herself a child of privilege, Gabriela is already part of an elite, because slightly less than half of all Guatemalan girls do not enroll in elementary school at all. If she perseveres in her studies, Gabriela could join an even more select group: the one out of eight Guatemalan girls who complete sixth grade.

Gabriela's chances are relatively good. Her mother is herself an elementary school graduate, and her father completed high school. Though their home has but a zinc roof, bare cement floors and no running water, Gabriela's parents are determined to keep her in school because they are convinced that education represents her best chance to escape poverty. Gabriela is also lucky because she lives near a city that offers relatively good access to roads, schools and income-generating work for her parents.

But for girls in Guatemala's rural areas, the outlook is much bleaker. Simply walking to and from a distant school each day can challenge a young girl's endurance and threaten her safety. In households where both parents must do full-time agricultural work, school can seem like a questionable luxury. Most girls end up staying home to care for younger siblings, cook and help wherever else they are needed. The pressures are such that even among girls in rural Guatemala who do enroll in first grade, 66 percent drop out before reaching third grade. And when families feel they can afford to send a child to school, they generally send a boy. In 1991, some 500,000 girls between 7 and 15 were estimated to be missing school in Guatemala, compared to only 300,000 boys. Overall, 60 percent of Guatemalan women are illiterate, and 80 percent of these are from the country's rural indigenous regions, according to official figures compiled early this decade.

Guatemala is hardly alone in this respect. Mayra Buvinic, chief of the IDB's Social Development Division, cites global literacy statistics showing that in 1990, there were only 74 literate women for every 100 literate men worldwide. "The same studies estimated that globally there were 77 million girls between the ages of 6 and 11 who were not attending school, compared to 52 million boys, and that does not take into account repetition, absenteeism and dropout rates that make the gap even wider," says Buvinic.

Although the bias against educating girls has complex social and cultural roots, it is almost universally exacerbated by poverty. The nations of Latin America and the Caribbean are a case in point. In the region's most developed countries and in its largest cities, the education gender gap is either small or nonexistent. But among the tens of millions of Latin Americans who live in acute poverty, even in the richest countries, the problem is pronounced.

HIDDEN COSTS

Societies pay a high price for the failure to educate girls. While investing in boys' education is obviously beneficial, there is evidence that the same investment in female education yields higher returns for society as a whole. Why? Because although both men and women who went to school are more likely to earn better wages and improve a country's productivity, education tends to affect aspects of women's lives that don't apply to men.

Educated women are more likely to obtain prenatal, delivery and postnatal care, which leads to lower rates of infant and maternal mortality. Indeed, a World Bank study of twenty-five countries found that an increase of one to three years in a mother's schooling reduced infant mortality in the first year of life by 15 percent. Among fathers, the same increase in schooling resulted in only a 6 percent reduction in infant mortality rates. Likewise, better-educated women in almost all societies wait longer before they get married and tend to have fewer children—two factors that lower the risk of birth-related health problems for both infants and mothers.

The children of women with as little as three to six years of formal education tend to be better nourished, and they are more likely to enroll and stay in school than the children of uneducated mothers. Educated women also tend to be more active and effective participants in local government, particularly in issues involving social services. In short, because of their multiple roles in the marketplace, the community, and the home, educated women can have a higher impact than educated men on the development and well-being of their societies.

NATIONAL CONCERN, LOCAL APPROACHES

In Guatemala, concern about girls' limited access to education has led to a unique effort to confront the problem head-on. Starting in 1991, a diverse group of educators, researchers, business leaders, civic groups, and donor organizations formed what would later become the National Association for Girls' Education. The association immediately began working with the Ministry of Education to develop a girls' education strategy within the ministry's broader program to strengthen elementary education.

In 1992, with support from the United States Agency for International Development and local foundations, the association commissioned a detailed diagnostic study that for the first time showed the extent of the shortfall in girls' education in Guatemala. The study identified the regions and municipalities where the problem was most severe and proposed a plan of action that included outlines of thirty-seven potential projects.

Soon thereafter, the Ministry of Education launched the Girls' Education Program, a multifaceted effort to develop and test practical ways of increasing enrollment and retention of girls through the sixth grade. The program included projects in four broad areas: technical assistance for the Ministry of Education, the National Association for Girls' Education and individual schools working to implement girls' education programs; training for government officials, teachers and parents; conducting original research on the problem of girls' education; and developing motivational books and other didactic materials in Mayan languages for use by rural schoolgirls.

From the outset, the program's organizers realized that a successful intervention would require coordinating the activities of students, parents, teachers, community leaders and high-level government officials who supported the effort. To find effective approaches, the program launched a pilot "Educate Girls Project," that tested different combinations of initiatives such as training teachers, offering scholarships to individual students, forming parents committees and providing supplementary curricula to schools. The project also hired indigenous women to work as education aides to provide special support to schoolgirls and their families.

The pilot project yielded a number of lessons. For example, project leaders discovered that although teachers were generally receptive to new ideas, they needed training on the theory and practice of reaching girls in the classroom, as well as appropriate teaching aids and materials.

Gabriela Núñez, a sociologist who coordinated the pilot project, believes the training sessions were important because they boosted teachers' sense of their importance in the process. "We found it was crucial to reinforce teachers' assessments of their own value as people, because only with a positive self-image can they transmit a sense of self-worth and recognition to their girl students," she says.

(continued)

(continued)

The pilot project also found that even modest scholarship grants, amounting to the equivalent of around five U.S. dollars per month, were a very cost-effective way of encouraging attendance because they helped compensate for the loss of a girl's labor around the house. Although scholarships were also found to improve long-term retention, project officials concluded that financial support would have to be complemented by a variety of other strategies to encourage girls to return to school year after year.

Núñez argues that efforts to improve educational opportunities for girls invariably benefit boys as well. "When boys see girls becoming more active in class and in school organizations, they get more involved themselves, because they don't want to be left out." Likewise, parent committees formed as part of the pilot project increased the parents' engagement in the education of all their children, regardless of gender.

Although it is hard to quantify the success of Guatemala's girls' education efforts to date, one fundamental accomplishment is clear. "The need to improve girls' access to education is now understood and considered a priority among policymakers at the national level," says Isabel Nieves, lead author of the Guatemalan diagnostic study and now a social development specialist at the IDB.

This new awareness became evident during the drafting of the 1996 Peace Accords that brought an end to Guatemala's civil war. The accords included specific mandates to end gender inequalities in education, a goal that was also specifically addressed in the Guatemalan government's 2000 action plan. Indeed, that plan set an ambitious target of 80 percent primary school enrollment for girls by the year 2000 as part of educational reform programs.

Now, the IDB is supporting that program through a $15 million loan approved last year for Guatemala's Ministry of Education. The funds will be used to pay for training teachers and supplying schools with bilingual and Spanish-language materials, implementing programs to reduce first grade repetition, consolidating community participation and replicating successful innovations from the Girls' Education Program.

"The IDB support is arriving at a crucial time," says Nieves. "These funds are allowing the Guatemalan government to mainstream many of the lessons learned during the girls' education pilot project into its overall educational reform program."

The IDB is supporting innovative girls' education efforts in other countries as well. In Bolivia, where illiteracy among women averages 67 percent and girls spend only 60 percent as much time in school as boys, a recent educational reform program partly financed by the Bank set out specifically to reduce dropout rates among girls. The program included a variety of incentives, including scholarships and day care centers where girls could drop off younger siblings in order to attend classes.

In Mexico, an IDB-funded program to assist up to three million children in extreme poverty is testing a different approach to easing the child-care duties of school-age children: letting them bring their younger siblings into the classroom. Though it is too early to judge the effectiveness of this concept, the aim is both to keep girls in school and to offer a more stimulating environment to preschool children.

The ultimate success of these kinds of programs depends, of course, on the perseverance of girls like Gabriela González Hernández and the commitment of parents, teachers and community leaders. But as the progress achieved in Guatemala illustrates, governments can help to create an environment where perseverance and commitment can bear fruit in the lives of individual girls.

Source: Reproduced from *IDB América*, April 1998, pp. 4–7.

Municipalities had the power to hire and fire teachers. Schools were encouraged to compete for funds, and allocations were based on student attendance under a school choice program.[48] Pegging grant payments to pupil days in school improved attendance records, and competition to attract students improved the quality of teaching.

Nonetheless, the market-driven spirit of the reforms was biased against poor communities with fewer resources and institutional capacities. After democratization, spending on education was increased to 3.2 percent of GDP, a 54-percent increase over the previous government. The P900 emergency program introduced in 1990 targeted teacher training and resources in Chile's 900 lowest-achieving schools. The MECE program, funded in part by the Chilean government ($73 million) and in part by the World Bank ($170 million), is designed to improve the physical and educational conditions of primary schools. Through a competitive application process, schools were awarded project funds from the central government to enhance computer learning. Teachers were empowered to make changes in their own classrooms. The program has been successful in enhancing the textbooks and teaching materials available to schools and encouraging innovative teaching methods and community involvement—the critical goals of the program.[49]

Chile has also experimented with the use of vouchers in the school systems. People can spend educational vouchers in public municipal or private subsidized schools. The demand registered by users is supposed to create a quasi-market in which the buyers of the good, education, can direct educational outcomes. School districts can also ask parents for contributions to costs. The results, however, have been problematic in light of the goal of greater equity. Markets for education devel-

---

Box 13.2.   Bolivia: Getting Kids Back in School

Samuel Ardaya Rivera, 13, knows firsthand how hard it is to attend school when you're dirt poor. The little he makes washing auto windshields on the streets of Santa Cruz, Bolivia, goes to help with home expenses and pay for school supplies, according to the newspaper *El Mundo*. Life is a struggle, and for many children like Rivera, school is an unaffordable luxury. Helping to get working children off the streets and into the classroom, and at the same time strengthen parental involvement in their children's education, is the aim of a new project being carried out by nongovernmental groups in Santa Cruz as well as the cities of La Paz, El Alto and Cochabamba. Financed with the help of a $2.65 million IDB grant, the program is benefiting 1,900 children from extremely poor families—21 percent of the total number of working children in those cities—with after-school tutoring, school supplies, clothing, snacks and meals. In Santa Cruz, each of the three institutions carrying out the program has contracted eight tutors. Their main job is to help the children keep on top of their school work as well as engage them in recreational, artistic, cultural and science activities. The program has resulted in a significant decline in school dropout and repetition rates. In fact, a year into the program, 90 percent of the 1,900 participating children completed the school year. An important side effect of the tutoring is strengthening the children's self-esteem, which in many cases has been damaged by their work experience and family situation.

Source: Reproduced from *IDB América*, November 1997, p. 14. Available online at www.iadb.org/English/projects/projects.html.

oped only in large towns and in less poor neighborhoods in which private subsidized schools were able to turn a profit. Municipal schools in less advantaged areas found it difficult to raise funds, contributing to budget pressures.[50] Poorly educated parents appeared more concerned with things like school appearance, whereas wealthier families demanded qualitative changes in curriculum. Many low-income families were not able to take advantage of access to schools in more affluent areas; the costs of transportation, uniforms, and the commuting time away from home or market work precluded participation.[51] The market may be a useful tool under certain socioeconomic circumstances, but it may have a high price in terms of equity under unequal conditions.

Brazil provides an example of what can be accomplished with strong political will that engages educational stakeholders and draws upon the interests of the public sector to improve a highly unequal and ineffective educational system. Since 1934 universal primary education has been the law for children ages seven to fourteen, yet Brazil has one of the highest illiteracy rates in the region. National adult literacy stood at 20 percent in the 1990s, with levels twice as bad in the poor Northeast. During the 1970s, the government invested lavishly in education, expanding on educational infrastructure. Schools popped up everywhere, but without funding for books, supplies, and teacher training, educational outcomes were dismal. Except in the richest of systems not every pupil has a book; in most schools books are kept in the school office. Most of the spending went to universities.

Brazil was a striking outlier in terms of the weakness of its primary school system. The educational attainment of upper-income compared to lower-income children was highly divergent. The issue is not the amount of money being spent. From 1980 to 1988 expenditure on education as a proportion of GNP doubled, and it also increased as a percentage of total federal government expenditure, from 6.1 to 8.2 percent. Despite these real increases in total expenditure, resources directed to primary education were reduced by 39 percent between 1986 and 1989, whereas those to higher education increased 59 percent over the period. The Brazilian education system is asymmetric. Rich students go to private primary and secondary schools and then attend free public universities. The poor attend public primary and secondary schools. Poorly prepared, few pass the tough exams to get into the strong government-funded university system.[52] In 1996 the Brazilian congress approved an amendment that mandated 25 percent of state and municipal revenues be spent on education, with at least 60 percent of the total money to be allocated to raising teachers salaries. But funding to federal universities, which receive 80 percent of all federal spending, was preserved, as congress was unwilling to touch such middle-class entitlements.[53] As a percentage of GDP, Brazilian spending on public education is the highest in the world; it also ranks among the most expensive higher education systems.[54] Because of unequal distribution of educational opportunity, Brazil has spending levels in education comparable to middle-income countries and educational outcomes similar to those in very poor countries. The problem is not a lack of resources but uneven distribution of educational spending.

The results of the skewed spending on education in Brazil are startling. The average worker in the São Paulo area has only a fourth-grade education. As shown in figure 13.1, less than 20 percent of the population has some high school, in con-

Figure 13.1.   Percentage of Population with Some High School Education

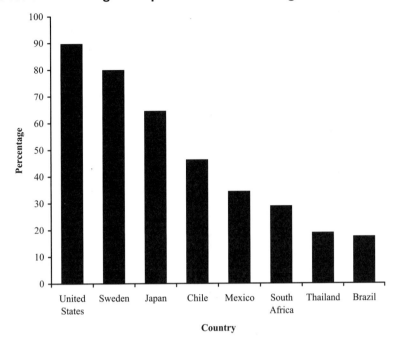

Source: Unesco, *Statistical Yearbook 1998* (Paris: UNESCO Publishing & Bernan Press, 1998), 1-44–1-S4.

trast to more than 40 percent in Chile, 35 percent in Mexico, 65 percent in Japan, and 90 percent in the United States. In the poorest regions in the Northeast, public school teachers earn less than $50 a month—drawing in the least talented in the society, many without secondary education themselves.[55]

Despite the difficulties in educational policies, some progress has been made. Figure 13.2 shows the gains in education since the 1970s. It also highlights, however, the unequal distribution by gender, region, and race. The Brazilian educational deficit in the face of global competitiveness was enormous. Radical changes in educational policy were implemented under the Cardoso administration. Under the astute political leadership of education minister Paulo Renato de Souza, responsibility for education was decentralized to the local level. Financing was devolved to the local level as well, where the demand for education could address local school board needs. A new role was set for the central government: establishing standards and assessing progress. Efforts are being made at computerization, installing 100,000 computers in the schools. Textbook distribution increased 83 percent over 1995, and there was an increase in school lunch programs as well as improvements in the TV school system for distance learning. One innovative program pays children to stay in school. In a suburb of Brasilia, 24,000 children draw one minimum wage of $110. A deposit is made each year that the student stays in school and can be touched only after four successful years of schooling. Enrollments are up and dropouts rare. The historical repeat rate in this district was 17 percent; it has now fallen to 8 percent.

Figure 13.2.   Average Years of Schooling in Brazil, 1970 versus 1990

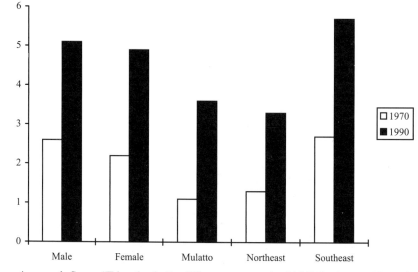

Source: Amaury de Souza, "Education in Brazil," paper presented at IADB Conference, November 1997.

In the Brazilian state of Minas Gerais, decentralization has improved efficiency and educational outcomes. The philosophy is that the school belongs to the community. Before decentralization, if a rural school wanted to buy a few new chairs, it would have to send a requisition to the state capital. Now local schools receive four quarterly payments for supplies and educational materials. School boards were formed to make personnel decisions, and competency exams for teachers were instituted. To overcome problems of patronage, principals are elected by the community among prequalified candidates using secret ballots.[56] The state has seen dramatic improvements in student scores: math scores have doubled, primary school graduation rates increased 47 percent, and repeaters fell from 29 to 17 percent.[57] Surprisingly, participation has been strongest among poor communities.

The overall results of educational reform have been dramatic. Illiteracy is down 15 percent, and test scores are rising. National teacher standards are improving, with nine out of ten teachers attaining a high school education or better. Nonetheless high repetition rates continue to plague the system.

What lessons can be drawn from educational reform in Brazil?[58] First, there was strong leadership from the top that was complemented by action from the bottom. Programs engaged stakeholders, bringing parents and the private sector together in the battle to keep kids in school. The leadership created a shared perspective on what needed to be done to reach common goals and engaged various levels of society to make it possible. The central government function performed well in producing and disseminating information while the local level had enough leeway for innovation and local experimentation. Much remains to be done in Brazil, but the educational future looks brighter.

Improving school materials and classroom conditions can promote better educational outcomes. *(Courtesy of David Mangurian and the Inter-American Development Bank.)*

THE PROCESS OF DECENTRALIZATION

As demonstrated in the Brazilian case, decentralization of education works best when it is supported by the following factors: political will at all levels of government; explicit guidelines delineating which functions of the educational system will be decentralized or provided by the private sector; an implementation timetable and strategy with clear operational guidelines; continuous training for educational administrators provided at the local level; development of performance indicators to measure outcomes; and adequate financial, human, and physical resources to sustain the process.[59] Incentives should be built into the system to encourage good management and discourage corruption at the local administrative level. Clear lines of responsibility should be defined to encourage accountability for poor standards and failed systems. Decentralization is a process that will take time to alter the rules of financing and delivery systems; it must be carefully monitored for efficiency and effectiveness. Decentralization may confront political obstacles, as centralized ministries lose power. Some countries might choose to decentralize particular components of the education system, rather than instituting a frontal attack. Decentralization that takes place too quickly could simply transfer the inefficiencies from central bureaucracies to the local level.[60]

Decentralization does not mean the abdication of responsibility for education at the national level. PREAL, the Partnership for Educational Revitalization in the Americas, recommends in its task force report, *The Future at Stake,* that governments establish clear standards for education, introduce national tests, and use results to revise programs and reallocate resources. Local governments should have the authority to run schools, but central administration of funds, standards, equity assurances, and monitoring of results is crucial. Better measures of assessment of educational outcomes must be developed to evaluate new directions in policy. Without effective assessment of outcomes, it is difficult to set clear goals. The few assessments that exist focus on inputs such as spending and the number of teachers rather than indicators of educational performance.[61] Assessment data should be disseminated to the local level to direct resources to the greatest need.[62] In Chile, for example, assessments were used to target schools at greatest educational risk. High- and medium-risk schools were eligible to apply for additional resources for reform. Decentralization does not necessarily mean less state involvement. Instead, it redefines responsibilities for different levels of government.

PUBLIC–PRIVATE PARTNERSHIPS

As businesses have worried about global competitiveness, the private sector has also assumed a role in education in the region. In Brazil, employees of Rigesa, a Brazilian subsidiary of Westvaco, a New York–based paper company and a blue jeans factory owned by a large Brazilian textile manufacturer, sponsor basic literacy classes after hours. A major Brazilian Bank, Bradesco, finances roughly fifty primary and secondary classes around the nation. The need to operate more sophisticated equipment drives the company programs.[63] A São Paulo cosmetics firm called Natura donated more than $3 million to train public school teachers. Embraer, Brazil's successful aircraft exporter, runs a technology institute to encourage young scientists. In Venezuela, a widow of a wealthy industrialist funded a school adjacent to the factory she owned to improve her workers' children's education. Another Venezuela-based firm, the Cisneros Group, is working with IBM and Microsoft in a project to use its Direct TV satellite to beam programs for teachers into 120 schools across the region.[64] Microsoft is working with the IADB in a program called Informatics 2000 to promote computer skills at the elementary and high school levels. To meet the skills gap to compete in the global economy, Mexico's private sector has taken steps by creating a National Commission of Normalization of Job Skills. Patterned on a Japanese program, it provides workers with a certification of job skill or knowledge level, regardless of how or where the skills were obtained.

Public-sector provision of early childhood programs may be complemented by private-sector initiatives. Partnerships of governments, NGOs, and communities should be encouraged. Informal programs such as the *hogares comunitarios* in Colombia have much lower salary and investment costs than formal programs. Public financing of preschool should start with the most deprived children in the urban and rural slums, and governments should resist middle-class pressures for general support of preschooling until the needs of the poor are met.[65] In Mexico, under the National Solidarity Program, PRONASOL, a poverty reduction program, the residents complemented state investments by providing half the funds and the labor for the building and refurbishing of schools. Local businesses contributed materials. Schoolchildren voted on which classmates were most deserving of funds to help their families while the children attended school.[66] Community participation matters in improving educational outcomes. Nonetheless, there is a long way to go in private participation in social efforts. With different sets of tax laws in the region, there is a limited tradition of corporate philanthropy in Latin America.

MULTILATERAL EFFORTS

As we discussed in chapter 8 in the section on the Free Trade Area of the Americas, at the 1994 Miami summit heads of Latin American governments ratified their commitment to guarantee universal access to **quality primary education by the year 2010,** a 100-percent primary school completion rate, and a rate of 75-percent inscription in secondary schools.[67] At the 1998 Santiago summit, heads of state from the region defined education and the so-called second generation of reforms as critical to strengthening Latin America's fragile political and economic system. Vulnerable groups, including women, indigenous people, geographically dispersed and migrant populations, urban marginalized communities, and the illiterate population over twenty-five, will be targeted through compensatory programs, preschool education, certificates of on-the-job training, and distance learning programs.[68]

Multilateral funding commitments make the achievement of these goals possible. The World Bank is the world's largest external funder of education, having provided $30 billion in loans and credits since its education funding began in 1963.[69] In 2001 the IADB allocated $711 million or 9 percent of the bank's loans for basic, secondary, and technical education. It emphasizes modernizing secondary education, supporting vocational and technical education and narrowing social inequalities by giving poor children more schooling.[70] The IADB has provided training for nearly 20 percent of the region's primary and secondary teachers through education loans. As a result of the summit, the World Bank and the IADB committed U.S.$8.2 billion over a three-year period to jump-start the process.[71] For the ILO (International Labor Organization), the focus is on equality of access. The ILO advocates setting basic education and vocational training as priority areas. The United Nations Educational, Scientific, and Cultural Organization (UNESCO)'s goals center on enhancing the role of national partners and developing strategies for national capacity in education planning, budgeting, and educational administration.[72]

New technologies offer new opportunities for education that both national governments and multilateral agencies are exploiting. The Internet brings a wide range of materials into even the most remote classroom. Students in rural classrooms can read the more than 1,000 national and international newspapers on the Internet. Wiring schools, even in remote areas, vastly enhances educational resources—and students often find it fun. Satellite classrooms and videotapes can work around the limitations of teacher training. In Brazil, Telecurso 2000 offers a basic high school equivalency program by television for young adults, with lessons broadcast at different times of day to accommodate work schedules. The workbook to accompany the course can be purchased at newsstands. Brazil is now moving to Internet-based courses to complement televised distance learning opportunities.

Nonetheless, technical solutions must be carefully evaluated for cost-effectiveness. Putting computers in classrooms is an expensive venture. Appropriate software must also be procured. If teachers are not adequately trained in the use of computers, their potential is wasted. Simply providing the hardware and software without clear plans to integrate computers into the classrooms increases the likelihood of failure.

EDUCATION AS SOCIAL CHANGE

Educational reform should not be limited to the walls of the classroom. In developing countries, adult learners play a large role in the educational challenge. Those who support education as a vehicle for social change argue that education should be used to empower the poor to participate in defining their own needs and transforming their physical world. Brazilian sociologist Paulo Freire, in his pathbreaking *Pedagogy of the Oppressed,* provided a methodology by which community-based groups, through the identification of common symbols, would become "consciencitized" to the causes of their poverty and empowered through education to change their situation. Freire rejects the "banking concept" of education, in which students are stocked with facts but rarely enter into a dialogue with instructors that is useful in transforming social reality.[73] Instead, through a process of community-based culture circles, Freire advocates the communal problematizing of local conditions and using education as a means of change and empowerment.

Ivan Illich, an Austrian-born social critic, in the 1960s and 1970s made Cuernavaca, Mexico, his home. He argued for "deschooling," or the breakup of the formal (and expensive) educational system in favor of creating mechanisms at the local level to transform the lives of the poor.[74] Nonformal education based on mass media, the distribution of printed materials, and group sessions animated by a local contact may cost a third or a fifth of the unit cost in primary education.[75] Adult education is a central element of the goal of Universal Access to Education for 2010 adopted by the Miami summit. Simply reforming the school will leave generations of the economically active population without the skills to compete in the global environment. Adult education and empowerment will contribute to human capital development in the region.

Key Concepts

decentralization
educational deficit
educational
   performance index

externalities
grade repetition
merit good

quality primary
education by
   the year 2010

Chapter Summary

- In comparison to other regions in the world, Latin America is deficient in the area of education.
- Primary education is segregated by class. Not only do the rich benefit from private schooling, but they are also allotted a greater share of public educational expenditure. In addition, schools suffer from high rates of grade repetition, thereby limiting resources for new educational opportunities.
- Although Latin America has made progress on gender bias in education, these benefits do not extend to indigenous communities. Language, cultural barriers, and high opportunity costs hinder indigenous groups from attending school. Improving educational opportunities and investing in human capital will contribute to economic growth.
- The educational deficit in Latin America is the result of ineffective demand by poor families and deficient quantity and quality of the supply offered by school systems. Strong educational infrastructure will contribute to significant economic progress. Educational programs that address the high opportunity costs of attending school and involve communities in decision making will effectively improve education in the region. The additional participation of international organization, NGOs, and respective governments will prove beneficial as well.
- Education does not have to be limited to younger students and the classroom. Informal education can be used as a vehicle for social change. Methods used to empower marginalized groups in defining their own educational needs may help to close the educational deficit in the region.

Notes

1. Unesco, *Education for All Year 2000 Assessment,* preparatory document for the World Education Forum, Dakar, Senegal, April 2000.

2. Statistics from Jeffrey M. Puryear, "Education in Latin America: Problems and Challenges," Partnership for Educational Revitalization in the Americas [PREAL], 7 May 1997. Presented to the Council of Foreign Relations, 27 February 1996, for the Latin America program study group, "Educational Reform in Latin America," New York. Available at www.preal.cl. Key FLACSO into your favorite search engine to get a sense of the broad range of activity in the region.

3. Laurence Wolff, Ernesto Schiefelbeing, and Jorge Valenzuela, *Improving the Quality of Primary Education in Latin America and the Caribbean: Toward the 21st Century* (Washington, D.C: World Bank, 1994), 12.

4. PREAL, "Lagging Behind: A Report Card on Education in Latin America," Task Force on Education, Equity and Economic Competitiveness in Latin America & the Caribbean, November 2001, www.preal.org, unweighted averages calculated from table A. 16.

5. PREAL, "Lagging Behind," 8.

6. World Education Forum, Dakar, Senegal, April 2000, Education for All Statistical Document, figure 3.10.

7. Samuel Morley, "Distribution and Growth in Latin America in an Era of Structural Reform: The Impact of Globalization," *OECD Technical Papers* no. 184, December 2001, 16, www.oecd.org.

8. Marcela Gajardo, "Reformas Educativas en América Latina—Balance de una década," *PREAL Working Paper* no. 15, September 1999, 9.

9. Fernando Reimers, "Educación para todos en América Latina en el siglo XXIL. Los desafíos de la estabilización, el ajuste y los mandatos de Jomtien," paper presented at UNESCO workshop, Peru, December 1990. Described in Carlos Alberto Torres and Adriana Puiggrós, "The State and Public Education in Latin America," *Comparative Education Review* 39, no. 1 (1995): 10.

10. "A Teacher's Lot," *The IDB* (May 1996): 9.

11. Amaury de Souza, "Redressing Inequalities: Brazil's Social Agenda at Century's End," in *Brazil under Cardoso*, ed. Susan Kaufman Purcell and Riordan Roett (Boulder, Colo.: Rienner, 1997), 71.

12. Peter Bate, "Education: The Gordian Knot," *IDB Today*. Online edition available at www.iadb.org.

13. Kevin Watkins, *The Oxfam Education Report*, Oxfam GB, 2000, accessed at www.oxfam.org, 10.

14. Wolff et al., *Improving the Quality of Primary Education*, 2.

15. Puryear, "Education in Latin America."

16. IADB, *Facing Up to Inequality in Latin America: Economic and Social Progress in Latin America, 1998–1999 Report* (Baltimore: Johns Hopkins University Press/IADB, 1998), 51.

17. Bate, "Education."

18. IADB, *Facing Up to Inequality*, 53.

19. PREAL, "Lagging Behind," 6.

20. PREAL, *The Future at Stake: Report of the Task Force on Education, Equity and Economic Competitiveness in Latin America and the Caribbean*, 7. Santiago, Chile: PREAL, in conjunction with the Inter-American Dialogue and CINDE, 1998. Available online at www.preal.cl/index-i.htm.

21. Wolff et al., *Improving the Quality of Primary Education*, 5.

22. Torres and Puiggrós, "The State and Public Education," 1.

23. Puryear, "Education in Latin America."

24. IADB, *Women in the Americas: Bridging the Gap* (Baltimore: Johns Hopkins University Press, 1995).

25. M. Anne Hill and Elizabeth M. King, "Women's Education in Developing Countries: An Overview," in *Women's Education in Developing Countries: Barriers, Benefits, and Policies*, ed. M. Anne Hill and Elizabeth M. King (Baltimore: Johns Hopkins University Press, 1993), 19.

26. Diane Steele, "Guatemala," in *Indigenous People and Poverty in Latin America*, ed. George Psacharopoulos and Harry Anthony Patrinos (Washington, D.C.: World Bank, 1994), 104.

27. Bill Wood and Harry Anthony Patrinos, "Urban Bolivia," in *Indigenous People and Poverty in Latin America*, ed. George Psacharopoulos and Harry Anthony Patrinos (Washington, D.C.: World Bank, 1994), 63.

28. Donna Macisaac, "Peru," in *Indigenous People and Poverty in Latin America*, ed. George Psacharopoulos and Harry Anthony Patrinos (Washington, D.C.: World Bank, 1994), 170.

29. William Myers, ed., *Protecting Working Children* (London: Zed, 1991); and Anthony Dewees and Steven Klees, "Social Movements and the Transformation of National Policy: Street and Working Children in Brazil," *Comparative Education Review* 39, no. 1 (1995).

30. Jere R. Behrman, Suzanne Duryea, and Migúel Szekely, "Schooling, Investment and Aggregate Conditions: A Household Survey-Based Approach for Latin America and the Caribbean," *IADB Working Paper* no. 40, November 29, 1999, 27.

31. Fernando Reimers, "The Impact of Economic Stabilization and Adjustment on Education in Latin America," *Comparative Education* 35, no. 2 (May 1991): 322.

32. Fernando Fajnzylber, "Education and Changing Production Patterns with Social Equity," *CEPAL Review* 47 (August 1992): 8.

33. Puryear, "Education in Latin America."

34. IADB, *Facing Up to Inequality,* 129.

35. Katherine Ellison, "Latin Summit's Focus: Education of Kids," *Miami Herald,* April 13, 1998, p. A1. Available online at www.alca-cupula.org.

36. A. Fiszbein and G. Psacharopoulos, *Income Inequality in Latin America: The Story of the Eighties,* Technical Department for Latin America Working Paper (Washington, D.C.: World Bank, 1995), as cited in IADB, *IDB Annual Report: Making Social Services Work* (Washington, D.C.: IADB, 1996), 245.

37. "Skills Gap May Be Biggest Trade Barrier," *Journal of Commerce,* April 20, 1998. Online edition available at www.alca-cupula.org.

38. Wolff et al., *Improving the Quality of Primary Education,* 1.

39. Lawrence J. Lau, Dean T. Jamison, Shucheng Liu, and Steven Rivkin, "Education and Economic Growth: Some Cross-Sectional Evidence," in *Education in Brazil,* ed. Nancy Birdsall and Richard H. Sabot (Washington, D.C.: IADB, 1996), 83–116. The large variation, between 5 and 20 percent, is a function of the existing educational infrastructure. If initial levels are low, large returns accrue after four years. The authors estimate that after this jump, the relationship will smooth out, with each year adding 5 percent in output.

40. Eduardo Lora and Felipe Barrera, "A Decade of Structural Reform in Latin America: Growth, Productivity, and Investment Are Not What They Used to Be," document for discussion at the IADB Barcelona seminar, "Latin America after a Decade of Reform: What Next?" 16 March 1997.

41. PREAL, *Future at Stake,* 10.

42. Christopher Colclough, "Education and the Market: Which Parts of the Neoliberal Solution Are Correct?" *World Development* 24, no. 4 (1996): 589–610.

43. Martin Carnoy, "Structural Adjustment and the Changing Face of Education," *International Labor Review* 134, no. 6 (1995): 653–73.

44. Rosemary T. Bellew and Elizabeth M. King, "Educating Women: Lessons from Experience," in *Women's Education in Developing Countries: Barriers, Benefits and Policies,* ed. Elizabeth M. King and Rosemary Bellew (Baltimore: Johns Hopkins University Press, 1993), 305.

45. George Psacharopoulos, Carlos Rojas, and Eduardo Velez, "Achieving Evaluation of Colombia's Escuela Nueva: Is Multigrade the Answer?" *Comparative Education Review* 37, no. 3 (1993).

46. Molly Moore, "Mayan Girls Make Fifth Grade History," *Washington Post,* 20 June 1996, p. A19.

47. Gary S. Becker, "Bribe the Third World Parents to Keep Their Kids in School." *BusinessWeek,* November 22, 1999, p. 15.

48. Taryn Rounds Parry, "Achieving Balance in Decentralization: A Case Study of Education Decentralization in Chile," *World Development* 25, no. 2 (February 1997): 211–25. For a review of the Pinochet period, see Tarsicio Castañeda, "Combating Poverty," in *Reforms in Education* (San Francisco: International Center for Economic Growth, 1992).

49. Alan Engell, "Improving the Quality and Equity of Education in Chile: The Programa 900 Escuelas and the MECE-Basica," in *Implementing Policy Innovation in Latin America: Politics, Economics and Techniques,* ed. Antonio Silva (Washington, D.C.: IADB, 1996), 94–117.

50. Emmanuel de Kadt, "Thematic Lessons from the Case Studies," in *The Public-Private Mix in Social Services*, ed. Elaine Zuckerman and Emanuel de Kadt (Washington, D.C.: Inter-American Development Bank, 1997), 131–143.

51. Carol Graham, *Private Markets for Public Goods: Raising the Stakes for Economic Reform* (Washington, D.C.: Brookings Institution Press, 1998), 45.

52. Eduardo Amedeo, José Márcio Camargo, Antônio Emílio S. Marques, and Cândido Gomes, "Fiscal Crisis and Asymmetries in the Education System in Brazil," in *Coping with Crisis: Austerity, Adjustment, and Human Resources*, ed. Joel Samoa (New York: UNESCO/ILO, 1994), 48.

53. De Souza, "Redressing Inequalities," 76.

54. Claudio de Moura Castro, "Education: Way Behind but Trying to Catch Up," *Daedalus* 129, no. 2 (Spring 2000): 304.

55. Diana Jean Schemo, "The ABC's of Doing Business in Brazil," *New York Times*, 16 July 1998, p. D7.

56. PREAL, *Future at Stake*, 12.

57. Mary Anastasia O'Grady, "A Brazilian State Shows How to Reform Schools," *Wall Street Journal*, 16 August 1997, p. A17.

58. Summarized from presentation of Juan Carlos Navarro, IADB conference, Washington, D.C., 12 November 1997.

59. Juan Prawda, "Educational Decentralization in Latin America: Lessons Learned," *International Journal of Educational Development* 13, no. 3 (1993): 253–64.

60. Council on Foreign Relations, "Reforming Education in America," study group on reforming education in Latin America, "The Second Wave of Reform," directed by Allison L. C. de Cerreño, New York, February–October 1996.

61. PREAL, *Future at Stake*, 11.

62. For a review of educational assessment instruments, see Laurence Wolff, "Educational Assessments in Latin America: Current Progress and Future Challenges," *Partnership for Educational Revitalization in the Americas*, June 1998, p. 11. Online publication available at www.preal.cl/index-i.htm.

63. Schemo, "The ABC's," D7.

64. Ellison, "Latin Summit's Focus."

65. Wolff et al., *Improving the Quality of Primary Education*, 8.

66. David E. Lorey, "Education and the Challenges of Mexican Development," *Challenge* 38, no. 2 (March–April 1995): 52.

67. Summit of the Americas Information Network Education. Available online at www.summit-americas.org.

68. *Action Plan for Universal and Quality Basic Education by the Year 2000*, Summit of the Americas. Available online at www.summit-americas.org.

69. The World Bank, education program objectives, www.worldbank.org.

70. IADB, *Annual Report 2001*, www.iadb.org.

71. "The Summiteers Go to School," *The Economist*, 25 April 1998, pp. 37–38.

72. Lucila Jallade, Eddy Lee, and Joel Samoff, "International Cooperation," in *Coping with Crisis: Austerity, Adjustment, and Human Resources*, ed. Joel Samoff (New York: UNESCO/ILO, 1994), 254–66.

73. Paulo Freire, *Pedagogy of the Oppressed* (New York: Seabury, 1970).

74. John A. Britton, ed., *Molding the Hearts and Minds: Education, Communications, and Social Change in Latin America* (Wilmington, Del.: Scholarly Resources, 1994), xxiv. For more on social change, see Carlos A. Torres, *Education and Social Change in Latin America* (Albert Park, Australia: James Nicolas, 1997).

75. Wolff et al., *Improving the Quality of Primary Education*, 4.

CHAPTER FOURTEEN

ENVIRONMENTAL CHALLENGES

Internalizing the Costs of Development

Automobiles are a major source of urban pollution. *(Courtesy of the Inter-American Development Bank.)*

Understanding environmental issues in Latin America is very much about understanding the broader pattern of development that has shaped the region. The environment is inextricably linked with past economic performance and social conditions, as well as local and global policy choices. In the context of our understanding of the history of the region, the import substitution model, the challenge of the debt crisis, and the transformations of the neoliberal model, we now turn our focus specifically to the environment.

The following questions inform our discussion:

- How do countries, grappling with problems of economic growth and stability, and burdened by poverty, address environmental concerns?
- Is there a trade-off between a brighter economic future for the millions of impoverished in Latin America and the health of the environment?
- How should countries weigh the pressing needs of present generations against a clean environment for the future?

Such environmental concerns have challenged and transformed the core of development economics. Traditional economic models neglected to account for externalities in the growth process or the finite nature of natural resources. Today development economics is being redefined by the concept of **sustainable development.** A simple definition of sustainable development offered by the World Commission on Environment and Development is that current generations should "meet their needs without compromising the ability of future generations to meet their own needs."[1] This vision has inspired local, national, and international organizations to work to define a development model that balances economic growth with environmental sensibility. The 1992 United Nations Conference on the Environment and Development held in Rio de Janeiro was a turning point for the region and the world in re-visioning the development process. Ten years later nations revisited the accomplishments and challenges in international environmental policy in Johannesburg South Africa. The 2002 meetings highlighted that although much has been accomplished in raising environmental consciousness, financing for sustainable development remains a huge obstacle to measurable progress.

Implementation of a development strategy that weighs the needs of current generations against the requirements of the future is complicated in practice. Difficult policy questions arise:

- How should competing needs of the present and the future, the economy and the environment, be prioritized?
- How can we think systematically about the complex interrelationships between social, economic, and eco systems in the region?
- What are the elements of an economically sound and politically viable environmental policy?
- How should global institutions promote financing for sound international environmental policy?

After exploring the concept of sustainable development in greater detail, we will consider its application in the region. Latin America is geographically diverse, ranging from deserts to rain forests, mountains to plains, from the most rural settlements to the most densely populated and extensive megacities in the world. Each area itself contains a huge variety of plants, animals (including humans), and minerals. The complexity of social and eco systems adds to the challenge of environmental management in Latin America. Priorities in environmental management vary from country to country, as does the institutional capacity to meet the challenge of sustainable development. This chapter will describe the diverse environmental concerns Latin America faces in terms of human standards of living as well as ecological conditions. It will then turn to consider the best policy mix and the options for financing to meet the standard of sustainable development in the region.

JUST WHAT IS SUSTAINABLE DEVELOPMENT?

The challenge set by the 1987 Brundtland Report of the World Commission on Environment and Development, which defined environmentally sustainable development as meeting the needs of the current generation without compromising the ability of future generations, is—perhaps like all great ideas—a deceivingly simple concept. Meeting the needs of a current generation involves integrating economic, social, environmental, and political concerns.[2] Sustainable development promotes the efficient use of resources in the service of a stable growth path. The growth pattern, however, is very much shaped by social conditions. Without attention to poverty and inequality, the basic needs of the current generation are not met. Attention must be paid to the ways gender shapes access to environmental assets. The Brundtland Report notes that a "world in which poverty is endemic will always be prone to ecological and other catastrophes."[3] All people, including marginalized groups, must be vested in the development process. How can people living in absolute poverty support the hard choices that sometimes must be made to postpone present consumption to favor future sustainability? Postponing consumption while living on the margins of existence threatens survival. Without participation of all segments of the population, a social consensus cannot be achieved to balance present and future needs.

For development to be sustainable, economic and social changes must be set against the capabilities of the physical environment to support human activity. Achieving sustainability therefore must delicately balance a growing population and the ability of the physical environment to absorb the waste of human activity.[4] Technical fixes are one way out of this bind. The capacity of the physical environment to support human life can be transformed by technological changes allowing people to do more with less. However, betting sustainability on potential technological change is fraught with uncertainty. We might hope that new (and cheap) technologies are developed to provide energy, recycle solid and hazardous wastes, purify sewage and industrial wastes before they hit the sea, and reduce emission from motor vehicles—but can we count on it?

Sound environmental policy involves hard choices. Who makes them? Identifying whose needs are met in the present and the future involves political decisions—

This Colombian recycling project contributes to urban clean-up and generates jobs.
(Courtesy of Willie Heinz and the Inter-American Development Bank.)

Figure 14.1.   The Complexity of Environmental Decision Making

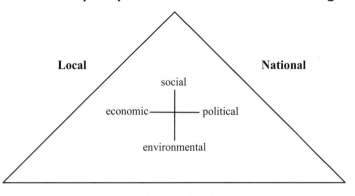

decisions in Latin America that historically have been made by male elites. As can be seen in figure 14.1, economic, environmental, political, and social factors influence policy at the local, national, and international levels. The priorities at each level might be in conflict. Although global concerns for biodiversity or greenhouse effects might dominate the agenda of the more industrialized nations, the interaction of poverty and the environment is likely to be of greater concern at the local and national levels.

When the problems of current generations are so pressing, it is tough (especially for elected officials) to postpone meeting today's needs in favor of the future. As one Salvadoran said, "There is no point in having a beautiful environment if there is nothing to eat."[5] Furthermore, it is difficult for governments to assess the well-being of present generations. How do we measure environmental quality? Is it measured by homes with sewer connections, clean air, the number of endangered species, or the acreage in protected national parks?[6] An accurate measure of environmental quality involves much better data collection and estimation of current and future resource stocks.[7] Better data would permit a more consistent estimation of the present value of future resource use. This tough calculation of society's willingness to pay today for future access to a sustainable environment is at the core of strong policy recommendations.

To assess the bundle of social and environmental capital that one generation should pass on to the next, some environmental economists promote the concept of a **safe minimum standard.**[8] The safe minimum is seen as a social compact that, in the face of high ecological uncertainty, provides a basis for sustainable growth. Of course the differing priorities of the industrialized North and the developing South make such a compact on global issues precarious. To a large degree, natural capital or biodiversity finds its home in the South, whereas social capital, including scientific and technical knowledge to preserve natural capital, is largely lodged in the North. Different valuations placed on the need to employ natural capital today versus desires to preserve ecological diversity for the future suggest that the North, having already depleted much of its natural stocks, will have to compensate the South to preserve biodiversity. But how much, and on whose terms?

The **Global Environmental Facility** (GEF) was formed after the 1992 Earth Summit Rio to address financial and technological transfers. Following the conference, the concept of sustainable development found expression in five basic agreements: the Rio Declaration, which articulated political principles for re-visioning development models; **Agenda 21,** a comprehensive agenda for action; the Convention on Biological Diversity; the Convention on Climate Change; and the Declaration of Principles on the Management, Conservation, and Sustainable Development of Forests. The 2002 **World Summit on Sustainable Development** (WSSD) in Johannesburg has underscored the patchy record in reversing environmental degradation while the South struggles under financial constraints. Despite clear goals there has been an implementation gap, driven by limited resources, policy incoherence, and a fragmented approach in connecting the environment to development.

Globalization has increased the negative externalities created by an integrated production structure. Direct environmental effects are generated by new agricultural and industrial techniques, the exploitation of hitherto untapped nonrenewable resources, and the release of new substances into the environment. Indirect effects are created by the social, economic, political, and demographic adjustments to globalization that have resulted in new forms of organizing work and new consumption patterns and the location and nature of human activities and settlements.[9] New technologies and sustainable social planning are necessary to manage increasing pressures on ecosystems, especially in fragile and remote areas.

Achieving sustainable development is therefore complicated by problems of measurement; the uncertainty of future technological change; and political will on local, national, and international levels to make and pay for hard choices. Yet for all its limitations, it is an extremely useful policy principle. Meeting the needs of the present for a better life without compromising the stock of assets available to future generations is an important criterion that can be applied to policies addressing industry, infrastructure development, or poverty. The accomplishment of the past decade has been to insert sustainable development as a clear frame of reference in macro, poverty, health, and industrial policy. How to bring this principle into the policy arena in a way that minimizes the economic costs and maximizes the environmental benefits will be addressed at the end of the chapter. But before we design policy, we must first better understand the nature of the environmental problem in the Latin American region.

ENVIRONMENTAL PRIORITIES IN LATIN AMERICA

What is the most pressing environmental problem in Latin America? In fact this is not a very good question. There is a broad array of environmental issues in the region that vary in importance based upon who you are, where you live, and what economic resources are available to you. The priority list depends on whether you are rich or poor, urban or rural, male or female. A middle-class resident of Santiago, Chile, is likely to complain most about air quality, while someone living in a shack along the Tietê River in São Paulo might be most affected by problems of water sanitation. A rubber tapper might ally with an international rain forest activist in

Table 14.1. Latin America and the Caribbean: Selected Environmental Indicators (cumulative percentage growth rates)

Physical Indicators	1980–1989	1990–1999
Arable farmland area	7.3	6.3[a]
Volume of agricultural output	26.8	28.3
Total fertilizer consumption	5.3	42.2[a]
Livestock	7.4	0.8
Volume of industrial roundwood production	25.4	18.1[a]
Firewood and coal production	12.3	0.4[a]
Marine fisheries production	17.9[b]	–24.3[a]
Marine fish farming production	165.0[b]	116.0
Physical volume of mineral production, including oil	25.9	43.1
Physical volume of mineral production, excluding oil	46.2	67.6
Carbon dioxide (CO_2) emissions	22.9	37.1
Carbon monoxide (CO) emissions	23.5	28.4
Cumulative percentage population growth	21.9	17.0[c]
Cumulative increase in gross domestic product (dollars)	14.0	33.2

Source: ECLAC, *Globalization & Development* (Santiago, Chile: ECLAC, 2002), table 9.1.
[a]1990–1998.
[b]1985–1990.
[c]1990–2000.

arguing that tropical deforestation is the most pressing issue, but for very different reasons. Problems in maintaining fishing stocks off the coast of Argentina might seem a long way from the concerns of the Indians in Peru's Altiplano. Women might worry about the ways communities struggle to overcome deficits with water or sewage. As Latin America is diverse, so are its environmental concerns. Table 14.1 gives an overview of environmental indicators in the region; you might identify priorities by comparing the data for the 1980s through the 1990s.

THE POOR: AGENTS AND VICTIMS OF ENVIRONMENTAL DESTRUCTION

Throughout Latin America—urban or rural, tropical or polar—it is clear that sustainable development is not possible without making progress toward alleviating poverty. The poor are both agents and victims of an unsafe environment. Lacking resources to invest in cleaner water or waste removal, or the assets necessary in agriculture to reinvest in soil quality, the poor promote environmental degradation. But they are also the worst victims of unhealthy water and air quality, and they are often financially unable to flee the worst zones of pollution.

Poverty, and its associated social and economic conditions of malnutrition, underdeveloped human capital, disease, and lack of savings, is linked to environmental damage. Loss of biodiversity, deforestation and desertification, soil erosion and nutrient depletion, and water pollution are in part caused by resource constraints of land scarcity, receding fuel wood and water supply, reduced agricultural productivity, and unhygienic sanitation.[10] Unable to postpone present consumption or invest in the future, the poor scrape to survive. Poverty can be exacerbated by population growth. If the economic pie is not growing, more inhabitants leave fewer people with the ability to sustain themselves today and invest in their futures. Population growth increases the demand for goods and services, as well as introduces more pollutants into the waste stream. In Latin America the population grew 2.4 percent from 1970 to 1980 and approximately 2 percent from 1980 until 1995. Over the lost decade of the 1980s, as gross domestic product (GDP) rose only 1.1 percent, population growth rates far outpaced the economy, leaving little for environmental progress. Over the next four decades Latin America's population will increase from 450 to 750 million—multiplying the demands on the carrying capacity of its fragile environmental infrastructure.

THE PROBLEMS OF THE URBAN ENVIRONMENT

Population growth rates outpaced the economy in the 1980s, but as the region has recovered in the 1990s, the environmental dividend has been far from evident. Why? In part this is due to the fact that population growth has taken place disproportionately in the urban sector. In 1965, 55.9 percent of the population in South America lived in cities; by 2000 this number reached 79.8 percent. This is higher than the U.S. ratio of 77.2 percent. Rates of **urbanization** of 89.9 percent in Argentina, 81.3 percent in Brazil, 86.9 percent in Venezuela, 91.3 percent in Uruguay, and 85.7 percent in Chile challenge the folkloric picture of a peasant in a small village or an Indian in the rain forest that many hold as typical of Latin America.[11] It is estimated that by 2025 Latin America will have the highest rate of urbanization in the world at approximately 85 percent.[12] The rate of transformation of urban centers has overwhelmed the capacity of municipalities to provide clean air and water or rapid and reasonable transportation and telecommunications infrastructure to their inhabitants. For example, as the population of Cancun mushroomed from a small town of 20,000 to a city of 340,000, only 60 percent of its urban zone had running water; those with piped access didn't have a steady twenty-four-hour supply. Waste water was worse; only 30 percent of the urban zone connected to sewerage systems.[13]

As Secretary-General of the United Nations Kofi Annan noted in the UN's State of the World's Cities,[14] cities are hubs of dynamism, change, and opportunity but also places of exploitation, disease, and unemployment. Urbanization in Latin America is compressed in a few megacities. In the United States 41.7 percent of urban dwellers live rather evenly spread over forty-three cities with at least 750,000 inhabitants; in Latin America the pattern, with the exception of Brazil, typically is one megacity per country. Forty percent of all Chileans live in Santiago, 25 percent living below the poverty line; 30 percent of Peruvians inhabit Lima. In 2000, São Paulo and Mexico City had populations of 17.8 million and 18.1 million, respectively, putting them in the top four megacities with Tokyo and Mumbai.[15] As anyone who has lived in or visited New York or Los Angeles knows, the air, water, and transport problems of the city overpower even the best of intentions. Imagine trying to solve the same set of problems with even fewer financial resources.

The *size of urban cities* makes environmental problems extraordinarily complex. Poverty is concentrated in urban areas, with poor urban dwellers living in substandard housing within informal settlements with limited or no access to basic services. Unsustainable human settlements, often in dangerous locations, generally lack basic municipal services such as safe drinking water, sanitation, public transport, schools, and clinics. A 1995 Pan American Health Organization (PAHO) survey of Brazil found that 57 percent of cities have open garbage dumps, a mere 14 percent have controlled landfills, and only 28 percent have sanitary landfills or other adequate methods of waste disposal. Furthermore, while 78 percent of waste disposal facilities are sanitary in Chile, this number falls to 30 percent in Mexico. In 1995, Bolivia, Ecuador, and Peru had no sanitary landfills outside the capital cities.[16] Lima, Peru, is home for approximately seven million of the country's inhabitants living in what the government euphemistically refers to as "emergency dwellings." The lack of running water, electricity, and sanitation make perfect conditions for the spread of infectious disease such as cholera.[17] Guatemala City collects only 65 percent of its municipal waste; the rest is disposed of in "unofficial" locations. Garbage collection is seen as outside formal-sector services or inaccessible through narrow, unpaved streets.[18] Ironies abound. Although Mexico can store 10 percent less garbage than it produces, 36,000 tons of toxic waste a year are imported from the United States.[19] Of course, if Latin Americans produced as much garbage as those who live in the United States, the result would simply be unbearable. For example, each person in Quito, Ecuador, produces about 281 kilograms of solid waste a year. In São Paulo per capita solid waste generation stands at 352 kilograms—low compared to the average resident in Washington, D.C., who produces 1,246 kilograms of solid waste.[20] Table 14.2 illustrates solid waste per capita, wastewater treatment, and households with waste collection service in selected Latin American cities.

Poor urban residents in Latin America struggle to cope with a host of these societal shortfalls making daily life an environmental battle. These deficits may be the result of inadequate urban planning under pressure from population changes, lack of

Table 14.2. Solid Waste Production, Wastewater Treatment, and Waste Collection in Selected Latin American Cities

City	Solid Waste per Capita (kg/year)	Wastewater Treated (percentage)	Households with Waste Collection Service (percentage)
Brasilia	182	54	95
Havana	584	100	100
La Paz	182	0	92
San Salvador	328	2	46
Santiago	182	5	57
Toronto[a]	511	100	100

Source: United Nations Environment Program and ECLAC, "The Sustainability of Development in Latin America and the Caribbean: Challenges and Opportunities," prepared for the Preparatory Conference of Latin America and the Caribbean for the World Conference on Sustainable Development (Johannesburg, South Africa, 2002), table IV.12, 81.
[a]For purposes of comparison.

investment in infrastructure, or indifference to the needs of the poor in elite-controlled political systems. Market criteria have dominated development planning, compounding weaknesses of environmental institutions and the lack of formal mechanisms for effective civil society participation.[21] Investments in the poor *favelas* or *barrios* in the region are critical to achieving environmental sustainability.

The costs of urban environmental problems are enormous. The World Bank estimates that the *welfare costs* of illness and death due to dirty air and water in the region range between $1 billion and $3 billion. Premature death and illness caused by environmental health risks account for one-fifth of the total burden of disease in the developing world, comparable to that of nutrition, and larger than all other preventable risk factors and groups.[22] Brazilians calculate that 70 percent of all hospital admissions are due to diseases related to lack of sanitation. The leading source of death among children under five in most Latin American countries is traceable to water-transmitted diseases such as cholera and diarrhea;[23] waterborne diseases are estimated to cause 60 percent of child mortality in the Latin America and Caribbean (LAC) region.[24] Failing to prevent disease costs money. One study estimated that the cost of water pollution in Mexico in terms of the incidence of diarrheal diseases and premature death was U.S.$3.6 billion—nearly 2 percent of total Mexican GDP in 1988.[25] The cost to Peru of the cholera epidemic was U.S.$1 billion, more than three times what it invested in water supply and sanitation during the entire 1980s. The urban environmental challenge in Latin America is a pressing health issue with overwhelming economic and human costs.[26]

Water quality is problematic in both the rural and the urban areas. A joint PAHO–United Nations Children's Fund (UNICEF) evaluation on the situation at the end of the 1990s revealed that of the 459 million inhabitants in Latin America in 1998, 70 million lacked drinking water, 95 million lacked sanitation, and 194 million were connected to sewerage systems where effluents do not receive treatment. Data released by the United Nations are slightly more daunting. As shown in table 14.3, 92 million inhabitants were without drinking water in 2000. While the number of rural inhabitants with access to drinking water appears to have dropped between 1990 and 2000, the number of urban dwellers without adequate water has risen sharply. In 2000, 128 million people were cited as not having sanitation services.[27] From 1990 to 1997, Paraguay, Nicaragua, and Bolivia exhibited the lowest levels of people with access to safe water, with 60 percent, 62 percent, and 63 percent respectively.[28] Most widespread contamination of water is from disease-bearing human waste, but in the rural areas agro-industrial effluent, especially fertilizer use, is particularly damaging. Toxic chemical buildup in rivers, including lead and mercury, lowers oxygen levels and also threatens fish and aquatic culture. Rapid urban growth will add more than 140 million to the region's inadequate urban infrastructure.[29] Box 14.1 illustrates how simple solar technologies can be used to address some of the water problems in the rural sector.

It has been estimated that more than eighty million dwellers, or 27 percent of the urban population and 19 percent of the total population, are exposed to *air pollution* levels exceeding World Health Organization (WHO) guidelines.[30] In the cities, a larger percentage of the population lives in the open air, with greater exposure to toxic pollutants.[31] Indoor pollution through poorly ventilated biomass stoves and the

Table 14.3. Drinking Water and Basic Sanitation in Latin America and the Caribbean

	1990			2000		
	Population	With Service	% Coverage	Population	With Service	% Coverage
Urban drinking water	313	283	90.4	391	353	90.3
Rural drinking water	128	72	56.4	128	74	57.6
Total drinking water	440	355	80.6	519	427	82.2
Urban sanitation	313	247	78.9	391	335	85.7
Rural sanitation	128	39	30.7	128	56	43.5
Total sanitation	440	286	64.9	519	391	75.3

Source: United Nations Environment Programme and ECLAC, "The Sustainability of Development in Latin America and the Caribbean: Challenges and Opportunities," prepared for Preparatory Conference of Latin America and the Caribbean for the World Conference on Sustainable Development (Johannesburg, South Africa, 2002), table IV.11, 79.

Box 14.1.   How Two Nonprofit International Development Organizations Are Using Solar Energy to Improve People's Quality of Life in Rural Latin America

ENERSOL

Enersol, a nonprofit international development organization, uses clean solar energy to improve the quality of life of Latin Americans while protecting the global environment. Specifically, Enersol assists rural communities with the application of solar electric technologies to improve health and education. In its models, the organization seeks to utilize local institutional and private-sector resources and to contribute to the global transition toward sustainable societies.

Over three million Dominicans and Hondurans currently live without access to clean water. Imagine always having to cook, wash, and drink with unsafe water. To combat the problem, Enersol has established solar-powered pumping systems in thirteen communities of the Dominican Republic. In 2000, the first solar-powered community water system was completed in Honduras. Clean Water for Health has effectively made clean water available to thousands of people. Families within each community pay into a fund for maintenance of their water systems, and Enersol trains members within each community to care for them. By training locals to care for their own clean water delivery and by establishing a financial reserve for maintenance of the system, sustainable water projects are created.

Enersol has also begun using solar energy to power computers in rural community schools that lack electricity and own very few books. Through the Information Technology for Education program, solar-powered laptops and educational software are bringing problem-solving skills and knowledge to both teachers and students. As in the case of providing clean water, family members within the community pay into a maintenance fund and Enersol provides community training to ensure that the new solar-powered technology can be cared for. Enersol has enabled children who have very little knowledge outside of their own communities to gain skills and knowledge they perhaps had never dreamed possible.

THE MESOAMERICAN DEVELOPMENT INSTITUTE (MDI)

During the coffee harvest throughout Latin America, coffee beans are shipped to centralized facilities where they are dried using wood or diesel-fired burners. This drying process contributes to the deforestation of the region. In Honduras, for example, an estimated 1,885 acres of forest (or 16 percent of the industrial consumption of wood) are cleared annually for coffee processing. In Central America, furthermore, an estimated 16,086 acres of forest are cleared for firewood to be used in coffee production. To combat, or at least partly curb this destructive process, the Mesoamerican Development Institute (MDI), founded by University of Massachusetts-Lowell alumni, has developed solar coffee-drying systems for use by small coffee farmers in Latin America. The new drying system uses a lower temperature for drying, which effectively preserves the quality of the coffee bean, as well as allows small growers to dry their own beans without outsourcing. Because the coffee can be dried at the farm where it was grown and not mixed with other varieties at centralized processing facilities, the coffee can be characterized according to variety, altitude, plantation, etc. Such production techniques not only contribute to goals of sustainable agriculture in the region, but they also allow for a higher quality coffee that can be sold in niche markets.

Source: Information on Enersol has been extracted from the Enersol website, available online at www.enersol.org. Information on MDI has been extracted from the Solar Energy Engineering, University of Massachusetts, Lowell, website, available online at energy.caeds.eng.uml.edu/coffee.html.

use of unprocessed solid fuels for cooking and heating expose people—mostly women and children in rural areas and slums—to high levels of suspended particulates. Between 1990 and 1999 emission of suspended particulates role by 6.2 percent; sulphur dioxide by 22 percent, nitrogen oxides by 41 percent, hydrocarbons by 45 percent, carbon monoxide by 28 percent, and carbon dioxide by 37 percent.[32] Pollution affects the health of more than eighty million Latin Americans, resulting in the lost of sixty-five million working days and causing 2.3 million cases of chronic breathing difficulties among children and over ten thousand cases of chronic bronchitis in adults.[33] A primary cause of poor air quality is motor vehicles. Concentrated in a few large cities, they account for 80 to 99 percent of carbon monoxide emissions.[34] Half the Mexican fleet operates in Mexico City, and one quarter of Brazilian cars are registered in São Paulo. More than in industrialized countries, motor vehicles are a significant source of airborne toxic pollutants because cars are in poor condition and lower-quality fuels are used. And it could get worst. Imagine the damage if instead of 67.9 cars per 1,000 residents in Latin America and the Caribbean, the 561 per 1,000 rate of the United States were matched.[35] Rising real incomes could result in an explosive growth in cars; in Santiago, Chile, the number of cars is doubling every five years, contributing negatively not only to pollution but also to urban productivity and quality of life.[36] Achieving sustainability may involve changing consumption patterns in both the North and the South.

Geographic characteristics compound the environmental problems of some cities. Mexico City sits in a basin surrounded by mountains. Ventilation is poor, and during winter thermal inversions occur up to twenty-five days per month. More than thirty thousand industries and twelve thousand service facilities are located in the valley, and 2.5 million motor vehicles—buses, minibuses, taxis, trucks, vans, private cars—operate in the area. WHO guidelines are exceeded regularly, especially during the morning rush hour when low temperature, atmospheric stability (inversion), and heavy traffic occur simultaneously.[37] Sadly, one should not be surprised that more than 25 percent of newborns had toxins in their blood at levels high enough to impair neurological and motor-physical development.[38]

Environmental fragility compounds the damage of *natural disasters*. Table 14.4 provides a history of natural disasters in Latin America. Hurricane Mitch was the most destructive disaster in the hemisphere's recorded history. Nine thousand deaths were reported in Central America, and three million people were left homeless. The destruction of social and economic infrastructure such as transportation routes, villages, schools, and crops resulted in an overwhelming $8 billion in damage. On average, coping with natural disasters costs 2 percent of Central America's GDP per year—many of these damages avoidable. Mitch is a perfect example of how a physical phenomena can destroy years of development progress. Meeting relief and reconstruction needs must take priority over long-term development goals, setting back progress on environmental sustainability.[39] The Economic Commission for Latin America and the Caribbean (ECLAC) notes that preventing natural disasters constitutes one of the region's main challenges. The return is substantial; a dollar spent on prevention can save seven in resulting damages. Prevention can deter damage escalation; the fire that results from dead material following a hurricane need never begin.[40]

Table 14.4.   Natural Disasters between 1972 and 2001

Country and Year	Type of Disaster	Deaths	Number of Persons Directly Affected	Millions of 1998 Dollars (total damage)
Nicaragua, 1972	earthquake	6,000	300,000	2,968
Honduras, 1974	Hurricane Fifi	7,000	115,000	1,331
Grenada, 1975	tropical storm			29
Guatemala, 1976	earthquake	23,000	1,550,000	2,147
Nicaragua, 1982	floods	80	70,000	599
El Salvador, 1982	earthquake, droughts, and flooding	600	20,000	216
Guatemala, 1982	heavy rains and drought	610	10,000	136
Nicaragua, 1982	floods and drought			588
Bolivia, Ecuador, and Peru 1982–1983	El Niño		3,840,000	5,651
Mexico, 1985	earthquake	8,000	150,000	6,216
Colombia, 1985	eruption of Nevado del Ruiz volcano	22,000	200,000	465
El Salvador, 1986	earthquake	1,200	520,000	1,352
Ecuador, 1987	earthquake	1,000	82,500	1,438
Nicaragua, 1988	Hurricane Joan	148	550,000	1,160
Nicaragua, 1992	eruption of Cerro Negro volcano	2	12,000	22
Nicaragua, 1992	Pacific tsunami	116	40,500	30
Costa Rica, 1996	Hurricane Cesar	39	40,260	157
Nicaragua, 1996	Hurricane Cesar	9	29,500	53
Costa Rica, 1997–1998	El Niño		119,279	93
Andean Community, 1997–1998	El Niño	600	125,000	7,694
Central America, 1998	Hurricane Mitch	9,214	1,191,908	6,008
Colombia, 1999	earthquake	1,185	559,401	1,580
Venezuela, 1999	torrential rain	—	68,503	3,237
Belize, 2000	Hurricane Keith	10	57,400	265
El Salvador, 2001	earthquakes	1,159	1,412,938	1,518
Total		84,249	13,625,086	50,365

Source: United Nations Environment Programme and ECLAC, "The Sustainability of Development in Latin America and the Caribbean: Challenges and Opportunities," prepared for Preparatory Conference of Latin America and the Caribbean for the World Conference on Sustainable Development (Johannesburg, South Africa, 2002), table V.2, 99.

The Energy Problem

Migration to the cities also pressures the efficient provision of energy to the population. Energy consumption packs a double environmental whammy. Not only is raw energy a scarce natural resource, but the consumption of energy also generates significant externalities. Table 14.5 dramatically portrays both the rapid rate of growth in demand for energy resources and the North–South imbalance in per capita energy consumption. The growth in energy consumption has been strong over the period 1970–1998. We can see from the data that in countries such as Honduras, Nicaragua, Guatemala, Bolivia, El Salvador, Ecuador, Paraguay, and Brazil per person energy consumption has increased more than 100 percent; the second group, including Colombia, Costa Rica, and Mexico, doubled the 1970–1998 growth rates

Table 14.5.   Energy Consumption per Capita (kg of oil equivalent)

Country	1970	1990	1998	% Change 1970–1998	% Change 1990–1998	% of U.S. per Capita Consumption, 1998
Honduras	191	501	542	162	8	5.42
Nicaragua	253	568	553	125	–3	5.53
Guatemala	170	500	579	194	16	5.79
Bolivia	183	441	581	141	32	5.81
El Salvador	157	527	640	236	21	6.40
Ecuador	216	639	737	196	15	7.37
Colombia	490	765	753	56	–2	7.53
Costa Rica	378	676	789	79	17	7.89
Paraguay	114	734	819	544	12	8.19
Uruguay	797	719	910	–10	27	9.10
Brazil	410	920	1,055	124	15	10.55
Mexico	786	1,492	1,552	90	4	15.52
Chile	867	1,059	1,594	22	51	15.94
Argentina	1,208	1,332	1,726	10	30	17.26
Venezuela	2,206	2,095	2,433	–5	16	24.33
United Kingdom	3,847	3,702	3,930	–4	6	39.30
Japan	2,654	3,552	4,035	34	14	40.35
Germany	3,077	4,478	4,199	46	–6	41.99
United States	7,665	7,720	7,937	7	3	100.00

Source: The World Bank, *World Development Report 1993* (New York: Oxford University Press/World Bank, 1993), 246–47; *World Development Report 2000/2001* (New York: Oxford University Press/World Bank, 2001), 292–94; The World Bank, *World Development Indicators 2001* (New York: Oxford University Press/World Bank, 2001), 152–54.

of Japan and Germany, whereas Argentina has limited increases in per capita energy consumption to under 15 percent and Venezuela and Uruguay have actually decreased consumption.

Low rates of growth of energy consumption are not unambiguously a good thing but may simply reflect a low level of economic development. The use of energy will naturally increase as a country is growing. Growth may result in electrical access for more homes, more appliances for the middle class, and greater industrial requirements. The World Bank projects increased demand for energy in less-developed countries due to growth of populations and per capita incomes, migration to urban areas (substituting energy for fuel wood), and adoption of energy-intensive products (such as fertilizers, petrochemicals, cements, vehicles, appliances, and motors), as well as poor energy efficiency.[41] Higher growth rates of energy consumption are expected at higher income levels. Energy intensity—the amount of energy used to produce a given unit of output—has been rising; in 1999 it took 7 percent more to produce the same output than in 1980, reflecting deterioration in efficient energy utilization.[42] Some of the lower energy consumption rates over the period 1970–1990 can sadly be attributed to severe economic contraction or the dislocation of energy supplies in the Central American war. A bright spot is Chile. Despite strong rates of growth throughout the period, Chileans were able to maintain relatively low rates of per capita energy consumption. The puzzle in this

Table 14.6.   Selected Energy and Carbon Dioxide (CO_2) Emission Indicators

Region	Supply per Capita[b]	Electricity Consumption[c]	CO_2[d]
OECD	4.63	7751.2	10.92
Middle East	2.22	2336.9	5.78
Former Soviet Union	3.06	3617.2	7.56
Rest of Europe	1.91	2925.1	4.83
China	0.84	895.2	2.32
Asia	0.55	508.5	1.03
Africa	0.61	490.5	0.96
Latin America[a]	1.10	1494.6	2.15
World total	1.64	2252.3	3.86

Source: United Nations Environment Programme and ECLAC, "The Sustainability of Development in Latin America and the Caribbean: Challenges and Opportunities," prepared for Preparatory Conference of Latin America and the Caribbean for the World Conference on Sustainable Development (Johannesburg, South Africa, 2002), table IV.14, 89.
[a]The data for Latin America do not include Mexico, which is categorized as part of the OECD.
[b]Tons of oil equivalent per inhabitant.
[c]Kilowatt hours per inhabitant.
[d]Carbon dioxide per inhabitant.

positive story may be resolved by a growth strategy that is accompanied by greater attention to energy efficiency.

Energy planning for efficient use of resources is clearly indicated—perhaps most for the United States! The last column in table 14.5 indicates the percentage of energy a person in each country uses as a proportion of the individual energy use in the United States. On a per person basis, a Brazilian uses approximately 10.55 percent of the electricity of someone living in the United States. Imagine if the Brazilians' appetite for energy continued to grow to emulate their northern neighbors. The demands on the Brazilian balance of payments, not to mention global resources, would be enormous. Conversely, imagine if those living in the United States were able to conserve even a portion of the apparent excess consumption of energy. Energy sustainability requires changing global consumption patterns.

Table 14.6 shows that Latin Americans on average consume roughly a fifth of the energy of people living in Organization for Economic Cooperation and Development (OECD) countries and 30 percent less than the world average. They also produce 5.07 fewer CO_2 units per inhabitant, creating a basis for potential trades in the greenhouse gas reductions. Nonetheless, CO_2 emissions were 34 percent higher in 1999 than in 1980, growing 18 percent between 1994 and 1999. In total, Latin America accounts for 5.4 percent of world greenhouse gas emissions, with the largest share attributed to Mexico and Brazil, registering 53 percent of the region's total. Nonetheless, although these two countries have roughly the same population as the United States, their combined emissions equal only 12 percent of the U.S. total.[43]

In the developing world there are important opportunities for enhancing energy efficiency. Energy sectors in developing countries have been characterized by pricing below costs; concentrated, often inefficient state-held enterprises; companies acting as a direct extension of government, with little distinction between ownership, regulation, and management; high information costs; weak management expertise; and the need for a more transparent regulatory process.[44] Pricing energy to market cost, promoting efficiency at the enterprise level, and increasing transparency in regulatory agencies should, as in Chile, encourage economic growth while holding down energy consumption and costs. There are also opportunities for small-scale changes. Nongovernmental organizations (NGOs) such as Enersol promote grassroots introduction of renewable energy technologies. Encouraging the use of solar-electric systems through financing and technical assistance, as we saw in box 14.1, Enersol helps local organizations install energy systems that are economically and environmentally sustainable over time.[45]

Some countries in the region are energy exporters. The development patterns of Mexico, Ecuador, and Venezuela have clearly been shaped by their oil sectors. In 2000 Venezuela produced approximately 2.95 million barrels of oil per day and Mexico 3.01 million.[46] Measured by known reserves, Mexico ranked ninth in the world in 2000 and Venezuela, a member of the Organization of Petroleum Exporting Countries (OPEC), sixth.[47] Together they account for more than a tenth of the world's reserves of oil.

Although the oil sectors have traditionally been under the arm of state control, foreign participation has recently increased.[48] Oil production can have devastating environmental costs. One analyst estimates that since oil production began in Ecuador in 1972, the trans-Andean pipeline has spilled one and a half times the oil spilled in the *Exxon Valdez* disaster and discharged 4.3 million gallons of toxic waste daily. There has been an increase in skin and intestinal disease, headaches, and fever, with contaminants in drinking water reaching 1,000 times the safety standards set by the U.S. Environmental Protection Agency. This is not to mention the cultural conflict of oil versus indigenous people in the region.[49] Box 14.2 discusses the oil and environment dilemma in Ecuador.

Given problems with the high cost and environmental problems of oil consumption and production, increasingly countries have turned to harness the enormous hydroelectric power in the region. But more needs to be done to offset the environmental costs of energy production and consumption. A strategy to minimize costs and consumption on a global level is critical to sustainable development.

DEFORESTATION OF TROPICAL RAIN FORESTS

Forest covers of 47 percent of the land area in Latin America, extending from the Mexican dry forests to the southern temperate forests of Chile and Argentina, including the Amazon Basin. Among issues relating to the natural environment, perhaps the most well-known and visible problem is the deforestation of the rain forests. A tropical rain forest is defined as an evergreen or partially evergreen forest located in an area that receives no less than four inches of precipitation per month for two out of three years. The mean annual temperature exceeds 24 degrees C with no frost.[50] The Amazon rain forest covers 7 percent of the Earth, has 15 to 20 percent of the unsalted water on the planet, and is home to more than half the world's biological wealth.[51] In addition, rain forests take CO_2 out the atmosphere and are a source of food and medicines as well as recreation.[52]

Box 14.2. Who Is Responsible for Oil Spills in the Ecuadorian Rain Forest?

As Latin America proceeds with the privatization of natural resource development, crucial questions emerge with respect to responsibility for ensuring environmentally safe and sustainable practices.

Ecuadorians in Shushufindi fear the black slime that forms in pools in their backyards and schools. Florinda Balla's cows have died from drinking the sludge thick with arsenic and other toxic wastes. Crops have been lost, and rivers used for drinking, bathing, and fishing have been contaminated by spills and poor extraction practices. The soil is contaminated, its salty crust crumbling when poked with a stick. Trees are defoliated, branches brittle. Roughly 17 million barrels of oil were spilled as 17 billion were extracted from Ecuador's rich petroleum reserves.

Residents are trying to make Texaco accountable for the damage to their ecosystem. The U.S.-based company began operations in Ecuador in 1964 but became a minority partner after the contract 1977 with Petroecuador, the state-owned company. Lawyers for the community group allege that although Texaco was not the lead company, all extraction technologies were under the supervision of the U.S. firm. The case is being filed in U.S. court, for more than a billion dollars in damages and cleanup costs, because the maximum fine for environmental damage in Ecuador is $12,500.

Texaco vehemently denies wrongdoing, claiming that it met all environmental and health regulations at the time, consistent with prevailing international practice. Furthermore, it signed a cleanup agreement with the Ecuadorian government in 1995, although activists charge that treatment has not taken place. Texaco pledged more than $1 million for reforestation, new schools, and medical dispensaries, but improvements have not yet materialized. Other pools with oil spills are not covered by the agreement.

Environmental officials in Ecuador contextualize the damage as a legacy of a pre-environmentally conscious age, and Petroecuador's involvement as following Texaco's instructions.

Texaco, which pulled out of Ecuador in 1990, argues that the responsibility for the remaining problems falls in the government's lap. Policy mistakes, including drawing settlers into the region to strengthen its border with Peru, remain the burden of the government.

The losers appear to be the people of Shushufindi, in the Oriente rain forest. Although Ecuador depends on oil and related products for 44 percent of its national budget, less than 3 percent returns to the region. In the town, fewer than 0.2 percent of the homes have tap water. Oil has done little to alleviate their poverty and immiseration.

How should Ecuador balance the need for foreign investment to develop its natural resources with its obligation to protect the environment? What options do Ecuadorians have when they believe their government is not acting in their best interest? Should environmental standards differ for U.S. citizens and Ecuadorians? Should responsibility for meeting international standards be imposed retroactively in a country?

Source: Adapted from Diana Jean Schemo, "Ecuadorians Want Texaco to Clear Toxic Residue," *New York Times,* 31 January 1998.

The approximately 7 million square kilometers of the Amazon territory cover eight sovereign states with 42,000 kilometers of highways, river networks, and airports.[53] Its expanse houses a great heterogeneity of climates, geological formations, soils, flora, fauna, and cultural history unparalleled in the world. Between five and thirty million existing species are estimated to inhabit the Amazon, of which 750,000 insects, 40,000 vertebrates, 250,000 plants, and 360,000 micro-biota have been identified. Of these, more than 2,000 species of plants have been found as useful for medicinal and nutritive properties and as producers of oils, greases, waxes, varnishes, aromas, tan-nins, saponin, latex, rubber, condiments, and toxins.

The Amazon River, longer than the Nile, is the most powerful river in the world, with considerable hydroelectric potential. Its many rivers, lakes, lagoons, and swamps contain varieties of mam-mals, birds, reptiles, fish, and inverte-brates. It is estimated that the Amazon River supports 2,500 to 3,000 fish species, ten times the number found in the great Mississippi.[54] Although there is some dis-pute as to whether the Amazon is truly the lungs of the earth, it carries approximately one-sixth of the fresh water flowing into the seas from all the rivers of the world.[55]

> **QUESTION FOR THOUGHT**
>
> Many of the environmental problems in Latin America have both domestic and international causes and consequences. Land deforestation, for example, is driven by internal land use forces but also by global demand for forest prod-ucts. Halting deforestation could have global benefits to reduce the pressures on global warming. How much should citizens of North America be willing to pay to help reduce environmental pres-sures in the South? Would you be willing to pay a global environmental tax? How much?

The Amazon's roughly twenty million human inhabitants are likewise diverse—the Indians, rubber tappers, woodland soci-eties engaged in logging and mining, and riverbank people, all with rich cultural tradi-tions. Between 1 and 1.25 million indigenous people of approximately 400 ethnic groups remain after the ravages of disease and displacement of centuries of coloniza-tion. Twenty percent of the Amazonian population is dedicated to farming, and 50 to 60 percent live in cities. Some of the Amazonian cities have suffered a more than fifty-fold increase in population since 1940, overwhelming local infrastructure.[56] The basin contains rich oil reserves as well as bauxite, gold, manganese, copper, and iron. *Garimpeiros,* or gold miners, roughly 30 percent of the basin's population, have attracted a good deal of environmental and social attention for the questions they raise about poverty and wealth and their conflicts with the indigenous peoples and the envi-ronment. The good news is that approximately 90 percent of the Amazon forest and its affiliated ecosystem is in a good state of preservation; nonetheless, it is subject to increasing risk and an accelerated pace of deforestation.

Despite its importance, it should be remembered that the Amazon is not the only forest area under threat in the region. As shown in table 14.7 the fastest rates of deforestation are occurring in Central America; the average annual percentage change of total forest between 1990 and 1995 has been between 2 and 4 percent—3.1 percent in Costa Rica, 3.33 percent in El Salvador, 2.34 percent in Honduras, and 2.65 percent in Paraguay. In the Mesoamerican region, the dry forests have been drastically reduced to only 4 percent of their original area.[57] In contrast to the Amazon basin, where larger commercial interests dominate, land degradation in Central America is tied to the desire of small holders to obtain property rights under uncertain economic conditions.

Natural resources, particularly forests, are being utilized beyond their regenera-

Table 14.7.   Forest Cover and Forest Change in Latin America and the Caribbean, 1980–1995

	Extent of Total Forest (in 1000s of hectares)			Average Annual % Change	
	1980	*1990*	*1995*	*1980–1990*	*1990–1995*
El Salvador	156	124	105	–2.3	–3.3
Costa Rica	1,925	1,455	1,248	–2.8	–3.1
Paraguay	16,886	13,160	11,527	–2.5	–2.6
Nicaragua	7,255	6,314	5,560	–1.4	–2.5
Honduras	5,720	4,626	4,115	–2.1	–2.3
Panama	3,764	3,118	2,800	–1.9	–2.2
Guatemala	5,049	4,253	3,841	–1.7	–2.0
Dominican Republic	1,432	1,714	1,582	1.8	–1.6
Ecuador	14,372		11,137	–1.7	–1.6
Bolivia	55,582	51,217	48,310	–0.8	–1.2
Venezuela	51,768	46,512	43,995	–1.1	–1.1
Mexico	55,423	57,927	55,387	0.4	–0.9
Brazil	600,762	563,911	551,139	–0.6	–0.5
Colombia	57,771	54,299	52,988	–0.6	–0.5
Chile	8,087	8,038	7,892	–0.1	–0.4
Argentina	36,527	34,389	33,942	–0.6	–0.3
Belize	2,048	1,995	1,962	–0.3	–0.3
Peru	70,714	68,646	67,562	–0.3	–0.3

Source: The World Resources Institute, *World Resources 1998–1999* (New York: Oxford University Press, 1998), table 11.1.

tive capacity. This presents particular problems for the poor, with limited access to a resource basis. Causes of deforestation throughout the region include the conversion of land to agriculture (approximately 64 percent of deforestation), commercial logging (18 percent), firewood gathering (10 percent), and cattle ranching (8 percent).[58] Primary agricultural or mining activity is not the only cause of destruction in the region. Secondary destruction results from road construction and the equipment necessary to sustain distant settlements. Inadequate property rights and unequal asset distribution contribute to the destructive human activity in the rain forest region. In the past, unintended policy outcomes were also to blame. For example, in Brazil during the late 1960s and early 1970s, government regional development programs provided incentives to ranchers and other farmers to move into Amazonia to relieve pressure on overcrowded cities. In addition, mining projects such as the Grande Carajas Program accelerated deforestation.[59]

Clearing forested land for agriculture is the main driving force behind deforestation. From 1961 to 2000, land used for agriculture has expanded by approximately 25 percent; with finite quantities of arable land, this has concentrated agricultural production in smaller, more fragile areas of greater ecological significance.[60] The Food and Agriculture Organization (FAO) estimates that some 5.8 million hectares of forests are lost in the region every year, with a yearly rate of .75 percent. However, in most cases agricultural use of these lands is not sustainable due to the generally nutrient-poor soils. The results include erosion and water pollution (especially through pesticide use), leaving behind nonproductive land, and a depleted resource base. The costs of deforestation are not limited to plant life. Of the six to nine million Indians once calling the Amazon home, only remnants of their tribes remain. The twentieth century saw ninety tribes go out of existence.[61] Box 14.3 describes the terrible clash of needs and cultures as local rubber tappers came in contact with the force of ranchers and loggers in the Brazilian Amazon.

BOX 14.3.   CHICO MENDES

On December 24, 1988, the *New York Times* reported the murder of Francisco "Chico" Alves Mendes. At the time of his death, he was the president of the Xapuri Rural Workers' Union and a committed spokesperson for the defense of the Amazon rain forest in Xapuri Acre in northwest Brazil. Chico Mendes became a martyr in the plight to prevent the deforestation of the Amazon forest.

Since the eighteenth century and through World War II, the Amazon was a major source of rubber. It is home to a species of trees from the genus *Havea,* which produces the best rubber in the world. Ninety-five percent of world rubber production comes from these trees, of which there are an estimated 300 million scattered throughout the Amazon and Orinoco River basins.

Until the 1960s, the rubber industry was based on rubber estates operating in a system of debt bondage. Rubber tappers, who were kept illiterate and innumerate, were obliged to sell their product at artificially low prices to the estate owners. Hence, as a son of a rubber tapper, Chico Mendes first went to school in the forest, where he learned the basic plant–animal relationships and the unique method of extracting rubber from *Havea* trees. It was not until the age of twenty that he began to read and write.

In the 1960s, the Brazilian government began to promote the settlement and development of Xapuri Acre by opening the BR-364 road. Incentives were given to cattle ranchers, and estate owners were bought out. The result was the eviction of many rubber tappers and a constant harassment of those who remained. Very often, the tappers were forced to labor for the cattle ranchers, engaging in clear-cutting and slash-and-burn techniques to adapt the land for cattle grazing. Western Brazil became like the American west of the nineteenth century, lawless and without order. Arguments of manifest destiny were used to justify the taking over of the land and the exploitation of its inhabitants.

To protect the rubber tappers and their lifestyle, the Rural Workers Union was founded in the mid-1970s. As the clear-cutting intensified and the evictions increased, the union actively began to stop the destruction of the forest. It assembled tappers and their families as human walls to prevent clear-cutting by cattle ranchers. This classic form of passive resistance was called an *empate,* frequently translated as a stalemate or draw. The *empates* became so successful by 1979 that the ranchers arranged for the murder of the union's founder, Wilson Pinheiro, leaving Chico with the leadership.

In 1985, the National Rubber Tappers Congress assembled in Brasilia to work out alternative development proposals for the protection of the Amazon and the rubber tappers. Chico wanted to justify the *empates* by providing an alternative development strategy for the forest. He came up with the idea of "Extractive Reserves." In the same manner that the Indians' traditional habitat and living style were protected, Chico proposed the creation of reserves to preserve the rain forests and continue rubber tapping.

(continued)

(continued)

Chico's proposal was the weapon that international environmental groups needed to persuade the Brazilian government to slow down the burning of the Amazon. These groups realized that the government might approve because it was not simply another U.S. proposal, but instead was a native initiative undertaken by grassroots groups who wanted to preserve their habitat. Thus, Chico was taken to testify before the Inter-American Development Bank's board of directors. He also met informally with members of the U.S. Senate Appropriations Committee to obtain funds for the protection of the rain forests in Xapuri Acre. In 1987, Chico was awarded the Global 500 Prize from the United Nations and the medal from the Society for a Better World for his fight to preserve Amazonia.

In 1988, the first extractive reserve was put in place in Xapuri Acre. This reserve fell on the land claimed by a prominent cattle rancher who previously had many encounters with the Union's *empates*. On 22 December 1988, the embittered son of this cattle rancher assassinated Chico Mendes in the doorway of his home. His death did not quiet the union but strengthened it by attracting more international attention. Chico Mendes's legacy is the expansion of extractive reserves in Brazil to protect the rain forest and the lifestyle of rubber tappers.

REFERENCES

Mendes, Chico. *Fight for the Forest.* London: Latin American Bureau, 1990.
Shoumatoff, Alex. *The World Is Burning.* Boston: Little, Brown, 1990.
More on Chico Mendes and the Amazon is available at the Environmental Defense Fund
    website at www.edf.org/programs/international/chico/chicotimeline.html.

Throughout the region forest conservation policies have concentrated almost exclusively on tropical rain forests, ignoring highly degraded areas where the value, potential, and possible extinction of species urgently needs evaluating. With the signature of the Amazon Cooperation Treaty in 1978 the countries of the region began coordination of development strategies to promote rational and sustainable use of resources. In addition to national and regional organizations, local and international nongovernmental groups are also active in the region. The good news is that the rate of deforestation has declined from a peak of 22 percent (average annual rate) between 1978 and 1988 to 11.1 percent in 1990–1991. The sad fact is that despite substantial progress, the area destroyed each year is still half the size of the state of Massachusetts.[62] Reforestation efforts have not kept pace with decline; for every hectare planted, twenty-five are deforested. Increasing pressures from population and agriculture and the rising demand for lumber will further threaten Latin America's forests, resulting in a loss of forest quantity and quality.

Forests are not the only ecosystem suffering under the weight of population pressures. *Coastal habitats,* one of the richest sources of marine biodiversity and a vital source of food supply, are threatened by the so-called progress of development. In South America 50 percent of the coastlines are under moderate or high potential threat.[63] Coastal development, overfishing, increased waste disposal, industrial pollution, oil spills, and population density have led to dramatic changes in habitat. A 97-percent increase in the use of fertilizers from 1980 to 1999 has contaminated rural water supplies.[64]

Environmental concerns in Latin America are clearly broad. From city sewage to mangrove swamps, from air pollution alerts to the felling of trees, questions of sustainability abound. Without change in current practice, future generations will not be as well-off. The environmental deficit in the region requires changes in policy formation, institutional capacity, and financing to promote sustainable development. Let's turn to these implementation issues.

POLICY FORMULATION: WHAT CAN BE DONE ABOUT ENVIRONMENTAL PROBLEMS IN THE REGION?

Given the wide range of problems as well as limited resources, what would constitute good environmental policy in Latin America? How can different groups with widely varied interests be brought together in the service of environmental sustainability? Who should pay for a cleaner environment in the region?

Environmental goodwill has been part of the political platform of Latin American governments in the 1990s. Yet progress has sometimes been frustratingly slow. Despite an expansion of pro-environmental legislation in the region and a broader participation by civil society, Latin America remains environmentally vulnerable. Why do policies fail? Policy failures, certainly not limited to the Latin American region, may be attributed to undervaluation of forest resources, inadequate understanding of affected groups, difficulty in analyzing policy impacts, administrative corruption, the lack of synergy among global environmental organizations, and operational difficulties.[65] Ineffective policies, or policies that do not achieve their objectives, most often result from a poor match between ends and means. The policy goal may have been too broad given available resources and institutional capacity. Inefficient policies are policies that could have been achieved at a lower cost. Effectiveness and efficiency gains are necessary to achieve sustainability.

Environmental policies have to make good economic sense to continue over time. Other policy failures have occurred because the goal was unidimensional, focusing on the environment to the exclusion of the economy or the social base. Ignoring gender issues—particularly the ways in which the division of labor by sex, the inequality between men and women in access to productive resources, and the political restrictions on public power that bar women—has limited the positive contributions women can make to sustainable development.[66] Environmental policies must consider the linkages between social, environmental, and economic objectives for success. Intersectoral linkages are also critical; infrastructure, mining, energy, trade, monetary, fiscal, and agricultural policies are linked. In analyzing potential policy outcomes, these complex linkages must be taken into account. Such environmental accounting is extremely tough but vitally important. Although it is difficult to assign monetary value to natural resources, estimate the effects on a variety of social groups, predict direct and indirect linkages, and account for administrative and operational weaknesses, not doing so will further compromise achievements in the environmental arena.

The design of policies can be broken down into three types: **direct government investment, market-based incentives** (MBI), and **command and control measures**

Box 14.4.   MBIs—Market-Based Instruments in Latin American Environmental Policy

BACKGROUND ON MBIs

Market-based instruments (MBIs), policies designed to reduce environmental degradation at the lowest possible social cost, are gaining wider attention in developing countries. Hundreds of individual instruments exist, ranging from fines or sanctions that are linked to traditional command-and-control mechanisms to laissez faire approaches that depend on consumer advocacy. More commonly used mechanisms include tax-and-subsidy approaches. Latin American countries have demonstrated relatively wide experimentation with MBIs. In Brazil, Colombia, and Mexico, credit subsidies are offered for abatement investments in the industrial sector. In Ecuador, taxation and tariff relief is offered for investments on mercury recovery in artisinal mining. Deposit-refund systems for consumers are well established throughout the region as well. Informal collection of beverage and beer cans in exchange for flat fees paid out by recycling operations are growing increasingly popular in Brazil and Venezuela, where beverage-packaging plants are common. Resource use charges, including forestry taxation, as well as water charges for use and pollution, are in place in the region as well.[67]

ORGANIZING FOREST COMMUNITIES IN MEXICO

In the early 1980s, indigenous communities in the poor, mountainous southern states of Mexico—angered by watching their forests degraded by outside loggers—formed a regional organization and succeeded in stopping the government from renewing timber concessions. Many of these communities went on to establish their own community forest enterprises. In 1997, the Proyecto de Conservación y Manejo Sostenable y Recursos Forestales (PROCYMAF), cofinanced by the government and the World Bank, began to operate in the pine-oak forests of the state of Oaxaca.

The project works on a demand basis, assisting 256 communities to become more organized and build capacity. Communities that are not actively engaged in commercial forestry first develop land-use plans and evaluate their land governance systems. Communities that are already engaged in forestry activities use project funds to either develop new management plans, establish new community-protected areas, or explore new business or marketing options. Training courses regularly provide information about silviculture, management, and marketing of wood and nonwood forest products. The project has a separate component that involves private-sector consulting services for communities.

Since the project's start, the area under forest management has expanded from 500,000 to 650,000 hectares, and total wood production has increased from 400,000 to 660,000 cubic meters annually. These communities currently sell their timber to a local door manufacturer at a premium of 15 percent. This new volume generates at least an additional $10 million in value annually. About 1,300 new permanent jobs in forest management and processing have resulted, and an additional 175 jobs have been generated in nontimber forest product activities including mushroom production and freshwater bottling. As a result, the state of Oaxaca is taking in an additional $1 million a year in tax revenue, and communities' social expenditures, apart from salaries and wages, have increased at least $1 million a year.

Forests are also better managed. Some 13,500 hectares of permanent old-growth reserves have been established. Some 90,000 hectares have already been certified by the Forest Stewardship Council.[68]

Roughly one-fourth of the world's poor depend fully or in part on forest resources for subsistence needs. However, many environmental policies designed to preserve the world's forests pose barriers for small, low-income producers. Prices are kept low, effectively limiting their ability to acquire capital and technology and therefore their income opportunities and livelihoods. New strategies must be designed to insure that small forest communities are able to capitalize on their forest assets. Without such strategies forest communities, who own some 25 percent of the world's forests, will have little incentive to protect them for future generations. Strengthening producer organizations, as illustrated in the southern states of Mexico, and establishing business services within Amazon communities can make markets work for local producers while simultaneously promoting sustainable forestry.

VENTURE CAPITAL FIRM BUILDS SUSTAINABLE INDUSTRY WITH AMAZON COMMUNITIES

Small and medium-sized Latin American companies are earning competitive profits while increasing biodiversity with the help of A2R's Terra Capital. The venture capital fund reflects a partnership between Axial RR of Brazil and GMO-RR of Boston. Investment areas include organic agriculture, sustainable forestry, nontimber forest products, ecotourism, and bioprospecting. Several Terra Capital investments involve community-based forestry in the Brazilian Amazon—including a processing plant for heart of palm, a babacu palm processing company, and a large production and processing enterprise for certified sustainable softwood. A2R is committed to improving local livelihoods and conserving forest resources as part of its core business strategy. An interdisciplinary team of financial and technical specialists from A2R visits the enterprises frequently to provide business support.

For example, A2R acquired a financial interest in a heart of palm processing plant on a remote island in Marajo, in the state of Parà, which was suffering from unreliable raw material supply and poor management. A2R helped to resolve local land conflicts and to secure local rights for growing palm fruits, thereby ensuring a regular and secure source for the processing plant. Within three years, the enterprise achieved sales of U.S.$4 million, supporting one hundred factory employees and increasing incomes and assets for 5,000 families in one of the poorest parts of the Amazon. A2R also has helped local people produce the palm fruits more sustainably. They have begun to seek Forest Stewardship Council certification, which would establish the first certification for heart of palm in Brazil.[69]

(CAC). The government may invest directly in infrastructure projects such as waste treatment plants or sewage lines to improve environmental quality. Market-based incentives encourage or discourage certain behaviors. For example, taxes have been used effectively to reduce industrial wastewater in Brazil by almost half, or incentives can reduce the consumption of energy. Box 14.4 demonstrates the wide applicability of MBIs in Latin America. Regulations, or CAC measures, are most effective when the risk to public health is severe and when the number of polluters is relatively limited.[70] When the regulatory arm is used, it is important that legislation be matched by institutional capacity for enforcement. Lofty environmental goals without the ability to implement and enforce regulations only contribute to a lack of credibility in government. A practical, pragmatic policy mix of government investment, CAC, and MBI gradually implemented will better serve long-run environmental interests.

The focus of environmental policy might differ in the rural and the urban sectors. Rural priorities include fuel plantations; tree nurseries; sapling distribution; fuel wood quasi-self-sufficiency; southern carbon sink forests fully paid for by the North; alternative small-scale energy systems such as solar, wind, and biogas; intensification of food production through terraces, fish ponds, and small livestock; perennial crops; wood processing from plantation forests; and improved water supply with wells and low-technology pumps, as well as social organizations and collective action by the poor to improve resource management. In the urban sector, low-technology sanitation; drinking water loss reduction for slums; promotion of cleaner slum fuels (methanol versus charcoal); solar stove and cooker efficiencies; garbage and biogas/methane digesters; garbage prevention; promotion of slum cooperatives and "fair price" shops; health, hygiene, breast-feeding, and family planning education campaigns; and pro bono medical aid for vaccines and oral rehydration, supported by social organization by the urban poor, are possible policy measures.[71]

How should this long list of policy options be prioritized? **Cost-effectiveness** is an important criterion to evaluate alternative policies. For example, water-related illness and death, the largest health impact of urban pollution, can be addressed at a reasonable cost. In contrast, although sewage and sanitation services are often demanded, they may have to be postponed until more vital needs are met. As the technology is available, solid waste problems may be solved by additional resources—but this might come at an opportunity cost to more pressing needs. Cost matters for policies to be sustainable over time. Governments might have the greenest of intentions, but without long-term financing, little of enduring value will be accomplished.

MBIs have the advantage of limiting fiscal impacts on cash-strapped governments. For example, in Argentina a competitive thirty-year concession for the provision of water services was awarded to the private firm Aguas Argentinas. It has expanded the water network to 600,000 new residents, eliminated shortages, and increased potable water production by 26 percent. Reductions in the workforce and better collection policies have transformed the financial performance from losses that strained state budgets to profits for the private provider of services. But market magic did not take place spontaneously. This successful transition to private provision of services was facilitated over a two-year period by a World Bank loan that supported repairs and rehabilitation of the water system as well as a portion of the voluntary retirement program.[72]

Addressing the problem of air pollution involves a mix of regulatory and market policies. Mexico City has a contingency program restricting vehicles and activity of highly polluting industries, including PEMEX refineries, on bad air days. This long-run strategy to substitute low- for high-polluting industries will, however, take time. Using outdated technology, domestically assembled automobiles in Latin America are half as fuel-efficient as best practices in the United States and Japan. The old-style Volkswagen Beetle is still in production in Mexico and Brazil. Only Brazil has succeeded in eliminating lead in gas.[73] Based on Latin American experience, the most cost-effective programs include inspection and maintenance programs to comply with emissions standards; the use of reformulated and alternative fuels (with fuels modified to accommodate seasonal geographical variations); traffic management, including bus policy regulations and liberalization, route restructuring, rationalization of truck and bus sizes, traffic signal improvements, area traffic bans, car pooling, and bikeways; road construction (paving decreases dust) and creating HOV lanes; fuel pricing; and a vehicle emissions tax.[74]

The Chileans used an innovative mix of regulation and market incentives to reduce air pollution levels in Santiago that were reaching critically unhealthy levels about once a week. Ironically, part of the problem had originated in an effort to make transportation more competitive. When bus routes were deregulated, thousands of cheap, old—and polluting—buses were imported. In 1991, 2,600 buses with pre-1972 engines, or 20 percent of the fleet, were banned. More stringent emission standards for new buses and limits on the kinds of buses permitted on downtown routes were implemented. The market came into play through the auction of bus transit rights in the city center. Routes were awarded based on fares to be charged and the type of buses to be operated. In this way private firms could make money through the exclusive right to operate in the downtown area, pollution was to be reduced by regulating the kinds of buses in the downtown area, and low fares would favor the use of public transportation. The result was a reduction in the number of winter days with critical pollution levels by approximately one-third. Although the number of buses permitted in the downtown area was limited, fleets needed fewer vehicles because each bus could make more round trips with reduced congestion. Average fares were reduced by 10 percent, and the auction yielded revenues to finance improvements in dust-reducing paved roads.[75] As described in box 14.5, a controversial example of private initiative arises in the case of Pumalin Park in Chile, where an American businessman proposed the set aside of Chilean lands.

Policies to promote sustainability of small farming in the Amazon likewise involve a mix of the market, direct investment, and regulation. Zoning and promoting settlements only where land is sufficiently productive, taxing capital gains to reduce speculative land sales, placing a stumpage tax on deforestation, diffusing appropriate technology, improving market and storage systems to help small farmers, and establishing credit and other institutions have been found to promote good farming frontiers and to help farmers stay where they are without pressuring virgin areas.[76] Environmental policy requires a partnership between the public and the private sectors.

A critical step toward good environmental policy is incorporating **environmental assessments** (EA) into development policy making. Environmental problems are most often the by-product of the development process. Encouraging environmental accounting before the damage is done will promote the goal of future sustainability. There are three steps in conducting an environmental assessment: data collection, the identification of the problem, and a CBA or cost-benefit analysis. Box 14.6 discusses the CBA technique and its limitations. Data collection is useful in establishing priorities for rational decision making in the environmental area. It is important when identifying the problem that both direct and indirect costs and benefits are included. For example, in assessing the Carajas project in Brazil, the Brazilian mining firm CVRD did a good job of working with FUNAI, the Brazilian Indian Protection Agency, to identify the direct effects on Indian lands. What were not accounted for, however, were the indirect costs. New roads led to squatter settlements that encroached on Indian property and brought new disease into the region. These indirect costs were the greatest source of environmental damage.

BOX 14.5.   PRIVATELY FUNDED CONSERVATION—PUMALIN PARK

On July 7, 1997, the U.S. businessman and environmental philanthropist Douglas Tompkins signed an agreement with former Chilean president Eduardo Frei to open a natural sanctuary in southern Chile. Four years later, however, the final approval is still pending. The 362,180 hectares-large park, which extends from the Argentinian border to the Pacific coast, is designed to protect ancient temperate rainforest and endangered animals. The ecosystem in the region is characterized by snow-capped mountains, crystal-blue glaciers, and meandering fjords, and is home to four-thousand-year-old *alerce* trees, the Andean condor, and the world's smallest deer, the southern *pudu*. Tompkins intends to make the conservation project sustainable by relying on ecotourism and apiculture (a low-impact, high-return agriculture that suits this environment) as primary sources of income. When discussing the plan with President Frei, Tompkins suggested investing U.S.$30 million of his personal fortune, earned as the founder of Esprit and The North Face, into the Pumalin Park project. His only stipulations were that the Chilean Government should commit by contributing a share of state-owned land and turn 100 km of road into Chile's first scenic highway.

Despite Tompkins' generous financial offer, he has since the signing of the agreement met with skepticism and disbelief from various interest groups. Among the rumors are accusations that Tompkins is harassing and underpaying local farmers for their land, building a nuclear base, planning a Jewish colony, developing a secret gold mine, and financing political opposition. Opponents argue that the project will jeopardize national interests and the rights of Chilean entrepreneurs. The Chilean armed forces have claimed that the park could be a threat to national security because it could divide the country in half and that the project would make Chile overly vulnerable due to the unpredictability of foreign direct investment. Meanwhile industries such as forestry, fishing, agriculture, and mining, which consider Pumalin their primary industrial territory, predict that the park will affect them adversely. Chile's minister of national property, Adriana Delpiano, challenges the natural sanctuary by arguing that the land ought to be used for industrial economic development.

The long-term, sustainable development plans for the land is Douglas Tompkins's fundamental concern. Knowing that Chile's "free-market economy is 90 percent based on the export of natural resources," he is particularly concerned with the overexploitation and destruction of Chile's native forest. Instead of wasting its four-thousand-year-old *alerce* trees on wood chip exports, Tompkins aspires to preserve and profit from these rare species through ecotourism. The success of his ambitions depends on the collaboration of powerful Chilean political and entrepreneurial interest groups.

Source: Adapted from "Armed Forces Oppose Tompkins Sanctuary," *Santiago Times,* June 20, 2001; "Natural Preserve," *Geographical Magazine* 73, issue 4 (April 2001): 65; "Tompkins Gets Green Light Pumalin Park to Become Natural Sanctuary," *Santiago Times,* July 3, 2001; "Tompkins Angers Local Politicians Opponents Respond to Allegations," *Santiago Times,* June 28, 2001; and Pablo Camus y Ernst R. Hajek, "Douglas Tompkins: El empresario/ecologista y su polemico proyecto de instalar en Chile el 'parque ecologico privado mas grande del mundo,'" *Ecology and Environment in Chile,* 1998, available online at www.hajek.cl/ecolyma/doc03k.htm.

EA is not cheap and is not always simple. It may be difficult to forecast the benefits of a project. How can one estimate all the benefits of a virgin forest or cleaner air? One approach that attempts to address this problem is called the **contingent valuation** method. A survey is undertaken, asking people's willingness to pay for a given policy. In São Paulo, for example, it was found that people were three times

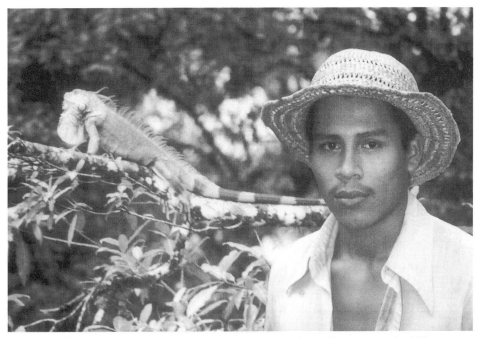

Ecotourism, well managed, can provide local income and contribute to sustainability. *(Courtesy of E. Drew McKechnie.)*

as willing to pay for sewage disposal than for a park.[77] Contingent valuation helps planners assess and measure the benefits of a given environmental project.

An alternative method to a CBA would be a CEA, or a cost-effectiveness analysis. A CEA approach gets around the problem of estimating willingness to pay for future programs by simply ranking projects on a basis of many environmental indicators rather than estimating a dollar benefit. This qualitative assessment, combined with environmental and conventional costs, is a useful, less expensive tool for decision makers. Difficulties in identifying full costs and benefits should not prevent policymakers from insisting on the best possible estimates of environmental impacts. Limited information is better than none at all in accounting for the environment.

Selecting the appropriate combination of policy instruments is a function of the institutional capacity of each country.[78] Policies are not implemented in a vacuum. Different instruments place different demands on the public sector to define a problem, design an instrument, and impose unpopular policies. It is important that agencies develop the technical skills for monitoring ambient conditions and the activities of regulated parties. Accurate data and record keeping are an important basis for the formulation of policy and midcourse corrections. The legal system must be sufficiently sophisticated to cover the forms of pollution discharge, renewable resource damage, and overharvesting that might be the target of policy. Institutions must be financially and technologically capable of turning laws into enforceable rules, with

Box 14.6.   Cost-Benefit Analysis: A Tool for Policy Effectiveness

THE GOAL OF COST-BENEFIT ANALYSIS

Cost-benefit analysis (CBA) is intended to improve public policy decision making. Used to rank policies on the basis of their potential improvements relative to likely costs, this tool helps policymakers select the option that best achieves a specified goal. It encourages decision makers to evaluate alternatives, making the best possible choice for the money. CBA encourages transparency. The enumeration of potential gains and losses versus alternatives encourages open consideration of various options. The framework relies on consistent data collection—and helps identify gaps in knowledge. Ignorance revelation is not an inconsequential outcome in policy making! CBA encourages comparability, encouraging the aggregation of dissimilar effect through the metric of money into one measure of net benefits.

THE FORMULA TO ARRIVE AT A CONSISTENT MEASURE

To arrive at a measure of the costs and benefits of a potential policy, one must list all potential benefits and costs, measured in currency units. This is not an easy task; sometimes it involves imputing a dollar cost on nonmonetized outcomes such as the willingness to pay for clean air. It is especially difficult to impute future gains from policies such as biodiversity, especially when the true risk of not pursuing a policy is unknown. Nonetheless, mathematics lends probability tools and other methods to calculate contingencies for policy outcomes. Risk assessment is a subset of CBA. Statistical techniques can help quantify risks such as the quantitative relationship between pollution exposure and human response. It is important to enumerate not only the direct effects of a program—for example building a road—but also indirect effects—perhaps in bringing disease to indigenous communities.

Once benefits and costs are established in money units, one takes the sum of all the benefits minus the costs, discounting these for future value as well as social gain. One must reduce the value of the future gains by the fact that their benefits may not accrue until some further point in time; there may also be a social discount rate that emphasizes the collective gain from pursuing a public good. The formula is:

$$NPV = \Sigma \, [\text{benefits} - \text{costs}]/[1 + r]^t$$

In the formula, r represents an interest rate (such as a prime rate) adjusted, perhaps for social gain, and t is time or the number of years that the project will produce benefits and costs.

PROBLEMS WITH THE CBA TECHNIQUE

Several problems arise with CBA. Some question the ability to express social well-being as a summation of individual welfare. Individual welfare—based upon the ability of agents to rationally assess preferences—is controversial in itself. Others worry about quantifying economic value when the outcome in question—such as the environment—is a public good. How can this value be measured? Solutions such as willingness to pay or contingent valuation measures are imperfect estimates. Nonetheless, if agencies are clear about the guesses employed in a calculation and estimates are subject to peer evaluation such as through something like the U.S. General Accounting Office, cost-benefit estimates can help policymakers through the very tough task of decision making, especially in the difficult arena of environmental preservation.

AN EXAMPLE OF CBA: SANTIAGO SEWAGE

CBA was used to evaluate whether or not the Chilean government should build sewage treatment plants in Santiago. It was proposed as a costly endeavor—and the investment would have to come from other social-sector investments. To decide if the investment was worth the reduction in waterborne disease, health benefits in terms of mortality (wage compensation and foregone earnings of those dying from cholera and typhoid), morbidity (the cost of illness, including medical outlays, pain and suffering, and averting behavior), production and consumption costs (including the effects on crops, forests, fisheries, and the municipal water supply), valuation of economic assets (such as materials and property values), and environmental assets (recreation use, visibility, biodiversity) were assessed against not only the direct investment costs of the sewage plant but also versus the cheaper alternatives of strict regulation and monitoring of runoff by farmers using untreated water in fertilizing fields. It was concluded that the direct costs of investing in the sewage plant were not compensated for by an estimation of benefits (leaving the option of tough regulation and education as more cost-effective). Nonetheless, when the uncertainties of the indirect reputational effect on sales of Chilean fruits and vegetables in the international market were factored into the formula, the Chileans chose to move ahead with the pricey investment of full treatment of sewage in Santiago.

skilled people to monitor compliance. The political will must be available to impose costs on sometimes powerful agents. The residue of import substitution industrialization and the *latifundia* agricultural system is a legacy of powerful, concentrated firms in both the industrial and agricultural sectors. Is the government willing to take on these dominant interests in exchange for returns that are likely to be diffuse and to spread into the future? Is the government capable of monitoring the urban and rural informal-sector participants contributing to environmental degradation? Strong and independent media are necessary both to present information to the citizenry on environmental costs and to act as a watchdog against corrupt government and business practices. The institutional capacity of government and public institutions in the face of commercial and agricultural interests is a binding constraint on good environmental policy. The use of market-based instruments, for example, is limited by the degree to which efficient market transactions have permeated all levels of economic activity. Countries may need to begin with simpler mechanisms and gradually phase in more complicated mixtures of incentives and tax-based instruments as the institutional capacity to enforce and monitor develops.

ENVIRONMENTAL POLICY AND THE ROLE OF THE STATE

Among our three schools of thought there is general consensus that when negative externalities from growth contribute to environmental degradation, market intervention by the state is warranted. The debate revolves around how much governments should deal with pollution given fiscal, institutional, and technical and monitoring constraints.[79]

Neoliberals would suggest limited intervention, relying principally on the concept "Do no harm." That is, the state should reverse harmful subsidies that promote inefficient energy use, resettlement initiatives that pressure fragile lands and increase deforestation, agricultural supports that encourage the overuse of fertilizers and pesticides, or policies that result in overexploitation of extractive resources or coastal life.

MBIs such as expanding markets for renewable forest products (perhaps Ben & Jerry's Rainforest Crunch or Body Shop natural products) or encouraging tradable permits through the Kyoto Protocol's Clean Development Mechanism (where, for example, a utility in the United States could buy and then not use logging rights in Bolivia, effectively purchasing clean air to offset its greenhouse emissions in Chicago) might also be encouraged by neoliberals. Neoliberals would also suggest that consumer advocacy measures and stockholders voting with their feet would drive away big polluters. MBIs carry the advantage of being cost effective and creating profit incentives for sustainable development.

Neoinstitutionalists would point to deficiencies in institutional capacity in managing environmental problems. Regionally, the implementation of environmental laws in Latin America has outpaced the institutional capability to enforce them. Latin American countries have set up the Forum Ministers of the Environment; their work is supported by an Inter-Agency Technical Committee created in 1999 by ECLAC, the United Nations Development Programme (UNDP), the United Nations Environmental Program (UNEP), the World Bank, and the Inter-American Development Bank (IADB). Subregional trade agreements have incorporated environmental provisions to promote the sustainable use of shared natural resources. Under the North American Free Trade Agreement (NAFTA), the Border Environmental Commissions is an example.

Nonetheless, on a national and regional basis environmental institutions are underfunded and ineffective. Despite a proliferation of divisions of global institutions following the Rio Earth Summit such as the UNEP or World Bank's Sustainable Development Unit, institutional governance is fragmented and weak. One controversial proposal is for the creation of a world environmental organization with powers of sanction like the World Trade Organization. Neoliberal opponents of this idea criticize the effectiveness of global mega-institutions; other critics worry about widening the gap between the environment and economic and social policy.[80]

Neoinstitutionalists would also point to the power of good information in improving market outcomes. They would applaud the developments on the Internet that allow the sharing of best practices—and of negative publicity surrounding polluters. Corporate environmental reports, often encouraged by NGOs and citizen groups, can help in encouraging responsible corporate behavior. Information gaps also persist in providing technical knowledge to firms desiring regulatory compliance. In Mexico, for example, the information gap is being addressed through increased technical assistance and environmental training targeted at noncompliant enterprises.

Neostructuralists would argue for a stronger role for direct investment on the part of the state in improving environmental outcomes. Pointing to market failures to deliver clean water, breathable air, or sustainable agricultural practices, neostructuralists would allocate larger outlays to improving government provision of infrastructure services. Although they would not necessarily reject MBIs, the neostructuralists' distrust of the power of large corporations would lead them toward stronger oversight and investment by the state. The constraint, of course, is financing. Environmental spending competes with other priorities such as health and education. Environmental protection expenditure in the region rarely reaches one percent of GDP, well below the European average of 2.3 percent.[81] Administrative decentralization has resulted in a devolution to provinces or states; municipalities must struggle with the direct costs of water and waste services. One possibility to reconcile budgetary constraints with environmental investments would be through taxes to prevent environmental damage and internalize the social cost of activities, levying charges for the use of natural resources to generate revenues, and designing tax reforms to encourage optimum use of natural resources.[82]

> **QUESTION FOR THOUGHT**
>
> How would a neoliberal, a new institutionalist, and a neostructuralist promote sustainable environmental development in the region?

WHO SHOULD PAY FOR A CLEAN ENVIRONMENT? FINANCING SUSTAINABLE DEVELOPMENT

The biggest constraint on good environmental policy in Latin America is financial. As countries struggle to reduce government budgets, it is difficult to legislate new programs of environmental action. Because the benefits of a clean environment accrue not only to Latin Americans, but also to the global community, this raises the question: How should the burden be shared?

Global financing must be used to strengthen local institutions. To improve the environment in Latin America one must change the behaviors of people—people who live in poor rural communities and in mushrooming megacities. Environmental action, to be sustainable, must empower localities and provide incentives for change.

Environmental policy making involves a wide range of local, national, and international actors, often with conflicting priorities. Addressing local problems will begin to contribute to global solutions. Where such local actions benefit global concerns (such as biodiversity), the developed world should pay. This ought not be perceived as aid but as a responsible policy of paying for environmental change demanded.[83] The responsibilities for sustainable development should be shared by North and South, as both will share in the gains.

Given budget constraints of most governments of the Latin American and Caribbean regions, there are limited resources for conservation projects with more global than local significance. The Global Environmental Facility (GEF) was a three-year experiment set up in 1991 with funds from three sources: a core of $800 million pledged by twenty-four countries, concessional financing of $300 million, and $200 million from the interim trust of the Montreal Protocol. This financial mechanism was replenished with more than $2 billion in 1994 and again in 1998 and 2002 to offer grants and concessional funds in four focal areas: climate change, biological diversity, international waters, and stratospheric ozone. Institutionally, GEF projects are managed through the UNDP, which provides technical assistance for the GEF; the UNEP, which provides the secretariat; and the World Bank, which is responsible for implementation.[84] Countries are eligible for GEF funds if they are eligible to borrow from the World Bank or receive technical assistance grants from the UNDP; they may apply through one of these implementing agencies.

As described in box 14.7, the most ambitious GEF biodiversity project in Latin America draws nine Central American countries together in an effort to consolidate the Mesoamerican biological corridor, a proposed network of protected areas and their buffer zones. In another effort, the GEF Honduras Protected Areas project is working with indigenous communities, particularly focused on the role of women's groups. Its goal is to address the link between natural resource management and women's double workload in the home and in the market. In Argentina a GEF grant is supporting rural electrification through photovoltaics, wind power, and mini-hydroelectric schemes as sustainable sources of energy. A Brazilian program has invested $40 million through the GEF to pioneer the commercialization of electricity-generating technology that uses wood chips from plantation forests for fuel.[85]

Lessons from the first years of GEF project experience indicate that stakeholder participation, especially by affected communities, is essential to change behaviors. NGOs play key roles in conducting participatory appraisals in projects designed to minimize conflicts as land use patterns change. It is also important to engage local scientists, contributing to national scientific capacity. Village-based community projects give local leaders the authority to design and implement successful biodiversity and conservation programs, encouraging self-sufficiency. Recognition of the trade-offs in difficult livelihood choices of communities is important to their resolution in culturally and economically acceptable ways. Finally, lessons indicate that bureaucracies are in need of reform to streamline national environmental policymaking.[86] As the GEF continues to evolve institutionally, its objective is to meet the enormous environmental needs of the developing world with financing from the global community in pursuit of the common goal of sustainable economic practices.

But the GEF is not enough.

Global institutions must work with national environmental agencies to protect the environment. Care must be taken to respect national sovereignty. Some Brazilians, particularly in the military, find the insistent zeal of international environmentalists a threat to national autonomy.[87] They maintain that Brazilians have as much right as the settlers of the Wild West to claim natural resources in the service of growth. Long-run change in the service of sustainable development must take local attitudes and political institutions into account or it will certainly fail over time.

Sustained financing for development is an essential ingredient for sustainable development. The new millennium development goals create additional resources for the implementation of Agenda 21, but more is needed to reach the target of .7 percent of GDP for official development assistance from developed countries. More innovative and efficient mechanisms for financing environmentally sound development strategies are critical to global health. There is a clear need to develop win-win solutions—for communities, nations, and the global system. Institutional deepening to develop an enabling framework for sustainable development is required, built

BOX 14.7.   MESOAMERICA: REVIVING NATURE WHILE MAKING A LIVING

BY FRANK A. CAMPBELL

Imagine a forest cover starting in South America, passing through Central America, and continuing all the way to North America and you've just imagined the way things used to be. Today, unfortunately, this rich manifestation of nature has been reduced to a large number of disconnected forests facing the ongoing threat of destruction.

Just in Mesoamerica—Southern Mexico and the seven countries of Central America—44 hectares of forest are lost every 60 seconds, mostly to satisfy the demand for firewood. If this were to continue unabated, the area would be virtually without forest in a decade and a half. At least 42 species of mammals, 31 species of birds, and 1,541 species of higher plants (not counting algae and mosses, for example) are believed to be en route to extinction.

This is a potential loss of biodiversity that neither the region nor the global community can afford. Although measuring only 768,990 kilometers, accounting for just about half of one percent of emerged lands, this area accounts for about 8 percent of the earth's biodiversity and is numbered among the greatest riches of the world.

Panama alone has 929 species of birds—more than Canada and the United States put together. Belize is only 22,965 square kilometers in area but is home to more than 150 species of mammals, 540 species of birds and 151 species of amphibians and reptiles. Costa Rica, with a smaller landmass than Denmark comprises more than 55 distinct biotic unit—communities of plants and animals with similar life forms and environmental conditions. It houses more than 365,000 species of arthropods (a large group of invertebrates, ranging from tiny mites to large crabs). Yes, that's 1,000 species for every day of the year! There are more than 800 species of orchids in Nicaragua. Some 70 percent of the vascular flora of the high mountains of Guatemala are endemic to that country.

Central America alone has 20,000 to 25,000 vascular plant species. That's as many as in Peru, which is four times as large, or in the United States, which is 15 times as large. Moreover, the principal archaeological sites and remains of the Mayan civilization are located within the Mesoamerican Biological Corridor.

The bad news is that the conservation status of a third of Mesoamerica's 33 ecoregions is judged "critical" and another third is regarded as "endangered." That leaves only one third of the area in an acceptable state of ecological health.

Fortunately, a major "Mesoamerican Biological Corridor" program has been launched to help save the biodiversity of this important corner of the earth's surface. "Today," says an April 11, 2000, note from the program's communications unit, "commences one of the most ambitious environmental and social program to be carried out in the Central America and Southern Mexico region." The goal of the program, the note adds, is the recovery of "the chain of forests that up to a few years ago united South and North America and which at this time appears as a series of barren patches threatened by indiscriminate felling."

This program, headquartered in Nicaragua, does more than project new hope in the environmental area. It projects a new Central America in the political realm. At the formal April 11 launching, Nicaragua's Minister for the Environment and Natural Resources, Roberto Stadthagen, declared, "This initiative reintroduces the Central American region in the world scene as a region of progress and sustainable development. After having been known for conflicts and wars, it emerges now as a brilliant example of international cooperation for peace, democracy and the environment."

Indeed, the Mesoamerica Biological Corridor program represents a study in international cooperation at the wider level. In his speech at the launching, Nicaraguan President Arnoldo Alemán expressed special recognition and appreciation to the Global Environ-

(continued)

(continued)

ment Facility (GEF), the United Nations Development Programme (UNDP) and the German government for their support for the program. GEF, for example, is contributing almost $11 million and this investment is being overseen on the ground by UNDP. Among other sources of support for the effort are the World Bank and DANIDA, the Danish Government aid agency.

The need for such an international collaboration for the rescue of nature in the region became more and more evident over the years as each country developed institutions, usually at the ministerial level, in a valiant effort to meet the twin challenges of economic poverty and environmental degradation. In the course of the last 30 years, the governments of Mesoamerica established 461 separate protected areas. These covered as much as 31 percent of the territory (in Belize) and as little as 2 percent (in Honduras, Nicaragua, El Salvador and Mexico).

Regionally, these protected areas totaled 18 million hectares. Only half of the protected areas had any kind of staffing. Some 88 percent were without any management plans. Most are not even well demarcated. Only about 40 of the 461 have been host to research programs. Few have at their disposal the institutional and legal frameworks to facilitate either biodiversity conservation or the sustainable production of goods and services to meet the region's development needs.

Moreover, 270—over half—are too small to make a meaningful impact on biodiversity without links to other protected areas. Hence the importance of the new approach to regional cooperation in Mesoamerica. This approach actually goes back at least as far as 1989 when Central American presidents signed the Central American Environmental Protection Agreement and established the Central American Commission on Environment and Development (CCAD). Since then, a culture of cooperation has characterized the work of environment ministries in the region. That the region speaks with one voice on environmental matters has been obvious from the development of the Central American Environmental Agenda. This agenda formed the basis for joint regional positions at the 1992 Rio Summit.

CCAD, elevated to an environmental secretariat within the Central American Integration System (SICA), a revived regional integration movement, has been instrumental in strengthening the united regional voice at international fora. It has also helped strengthen the countries' environment ministries and has been the prime mover behind a number of regional activities, including the Mesoamerican Biological Corridor initiative.

While directed towards revitalizing the natural corridor from Mexico in the north to Panama in the southeast, the initiative, according to its website, "is by no means focused exclusively on protecting the animals, plants and microorganisms which inhabit the tropical forests, but will provide benefit on a priority basis to the people who live there, to all Mesoamericans and, by extension, to the entire world."

To achieve all these things, the program is being built upon two main pillars. The first and better known is biodiversity conservation. This includes strengthening the existing protected areas and building links among them.

The second pillar is the sustainable use of the resources of the region. Rather than focusing on a policing role by telling people what they cannot do with the forests, for example, the program will educate them on what they can do and how they can do it without causing ecological harm. Environmentally friendly agricultural pursuits—including organic food production—as well as ecotourism, pharmaceutical prospecting and reforestation have been identified as possible areas of activity and investment.

The region's governments hope that through the revival of the forests, they will contribute their "grain of sand," to borrow the words of Minister Stadthagen, to help reverse the trend of global warming.

In summary, the supporters and managers of the program hope that by their efforts to recreate the future, they will make it easier to imagine it. UNDP's Carmelo Angulo sought to capture this vision of the future for the benefit of participants at the launching of the program.

"Personally," said Angulo, "I wish to imagine many of those here present, within six years, when the evaluation of the successes and advances achieved by this great regional program is being carried out. I am completely certain that in that moment the region will have changed for the better, the panorama of human development will be clearer, and new opportunities will have opened so that a lasting and worthwhile life will be accessible to all."

upon consistent and transparent regulatory regimes. A clean environment is an international public good with global benefits; developing countries can only fulfill sustainable development goals with adequate financing, debt relief, technology transfer, and poverty eradication—a tall order, but a necessary one.

Key Concepts

Agenda 21
command and
    control measures
contingent
    valuation
cost-effectiveness

direct government
    investment
environmental assessments
Global Environmental
    Facility
market-based incentives

safe minimum standard
sustainable development
urbanization
World Summit on
    Sustainable
    Development

Chapter Summary

Sustainable Development

- Sustainable development requires the recognition of environmental, economic, social, and political concerns. Problems of measurement, the uncertainty of future technological change, and the political will on local, national, and international levels complicate the implementation of sustainable policies.

Environmental Problems in Latin America

- Poverty perpetuates environmental degradation. The poor are both agents and victims of unsafe environments. Urbanization in Latin America exacerbates environmental problems including insufficient garbage collection, increasing air pollution, and inadequate water supply.

- High energy consumption can be environmentally unsustainable. While energy is scarce and produces negative externalities, it is crucial for economic growth. Pricing energy at market cost, promoting efficiency at the enterprise level, and increasing transparency and regulatory agencies should encourage economic growth while holding down energy consumption and costs. The alarming rate of deforestation is caused by conversion of land to agriculture, commercial logging, firewood gathering, and cattle ranching.

Environmental Policy

- The most effective type of environmental policies are those that combine direct government investment, market-based incentives (MBI), and command and control (CAC) measures. Environmental policymakers should recognize the differences between rural and urban environmental concerns. Governments should evaluate the cost-effectiveness of alternative environmental policies and make choices accordingly. Furthermore, when formulating sustainable development policies, environmental assessments (EA) should be used to analyze the environmental implications of projects before they are implemented. Sustainable development policies can be costly. Cooperation between local, national, and international organizations is needed to attain the goal of sustainable development.

Notes

1. World Commission on Environment and Development, *Our Common Future* (Oxford: Oxford University Press, 1987), 43.

2. Adapted from Mohan Munainghe and Wilfrido Cruz, *Economy Wide Policies and the Environment: Lessons from Experience* (Washington, D.C.: World Bank, 1995).

3. World Commission on Environment and Development, *Our Common Future*, 8.

4. Dennis Pirages, "Sustainability as an Evolving Process," *Futures* 26, no. 2 (1994): 197–205.

5. Salvadoran representative to the PrepCom for the WSSD. Wendy Jackson, "ECLAC Final Summary," *Earth Negotiations Bulletin* published by the International Institute for Sustainable Development (IISD) VI, vol. 22, no. 06, Saturday, 27 October 2001. Online at: www.iisd.ca/linkages/2002/wslac.

6. John M. Antle and Gregg Heidebrink, "Environment and Development: Theory and International Evidence," *Economic Development and Cultural Change* 43, no. 3 (April 1995): 604.

7. Jerry Taylor, "The Challenge of Sustainable Development," *Regulation* 17, no. 1 (1994): 35–50.

8. Michael A. Toman, "Economics and 'Sustainability': Balancing Trade-offs and Imperatives," *Land Economics* 70, no. 4 (November 1994): 399–413.

9. ECLAC, *Globalization and Development*, 29th Session, Brasilia, Brazil, May 6–10, 2002: 260.

10. Robert Goodland and Herman Daly, *Poverty Alleviation Is Essential for Environmental Sustainability,* World Bank, Environment Department, Divisional Working Paper no. 1993-42 (Washington, D.C.: World Bank, 1993).

11. Population Division of the Department of Economic and Social Affairs of the United Nations Secretariat as found at the World Resources Institute website earthtrends.wri.org.

12. World Resources Institute, *World Resources, 1996–7* (New York: Oxford University Press, 1997), 3.

13. Henry Lee and Gustavo Merino Juarez, "Cancún, Mexico: Water System Privatization," Harvard University, JFK School of Government case #1593, August 2000.

14. United Nations Centre for Human Settlements (Habitat), *State of the World's Cities, 2001,* available online at www.un.org/ga/Instanbul+5/statereport.htm.

15. Data from World Resources Institute, *World Resources 1994–5* (New York: Oxford University Press, 1995).

16. United Nations Environmental Program, *Global Environment Outlook 2000,* available online at www.grida.no/geo2000.

17. "Latin America Struggles to Find Solutions to Megacity Woes," *Agence France Presse,* 2 June 1992. Available online in the LEXIS-NEXIS database.

18. World Resources Institute, *World Resources, 1996–7,* 23.

19. Diego Cevallos, "Environment-Mexico: Toxic Waste, a Dirty Problem," *Inter Press Service,* 11 August 1995. Available online in the LEXIS-NEXIS database.

20. World Resources Institute, *World Resources, 1996–7,* 70.

21. UN, ECLAC, and UNEP, "Report of the Preparatory Meeting of the Southern Cone for the World Summit on Sustainable Development," Santiago, Chile 14–15 June 2001, 14 September 2001.

22. "Toward an Environment Strategy for the World Bank Group," Progress Report/Discussion Draft, April 2000. Available online at lnweb18.worldbank.org/essd/essd.nsf/Global View/Consultationdraft.pdf/$File/Con sultationdraft.pdf.

23. John Dixon, *The Urban Environmental Challenge in Latin America,* LATEN Dissemination Note no. 4, World Bank Latin America Technical Department, Environment Division (Washington, D.C.: World Bank, 1993), 8.

24. "Environmental Protection in an Era of Dramatic economic Growth in Latin America," Hearing before the Subcommittee on Western Hemisphere, Peace Corps, Narcotics, and Terrorism of the Committee on Foreign Relations, United States Senate, One Hundred Sixth Congress, Second Session, July 25, 2000. Washington: U.S.G.P.O.: 2001. Available online at frwebgate.access.gpo.gov.

25. Margolis, cited by Dixon, *The Urban Environmental Challenge,* 9.

26. Dixon, *The Urban Environmental Challenge,* 19.

27. UNEP, "The Sustainability of Development in Latin America and the Caribbean: Challenges and Opportunities," prepared for the Regional Preparatory Conference of Latin America and the Caribbean for the World Conference on Sustainable Development (Johannesburg, South Africa, 2002).

28. Data from World Resources Institute, *Earth Trends,* 2002, available online at earthtrends.wri.org.

29. Dixon, *The Urban Environmental Challenge.*

30. Asif Faiz, Surhid Gautam, and Emaad Burki, "Air Pollution from Motor Vehicles: Issues and Options for Latin American Countries," *The Science of the Total Environment* 169 (1995): 303–10.

31. World Bank, *Energy Efficiency and Conservation in the Developing World: The World Bank's Role* (Washington, D.C.: World Bank, 1993), 66.

32. UNEP 2001 unpublished paper as presented in ECLAC and UNEP, "The Sustainability of Development in Latin America and the Caribbean: Challenges and Opportunities,"

Regional Preparatory Conference of Latin American and the Caribbean for WCSD, Rio de Janeiro, 23–24 October 2001: 77.

33. ECLAC and UNEP, "The Sustainability of Development," 79.

34. Faiz, Gautam, and Burki, "Air Pollution," 303–10.

35. World Resources Institute, *World Resources, 1996–7,* 82.

36. ECLAC and UNEP, "The Sustainability of Development," 78.

37. "Mexico City: A Topographical Error," *Environment* 36, no. 2 (1994): 25–26.

38. World Resources Institute, *World Resources, 1996–7,* 47.

39. "Environmental Protection in an Era of Dramatic Economic Growth in Latin America," hearing before the Subcommittee on Western Hemisphere, Peace Corps, Narcotics, and Terrorism of the Committee on Foreign Relations, United States Senate, One Hundred Sixth Congress, Second Session, July 25, 2000. Publisher Washington: U.S.G.P.O. (U.S.G.P.O., Supt. Of Docs., Congressional Sales Office, distributor), 2001. Available online at frwebgate.access.gpo.gov.

40. "Challenges and Opportunities for Sustainable Development," *CEPAL News* XXI, no. 11 (November 2001): 3. Available at www.eclacwash.org.

41. World Bank, *Energy Efficiency.*

42. ECLAC and UNEP, "The Sustainability of Development in Latin America and the Caribbean: Challenges and Opportunities," 88.

43. ECLAC and UNEP, "The Sustainability of Development in Latin America and the Caribbean: Challenges and Opportunities," 91.

44. ECLAC and UNEP, "The Sustainability of Development in Latin America and the Caribbean: Challenges and Opportunities," 38.

45. Visit Enersol's website at www.enersol.org to learn about some of its projects. Following Hurricane Mitch, for example, Enersol worked to install ultraviolet water disinfection systems to provide clean water.

46. Energy Information Administration, *International Petroleum Monthly,* World Crude Oil Production, 1970–2001, tables 4.1a and 4.1c, available online at www.eia.doe. gov/emeu/ipsr/supply.html.

47. Energy Information Administration, *International Energy Annual 1999* (Washington D.C., 2001), table 8.1. (Original Source: PennWell Publishing Company, *Oil and Gas Journal.*)

48. "Energy in Latin America: Even Oil Is Growing Less Sacred," *The Economist,* 1 June 1996, p. 63.

49. Judith Kimerling, cited by Suzana Sawyer, "Indigenous Initiatives and Petroleum Politics in the Ecuadorian Amazon," *Cultural Survival* (Spring 1996): 27.

50. John Vandermeer and Ivette Perfecto, *Breakfast of Biodiversity: The Truth about Rain Forest Destruction* (Oakland, Calif.: Institute for Food and Development Policy, 1995), 19.

51. Commission on Development and Environment for Amazonia, *Amazonia without Myths* (Washington, D.C.: IADB, 1992), xii.

52. Vandermeer and Perfecto, *Breakfast,* 3.

53. The countries and the percentage held of the Amazon are as follows: Bolivia (11.20 percent), Brazil (67.79 percent), Colombia (5.52 percent), Ecuador (1.67 percent), Guyana (0.08 percent), Peru (13.02 percent), and Venezuela (0.72 percent). Suriname and the territory of French Guiana are considered to be part of the "greater Amazon," not countries of the hydrographic watershed (Commission on Development and Environment for Amazonia, *Amazonia without Myths*).

54. Goulding in Bradley Bennett, "Plants and People of the Amazonian Rainforests: The Role of Ethnobotany in Sustainable Development," *BioScience* 42, no. 8 (1992): 599.

55. Commission on Development and Environment for Amazonia, *Amazonia without Myths,* 6.

56. Commission on Development and Environment for Amazonia, *Amazonia without Myths,* 37.

57. CIAT 1998 in the *Global Environmental Outlook 2000,* Latin American and the Caribbean, online at www.grida.no/geo2000.

58. First appeared in Brian Johnson, *The Great Fire of Borneo: Report of a Visit to Kalimantan-Timur a Year Later, May 1994* (London: World Wildlife Fund, 1991); also see Carlos Alberto Primo Braga, "Tropical Forests and Trade Policy: The Case of Indonesia and Brazil," in *International Trade and the Environment,* ed. Patrick Low (Washington, D.C.: World Bank, 1992), 177.

59. Braga, "Tropical Forests," 178.

60. Food and Agriculture Organization (FAO), www.fao.org.

61. Commission on Development and Environment for Amazonia, *Amazonia without Myths.*

62. Phillip Fearnside, "Deforestation in Brazilian Amazonia: The Effect of Population and Land Tenure," *Ambio* 22, no. 8 (December 1993): 542.

63. World Resources Institute, *World Resources, 1996–7,* 250.

64. ECLAC, *Statistical Yearbook for Latin America and the Caribbean 2001,* table 357, p. 684, accessed at www.eclac.org.

65. Hernán Cortés-Salas, Ronnie de Camino, and Arnoldo Contreras, *Readings of the Workshop on Government Policy Reform for Forestry Conservation and Development in Latin America,* June 1–3, 1994 (Washington, D.C.: Inter-American Institute for Cooperation on Agriculture, 1995).

66. Maria Nieves Rico, "Gender, the Environment and the Sustainability of Development," Women and Development Unit, ECLAC discussion paper, Serie mujer y Desarrollo no. 25, October 1998.

67. Richard M. Huber, Jack Ruitenbeck, and Renaldo Seroa DaMotta, "Market-Based Instruments for Environmental Policy Making in Latin America and the Caribbean: Lessons Learned from Eleven Countries," World Bank Discussion Paper no. 381 (Washington, D.C.: World Bank, 1998).

68. Excerpted from Scherr, White, and Kaimowitz, "Making Markets Work for Forest Communities." Original source: PROCYMAF (2000). Proyecto de conservación y manejo sostenable de recursos forestales en México. Informe y avance 1998–2000. Misión de avaluación de medio terino. SEMARNAP, Mexico; B. DeWalt, F. Olivera, and J. Betancourt Correa *Mid-term Evaluation of the Mexico Community Forestry Projects* (Washington, D.C.: World Bank, 2000).

69. Excerpted from Scherr, White, and Kaimowitz, "Making Markets Work for Forest Communities." Original source: Moles, P, A2R, personal communication, 2000.

70. World Bank, *Environment and Development in Latin America and the Caribbean: The Role of the World Bank* (Washington, D.C.: World Bank), 21.

71. Goodland and Daly, *Poverty Alleviation,* 28.

72. World Bank, *Privatization Principles and Practice,* IFC Lessons of Experience Series (Washington, D.C.: World Bank, 1995), 44.

73. Faiz, Gautam, and Burki, "Air Pollution," 303–10.

74. Faiz, Gautam, and Burki, "Air Pollution," 303–10.

75. World Bank, *Environment and Development.*

76. Anna Luíza Ozório de Almeida and João S. Campari, *Sustainable Settlement in the Brazilian Amazon* (Oxford: Oxford University Press, 1995), 75–80.

77. World Bank, *Environment and Development.*

78. The argument for this paragraph is distilled from Clifford S. Russell and Philip T. Powell, *Choosing Environmental Policy Tools: Theoretical Cautions and Practical Considerations,* no. ENV-102 (Washington, D.C.: Inter-American Development Bank, June 1996).

79. Environmental policy measures regarding the state are extracted from Allen Blackman, Mitchell Mathis, and Peter Nelson, "The Greening of Development Economics: A Survey," Resources for the Future Discussion Paper 01-08, January 2001, and then applied to our three schools of thought.

80. ECLAC, Globalization and Environmental Sustainability, in *Globalization and Development,* 29th session report, Brasilia, 6–10 May 2002, 281.

81. ECLAC/UNDP, *Financing for Sustainable Development in Latin America and the Caribbean,* Joint document prepared for the World Summit on Sustainable Development, August 2002.

82. ECLAC, Globalization and Environmental Sustainability, 281.

83. World Bank, *Environment and Development.*

84. More on the GEF is available at www.gefweb.com.

85. Mohamed T. El-Ashry, *Statement to the Fourth Session of the Conference of the Parties to the United National Framework Convention on Climate Change,* Buenos Aires, 11 November 1998 (Washington, D.C.: Global Environment Facility, 1998). El-Ashry is CEO and chair of the Global Environment Facility.

86. "Participation Means Learning through Doing: GEF's Experience in Biodiversity Conservation and Sustainable Use," GEF Lessons Notes 12, July 2001, 1–4. Available at ww.gefweb.org.

87. Margaret E. Keck, "Dilemmas for Conservation in the Brazilian Amazon," Environmental Change and Security Project Report, Woodrow Wilson International Center for Scholars, Issue 7:33.

CHAPTER FIFTEEN

LESSONS LEARNED

Cycles in Latin American Development

The devastation of Hurricane Mitch underscored the fragility of life, especially for the poor. *(Courtesy of David Mangurian and the Inter-American Development Bank.)*

Nearing his seventy-second birthday, Colombian Nobel laureate Gabriel García Márquez bought a newspaper company, *El Cambio*. He jokingly noted that after his 1982 Nobel Prize, no one would employ him as a journalist because he was too expensive. His reentry into journalism has promoted a greater spirit of open press in his native country, a critical component of accountable government policy. Unfortunately, the magical realism of his novels finds stark parallels in contemporary life in Latin America, giving him much to write about. As he said in a *New York Times* interview describing his political activism as a writer, his engagement in critical issues is driven by the fact that "underdevelopment is total, integral, it affects every part of our lives."[1] Life has imitated art in Latin America.

Many of the political obstacles to underdevelopment that concerned Marquez at the time of his award have changed. Most importantly, the region has gone from one dominated by repressive military regimes to one of open democracy. The economic model has radically been altered from state-centered import substitution industrialization to a market-driven approach. But political and economic openness have not yet transformed the devastating landscape of underdevelopment in the region. The cycle of poverty and oppression in Marquez's literature and his contemporary world remain a sad reminder of unresolved developmental challenges. Social protest and strikes mark the degree of dissatisfaction that many Latin Americans feel regarding the lack of improvement in their material lives. Sixty percent of Latin Americans think the economy is in trouble, and 70 percent see no hope for improvement in the near future. Seventy-five percent perceive themselves as poorer today than five years ago, and 86 percent believe income distribution is unjust. Two out of three are dissatisfied with the results of democracy.[2] Such dismal views complicate the generation of confidence in the future of the region. Social protest and strikes across Latin America register the level of dissatisfaction with the neoliberal development model. Regional output contracted in the first half of 2002 by 2.5 percent, and financial conditions are extremely fragile.

As an example of the cycles of poverty, consider the challenges facing Honduras and Ecuador as they move into the twenty-first century. Honduras, along with its Central American neighbors, was ravaged by Hurricane Mitch late in 1998. Decades of development were turned back by this powerful storm. Schools and hospitals were decimated, and the loss of life was staggering. Swelling rivers washed away homes, farms, and factories. Honduras lost export crops such as bananas, coffee, shrimp, and melons; its small farms have no arable soil left to grow sources of domestic sustenance, including rice and corn.

Honduras was terribly unlucky to be in the path of Mitch, but its own development path had made it more vulnerable to the destruction of the storm. Its fragile ecosystem, weakened from overfarming, overlogging, and overpopulation, left little resistance to wind and water. As noted by Edwin Mateo Molina, a Honduran sociologist specializing in environmental issues for the Inter-American Development Bank (IADB), "Everyone realizes that the damage was magnified by the misuse of resources. It will happen again, and will be even worse unless we look for a way to use the land in a more responsible manner."[3]

In Argentina the damage has come from political and economic forces as opposed to those from nature. Argentina has gone from the darling of international capital markets to a financial pariah. Successive economic shocks from the Asian, Russian, and Brazilian crises of 1998–1999 combined with the devaluation of the Brazilian *real* took their toll on a banking structure riddled with debt. A fall in the terms of trade of Argentina's exports further pressured external adjustment. Unsustainable domestic public sector finances—particularly pension commitments by the powerful provinces—compounded the crisis. Argentine credibility evaporated, and capital markets closed as political risk escalated. Last-ditch efforts to cut public sector wages and reduce government expenditures were insufficient to generate confidence in the Argentine economy. In November of 2001 the government announced a restructuring of debt—but this was not enough to forestall default on $140 billion of bonds to private investors. Argentina was forced to break its 1991 convertibility law linking the *peso* to the dollar after high unemployment and negative growth sent protestors to the streets. Argentina faces enormous political and economic challenges in reconstructing what had once been among the most prosperous economies in the world.[4] Its output is expected to contract at twice the level of the Great Depression; investment has fallen sharply, and unemployment hovers at a staggering 25 percent. Argentina is suffering an economic contraction unprecedented in its economic history.[5]

The news is not, however, all bad. After a decade of economic reform, Latin America is more squarely following a sustainable development path. Decentralization has placed more power in the hands of local governments. Women and indigenous groups have achieved greater recognition in the design of development strategies, although many tangible gains will accrue only over time. Environmental projects have sprung up throughout the region to support sustainable practices. Macroeconomies are better balanced, and the region is integrating through bilateral and regional accords. Cycles have persisted, but Latin America may have reversed some of the practices promoting downward cycles and replaced them with new directions in its unfolding development story.

CHALLENGES FOR DEVELOPMENT POLICY IN LATIN AMERICA REVISITED

In thinking about the progress and the prospects of development in Latin America, we will find it useful to recall the five critical issues for development policy in Latin America introduced in chapter 1:

- How can a balance be achieved between internal and external constraints on development?
- How can change be promoted even as stability is encouraged?
- Whose interests should economic policy serve—the needs of the poor or the investment requirements of the industrialists?
- What role should the state play in promoting a development agenda? What are the appropriate roles for the market?
- How should the needs of people today be addressed while leaving future generations as well-off?

We noted that it is important to understand how economies have resolved these issues to avoid negative historical cycles. What have we learned from our study of Latin American economic development with respect to how these issues have been dealt with across the different periods of development? What lessons can we bring to bear on understanding whether the future of economic development in the region will reflect the cycles of the past?

THE ECONOMIC LABORATORY OF LATIN AMERICA

Latin America has been a virtual economic laboratory to analyze imbalances across the domestic and international sectors. Our study of import substitution industrialization showed that an internal focus was implemented because of the dissatisfaction with the primary product export model in the late 1880s and early 1900s. Despite comparable starts, it appeared that the region was falling behind relative to Europe and North America. The surprising progress of Latin America as it was isolated during World War II from the international economy led analysts to believe that international capitalism was a cause of the underdevelopment of the region. According to the dependency theorists, powerful industrial countries were draining Latin America of its wealth. Alliances between elites in the center and the periphery perpetuated a model that privileged a few but immiserized the masses. Patterns of asset distribution in large *latifundia* or estate production determined by colonial decree were reproduced in industrial circles. Internal dynamism was lacking, with weak linkages between the export-oriented agricultural sector and the fragile and thin industrial sector. Technological prowess was building in the North, to the exclusion of the South. The perception was that the international economy was strangling dynamic domestic development.

To move beyond dependent development, import substitution industrialization constructed the state as the defined agent of change. Employing planning tools and the aggressive arm of state-led firms, governments opened new sectors to industrial activity. A focus on linkages and breaking down bottlenecks of production led the state to target key sectors. High tariffs kept multinational firms at bay, unless special technological licensing agreements or local production were negotiated to provide critical inputs of production. Monetary policy was essentially passive, with central banking authorities accommodating the expansionist thrust of the model. An initial euphoria surrounded the ability to promote development in the region. The ambitious plan to build Brasilia, moving it inland as a heartland capital to integrate diverse regions, was a symbol of the unbounded power of state energy. New light and heavy manufacturing sectors developed to meet the needs of domestic consumers. The labor movement strengthened, as unions promoted workers' rights. Public utilities were expanded, providing electricity and telephone services throughout the region. Ambitious projects such as the trans-Amazonian highway and the Itaipu Dam were begun with financing from capital markets bullish on Latin America. Latin American nations were transforming their economic landscape.

Unraveling Import Substitution Industrialization

But signs of disequilibrium began to surface. Balance of payments accounts were pressured by the need to import costly intermediate machinery for final goods production. As import bills surged, the exchange rate bias worked against exports. The state's attempt to do too much too fast resulted in an inflationary tendency in the economy. Rapid change meant frequent supply shortages, and state-led megaprojects required high levels of public finance. Powerful firms and powerful unions passed cost increases around. It was not a total coincidence that as the economies began to twist and crack, militaries around the region were called by industrial elites to govern and maintain order and progress. Stability was threatened by an uneven and unbalanced development process.

Given highly unequal income distributions and a model that had promoted a new urban privileged class, it was risky to begin tinkering too much with the internal and external balance. Rapid structural change made the management of economic outcomes unpredictable. Populist policies to buy off labor and business without strong regard for external constraints dominated the region. Corruption was encouraged by the ability of agents within the state to control economic property rights. Many abused privileges for personal gain in protected state jobs. Quotas on foreign exchange or technology import licenses led to under-the-table payments to grease the economic wheels. Sadly but predictably, the poor were largely neglected, the rural sector was nearly abandoned, and the environment was devastated.

International price shocks dislodged the inward-looking system of import substitution industrialization. Global interest rate hikes to restrain worldwide inflation triggered a massive debt crisis across the region. Countries faced default in adjusting to high real interest rates after the artificial luxury of low to negative rates over several years. External constraints became overwhelming when the price of international capital rose. Consumption or investment imports could no longer be cheaply financed. Countries could no longer support living beyond their means. A radical reorientation of the development model was required.

Neoliberal Reforms

Import substitution industrialization was replaced by variants of the neoliberal model throughout the region. The state itself was delegitimized as the economic guardian. Instead, markets became the primary allocators of resources. State spending was slashed to maintain fiscal balance, and state firms were privatized to promote profit and efficiency as the way to provide goods and services in the market. Privatization created enormous profit potential, which enticed international capital back to the region. Tariff walls came tumbling down, exposing firms to competition in the international market. Openness to international competition rooted out inefficiencies in production, and formerly protected firms scrambled to find new market niches. Nontraditional exports penetrated new markets. Agriculture and agro-industries got a boost from international demand. Cheaper imports from the global market provided consumers with new choices of goods at lower prices. Multinational firms established local production to meet the needs of consumers with real purchasing power for the first time in years. As countries looked outward and a democratic revolution swept the hemisphere, subregional integration efforts gained momentum. The external sector was again seen as the engine of development.

Latin American nations once again became darlings of international capital. With inflation in retreat throughout the region and democratic governments installed in all nations save Cuba, stability encouraged investor confidence. Money flowed back to the region, this time through bond and stock markets rather than commercial bank lending. Foreign direct investment blossomed because multinationals were enthusiastic about long-term development prospects. Not every country, however, benefited equally. Larger countries attracted the bulk of capital while smaller and poorer economies struggled. Nonetheless, the experiences of countries such as Costa Rica demonstrate that small countries that have invested in technology and work-force development can indeed succeed.

The Compelling Social and Environmental Agenda

Opening to the external economy also exposed weaknesses in the domestic political economy. Global attention to environmental and social issues promoted by new actors on the global stage, the nongovernmental organizations, directed some attention to issues of sustainable development and labor standards. Protests on the negative social and environmental effects of IMF- and World Bank–type conditionality packages led to a rethinking of the sustainability of short-term stabilization measures. Short-term export targets for the release of funds resulted in further deforestation; sweatshops started to spring up throughout the region as multinationals took advantage of cheaper, often female labor. In response to international outcries, new units were set up in multilateral organizations to safeguard environmental concerns and promote the interests of the least advantaged in society. Greater attention was paid to issues of gender and ethnicity in development. Recognition of the economic and social contributions of women and indigenous peoples began to inform decision making. But institutional change is slow and incomplete, and the intermediate environmental and social costs have been high.

There was an extraordinary degree of financial dislocation in the process of rapid transformation from closed to open economies. Some governments have been better able to manage this process than others. Mistakes such as the Mexican management of the 1994 *peso* overvaluation were made, with devastating financial costs. Brazil weathered its 1998–1999 crisis after a bungled devaluation, fiscal imprudence, and political infighting that shook market confidence. The Argentine economy has collapsed under the weight of external debt that was unmatched by increases in international competitiveness. Changing policies and outcomes have challenged the ability of governments to maintain credibility with their citizens and with international investors. Citizens have placed left-leaning politicians in Brazil and Venezuela to address the perceived social deficits. Social protest has gripped Ecuador, Argentina, and Guatemala. Pleasing one segment of society has sometimes come at a cost to another. Labor-market reform hasn't moved quickly for fear of upsetting domestic labor coalitions. Privatization may have taken place too rapidly, allowing some firms to be sold for less than market value. Appropriate regulatory measures were not always in place to protect consumer and environmental interests in the face of newly privatized monopolies. Finance ministers have had to manage not only money supplies but also extensive public relations efforts with the major brokerage houses around the world. Increasing transparency and credibility in policy making has been critical to maintaining confidence in Latin American markets.

ADDRESSING THE SOCIAL DEFICIT

At the same time that the economies have grappled with both the costs and the benefits of globalization, the Latin American state has had to figure out how to do more with less. The accumulated social and environmental deficits are huge impediments to sustained future growth. Radical structural change shook up the system, energizing productive potential. Realizing this potential in the long run, however, is a function of enhancing investments in human capital. Health and education systems must be revamped. Latin America must contend with its epidemiological backlog, eradicating traditional diseases linked to poor living conditions and inadequate nutrition as well as making headway against the ills of modern society such as violence, AIDS, and heart disease. Quality improvements in the supply of educational services, including better teacher training, appropriate texts, and computer-based learning, are critical to compete in the global economy. Environmental decision making must be systematically incorporated at the local level because people themselves demand it. The complex host of environmental problems borne of insufficient infrastructure and unmanaged economic expansion must be reconciled with communities' needs today and for the future.

Yet governments are not able to spend their way out of these challenges; the money just isn't there. Instead, with diligent attention to the fiscal bottom line, states are attempting to create incentives for the market to pull some weight in the social arena. Public–private partnerships to improve delivery of health and educational services are being employed to reinvigorate moribund systems. Decentralization of social services allows for more local ownership of projects. Local governments are partnering with businesses in communities that have a vested interest in the development of better-educated, healthier workforces and cleaner work environments. Nonetheless, the market is not a substitute for good policy or hard choices, particularly in the areas of public goods provision. It can complement good governance, but it cannot replace it.

THE BALANCING ACT OF THE STATE

In balancing between global demands and local needs, the tricky policy issue is deciding just how much government is enough. We have devoted a great deal of attention in this text to discussing the positions of neoliberals, new institutionalists, and neostructuralists. The latter two groups might argue that the pendulum may have swung too far toward the market, in the light of the weakness of market institutions in guaranteeing property rights, overseeing competition policy, and promoting social welfare. Although public–private partnerships are useful to attend to unmet needs, the invisible hand of the market may not work its magic when economic agents are unable to make rational, self-interested decisions because they simply don't have the minimal level of social assets to invest in themselves. States must be vigilant in their attempts to promote incentives for the formation of a domestic economy oriented not necessarily toward short-term consumption but rather to long-term investments in social and environmental systems. Incentives must be structured to change time horizons to preserve choices in the future.

However noble this task may be, its feasibility may be legitimately questioned. Orientation to the international arena drives countries to focus on short-term macroeconomic performance variables: prices, exchange rates, and fiscal and current account balances. The room to maneuver is extremely limited. Once international investors get a sniff of disequilibrium or social discontent, they quickly shift to another, more stable investment. One of the downsides of the broadening of the stock market to include a large number of smaller players is that the day trader or the middle America investors' circle is unlikely to have a profound understanding of the complexity and the diversity of Latin American economies. An increase in the current account can mean many things, some of which threaten stable growth (such as luxury consumption) and others that may promote change (business investment). Sorting out the causes of imbalances and placing them in a historical context requires information unavailable to many small investors.

Development is not a process of harmonious equilibrium. Much like people, economies may grow in fits and starts, taking new and unintended directions. Yet the costs today of short-term disequilibrium are loss of investor confidence and instantaneous capital flight. We may have arrived at a kind of MTV international economy with an attention span that is limited to sixty-second sound bites. Economic policymakers have to learn tools of international marketing to sell information about the national product in the global marketplace. The message must be clear and consistent. But the message in Latin America won't be a pleasant one unless the problems of inequality and poverty are resolved. Unfortunately, short-term policy making doesn't encourage the necessary social investments to reverse the plight of the poor, reduce inequality, and promote sustainable development. Latin America is precariously poised with one foot in the fast-moving international arena and the other stuck in a complicated web of unequal social relations that act as a drag on productivity and change.

MULTILATERAL SUPPORT

As the world has become more tightly integrated and the ability to make economic mistakes has become more circumscribed, there may be a stronger role warranted for multilateral institutions. In the wake of the Asian, Russian, and Brazilian currency crises, there have been calls for a re-visioning of the International Monetary

Fund to become more than an institution of last resort. Multilateral development banks such as the World Bank and the IADB can also play important roles in promoting systematic attention to investments in the social and environmental agendas. The Global Environmental Fund is an innovative financial mechanism to transfer funds from North to South and share responsibility for global sustainability. Nongovernmental organizations are key not only in raising awareness of issues but also as local conduits between bi- or multilateral organizations and the local community.

As a consumer of goods produced in the international economy, you too have a role in articulating your social preferences. Public attention is directed not only to governments; the international media and the Internet provide important devices to articulate demands for socially and environmentally sound production. In the least, it is hoped that by reading this book you have become more aware of the problems facing people in other parts of the world, better able to interpret and contextualize the enormous challenges of development, and better prepared, should you so choose, to participate in this arena as a more informed manager, policymaker, activist, or consumer in the international economy.

REVISITING OUR FIVE ISSUES

To summarize, we can perhaps conclude that because development is a continuous but not smooth process, the five factors we have considered will be found in constant tension. As firms expand when markets are incomplete, they are likely to require imported components. Consumers, facing strong employment prospects in expanding markets, euphorically accelerate purchases with a consumption boom. With relatively weak domestic macroeconomic tools to fine-tune the economy, external disequilibrium mounts, pressuring the exchange rate. Capital flees, creating an external crisis that is resolved by painful domestic austerity.

Economic change can be disruptive, challenging stability. It can also threaten ruling elites, if formulated to attend to the marginalized masses. Ironically, if policy does not include those most needy of government attention to raise living, health, and education standards to a level consistent with human dignity and self-empowerment, the development prospects will confront a human capital deficit that is unsustainable in the modern global economy. State intervention in promoting human development is circumscribed by the domestic constraints of financing as well as by the role of the state as an institutional actor. Recent changes in Latin America have shifted this debate to question the appropriate role of state participation at various levels of governance. Centrally funded and monitored local action plans can reduce inefficiency and benefit from local entrepreneurial partnerships. As decentralization plays out, however, it would not be surprising to see a swing back in the activity of the state in certain arenas. As priorities in environmental management shift from locally based sewage and sanitation to industrial pollutants that are not bounded by municipalities, the locus of action might shift as well. Changing development problems require dynamic solutions.

STAGES OF ADJUSTMENT

The resolution of the key issues of internal and external balance, development for whom, confidence and stability in the face of change, the role of the state, and future sustainability has varied with the different stages countries have passed through in their economic adjustment processes. Development, as we defined it in our first chapter, is a process of meeting the basic human needs of the population while enhancing options for how economic resources will be allocated today and in the future to increase the choices citizens have in their daily lives. As we have investigated issues of stabilization, adjustment, and growth, we can identify three contemporary stages that countries have passed through on this development journey. The first stage, immediately following the debt crisis, was characterized by often **severe stabilization** measures designed to bring macrofundamentals into line. Macroeconomic stabilization efforts were shaped by the financial constraints of the debt crisis as well as the historical legacy of asset distribution and policy making that constrained policy options. Restraining internal spending to achieve external balance became the dominant concern. Without external finance, countries no longer had the option of pursuing expansionary, inward-looking development strategies. Yet the earlier experience with export orientation left lingering doubts as to the social and environmental effects of active participation in the global economy.

But these questions were of necessity tabled. At the time of the crisis, macroeconomic considerations were primary. In the second phase, **structural transformation** was initiated. The shape of the economy changed with respect to the relative balance of internal and external orientation as well as the roles of the state and the market. Trade reforms, financial liberalization, integration, and privatization have changed the economic rules of the game in the region. The international market has been placed at the center of the development process. International capital flows, both short-term portfolio as well as long-term foreign direct investment, have become important arbiters of international growth. Liberalization of trade and the accompanying process of economic integration have become the drivers of change. State ownership in the economy has been severely curtailed, with local and multinational firms providing not only traditionally traded products but also many of the services, such as transportation and power, that had been the purview of public utilities. The goal of international competitiveness has prompted countries to think differently about labor relations, the generation of technology, and the provision of infrastructure. The agricultural sector has been infused with market-based policies, including the use of profit incentives for the provision of extension services and water. The structure of economies across the region has been radically altered over the past decade.

Having readjusted the orientation of the economy and the roles of key actors, the challenge of stage three is a long-term process of **capacity building** of human capital, improving productivity, and promoting sound use of natural resources, including land.[6] In short, stage three seeks to enlarge the options each society faces in allocating scarce resources, as well as to promote economically and environmentally sustainable development. These are no easy tasks. These reforms profoundly shape the ways people interact within institutions. **Institutions** are the rules that shape the behavior

Capacity building at the local level can promote more equitable and efficient use of resources. *(Courtesy of the Inter-American Development Bank.)*

of organizations and individuals. **Formal rules,** such as constitutions, laws, and regulations, or **informal rules,** such as values and norms, condition and are conditioned by the process of economic change.[7] Old or brittle institutions may collapse under the weight of new economic challenges. The 2001 World Development Report highlighted the importance of institutions in conditioning the ability of markets to function efficiently. The private sector, for example, has demanded changes in the quality and efficiency of financial and public services and judicial reform as it now perceives competitiveness to hinge on strong social, financial, and legal institutions. Institutional reform may also promote changes in the way economic agents behave. Increased transparency in judicial systems, for example, will encourage accountability in business dealings and foster international confidence in economic transactions. Institutional reform poses significant political and technical challenges. Losers in the political systems must somehow be convinced that the long-run gains are worth the cost. It is clear that new models of institutional reform are difficult to implement in economies struggling with a range of unresolved social and economic issues. Nonetheless, the resolve of the regional presidents at the Santiago summit in 1998 and Quebec in 2001 heralds an optimistic commitment to a new institutional structure in the region. The ability to reach the new millennium goals established by the 2000 UN Millennium Summit of reducing world poverty by half by 2015 rests on the ability to provide the technical assistance to countries to overcome the institutional obstacles to sustainable development.[8]

As governments move away from crisis management and radical economic restructuring toward the hard, slow process of deepening market institutions and their political environment, they must simultaneously balance issues of credibility and fairness in reform. Given the globalization of international capital, markets must be assured that macrofundamentals remain in place. Confidence is the name of the game.

At the same time, economic actors are beginning to sort out the welfare implications of the radical structural changes of economies. When economies were in crisis, people were willing to make sacrifices. There seemed to be little choice but to reform. As tariff walls came down, international capital found new opportunities, and private capital began to provide the water, telecommunications, and productive services of the region. There have been winners and losers. As growth has accelerated in some sectors, others have felt left behind. As different sectors of society have the opportunity to sort out the effects of reform, new claims will likely be made on the political and economic systems of the region. In many countries these systems are newly democratized, with evolving practices.

Changes in the economy necessarily call into question the perceived fairness of the results for citizens of the region. Balancing competing demands in newly consolidating democracies is a tricky act. Several questions define policy approaches to emerging concerns:

- As Latin America continues to move forward in the consolidation of economic and political reform, what are likely to be the pressure points constraining the evolution of a model of sustainable economic development?
- How can policymakers balance the need for confidence and credibility against the sometimes dislocating process of promoting dynamic growth?
- How can political momentum be maintained if outcomes are moderate at best, or at worst, when crisis rocks the hard-won gains of stabilization? Will economic frustrations burst the seams of democratic society?
- Can Latin American nations define a social compact on the responsibilities of the state and the market to resolve the deep inequalities in the region, or are the social divisions simply too great?
- Can the enthusiasm for outward-looking development be maintained, and the landscape of integration be practically and pragmatically defined beyond this first, relatively easy state of integration? Can and should the commitment to a free trade area be realized? What will the costs be if it is not?
- Can the fledgling environmental movement in the region be sustained through an era of thin financing? Can a kind of cost-effective environmentalism be promoted in Latin America that will be supplemented by the energies of public–private partnerships?

> **QUESTION FOR THOUGHT**
>
> Have recent economic, political, and social events in Latin America begun to provide answers to these questions?

The first stage of reform was crisis driven. Emergency measures were taken to address short-term goals of inflation stabilization and external balance. There was little choice but to take a deep breath and move ahead with macroeconomic stabilization as

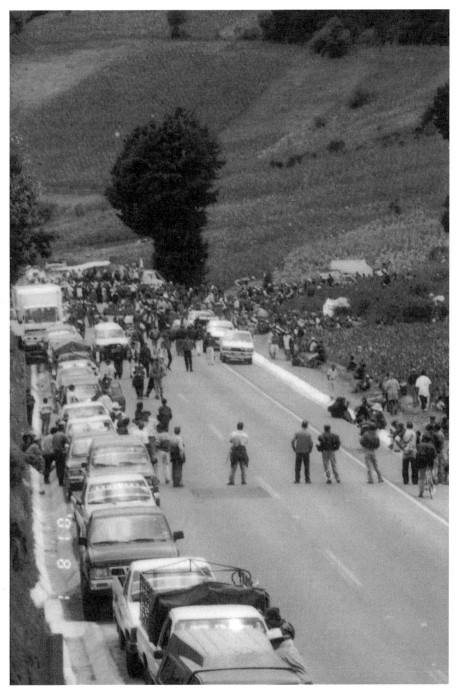

Unfulfilled promises of economic growth and political reform have led to social protest—such as this strike blocking roads in Guatemala—as people desperately search for just recourse. *(Photograph by Patrice Franko.)*

economies had spun out of control. Stage two has largely changed the structure of the game. The private sector now controls a larger portion of the economy, and internationalized production and finance regimes shape outcomes. But changes in the rules with respect to who plays in the international arena are more easily implemented than the long-term qualitative changes necessary in social systems of health and education or information. It is simpler to pass a law reflecting lower tariff rates, open the doors to international capital, or put a state enterprise on the auction block than to engage in the painfully slow process of building institutions to promote social fairness. We know less about changes in social systems and how to gauge results. Reforms in health care, education, and environmental management are less clear-cut, and the results take longer to materialize. Yet without this third stage of capacity building and institutional deepening, Latin America is doomed to repeat the cycle of unstable growth that has characterized its economic performance for centuries. Investment in human capital and promotion of more equitable and sustainable growth paths may help solve the puzzle of Latin American economic development.

Key Concepts

capacity building	informal rules	severe stabilization
formal rules	institutions	structural transformation

Chapter Summary

- Cycles of development have persisted in Latin America, calling into question the resolution of internal and external constraints, the problem of stability in the face of change, the target of economic policy, the role of the state, and the tension between current needs and sustainable future development.
- The periods of primary product exports, import substitution development, and the neoliberal model have addressed these issues differently. The economic contradictions of one period cause the pendulum to swing to a different degree of openness and state intervention.
- In analyzing periods of adjustment, three stages can be identified: severe adjustment, structural transformation, and institutional capacity building. The ability of Latin American countries to promote equitable growth hinges on progress in the third stage, creating stronger and more transparent institutions to support equitable, sustainable growth.

Notes

1. Marlise Simons, "A Talk with Gabriel García Márquez," *New York Times,* 5 December 1982, sec. 7, p. 7. Available at www.nytimes.com/books/97/06/15/reviews/marquez-talk.html and in the LEXIS-NEXIS database.

2. IADB, "Is Growth Enough?" *Latin American Economic Policies,* Second Quarter, vol. 14, 2001.

3. Dudley Althaus, "Deforestation Contributed to Tragedy by Mitch in Honduras, Experts Claim," *Houston Chronicle,* 30 December 1998, p. A. 1, as found in the LEXIS-NEXIS database.

4. IADB, "The Argentine Saga," *Latin American Economic Policies,* Fourth Quarter, vol. 16, 2001.

5. IMF, *World Economic Outlook 2002,* www.imf.org.

6. Alejandro Foxley uses these three stages in his preface to *The New Economic Model in Latin America and Its Impact on Income Distribution and Poverty,* ed. Victor Bulmer Thomas (New York: St Martin's, 1996).

7. World Bank, *Beyond the Washington Consensus: Institutions Matter,* Regional Brief (Washington, D.C.: World Bank, 1998). Available at www.worldbank.org.

8. Carol Graham, "Strengthening Institutional Capacity in Poor Countries," *The Brookings Institution Policy Brief,* no. 98, April 2002 at www.brookings.edu.

A Sampling of Institutional Actors in Latin American Economic Policy

As we move forward in our study of the region, it is useful to have a guide to the key governmental and nongovernmental actors in the region. What follows is a sampling of both multilateral and U.S.-based organizations. You are encouraged to visit their websites (at which much of this information was garnered) for further exploration. This is a sampling, not a comprehensive list, to give you an idea of the multilateral, U.S. governmental, and nongovernmental policymakers in the region.

REGIONAL MULTILATERAL ORGANIZATIONS

Inter-American Development Bank (IDB or IADB)

Headquarters: Washington, D.C.
www.iadb.org

The IADB, the largest regional multilateral institution, was established in 1959 to accelerate social and economic change in the region. Its membership is composed of forty-six nations, including twenty-six Latin American and Caribbean countries, the United States, Canada, and eighteen nonregional countries. Its mission is to raise funds in financial markets for development in Latin American and Caribbean member countries, to supplement private investment where private capital is not available, and to provide technical assistance for the preparation, financing, and implementation of projects. Its first loan was made in 1961 to improve the water and sewerage system of Arequipa, Peru. In 1994 the Multilateral Investment Fund (MIF) was created to assist investment reforms and promote private development throughout the region. Bank lending totalled $4.5 billion in 2002, well below the $7.9 billion in 2001, largely due to restrictions on borrowing in indebted countries.

United Nations Economic Commission for Latin America and the Caribbean (ECLAC or CEPAL)

Headquarters: Santiago de Chile
www.eclac.cl

The Economic Commission for Latin America (ECLA) was established by the U.N. Economic and Social Council in 1948 and was redesignated the Economic Commission for Latin America and the Caribbean in 1984. It disseminates economic and social information. It has little decision-making power but provides a second opinion for governments' economic and social policy. The functions established by its mandate are to promote economic and social development through regional and subregional cooperation; to gather, organize, interpret, and disseminate economic and social development information; to provide advisory services to governments; to plan and advocate development assistance activities; to organize intergovernmental conferences, seminars, workshops, and expert group meetings; and to help bring a regional perspective to global problems. ECLAC's influence is best known for the ISI strategy and the dependency theories of its first secretary-general, Raúl Prebisch. Today, the commission has adopted a more centrist approach.

The Organization of American States (OAS)

Headquarters: Washington, D.C.
www.oas.org

The OAS is the oldest regional organization in the world, finding its roots in the first International Conference of American States, held in Washington, D.C., in 1890. The OAS charter was signed in 1948. Its members include all thirty-five states of the Americas. The function of the organization is to strengthen the peace and security of the region; to ensure the peaceful settlement of disputes among member states; to promote and consolidate representative democracy; to provide common action on part of a member state in the case of aggression; to seek the solution to economic, juridical, and political problems that may arise among the states; and to promote through cooperative action the economic, social, and cultural development of member states. In the Miami summit of 1994, the leaders of the hemisphere's democratic nations agreed to establish a free trade area of the Americas by 2005; the OAS is providing institutional support in this effort. The OAS's most important roles have been to promote the pacific settlements of disputes among and within member states and to actively participate in democratization.

Pan American Health Organization (PAHO)

Headquarters: Washington, D.C.
www.paho.org

PAHO is an international health association that provides a forum for the consolidation and cooperation of health efforts by countries within the Americas region. Together, the thirty-five member countries work to promote physical and mental health, lengthen life, and fight diseases within their countries. PAHO dates back to the 1902 establishment of the International Sanitary Bureau. Since then its name has been changed several times. It operates under a budget consisting of member quotas and other outside extra budgetary funds.

GLOBAL MULTILATERAL ORGANIZATIONS

International Labor Organization (ILO)

Headquarters: Geneva, Switzerland
www.ilo.org

The ILO is an independent agency in the UN system with a mandate to improve working conditions, create employment, and promote human rights around the world. It has 173 member countries, of which 70 percent are LDCs. It is the only UN agency in which the private sector works actively with government in decision making. Its activities involve setting international labor standards, carrying out technical assistance and training programs, and providing information on products and services.

International Bank of Reconstruction and Development (IBRD or The World Bank)

Headquarters: Washington, D.C.
www.worldbank.org

The World Bank, a product of the 1944 Bretton Woods Conference, provides capital, technical assistance, and policy advice to developing countries. Like the IADB, it raises funds from capital markets to help finance development where private capital is not available. All of its monetary assistance comes in the form of loans. There are two forms of loans. The first type is for countries able to pay near-market interest rates. Money for these loans comes from private investors who purchase World Bank bonds. The second type of lending is for the poorest countries and is issued by the International Development Association, a World Bank affiliate. Money for these loans does not come from capital markets, but rather from thirty donor countries. There is no interest on these loans except for a 0.75 percent administrative charge, and they have thirty-five to forty-year terms. In addition to providing loans, the bank has become one of the most important sources of development information and publications.

International Monetary Fund (IMF)

Headquarters: Washington, D.C.
www.imf.org

The IMF, a result of the 1944 Bretton Woods Conference, was formally established in 1945 as an institution dedicated to the supervision of international monetary systems. It works to coordinate efforts and to encourage cooperation among its 181 voluntary member countries in the creation of economic policies. Acting as a forum for international monetary exchange, the IMF oversees transactions between countries to ensure that they occur smoothly and quickly. Additionally, through temporary emergency lending, the IMF provides access to the different international capitals made available through their quota subscriptions, or membership fees.

United Nations Development Programme (UNDP)

Headquarters: New York
www.undp.org

The UNDP is a network of 134 country offices that administers service to 174 countries and territories. Working together, the UNDP network countries work to promote sustainable development through sound governance and market development. Priorities are placed on poverty elimination, job creation, the advancement of women, and environmental regeneration.

U.S.-Based Governmental and Quasi-Governmental Organizations

Inter-American Foundation (IAF)

Headquarters: Washington, D.C.
www.iaf.gov

The IAF is a public–private bipartisan U.S. agency supporting programs in Latin America that promote grassroots development, self-reliance, and popular empowerment. It responds to requests for grants by indigenous nongovernmental organizations that provide assistance to peasant cooperatives, small enterprises, trade unions, women's collectives, human rights organizations, and cultural groups. Established in 1969, it was created as a small organization with no overseas staff to reduce costs and maximize program returns. It is viewed by many as a risk taker and groundbreaker for development assistance with its focus on supporting innovative and experimental programs. Since 1972, the IAF has funded more than 4,300 grants for over $500 million.

United States Agency for International Development (USAID)

Headquarters: Washington, D.C.
www.info.usaid.gov

USAID is an independent government agency established by President John F. Kennedy in 1961 to respond to the threat of communism and help poorer nations. In the post-Cold War era its mission is to ensure U.S. national security by promoting economic, political, environmental, and social development of developing nations. USAID views underdevelopment as a major threat to global stability. It aids participatory development with the aim of building indigenous capacity, enhancing participation, and encouraging transparency, decentralization, and the empowerment of communities and individuals. USAID is formally part of the U.S. Department of State.

NGO and Advocacy Groups

Inter-American Dialogue

www.iadialog.org

Started in 1982, the Inter-American Dialogue is a distinguished U.S. center for policy analysis, study, and commentary on Western Hemispheric affairs. Membership consists of one hundred leading citizens throughout the Americas who together seek to promote economic and political cooperation and communication through informed policy issue debate. The Dialogue is noted for its influence in shaping the agenda of inter-American relations.

Latin American Working Group (LAWG)

www.lawg.org

A coalition of activist groups that dedicates its efforts to lobbying the U.S. Congress on Latin American issues. Since 1983 LAWG has worked to craft common policies through public education. The LAWG provides information to NGOs, congressional offices, the media, and citizens concerned with U.S. policy toward Latin America.

Woodrow Wilson Center Latin American Program

wwics.si.edu

The Woodrow Wilson Center Latin American Program was established in 1977 to encourage academic-style research and discussion on inter-American issues facing the region as well as specifically Latin American topics. The center provides the opportunity for research and writing on issues of concern to Washington policymakers.

Center for Strategic and International Studies (CSIS)

www.csis.org

The Center for Strategic and International Studies, founded in 1962, is a prominent institution dedicated to effective analysis and recommendations of policies worldwide. The Americas Program focuses efforts on Latin American policy impact as well as U.S. and Canadian influences throughout the Americas. Policy study is considered from a variety of viewpoints covering issues as market integration, threats of narcotics trafficking, and political and economic reform.

Washington Office on Latin America (WOLA)

www.wola.org

The Washington Office on Latin America is an advocacy group with particular interests in human rights and counternarcotics policy. Funded in 1974, it facilitates dialogue between governmental and nongovernmental actors and monitors the impact of their policies and programs.

ACCION International

www.accion.org

ACCION International, established in 1961, is a nonprofit organization dedicated to providing microentrepreneurs with critical access to working capital in the form of credit and training. Through short-term loans, "solidarity group" lending, and technical business support, self-employed poor throughout Latin America are able expand their businesses, which indirectly leads to the creation of more jobs. ACCION works with affiliates in fourteen countries, and in 1998, ACCION disbursed nearly $577 million in loans, with about 447,000 small business recipients receiving an average of nearly $1,300 per loan.

Council of the Americas

www.counciloftheamericas.org

Founded in 1965 under the leadership of David Rockefeller and other business-people, the Council for the Americas encourages free markets and private enterprise throughout the Americas according to the belief that these policies encourage economic growth. The council acts in strategic ways through the advocacy of public discourse as well as through collaboration with private sector organizations in hopes of achieving economic prosperity. Membership consists of more than 240 firms that share an interest in Latin American investment.

Glossary

absorption Absorption is domestic consumption of goods both produced at home and imported from abroad. The IMF promoted the absorption approach, or the reduction of domestic utilization of resources to release them for export to earn hard currency to finance a country's debt.

adverse selection A situation where one side of a deal has more information than another, leading to the selection of an undesirable outcome.

Agenda 21 A comprehensive agenda for environmental action established at the 1992 United Nations Conference on the Environment and Development held in Rio de Janeiro.

agricultural extension programs Programs to introduce new agricultural practices to peasant farming communities.

Andean Community Signed in 1960, the Andean Community treaty allowed for free commerce among Bolivia, Ecuador, Colombia, Venezuela, and Peru, with a common external tariff.

Austral plan Argentina's Austral plan, named after the new currency put in place in 1985, was designed to combat inflation. The Austral plan was labeled as heterodox but also included some orthodox measures. To attack the inertial component of inflation, the administration declared a price freeze in June of 1985, froze wages, and implemented exchange-rate controls. These measures were taken to convince the population that prices would not increase, but the plan fell apart after people lost confidence in the ability of the government to manage the economy.

backward linkage As industry A grows, demand for inputs to produce industry A's product will increase. This increase in demand can spur investment in a new industry B that will produce inputs for industry A. Central to the thought of A. O. Hirschman, investing in industries with strong backward linkages on the supply chain should promote growth.

Bresser plan A follow-up to the *Cruzado* plan, the Brazilian use of heterodox policy to combat inflation in 1987. Wages were frozen, mini-devaluations were used to manage the exchange rate, and interest rates were targeted above the rate of inflation. Citizens were deputized as price inspectors. Despite initial success, shortages and external balance problems caused by excess consumer spending reignited inflation once again.

caciques Spanish word for the landlords of large agricultural estates prevalent in the Latin American colonial period.

capacity building   Refers to investments in human capital, improvements in productivity and system design, and greater efficiency in the use of resources within economic, political, and social institutions.

capital controls   Mechanisms such as licensing of foreign exchange used to limit imports or reduce capital flight, or taxation on short-term foreign investments to reduce the volatility of short-term capital flows.

capital flight   Large outflows of domestic capital into safer or more stable foreign banks and foreign stock markets to protect the value of that capital. This phenomenon is associated with countries suffering from severe inflation or the likelihood of devaluation. Individuals opt to invest abroad when they lose confidence in their country's currency.

Central American Common Market   Formed early in the 1960s, this attempt at integration among Central American countries to take advantage of economies of scale in production was set back in the 1970s and 1980s by political strife. The 1990s saw new commitment to strengthening the legal and institutional framework, joint actions to reduce debt, and cooperation on sectoral issues.

Chicago School   This free market school of thought, a precursor to the neoliberal model, advocated a hands-off role for the state. Adherents believe that the market and open international trade are the main engines behind development.

Collor plan   Economic policy engineered by Brazil's president, Fernando Collor de Mello in 1990 to address inertial inflation through orthodox and heterodox measures. Assets were frozen and a thirty-day price freeze instituted. These measures initially restrained inflation, but pressures such as increasing oil prices and shortages of goods, in addition to a lack of credibility in the government, caused an acceleration in inflation soon afterward.

command and control measures   Government regulations and penalties used to reduce environmental pollution.

commodity lottery   A term used by Victor Bulmer-Thomas that describes the export-oriented pattern of the late 1800s, when most Latin American countries were dependent on one export good, such as nitrates in Chile, coffee in Brazil, and tin in Bolivia.

common market   A form of integration in which countries coordinate policy-making measures in such areas as agriculture and the social sector, along with establishing a common external tariff.

conditionality   A term associated with the prerequisites necessary for disbursal of IMF funds to developing countries. Countries seeking loans from the IMF must first implement tough stabilization policies such as a decrease in fiscal spending, tight monetary policy, and strict trade policies. Conditionality is strongly debated because it forces a government to contract its economy and imposes social costs.

contingent valuation   A form of environmental assessment that asks people to assign a value to their willingness to pay to preserve a natural resource.

convertibility plan   Introduced in 1991 in Argentina, this policy to combat infla-tion tied the Argentine *peso* to the U.S. dollar and used a currency board to constrain monetary policy by law. The money supply could not increase unless there was a parallel increase in dollar reserves. Inflation was almost eliminated, but at a high cost in terms of recession and unemployment.

cost-effectiveness   A criterion used to decide among competing priorities, espe-cially in the environmental arena. Programs with broad impact and low cost are more desirable than programs of limited scope and high cost.

cost-push elements   Certain conditions or external shocks such as food shortages or increasing oil prices that will fuel inflation through the interaction with powerful labor organizations or a concentrated industry structure. Rising costs are seen as pushing up prices.

Cruzado **plan**   Based on a structural diagnosis of inflation, the first *Cruzado* plan in Brazil, in 1986, focused on the inertial component of inflation and implemented heterodox measures by freezing prices, wages, and exchange rates. Brazilians were deputized as *fiscais,* or price inspectors, to police the price freeze in supermarkets and shopping malls. Indexation of contracts with less than one year's duration was prohibited. A new currency, the *cruzado,* was created at a value of 1,000 *cruzeiros.* After a devaluation, the *cruzado* was fixed at 13.84 *cruzados* to the dollar. A neglect of tough fiscal adjustments combined with passive monetary policy that accommo-dated domestic deficits resulted in the re-eruption of inflation.

customs union   A form of regional trade integration in which a common external tariff is established for the group.

debt-for-equity swap   A win-win method used by firms, banks, and indebted countries to reduce exposure to the debt crisis. A firm wishing to invest in a partic-ular country would buy the country's debt at a discount from a bank through the secondary market. Owing the firm and not the bank, the country could pay the firm in local currency, as opposed to dollars, which the firm then used to buy local sup-plies and pay workers. Banks got risky loans off their books, countries were released from the need to earn hard currency to service the debt, and firms were repaid the full value of the loan bought at a discount. The plan was limited, how-ever, by inflationary risk and the demand for equity investments.

debt-for-nature swap   An environmental twist on debt-for-equity swaps, in which international organizations buy a country's discounted debt from the secondary market. Debts are reduced or canceled in exchange for a country establishing nature preserves or otherwise protecting the environment. A financial commitment to long-term management of the parks, sometimes through a trust fund, was an important element of success.

debt trap   When long-term projects are financed through short-term debt issues, countries may find themselves paying more in interest and principal than they are receiving in new money. Initially, the borrower is able to finance the project as well as pay the principal and interest with new lending each year. With each coming year, new lending available for investment dwindles because some of the money from new loans is used to pay the principal and interest on previous loans. The debt trap sets in when the new lending is not enough to pay for the principal and interest and the project is not yet generating significant returns to make up the difference.

decentralization   A devolution of governmental responsibilities from centralized bureaucracies to state and local levels. The ability to raise revenues is sometimes also moved to the local level, although systems of fiscal accountability need to be tightened to improve internal balance.

declining terms of trade   Terms of trade are the price of exports relative to the price of imports, mathematically expressed as Px/Pm, an index of export prices divided by an index of import prices. Declining terms of trade are reflected in a decrease in the ratio, meaning that the price of imports is increasing relative to the price of exports. Under these conditions, countries must export increasing amounts of their own goods (often agricultural goods or commodities) to pay for imports (more likely to be machinery and high-tech items).

demand-driven rural investment funds (DRIFs)   The allocation of central government funds to local governments or communities to promote local control of agricultural development. Certain eligibility requirements must be met, and beneficiaries must contribute to the cost of the projects, often through volunteer labor.

dependency theory   Despite different emphases by scholars, the central theme behind dependency is the proposition that a country does not develop because of its natural endowments; its growth is constrained by centers of power in the international system. Industrialized countries (the center) advance at the expense of the third world (the periphery), causing underdevelopment in the region through exploitation of cheap labor and extraction of resources. Underdevelopment was seen as linked to the relationship between the elite of Latin America and the center in their search for short-term profits as opposed to long-term growth.

development   The process of meeting the basic needs of the population and enhancing options for how economic resources will be allocated today and in the future to increase the choices citizens have in their daily lives.

direct government investment   In addition to command and control measures and market-based initiatives, this is a third policy option available to states to promote sound environmental practices. Governments might choose to invest in infrastructure such as sanitation or water projects to promote a cleaner environment.

dualism   The simultaneous existence of modern and traditional economies, usually characterized by an expanding industrial sector and a large self-subsistence agricultural sector. Dualistic models tend to benefit the elite and marginalize the poor.

dualistic structure of production   A bimodal pattern of agricultural production in which large corporate farming practices crowd out peasant farming, lowering employment and the production of basic foodstuffs in favor of lucrative export crops.

Dutch disease Named after Holland's experience with natural gas, the term describes a country's inclination to concentrate its financial resources into a few profitable sectors. This behavior was prevalent throughout Latin American history with investments in oil and sugar, and it contributed to the unbalanced development of the region as other important sectors were ignored.

economic populism Economic populism is patterned after the behavior of many charismatic Latin American leaders, such as Juan Perón in Argentina, whose programs were symbolically designed to attend to the needs of the poor. Industry was pacified with large subsidies. The welfare of future generations is sacrificed for the welfare of current generations through excessive current spending to satisfy pressure groups. In a desire to increase the standard of living today, this kind of behavior ignores external balance of payments constraints and large fiscal deficits, conditions that make inflation nearly inevitable.

economic union A group of countries that have moved beyond a common market to embrace common sectoral policies. Common monetary policies and a common currency constitute an additional step toward an economic community. Mercosur is therefore an economic union, whereas the European Community has moved a step beyond.

educational deficit The gap between Latin America and the rest of the world in educational attainment and years of schooling. The 4.2 years of schooling Latin American children receive is roughly half of that of counterparts in the United States, Japan, and Germany, and two-thirds those in the Asian newly industrialized countries.

educational performance index Measure developed by the international NGO Oxfam using weighted values of school enrollment, gender equity, and completion rates.

effective rate of protection The nominal tariff adjusted for the tariff on intermediate goods. If the garment industry faced a 10-percent tariff and the sewing machines to make clothing faced a 5- percent tariff, the effective rate of protection (adjusted for the importance of the machine in production) would be 15 percent.

effective selectivity A policy approach advocated by the neostructuralists that promotes prioritizing and allocating limited government funds to areas that will produce the highest social returns.

ejidos Land that had been held communally for centuries before the introduction of private property. This is the predominant form of peasant landholding in Mexico.

empowerment The full participation of beneficiaries in their own development process.

enclaves Industries, in isolation from the rest of the economy, that fail to spur domestic investment, employment, and income.

encomienda Land received by conquistadors or other Spanish settlers from the Spanish Crown that was accompanied by the deeding of Indian labor to work this land.

Engel's Law   When the increase in the demand for agricultural goods is slower than an increase in income (that is, there is a low income elasticity of demand), exporters of agricultural goods lose ground to producers of manufactured goods. When a low income elasticity for agricultural products exists, this means that if individuals experience an increase in their income, they will not increase their consumption of food or commodities by the same proportion. There is, for example, only so much coffee or sugar one will consume, no matter the increase in income. Engel's Law was used by economists such as Raúl Prebisch to explain why the developing world, which tends to export agricultural commodities, experiences declining terms of trade.

environmental assessment   An impact statement identifying the likely environmental effects of a development policy. Most new development projects today require environments assessments prior to approval.

epidemiological backlog   The simultaneous health challenge of addressing traditional diseases (such as cholera or dysentery tied to inadequate infrastructure and malnutrition) and the diseases of modern society (such as cancer and heart disease).

epidemiological transition   The transition from a focus on fighting traditional diseases such as cholera to a focus on more modern concerns such as heart disease.

equity   The access to equal opportunities within a nation. Although growth may increase inequality, models of growth with equity attempt to promote a more equal distribution of income. Equity also refers to ownership of capital—a very different use of the same term.

equity investments   The purchase of stock by foreigners.

expenditure switching   Changes in the prices of products, most often through an exchange-rate adjustment, that make imports more expensive and exports cheaper. The higher price of imports switches people away from them, helping to balance trade.

export pessimism   A term associated with the Prebisch–Singer thesis, stating that exports alone cannot be the engine of growth because of the effect of declining terms of trade.

externalities   A cost or a benefit that results from an activity or transaction that is imposed on parties outside the transaction. Pollution is a negative externality of production; reducing the spread of disease is a positive externality of education.

extreme poverty   Although levels vary by the local cost of living, those subsisting on roughly less than $1 a day are considered to be living in extreme poverty. Moderate poverty is roughly $2 per day, or between $50 (World Bank benchmark) and $60 a month (ECLAC level).

factor price equalization   As a country opens up to trade, the demand for its products, made with its most abundant (and cheap) factor, should in theory over time result in an increase in the price of this factor to world levels. Global factor prices should therefore become more uniform.

fazenda   Large feudal estates, similar to the *hacienda* in Spanish America, during the colonial period in Brazil.

fiscal austerity measures   Policy initiatives such as decreasing government spending, privatization, increasing tax revenues, and reducing subsidies to relieve pressure on domestic budgets. The IMF often recommends fiscal austerity measures.

fiscal covenant   A term coined by ECLAC to reflect a socioeconomic agreement between a government and civil society. This fiscal covenant incorporates consolidation of the ongoing fiscal adjustment, increases in the productivity of public management, transparency of fiscal activity, promotion of social equity, and development of democratic institutions.

foreign direct investment (FDI)   Describes the investment by foreigners through ownership of equity shares or setting up production facilities within a country. The most common type of foreign direct investor is the multinational corporation.

formal rules   The constitutions, laws, and written regulations that structure economic activity and guarantee property rights.

forward linkage   The production of a good that is complementary to another industry may spur the development of that new sector; such development is called a forward linkage. As opposed to a backward linkage, which calls for the production of critical inputs, a forward linkage moves ahead in the production chain. Roadside restaurants might be a forward linkage to automobile production, whereas tires would be considered a backward linkage.

free trade area   A form of regional integration in which trade restrictions are abolished between participating countries, but each country maintains an independent trade policy and separate tariff rates with the rest of the world.

gender development index (GDI)   The GDI discounts the human development index for gender inequality in life expectancy, educational attainment, and income, by assigning a penalty for inequality. The greater the gender disparity, the lower the GDI.

gender empowerment index (GEM)   The GEM concentrates on economic, political, and professional participation by incorporating variables such as female share of income, access to professional and managerial jobs, and seats in public office. The GEM therefore measures the degree to which society's opportunities are open to women.

Gini coefficient   A measure of income inequality that gauges the difference between a hypothetical society where income is perfectly equal and the actual income distribution. It is derived from the Lorenz curve. The higher the Gini coefficient, the more extensive is income inequality.

Global Environmental Facility (GEF)   Assists developing countries in funding projects and programs to protect the global environment and promote sustainable development. Established in 1991, GEF is the designated financial mechanism for international agreements on biodiversity, climate change, and persistent organic pollutants. GEF also supports projects that combat desertification and protects international waters and the ozone layer.

golden age of primary product exports   The period in Latin American history from the late 1800s to the early 1900s, when primary product exports boomed and contributed to the economic growth of the region.

grade repetition   A pervasive problem of educational systems in Latin America. Nearly one third of all school children repeat their grades annually, primarily because of poor educational inputs.

growth   A simultaneous gradual increase in quantities such as GDP, population, saving, and wealth. If the benefits of growth are not widely shared, it may not be considered development.

headcount ratio   The proportion within a country's population falling below the poverty line.

Heckscher–Ohlin theorem   A key theoretical construct in international trade that suggests that a country should trade the good that uses relatively intensively that country's most abundant factor.

heterodox policies   Monetary and fiscal policies grounded in the belief that one of the primary components of inflation is the inertia built into an economic chain, with wages increased in anticipation of future price increases, making inflation a self-fulfilling prophecy. Heterodox policies attempt to combat inflation by neutralizing expectations through price and wage freezes.

HFA   A program promoted by the World Health Organization mobilizing efforts to provide basic health services for all by the year 2000.

human development index (HDI)   The United Nations Human Development Report calculates the HDI as a composite of life expectancy at birth, educational attainment (measured by adult literacy and school enrollments), and income.

illiquidity   A condition in which cash flow does not match financial obligations. As opposed to insolvency, when an economic entity cannot and will not ever likely meet its obligations, illiquidity may be a temporary condition in which revenues do not cover costs of debt service. In the first stage of the debt crisis, countries were thought to have temporary liquidity problems; it was later seen that fundamental restructuring and debt relief were called for.

import substitution industrialization (ISI)   ISI was the dominant economic policy in Latin America during the 1950s, 1960s, and 1970s as a response to dependency and structuralist theories. It represented a shift away from the outward orientation of export promotion, to an inward-looking orientation. ISI was designed to replace imports with domestic production under the guiding hand of the state. Governments used activist industrial, fiscal, and monetary policy to achieve growth.

income gap   A measure of poverty that captures the difference between actual incomes and incomes at the officially designated poverty line.

incomplete markets   Markets in developing countries may be incomplete in the sense that they do not efficiently convey price signals to buyers or sellers. This may be due to lack of information, a limited number of participants, or the market infrastructure. When markets do not adjust smoothly, transactions costs rise and economic activity is compromised. Neostructuralists and new institutionalists suggest a role for the state in supplementing economic activity where markets are incomplete.

indexation   Under a system of indexation, countries will revise wages and financial prices upward by taking into account expected as well as past inflation. When indexation occurs, countries have embraced inflation and it becomes a part of daily life. Because incomes are protected, the inflation is less painful.

inertial inflation   Implies that inflation is not driven solely by an increase in the money supply, but by expectations as well. As individuals anticipate inflation, they will demand higher wages or set prices accordingly, which will push prices upward.

inflationary expectations   The expectations of a society, based on past experience, of future rates of inflation. When they anticipate future price increases, economic actors demand higher wages or set prices higher to cover the inflation they expect in the future, making the expectations a self-fulfilling prophecy. Inflationary expectations are a large part of inertial inflation.

informal rules   Values and norms that condition and are conditioned by the process of economic change.

informal sector   Small-scale business operations such as selling goods on street corners or providing cleaning services in homes. The informal sector operates outside the official, taxed economy. It is characterized by a low capital-labor ratio, family-intensive production, and worker-owned means of production. The informal sector can be divided into three areas—microenterprise employment, own-account workers, and domestic service.

insecure property rights   When owners of property are not sure of their rights to use or dispose of their property. When institutions guaranteeing land titles are inefficient or nonexistent, farmers may underinvest in developing property because there is a good chance that the returns from efforts will be appropriated by another. Insecure property rights are an important cause of environmental damage, because economic actors may exploit land and natural resources now if they assume that they will not, or may not, continue to have access to these inputs in the future.

institutionalist tradition   A vision of development policy that accords a strong role for nonmarket institutions. Institutionalists assume that markets are not perfect; that people are not purely rational, self-interested maximizers; and that economic power rather than efficiency will shape outcomes. For institutionalists, access to and control over technology is an important ingredient of dynamic (or sluggish) growth.

institutions   Rules that shape the behavior or organizations and individuals engaged in economic activity.

integrated approach   Addressing poverty by means of growth policy and social policy, as suggested by the Economic Commission for Latin America and the Caribbean (ECLAC).

integrated rural development   An holistic approach in the rural sector that takes into account the multidimensional nature of rural poverty, focusing on the well-being of rural people by building their productive, social, and environmental assets.

involuntary lending   During the debt crisis, involuntary lending described the process of rolling over the principal and interest payments due on a loan into new (usually more expensive) loans to give countries breathing room to meet their financial obligations. It was believed that after their economies became more productive through the tough measures required by the IMF, these countries would then be able to pay off their debt. Banks preferred to package the interest and principal due into a new loan because it kept the loan in the "performing" category rather than having a past-due amount trigger a classification of this asset as nonperforming and therefore worth less.

Kuznets curve   A graphical, U-shaped representation that illustrates income inequality initially increasing with economic growth, but later decreasing after economic growth has reached a certain level. At first economies may be equal but poor; equality may fall during rapid growth, but as economies mature, equality should rise again.

labor productivity   A measure of output produced by workers. The productivity of workers, conditioned by their education, health, and access to complementary inputs such as machinery and technology, is an important ingredient of growth. If productivity is rising faster than prices and population, a society will have more goods to distribute and welfare should improve.

land reform   Given unequal patterns of landholdings created by colonial patronage, some governments have attempted to redistribute land. These movements have been revolutionary at times, taking tracts of land from the rich and giving them to the poor, as well as progressive, where only land that has been idle or unproductive is reassigned to those who might use it more intensively.

latifundia   Feudal estates in Spanish Latin America, which stood in great contrast to the small parcels of land (known as *minifundias*) used by peasant farmers. The *latifundia* also served as a form of political, social, and economic organization and later contributed to a pattern of concentrated landholdings and power.

Lorenz curve   A graphical representation of income distribution. The population is sorted by income, usually deciles, and the percentage of income that each portion of the population holds is plotted. For example, in the Lorenz curve for Latin America, the first 20 percent of the population holds 2.5 percent of the income, and the first 40 percent a cumulative 8.6 percent. Altogether, the bottom 60 percent accounts for 19.6 percent of income, with the top 20 percent holding nearly two-thirds of the total.

mandamiento   A system by which communities, most often indigenous, were forced to provide workers for harvest when there were labor shortages, often under brutal working conditions.

market-based incentives In addition to command and control measures and direct government investment, one of three types of tools used in environmental policy. Instruments such as tax incentives are used to encourage market investments in such areas as recycling and use of solar power as a means of promoting sustainable development. The premise behind market-based initiatives is that if someone can profit from doing environmental good, the policy is more likely to endure over time.

market failure Neoclassical economic theorists believe that when left on its own, the market will promote economic growth. When the market fails to promote growth, primarily because of information constraints or ineffective price signals, market failure occurs.

Mercosur The South American common market comprising Argentina, Brazil, Uruguay, and Paraguay as well as associate members Chile and Bolivia.

merit good Investment in public goods such as education and health that have benefits for society in general.

microcredit Banking services that reach down to the small-scale entrepreneur. Collateral for loans is often provided by an investment circle that guarantees repayment of members. Microlending makes investment over time possible for the poor, but some question whether, because of the amounts involved and the repayment structure, microcredit makes a significant difference in people's lives.

minifundia The small parcels of land used for subsistence farming by Latin American peasants during the colonial period and whose remnants can still be seen today.

moderate poverty A standard of living corresponding to income of about $50–60 dollars a month, or $2 a day. Roughly 40 percent of the population of Latin America lives in moderate poverty.

moral hazard A situation that occurs when borrowers have more information than lenders about their own likely behavior after the sale. If sufficient collateral is not secured prior to the loan, the borrower has an incentive to pursue high-risk behavior because the gains will be high if the project succeeds but will be shared by the lender if it fails. Can also be applied to other situations when agents are not forced to internalize costs.

NAFTA The North American Free Trade Agreement was signed by the United States, Canada, and Mexico in 1994. It sought to reduce tariffs within a ten-year period, increase trade in the region, promote cross-border investment, and introduce environmental and labor standards across the region.

neoclassical tradition Belief among some economists that rational, self-interested maximizers, if left alone by governments to operate within markets, will generate the greatest quantity of goods for society.

neostructuralists Adherents of this school of economic thought do not believe that the market alone will spur development; the state should intervene in those areas where there has been market failure. Concentration of economic power in both the domestic and international arenas requires selective intervention to promote equitable development. The principal difference between structuralists and neostructuralists is that the latter group places a greater emphasis on outward-looking export development as opposed to the inward-looking policies that defined import substitution industrialization.

new institutional economics   New institutionalists argue that culture matters in defining the ways the economy provides for society. New institutionalists claim that certain institutional arrangements are necessary to reduce transaction costs that arise in imperfect markets. The arrangements may include improving property rights, providing effective and impartial judicial systems, and instituting transparent regulatory frameworks.

new political economy   The new political economy grounds its assumptions in the material self-interest and rational calculus of economic actors. Intervention by the state will serve only to interfere with market signals and the allocation of resources. The state should, therefore, play a minimal role in the market.

nontraditional export production   Policies such as agricultural extension training or preferential credit to promote goods that are not in the traditional export profile. By diversifying exports, countries are able to capture new markets and be less dependent on price swings in traditional commodities.

Olivera–Tanzi effect   The process by which inflation erodes the true value of tax receipts because of the time lag between assessment of tax liability and actual collection.

open regionalism   Promoted by ECLAC, this policy encourages the formation of regional and subregional trading units without excluding trade initiatives with other parts of the world.

orthodox theory of inflation   For the orthodox theorist, inflation is a monetary phenomenon. Too much money chasing too few goods increases the overall price level. This phenomenon is usually the result of governments trying to finance their budget deficits in one of three ways: raising money domestically, borrowing from abroad, and/or seignorage (printing money). To reduce inflation, the orthodox economists would attack not only the increase in the money supply but also large budget deficits. For the orthodox school, letting the markets work and limiting government intervention is the key to reducing inflation. The purpose behind tight monetary policy and a decrease in expenditures is to reduce aggregate demand that would otherwise lead to higher prices and not higher output.

overvalued exchange rates   Under a fixed exchange rate system, a rate is overvalued when inflation has eroded the true value of the money but a new par or official rate has not been established. For example, if inflation in country A is 25 percent a year higher than in country B and their currencies are fixed in terms of each other, the country experiencing inflation will have a currency that is 25 percent overvalued at the end of one year. Overvaluation of a currency is not sustainable because it encourages imports and discourages exports. If it is not corrected by contracting the economy, people will expect a devaluation, or adjustment in the currency price. As reserves to pay for the current account imbalance are drawn down, people will begin to vote with their feet, moving capital to currencies without the risk of devaluation.

Pact for Economic Solidarity Also known as *El Pacto,* this was an agreement between the Mexican state, business, and labor to limit price increases as a way to combat inflation.

planning model A vision of development policy that accords a strong role to a nation's government to jump start economic change.

portfolio bonds Short-term financial instruments held in emerging market portfolios that make a country vulnerable to quick movements of international capital flows.

portfolio investors Refers to certain types of investor, such as mutual funds or insurance companies, that generally invest with a short-term outlook.

poverty line The minimum income required to purchase the goods necessary for subsistence. Although this varies by location, $2 per day is the global benchmark for moderate poverty and $1 a day for extreme poverty.

preferential trade agreements Trade agreements such as free trade arrangements or customs unions that promote economic activity within a region by favoring trading partners within that region over those outside it.

primary health care Health care that promotes basic sanitation and nutrition practices to increase people's control over improvements in their environment so as to maintain a decent quality of life and achieve human and social potential.

productivity A measure of output in relation to inputs. Rising productivity is a key to economic growth.

provisioning A response by banks to the debt crisis whereby they would set aside profits (before dividend payments) against risky loans so as to reduce their exposure to debt.

purchasing power parity A good sold in two markets should sell for the same price, adjusted for the exchange rate, in both locations. If it does not, this suggests that one currency is overvalued.

quality primary education by the year 2010 The goal of 100 percent primary-school completion rates and 75 percent secondary-inscription rates agreed to by the presidents of the region at the 1994 Miami summit; action items to promote this goal were elaborated at the 1998 Santiago summit, including targeting vulnerable groups through compensatory programs, preschool education, and distance learning.

Real **plan** Introduced by Brazilian president Henrique Fernando Cardoso when he was minister of the economy, the *Real* Plan redenominated wages, prices, taxes, and the exchange rate in a new accounting unit called the *urv.* Later, a new currency, the *real,* was introduced. Contractionary monetary policies were undertaken. Unlike many previous attempts, the *Real* Plan proved to be successful, neutralizing inflationary expectations and curbing inflation.

regional integration   Regional integration is the matching of economic and other policies within a region. The simplest form of integration is a free trade area (FTA) covering goods, with lower (or no) tariffs on goods exchanged within the region. The next level would include an FTA with services and perhaps regulations in other areas such as the environment or social concerns. A customs union deepens the commitment with a common external tariff. A common market permits the movement of factors of production among member countries, and an economic union expands on this to cede sovereignty over commercial, fiscal, and monetary policy to a supranational authority. Regional integration may make the liberalization process politically palatable through playing on sentiments of reciprocity of neighbor markets, and it may improve the confidence of investors because policies of openness have been locked in by treaty.

repartida   Monopoly control over mines and land in the New World was accorded through the *encomienda* system, which gave land rights to colonists, with a share of the output or *repartida* owed in return back to the home country.

returned value   Revenue earned through exports that is retained by a country.

safe minimum standard   The highest level of pollution that a society can safely tolerate with the reasonable expectation that future generations will not be made worse off by the choice.

secondary market   A market for a financial instrument that separates the initial debt issuer from the eventual lender. During the debt crisis, many banks were pessimistic about the ability of Latin American countries to repay loans. In particular, small and medium-sized banks wanted to unload risky loans and offered them for resale below their face value in the secondary market. Larger banks (with a greater likelihood of being repaid) or multinational corporations interested in operating in a foreign market might choose to assume this credit risk at a discounted price. The larger bank or firm might, for example, pay 50 cents for a piece of paper saying that the borrowing country owed it a dollar. The greater the risk of default, the lower the secondary market price. Buyers of the debt could earn a substantial profit if a Latin American country paid off its debt in full, or in any proportion higher than what the debt was bought for.

segmented credit markets   Different groups of borrowers are assigned different prices for loans, and barriers between the groups prevent arbitrage from evening out the spread in interest rates. These barriers might be geographic distances or may be cultural or social differences that keep one group—perhaps poor minority women—separated from another portion of the population.

seignorage   An increase in the money supply by the mere printing of more currency, usually for the purpose of financing government spending. A government can profit from such an operation because it results in inflation. The government then is able to repay its debts in currency that is worth less than the currency that was borrowed. The result of monetary expansion might be short-run expansion of output, but eventually the increase in money will mean only an increase in prices.

severe stabilization   The first and often very painful stage of macroeconomic adjustment designed to bring macroeconomic fundamentals into line.

short-term money   This includes the "hot" capital flow of portfolio bonds and stocks that may be moved from country to country in an internationally linked global financial system with the stroke of a keyboard.

social investment funds   Targeted emergency aid for poverty reduction.

sovereign guarantee   The backing of a national government (collateralized by national assets) in the extension of a loan.

Stolper–Samuelson effect   As the price of the more abundant (and cheaper) factor rises after an opening of trade, the owners of this factor—in the case of the developing countries, labor—will accrue the largest gain. Trade should therefore make owners of the cheapest factor better off.

structural adjustment programs   Often supported by the World Bank and the IMF, these programs are designed to address internal and external balance by decreasing domestic expenditure, enhancing revenue collection, promoting exports, and limiting luxury imports. These programs changed the shape or structure of economies from the inward-oriented import substitution model to an externally oriented export promotion program, simultaneously privatizing state industries, decreasing government expenditures, and encouraging inflows of foreign capital.

structural transformation   The second stage of economic adjustment designed to change the shape of the economy, particularly with respect to decreasing the active role of the state and increasing the economy's orientation to the international market.

structuralists   Drawing on the work of the Economic Commission for Latin America (ECLA) under Raúl Prebisch, structuralists begin from the assumption that the underlying structure of developing economies differs from that of more industrialized nations. Macro policy for structuralists rests on the premise that relatively concentrated industrial elites can pass on price increases, resulting in inertial inflation. Structuralists tend to downplay the importance of fiscal balance in favor of an activist state policy to redress production bottlenecks. Structuralists and their intellectual descendants, the neostructuralists, have little faith in the ability of the market to generate spontaneous or equitable growth. Borrowing from dependency analysts, structuralists believe that the position of countries in the international system, especially their access to technology, limits possibilities for autonomous growth. Although neostructuralists appreciate the benefits of international trade and finance, they caution that states should intervene to mitigate the social and environmental costs of openness.

sustainable development   Development strategies that will meet today's needs without sacrificing the ability of future generations to meet their own needs.

targeting   A method of allocating social expenditures by identifying and distributing funds to those most in need. Targeted policies have often replaced general programs such as price subsidies on tortillas or milk that could not distinguish between the needy and the well-off. An example of a targeted policy would be a food debit card that is replenished when a mother brings a child to a clinic for preventive child care.

technological change   The key to economic development, technological change allows for new combinations of capital and labor to create more efficient production.

tesobono   A dollar-denominated treasury bond offered by the Mexican government during the Mexican financial crisis. The bonds were structured to convince investors to keep their capital in Mexico by eliminating exchange risk. After a series of political events that deepened the crisis and scared capital away, the *tesobono* led to a further depletion of dollar reserves because the Mexican government had to cover its dollar-based obligations.

theory of comparative advantage   This theory states that to maximize global output, each country should apply its resources to producing those goods that it can produce relatively most efficiently.

trade creation   A benefit of economic integration whereby a trade agreement leads to an increase in overall trade. An integration agreement has positive effects if trade creation exceeds trade diversion.

trade diversion   An effect of economic integration, when trade with a more efficient global producer is discontinued in favor of products from a regional trading partner.

transnational corporations   Transnational corporations, also known as multinational corporations (MNCs) and transnational enterprises (TNEs), are firms with central offices located in one country but with operations abroad. Transnational corporations are the primary form of foreign direct investment. TNCs bring capital, expertise, and jobs but also may thwart the growth of local industries and have been accused of exploiting low-wage workers.

urbanization   The growth of large cities. The high levels of urban living in Latin America, with rates in Argentina, Brazil, Venezuela, Uruguay, and Chile higher than that of the United States, create enormous environmental difficulties.

value added tax (VAT)   A consumption tax levied on the value added at each stage of production. The advantage of the VAT over other tax instruments is its self-regulating mechanism. Each producer requires a receipt from its supplier to demonstrate that taxes already have been paid on the earlier levels of production.

velocity of money   The amount of national output supported by the money supply; mathematically, it is expressed as GDP/M, or gross domestic product divided by the money supply. Velocity is higher when a small stock of money supports a higher level of output. The higher the velocity, the larger the effect of any increase in the money supply.

water rights   a critical element in agricultural policy. Access to water rights, if accrued on the basis of seniority or local power, often interferes with the efficient allocation of resources in an agricultural community.

World Summit on Sustainable Development (WSSD)   In Johannesburg during 2002, the WSSD brought together tens of thousands of participants, including heads of state and government, national delegates and leaders from NGOs, businesses, and other major groups to focus global attention and direct action toward meeting difficult development challenges, including improving people's lives and conserving our natural resources in a world that is growing in population, with ever-increasing demands for food, water, shelter, sanitation, energy, health services, and economic security.

BIBLIOGRAPHY

Abdelal, Rawi. *The State*. Harvard Business School case #9-701-077. Boston: Harvard Business School, 2001.

Acevedo, Carlos, Deborah Barry, and Herman Rosa. "El Salvador's Agricultural Sector: Macroeconomic Policy, Agrarian Change and the Environment." *World Development* 23, no. 12 (1995).

Action Plan for Universal and Quality Basic Education by the Year 2000, Summit of the Americas. Available online at www.summit-americas.org.

Adelman, Irma, and Cynthia Taft Morris. "Development History and Its Implications for Development Theory." *World Development* 25, no. 6 (June 1997): 841–40.

Adriance, Jim. "Living with the Land in Central America." *Grassroots Development* 19, no. 1 (1995).

Agarwala, A. N., and S. P. Singh, eds. *The Economics of Underdevelopment*. New York: Oxford University Press, 1963.

Alderman, Harold, and Victory Lavy. "Household Responses to Public Health Services: Cost and Quality Tradeoffs." *World Bank Research Observer* 11, no. 1 (February 1996): 3–22.

Althaus, Dudley. "Deforestation Contributed to Tragedy by Mitch in Honduras, Experts Claim." *Houston Chronicle,* 30 December 1998, A1, as found in the LEXIS-NEXIS database.

Amedo, Eduardo, José Márcio Camargo, Antônio Emilío S. Marques, and Cândido Gomes. "Fiscal Crisis and Asymmetries in the Education System in Brazil." In *Coping with Crisis: Austerity, Adjustment, and Human Resources,* edited by Joel Samoff. New York: UNESCO/ILO, 1994.

Ameur, Charles. *Agricultural Extension: A Step beyond the Next Step.* World Bank Technical Paper no. 247. Washington, D.C.: World Bank, 1994.

Anayiotos, George, and Jaime de Piniés. "The Secondary Market and the International Debt Problem." *World Development* 18, no. 2 (1990): 1655–60.

Anderson, Sarah, and John Cavanagh. *The Rise of Corporate Global Power.* Institute for Policy Studies, December 2000.

Anderson, Sarah, and Karen Hansen-Kuhn. *America's Plan for the Americas.* Washington, D.C.: Alliance, February 2001.

Aninat, Eduardo. "Growth and Stability in Latin America and the Caribbean: Challenges for the Epoch of Globalization." Lecture presented for the IMF in Port of Spain. 26 May 2000.

Anonymous. "Health of Indigenous Peoples." *Pan American Journal of Public Health* 2, no. 25 (1997): 357–62.

Antle, John M., and Gregg Heidebrink. "Environment and Development: Theory and International Evidence." *Economic Development and Cultural Change* 43, no. 3 (April 1995).

Argentina Business: The Portable Encyclopedia for Doing Business with Argentina. San Rafael, Calif.: World Trade Press, 1995.

Argentina: Selected Issues and Statistical Annex. Report No. 00/160. Washington, D.C.: IMF, December 2000.

"Argentina's New Struggle for Confidence and Growth." *The Economist,* 18 November 2000.

"Argentine Leader Races to Prop Economy." The Associated Press. *New York Times,* 16 July 2001.

Arriagada, Irma. "Unequal Participation by Women in the Working World." *CEPAL Review* 40 (April 1990): 83–98.

"Auto Industry Delivers Vote of Confidence in Brazil and Mercosur." *Latin American Weekly Report,* 3 February 1998.

Ayres, Robert L. *Crime and Violence as Development Issues in Latin America.* Washington, D.C.: World Bank, 1998.

Baer, Werner. "Changing Paradigms: Changing Interpretations of the Public Sector in Latin America's Economies." *Public Choice* 88 (1996): 365–79.

———. "Latin America and Europe in the Nineteenth Century: The Impact of an Unequal Relationship." In *Development and Underdevelopment in America,* edited by Walther Bernecker and Hans Werner Tobler. New York: Walter de Gruyter, 1993.

———, and Melissa Birch, eds. *Privatization in Latin America.* Westport, Conn.: Praeger, 1994.

Baer, Werner, and Annibal V. Villela. "Privatization and the Changing Role of the State in Brazil." In *Privatization in Latin America,* edited by Werner Baer and Melissa Birch. Westport, Conn.: Praeger, 1994.

Baker, Gerard. "Argentina Awakens US Pragmatism." *Financial Times,* 7 August 2001.

Baran, Paul A. "On the Political Economy of Backwardness." *Manchester School* 20, no. 1(1952). Reprinted in *The Economics of Underdevelopment,* edited by A. N. Agarwala and S. P. Singh. New York: Oxford University Press, 1963, and *Political Economy of Development and Underdevelopment,* edited by Charles K. Wilber. New York: Random House, 1973.

Barro, Robert J. "The Dollar Club: Why Countries Are So Keen to Join." *BusinessWeek,* 11 December 2000.

———. "From Seattle to Santiago, Let the Dollar Reign." *Hoover Digest* no. 3 (1999).

Bartlett, Christopher A., and Sumantra Ghoshal. "Going Global: Lessons from Late Movers." *Harvard Business Review* (March–April 2000).

Bastianensen, Johan. "Non-Conventional Rural Finance and the Crisis of Economic Institutions in Nicaragua." In *Sustainable Agriculture in Central America,* edited by Jan P. de Groot and Ruerd Ruben. New York: St. Martin's, 1997.

Bate, Peter. "Education: The Gordian Knot." *IDB Today.* Online edition available at www.iadb.org/idbamerica.

———. "Dollars for Everyone?" *IDB América* (May–June 1999).

Bauer, P., and B. Yamey. *The Economics of Underdeveloped Countries.* New York: Cambridge University Press, 1967.

Bellew, Rosemary T., and Elizabeth M. King. "Educating Women: Lessons from Experience." In *Women's Education in Developing Countries: Barriers, Benefits and Policies,* edited by Elizabeth M. King and Rosemary Bellew. Baltimore: Johns Hopkins University Press, 1993.

Bellos, Alex. "Ronaldo's Fame Hasn't Hit Home." *Minneapolis Star Tribune,* 10 July 1998, C6.

Benavente, José Miguel, Gustavo Crespi, Jorge Katz, and Giovanni Stumpo. "Changes in the Industrial Development of Latin America." *CEPAL Review* 60 (December 1996).

"The Benefits and Risks of Short-Term Borrowing." *Global Development Finance.* Washington, D.C.: World Bank, 2000.

Bennett, Bradley. "Plants and People of the Amazonian Rainforests: The Role of Ethnobotany in Sustainable Development." *BioScience* 42, no. 8 (1992).

Berg, Andrew and Eduardo Borensztein. "The Dollarization Debate." *Finance & Development* (March 2000).

————. "Full Dollarization—The Pros and Cons." *International Monetary Fund Economic Issue* no. 24. (December 2000).

Berger, Marguerite. *Microfinance: An Emerging Market within the Emerging Markets.* Draft. Washington, D.C.: IADB, 2000.

Bergsten, Fred C. "American Politics, Global Trade." *The Economist,* 27 September 1997.

Bernstein, H., ed. *Underdevelopment and Development.* Harmondsworth, U.K.: Penguin, 1973.

Berstein, Aarn. "Sweatshop Reform: How to Solve the Standoff." *BusinessWeek,* 3 May 1999.

Bhagwati, Jagdish. "The FTAA Is *Not* Free Trade." In *Trade: Towards Open Regionalism,* proceedings of the 1997 World Bank Conference on Development in Latin America and the Caribbean. Washington, D.C.: World Bank, 1998.

————. "Fast Track to Nowhere." *The Economist,* 18 October 1997.

Biersteker, Thomas J. *Dealing with Debt.* Boulder, Colo.: Westview, 1993.

————. *Distortion or Development? Contending Perspectives on the Multinational Corporation.* Cambridge, Mass.: MIT Press, 1978.

Binswanger, Hans P., and Klaus Deininger. "Explaining Agricultural and Agrarian Policies in Developing Countries." *Journal of Economic Literature* 35 (December 1997).

Birdsall, Nancy, and Carlos Lozada. "Prebish Reconsidered: Coping with External Shocks in Vulnerable Economies." *CEPAL Review* (October 2000).

————. "Recurring Themes in Latin American Economic Thought: From Prebisch to the Market and Back." In *Securing Stability and Growth in Latin America,* edited by Ricardo Hausmann and Helmut Reisen. Paris: OECD Publications, 1996.

Bitran, Eduardo, and Pablo Serra. "Regulation of Privatized Utilities: The Chilean Experience." *World Development* 26, no.6 (1998): 945–62.

Blackwood, D. L., and R. G. Lynch. "The Measurement of Inequality and Poverty." *World Development* 22, no. 4 (1994): 567–78.

Blomström, Magnus, and Ari Kokko. *Regional Integration and Foreign Direct Investment.* National Bureau of Economic Research Working Paper no. 6019. Cambridge, Mass.: National Bureau of Economic Research, 1997.

Blomström, Magnus, and Edward N. Wolff. "Multinational Corporations and Productivity Convergence in Mexico." In *Convergence of Productivity: Cross-National Studies and Historical Evidence,* edited by William Baumol, Richard R. Nelson, and Edward N. Wolff. New York: Oxford University Press, 1994.

Bloomberg Latin America. "Argentine Markets Climb after IMF, Banks Move to Shore Up Confidence." Retrieved from the Internet, 14 July 1999, at www.quote.bloomberg.com.

Blumenstein, Rebecca. "GM to Build a Low-Priced Car in Brazil." *Wall Street Journal,* 19 March 1997.

Blustein, Paul. "Currencies in Crisis." *Washington Post,* 7 February 1999.

"Bolivia: Getting Kids Back in School." *IDB América* (November 1997): 14. Available online at wwwiadb.org/English/projects/projects.html.

Bonior, Congressman David. "I Told You So." *New York Times,* editorial, 13 July 1997.

Borenstein, E, J. De Gregorio, and J. W. Lee. "How Does Foreign Investment Affect Economic Growth?" *Journal of International Economics* 45 (1998): 115–35.

Bowman, Kirk, and Jesus Felipe. *Convergence, Catch Up, and the Future of Latin America* (Atlanta: Georgia Institute of Technology.) Unpublished paper, 17 October 2000. Access at pro.harvard.edu/papers/020/020015BowmanKirk.pdf.

Bowman, Kirk S. "Should the Kuznets Effect Be Relied on to Induce Equalizing Growth?" *World Development* 25, no.1 (1997): 127–43.

Boyd, Stephanie. "A Natural Weapon for Preventing Malaria in the Peruvian Amazon." *Science from the Developing World,* 19 January 2001.

Bradford, Colin, Jr. "Future Policy Directions and Relevance." In *The Legacy of Raúl Prebisch,* edited by Enrique V. Iglesias. Washington, D.C.: IADB, 1994.

Braga, Carlos Alberto Primo. "Tropical Forests and Trade Policy: The Case of Indonesia and Brazil." In *International Trade and the Environment,* edited by Patrick Low. Washington, D.C.: World Bank, 1992.

Brainard, S. Lael, and David Riker. *Are U.S. Multinationals Exporting U.S. Jobs?* National Bureau of Economic Research Working Paper no. 5958. Cambridge, Mass: National Bureau of Economic Research, 1997.

Braverman, Avishay, and J. Luis Guasch. "Administrative Failures in Government Credit Programs." In *The Economics of Rural Organization,* edited by Karla Hoff, Avishay Braverman, and Joseph Stiglitz. New York: Oxford University Press/World Bank, 1993.

"Brazil: Domestic Debt Dynamics and Implications." *ING Barings Emerging Markets Weekly Report,* 5 March 1999, 1–3.

"Brazil's Affluent Are Hurt by Crisis." *Washington Post,* 25 January 1999.

"Brazil's Iron King." *Financial Times,* 29 June 1998.

"Brazil's Neighbors Are Very Nervous." *BusinessWeek,* 17 November 1997.

Britan, Ricardo, and Keith McInnes. *The Demand for Health Care in Latin America.* Economic Development Institute Seminar Paper no. 46. Washington, D.C.: World Bank, 1993.

Britton, John A., ed. *Molding the Hearts and Minds: Education, Communications and Social Change in Latin America.* Wilmington, Del.: Scholarly Resources, 1994.

Brooke, James. "Home, Home on the Range, in Brazil's Heartland." *New York Times,* 26 April 1995.

The Brookings Institution, World Bank, and IMF. *Emerging Market Economies Recover, but Debt Restructuring Problems Linger On.* News Release. Available online at www.brookings.edu/com/news/0004WBIMF.htm. 2001.

Bruton, Henry. "A Reconsideration of Import Substitution." *Journal of Economic Literature* 36 (June 1998).

———. "Import Substitution." In *Handbook of Development Economics,* vol. 2, 3rd ed., edited by Hollis Chenery and T. N. Srivivasan. New York: Elsevier, 1996.

Bulmer-Thomas, Victor. "The Brazilian Devaluation: National Responses and International Consequences." *International Affairs* 75, no. 4 (1999).

———. *The Economic History of Latin America since Independence.* New York: Cambridge University Press, 1994.

Buntin, John, and Christine Letts. *Accion International: Where Latin America Meets Brooklyn.* Cambridge, Mass.: John F. Kennedy School of Government, 1996.

Burbach, Roger, and Peter Rosset. "Chiapas and the Crisis of Mexican Agriculture." *Food First Policy Brief* no. 1. San Francisco: Institute for Food and Development, 1994.

Burki, Shahid Javed, and Sebastian Edwards. *Dismantling the Populist State.* Washington, D.C.: World Bank, 1996.

———. *Latin America after Mexico: Quickening the Pace.* Washington, D.C.: World Bank, 1996.

Burns, Bradford E., ed. *Latin America: Conflict and Creation: A Historical Reader.* Englewood Cliffs, N.J.: Prentice Hall, 1992.

Burns, Tom. "Telefonica Moviles Expands Its Latin American Empire: Mexican Purchase Sharpens Interest Ahead of Listening." *Financial Times,* 5 October 2000.

Buvinic, Mayra, and Andrew Morrison. "How Can We Measure Violence." *Social Development* (July 2000).

———. *Women in Poverty: A New Global Underclass.* Washington, D.C: IADB, Women in Development, N WID-101 Page 2. www.iadb.org/sds/doc/767eng.pdf. July 1998.

Byrnes, H., and B. Spencer. "U.S. Must Aid Guatemala's Shift to Peace." *St. Louis Post-Dispatch,* 20 December 1996.

Caballero, Ricardo J. *Macroeconomic Volatility in Latin America: A View and Three Case Studies.* Working Paper 7782. Massachusetts: National Bureau of Economic Research, July 2000.

Calcagno, Alfredo, Sandra Manuelito, and Gunilla Ryd. *Proyecciones Latinoamericanos 2000–2001.* Santiago, Chile: United Nations and ECLAC, January 2001.

Caldwell, Laura. "Swapping Debt to Preserve Nature." *Christian Science Monitor,* 11 September 1990.

Camdessus, Michel. "The Private Sector in a Strengthened Global Financial System." Remarks at the International Monetary Conference, Philadelphia, 8 June 1999. Available online at www.imf.org/external/speeches.

"CANTV in 1994." *Harvard Business School Case Studies,* 28 February 1996.

"Capital Controversies." *The Economist,* 23 May 1998.

Cardoso, Fernando Henrique. Interview on the occasion of the second anniversary of the *Real* Plan, as reported in FBIS-LAT-96-129 (Foreign Broadcast Information Services, Latin America), 3 July 1996. Originally appeared on the Rede Globo website, 1 July 1996.

Carnegie Endowment for International Peace. *Working Papers—Breaking the Labor–Trade Deadlock,* no. 17. Washington, D.C.: Inter-American Dialogue and the Carnegie Endowment for International Peace. (February 2001).

Carnoy, Martin. "Structural Adjustment and the Changing Face of Education." *International Labor Review* 134, no. 6 (1995): 653–73.

Cartaya, Vanessa F. "El Confuso mundo del sector informal." *Nueva Sociedad* 90 (July–August 1987): 81–84.

Carter, Michael, and Bradford Barham. "Level Playing Fields and Laissez Faire: Postliberal Development Strategy in Inegalitarian Agrarian Economies." *World Development* 24, no. 7 (July 1996).

Carter, Michael, and Dina Mesbah. "State-Mandated and Market-Mediated Reform in Latin America." In *Including the Poor,* edited by Michael Lipton and Jacques van der Gaag. Baltimore: Johns Hopkins University Press/World Bank, 1993.

Case, Brendan M. "Mexican Tariff on U.S. Beef Ignites Trade Dispute." *Dallas Morning News,* 3 August 1999.

Castañeda, Tarsicio. "Combating Poverty." In *Reforms in Education.* San Francisco: International Center for Economic Growth, 1992.

Catán, Thomas. "Argentina Looks to $6bn IMF Injection." *Financial Times,* 6 August 2001.

Caves, Richard E. *Multinational Enterprise and Economic Analysis.* 2nd ed. Cambridge: Cambridge University Press, 1996.

Center for International Health Information. *Country Health Profile/Bolivia.* Arlington, Va.: Center for International Health Information, December 1996. Available online at www.cihi.com.

Central Intelligence Agency. *The World Fact Book.* Available online at www.odci.gov/cia.

Cevallos, Diego. "Environment-Mexico: Toxic Waste, a Dirty Problem." Inter Press Service. 11 August 1995. Available on the LEXIS-NEXIS database.

Chile Info. *Chile Facts on Demand.*

Chipman, Andre. "U.S., Latin-American Oil Companies Build Alliance as Mideast Clout Fades." *Wall Street Journal,* 9 March 1998.

Choque Schulter, Sidney, and Ruth Choque Schulter. "Misinformation, Mistrust, and Mistreatment: Family Planning among Bolivian Market Women." *Studies in Family Planning* 25 (1994).

"Chronology of FTAA Process." Free Trade Area of the Americas. "Citizen's Guide to Dollarization." Committee Documents Online—106th Congress. Senate Banking Committee. Available online at www.banking.senate.gov/docs/reports/doillar.htm, 2000.

Clements, Benedict. "The Real Plan, Poverty, and Income Distribution in Brazil." *Finance and Development* (September 1997).

Coatsworth, John. "Notes on the Comparative Economic History of Latin America and the United States." In *Development and Underdevelopment in America,* edited by Walther Bernecker and Hans Werner Tobler. New York: Walter de Gruyter, 1993.

Coes, Donald V. *Macroeconomic Crises, Policies, and Growth in Brazil, 1964–90.* Washington, D.C.: World Bank, 1995.

Colclough, Christopher. "Education and the Market: Which Parts of the Neoliberal Solution Are Correct?" *World Development* 24, no. 4 (1996): 589–610.

Colitt, Raymond. "Banking and Telecom Sectors Lead the Way: Brazil's New IT Markets." *Financial Times,* 1 November 2000.

Comision Económica Para América Latina. *Indicadores Económicos.* Santiago, Chile: Comision Económica Para América Latina, 1997.

"Commercial Debt Restructuring." *Global Development Finance.* Washington, D.C.: World Bank.

Commission on Development and Environment for Amazonia. *Amazonia without Myths.* Washington, D.C.: IADB, 1992.

"Competitiveness Is Vital." *Financial Times,* 14 December 2000.

Conger, Lucy. "A Fourth Way? The Latin American Alternative to Neoliberalism." *Current History,* November 1998.

Constance, Paul. "Lousy Deal." *IDB América,* May–June 2000.

———. "A Seat at the Table: Union Leaders Urge IDB to Include Workers' Concerns in Reform Programs and Free Trade Negotiations." *IDB América,* April 1998. Available at the IADB homepage at www.iadb.org.

———. "The New Referees." *IDB América,* January–February 1998.

———. "A High Technology Incubator." *IDB América,* 1997. Available at the IADB homepage at www.iadb.org.

Contreras Murphy, Ellen. "La Selva and the Magnetic Pull of Markets: Organic Coffee-Growing in Mexico." *Grassroots Development* 19, no. 1 (1995): 27–34.

Corbo, Vittorio. "Economic Policies and Performance in Latin America." In *Economic Development: Handbook of Comparative Economic Policies,* edited by Enzo Grilli and Dominick Salvatore. Westport, Conn.: Greenwood, 1994.

Cortés-Salas, Hernán, Ronnie de Camino, and Arnoldo Contreras. Readings of the *Workshop on Government Policy Reform for Forestry Conservation and Development in Latin America,* 1–3 June 1994. Washington, D.C.: Inter-American Institute for Cooperation on Agriculture, 1995.

"Cost Information and Management Decision in a Brazilian Hospital." In *World Development Report 1993.* New York: Oxford University Press/World Bank, 1993.

"Cost-Cutting Takes a Private Road." *Euromoney,* September 1996.

Council on Foreign Relations. "Reforming Education in America." Study group on reforming education in Latin America, "The Second Wave of Reform," February–October 1996.

"Creating Jobs Is Main Headache." *Latin American Weekly Report,* 5 January 1999.

"Crime Could Drive Sony From Mexico." *Gazette,* 10 May 2000.

Cuddington, John T. *Capital Flight: Estimates, Issues, and Explanations.* Princeton Studies in International Finance no. 58. Princeton, N.J.: Princeton University Press, 1986.

Cypher, James, and James Dietz, *The Process of Economic Development* (New York: Routledge, 1997), cited by Miguel D. Ramirez, "Foreign Direct Investment in Mexico and

Chile: A Critical Appraisal ." In *Foreign Direct Investment in Latin America,* edited by Werner Baer and William R. Miles. New York: The Hayworth Press, 2001.

Dadus, Uri, Dipak Dasgupta, and Dilip Ratha. "The Role of Short-Term Debt in Recent Crises." *Finance & Development,* December 2000.

De Gortari, Carlos Salinas, and Roberto Mangabeira Unger. "The Market Turn without Neoliberalism." *Challenge* 42, no. 1 (January–February 1999).

De Janvry, Alain, and Elisabeth Sadoulet. "NAFTA and Mexico's Maize Producers." *World Development* 23, no. 8 (August 1995): 1349–62.

———. "Rural Development in Latin America: Relinking Poverty Reduction to Growth." In *Including the Poor,* edited by Michael Lipton and Jacques van der Gaag. Washington, D.C.: World Bank, 1993.

De Souza, Amaury. "Redressing Inequalities: Brazil's Social Agenda at Century's End." In *Brazil under Cardoso,* edited by Susan Kaufman Purcell and Riordan Roett. Boulder, Colo.: Rienner, 1997.

"Debt Relief for Poor Countries (HIPC): What Has Been Achieved?—A Factsheet." *International Monetary Fund* (April 2001).

"Declaration and Action Plan for Latin American Economic Recovery." *UN Chronicle* 21, no. 3 (March 1984): 13–17.

Deere, Carmen D., and Magdalena León. "Institutional Reform of Agriculture under Neoliberalism." *Latin American Research Review* 36, no. 2 (2001).

della Paolera, Gerardo, and Alan Taylor. *Finance and Development in an Emerging Market: Argentina in the Interwar Period.* National Bureau of Economic Research Working Paper Series no. 6236. Cambridge, Mass.: National Bureau of Economic Research, 1997.

Delovitch, Emanuel, and Klas Ringskog. *Private Sector Participation in Water Supply and Sanitation in Latin America.* Washington, D.C.: World Bank, 1995.

Delph, Yvette M. "Health Priorities in Developing Countries." *Journal of Law, Medicine, & Ethics* 21, no. 1 (1993).

DePalma, Anthony. "Free Trade's Promise in Latin America; the Poor Survive It All. Even Boom Times." *New York Times,* 24 June 2001.

———. "Passing the Torch on a Chile Trade Deal." *New York Times,* 7 January 2001.

Devlin, Robert, and Ricardo French-Davis. *Toward an Evaluation of Regional Integration in Latin America in the 1990s.* Working Paper 2. Buenos Aires: INTAL and ITD, 1998.

Devlin, Robert, Ricardo Ffrench-Davis, and Stephany Griffith-Jones. "Surges in Capital Flows and Development: An Overview of Policy Issues." In *Coping with Capital Surges,* edited by Ricardo Ffrench-Davis and Stephany Griffith-Jones. Boulder, Colo.: Rienner, 1995.

Dewees, Anthony, and Steven Klees. "Social Movements and the Transformation of National Policy: Street and Working Children in Brazil." *Comparative Education Review* 39, no. 1 (1995).

Diáz Alejandro, Carlos. "International Markets for LDCs: The Old and the New." *American Economic Review* (May): 254–69.

Diaz Bonilla, Eugenio, and Hector E. Schamis. *The Political Economy of Exchange Rate Policies in Argentina 1950–1998.* Working Paper #R-379. IADB (April 1999).

Dietz, James L., and James H. Street, eds. *Latin America's Economic Development: Institutionalist and Structuralist Perspectives.* Boulder, Colo.: Rienner, 1987.

Dillin, John. "Crime Down, but Many Still Edgy." *Christian Science Monitor,* 19 June 2001.

Dixon, John. *The Urban Environmental Challenge in Latin America.* LATEN Dissemination Note no. 4, World Bank Latin America Technical Department, Environment Division. Washington, D.C.: World Bank, 1993.

"Dollarization: Fad or Future for Latin America." IMF Economic Forum. Washington, D.C.: International Monetary Fund, 24 June 1999.

Dornbusch, Rudiger. *Stabilization, Debt, and Reform: Policy Analysis for Developing Countries.* Englewood Cliffs, N.J.: Prentice Hall, 1993.

———, and Sebastian Edwards. "The Political Economy of Latin America." In *The Macroeconomics of Populism in Latin America* (a National Bureau of Economic Research conference report), edited by Rudiger Dornbusch and Sebastian Edwards. Chicago: University of Chicago Press, 1991.

Dos Santos, Theodoro. "La crisis de la teoría del desarollo y las relaciones de dependencia en América Latina." *Boletin de CESO* 3 (1968). English translation in H. Bernstein, ed., *Underdevelopment and Development.* Harmondsworth, U.K.: Penguin, 1973.

Drabek, Zdenek, and Warren Payne. "The Impact of Transparency on Foreign Direct Investment." IMF Staff Working Paper ERAD-99-02. Geneva: The World Trade Organization, 1999.

Druckerman, Pamela. "Argentina Wants to Speed or Boost Aid." *Wall Street Journal,* 3 August 2001.

———. "Argentine Bank Depositors Hold Reins of Nation's Fate. *Wall Street Journal,* 17 July 2001.

———, Michael Phillips, Jonathan Karp, and Hugh Pope. "IMF Acts to Preempt Emerging-Market Crisis." *Wall Street Journal,* 6 August 2001.

Dyer, Geoff. "Brazil Markets Maintain Boost from IMF Deal." *Financial Times,* 7 August 2001.

———. "Brazil's Star Pupil Status Gets a Caning." *Financial Times,* 5 August 2001.

Eakin, Ken. "Monitoring and Evaluating Poverty Alleviation Programs in Peru. *Science from the Developing World,* 4 September 2001.

Eberlee, John. "Agenda Peru: Charting a Shared National Vision for the Future." *Science from the Developing World,* 23 March 2001.

Echavarría, Juan José. "Trade Flow in the Andean Countries: Unilateral Liberalization or Regional Preferences." In *Trade: Towards Open Regionalism,* proceedings of the 1997 World Bank Conference on Development in Latin America and the Caribbean. Washington, D.C.: World Bank, 1998.

ECLAC/UNDP, *Financing for Sustainable Development in Latin America and the Caribbean,* Joint document prepared for the World Summit on Sustainable Development, August 2002.

Economic Commission for Latin America and the Caribbean. *Notes* N. 13. November 2000.

———. *Notes* N. 12. September 2000.

———. *Foreign Investment in Latin America and the Caribbean, 2000*: table I.12, 65.

———. *Preliminary Overview of the Economies of Latin America and the Caribbean, 1999.* Santiago, Chile: United Nations and ECLAC, December 1999.

———. *Communique on the International Financial Crises.* 15 September 1998. Available online at www.cepal.org.english/coverpage/financialcrisis.htm.

———. *Preliminary Overview of the Economies of Latin America and the Caribbean, 1999.* Santiago, Chile: United Nations and ECLAC, 1998.

———. *The Equity Gap: Latin America, the Caribbean, and the Social Summit.* Santiago, Chile: ECLAC, 1997.

———. *The Fiscal Covenant: Strengths, Weaknesses, Challenges.* Santiago, Chile: ECLAC, 1997.

———. *Indicadores Económicos.* Santiago, Chile: ECLAC, 1997.

———. *Panorama de la Insercion Internactional de América Latina y el Caribe, 1996.* Santiago, Chile: ECLAC, 1996.

———. *Statistical Yearbook for Latin American and the Caribbean, 1996.* Chile: ECLAC, 1996.

————. *Strengthening Development: The Interplay of Macro- and Microeconomics.* Santiago, Chile: ECLAC, 1996.

————. *Policies to Improve Linkages with the Global Economy.* Santiago, Chile: ECLAC, 1995.

————. *Economic Survey of Latin America and the Caribbean.* Santiago, Chile: ECLAC, various years.

"Ecuador Drifts between Opportunity and Deadlock." *The Economist,* 23 December 2000.

Edwards, Sebastian. *Capital Flows into Latin America: A Stop-Go Story?* National Bureau of Economic Research Working Paper no. 6441. Cambridge, Mass. National Bureau of Economic Research, 1998. Available online at www.nber.org/papers/w6441.

————. "The Mexican Peso Crisis: How Much Did We Know? When Did We Know It?" *World Economy* 21, no. 1 (1998).

————. *Crisis and Reform in Latin America: From Despair to Hope.* New York: Oxford University Press, 1995.

————. "The Political Economy of Inflation and Stabilization in Developing Countries." *Economic Development and Cultural Change* 42, no. 2 (January 1994): 235–66.

————, and Daniel Lederman. *The Political Economy of Unilateral Trade Liberalization: The Case of Chile.* National Bureau of Economic Research Working Paper no. 6510. Cambridge, Mass.: National Bureau of Economic Research, 1998. Available online at www.nber.org/papers/w6510.

Edwards, Sebastian, and Nora Claudia Lustig, eds. *Labor Markets in Latin America: Combining Social Protection with Market Flexibility.* Washington, D.C.: Brookings Institution, 1997.

Eichengreen, Barry. "When to Dollarize." Presented for the ITAM Dollarization Project Meeting in Mexico City (3 December 1999).

El-Ashry, Mohamed T. *Statement to the Fourth Session of the Conference of the Parties to the United Nations Framework Convention on Climate Change.* Buenos Aires, 11 November 1998. Washington, D.C.: Global Environment Facility, 1998.

Ellison, Katherine. "Latin Summit's Focus: Education of Kids." *Miami Herald,* 13 April 1998, A1. Available online at www.alca-cupula.org.

"Emerging-Market Indicators." *The Economist,* 4 November 2000.

Emmott, Robin, "Bribery Costs Mexicans Up to 14% of Income. "*Financial Times,* October 31, 2001.

Employment Policy Foundation. "Open Trade: The 'Fast Track' to Higher Living Standards." *Contemporary Issues in Employment and Workplace Policy* 111, no. 10 (October 1997). Internet publication available at epfnet.org.

"Energy in Latin America: Even Oil Is Growing Less Sacred." *The Economist,* 1 June 1996.

Energy Information Administration. *Petroleum Supply Annual, 1995.* Washington, D.C.: U.S. Department of Energy, 1995.

The Equity Gap—A Second Assessment. Prepared by the ECLAC Secretariat for the Second Regional Conference. ECLAC, 2000.

Estache, Antonio, and Danny Leipziger, "Utilities Privatization and the Poor: Lessons and Evidence from Latin America." *World Development* 29, no. 7 (2001): 1181.

Engell, Alan. "Improving the Quality and Equity of Education in Chile: The Programa 900 Escuelas and the MECE-Basica." In *Implementing Policy Innovation in Latin America: Politics, Economics and Techniques,* edited by Antonio Silva. Washington, D.C.: IADB, 1996.

Evans, Peter. "The Eclipse of the State?: Reflection on Stateness in an Era of Globalization." *World Politics* 50 (October 1997).

————. *Dependent Development.* Princeton, N.J.: Princeton University Press, 1979.

————, ed. "State–Society Synergy: Government and Social Capital in Development," *World Development* 24, no. 6, special edition (June 1996).

Faiz, Asif, Surhid Gautam, and Emaad Burki. "Air Pollution from Motor Vehicles: Issues and Options for Latin American Countries." *The Science of the Total Environment* 169 (1995): 303–10.

Fajnzylber, Fernando. "Education and Changing Production Patterns with Social Equality." *CEPAL Review* 47 (August 1992).

Fanelli, José María, and Roberto Frenkel. "Macropolicies for the Transition from Stabilization to Growth." In *New Directions in Development Economics: Growth, Environmental Concerns, and Government in the 1990s,* edited by Mats Lundahl and Benno J. Ndulu. London: Routledge, 1996.

Fanelli, José Maria, and José Luis Machinea. "Capital Movements in Argentina." In *Coping with Capital Surges: The Return of Finance to Latin America,* edited by Ricardo Ffrench-Davis and Stephany Griffith-Jones. Boulder, Colo.: Rienner, 1995. Farber, Daniel. *Environment under Fire.* New York: Monthly Review Press, 1993.

Fauriol, Georges A., and Sidney Weintraub. "The Century of the Americas: Dawn of a New Century." *The Washington Quarterly* 24, no. 2 (Spring 2001).

Fearnside, Phillip. "Deforestation in Brazilian Amazonia: The Effect of Population and Land Tenure." *Ambio* 22, no. 8 (December 1993).

Federal Reserve Bank of Atlanta. "Imbalances in Latin American Fiscal Accounts: Why the United States Should Care." *EconSouth* 2, no. 4 (2000).

Fernández-Arias, Eduardo. "The New Wave of Capital Inflows: Sea Change or Tide?" Presented at the Annual Meeting of the Board of Governors, IADB and Inter-American Investment Corporation (26 March 2000).

———, and Ricardo Hausmann. *Getting It Right: What to Reform in International Financial Markets.* Working Paper #428. Presented at the Tenth International Forum on Latin American Perspectives in Paris. IADB, November 1999.

———. *What's Wrong with International Financial Markets?* Working Paper #429. Presented at the Tenth International Forum on Latin American Perspectives in Paris. IADB, November 1999.

———. *International Initiatives to Bring Stability to Financial Integration.* IADB. March 1999.

Ffrench-Davis Ricardo. "Policy Implications of the Tequila Effect." *Challenge.* March–April 1998.

———. Comment on L. Allan Winters, "Assessing Regional Integration." In *Trade: Towards Open Regionalism,* proceedings of the 1997 World Bank Conference on Development in Latin America and the Caribbean. Washington, D.C.: World Bank, 1998.

———, Manuel Agosin, and Andras Uthoff. "Capital Movements, Export Strategy and Macroeconomic Stability in Chile." In *Coping with Capital Surges: The Return of Finance to Latin America,* edited by Ricardo Ffrench-Davis and Stephany Griffith-Jones. Boulder, Colo.: Rienner, 1995.

"Fifty Years On." *The Economist,* 16 May 1998, 22.

"The Fiscal Mire." *The Economist,* 4 May 1996.

Fisher, Stanley. "Reforming World Finance." *The Economist,* 3–9 October 1998. Reproduced at www.imf.org.

———. "Remarks to the Argentine Bankers Association." Presented at the Argentine Bankers Association Meeting." Buenos Aires: IMF.

Fiszbein, A., and G. Psacharopoulos. *Income Inequality in Latin America: The Story of the Eighties.* Technical Department for Latin America Working Paper. Washington, D.C.: World Bank, 1995.

Foley, Michael. "Agenda for Mobilization: The Agrarian Question and Popular Mobilization in Contemporary Mexico." *Latin American Research Review* 26, no. 2 (1991): 39–74.

Food and Agriculture Organization of the United Nations. *The State of Food and Agriculture.* Rome: Food and Agriculture Organization of the United Nations, 1994.

Foxley, Alejandro. "Preface." In *The New Economic Model in Latin America and Its Impact on Income Distribution and Poverty,* edited by Victor Bulmer-Thomas. New York: St. Martin's, 1996.

Fraga, Arminio. "Monetary Policy during the Transition to a Floating Exchange Rate: Brazil's Recent Experience." *Finance & Development* 37, no. 1 (March 2000).

Frank, Andre Gundar. *Capitalism and Underdevelopment in Latin America.* New York: Monthly Review Press, 1967.

Free Trade Area of the Americas. "Free Trade Area of the Americas Declaration of Ministers Fifth Trade Ministerial Meeting." Canada: Free Trade Area of the Americas. 4 November 1999.

"Free Trade Area of the Americas Sixth Meeting of Ministers of Trade of the Hemisphere." Ministerial Declaration in Buenos Aires. Argentina: Free Trade Area of the Americas. 7 April 2001.

Freire, Paulo. *Pedagogy of the Oppressed.* New York: Seabury, 1970.

Friedland, Jonathan. "Their Success Earns Chileans a New Title: Ugly Pan-Americans." *Wall Street Journal,* 3 October 1996.

———. "Argentina's Tax Collector Names Names" *Wall Street Journal,* 13 April 1995.

"From Sandals to Suits." *The Economist,* 1 February 1997.

From Santiago to Quebec City—*Report on the Achievements of the Inter-American System.* Washington, DC: Summits of the Americas Information Network, Office of Summit Follow-up March 2001 www.summit-americas.org.

Fuerbringer, Jonathan. "Trouble in Argentina May Help Other Emerging Markets." *New York Times,* 15 July 2001.

———. "Economic Troubles Worsen in Argentina." *New York Times,* 11 July 2001.

"Funds for Farmers Needed for Future." *Financial Times,* 14 December 2000.

Furtado, Celso. *Development and Underdevelopment.* Translated by Ricardo W. Agruar and Eric Charles Drysdale. Berkeley: University of California Press, 1965.

Gagné, Gilbert. "North American Free Trade, Canada, and the US Trade Remedies: An Assessment After Ten Years." *World Economics* 23, no. 1 (January 2000).

Galal, Ahmed, Leroy Jones, Pankaj Tandon, and Ingo Vogelsang. "Divestiture: Questions and Answers." In *Welfare Consequences of Selling Public Enterprises.* Washington, D.C.: World Bank 1994.

García, María Isabel. "Forecast Bright for 'Clean' Agriculture." *Tierramérica,* 24 July 2001.

Garfield, Elsie, Maurizio Guadagni, and Daniel Moreau. *Colombia—Decentralization of Agricultural Extension Services.* In *Agricultural Extension: Generic Challenges and Some Ingredients for Solutions,* by Gershon Feder, Anthony Willett, and Willem Zijp. Washington, D.C.: The World Bank, 1999.

"A Gathering Twilight." *The Economist,* 14 July 2001.

Gavin, Michael. "Surviving Economic Surgery." *The IDB* (December 1996): 4–5.

———. "Hearing on Official Dollarization in Latin America." Presented to the Senate Banking Committee (15 July 1999).

———, Ricardo Hausmann, Roberto Perotti, and Ernesto Talvi. *Managing Fiscal Policy in Latin America and the Caribbean: Volatility, Procyclicality, and Limited Creditworthiness.* IADB, Office of the Chief Economist Working Paper no. 326. Washington, D.C.: IADB, 1996.

Gelbard, Alene H. *An Action Plan for Population, Development, and the Environment: Woodrow Wilson Center Spring 1996 Report.* Washington, D.C.: Woodrow Wilson Center, 1996.

Gereffi, Gary, and Peter Evans. "Transnational Corporations, Dependent Development, and State Policy in the Semiperiphery." *Latin American Research Review* 16, no. 3 (1981): 31–64.

Global Development Finance 2001, Washington, D.C.: World Bank Publications, 2001, 186, table A42.

Global Environmental Fund, "Participation Means Learning through Doing: GEF's Experience. in Biodiversity Conservation and Sustainable Use," *GEF Lessons Notes* 12, July 2001, 1–4. Available at ww.gefweb.org.

"Gloom over the River Plate." *The Economist,* 14 July 2001.

"Going Too Far in Support of Trade." *The Economist,* 16 December 2000.

Gómez, Ricardo. "The Hall of Mirrors: The Internet in Latin America." *Current History* 99, no. 634 (2000).

Gonzalez, David. "Gaining Dollars, Town Is Losing Its Folkways." *New York Times,* 1 January 2001.

Goodland, Robert, and Herman Daly. *Poverty Alleviation Is Essential for Environmental Sustainability.* World Bank, Environment Department, Divisional Working Paper 1993-42. Washington, D.C.: World Bank, 1993.

Gori, Graham. "Mexicans Wait More for a Phone." *New York Times,* 24 January 2001.

———. "Mexico's Heavy Industries threatened by Natural Gas Costs." *New York Times,* 5 January 2001.

Goulet, Denis. *The Cruel Choice: A New Concept in the Theory of Development.* New York: Atheneum, 1971.

Graham, Carol. "Strengthening Institutional Capacity in Poor Countries," *The Brookings Institution Policy Brief,* No. 98, April 2002; www.brookings.edu.

———. *Private Markets for Public Goods: Raising the Stakes for Economic Reform.* Washington, D.C.: Brookings Institution Press, 1998.

———. *Safety Nets, Politics, and the Poor: Transitions to Market Economies.* Washington, D.C.: Brookings Institution, 1994.

Graham, Edward, M. and Erika Wada. *Domestic Reform, Trade and Investment Liberalisation, Financial Crisis, and Foreign Direct Investment into Mexico.* Washington, D.C.: Institute for International Economics, 2000.

"Green, as in Greenbacks." *The Economist,* 1 February 1997.

Greig, Alan, Michael Kimmel, and James Lang. *Men, Masculinities & Development: Broadening Our Work towards Gender Equality.* UNDP Gender in Development Monograph Series #10. May 2000.

Griffith-Jones, Stephany. "The Mexican Peso Crisis." *CEPAL Review* 60 (December 1996).

Grilli, Enzo, and Dominick Salvatore, eds. *Economic Development: Handbook of Comparative Economic Policies.* Westport, Conn.: Greenwood, 1994.

Grosh, Margaret E. *Administering Targeted Social Programs in Latin America.* Washington, D.C.: World Bank, 1994.

"Guadalajara Takes High-Tech Route." *Financial Times,* 14 December 2000.

Guerguil, Marinte. "Some Thoughts on the Definition of the Informal Sector." *CEPAL Review* 35 (August 1988).

Gunnarsson, C., and M. Lundahl. "The Good, The Bad, and the Wobbly." In *New Directions in Development Economics: Growth, Environmental Concerns, and Government in the 1990s,* edited by Mats Lundahl and Benno J. Ndulu. London: Routledge, 1996.

Gutierrez, Luish H., and Sanford Berg. "Telecommunications Liberalization and Regulatory Governance: Lessons from Latin America." *Telecommunications Policy* 24 (December 2000): 865–84.

Haass, Richard N., and Robert E. Litan. "Globalization and Its Discontents." *Foreign Affairs* 77, no. 3 (1998).

Hall, Susan E. A. "Conoco's Green Strategy." Harvard Business School Case #9-394-001. 4 October 1993.

Hammergren, Linn. "The Development Wars: Analyzing Foreign Assistance Impact and Policy." *Latin American Research Review* 34, no. 2 (1999).

Hanshaw, Margaret. "Venture Philanthropist." *Harvard Business Review* (July–August 2000).

Hanson, Simon. *Economic Development in Latin America.* Washington, D.C.: Inter-American Affairs Press, 1951.

Harriss, John, Janet Hunter, and Colin M. Lewis, "Introduction: Development and Significance of the NIE." In *The New Institutional Economics and Third World Development,* ed. John Harriss, Janet Hunter, and Colin M. Lewis, 1. London: Routledge, 1995.

Harriss-White, Barbara. "Maps and Landscapes of Grain Markets in South Asia." In *The New Institutional Economics and Third World Development,* edited by John Harriss, Janet Hunter, and Colin M. Lewis. London: Routledge, 1996.

Hartshorn, Gary S. "Natural Forest Management by the Yanesha Forestry Cooperative in Peruvian Amazonia." In *Alternatives to Deforestation: Steps toward Sustainable Use of the Amazon Rain Forest,* edited by Anthony B. Anderson. New York: Columbia University Press, 1990.

"Harvesting Farming's Potential." *The Economist,* 9 September 2000.

Hasan Khan Mahmood. "Rural Poverty in Developing Countries—Implications for Public Policy." *IMF Economic Issues* 26 (March 2001).

Hausmann, Ricardo, and Helmut Reisen, eds. *Securing Stability and Growth in Latin America.* Paris: OECD Publications, 1996.

Hausmann, Ricardo, and Ernesto Stein. "Searching for the Right Budgetary Institution for a Volatile Region." In *Securing Stability and Growth in Latin America,* edited by Ricardo Hausmann and Helmut Reisen. Paris: OECD Publications, 1996.

"Heading Off Contagion." Editorial Comment. *Financial Times,* 7 August 2001.

Helleiner, Gerald K. "Toward a New Development Strategy." In *The Legacy of Raúl Prebisch,* edited by Enrique V. Iglesias. Washington, D.C.: IADB, 1994.

Hellinger, Daniel. "Understanding Venezuela's Crisis—Dutch Diseases, Money Doctors, and Magicians." *Latin American Perspectives* 27, no. 1 (January 2000.).

Helwege, Ann. "Poverty in Latin America: Back to the Abyss?" *Journal of Inter-American Studies and World Affairs* 37, no. 3 (Fall 1995).

———. "Poverty and Inequality in Latin America and the Caribbean." *CEPAL Review* 47 (August 1992).

Hemispheric Social Alliance. *Alternatives for the Americas.* Prepared for the 2nd Peoples Summit of the Americas. Canada: Hemispheric Social Alliance, April 2001.

Henriot, Peter J. "Development Alternatives: Problems, Strategies, Values." In *The Political Economy of Development and Underdevelopment,* 2nd ed., edited by Charles K. Wilbert. New York: Random House, 1979.

Hey, Jeanne A. K., and Thomas Klak. "From Protectionism towards Neoliberalism: Ecuador across Four Administrations (1981–1996)." In *Studies in Comparative International Development* (Fall 1999).

Higgins, B. *Economic Development: Problems, Principles, and Policies.* New York: Norton, 1968.

Hikino, Takashi, and Alice Amsden. "Staying Behind, Stumbling Back, Sneaking Up, Soaring Ahead: Late Industrialization in Historical Perspective." In *Convergence of Productivity: Cross-National Studies and Historical Evidence,* edited by William Baumol, Richard R. Nelson, and Edward N. Wolff. New York: Oxford University Press, 1994.

Hill, M. Anne, and Elizabeth M. King. "Women's Education in Developing Countries: An Overview." In *Women's Education in Developing Countries: Barriers, Benefits, and Poli-*

cies, edited by M. Anne Hill and Elizabeth M. King. Baltimore: Johns Hopkins University Press, 1993.

Hinds, Manuel E. "Hearing on Official Dollarization in Latin America." Presented to the Senate Banking Committee. (15 July 1999).

Hirata, Helena, and John Humphrey. "Workers' Response to Job Loss: Female and Male Industrial Workers in Brazil." *World Development* 19, no. 6 (1991): 671–82.

Hoff, Karla. "Designing Land Policies: An Overview." In *The Economics of Rural Organization,* edited by Karla Hoff, Avishay Braverman, and Joseph Stiglitz. New York: Oxford University Press/World Bank, 1993.

———, Avishay Braverman, and Joseph Stiglitz. "Introduction." In *The Economics of Rural Organization,* edited by Karla Hoff, Avishay Braverman, and Joseph Stiglitz. New York: Oxford University Press/World Bank, 1993.

———, eds. *The Economics of Rural Organization.* New York: Oxford University Press/World Bank, 1993.

Holmes, Michael. "TDA Urges Mexico to Reconsider Beef Tariffs." *AM Cycle,* 4 August 1999.

Holm-Nielsen, Lauritz, Michael Crawford, and Alcyone Saliba. *Institutional and Entrepreneurial Leadership in the Brazilian Science and Technology Sector.* World Bank Discussion Paper no. 325. Washington, D.C.: World Bank, 1996.

"Hope for the No-Hopers." *The Economist,* 23 December 2000.

Hsiao, William C. "Marketization—The Illusory Magic Pill." *Health Economics* 3 (1994): 351–57.

Huber, Richard M., Jack Ruitenbeck, and Renaldo Serra De Motta. "Market-Based Instruments for Environmental Policy Making in Latin America and the Caribbean: Lessons Learned from Eleven Countries." World Bank Discussion Paper no. 381. Washington, D.C.: World Bank, 1998.

Hufbauer, Gary, and Diana Orejas. *NAFTA and the Environment: Lessons for Trade Policy.* Speech delivered at the International Policy Forum organized by the Bildner Center. Washington, D.C.: Institute for International Economics. 28 February 2001.

Hufbauer, Gary C. *NAFTA in a Skeptical Age: The Way Forward.* Washington, D.C.: Institute for International Economics, 2000.

"Human Development Index." In *Human Development Report, 1997,* edited by United Nations Development Program. New York: Oxford University Press, 1997.

Idelovitch, Emanuel, and Klas Ringskog. *Private Sector Participation in Water Supply and Sanitation in Latin America.* Washington, D.C.: World Bank, 1995.

"If Not for NAFTA, When?" *The Economist,* 28 October 2000.

"IFC: Making a Positive Difference for Sustainable Development." Washington, D.C.: The World Bank Group.

Iglesias, Enrique V. "The Search for a New Economic Consensus in Latin America." In *The Legacy of Raúl Prebisch,* edited by Enrique V. Iglesias. Washington, D.C.: IADB, 1994.

———, ed. *The Legacy of Raúl Prebisch,* Washington, D.C.: IADB, 1994.

Ignatius, David. "'Dollarization' in Latin America." *World News,* 28 April 1999, A26.

"IMF Completes Brazil Fifth Review." IMF News Brief No. 00/33. Washington, D.C.: IMF, 31 May 2000.

"IMF Concludes Article IV Consultation with Argentina." Public Information Notice No. 00/84. Washington, D.C.: IMF, 3 October 2000.

"IMF Lending to Poor Countries—How Does the PRGF Differ from the ESAF?" Washington, D.C.: IMF, April 2001.

"IMF Managing Director Köhler Welcomes Argentine Senate Action." News Brief No. 01/67. Washington, D.C.: IMF, 30 July 2001.

"IMF Press Conference on Exchange Rate Regimes in an Increasingly Integrated World Economy." Washington, D.C.: IMF, 14 April 2000.

"IMF Lending to Poor Countries—How does the PRGF differ from the ESAF?" Washington, D.C.: IMF, April 2001.

"The IMF's Poverty Reduction and Growth Facility (PRGF)—A Factsheet." *International Monetary Fund,* March 2001.

"In the Gap and Sweatshop Labor in El Salvador." *NACLA Report on the Americas* 29, no. 4 (January–February 1996): 37.

Inter-American Development Bank. *Disaster Prevention Sector Facility.* Document GN-2085-5. March 2001.

———. Annual Report 2001, www.iadb.org.

———. "The Argentine Saga." *Latin American Economic Policies,* Fourth Quarter, vol. 16, 2001.

———. "Is Growth Enough?" *Latin American Economic Policies,* Second Quarter, vol. 14, 2001.

———. *Group Support to the Microenterprise Sector (1990–2000).* IADB. February 2001.

———. *Facing Up to Inequality in Latin America: Economic and Social Progress in Latin America, 1998–1999* Report. Washington, D.C.: Johns Hopkins University Press/IADB, 1998.

———. *Intra-Hemispheric Exports by Integration Group.* 12 July 1997. Available online at www.iadb.org.statistics/notaest.htm.

———. *Latin America after a Decade of Reforms: Economic and Social Progress 1997 Report.* Washington, D.C.: Johns Hopkins University Press/IADB, 1997.

———. *Economic and Social Progress in Latin America 1996 Report: Making Social Services Work.* Washington, D.C.: IADB, 1996.

———. *Economic and Social Progress in Latin America 1995 Report: Overcoming Volatility.* Washington, D.C.: IADB, 1995.

———. *Women in the Americas: Bridging the Gap.* Baltimore: Johns Hopkins University Press, 1995.

———. "Invisible Farmers." In *IDB Extra: Investing in Women.* Washington, D.C.: IADB, 1994.

———. "Argentina—Country Paper."

International Labor Organization. *World Employment Report 2001. The World Employment Report 2001: Life at Work in the Information Economy.* Geneva, Switzerland.

International Monetary Fund. *World Economic Outlook 2002,* www.imf.org.

———. *Key Features of IMF Poverty Reduction and Growth Facility (PRGF) Supported Programs.* Prepared by the Policy Development and Review Department. 16 August 2000.

———. *International Financial Statistics, 1997.* Washington, D.C.: IMF, 1997.

———. *Bolivia—Interim Poverty Reduction Strategy Paper.* Prepared by the Bolivian Authorities.

International Trade Administration, U.S. Department of Commerce, *U.S. Foreign Trade Highlights,* 1995. Washington, D.C.: U.S. Department of Commerce, 1995.

"Involving the Private Sector and Preventing Financial Crises." *IMF Survey* 28, no. 12 (21 June 1999).

"It's Time to Bite the Bullet." *Euromoney,* September 1996.

Jallade, Lucila, Eddy Lee, and Joel Samoff. "International Cooperation." In *Coping with Crisis: Austerity, Adjustment, and Human Resources,* edited by Joel Samoff. New York: UNESCO/ILO, 1994.

Jameson, Kenneth P. "The Financial Sector in Latin American Restructuring." In *Privatiza-*

tion in Latin America, edited by Werner Baer and Melissa Birch. Westport, Conn.: Praeger, 1994.

Jenkins, Rhys. "Car Manufacture in East Asia and Latin America." *Cambridge Journal of Economics* October 1995: 625–46.

————. *Transnational Corporations and the Latin American Automobile Industry.* Pittsburgh: University of Pittsburgh Press, 1987.

————. *Transnational Corporations and Industrial Transformation in Latin America.* New York: St. Martin's, 1984.

Jessen, Anneke, et al. *Integration and Trade in the Americas.* Washington, D.C.: IADB, 1999.

Jewett, Dale. "Magna Touts Lower-Cost Navigational System." *Automotive News,* 23 October 2000.

Jimenez de la Jara, Jorge, and Thomas J. Bossert. "Chile's Health Sector Reform: Lessons from Four Reform Periods." In *Health Sector Reform in Developing Countries: Making Health Development Sustainable,* edited by Peter Berman. Cambridge: Harvard University Press, 1995.

Johnson, Brian. *The Great Fire of Borneo: Report of a Visit to Kalimantan-Timur a Year Later, May 1994.* London: World Wildlife Fund, 1991.

Jonakin, Jon. "The Interaction of Market Failure and Structural Adjustment in Producer Credit and Land Markets: The Case of Nicaragua." *Journal of Economic Issues* 31, no. 2 (June 1997).

"Just Don't Call It Downsizing." *IADB América* (September–October 2000): 10–11.

Kadt, Emanuel de. "Thematic Lessons from the Case Studies." In *The Public–Private Mix in Social Services,* edited by Elaine Zuckerman and Emanuel de Kadt. Washington, D.C.: IADB, 1997.

Kahn, Joseph. "Congressional Leadership Agrees to Debt Relief for Poor Nations." *New York Times,* 18 October 2000.

Kaltenheuser, Skip. "Fitting Microcredit into a Macro Picture." *Christian Science Monitor,* 5 February 1997.

Kapstein, Ethan. "Global Rules for Global Finance." *Current History,* November 1998.

Karp, Jonathan. "Brazilian Central Banker Plays It Cool." *Wall Street Journal,* July 18, 2001, Section A: page 12, column 3.

Kate, Adriaan ten, and Robert Bruce Wallace. "Nominal and Effective Protection by Sector." In *Protection and Economic Development in Mexico,* edited by Adriaan ten Kate and Robert Bruce Wallace. Hampshire, U.K.: Gower, 1980.

Katz, Elizabeth G. "Gender and Trade within the Household: Observations from Rural Guatemala." *World Development* 23, no. 2 (1995): 327–42.

Katz, Ian. "Snapping up South America." *BusinessWeek,* 18 January 1999.

Kay, Stephen J. "Privatizing Pensions: Prospects for the Latin American Reforms." In *Journal of Interamerican Studies and World Affairs* 42, no. 1 (Spring 2000).

Keen, Benjamin. *Latin American Civilization.* 3rd ed. Boston: Houghton Mifflin, 1974.

Kepp, Michael. "Refining Mining," *Latin Trade,* April 2002, p.30.

Key, Cristóbal. "Rural Development and Agrarian Issues in Contemporary Latin America." In *Structural Adjustment and the Agricultural Sector in Latin America and the Caribbean,* edited by John Weeks. New York: St. Martin's, 1995.

"The Key Points of the FTAA Agenda." *Latin American Weekly Report,* WR-97-20, 1997.

Keynan, Gabriel, Manuel Olin, and Ariel Dinar. "Cofinanced Public Extension in Nicaragua." *World Bank Research Observer* 12, no. 2 (August 1997).

Klitgaard, Robert. "Subverting Corruption." *Finance & Development* (June 2000).

Knight, Alan. "Populism and Neo-Populism in Latin America, Especially Mexico." *Journal of Latin American Studies* 30 (1998): 223–48.

"Kóhler Says IMF Management to Recommend Accelerated Disbursement of US $1.2 Billion for Argentina." News Brief No. 01/17. Washington, D.C.: IMF, 3 August 2001.

"Kóhler Says IMF Management to Recommend US $15 Billion Stand-By for Brazil." News Brief No. 01/72. Washington, D.C.: IMF, 3 August 2001.

Krauss, Clifford. "Argentina's Austerity Plan Provokes Nationwide Strike." *New York Times,* 20 July 2001.

————. "Argentine With a Headache: The Economy." *New York Times,* 18 July 2001.

————. "Poll-Whipped and Pilloried, Chief Endures in Argentina." *New York Times,* 8 July 2001.

————. "Economy Aide to the Rescue, as Argentina Fights Default." *New York Times,* 30 March 2001.

————. "Where the Coca Trade Withers, Tourism Sprouts." *New York Times,* 2 November 2000.

————. "Bolivia Wiping Out Coca, at a Price." *New York Times,* 23 October 2000.

————. "When Even an Economic Miracle Isn't Enough." *New York Times,* 12 July 1998.

————. "Argentina to Hasten End of a Phone Monopoly." *New York Times,* 11 March 1998.

Krawczyk, Miriam. "Women in the Region: Major Changes." *CEPAL Review* 49 (April 1993).

Kronish, Rich, and Kenneth S. Mericle. "The Development of the Latin American Motor Vehicle Industry, 1900–1980: A Class Analysis." In *The Political Economy of the Latin American Motor Vehicle Industry,* ed Rich Kronish and Kenneth S. Mericle. Cambridge: MIT Press, 1984.

Krueger, Anne O. *NAFTA's Effects: A Preliminary Assessment.* Oxford: Blackwell Publishers, 2000.

Krugman, Paul. "Other People's Money." *New York Times,* 18 July 2001.

————. "A Latin Tragedy." *New York Times,* 15 July 2001.

Krugman, Paul R., and Maurice Obstfeld. *International Economics: Theory and Policy.* 3rd ed. New York: HarperCollins, 1994.

Kuttner, Robert. "What Sank Asia? Money Sloshing Around the World." *BusinessWeek,* 27 July 1998.

Kuznets, Simon. "Modern Economic Growth: Findings and Reflections." *American Economic Review* 63, no. 3 (June 1973).

Kwast, Barbara. "Reeducation of Material and Peri-natal Mortality in Rural and Peri-urban Settings: What Works?" *European Journal of Obstetrics and Gynecology and Reproductive Biology* 609 (1996).

Lamb, James J. "The Third World and the Development Debate." *IDOC-North America* January–February 1973.

"Land for the Landless." *The Economist,* 13 April 1996.

Lanjouw, Peter. "Nonfarm Employment and Poverty in rural El Salvador." *World Development* 29, no. 3. 2001.

La Porta, Rafael, Florencio Lopez-de-Silanes, and Andrei Shleifer, 1999, as summarized in William Megginson and Jeffry M. Netter, "From State to Market: A Survey of Empirical Studies of Privatization," *Journal of Economic Literature* XXXIX (June 2001).

Lapper, Richard. "Policy under Pressure," *Financial Times,* October 6, 2002, weekend I.

Larner, Monica, and Ian Katz. "It's Ronaldo's World." *BusinessWeek,* 22 June 1998: 204.

Larraín, Felipe B., and Luis F. López-Calva, "Privatization: Fostering Economic Growth through Private Sector Development." Chapter 13 in *Economic Development in Central America. Vol. 2: Structural Reform.* Cambridge, Mass.: Harvard University Press, 2001), 68.

————, and Andrés Rodriguez-Clare. *Intel: A Case Study of Foreign Direct Investment in Central America.* CID Working Paper No. 58. Center for International Development at Harvard University. December 2000.

Larraín, Felipe B., ed. *Capital Flows, Capital Controls and Currency* Ann Arbor: The University of Michigan Press, 2000), 12.

Latin America Research Review 35, no. 3 (2000).

"Latin America Struggles to Find Solutions to Megacity Woes." *Agence France Press,* 2 June 1992. Available on the LEXIS-NEXIS database.

Latin America Weekly Report. 26 May 1998. "Latin America's Car Industry Revving Up." *The Economist,* 27 April 1996.

"Latin America's Export of Manufactured Goods." Special section of *Economic and Social Progress in Latin America 1992 Report.* Washington, D.C.: IADB, 1992.

Latin Watch. Banco Bilbao Vizcaya Agentaria. (December 2000).

Lau, Lawrence J., Dean T. Jamison, Shucheng Liu, and Steven Rivkin. "Education and Economic Growth: Some Cross-Sectional Evidence." In *Education in Brazil,* edited by Nancy Birdsall and Richard H. Sabot. Washington, D.C.: IADB, 1996.

Lehmann, David, ed. *Agrarian Reform and Agrarian Reformism: Studies of Peru, Chile, China, and India.* London: Faber & Faber, 1974.

Lepziger, Danny, Claudio Frischtak, Homi J. Kharas, and John F. Normand. "Mercosur: Integration and Industrial Policy." *World Economy* 20, no. 5 (1997).

Lewis, Colin M. "Industry in Latin America." In *Dependency and Development,* edited by Fernando Henrique Cardoso and Enzo Faletto, translated by Marjory Mattinglly Urguidi. Berkeley: University of California Press, 1979.

Lewis, Paul. "Latin Americans Say Russian Default Is Hurting Their Economies." *New York Times,* 6 October 1998, A13. Online edition.

Lippert, John. "'Going Zunion' Is the Buzz at Magna Auto Parts Giant Pays Wages Half the Big Three's." *Toronto Star,* 15 August 1998.

Lizano, Eduardo, and José M. Salazar-Xirinach. "Central American Common Market and Hemispheric Free Trade." In *Integrating the Hemisphere, 1997: The Inter-American Dialogue,* edited by Ana Julia Jatar and Sidney Weintraub. Santa Fé de Bogotá, Colombia: Tercer Mundo, 1997.

Lizondo, S., et al. Chile: Selected Issues. IMF Country Report No. 01/120. Washington, D.C.: IMF, July 2001.

"Loan 'Club' Is a Useful Model." *Financial Times,* 14 December 2000.

Londoño, Juan Luis, and Miguel Székely. "Distributional Surprises after a Decade of Reforms: Latin America in the Nineties." Paper prepared for the annual meetings of the IADB. Barcelona, March 1997.

———. *Persistent Poverty and Excess Inequality: Latin America, 1970–1995.* Office of the Chief Economist. IADB Working Paper no. 357. Washington, D.C.: IADB, 1997.

López, Ramón. *Policy Instruments and Financing Mechanisms for the Sustainable Use of Forests in Latin America.* No. ENV-16. Washington, D.C.: IADB, 1996.

Lora, Eduardo, and Felipe Barrera. "A Decade of Structural Reform in Latin America: Growth, Productivity, and Investment Are Not What They Used to Be." Document for discussion at the IADB Barcelona seminar, "Latin America after a Decade of Reform: What Next?" 16 March 1997.

Lorey, David E. "Education and the Challenges of Mexican Development." *Challenge* 38, no. 2 (March–April 1995): 51–55.

Loser, Claudio M. "The Long Road to Financial Stability." *Finance and Development,* March 2000.

Loser, Claudio M., and Jesús Seade. *Second Review under the Stand-by Arrangement and Request for Augmentation.* Report No. 01/26. Washington, D.C.: IMF,. January 2001.

———. *Staff Report for the 2000 Article IV Consultation, First Review under the Stand-By Arrangement, and Request for Modification of Performance Criteria.* Report No. 00/164. Washington, D.C.: IMF, December 2000.

"Lousy Deal." *IDB América* May–June 2000: 2.

Loyola, Gustavo. "Elusive Tax Reform: 'President Must Lead the Way.'" *UNICEF—Info-Brazil,* September 2001.

Lustig, Nora. *Coping with Austerity.* Washington, D.C.: Brookings Institution, 1995.

———, and Ruthanne Deutsch. The *Inter-American Development Bank and Poverty Reduction: An Overview.* Washington, D.C.: IADB, 1998. Available online at www.iadb.org.

Lustig, Nora C. *NAFTA: Setting the Record Straight.* Brookings Policy Brief No. 20.

MacCulloch, Christina. "Will She Make It? Guatemala Finds New Ways to Keep Girls in School." *IDB América* (April 1998): 4–7.

Macisaac, Donna. "Peru." In *Indigenous People and Poverty in Latin America*, edited by George Psacharopoulos and Harry Anthony Patrinos. Washington, D.C.: World Bank, 1994.

Maddison, Angus. *Monitoring the World Economy, 1820–1992.* Washington, D.C.: OECD Publications and Information Center, 1995.

———. "Economic and Social Conditions in Latin America, 1913–1950." In *Long-Term Trends in Latin American Economic Development,* edited by Miguel Urrutia. Washington, D.C.: IADB/Johns Hopkins University Press, 1991.

"Magna Auto Parts Boss on $33m a Year Roll." *Canadian Press Newswire,* 10 April 2000.

"Magna Forms Mexican Joint Venture." *Canada Newswire,* 20 August 1997.

"Magna International Inc.—Online Earnings Conference Call Notification." *Canada Newswire,* 17 August 2000.

Mahon, James E., Jr. "Was Latin America Too Rich to Prosper? Structural and Political Obstacles to Export-Led Industrial Growth." *Journal of Development Studies* 28, no. 2 (1992).

"Making Money from Microcredit." *IDB América,* June 1998.

Malpass, David. "Hearing on Official Dollarization in Emerging-Market Countries." Presented to the Senate Banking, Housing and Urban Affairs Committee. 15 July 1999.

"The Man from Whom Miracles Hang." *The Economist,* 28 October 2000.

Mandel-Campbell, Andrea. "I Bet the Ranch, and I Won—Absolutely." *BusinessWeek,* 22 June 1998: 64–65.

Mangurian, David. "Against the Odds: How a Seemingly Hopeless Energy Project Became a Model for Investors." *IDB América.* March 1998. Available online at www.iadb.org.

Margolis, Mac. "Hat in Hand." *Newsweek,* 12 October 1998.

Martinussen, John. *Society, State, and Market: A Guide to Competing Theories of Development.* London: Zed, 1997.

Maxwell, Kenneth. "Latin America: Sustaining Economic & Political Reform—A Working Conference on the Underlying Realities." Conference Overview. The Council on Foreign Relations. 18 May 2000.

Mayer-Serra, Carlos Elizondo. "Tax Reform under the Salinas Administration." In *The Changing Structure of Mexico,* edited by Laura Randall, Armonk, N.Y.: Sharpe, 1996.

Mayorga, Román. *Closing the Gap.* IADB Working Paper SOC97-101. Washington, D.C.: IADB, 1997.

McKee, Colin. "Realizing the Potential of the Internet in Latin America." Unpublished paper, Colby College, Waterville, Maine, 2001.

McKinsey Global Institute. *Productivity: The Key to an Accelerated Development Path for Brazil 1998.* São Paulo: McKinsey and Company, 1998.

McLarty, Thomas F. "Hemispheric Free Trade Is Still a National Priority." *Wall Street Journal,* 26 May 1995.

McQuerry, Elizabeth, Michael Chriszt, and Stephen Kay. "Patterns in Latin American Public Sector Accounts." Federal Reserve Bank of Atlanta. Available online at www.frbatlanta.org/econ_rd/larq/fiscal_policy/public_sector/patterns/htm, 2001.

Meerman, Jacob. *Reforming Agriculture: The World Bank Goes to Market.* Washington, D.C.: World Bank, 1997.

Meier, Gerald M. *Leading Issues in Economic Development.* 6th ed. Oxford: Oxford University Press, 1995.

———, and Dudley Seers. *Pioneers in Development.* Oxford: Oxford University Press, 1984.

Meller, Patricio. "IMF and World Bank Roles in the Latin America Foreign Debt Problem." In *The Latin American Development Debate: Neostructuralism, Neomonetarism, and Adjustment Processes,* edited by Patricio Meller. Boulder, Colo.: Westview, 1991.

"Memorandum of Economic Policies." International Monetary Fund. Public Information Notice No. 00/84. Washington, D.C.: IMF, 1999.

Mendez, Chico. *Fight for the Forest.* London: Latin American Bureau, 1990.

Mercosur Consulting Group Limited. "Recent Developments Affecting the Mercosur Economic Integration Project." *Thunderbird International Business Review* vol. 42, no. 1 (January–February 2002): 1–7; www.mercosurconsulting.net.

"Mercosur Survey." *The Economist,* 12 October 1996.

"Mexico City: A Topographical Error." *Environment* 36, no. 2 (1994): 25–26.

"Mexico Domestic Sales Rise Sharply." *Reuters Financial Service,* 4 June 1997. U.S. Department of State, "Mexico FY 2000 Country Commercial Guide," July 1999. Available online on the LEXIS-NEXIS.

"Mexico FY 2000 Country Commercial Guide." Washington, D.C.: U.S. Department of State.

Mezzera, Jaime. "Abundancia como efecto de la escasez. Oferta y demanda en el Mercado laboral urbano." *Nueva Sociedad* 90 (1997): 106–17.

Miller, Eric. *Financial Services in the Trading System: Progress and Prospects.* Washington D.C.: IADB, 1999.

Mishkin, Frederick. "Understanding Financial Crises: A Developing Country Perspective." In *The Annual World Bank Conference Report on Development Economics, 1996.* Washington, D.C.: World Bank, 1997.

Moffett, Matt. "Deep in the Amazon, an Industrial Enclave Fights for Its Survival." *Wall Street Journal,* 9 July 1998.

Molano, Walter. *Financial Reverberations: The Latin American Banking System during the Mid-1990s.* Working paper, SBC Warburg. April 1997.

Moody-Stuart, Mark. *Putting Principles into Practice: The Ethical Challenge to Global Business.* Presented at the World Congress of the International Society of Business, Economics and Ethics in São Paolo, Brazil, 19 July 2000.

Mooney, Elizabeth. "South American Economic Crisis Hits Telecom Operators." *RCR Wireless News,* April 2002, p. 25.

Moore, Mick. "Toward a Useful Consensus." In *The Bank, the State, and Development: Dissecting the World Development Report, 1997. IDS Bulletin* 29, no. 2, special issue (1998).

Moore, Molly. "Mayan Girls Make Fifth Grade History." *Washington Post,* 20 June 1996.

Morales, Juan Antonio, and Jeffrey Sachs. "Bolivia's Economic Crisis." In *Developing Country Debt and the World Economy,* edited by Jeffrey Sachs. Chicago: University of Chicago Press, 1989.

Morandé, Felipe G. "Savings in Chile: What Went Right?" *Journal of Development Economics* 57, no. 1 (1998).

Morris, Valerie, and Donald Van De Mark. "Magna Auto Parts Ceo." *Cable News Network Financial,* 11 March 1998.

Mosbacher, Robert, chairman, Council of the Americas. "Trade Expansion within the Americas: A U.S. Business Perspective." Remarks at the Chile–United States Issues Round Table, Crown Plaza Hotel, Santiago, Chile, 17 April 1998. Available at 207.87.5.23/sr.html; accessed 12 July 1999.

Moseley, Paul, and David Hulme. "Microenterprise Finance: Is There a Conflict between Growth and Poverty Alleviation?" *World Development* 26, no. 5 (1988): 783–90.

Moser, Caroline. "Gender Planning in the Third World: Meeting Practical and Strategic Gender Needs." *World Development* 17, no. 11 (1989): 1799–825.

Moser, Titus. "MNCs and Sustainable Business Practice: The Case of the Colombian and Peruvian Petroleum Industries." *World Development* 29, no. 2 (2001).

Mulligan, Mark. "Honeymoon over for Cavallo." *Financial Times,* 19 July 2001.

———. "Argentine Opposition Backs Government Austerity Package." *Financial Times,* July 18 2001.

———. "Protests Flare over Argentina Austerity Plan." *Financial Times,* 18 July 2001.

Munainghe, Mohran, and Wilfrido Cruz. *Economy Wide Policies and the Environment: Lessons from Experience.* Washington, D.C.: World Bank, 1995.

Myers, William, ed. *Protecting Working Children.* London: Zed, 1991.

"NAFTA Key Provisions." NAFTA Facts Document #3001.

"NAFTA: Where's That Giant Sucking Sound?" *BusinessWeek,* 7 July 1997, 45.

Naim, Moises. "Fads and Fashion in Economic Reforms: Washington Consensus or Washington Confusion?" *Foreign Policy Magazine,* 26 October 1999.

Nasar, Sylvia. "The Cure That Can Sometimes Kill the Patient." *New York Times,* 19 July 1998.

"National Trade Estimate Reports—1998 Country Report." Trade Compliance Center.

"National Trade Estimate 2000—Mexico." Trade Compliance Center.

Nazmi, Nader. "The Internationalization of Capital in a Small and Vulnerable Economy: The Case of Ecuador." In Werner Baer and William R. Miles, *Foreign Direct Investment in Latin America,* 119–39. New York: The Hayworth Press, 2001.

———. *Economic Policy and Stabilization in Latin America.* New York: Sharpe, 1996.

Nelson, Richard R. "Schumpeterian Competition." In *The Sources of Economic Growth.* Cambridge, Mass.: Harvard University Press, 1996.

"The New Entrepreneurs: Preparing the Ground for Small Business." *IDB América* 1997. Available online at the IADB homepage at www.iadb.org.

"New Era Dawns with Great Expectations." *Financial Times,* 14 December 2000.

"New Farms for Old." *The Economist,* 10 January 1998.

"A New Risk of Default." *Euromoney,* September 1996.

Newfarmer, Richard S. *Profits, Progress, and Poverty.* South Bend, Ind.: University of Notre Dame Press, 1984.

Noll, Roger G. *Telecommunications Reform in Developing Countries.* Working Paper 99-10. AEI-Brookings Joint Center for Regulator Studies. November 1999.

"The North American Free Trade Agreement Is Good for US Agricultural Trade." *World Food Chemical News,* 23 July 1997.

North, Douglas C. "The New Institutional Economics and Third World Development." In *The New Institutional Economics and Third World Development,* edited by John Harriss, Janet Hunter, and Colin M. Lewis. London: Routledge, 1995.

"North Is North and South Is South." *The Economist,* 28 October 2000.

"Nuts in Brazil." *The Economist,* 9 October 1999.

"Obstacles to Business Development." *Latin American Economic Policies* 13, no. 1 (2001).

Ocampo, José Antonio. "The Pending Agenda: A Decade of Light and Shadow." *ECLAC Notes* 20 (March 2001).

———. "Rethinking the Development Agenda." Presented at the American Economic Association Annual Meeting Panel "Toward a Post-Washington Consensus on Development and Security" in New Orleans. 5 January 2001.

———. "Towards a Global Solution." *ECLAC Notes* 1 (November 1998).

"Of Cranes, Aid and Unintended Consequences." *The Economist,* 5 October 1996.

"Official Debt Restructuring." *Global Development Finance.* Washington, D.C: World Bank.

O'Grady, Mary Anastasia "What Argentina Needs." *Wall Street Journal,* 17 July 2001.

_____. "A Brazilian State Shows How to Reform Schools." *Wall Street Journal,* 16 August 1997.

"Oil Chief & Leading Candidate Breach Taboo on Privatisation of PDVSA." *Latin American Weekly Report,* WR-98-30. 4 August 1998.

Olpadwala, Porus, and William Goldsmith. "The Sustainability of Privilege: Reflection on the Environment, The Third World City and Poverty." *World Development* 20, no. 4 (1992).

Önis, Ziya, and Ahmet Faruk Aysan. "Neoliberal Globalisation, the Nation-State and Financial Crises in the Semi-Periphery: A Comparative Analysis." *Third World Quarterly* 21, no. 1 (2000).

Ortega, Emiliano. "Evolution of the Rural Dimension in Latin America and the Caribbean." *CEPAL Review* 47 (August 1992).

Ostrovsky, Arkady. "Mexico Bucks Trend and Issues $1bn Bond." *Financial Times,* 6 August 2001.

Otteman, Scott. "Trade Policy Today." *Latin American Advisor,* 2 July 2001.

Overhold, Catherine, and Margaret Saunders. *Policy Choices and Practical Problems in Health Economics: Cases from Latin America and the Caribbean.* Economic Development Institute Resources Series. Washington, D.C.: World Bank, 1996.

Ozório de Almeida, Anna Luiza, and João S. Campari. *Sustainable Settlement in the Brazilian Amazon.* Oxford: Oxford University Press.

Paarlberg, Robert L. "The Politics of Agricultural Resource Abuse." *Environment* 36, no. 8 (October 1994).

Palma, Gabriel. "Dependency: A Formal Theory of Underdevelopment or a Methodology for the Analysis of Concrete Situations of Underdevelopment?" *World Development* 6, no. 7–8 (July–August 1979): 881–924.

Palmer, Ingrid. "Public Finance from a Gender Perspective." *World Development* 23, no. 11 (1995).

Pan American Health Organization. "Mexico." In *Health in the Americas,* vol. 2. Washington, D.C.: PAHO, 1998.

————. *Strategic and Programmatic Orientations, 1995–1998.* Presented at the Inter-American Meeting, Washington, D.C., 25–27 April 1995. Available online at www.paho.org.

————. *Implementation of the Global Strategy: Health for All by the Year 2000,* vol. 3. Washington, D.C.: PAHO, 1993.

————. *PAHO Resolution V: Health of Indigenous Peoples.* Series HSS/SILOS, 34. Washington, D.C.: PAHO, 1993. Available online at www.paho.org.

Panagariya, Arvind. "The Free Trade Area of the Americas: Good for Latin America?" *World Economy* 19, no. 5 (1996).

"Panel Finds Mexican Antidumping Order Violates WTO Rules." Press Release. Office of the United States Trade Representative. Washington, D.C.: WTO. 27 January 2000.

Panizza, Ugo. "Financial Contagion in Latin America: Measuring Morbidity." *Latin American Economic Policies* 6, no. 1 (1999).

Pánuco-Laguette, Humberto, and Miguel Székely. "Income Distribution and Poverty in Mexico." In *The New Economic Model in Latin America and Its Impact on Income Distribution and Poverty,* edited by Victor Bulmer-Thomas. New York: St. Martin's, 1996.

Parry, Taryn Rounds. "Achieving Balance in Decentralization: A Case Study of Education Decentralization in Chile." *World Development* 25, no. 2 (1997).

Partnership for Educational Revitalization in the Americas. *The Future at Stake: Report of the Task Force on Education, Equity and Economic Competitiveness in Latin America and the Caribbean.* Santiago, Chile: PREAL, in conjunction with the Inter-American Dialogue and CINDE, 1998. Available on-line at www.preal.cl/index-i.htm.

Pastor, Robert A. *Lessons from the Old World for the New: The European Union and A Deeper, Wilder American Community.* HEL-Excerpts. 5 May 2000.

"Patience Runs Out in Bolivia." *The Economist,* 21 April 2001.

Patterson, Allen. "Debt for Nature Swaps and the Need for Alternatives." *Environment* 21 (December 1990): 5–32.

Peach, James T., and Richard V. Adkisson. "Enabling Myths and Mexico's Economic Crises (1976–1996)." *Journal of Economic Issues* 31, no. 2 (June 1997).

Pereira Leite, Sérgio. "International Capital Flows: A Challenge for the 21st Century." *Revista ILO,* 1 July 2001.

Perez-Aleman, Paola. "Learning, Adjustment and Economic Development: Transforming Firms, the State and Associations in Chile." *World Development* 28, no. 1 (2000).

"The Permanent Crisis in Argentina." *Latin American Weekly Report,* no. 24 (21 June 2001).

Perry, Guillermo, and Ana Maria Herrera. *Public Finance, Stabilization, and Structural Reform in Latin America.* Washington, D.C.: Johns Hopkins University Press/IADB, 1994.

Peterson, Jim. "Commentary: Don't Buy into the Import Hype." *A Monthly Journal from the Lemhi Mountains* (September 2000).

Phillip, Michael. "South American Trade Pact Is under Fire." *Wall Street Journal,* 23 October 1996.

Picciotto, Robert. *Putting Institutional Economics to Work: From Participation to Governance.* World Bank Discussion Papers, no. 304. Washington, D.C.: World Bank, 1995.

———, and Jock Anderson. "Reconsidering Agricultural Extension." *World Bank Research Observer* 12, no. 2 (August 1997).

Pirages, Dennis. "Sustainability as an Evolving Process." *Futures* 26, no. 2 (1994): 197–205.

Pleskovic, Boris, and Joseph E. Stiglitz, eds. *Annual World Bank Conference on Development Economics, 1997.* Washington, D.C.: World Bank, 1998.

Pou, Pedro. "Argentina's Structural Reforms of the 1990s." *Finance & Development* (March 2000).

Poverty Reduction and the World Bank: Progress in Fiscal 1996 and 1997. Washington, D.C.: World Bank, 1998. Available online at www.worldbank.org.

"Poverty Reduction Strategy Papers and the HIPC Initiative." Statement of U.S. Treasury Secretary Lawrence H. Summers at the Joint Session of the International Monetary and Finance Committee and the Development Committee. Washington, D.C.: International Monetary Fund. 24 September 2000.

Powell, Robert. "Debt Relief for Poor Countries." *Finance & Development* (December 2000).

Prawda, Juan. "Educational Decentralization in Latin America: Lessons Learned." *International Journal of Educational Development* 13, no. 3 (1993): 253–64.

"Pride before the Fall." *The Economist,* 28 October 2000.

"Privatization." *Euromoney,* September 1996.

PROCYMAF. 2000. Proyecto de conservación y manejo sostenible de recursos forestales en México. Informe y avance 1998–2000. Misión de avaluación de medio terino. SEMARNAP, Mexico; B. DeWalt, F. Olivera, and J. Betancourt Correa *Mid-term Evaluation of the Mexico Community Forestry Projects* (Washington, D.C.: World Bank, 2000).

"Progress in Privatization." *Global Development Finance.* Washington, D.C.: World Bank, 2001.

Psacharopoulos, George, and Harry Anthony Patrinos, eds. *Indigenous People and Poverty in Latin America.* Washington, D.C.: World Bank, 1994.

Psacharopoulos, George, Carlos Rojas, and Eduardo Velez. "Achieving Evaluation of Colombia's Escuela Nueva: Is Multigrade the Answer?" *Comparative Education Review* 37, no. 3 (1993).

Psacharopoulos, George, et al. *Poverty and Income Distribution in Latin America: The Story of the 1980s.* World Bank Technical Paper no. 351. Washington, D.C.: World Bank, 1997.

Puder, Don. "U.S. Bill Would Country-of-Origin Labeling for Beef." *Times,* 17 April 2000.

Puryear, Jeffrey M. "Education in Latin America: Problems and Challenges." Presented to the Council of Foreign Relations, 24 February 1996, for the Latin American Program Study Group, "Educational Reform in Latin America," New York. Available online at www.preal.cl/index-i.htm.

"Putting 'Missed' Chances Behind." *Financial Times,* 14 December 2000.

Rajapatirana, Sarath. *Trade Policies in Latin America and the Caribbean: Priorities, Progress, and Prospects.* San Francisco: International Center for Economic Growth, 1997.

Ramos, Joseph. "Poverty and Inequality in Latin America: A Neostructuralist Perspective." *Journal of Inter-American Studies and World Affairs* 38, no. 2–3 (Summer–Fall 1996).

Randall, Laura, ed. *Changing Structure of Mexico: Political, Social and Economic Prospects.* Armonk, N.Y.: Sharpe, 1996.

"Rate of Growth Moves Up a Gear." *Financial Times,* 14 December 2000.

Reardon, Thomas. "Rural Nonfarm Employment and Incomes in Latin America: Overview and Policy Implications." *World Development* 29, no. 3 (2001).

Redclift, Michael. "The Environment and Structural Adjustment: Lessons for Policy Intervention." In *Structural Adjustment and the Agricultural Sector in Latin America and the Caribbean,* edited by John Weeks. New York: St. Martin's, 1995.

The Reform of the Mexican Health Care System. OECD Economic Surveys: Mexico. Paris: OECD, 1998.

"Regional Overview of Foreign Investment in Latin America and the Caribbean." *Chapter I of the 2000 Report on Foreign Investment in Latin American and the Caribbean.* ECLAC, United Nations (18 April 2001).

"The Regulation of Foreign Capital Flows in Chile." Report by *Innovative Experiences.* Available online at the United Nations Development Program homepage at www.undp.org.

Reimers, Fernando. "The Impact of Economic Stabilization and Adjustment on Education in Latin America." *Comparative Education* 35, no. 2 (May 1991).

———. "Educacion para todos en América Latina en el Siglo XXIL. Los desafíos de la estabilización, el ajuste y los mandatos de Jomtien." Paper presented at UNESCO workshop, Peru, December 1990.

Report on the Binational Commission, International Studies Association meetings, Washington, D.C., 20 February 1999.

"Responsible Regionalism." *The Economist,* 2 December 2000.

"Revolution Ends, Change Begins." *The Economist,* 28 October 2000.

"Rich Is Rich and Poor Is Poor." *The Economist,* 28 October 2000.

"Rich, Jennifer L. "Compressed Data: Brazilians Think Basic to Bridge the Digital Divide." *New York Times,* 12 February 2001.

Richards, Michael. "Alternative Approaches and Problems in Protected Area Management and Forest Conservation in Honduras." In *Sustainable Agriculture in Central America,* edited by Jan P. de Groot and Ruerd Ruben. New York: St. Martin's, 1997.

Rodriguez-Garcia, Rosalia, and Ann Goldman, eds. *The Health-Development Link.* Washington, D.C.: PAHO, 1994.

Rodriguez-Mendoz, Miguel. "The Andean Group's Integration Strategy." In *Integrating the Hemisphere, 1997: The Inter-American Dialogue,* edited by Ana Julia Jatar and Sidney Weintraub. Santafé de Bogotá, Colombia: Tercer Mundo, 1997.

Rodrik, Dani. "Growth and Poverty Reduction: What Are the Real Questions?" *Finance & Development* (August 2000).

———. "Institutions for High-Quality Growth: What They Are and How to Acquire Them." *International Monetary Fund 1999.* Available online at www.imf.org/external/pubs/ft/seminar/1999/reforms/rodrik/htm.

———. "Why Do More Open Economies Have Bigger Governments?" *Journal of Political Economy* 16, no. 5 (1998).

———. *King Kong Meets Godzilla. The World Bank and the East Asian Miracle.* CEPR Discussion Paper no. 944. London: Centre for Economic Policy Research, 1994.

Rohloff, Greg. "Beef Processor IBP Inc. Agrees to Buyout by Investment Bank." *Amarillo Daily News,* 5 October 2000.

Rohter, Larry. "Brazilians Uneasy Despite Help by I.M.F. *New York Times,* 6 August 2001.

———. "Bush and Brazil Chief Have Politics, if Not Trade, to Discuss." *New York Times,* 30 March 2001.

———. "For Brazil's College-Bound, a Brutal Test of Mettle." *New York Times,* 29 December 2000.

———. "Where Darwin Mused, Strife Over Ecosystem." *New York Times,* 27 December 2000.

———. "U.S. Aid to Colombia worries Hemisphere's Defense Leaders." *New York Times,* 18 October 2000.

———. "Ecuadorian President Imposes Sweeping Austerity Measures." *New York Times,* 21 March 1999.

———. "Crisis Whipsaws Brazilian Workers." *New York Times,* 16 January 1999. Online edition.

Rojas, Eduardo. *The IDB in Low-Cost Housing the First Three Decades.* Strategic Planning and Operational Policy Department. February 1995.

Rojas-Suarez, Liliana. "Dollarization in Latin America." Presented to the Hearing on Official Dollarization in Latin America for the Senate Banking Committee. (15 July 1999).

———, and Steven R. Weisbrod. "Building Stability in Latin American Financial Markets." In *Securing Stability and Growth in Latin America,* edited by Ricardo Hausmann and Helmut Reisen. Paris: OECD Publications, 1996.

Roldán, Jorge. Interview. *IDB Extra.* 14 June 1998. Online edition.

Romero, Simon. "Where the Risk Is Riskier Yet." *New York Times,* 16 December 1999.

Rosegrant, Susan. *Banana Wars: Challenges to the European Union's Banana Regime.* Abstract. 1999.

Rosenthal, Gert. "Development Thinking and Policies: The Way Ahead." *CEPAL Review* 60 (December 1996).

———. "On Poverty and Inequality in Latin America." *Journal of Inter-American Studies and World Affairs* 38, no. 2–3 (Summer–Fall 1996).

Rothkopf, David J. "Rising Above the Moment." *The New Democrat* (September/October 1997).

Russell, Clifford S., and Philip T. Powell. *Choosing Environmental Policy Tools: Theoretical Cautions and Practical Considerations.* No. ENV-102. Washington, D.C.: IADB, June 1996.

Ryan, John. "The Shrinking Forest." *NACLA Report on the Americas* 25, no. 2 (September 1991).

Sachs, Jeffrey, and Alvaro Zini. "Brazilian Inflation and the Plano Real." *World Economy* 19, no. 1 (January 1996).

Sachs, Jeffrey D. *Tropical Underdevelopment.* CID Working Paper No. 57. Cambridge, Mass.: Harvard University Press, December 2000.

Sachs, Wolfgang, ed. *The Development Dictionary: A Guide to Knowledge as Power.* London: Zed, 1992.

"Safeguarding against Crisis: The Near-Term Agenda." *Global Development Finance,* Washington, D.C.: World Bank, 2000.

Salzinger, Leslie. "Making Fantasies Real—Producing Women and Men on the Maquila Shop Floor." *NACLA Report on the Americas* 34, no. 5 (March/April 2001).

"The Samba and the Tango." *The Economist,* 24 February 1996.

Sampaio Malan, Pedro, and Arminio Fraga Neto. "Brazil—Memorandum of Economic Policies." Washington, D.C.: IMF, 20 April 2000.

Samuelson, Robert J. "Dollarization—a Black Hole." *Washington Post,* 12 May 1999, A27.

Sánchez, M., R. Corona, L. F. Herrera, and O. Ochoa. "A Comparison of Privatization Experiences: Chile, Mexico, Colombia, and Argentina." In *Privatization in Latin America,* edited by M. Sánchez and R. Corona. Baltimore: Johns Hopkins University Press, 1994.

Santiso, Javier. "Political Sluggishness and Economic Speed: A Latin American Perspective." *Social Science Information* 39, no. 2 (2000).

Savedoff, William, Antonio Giuffrida, and Roberto Iunes, *Economic and Health Effects of Occupational Hazards.* IADB, Sustainable Development Department, June 2001.

Sawyer, Suzana. "Indigenous Initiatives and Petroleum Politics in the Ecuadorian Amazon." *Cultural Survival* (Spring 1996).

Schemo, Diana Jean. "A Latin Bloc Asks U.S. and Europe to Ease Trade Barriers." *New York Times,* 23 February 1999. Online edition.

———. "Brazilians Fret as Economic Threat Moves Closer." *New York Times,* 20 September 1998. Online edition.

———. "The ABC's of Doing Business in Brazil." *New York Times,* 16 July 1998. Online edition.

———. "Brazil Farmers Feel Squeezed by Tobacco Companies." *New York Times,* 6 April 1998. Online edition.

———. "Ecuadorians Want Texaco to Clear Toxic Residue." *New York Times,* 31 January 1998.

Scherr, Sara J., Andy White, and David Kaimowitz. "Making Markets Work for Forest Communities." *Forest Trends.* Washington, D.C., 2002.

Schiesel, Seth. "Brazil Sells Most of State Phone Utility." *New York Times,* 30 July 1998, p. D1.

Schiff, Maurice, and Alberto Valdes. "The Plundering of Agriculture in Developing Countries." 1994 draft paper, available at the World Bank homepage at www.worldbank.org/html/extpb/PlunderingAgri.html.

Schmitz, Hubert, and José Cassiolato. *Hi-Tech for Industrial Development: Lessons from the Brazilian Experience in Electronics and Automation.* London: Routledge, 1992.

Schott, Jeffrey J. "NAFTA: An Interim Report." In *Trade: Towards Open Regionalism,* proceedings of the 1997 World Bank Conference on Development in Latin America and the Caribbean. Washington, D.C.: World Bank 1998.

Sedelnik, Lisa. "CANTV: Inside the IPO." *Latin Finance* 83 (1997): 43–46.

Seers, Dudley. "What Are We Trying to Measure?" *Journal of Development Studies* (April 1972).

Sen, Amartya. "The Concept of Development." In *Handbook of Development Economics,* vol. 1. Netherlands: North-Holland, 1988.

Serant, Claire. "Sony Will Play Solectron—Sale of Two Plants May Fling Open Japan's Doors." *Electronic Buyers News,* 23 October 2000.

Shah, Fared, David Zilberman, and Ujjayant Chakravorty. "Water Rights Doctrines and Technology Adoption." In *The Economics of Rural Organization,* edited by Karla Hoff, Avishay Braverman, and Joseph Stiglitz. New York: Oxford University Press/World Bank, 1993.

Shapiro, Helen. *Engines of Growth: The State and Transnational Auto Companies in Brazil.* Cambridge: Cambridge University Press, 1994.

———. *North American Free Trade Agreement: Free for Whom?* Harvard Business School case #5-792-059. Boston: Harvard Business School, 1993.

———. *Mexico: Escaping the Debt Crisis.* Harvard Business School Case. Boston: Harvard Business School, 1991.

Shatz, Howard, "Expanding Foreign Direct Investment in the Andean Countries," CID Working Paper no. 64. Cambridge, Mass.: Center for International Development at Harvard University, March 2001, 3.

Sheahan, John, and Enrique Iglesias. "Kinds and Causes of Inequality in Latin America." In *Beyond Trade-Offs: Market Reform and Equitable Growth in Latin America,* edited by Nancy Birdsall, Carol Graham, and Richard Sabot. Washington, D.C.: Brookings Institution Press/ IADB, 1998.

Shinkai, Naoko. *Does Stolper–Samuelson Theorem Explain the Movement in Wages?: The Linkage between Trade and Wages in Latin American Countries.* Working Paper #436. Washington, D.C.: IADB, November 2000.

Shore, Keane. *Harvard Economist Calls for New Approach to International Development.* IRDC report. 9 August 2001.

Shoumatoff, Alex. *The World Is Burning.* Boston: Little, Brown, 1990.

Sillars, Les. "A Bull Market for Beef and Pork: Investment in Western Meat Processing Continues to Surge." *Alberta Report,* 14 April 1997.

Simons, Marlise. "A Talk with Gabriel García Marquez." *New York Times,* 5 December 1982, sec. 7, p. 7. Available at www.nytimes.com/books/97/06/15/reviews/marquez-talk.html and in the LEXIS-NEXIS database.

Sims, Calvin. "Peruvians Climb onto the Web." *New York Times,* 27 May 1996.

"Skills Gap May Be Biggest Trade Barrier." *Journal of Commerce.* April 20, 1998. Online edition. Available at www.alca-cupula.org.

"Slicing the Cake: What Is the Relationship between Inequality and Economic Growth?" *The Economist,* 19 October 1996.

"The Slow Road to Reform." *The Economist,* 2 December 2000.

Smith, James F. "Mexican Beef Growers Decry Duties on U.S. as Too Low." *Los Angeles Times,* 4 August 1999.

Sola, Lourdes, Christopher Garman, and Moises S. Marques. *Central Reform and Overcoming the Moral Hazard Problem: The Case of Brazil.* Paper Presented for the XXII International Latin American Studies Association Congress, 2000.

"Some Mutual Funds Go Back Full Throttle to Emerging Markets." *Wall Street Journal,* 12, November 1996.

"Something for a Refresco." *The Economist,* 28 October 2000.

Spar, Debora. *Regarding NAFTA.* Harvard Business School Case #5-798-122. Boston: Harvard Business School, 1998.

Sprague, Courtnay. *Debt Restructuring Under the Brady Plan.* Harvard Business School case #9-796-130. Boston: Harvard Business School, 1998.

"The Sputtering Spark from South America's Car Industry." *The Economist,* 15 April 1995.

Stahl, Karin. "Anti-Poverty Programs: Making Structural Adjustment More Palatable." *NACLA Report on the Americas* 29, no. 6 (May–June 1995).

Stallings, Barbara, and Wilson Peres. *Growth, Employment, and Equity: The Impact of the Economic Reforms in Latin America and the Caribbean.* Summary. ECLAC, Spring 2000.

Stauder, Monique. "Colombian Cocaine Runs through It." *Christian Science Monitor,* 13 June 2001.

Steele, Diane. "Guatemala." In *Indigenous People and Poverty in Latin America,* edited by George Psacharopoulos and Harry Anthony Patrinos. Washington, D.C.: World Bank, 1994.

Stein, Elizabeth. *Regarding NAFTA.* Harvard Business School Case #9-797-013. Boston: Harvard Business School, 1998.

Stein, Ernesto, Ernesto Talvi, and Alejandro Grisanti. *Institutional Arrangements and Fiscal Performance: The Latin American Experience.* National Bureau of Economic Research Working Paper no. 6358. Cambridge, Mass.: National Bureau of Economic Research, 1998.

Stewart, Frances. *Adjustment and Poverty: Options and Choices.* London: Routledge, 1995.

Stiglitz, Joseph. "More Instruments and Broader Goals: Moving toward the Post-Washington Consensus." *The 1998 WIDER Annual Lecture.* The World Bank Group, Washington, D.C.: 1998.

———. "The Role of Government in Economic Development." In *Annual World Bank Conference on Development Economics 1996.* Washington, D.C.: World Bank, 1997.

"Stopping the Rot in Public Life." *The Economist,* 16 September 2000.

Streeten, Paul. "From Growth to Basic Needs." In *Latin America's Economic Development: Institutionalist and Structuralist Perspectives,* edited by James L. Dietz and James H. Street. Boulder, Colo.: Rienner, 1987.

———. "A Basic Needs Approach to Economic Development." In *Directions in Economic Development,* edited by Kenneth P. Jameson and Charles K. Wilber. Notre Dame, Ind.: University of Notre Dame Press, 1979.

Sturzenegger, Federico A. "Description of a Populist Experience: Argentina, 1973–1976." In *The Macroeconomics of Populism in Latin America,* edited by Rudiger Dornbusch and Sebastian Edwards. Chicago: University of Chicago Press, 1991.

"Summing Up by the Chairman of the IMF Executive Board Enhanced Initiative for Heavily Indebted Poor Countries (HIPC) and Poverty Reduction Strategy Papers (PRSP)—Progress Reports and Review of Implementation. Executive Board Meeting of September 5, 2000. Washington, D.C.: IMF. 11 September 2000.

"The Summiteers Go to School." *The Economist,* 25 April 1998, 37–38.

Sunkel, Osvaldo. *Development from Within: Toward a Neostructuralist Approach for Latin America.* Boulder, Colo.: Rienner, 1993.

Swafford, David. "A Healthy Trend: Health Care Reform in Latin America." *Latin Finance* 83 (December 1996).

Sylos Labini, Paolo. "The Classical Roots of Development Theory." In *Economic Development: Handbook of Comparative Economic Policies,* edited by Enzo Grilli and Dominick Salvatore. Westport, Conn.: Greenwood, 1994.

"A System That Needs Some Simplifying." *Financial Times,* 14 December 2000.

Székely, Miguel, *The 1990s in Latin America: Another Decade of Persistent Inequality, but with Somewhat Lower Poverty.* Working Paper no. 454. IADB, June 2001.

———, Nora Lustig, Martin Cumpa, and José Antonio Mejía. *Do We Know How Much Poverty There Is?* Working Paper 437. IADB, December 2000.

Tanzi, Vito, "Fiscal Federalism and Decentralization: A Review of Some Efficiency and Macroeconomic Aspects." Paper presented at the World Bank Conference on Development Economics, World Bank, May 1995 (As summarized by *The Economist,* 3 June 1995).

———, and Howell Zee. *Tax Policy for Developing Countries.* Washington, D.C.: IMF, 2001.

Tardanico, Richard, and Rafael Menjívar Larraín. "Restructuring, Employment, and Social Inequality: Comparative Urban Latin American Patterns." In *Global Restructuring, Employment, and Social Inequality in Urban Latin America,* edited by Richard Tardanico and Rafael Menjívar Larraín. Miami: University of Miami North-South Center Press, 1997.

"A Taxing Problem." *The Economist,* 3 June 1995.

Taylor, Alan M. "On the Costs of Inward-Looking Development: Price Distortions, Growth and Divergence In Latin America." *Journal of Economic History* 58, no. 1 (March 1998).

———. *Argentina and the World Capital Market: Saving, Investment and International Capital Mobility in the Twentieth Century.* National Bureau of Economic Research Working Paper no. 6302. Cambridge, Mass.: National Bureau of Economic Research, 1997.

Taylor, Jerry. "The Challenge of Sustainable Development." *Regulation* 17, no. 1 (1994): 35–50.

Taylor, Lance, and Ute Piper. *Reconciling Economic Reform and Sustainable Human Development: Social Consequences of Neo-Liberalism.* UNDP Discussion Paper Series. New York: United Nations Development Programme, 1996.

"A Teacher's Lot." *The IDB,* May 1996.

Teichman, Judith. "Policy Networks and Policy Reform in Mexico: Technocrats, the World Bank and the Private Sector." Paper presented to the Congress of the Latin American Studies Association (16 March 2000).

"Telebras Sold for US$19.lB." *Latin American Weekly Report,* 4 August 1998.

Templeman, John. "Is Europe Elbowing the U.S. Out of South America?" *BusinessWeek,* 4 August 1997: 56.

Tendler, Judith. *Good Government in the Tropics.* Baltimore: Johns Hopkins University Press, 1997.

"Tequila Freeways." *The Economist,* 16 December 1996.

Thatcher, Peter S. "The Role of the United Nations." In *The International Politics of the Environment: Actors, Interests, and Institutions,* edited by Andrew Hurrell and Benedict Kingsbury. Oxford, U.K.: Clarendon, 1992.

Thomas, Vinod. "Why Quality Matters." *The Economist,* 7 October 2000.

Thompson, Ginger. "At Home, Mexico Mistreats Its Farmhands." *New York Times,* 6 May 2001.

———. "Chasing Mexico's Dream Into Squalor." *New York Times,* 11 February 2001.

Thorp, Rosemary. *Progress, Poverty, and Exclusion: An Economic History of Latin America in the 20th Century.* Baltimore: Johns Hopkins University Press/IADB, 1998.

———. "Import Substitution: A Good Idea in Principle." In *Latin America and the World Economy: Dependency and Beyond,* edited by Richard J. Salvucci. Lexington, Mass.: Heath, 1996.

Thorpe, Andy. "Sustainable Agriculture in Latin America." In *Sustainable Agriculture in Central America,* edited by Jan P. de Groot and Ruerd Ruben. New York: St. Martin's, 1997.

Thrupp, Lori Ann. *Bittersweet Harvests for Global Supermarkets: Challenges in Latin America's Agricultural Export Boom.* Washington, D.C.: World Resources Institute, 1995.

"'Til Debt Do Us Part." *The Economist,* 28 February 1987.

Todaro, Michael P. *Economic Development.* 5th ed. White Plains N.Y.: Longham, 1994.

Tokman, Victor E. "Jobs and Solidarity: Challenges for Post-Adjustment in Latin America." In *Economic and Social Development in the XXI Century,* proceedings of the 1997 IADB conference, ed. Louis Emmerij. Available online at www.iadb.org/exr/pub/xxi/sec4.htm, 1998.

Tokman, Viktor. *Beyond Regulation: The Informal Economy in Latin America.* Boulder, Colo.: Rienner, 1992.

———. "Policies for a Heterogeneous Informal Sector." *World Development* 17, no. 7 (1989): 1067–76.

Toman, Michael A. "Economics and 'Sustainability': Balancing the Trade-offs and Imperatives." *Land Economics* 70, no. 4 (November 1994): 399–413.

Toomy, Gerry. "Combining Environmental Protection and Poverty Alleviation in Colombia." *Science from the Developing World,* 7 August 2001.

Torres, Carlos A. *Education and Social Change in Latin America.* Albert Park, Australia: James Nicolas, 1997.

Torres, Carlos Alberto, and Adriana Puiggrós. "The State and Public Education in Latin America." *Comparative Education Review* 39, no. 1 (1995).

"Trade in the Americas." *The Economist,* 21 April 2001.

Transparency International, Global Corruption Reports 2001, www.transparency.org.

Trebat, Thomas. *Brazil's State-Owned Enterprises: A Case Study of the State as Entrepreneur.* New York: Cambridge University Press, 1983.

Tricks, Henry. "Electronic Expansion for Cemex." *Financial Times,* 13 December 2000.

Trivelli, Carolina, Javier Alvarado, Francisco Galarza. *Increasing Indebtedness, Institutional Change and Credit Contracts in Peru.* IADB, Office of the Chief Economist. Working paper #R-378. Washington, D.C.: IADB, 1999.

"Trouble Brewing." *The Economist,* 10 March 2001.

Tuillo, G., and M. Ronci. "Brazilian Inflation from 1980 to 1993: Causes, Consequences and Dynamics." *Journal of Latin American Studies* 28 (October 1996): 635–66.

Tussie, Diana. *The Inter-American Development Bank.* Vol. 4 of *The Multilateral Development Banks.* Ottawa: North-South Institute, 1995.

———, and María Fernanda Tuozzo. Multilateral Development Banks and Civil Society Participation in Latin America." Presented to Facultad Latinoamericana de Ciencias Sociales for the LASA Conference. (March 2000).

Twomey, Michael J. *Multinational Corporations and the North American Free Trade Agreement.* Westport, Conn.: Praeger, 1993.

"Unfinished Business." *The Economist,* 2 March 1996.

United Nations. *World Investment Report 1994.* New York: United Nations, 1994.

United Nations Development Programme. *Human Development Report, 1997.* New York: Oxford University Press.

United Nations Office for Drug Control and Crime Prevention. *World Drug Report 2000.* Oxford University Press, 2000, Annex 1, www.odccp.org/pdf/world_drug_report_2000/report_2001-01-22_1.pdf.

"U.S. and Mexican Labor Secretaries Sign Consultation Agreements." *PR Newswire,* 22 May 2000.

U.S. Department of State. *1996 Country Reports on Economic Policy and Trade Practices.* January 1997. Available online at www.state.gov/www/issues/trade_reports/latin_america99/costarica96.html and www.state.gov/www/issues/economic/trade_reports/latin_america96/panama96.h tml.

U.S. Trade Representative "Mexico." Foreign Trade Barriers. 2000 National Trade Estimate Report. www.ustr.gov.

Valcarel, Juan Manuel. "Calling Someone in Argentina: Dial M for Monopoly." *Wall Street Journal,* 16 August 1996.

Van der Hoeven, Rolph, and Gyorgy Sziraczi. *Lesson from Privatization.* Geneva: International Labour Office, 1997.

Vandermeer, John, and Ivette Perfecto. *Breakfast of Biodiversity: The Truth about Rain Forest Destruction.* Oakland, Calif.: Institute for Food and Development Policy, 1995.

Varo, Vicente. "Argentine Stocks Rebound on Budget Cut Accord." *Financial Times,* 17 July 2001.

Velzboer-Salcedo, Markjke, and Julie Novick, "Violence Against Women in the Americas," *PAHO Perspectives in Health,* vol. 5, no. 2 (2000), www.paho.org.

Vera-Vassallo, Alejandro C. "Foreign Investment and Competitive Development in Latin America and the Caribbean." *CEPAL Review* 60 (December 1996).

Verhovek, Sam Howe. "Pollution Problems Fester South of the Border." *New York Times,* 4 July 1998. Online edition.

Vetter, Stephen G. "The Business of Grassroots Development." *Grassroots Development* 19, no. 2 (1995): 2–12.

Vives, Antonio. *Private Infrastructure: Ten Commandments for Sustainability.* The IADB, Sustainable Development Department, February 1997, www.iadb.org/SDS/doc/ifm%2D303e.pdf.

Vogel, Thomas T., Jr. "Venezuela Privatization Proves Paltry." *Wall Street Journal,* 17 July 1996.

Wade, Robert. "The Asian Crisis and the Global Economy: Causes, Consequences and Cure." *Current History,* November 1998.

Wallace, Robert Bruce. "Policies of Protection in Mexico." In *Protection and Economic Development in Mexico,* edited by Adriaan ten Kate and Robert Bruce Wallace. Hampshire, U.K.: Gower, 1980.

Walsh, Sharon. "Tyson Foods to Buy Competitor Hudson; Rival Had Been Hit by Massive Beef Recall." *Washington Post,* 5 September 1997.

Warburg Dillon Read. "The Impact of the Asian Crisis on Latin America." Fax newsletter, 14 July 1998, p. 2.

———. *The Latin American Adviser.* Fax newsletter, 9 July 1998.

———. *The Latin American Adviser.* Fax newsletter, February 1998.

Warts, Tom. "Protection and Private Foreign Investment." In *Protection and Economic Development in Mexico,* edited by Adriaan ten Kate and Robert Bruce Wallace. Hampshire, U.K.: Gower, 1980.

"Water Works in Buenos Aires." *The Economist,* 24 February 1996.

Weeks, John. "The Manufacturing Sector in Latin America and the New Economic Model." In *The New Economic Model in Latin America and Its Impact on Income Distribution and Poverty,* edited by Victor Bulmer-Thomas. New York: St. Martin's, 1996.

———. "Macroeconomic Adjustment." As noted in *Economic and Social Progress in Latin America 1992 Report,* special section, "Latin America's Export of Manufactured Goods." Washington, D.C.: IADB, 1992.

Weersma-Haworth, Teresa S. "Export Processing Free Zones as Export Strategy." In *Latin America's New Insertion in the World Economy,* edited by Ruud Buitelaar and Pitou Van Dijck. New York: St. Martin's, 1996.

Weinberg, Bill. *War on the Land: Ecology and Politics in Central America.* Atlantic Highlands, N.J.: Zed, 1991.

Weiner, Tim. "Terrific News in Mexico City: Air Is Sometimes Breathable." *New York Times,* 5 January 2001.

Weintraub, Sidney. "In the Debate about NAFTA, Just the Facts, Please." *Wall Street Journal,* 20 June 1997, p. A19.

———. "Ideological Generalizations about Financial Rescue Packages." *Issues in International Political Economy* no. 15. Washington, D.C.: CSIS.

Welch, John. "The New Face of Latin America: Financial Flows, Markets, and Institutions in the 1990s." *Journal of Latin American Studies* 25 (1993): 1–24.

Wheeler, David, "Racing to the Bottom? Foreign Investment and Air Pollution in Developing Countries," Washington, D.C.: World Bank, Environmental Division.

White, Allen T. "Venezuela's Organic Law: Regulating Pollution in an Industrializing Country." *Environment* 33, no. 7 (September 1991).

Wilber, Charles K., *The Political Economy of Development and Underdevelopment.* New York: Random House, 1973.

———, and Steven Francis. "The Methodological Basis of Hirschman's Development Economics: Pattern Modeling vs. General Laws." *World Development* 14, no. 2, special issue (February 1986): 181–91.

Williams, Frances, and Michael Mann. "Delay Threat to US and EU Banana Deal." *Financial Times,* 1 August 2000.

Williamson, John. *Dollarization Does Not Make Sense Everywhere.* Institute for International Economics. Available online at www.iie.com/TESTMONY.jwdollar.htm, 2001.

Willis, Eliza, Christopher da C.B. Garman, and Stephan Haggard. "The Politics of Decentralization in Latin America." *Latin American Research Review* 43, no. 1 (1999).

Wills, Rick. "Mexico Beef Dispute." *New York Times,* 3 August 1999.

Winters, L. Allan. "Assessing Regional Integration." *In Trade: Towards Open Regionalism,* proceedings of the 1997 World Bank Conference on Development in Latin America and the Caribbean. Washington, D.C.: World Bank, 1998.

Wise, Carol. "Latin America and the State–Market Debate: Beyond Stylized Facts." Paper presented to the Latin American Studies Association (16 March 2000).

Wolfensohn, James D. *Building an Equitable World—Address to the Board of Governors.* Prague: The World Bank Group. 26 September 2000.

———. Remarks to the Board of Governors of the World Bank Group, 1 October 1996. Available online in the LEXIS-NEXIS database.

Wolff, Laurence. "Educational Assessments in Latin America: Current Progress and Future Challenges." *Partnership for Educational Revitalization in the Americas.* June 1998. Online publication, available at www.preal.cl/index-i.htm.

———, Ernesto Schiefelbeing, and Jorge Valenzuela. *Improving the Quality of Primary Education in Latin America and the Caribbean: Toward the 21st Century.* Washington, D.C.: World Bank, 1994.

Wood, Bill, and Harry Anthony Patrinos. "Urban Bolivia." In *Indigenous People and Poverty in Latin America,* edited by George Psacharopoulus and Harry Anthony Patrinos. Washington, D.C.: World Bank, 1994.

Woodruff, David, Ian Katz, and Keith Naughton. "VW's Factory of the Future." *BusinessWeek,* 7 October 1996.

World Bank. Mexico–"Municipal Development in Rural Areas Project." July 2002, www.worldbank.org.

———. Education Program Objectives, www.worldbank.org.

———. *Update on Implementation of HIPC Debt Relief Programs and Poverty Reduction Strategy Papers.* Press Conference. Washington, D.C.: The World Bank Group. (23 April 2001).

———. *Fighting Poverty in Latin America and the Caribbean.* The World Bank Group. September 2000.

———. *Ecuador—Public Enterprise Reform and Privatization Technical Assistance Project.* June 1999.

———. *Global Development Finance 1999.* Washington, D.C.: World Bank, 1999.

———. *Beyond the Washington Consensus: Institutions Matter.* Regional Brief. Washington, D.C.: World Bank, 1998. Available online at www.worldbank.org.

———. *Global Development Finance 1998.* Washington, D.C.: World Bank, 1998.

———. *Trade: Towards Open Regionalism,* proceedings of the 1997 World Bank Conference on Development in Latin America and the Caribbean. Washington, D.C.: World Bank, 1998.

———. *Global Development Finance.* Washington, D.C.: World Bank, 1997.

———. *Guatemala—Infrastructure, Privatization, Technical Assistance Loan.* April 1997.

———. *Rural Development: From Vision to Action.* Environmentally and Socially Sustainable Development Studies and Monographs Series no. 12. Washington, D.C.: World Bank, 1997.

———. *World Development Indicators, 1997.* Washington, D.C.: World Bank 1997.

———. *Economic Growth and Returns to Work.* Washington, D.C.: World Bank, 1995.

———. *Labor and Economic Reforms in Latin America and the Caribbean: Regional Perspectives on World Development Report.* Washington, D.C.: World Bank, 1995.

———. *Energy Efficiency and Conservation in the Developing World: The World Bank's Role.* Washington, D.C.: World Bank, 1993.

———. *Meeting the Infrastructure Challenge in Latin America and the Caribbean.* Washington, D.C.: World Bank, 1995.

———. *Privatization Principles and Practice.* IFC Lessons of Experience Series. Washington, D.C.: World Bank, 1995.

———. *World Development Report 1995.* New York: Oxford University Press/World Bank, 1995.

———. *World Development Report 1994.* New York: Oxford University Press/World Bank, 1994.

———. *World Development Report 1992.* New York: Oxford University Press/World Bank, 1992.

———. *World Development Report 1988/9.* New York: Oxford University Press/World Bank, 1989.

———. *Environment and Development in Latin America and the Caribbean: The Role of the World Bank.* Washington, D.C.: World Bank.

———. *IFC: Making a Positive Difference for Sustainable Development.* Issue Brief. Washington, D.C.: The World Bank Group.

———. *Other Financial Mechanisms: Debt-for-Nature Swaps and Social Funds.* Available online at www-esd.worldbank.org/html/esd/env/publicat/edp/edp1116.htm.

———. *Ten Things You Never Knew about the World Bank.* Issue Brief. Washington, D.C.: The World Bank Group.

———. *World Debt Tables.* Washington, D.C. World Bank, various years. "World Bank and the IMF Agree on Debt Relief for Poor Countries."

World Bank Staff and IMF Staff. *100 Percent Debt Cancellation? A Response from the IMF and the World Bank.* Washington, D.C.: IMF, July 2001.

World Commission on Environment and Development, *Our Common Future.* Oxford: Oxford University Press, 1987.

World Health Organization. *Report on the Global HIV/AIDS Epidemic, June 1998.* Geneva: UNAIDS, 1998. Available online at www.who.int/emc-hiv.

———. *Integration of Health Care Delivery: Report of a WHO Study Group.* WHO Technical Report Series 861. Geneva: World Health Organization, 1996.

World Resources Institute. *World Resources: A Guide to the Global Environment 1996–7.* New York: Oxford University Press, 1997.

———. *World Resources, 1994–5.* New York: Oxford University Press, 1995.

World Trade Organization, "World Merchandise Trade in 1996 by Region and Leading Trader," *International Trade,* 30 July 1997, available at www.wto/intltrad/iiworld.htm.

Wrobel, Paulo. "A Free Trade Area of the Americas in 2005?" *International Affairs* 74, no. 3 (1998).

"WTO Adopts Panel Findings Against Mexican Measure on High-Fructose Corn Syrup." Press Release. Office of the United States Trade Representative. Washington, D.C.: World Trade Organization. 28 February 2000. www.iadb.org.

Yeager, Timothy. "Encomienda or Slavery? The Spanish Crown's Choice of Labor Organization in Sixteenth-Century Spanish America." *Journal of Economic History* 55, no. 4 (December 1995).

Young, Kate. *Planning Development with Women: Making a World of Difference.* New York: St. Martin's, 1993.

Zimbalist, Andrew. "Costa Rica." In *Struggle against Dependence: Nontraditional Export Growth in Central America and the Caribbean,* edited by Eva Paus. Boulder, Colo.: Westview, 1988.

Zoninsein, Jonas. *The Economic Case for Combating Racial and Ethnic Exclusion in Latin America and Caribbean Countries.* Research Report. Washington, D.C.: IADB, May 2001.

Zuckerman, Laurence. "In South America Car Makers See One Big Showroom." *New York Times,* 25 April 1997.

Index

Page references followed by b, f, n, or t refer to boxes, figures, endnotes, and tables, respectively. Numbers in *italic* refer to maps or photographs.

557

About the Author

Patrice Franko is Grossman Professor of Economics and professor of international studies at Colby College (Waterville, Maine) where she teaches international finance, Latin American economic policy, and microeconomics. She was a Pew Faculty Fellow in International Affairs and an American Association for the Advancement of Science Fellow in International Security Affairs. She has served as a consultant for the National Academy of Sciences, the Center for Hemispheric Studies at the National Defense University, and the Office of Inter-American Affairs, the Pentagon. She also holds a position as an adjunct fellow at the Center for Strategic and International Studies in Washington, D.C., in the Americas Program.

A specialist on economics and security relations in South America, she has authored *The Brazilian Defense Industry* (Westview Press, 1992) and numerous journal articles. She lives in Rome, Maine, with her husband, L. Sandy Maisel.